empowerment series

Social Work with Groups

COMPREHENSIVE PRACTICE AND SELF-CARE

Tenth edition

Charles H. Zastrow, MSW, PhD
Professor Emeritus
University of Wisconsin–Whitewater

Sarah L. Hessenauer
Associate Professor
University of Wisconsin–Whitewater

CENGAGE

Australia • Brazil • Mexico • Singapore • United Kingdom • United States

Social Work with Groups: Comprehensive Practice And Self-Care, **Tenth Edition**
Charles H. Zastrow and Sarah L. Hessenauer

Product Director: Marta Lee-Perriard

Product Manager: Julie A. Martinez

Project Manager: Ronald D'Souza

Content Developer: Nicky Montalvo

Product Assistant: Allison Balchunas

Marketing Manager: Zina Craft

Manufacturing Planner: Karen Hunt

Text Researcher: Lumina Datamatics Limited

Production Management and Composition: MPS Limited

Art Director: Vernon Boes

Text and Cover Designer: Jennifer Wahi

Cover Image: Peopleimages/Getty Images

For product information and technology assistance, contact us at **Cengage Customer & Sales Support, 1-800-354-9706.**

For permission to use material from this text or product, submit all requests online at **www.cengage.com/permissions.** Further permissions questions can be emailed to **permissionrequest@cengage.com.**

Library of Congress Control Number: 2017949429

Student Edition:
ISBN: 978-1-337-56791-6

Loose-leaf Edition:
ISBN: 978-1-337-56668-1

Cengage
20 Channel Center Street
Boston, MA 02210
USA

Cengage is a leading provider of customized learning solutions with employees residing in nearly 40 different countries and sales in more than 125 countries around the world. Find your local representative at: **www.cengage.com.**

Cengage products are represented in Canada by Nelson Education, Ltd.

To learn more about Cengage platforms and services, visit **www.cengage.com.**

To register or access your online learning solution or purchase materials for your course, visit **www.cengagebrain.com.**

Printed at CLDPC, USA, 12-21

To Kathy, My wife and soul mate

Contents

Chapter 3
Group Dynamics: Leadership   72

Chapter 4
Group Dynamics: Goals and Norms 106

Chapter 5
Verbal and Nonverbal Communication 138

Chapter 6
Task Groups 178

Chapter 7
Working with Diverse Groups 217

Chapter 8
Self-Help Groups 252

Chapter 9
Social Work with Families 266

Chapter 10
Organizations, Communities, and Groups 297

Chapter 11
Educational Groups: With a Focus on Self-Care 332

Chapter 12
Treatment Groups   363

Chapter 13
Treatment Groups with Diverse and Vulnerable Populations   400

Chapter 14
Termination and Evaluation of a Group   451

Appendix 2
Answers to Group Exercises D–F in Chapter 6   573

Preface

What inspired this book? In the spring of 1983, I was teaching my first group work course to an undergraduate social work class. Before the start of the semester, I wrote a number of lectures about group dynamics and how groups are used in social work practice with socialization groups, task groups, decision-making and problem-solving groups, self-help groups, and therapy groups. At the start of the semester, I dutifully began giving these lectures. Soon, however, I began sensing that the lectures were not being well received. During the third week, a student stayed after class and said, "I'm afraid this may hurt my grade, but most of the students in this class feel that you can't teach a group work class with only lectures. The only way students will learn how to run groups is by having the experience (in class or out of class) of leading groups." I thought about it for a few days and decided the student was exactly right. With the students' consent, I redesigned the whole course, with the basic thrust being to have the students take turns in leading the class on group work topics that we mutually agreed upon. Because at that time there was no social work group text to facilitate this process, I attempted to write one. The first edition of this text was published in 1985.

The basic assumption of this text is that the best way for students to learn how to run groups is by leading groups in class. The classroom thus becomes a laboratory for students to practice and develop their group leadership skills. This text is designed to facilitate this laboratory approach to undergraduate and graduate group work courses.

This edition provides a number of opportunities for students to gain proficiency in social group work skills through the inclusion of numerous "skill-building" exercises in various sections of each chapter. This book is a "worktext" that focuses on using skill-building exercises to facilitate student development of group leadership skills.

A major focus of this edition is to provide text content and skill-building exercises that focus on students acquiring the 9 competencies and 31 behaviors of the 2015 EPAS (*Educational Policy and Accreditation Standards*) of the Council on Social Work Education (CSWE).

The advantage of using the exercises from this workbook is that the exercises are explicitly connected to the competencies and behaviors of 2015 EPAS. In addition, there is an assessment process in this workbook that will facilitate the evaluation of students on the extent to which they are attaining the competencies and behaviors of 2015 EPAS. The higher a student is assessed in attaining these competencies and behaviors, the more likely it is that the student is becoming a competent social worker. A table that identifies the chapters in the text and the practice exercises in this workbook that relate to the 31 behaviors in 2015 EPAS can be found on the inside covers of the text. (Students will progress in developing the knowledge, values, skills, and cognitive and affective processes needed to become a competent social worker by conscientiously completing these exercises.)

An additional advantage of this text is that it may be used in preparing self-study documents for accreditation—as documentation that the course in which *Social Work with Groups* is being used is covering the competencies and behaviors of 2015 EPAS. Coverage is provided with text content and with exercises.

A SELF-CARE EMPHASIS

This edition of *Social Work with Groups* has an emphasis on self-care; that is, the importance of social workers setting the highest priority in taking care of their own physical, emotional, intellectual, social, and spiritual well-being. Why? It is axiomatic that if social workers do not care for themselves, their ability to care for others will be sharply diminished or even depleted. The more that social workers maximize their physical, emotional, intellectual, social, and spiritual well-being, the more energy, knowledge, skills, cognitive, and emotional resources they will have in providing services to clients.

It is also axiomatic that the same intervention strategies that social workers learn to maximize their own physical, emotional, intellectual, social, and spiritual well-being are the same strategies that social workers can convey to clients so that clients can use these strategies to learn to better care for themselves and improve their well-being!

A social worker primarily works as a "change agent" (i.e., someone who facilitates positive changes) in individuals, groups, families, organizations, and communities. Why is self-care essential in working with individuals, groups, families, organizations, and communities? A social worker who sets the highest priority on taking care of his or her physical, emotional, intellectual, social, and spiritual well-being learns an immense number of intervention strategies to improve his or her life. These strategies are precisely the strategies that the worker can convey to individuals, members of treatment groups, and family members, which these clients can then use to improve their lives.

A social worker who has excelled in self-care also has the critical resources (physical energy, positive mind-set, emotional poise, intellectual capacities, problem-solving skills, and social skills) to effectively work with organizations and communities to facilitate positive changes.

Self-care content and exercises to facilitate self-care for social work students and practicing social workers is contained in the following materials in this text:

This text obviously has considerable theories on how social workers can improve the lives of the clients they serve. In addition, there are a plethora of exercises that social work students can utilize to learn how to apply these theories. Equally important is the fact that these theories and exercises can and should be used by social work students to maximize their physical, emotional, intellectual, social, and spiritual well-being.

PLAN OF THE BOOK

Each chapter is designed according to the following format:
1. The learning objectives of the chapter are stated.
2. Theoretical material is presented on how the learning objectives can be achieved. If the learning objective is to learn how to handle disruptive members of a group, for example, the chapter describes appropriate strategies.
3. Several "skill-building" exercises are then interspersed throughout each chapter and at the end of each chapter. These exercises give students practice in acquiring the skills described in the chapter.

At the end of the book is a Group Treatment Theories Resource Manual (GTTRM). To highlight the uniqueness of the GTTRM, material is presented in modules rather than chapters. This GTTRM presents prominent theories of counseling that are widely used by social workers in working with treatment groups.

USING THE BOOK

After the instructor covers the introductory material contained in the first chapter, it is suggested that students (either individually or in small groups) take turns preparing and conducting future class sessions by summarizing the theoretical material in the chapters and leading the class in related exercises. (Students may also be given the opportunity to select a topic not covered in the text.)

The skill-building exercises in this text may be used in a variety of ways. The assigned leader (who may be the instructor, a student, or a small group of students) for a chapter may use the exercises in the following ways: (1) The assigned leader may request that the other students complete certain exercises as a homework assignment prior to the next class period; the exercises are then reviewed when the class next meets. (2) The assigned leader may have the other students complete one or more exercises during the class. (3) The

instructor may assign certain exercises as written homework to be submitted for evaluation. (4) The instructor may have each student complete several exercises and then place them in a portfolio, which the instructor may periodically review for evaluation purposes.

Students should make their presentations stimulating, interesting, and educational by speaking extemporaneously rather than reading and by adapting chapter topics using personal observations or research. Students should also prepare and distribute handouts that summarize the key points of their presentations and should move around the classroom to maintain and increase the interest of the class. The use of technological resources, such as Microsoft PowerPoint, is also suggested.

About the Authors

Charles H. Zastrow, MSW, PhD, is Professor Emeritus in Social Work at the University of Wisconsin-Whitewater. He chaired the Social Work Department for six years at this campus. He has also been the Assistant Director and Professor in the Social Work Program at George Williams College of Aurora University at Williams Bay, Wisconsin. He has worked as a practitioner in a variety of public and private social welfare agencies and has chaired 28 social work accreditation site visit teams for the Council on Social Work Education (CSWE).

He was a member of the Commission on Accreditation of CSWE for six years. He is a member of the International Association for Social Work with Groups, the National Association of Social Workers, the Council on Social Work Education, and the NASW Register of Clinical Social Workers. He is licensed as a clinical social worker in Wisconsin. In addition to *Social Work with Groups*, he has written several other books, including the following textbooks: *Introduction to Social Work and Social Welfare* (12th ed.), *Generalist Social Work Practice* (11th ed.), and *Understanding Human Behavior and Social Environment* (10th ed.) (with Dr. Karen Kirst-Ashman).

Sarah L. Hessenauer, BSW, MSW, PhD, is an associate professor in social work at the University of Wisconsin-Whitewater. She has been in the department for 10 years and is chair of the department. She earned her BSW degree in 1990 from the University of Wisconsin-Whitewater, her MSW in 1991 from UW-Milwaukee, and her PhD in 2011 from Loyola University of Chicago. She is a certified licensed clinical social worker in the state of Wisconsin. She has worked as a practitioner and administrator in a variety of mental health and addictions agencies. She is a Council on Social Work Education (CSWE) accreditation site visitor. She is a current member of NASW, BPD, and CSWE. She has authored several articles and is a reviewer for several social work journals.

CONTRIBUTING AUTHORS

Katherine Drechsler, MSW
Lecturer
University of Wisconsin–Whitewater
Doctoral Student in Social Work
George Williams College of Aurora
University

Jacob Dunn, MSW, LCSW
Associate Lecturer
University of Wisconsin–Madison
Social Worker, Stoughton Hospital
Geriatric Psychiatry Unit
Stoughton, WI

Rachel Dunn, MSW, LCSW
Associate Lecturer
University of Wisconsin–Madison
Psychotherapist, Crossroads Counseling
Janesville, WI

Craig Mead, MSW, LSW
Licensed Social Worker at Presence
St. Mary and Elizabeth Medical
Center
Chicago, IL

Michael Wallace, MSSW, LCSW
Clinical Social Worker and Lecturer
(Retired)
Social Work Department
University of Wisconsin–Whitewater

Mary R. Weeden, LCSW, PhD
Clinical Therapist for Eating Disorders
Instructor, University of Wisconsin–
Oshkosh

1

Groups: Types and Stages of Development

LEARNING OBJECTIVESLEARNING
OBJECTIVES

Each group develops a unique character or personality because of the principles of group dynamics. This chapter will help prepare students to:

LO 1
Understand the history of social group work.

LO 2
Identify the primary types of groups in social work.

LO 3
Understand four models of group development over time.

LO 4
Describe the differences between reference groups and membership groups.

LO 5
Comprehend guidelines on how to conduct classroom exercises.

Every social service agency uses groups, and every practicing social worker is involved in a variety of groups. Social work with groups is practiced in adoption agencies, correctional settings, halfway houses, substance abuse treatment centers, physical rehabilitation centers, family service agencies, private psychotherapy clinics, mental hospitals, nursing homes, community centers, public schools, and many other social service settings. To effectively serve clients in human service systems today, social workers in generalist practice positions must be trained in group methods. Often, social workers serve as leaders and participants in myriad groups requiring skills ranging from simple to complex. The beginning social worker is likely to be surprised at the diverse groups in existence and excited by the challenge of practicing social work in many different settings.

LO 1   Understand the History of Social Group Work

HISTORICAL DEVELOPMENT OF GROUP WORK

The roots of group social work began in the settlement houses, the Young Men's and Young Women's Christian Associations (YMCAs and YWCAs), Boy Scouts and Girl Scouts, and Jewish centers of the 1800s.[1] These agencies focused on providing group programs for people considered "normal." Recipients of early group services came for recreation, informal education, friendship, and social action. Euster notes that these recipients "learned to cooperate and get along with others socially; they enriched themselves through new knowledge, skills, and interests, and the overall state of society was bettered through responsible involvement in community problems."[2]

Settlement Houses

The first settlement house, Toynbee Hall, was established in London in 1884; many others were soon formed in large U.S. cities.[3]

Many of the early settlement-house workers were daughters of ministers. Usually from middle- and upper-class families, they would live in a poor neighborhood so they could experience the harsh realities of poverty. Using the missionary approach of teaching residents how to live moral lives and improve their circumstances, early settlement workers sought to improve housing, health, and living conditions; find jobs for workers; teach English, hygiene, and occupational skills; and improve living conditions through neighborhood cooperative efforts. The techniques settlement houses used to effect change are now called social group work, social action, and community organization.

Settlement houses not only emphasized "environmental reform," but they also "continued to struggle to teach the poor the prevailing middle-class values

1

of work, thrift, and abstinence as the keys to success."[4] In addition to dealing with local problems through local action, settlement houses played important roles in drafting legislation and organizing to influence social policy and legislation.

The most noted leader in the settlement-house movement was Jane Addams of Hull House in Chicago. She was born in 1860 in Cedarville, Illinois, the daughter of parents who owned a successful flour mill and wood mill.[5] After graduating from Rockford Seminary in Rockford, Illinois, she attended medical school briefly but was forced to leave due to illness. She then traveled for a few years in Europe, perplexed as to what her life work should be. At the age of 25, she joined the Presbyterian Church, which helped her find a focus for her life: religion, humanitarianism, and serving the poor. (She later joined the Congregational Church, now known as the United Church of Christ.) Addams heard about the establishment of Toynbee Hall in England and returned to Europe to study the approach. The staff of college students and graduates, mainly from Oxford, lived in the slums of London to learn conditions firsthand and to improve life there with their own personal resources, including financial ones.

Jane Addams returned to the United States and rented a two-story house, later named Hull House, in an impoverished neighborhood in Chicago. With a few friends, Addams initiated a variety of group and individual activities for the community. Group activities included a literature reading group for young women; a kindergarten; and groups that focused on social relationships, sports, music, painting, art, and discussion of current affairs. Hull House also provided services to individuals who needed immediate help, such as food, shelter, and information on and referral for other services. A Hull House Social Science Club studied social problems in a scientific manner and then became involved in social action efforts to improve living conditions. This group worked successfully for passage of Illinois legislation to prevent the employment of children in sweatshops. Addams also became interested in the various ethnic groups in the neighborhood. She was fairly successful in bringing the various nationalities together at Hull House, where they could interact and exchange cultural values.

The success of Hull House served as a model for the establishment of settlement houses in other areas of Chicago and many other large cities in the United States. Settlement-house leaders believed that by changing neighborhoods, they could improve communities, and by altering communities, they could develop a better society. For her extraordinary contributions, Jane Addams received the Nobel Prize for Peace in 1931.

Young Men's Christian Association (YMCA)

The founder of the Young Men's Christian Association (YMCA), George Williams,[6] was born and reared on a small farm in England. He stopped attending school at the age of 13 to work on his father's farm, but at 14, he became an apprentice to a draper (a manufacturer and dealer of cloth and woolen materials) and learned the trade. He grew up in a religious environment and joined the Congregational Church at the age of 16. At 20, he moved to London and worked for another drapery firm. Like Williams, the business owner, George Hitchcock, was deeply religious and allowed his new employee to organize prayer meetings at work.

The size of the prayer circle gradually grew, and the meetings featured Bible reading as well as prayers. The success of this group inspired Williams and his associates to organize similar groups at other drapers' establishments. The prayer circle Williams formed with 12 fellow employees marked the beginning of YMCAs. In 1844, the resulting prayer circles at 14 businesses formed an association called the Young Men's Christian Association. Each group conducted weekly religious services that included prayer, Bible readings, and discussions of spiritual topics.

The YMCA soon began to expand its activities. Prominent speakers from various fields of public and scholarly life addressed its members. An office was selected, and Protestant clergy in France, Holland, and other countries were persuaded to form YMCAs. Gradually, the programs were expanded to meet the unique needs of the communities in which the YMCAs were located.

In 1851, Thomas V. Sullivan, a retired mariner, picked up a religious weekly in Boston and read about the YMCA movement in London.[7] Sullivan gathered a few friends and established the first YMCA in the United States. Similar to the London association, the U.S. movement spread quickly to other communities. In only 7 years, YMCAs were serving communities throughout the United States.

The U.S. YMCA had many firsts. It was the first organization to aid troops during wartime in the field and in prison camps. It pioneered community sports and athletics, invented volleyball and basketball, and taught water safety and swimming. It devised an international program of social service similar to that of the Peace Corps. It originated group recreational camping, developed night schools and adult education, initiated widespread nondenominational Christian work for college students, and reached out to assist foreign students. From an origin that involved a narrowly focused religious objective, YMCAs have expanded their objectives in a variety of directions. The success of YMCAs helped spur the first Young Women's Christian Association (YWCA), formed in Boston in 1866.[8]

LO 2   Identify the Primary Types of Groups in Social Work

TYPES OF GROUPS

A variety of groups occur in social work—social conversation, recreation skill building, educational, task, problem solving and decision making, focus, self-help, socialization, treatment, and sensitivity and encounter training. According to Johnson and Johnson, a group may be defined as two or more individuals in face-to-face interaction, each aware of positive interdependence as they strive to achieve mutual goals, each aware of his or her membership in the group, and each aware of the others who belong to the group.[9]

Social Conversation

Social conversation is often employed to determine what kind of relationship might develop with people we do not know very well. Because talk is often loose and tends to drift aimlessly, there is usually no formal agenda for social conversations. If the topic of conversation is dull, the subject can simply be changed. Although individuals may have a goal (perhaps only to establish an acquaintanceship), such goals need not become the agenda for the entire group. In social work, social conversation with other professionals is frequent, but groups involving clients generally have objectives other than conversation, such as resolving personal problems.

Recreation/Skill Building

Recreational groups may be categorized as **informal recreational groups** or **skill-building recreational groups**.

A recreational group service agency (such as the YMCA, YWCA, or neighborhood center) may offer little more than physical space and the use of some equipment to provide activities for enjoyment and exercise. Often activities such as playground games and informal athletics are spontaneous, and the groups are practically leaderless. Some agencies claim that recreation and interaction with others help build character and prevent delinquency among youths by providing an alternative to street life.

In contrast to informal recreational groups, a skill-building recreational group has an increased focus on tasks and is guided by an adviser, coach, or instructor. The objective is to improve a set of skills in an enjoyable way. Examples of activities include arts and crafts and sports such as golf, basketball, and swimming, which may develop into competitive team sports with leagues. These groups are frequently led by professionals with recreational training rather than social work training, and the agencies involved include the YMCA, YWCA, Boy Scouts, Girl Scouts, neighborhood centers, and school recreational departments.

Education

Although the topics covered vary widely, all educational groups teach specialized skills and knowledge, such as classes on childrearing, stress management, parenting, English as a foreign language, and assertiveness training. Orientations offered by social service organizations to train volunteers fall into this category as well. Educational groups usually have a classroom atmosphere, involving considerable group interaction and discussion; a professional person with expertise in the area, often a social worker, assumes the role of teacher.

Task

Task groups are formed to achieve a specific set of tasks or objectives. The following examples are types of task groups that social workers are apt to interact with or become involved in. A **board of directors** is an administrative group charged with responsibility for setting the policy governing agency programs. A **task force** is a group established for a special purpose and

A Problem-Solving and Decision-Making Group: Family Group Conferencing

The family group conferencing approach with abused or neglected children originated in New Zealand. The approach has now been adopted in many other countries, including in the United States.

When evidence of child abuse by child protective services or the police has been documented, some child protective services agencies are now offering the parents of the affected children the option of using the family group conferencing approach to attempt to improve the parenting and end future abuse. The process is first explained to the parents. If the parents agree to involve their extended kinship network in planning, the process is then implemented.

The family decision-making conference is facilitated by a professional person (often associated with child protective services). The professional person is usually called the "family group coordinator." Three characteristics are central to family group conferencing:

1. Family is widely defined to include extended family members, as well as other people who are significant to the family.
2. The family is given the opportunity to prepare the plan.
3. The professionals involved with the family must agree to the plan unless it is thought to place the child at risk.

The coordinator prepares and plans for the first meeting of the extended family. Such planning may take weeks.

Downs, Moore, McFadden, and Costin describe the initial planning process:

> This involves working with the family; identifying concerned parties and members of the extended kinship network; clarifying their roles and inviting them to a family group meeting; establishing the location, time, and other logistics; and managing other unresolved issues. At the meeting the coordinator welcomes and introduces participants in a culturally appropriate manner, establishes the purpose of the meeting, and helps participants reach agreement about roles, goals, and ground rules. Next, information is shared with the family, which may involve the child protection workers and other relevant professionals such as a doctor or teacher involved with the child.[a]

In the New Zealand model, the coordinator and other professional withdraw from the meeting in the next stage to allow the family privacy for their deliberations. (Some programs in the United States and other countries allow the coordinator to remain in the meeting.) The kinship network makes plans to respond to the issues that are raised, including developing a plan for the safety and the care of the child. The coordinator and/or protective services retain the right to veto a family plan if they believe the child will not be protected. (In reality, a veto is rarely used.) Several meetings over several days may be necessary to develop the family plan.

Downs and colleagues summarize the challenges faced by social workers with this approach:

> Working with family group decision making requires a new approach to family-centered practice. The social worker must expand his or her ideas about the family to recognize the strength and centrality of the extended kinship network, particularly in communities of color. Use of the strengths perspective is critical. The worker must understand the greater investment of kin in the well-being of the child and should also understand that, even when parts of the kinship system may seem to be compromised or dysfunctional, the healthier kinfolk can assess and deal with the problem. One of the greatest challenges for the social worker is incorporating the sharing of power or returning of power to the kinship network. Many social workers trained as family therapists or child welfare workers have assumed a power role and may find it difficult to relinquish a sense of control.[b]

There are several advantages of family group conferencing. It facilitates getting the extended family involved in meeting the needs of the abused/neglected child or children and in meeting the needs of their parents. It reduces government intervention in people's lives. It recognizes the strengths of kinship networks to provide assistance to at-risk families. It reduces the number of children placed in foster homes. (Frequently with this approach one or more extended family members temporarily take in the child, giving the parents an opportunity to receive whatever they need to become more stable and to learn better parenting skills.)

Family group conferencing has also been adapted to respond to other family issues, such as families with an adjudicated delinquent.

---

a. Downs, S. W., Moore, E., McFadden, E. J., & Costin, L. B. (2000). *Child welfare and family services.* (6th ed., p. 295). Boston, MA: Allyn & Bacon.
b. Ibid., p. 295.

is usually disbanded after the task is completed. A **committee** of an agency or organization is a group that is formed to deal with specific tasks or matters. An **ad hoc committee**, like a task force, is set up for one purpose and usually ceases functioning after completion of its task.

Problem Solving and Decision Making

Both providers and consumers of social services may become involved in groups concerned with problem solving and decision making. (There is considerable overlap between task groups and these groups; in fact, problem-solving and decision-making groups can be considered a subcategory of task groups.)

Social service providers use group meetings for objectives such as developing a treatment plan for a client or a group of clients, or deciding how best to allocate scarce resources. Potential consumers of services may form a group to meet a current community need. Data on the need may be gathered, and the group may be used as a vehicle, either to develop a program or to influence existing agencies to provide services. Social workers may function as stimulators and organizers of these group efforts.

In problem-solving and decision-making groups, each participant normally has some interest or stake in the process and stands to gain or lose personally by the outcome. Usually, there is a formal leader, and other leaders sometimes emerge during the process.

Focus

Focus groups are closely related to task groups and problem-solving and decision-making groups. They may be formed for a variety of purposes, including (1) to identify needs or issues, (2) to generate proposals that resolve an identified issue, and (3) to test reactions to alternative approaches to an issue. A focus group is a group convened to discuss a specific issue or single topic, often with the aid of questionnaires, and a moderator who actively keeps the conversation oriented to that topic. Such groups are often established to acquire information and generate ideas that would not be as accessible through individual interviews.[10]

Two examples of a focus group are a nominal group (described in Chapter 4) and a brainstorming session (described in Chapter 6).

A **representative group** is another version of a focus group. Its strength is that its members have been selected specifically to represent different perspectives and points of view in a community. At best, the representative group is a focus group that reflects the cleavages in the community and seeks to bring diverse views to the table; at worst, it is a front group for people who seek to make the community *think* it has been involved.

Self-Help and Mutual Aid

Self-help groups are increasingly popular and often successful in helping individuals overcome social or personal problems. Katz and Bender provide a comprehensive definition:

> Self-help groups are voluntary, small group structures . . . usually formed by peers who have come together for mutual assistance in satisfying a common need, overcoming a common handicap or life-disrupting problem, and bringing about desired social and/or personal change. The initiators and members of such groups perceive that their needs are not, or cannot be, met by or through existing social institutions. . . . They often provide material assistance as well as emotional support, they are frequently "cause"-oriented, and promulgate an ideology or [set of] values through which members may attain an enhanced sense of personal identity.[11]

Alcoholics Anonymous, developed by two recovering alcoholics, was the first self-help group to demonstrate substantial success. In *Self-Help Organizations and Professional Practice*, Powell describes numerous self-help groups that are now active.[12]

Closely related to self-help groups are mutual-aid groups, and the terms are sometimes interchangeable. Mutual-aid groups are informal or formal associations of people who share certain problems and meet regularly in small groups with professional leaders to provide emotional support, information, assistance in problem solving, and other help for each other.

A Self-Help Group: Parents Anonymous

Parents Anonymous (PA), a national self-help organization for parents who have abused or neglected their children, was established in 1970 by Jolly K. in California. For 4 years before forming the group, Jolly had struggled with an uncontrollable urge to severely punish her daughter. One afternoon she attempted to strangle the child. Desperate, she sought help from a local child-guidance clinic and was placed in therapy. When asked by her therapist what she could do about her problem, Jolly developed an idea. As she explained, "If alcoholics could stop drinking by getting together, and gamblers could stop gambling, maybe the same principle would work for [child] abusers, too." With her therapist's encouragement she formed "Mothers Anonymous" in 1970 and organized a few chapters in California. Nearly every major city in the United States and Canada now has a chapter, and the name has been changed to Parents Anonymous because fathers who abuse their children are also eligible to join.

PA is a crisis intervention program that offers two main forms of help: a weekly group meeting and personal and telephone contact. Members share experiences and feelings during weekly meetings and learn to better control their emotions. During periods of crisis, personal and telephone contact is especially important, particularly when a member feels a nearly uncontrollable desire to take anger or frustration out on a child. Parents may be referred to PA by a social agency (including protective services) or be self-referred as parents who recognize that they need help.

Cassie Starkweather and S. Michael Turner describe why abusive parents would rather participate in a self-help group than receive professional counseling:

It has been our experience that most [abusive] parents judge themselves more harshly than other, more objective people tend to judge them. The fear of losing their children frequently diminishes with reassurance from other members that they are not the monsters they think they are.

Generally speaking, PA members are so afraid they are going to be judged by others as harshly as they judge themselves that they are afraid to go out and seek help. Frequently our members express fears of dealing with a professional person, seeing differences in education, sex, or social status as basic differences that would prevent easy communication or mutual understanding.

Members express feelings of gratification at finding that other parents are "in the same boat." They contrast this with their feelings about professionals who, they often assume, have not taken out the time from their training and current job responsibilities to raise families of their own.[a]

PA emphasizes honesty and directness, as parents who are prone to abuse their children have learned to hide this problem because society finds it difficult to acknowledge. In contrast to society's tendency to deny the problem, the goal of PA is to help parents admit that they are abusive. The term *abuse* is used liberally at meetings, and this insistence on frankness has a healthy effect on members. Abusive parents are relieved because they have finally found a group of people able to accept them as they are. Furthermore, only when they are able to admit they are abusive can they begin to find ways to heal themselves.

During meetings, parents are expected to actually admit to beating their child or engaging in other forms of abuse, and the members challenge each other to find ways to curb these activities. Members share constructive approaches to anger and other abuse-precipitating emotions and help each other develop specific plans for dealing with situations that have resulted in abusive episodes. Members learn to recognize danger signs and to take action to avoid abuse.

Leadership is provided by a group member selected by other members. The leader, called a chairperson, is normally assisted by a professional sponsor who serves as resource and back-up person to the chair and the group. The social worker who assumes the role of sponsor must be prepared to perform a variety of functions, including teacher-trainer, broker of community services needed by parents, advocate, consultant, and counselor.[b]

SOURCE: Adapted from *Introduction to Social Work and Social Welfare*, 8th ed., by Zastrow © 2004. Reprinted with permission of Brooks/Cole.

a. Starkweather, C. L., & Turner, S. M. (1975). Parents Anonymous: Reflections on the development of a self-help group. In N. C. Ebeling & D. A. Hill (Eds.), *Child abuse: Intervention and treatment* (p. 151). Acton, MA: Publishing Sciences Group.

b. Check the Parents Anonymous website at http://parentsanonymous.org.

Many self-help groups use individual confession and testimony techniques. Each member explains his or her problem and recounts related experiences and plans for handling the problem. When a member encounters a crisis (for example, an abusive parent having an urge to abuse a child), he or she is encouraged to call another group member, who helps the person cope. Having experienced the misery and consequences of the problem, group members are highly dedicated to helping themselves and then fellow sufferers. The participants also benefit from the "helper therapy" principle; that is, the helper gains psychological rewards.[13] Helping others makes a person feel worthwhile, enabling the person to put his or her own problems into perspective.

Most self-help groups are "direct service" in that they help members with individual problems. Other self-help groups work on community-wide issues and tend to be more social action oriented. Some direct service self-help groups attempt to change legislation and policy in public and private institutions. Others (parents of children with a cognitive disability, for example) also raise funds and operate community programs. However, many people with personal problems use self-help groups in the same way others use social agencies. An additional advantage of self-help groups is that they generally operate with a minimal budget. (For further discussion, see Chapter 8.)

Socialization

The primary objective of most socialization groups is to develop attitudes and behaviors in group members that are more socially acceptable.[14] Developing social skills, increasing self-confidence, and planning for the future are other focuses. Leadership roles in socialization groups are frequently filled by social workers who work with groups for predelinquent youths to curb delinquency; youths of diverse racial backgrounds to reduce racial tensions; and pregnant, unmarried young females to help them make plans for the future. Older residents in nursing homes are often remotivated by socialization groups and become

A Socialization Group: A Group at a Runaway Center

New Horizons, located in an older home in a large Midwestern city, is a private, temporary shelter where youths on the run can stay for 2 weeks. The facility is licensed to house up to eight youths; however, state law requires that parents be contacted and parental permission received before New Horizons can provide shelter overnight. Services include temporary shelter, individual and family counseling, and a 24-hour hotline for youths in crisis. Because the average stay at New Horizons is 9 days, the population is continually changing. During their stay, youths (and often their parents) receive intensive counseling, which focuses on reducing conflicts between the youths and their parents and on helping them make future living plans. The 2-week limit conveys the importance to residents and their families of resolving the conflicts that keep them apart.

Every evening at 7 P.M., a group meeting allows residents to express their satisfactions and dissatisfactions with the facilities and program at New Horizons. All the residents and the two or three staff members on duty are expected to attend. The meetings are convened and led by the staff, most of whom are social workers. Sometimes, the group becomes primarily a "gripe" session, but the staff makes conscientious efforts to improve or change situations involving legitimate gripes. For example, a youth may indicate that the past few days have been "boring," and staff and residents then jointly plan activities for the next few days.

Interaction problems that arise between residents, and between staff and residents, are also handled during a group session. A resident may be preventing others from sleeping; some residents may refuse to share in domestic tasks; there may be squabbles about which TV program to watch; some residents may be overly aggressive. Because most of the youths face a variety of crises associated with being on the run, many are anxious and under stress. In such an emotional climate, interaction problems are certain to arise. Staff members are sometimes intensely questioned about their actions, decisions, and policies. For example, one of the policies at New Horizons is that each resident must agree not to use alcohol or narcotic drugs while at the shelter. The penalty is expulsion. Occasionally, few youths use some drugs, are caught, and are expelled. Removing a youth from this facility has an immense impact on the other residents, and at the following meetings staff members are expected to clarify and explain such decisions.

The staff also presents material on topics requested by residents during meetings. Subjects often covered include sex; drugs; homosexuality; physical and sexual abuse (a fair number of residents are abused by family members); avoiding rape; handling anger, depression, and other unwanted emotions; legal rights of youths on the run; being more assertive; explaining running away to relatives and friends; and human services available to youths in the community. During such presentations, considerable discussion with residents is encouraged and generally occurs.

The final objective of the group is to convey information about planned daily activities and changes in the overall program at New Horizons.

involved in various activities. Teenagers at correctional schools are helped to make plans for returning to their home community. Leadership of all the groups mentioned in this section requires considerable skills and knowledge to help the group to foster individual growth and change.

Treatment

Treatment groups are generally composed of members with severe emotional, behavioral, and personal problems. Leaders of such groups must have superb counseling and group leadership skills, including the ability to accurately perceive the core of each member's response to what is being communicated. Group leaders must also have the personal capacities to develop and maintain a constructive atmosphere within a group. As in one-on-one counseling, the goal of treatment groups is to have members explore their problems in depth and then develop strategies for resolving them. Three treatment approaches (reality therapy, behavior therapy, and rational therapy) are described in the Group Treatment Theories Resource Manual (located at the end of the text). These three treatment approaches can be used to change dysfunctional behaviors and unwanted emotions of group members. There are a variety of treatment groups. (See "Common Types of Treatment Groups.")

COMMON TYPES OF TREATMENT GROUPS*

Social workers are likely to encounter treatment groups in a wide variety of settings, such as outpatient mental health clinics, community-based social service agencies, inpatient psychiatric units, intensive outpatient programs, substance abuse programs, residential programs, domestic violence programs, special education programs, therapeutic day schools, veterans' programs, day treatment programs, correctional institutions, juvenile justice programs, and other institutional programs. Most treatment groups in these settings are based upon a recovery model emphasizing that clients can achieve long-term recovery from serious mental illness, developmental and social problems, and behavioral health issues. This recovery is facilitated and achieved through skill building and psychosocial rehabilitation, which improves clients' abilities to self-manage symptoms and problems in their current environment. These groups are often called psychosocial rehabilitation or community support groups and focus on changing behavior, skill building, and increasing natural supports. Groups are frequently structured using cognitive and behavioral therapy approaches (see modules at the end of the text), and facilitators are often given substantial latitude as to the content and structure of specific group sessions. Next we'll look at some of the more common treatment groups social workers may encounter and be asked to facilitate. The types of groups an agency provides and the group names used will vary depending on agency, mission, population, and client needs.

Psychoeducational Groups

Psychoeducational groups are becoming increasingly common in many community-based agencies and institutional settings. These groups are designed to educate and empower clients, families, caregivers, and support systems to be able to better manage a client's psychiatric symptoms, mental illness, or behavioral health problems. They often center on a specific diagnosis, such as depression, anxiety, attention-deficit/hyperactivity disorder (ADHD), bipolar disorder, posttraumatic stress disorder (PTSD), substance dependence, or obsessive-compulsive disorder. The primary goal is to educate and improve understanding about common symptoms; recognize early warning signs; improve symptom management; and enhance relapse prevention, effective intervention, coping skills, and effective supports. An additional goal is to improve insight, which enhances recovery, reduces inpatient hospitalizations, and improves family stress levels and well-being. Sometimes psychoeducational groups are specifically geared toward family members and client support systems. Often these are facilitated self-help groups that emphasize peer support and encouragement.

---

* This material was written by Craig Mead, MSW, LSW, Licensed Social Worker at Presence St. Mary and Elizabeth Medical Center, Chicago, IL.

For example, an ADHD parents group would focus on educating parents on symptoms to improve their ability to distinguish true symptoms from other oppositional, defiant, or age-appropriate behaviors. Parents also benefit from hearing about others' struggles and may subsequently feel less self-blame and alienation. They can provide each other encouragement and support and share successful parenting skills and behavior interventions.

Symptom Management Groups

Symptom management groups focus on helping individuals cope with specific types of disorders. These groups are structured for people who struggle with specific diagnoses, such as depression, anxiety, bipolar disorder, eating disorders, obsessive-compulsive disorder, borderline personality, ADHD, or addictions. For example, a depression group would focus on specific symptoms and issues that are unique to people who struggle with depression. Often they include a significant psychoeducational segment and then focus on skill improvement. Skill instruction is tailored to the unique needs of the group. These groups frequently focus on improving the use of coping skills and strategies to manage feelings, control impulses, reduce problematic thinking patterns, and effectively solve interpersonal problems. The group process is used to help empower participants to make meaningful changes, view problems in perspective, and enhance their overall well-being. Managing symptoms is viewed as an important action step in the recovery process.

Anger Management Groups

An anger management group is one of the most common types of groups found in treatment settings. An inability to manage one's feelings is a common deficit, especially in people with emotional problems. The emotion of anger is given special attention because of the unhealthy behavior choices people often make when they are angry. Verbal or physical aggression is a common behavioral manifestation of anger. These groups often focus on finding healthier ways to channel feelings, learning more effective coping skills, building better assertiveness skills, improving problem-solving ability, challenging distorted thinking patterns, resolving conflicts collaboratively, and learning to express feelings without aggression. The group process is used as an opportunity to practice these skills with the assistance of the facilitator and other participants.

Life Skills Groups

A life skills group is also often called an independent living skills or daily living skills group. This group is most commonly used with adults with chronic mental illness, adults with developmental or cognitive disabilities, and teenagers and young adults. The focus is on teaching skills to improve the participant's ability to live independently. These groups tend to be much more didactic in nature but utilize the group process for collaborative learning and support-system building. Individual group sessions may focus on managing money, budgeting, accessing public transportation, securing and maintaining housing, housekeeping, laundry, grocery shopping, cooking, accessing healthcare and prescriptions, finding employment, job skills, and healthy living. Groups may cover a myriad of topics and be customized to the specific needs and developmental and skill levels of participants.

Social Skills Groups

Social skills groups focus on improving the participant's interpersonal effectiveness skills. Topics often include improving assertiveness, problem solving, conflict resolution, building healthy relationships, boundaries, manners, making friends, empathy, and building natural supports. Participants may be challenged to improve their self-awareness of problematic and unhealthy behaviors. Role-play is frequently used to practice new skills and improve the client's ability to self-manage relationships. At times participants may process specific problems expressed by group members and discuss potential changes that group members might make. Group members are encouraged to provide positive and negative feedback, which enhances participants' understanding of others' perception of them.

Process Groups

Process groups are often used in inpatient, residential, and other settings where group members spend significant amounts of time together. They are also used in other settings when one group participant has a major issue to resolve that would be beneficial and relevant for all members to discuss. Sometimes these groups are prescheduled, such as a daily reflection group at a group home or inpatient facility. Other times a group session may be called spontaneously to resolve a major conflict or problem within the milieu. The specific issue is brought to the attention of the group, and participants are encouraged to process through their thoughts and feelings, provide each other with feedback and support, and collaboratively problem-solve as a group. Sometimes group members may be confrontational and challenging, which can be a healthy process when facilitated properly. In some settings, this group is used to help participants process thoughts and feelings about a major life event, such as the death of a loved one or a suicide attempt by a group member. Participants are assisted with managing feelings, reframing unhealthy thought patterns, and integrating life's challenges.

Stress Management Groups

Stress management groups focus on learning healthier and more effective strategies for dealing with stress. Participants may be encouraged to make lifestyle changes and take a more proactive role in reducing stress before it happens. Group facilitators often instruct on a variety of relaxation techniques and lead participants in practice exercises. Breathing exercises, guided meditation, yoga, positive imagery, and healthy living are common themes. Participants are encouraged to practice relaxation techniques at home, which will improve their ability to use the skills at times of increased stress. Skill development, such as time management, problem solving, or assertiveness training, may also be a topic for specific sessions. The group process may also be used to challenge and change thinking patterns and beliefs that contribute to stress. Psychoeducation may be used to assist participants to recognize how stress contributes to their disorders. Other areas of discussion could include exercise, healthy eating, and avoiding substance use. (A stress management group is sometimes also called an educational group. See Chapter 11 for a detailed discussion of stress management groups.)

Specialty Groups

Specialty groups address specific topics or problems that are unique to certain client populations and settings. The focus of the group and topics discussed will vary depending on client needs. For example, substance abuse programs have a number of different groups geared specifically toward alcohol and drug addiction recovery. Different groups may focus on drug and alcohol education, relapse prevention, recovery and lifestyle changes, or 12-step programs. Other examples would include eating disorder program groups, grief counseling and support groups, veteran PTSD recovery groups, domestic violence recovery groups, and healthcare-focused groups for psychological challenges related to patients with cancer, heart disease, or other major illnesses. (Treatment groups are discussed more fully in Chapter 12.)

In summary, to be a competent group therapist, the professional should have superb interviewing and counseling skills, a working knowledge of the principles of group dynamics (described in Chapters 1 through 6 of this text), and a working knowledge of contemporary therapy approaches, three of which are described in the Group Treatment Theories Resource Manual, located at the end of this text.

Group treatment has several advantages over one-on-one therapy. The "helper" therapy principle generally is operative. Members at times interchange roles and become the helper for someone else, receiving psychological rewards and putting their own problems into perspective in the process. Group treatment also allows members with interaction problems to test new approaches. In addition, research has shown it is generally easier to change the attitudes of an individual in a group than one on one.[15] Group treatment permits a social worker to treat more than one person at a time and represents a substantial savings of professional time. (See "Group Therapy with Substance Use Disorders.")

Group Therapy with Substance Use Disorders*

ADVANTAGES OF GROUP TREATMENT

Group therapy is one of the therapeutic tools used for treating people with substance use disorders. A benefit of using groups for treating people with substance use disorders is that groups intrinsically reduce feelings of isolation of group members, and participation in the group allows members of the group to realize that they are not the only ones dealing with the process of recovery. These qualities experienced by the group members can draw them into the culture of recovery. People who abuse substances often are more likely to remain abstinent and committed to recovery when treatment is provided in groups because of rewarding and therapeutic forces such as affiliation, confrontation, support, gratification, and identification. Groups provide positive peer support and pressure to abstain from substances of abuse. Another reason groups work as a mode of treatment for substance use is that factors associated with substance use, such as depression, isolation, and shame, can be addressed. Great emphasis is placed on interpersonal process within the groups, which helps substance use clients resolve problems in relating to other people, problems that they may have attempted to avoid by means of addictive substances.[a]

DEFINING THERAPEUTIC GROUP MODELS IN SUBSTANCE USE TREATMENT

Five models of groups are used in substance use treatment:

- Psychoeducational groups
- Skills-development groups
- Cognitive-behavioral groups
- Support groups
- Interpersonal process group psychotherapy

Treatment providers routinely use the first four models and various combinations of them. Interpersonal process groups are not widely used because of the extensive training required to lead these groups and the long duration to complete this type of group. This demands a high level of commitment from both the providers and the clients.[b] The major purpose of psychoeducational groups is to create and expand awareness about the behavioral, medical, and psychological consequences of substance use. This type of group is highly structured and presents group-specific content. The information presented is designed to have a direct application to the clients' lives to help instill self-awareness. This self-awareness presents options for growth and change, identifies community resources that can assist in the recovery process, and attempts to motivate clients to take action on their own to attend treatment. An example of a psychoeducational group activity would be to have group members read and discuss a handout on the potential physiological effects of alcohol.[c]

Skills-development groups are primarily developed from a cognitive-behavioral approach. This approach is most often used in conjunction with psychoeducational elements. The most common type of skills-development group is one that teaches and helps group members develop coping skills. These skills may be directly related to substance use, such as learning refusal skills when offered drugs, or to broader areas in the client's life, such as ways to manage anger or anxiety. Many of the skills that people with substance use heed to develop are interpersonal in nature, so group therapy is a place for them to practice these skills.[d]

Cognitive-behavioral groups identify that the substance use of the individual is a learned behavior that can be modified through various interventions. These interventions include identification of conditioned stimuli associated with the specific addictive behaviors, avoidance of such stimuli, development of enhanced contingency management strategies, and response desensitization. The cognitive-behavioral group works to change the learned behavior by changing thinking patterns, beliefs, and perceptions (see Modules 1 and 3). The group activities help the individual develop social networks that will help support the individual's recovery. Cognitions developed by psychological elements such as thoughts, beliefs, decisions, opinions, and assumptions are challenged and strategies are learned to change these thought patterns. Cognitive-behavioral groups are most helpful in the beginning stages of recovery.[e]

Participation in support groups helps members strengthen their ability to manage their thinking and emotions and to develop interpersonal skills by interacting with group members. Group members help each other out by discussing pragmatic concerns members may currently be having. An example of this would be group members coaching an individual on how to manage current triggers of wanting to use a substance as a way of coping. These groups are used to improve group members' self-esteem and self-confidence. Group leaders and group members offer words of support and encouragement to each other. Support groups can be found in all stages of substance use treatment. Learning specific recovery tools, such as relapse-prevention skills, can be the basis of forming a substance use support group.[f]

Interpersonal process groups use psychodynamics, or knowledge of the way people function psychologically, to promote change in substance use recovery. The psychodynamic approach recognizes that unresolved conflicts in the mind (some that may be out of the person's awareness) may be influencing the person's behavior. Early experiences in the person's life may be influencing the person's substance rise. The

(continued)

Group Therapy with Substance Use Disorders* (*continued*)

individual's perceptions may be distorting his or her reality, and behaviors, such as the use of a substance, may be chosen to deal with the situation.[g]

STAGES-OF-CHANGE THERAPY FOR SUBSTANCE USERS

The stages-of-change therapy model can be used for group therapy for substance users. This model uses the transtheoretical model of change to describe how people make successful changes in their lives. The transtheoretical model of change is based on research completed by Prochaska and Diclemente.[h] This model agrees that change does not happen all at once and it takes time and energy to change. This model notes five distinct stages of change: precontemplation, contemplation, preparation, action, and maintenance. (See Chapter 12 for an expanded description of this approach.) Treatment strategies for the group are based on the stages-of-change model. It is important for the leaders of the group to be aware of the stages of change, determine what stage of change group members are in, and then develop activities to motivate individuals to move along the stages of change.[i]

The change process starts with an individual not knowing that a change needs to take place. This stage is called the precontemplation stage. In this stage substance abuse users do not see their using as a problem. If there is a problem, the person is probably ignoring it or does not consider the problem as something that is important. When the problem can no longer be ignored—for example, a partner no longer wants to be with the user because of the using behavior—the individual may begin to consider that he or she needs to do something about his or her using. This stage is seen as the contemplation stage of change. If the problem continues to grow and the individual begins to make plans to change, this is considered the preparation stage of the change process. When individuals start the action stage of change, their mental, physical, and social forces have been organized and they begin to take steps to make the change. If the clients continue to maintain the change, it is said that they are in the maintenance stage of change. This model does expect and prepares for individuals to possibly go back to the problem behavior.[j]

EXERCISE: "A DAY IN THE LIFE"

An example of an exercise that could be completed in a group setting with clients who are in the precontemplation or contemplation stage of change with their substance use is as follows:

Goal

The name of the exercise is called "A Day in the Life." The change-process objective for the exercise is for group members

to raise consciousness of their drinking during the day. This exercise helps raise consciousness about the quantity and frequency of their substance use. Clients in the early stages of change are often unaware of how much and how often they are drinking. Students could complete this exercise by thinking about something that they would like to change in their lives.

Step 1

The facilitator of the group explains in a nonthreatening way that sometimes it is difficult for people to realize how much they are using in a day.

Step 2

The facilitator hands out a worksheet and has the clients answer the following questions: describe your use from the time you wake up in the morning until around noon; describe your using from noon until early evening, and describe your use from around 6 P.M. until you go to bed. Students could answer the same questions about the identified behavior that they would like to change.

Step 3

Ask the clients to discuss what they have learned about their substance use by doing the exercise. Discuss with the group members when this use may be less or may be more. Students could discuss what they have learned about their desired behavior they want to change and reflect on what they learned about the duration and frequency of the behavior they would like to change. Students could discuss the importance of raising consciousness of a behavior in the early stages of the change process.[k]

---

*   This material was written by Katherine Drechsler and Dr. Sarah Hessenauer. Ms. Drechsler is a lecturer at the University of Wisconsin–Whitewater and is a doctoral student in social work at George Williams College. Dr. Hessenauer is an associate professor and chair of the Social Work Department at the University of Wisconsin–Whitewater.

a.   Harris, J., & Hill, R. (2011). *Principles and practice of group work in addictions.* New York, NY: Routledge.

b.   Center for Substance Abuse Treatment. (2005). *Substance abuse treatment group therapy.* Rockville, MD: Substance Abuse and Mental Health Services Administration. (Treatment Improvement Protocol [TIP] Series, No. 41.) Retrieved from http://www.ncbi.nlm.mh.gov/books/NBK64220/.

c.   Ibid.

d.   Ibid.

e.   Ibid

f.   Ibid.

g.   Ibid.

h.   Prochaska, J. O., & DiClemente, C. C. (1982). Trans-theoretical therapy toward a more integrative model of change. *Psychotherapy Theory, Research and Practice 19*(3), 276–288.

i.   Crouch, C., DiClemente, C., Maner, G., & Velasquez, M. (2001). *Group treatment for substance abuse: A stages-of-change therapy manual.* New York, NY: The Guilford Press.

j.   Ibid.

k.   Ibid.

Sensitivity and Encounter Training

Encounter groups, sensitivity training groups, and T (training) groups all refer to a group experience in which people relate to each other in a close interpersonal manner and self-disclosure is required. The goal is to improve interpersonal awareness. The goal of sensitivity training groups is to have members develop an increased sensitive awareness and understanding of oneself and one's relationships with others. Members participate in discussions and experiential activities to improve interpersonal awareness.[16]

An encounter group may meet for a few hours or over a few days. Once increased interpersonal awareness is achieved, it is anticipated that attitudes and behaviors will change. For these changes to occur, a three-phase process generally takes place: **unfreezing**, **change**, and **refreezing**.[17]

Unfreezing occurs in encounter groups through a deliberate process of interacting in nontraditional ways. Our attitudes and behavior patterns have been developed through years of social experiences. Such patterns, following years of experimentation and refinement, have now become nearly automatic. The interpersonal style we develop through years of trial and error generally has considerable utility in our everyday interactions. Deep down, however, we may recognize a need for improvement but are reluctant to make the effort, partly because our present style is somewhat functional and partly because we are afraid to reveal things about ourselves. Unfreezing occurs when we decide certain patterns of our present behavior need to be changed and we are psychologically ready to explore ways to make changes.

Tubbs and Baird describe the unfreezing process in sensitivity groups:

> Unfreezing occurs when our expectations are violated. We become less sure of ourselves when traditional ways of doing things are not followed. In the encounter group, the leader usually does not act like a leader. He or she frequently starts with a brief statement encouraging the group members to participate, to be open and honest, and to expect things to be different. Group members may begin by taking off their shoes, sitting in a circle on the floor, and holding hands with their eyes closed. The leader then encourages them to feel intensely the sensations they are experiencing, the size and texture of the hands they are holding, and so forth.
>
> Other structured exercises or experiences may be planned to help the group focus on the "here-and-now" experience. Pairs may go for "trust walks" in which each person alternately is led around with eyes closed. Sitting face to face and conducting a hand dialogue or a silent facial mirroring often helps to break the initial barriers to change. Other techniques may involve the "pass around" in which a person in the center of a tight circle relaxes and is physically passed around the circle. Those who have trouble feeling a part of the group are encouraged to break into or out of the circle of people whose hands are tightly held. With these experiences, most participants begin to feel more open to conversation about what they have experienced. This sharing of experiences or self-disclosure about the here and now provides more data for the group to discuss.[18]

The second phase of the process involves making changes in attitudes and behavior patterns, which are usually facilitated by spontaneous feedback as to how a person "comes across" to others. In everyday interaction, spontaneous feedback seldom occurs, so ineffective interaction patterns are repeated. In sensitivity groups, feedback is strongly encouraged, as the following interaction illustrates:

Carl: All right (in *a sharp tone*), let's get this trust walk over with and stop dillydally-
ing around. I'll lead the first person around—who wants to be blindfolded first?

Judy: I feel uncomfortable about your statement. I feel you are saying this group is
a waste of your time. Also, this appears to be your third attempt this evening to
"boss" us around.

Jim: I also feel like you are trying to tell us peons what to do. Even the tone of your
voice is autocratic and suggests some disgust with this group.

Carl: I'm sorry. I didn't mean it to sound like that. I wonder if I do that outside the
group too?

Such feedback provides us with new insights on how we affect others. Once problem interactions are identified, that member is encouraged to try out new response patterns in the relative safety of the group.

The third and final phase involves "refreezing," a term that is not an accurate description because it implies rigidity within a new set of response patterns. On the contrary, by experimenting with new sets of behaviors, a group member becomes a growing, continually changing person who becomes increasingly effective in interacting with others. In terminating a sensitivity group, the leader may alert the participants to be "on guard" as old behavior patterns tend to creep back in.

Sensitivity groups usually generate an outpouring of emotions, as do treatment groups. Sensitivity groups provide an interesting contrast to treatment groups. In treatment groups, each member explores personal and emotional problems in depth and then develops strategies to resolve them. Sensitivity groups generally do not directly attempt to identify and change specific emotional or personal problems, such as drinking, feelings of depression, or sexual dysfunctions. The philosophy behind sensitivity groups is that by simply increasing personal and interpersonal awareness, people will be better able to avoid, cope with, and handle specific personal problems that arise.

Despite their popularity, sensitivity groups remain controversial. In some cases, inadequately trained and incompetent individuals have become self-proclaimed leaders and enticed people to join through sensational advertising. If handled poorly, the short duration of some groups may intensify personal problems; for example, a person's defense mechanisms may be stripped away without first developing adaptive coping patterns. Many authorities on sensitivity training disclaim the use of encounter groups as a form of psychotherapy and discourage those with serious personal problems from joining such a group. Carl Rogers, in reviewing his own extensive experience as leader/participant, echoes these concerns:

> Frequently the behavior changes that occur, if any, are not lasting. In addition, the individual may become deeply involved in revealing himself and then be left with problems which are not worked through. Less common, but still noteworthy, there are also very occasional accounts of an individual having a psychotic episode during or immediately following an intensive group experience. We must keep in mind that not all people are suited for groups.[19]

In some cases, the popularity of sensitivity groups has led some individuals to enter harmful groups with incompetent leaders where normal ethical standards have been abused. Shostrom has identified some means by which those interested in encounter groups can prevent exploitation: (1) Never participate in a group of fewer than a half-dozen members. The necessary and valuable candor generated by an effective group cannot be dissipated, shared, or examined by too small a group, and scapegoating or purely vicious ganging up can develop. (2) Never join an encounter group on impulse—as a fling, binge, or surrender to the unplanned. (3) Never stay with a group that has a behavioral ax to grind. (4) Never participate in a group that lacks formal connection with a professional who has proper credentials.[20]

After reviewing the research on the outcome of sensitivity groups, Lieberman, Yalom, and Miles provide an appropriate perspective for those interested in the intensive group experience:

> Encounter groups present a clear and evident danger if they are used for radical surgery to produce a new man [person]. The danger is even greater when the leader and the participants share this misconception. If we no longer expect groups to produce magical, lasting change and if we stop seeing them as panaceas, we can regard them as useful, socially sanctioned opportunities for human beings to explore and to express themselves. Then we can begin to work on ways to improve them so that they may make a meaningful contribution toward solving human problems.[21]

Contrasting Goals of Treatment Groups versus Sensitivity Groups

TREATMENT GROUPS

Step 1: Examine problems in depth.
Step 2: Develop and select from various resolution approaches a strategy to resolve the problem.

SENSITIVITY GROUPS

Step 1: Help each person become more aware of himself or herself and how he or she affects others in interpersonal interactions.
Step 2: Help a person develop more effective interaction patterns.

INITIAL DEVELOPMENT OF GROUPS

The process of establishing and conducting groups varies significantly, depending on the type of group and the specific purposes to be achieved. However, for a group to reach its maximum potential, some unifying or common elements still need to be addressed prior to establishing the group. These factors described in this section include determining a group's objectives, size, open-ended or closed-ended status, and duration. In addition, because specific pitfalls or dilemmas characterize certain types of groups, plans must be made to prevent or handle problems should they arise.

Determining Objectives

Careful consideration must be given to the objectives for a group being formed in order to select effective members. For example, problem-solving groups often require the expertise of professionals in other disciplines—professionals whose skills and knowledge directly contribute to the accomplishment of group goals; some of these professionals may have backgrounds, training, and perceptions that differ from those of the social worker. Although this approach produces a group with a wealth of expertise, it creates additional demands on the leader. When the members have diverse backgrounds and interests, other difficulties include problems encountered in setting goals, prioritizing goals, and determining tasks to be performed. Educational groups, on the other hand, are usually composed of members who share a common interest in a particular area, such as childrearing skills. Individuals with similar needs join an educational group primarily to gain rather than dispense information. This tends to make leadership easier. Because potential members of treatment groups (unlike those of problem-solving or educational groups) often have diverse problems and may also have interactional difficulties, a much more thorough screening of members is required. Therefore, it is essential that the objectives or purposes of each group be established at the beginning because they have a significant impact on the process of membership selection and other aspects of functioning.

Size

The size of a group affects members' satisfaction, interaction, and the amount of output per member. Although smaller groups are generally rated more favorably, larger groups are often more successful in resolving complex problems.[22] Although members in larger groups experience more stress and greater communication difficulties, they usually bring a greater number of problem-solving skills and resources to the group as a whole. Because each person has fewer opportunities to interact in a large group, some members feel inhibited and reluctant to talk. As the size of the group increases, discussion generally hinges on the input of the most frequent contributor, who assumes a dominant role. As a result, the gap in participation widens between the most frequent contributor and the other members of the group.

In his research on group size, Slater found that groups of five people were considered most satisfactory by members themselves and most effective in dealing with an intellectual task involving the collection and exchange of information about a situation; the coordination, analysis, and evaluation of this information; and a group decision regarding the appropriate administrative action to be taken.[23] In a group of five members, a number of different relationships can be formed with a moderate level of intimacy. Several individuals can also act as "buffers" who deal with strained situations or power plays. If a vote is needed to resolve a dispute, obviously a two-two split can be avoided. In groups smaller than five, Slater observed, the members were inhibited from expressing their ideas through fear of alienating one another and thereby destroying the group. In groups of more than five, members also felt inhibited and participated less often.

Groups with an even number of members tend to have higher rates of disagreement and antagonism than those with an odd number, apparently because of the possible division of the group into two equal subdivisions.[24] For each task to be accomplished, there is probably an optimal group size. The more complex the task, the larger the optimal size, so that the knowledge, abilities, and skills of many members are available to accomplish the task. A group should be large enough to allow members to speak freely without being inhibited and small enough to permit a moderate level of intimacy and involvement.

Open-Ended versus Closed-Ended Groups

Whether the group will be open ended, with new members added as old members leave, or whether the membership will remain constant until termination (closed ended) should be determined at the outset. **Open-ended groups** provide a measure of synergism through the addition of new members. As new individuals join, they provide a different viewpoint, even though they usually are gradually socialized into group norms and practices by the older members. The impact of such changes is not all beneficial, however. The constant change in membership may inhibit openness and detract from the sense of trust needed before certain subjects are broached. In addition, open groups are likely to "have members at different levels of commitment to the process and members [who are not] at the same stages of development."[25]

A **closed-ended group** can often function more effectively because it has a relatively constant population and often operates within a specified time frame.[26] Although the premature loss of members can seriously damage such a group's effectiveness, a leader must deal with member termination in both open and closed groups and plan for this eventuality.

Duration

The duration of a group has two related components: the number of sessions and the length of each session. Many groups meet for 1 to 2 hours once or twice a week for a specified number of weeks. Meeting for 1 to 2 hours tends to optimize productive activity and behavior. Meeting lengths shorter than 1 hour usually do not allow sufficient time to thoroughly discuss the issues that are raised. In meetings that last longer than 3 hours, members tend to become drowsy, frustrated, and unable to concentrate. Although a meeting length of 1 to 2 hours appears to be a guideline for optimal functioning in many groups, at times pressing issues may necessitate a longer meeting to process and conclude group business. Obviously, if a crisis occurs 5 minutes before the end of the meeting, the group leader should not conclude the session. By the same token, some discussions can become so intense that they could last indefinitely and accomplish little. A pragmatic approach to terminating each meeting or series of meetings within a set time frame will enhance the group's respect for the leader and foster the group's development.

Setting meetings in which there are 3 or 4 (or more) days between meetings usually allows the members some time to work on tasks that are designed to accomplish their personal goals and the goals of the group. For example, in educational groups, members can study and complete homework assignments between meetings. In treatment groups, members can carry out homework assignments designed to reduce or resolve personal problems.

STAGES OF GROUPS

The steps involved in planning and implementing educational, treatment, and socialization groups are similar to the procedures followed by social workers who deal with individual clients:

GROUPS	INDIVIDUALS
intake	intake
selection of members	assessment and planning
assessment and planning	intervention
group development and intervention	evaluation and termination
evaluation and termination	

Inexperienced group leaders usually expect a smooth transition from one stage to another and are disappointed if this does not occur. Therefore, many new practitioners tend to force the group out of one stage into another instead of allowing the natural growth process to evolve. Experience will demonstrate the futility of these efforts as, barring unforeseen circumstances, each group will move at its own pace and eventually arrive at the same destination. Groups that skip stages or whose development is otherwise thwarted will often return to a previous stage to complete unfinished business. Although groups do sometimes become mired in one stage, these occurrences are less common than generally thought. The procedures for establishing socialization, educational, and treatment groups are briefly summarized in the following material and expanded upon throughout the text.

Intake

During intake, the presenting concerns and needs of prospective members are identified. Judgments that some or all of these people could benefit from a group approach are made. An agreement is often formulated between the members of the group and the group leader about tentative group goals (see Chapter 4). This stage may also be referred to as the contract stage, as the leader and the members make a commitment to pursue the situation to the next step.

Selection of Members

Individuals most likely to benefit from a group should be selected as members. Selecting a group requires attention to both descriptive and behavioral factors.[27] A decision needs to be made whether to seek homogeneity or diversity in these factors. There are few guidelines as to when diversity and when homogeneity of these factors will be most effective and efficient. Age, sex, and level of education are **descriptive factors** that may create homogeneity or foster diversity within the group. In groups of children and adolescents, the age span among members must be kept relatively small because levels of maturity and interests can vary greatly. Similarly, same-sex groupings may facilitate achieving group goals for preadolescents, but for middle-adolescent groups there may be specific advantages to having representation from both sexes.

The **behavioral attributes** expected of a group member will also have a major effect on the attainment of group objectives. For example, placing several hyperactive or aggressive youngsters in a group may be a prelude to failure. Members may be selected for their value as models for appropriate behavior or because they possess other personal characteristics expected to enhance the group. As a general rule, the best judgment regarding a member's potential contribution to the group is obtained by looking at past behavioral attributes.[28]

Assessment and Planning

A more in-depth assessment and statement of goals and plans for action occur during this phase. In reality, this step is completed only when the group ends because the dynamic nature of most groups requires an ongoing adjustment of goals and intervention plans. Goals should be time limited with a reasonable chance for attainment, and the leader should ensure that all goals are clearly stated to aid in later evaluations. Clarification of goals also eliminates hidden agendas.

Group Development and Intervention

Numerous models of group development have evolved. Four of these models are described in the following section of this chapter, entitled "Models of Group Development over Time."

Evaluation and Termination

To think of evaluation as a specific point in the life of a group is perhaps not realistic because evaluation must be an ongoing process. The decision to terminate a group may be based on the accomplishment of group or individual goals, the expiration of a predetermined period of time, the failure of the group to achieve desired ends, the relocation of the leader of the group, or a shortage of funds to keep the group going.

The termination of a group often produces the same reactions that characterize the termination of other significant relationships, including the feeling of being rejected. The group leader must be aware of these potential feelings and help group members terminate with a minimum of difficulty. Additional material on how to terminate a group is presented in Chapter 14.

LO 3   Understand Four Models of Group Development over Time

EP 6a
EP 7b

MODELS OF GROUP DEVELOPMENT OVER TIME

Groups change over time. Numerous framework models have been developed to describe these changes. The models of group development described here are (1) the Garland, Jones, and Kolodny Model; (2) the Tuckman Model; (3) the Northen and Kurland Model; and (4) the Bales Model.

Garland, Jones, and Kolodny Model

Garland, Jones, and Kolodny developed a model that identifies live stages of development in social work groups.[29] By describing and understanding the various kinds of developmental problems in groups, leaders can more effectively anticipate and respond to the reactions of group members. The conceptualization of Garland et al. appears particularly applicable to socialization, therapeutic, and encounter groups; to a lesser extent, the model is applicable to self-help, task, problem-solving and decision-making, educational, and recreation/skill groups.

Emotional closeness among members is the central focus of the model and is reflected in **struggles** that occur at five stages of group growth: preaffiliation, power and control, intimacy, differentiation, and separation.

Preaffiliation   In the first stage, **preaffiliation**, members are ambivalent about joining the group and interaction is guarded. Members test out, often through approach and avoidance behavior, whether they really want to belong. Because new situations are often frightening, members attempt to protect themselves from being hurt or taken advantage of, maintaining a certain amount of distance and attempting to get what they can from the group without taking many risks. Even though individuals are aware that group involvement will make demands that may be frustrating or even painful, they are attracted because of rewards and satisfying experiences in other groups. These former positive ramifications are transferred to the "new" group. During this first stage, the leader tries to make the group appear as attractive as possible "by allowing and supporting distance, gently inviting trust, facilitating exploration of the physical and psychological milieu, and by providing activities if necessary and initiating group structure."[30] This stage ends gradually as members begin to feel safe and comfortable within the group and to view its rewards as worth a tentative emotional commitment.

Power and Control   In the second stage, **power and control**, the character of the group begins to emerge. Patterns of communication, alliances, and subgroups begin to develop.

Individuals assume certain roles and responsibilities, establish norms and methods for handling group tasks, and begin to ask questions. Although these processes are necessary to conduct meetings, they also lead to a power struggle, in which each member attempts to gain greater control over the gratifications and rewards to be received from the group. A major source of gratification for any group is the leader, who influences the direction of the group and gives or withholds emotional and material rewards. At this point, members realize that the group is becoming important to them. This second stage is transitional, with certain basic issues requiring resolution: Does the group or the leader have primary control? What are the limits of the power of the group and of the leader, and to what extent will the leader use his or her power?

This uncertainty results in anxiety and considerable testing by group members to gauge limits and establish norms for the power and authority of both the group and the leader. Rebellion is not uncommon, and the dropout rate in groups is often highest at this stage. During this struggle the leader should (1) help the members understand the nature of the power struggle, (2) give emotional support to help members weather the discomfort of uncertainty, and (3) help establish norms to resolve the uncertainty. Group members must trust the leader to maintain a safe balance of shared power and control. When that trust is achieved, group members make a major commitment to become involved.

Intimacy   In the third stage, **intimacy**, the likes and dislikes of intimate relationships are expressed. The group becomes more like a family, with sibling rivalry exhibited and with the leader sometimes referred to as a parent. Feelings are more openly expressed and discussed, and the group is viewed as a place where growth and change take place. Individuals feel free to examine and make efforts to change personal attitudes, concerns, and problems, and there is a feeling of "oneness" or cohesiveness. Members struggle to explore and make changes in their personal lives and to examine "what this group is all about."

Differentiation   During the fourth stage, **differentiation**, members are freer to experiment with new and alternative behavior patterns because they recognize individual rights and needs, and they communicate more effectively. Leadership is more evenly shared, roles are more functional, and the organization itself is more efficient. Power problems are now minimal, and decisions are made and carried out on a less emotional and more objective basis. Garland and Frey note:

> This kind of individualized therapeutic cohesion has been achieved because the group experience has all along valued and nurtured individual integrity. . .
>
> The worker assists in this stage by helping the group to run itself and by encouraging it to act as a unit with other groups or in the wider community. During this time the [social] worker exploits opportunities for evaluation by the group of its activities, feelings and behavior.[31]

The differentiation stage is analogous to a healthy functioning family in which the children have reached adulthood and are now becoming successful in pursuing their own lives. Relationships are more often between equals, and members are mutually supportive and able to relate to each other in more rational and objective ways.

Separation   The final stage is **separation**. Group purposes have been achieved, and members have learned new behavioral patterns to enable them to move on to other social experiences. Termination is not always easily accomplished, as members may be reluctant to move on and may display regressive behavior to prolong the existence of the group. Members may express anger or may psychologically deny that termination is approaching. Garland and Frey describe the leader's (or social worker's) role this way:

> To facilitate separation the [social] worker must be willing to let go. Concentration upon group and individual mobility, evaluation of the experience, help with the expression of the ambivalence about termination and recognition of the progress which has

EXERCISE 1.1   The Garland, Jones, and Kolodny Model

GOAL: This exercise is designed to help you analyze groups in terms of the Garland, Jones, and Kolodny Model.

Write a description of a group that you have participated in that has at least some of the group development stages identified by the Garland, Jones, and Kolodny Model. Identify the stages of your group that are consistent with the model. Also describe any developmental stages of your group that are inconsistent with this model.

been made are his major tasks. Acceptance of termination is facilitated by active guidance of members as individuals to other ongoing sources of support and assistance.[32]

Tuckman Model

Tuckman reviewed more than 50 studies, primarily of limited-duration therapy and sensitivity groups, and concluded that these groups go through the following five predictable developmental stages: forming, storming, norming, performing, and adjourning.[33] Each stage will be briefly described.

Forming   Members become oriented toward each other, work on being accepted, and learn more about the group. This stage is marked by a period of uncertainty in which members try to determine their places in the group and learn the group's rules and procedures.

Storming   Conflicts begin to arise as members resist the influence of the group and rebel against accomplishing their tasks. Members confront their various differences, and the management of conflict often becomes the focus of attention.

Norming   The group establishes cohesiveness and commitment. In the process, the members discover new ways to work together. Norms are also set for appropriate behavior.

Performing   The group works as a unit to achieve group goals. Members develop proficiency in achieving goals and become more flexible in their patterns of working together.

Adjourning   The group disbands. The feelings that members experience are similar to those in the "separation stage" of the Garland, Jones, and Kolodny Model described in the previous section.

EXERCISE 1.2   The Tuckman Model

GOAL: This exercise is designed to help you analyze groups in terms of the Tuckman Model.

Write a description of a group that you have participated in that has at least some of the group development stages identified by the Tuckman Model. Identify the stages of your group that are consistent with the model. Also describe any developmental stages of your group that are inconsistent with this model.

Northen and Kurland Model*

Northen and Kurland focus on stages of group development and point out that each stage has its own developmental issues that must be attended to and at least partially resolved before the group can move into the next stage.[34] Northen and Kurland propose a four-stage model with emphasis on socioemotional themes.

Inclusion-Orientation   The main socioemotional theme of this stage, as the title implies, is whether or not group members will feel included. This stage is typically marked by anxiety and uncertainty as group members become acquainted with the group leader and each other. "The major task for the members is to become oriented to the group and to decide to be included in the group's membership."[35]

Uncertainty-Exploration   The major theme of this stage has to do with group members' uncertainty regarding issues of power and control. The socioemotional issue pertains to conflict, especially in relation to the group leader. Group members at this stage explore and test their relationships with the leader and each other in order to establish roles and develop trust and acceptance.

Mutuality-Goal Achievement   At this stage, the group is characterized by mutual aid and problem solving. Socioemotional patterns among group members show greater self-disclosure, empathy, and mutual acceptance. Conflict and differences are dealt with as a means to achieve both individual and group goals.

Separation-Termination   The final stage focuses on the socioemotional issues of separation and termination. Members at this stage may be reluctant to leave the leader and the group. The task here is to help prepare members for termination, deal with any unfinished business, and, most important, help group members transfer what they have learned in group to life outside the group.

---

*   The description of this model was written by Michael Wallace, MSW, retired instructor of the University of Wisconsin–Whitewater.

EXERCISE 1.3   The Northen and Kurland Model

GOAL: This exercise is designed to help you analyze groups in terms of the Northen and Kurland Model.

Write a description of a group that you have participated in that has at least some of the group development stages identified by the Northen and Kurland Model. Identify the stages of your group that are consistent with the model. Also describe any developmental stages of your group that are inconsistent with this model.

Sequential-Stage Models of Group Development

The three models of group development that were just described are sequential-stage models. Despite the variable nature of the stages of group development described in these three models, these models contain similar stages. As can be seen in Table 1.1, the various phases of group development can be divided into three phases: beginning, middle, and end.

In sequential models, the beginning stages of groups are concerned with planning, organizing, convening, and orientation. The beginnings of groups tend to be characterized by an emergence of group feeling. However, group feeling does not emerge without a struggle. Power issues and conflicts between members often emerge. The leader can help resolve power issues and conflicts by encouraging members to discuss and seek to resolve the power issues and conflicts that arise. (Strategies to resolve conflicts and power issues are described in Chapter 6.)

TABLE 1.1   Sequential-Stage Models of Group Development

Development Stage	Garland, Jones, and Kolodny	Tuckman	Northen and Kurland
Beginning	Preaffiliation Power and control	Forming	Inclusion–Orientation Uncertainty–Exploration
Middle	Intimacy	Storming	Mutuality–Goal Achievement
	Differentiation	Norming Performing	
End	Separation	Adjourning	Separation–Termination

Although some work is accomplished in all stages of a group's development, most occurs in the middle stage. At the beginning of the middle stage, the conflicts over roles, norms, and power issues found in the later part of the beginning stage give way to the members' learning effective patterns of working together. Greater group cohesion appears. When this occurs, members concern themselves with the work necessary to accomplish the specific tasks (and achieve the goals) that have been agreed upon.

The end stage of a group is characterized by the completion and evaluation of the group's efforts and by members terminating their contact with one another in this specific group. In this stage, task groups tend to make decisions, finish their business, produce the results of their efforts, and celebrate the accomplishments. On the other hand, treatment group members (because they have focused on emotional and behavioral issues) often experience the termination of the group as an emotional loss. They are pleased that they have made progress in resolving their issues but have a reluctance to lose the support they have received from the group. Termination is described in more detail in Chapter 6 and in Chapter 12.

For the interested reader, a relational model of group development stages in women's groups is described in Chapter 7.

Bales Model

The stages described in the models of group development that were just discussed are sequential-stage models, as they specify sequential stages of group development. In contrast, Robert F. Bales developed a recurring-phase model.[36] Bales asserted that groups continue to seek an equilibrium between task-oriented work and emotional expressions in order to build better relationships among group members. (Task roles and social/emotional roles performed by members of a group are specified at some length in Chapter 3.) Bales asserts that groups tend to oscillate between these two concerns. Sometimes a group focuses on identifying and performing the tasks that will lead to achievement of its goals. At other times, the group focuses on building the morale and improving the social/emotional atmosphere of the group.

The sequential-stage perspective and the recurring-phase perspective are not necessarily contradictory. Both are useful for understanding group development. The sequential-stage perspective assumes that groups move through various stages while dealing with a series of basic themes that surface when they are relevant to the group's work. The recurring-phase perspective assumes that the issues underlying these basic themes are never completely resolved and tend to recur later.

GROUP COHESION

Group cohesion is the sum of all the variables influencing members to stay in a group. It occurs when the positive attractions of a group outweigh the negative implications a member might encounter. The word **cohesion** is derived from Latin and can be translated literally as the "act of sticking together." A group's level of cohesion is constantly changing as events alter each member's feelings and attitudes about the group.

The extent of a member's attraction to and involvement in a group can be measured by his or her perceptions of the payoffs and costs. They are infinite because they vary from individual to individual, but the following lists offer a brief indication of possibilities:

PAYOFFS	COSTS
companionship	being with people one dislikes
attaining person1al goals	expending time and effort
prestige	criticism
enjoyment	distasteful tasks
emotional support	boring meetings

The higher the level of attraction (payoffs), the greater the attractive qualities of cohesion.

An individual's willingness to risk and to become involved in a group depends to a large extent on the degree to which his or her needs for belonging are met. Often, members join groups to help meet the need to belong. Membership in a group or a person's willingness to share himself or herself often hinges on the degree of acceptance experienced in the group. The climate in a group is a crucial factor in determining the actual sense of belonging that members achieve. Clearly, the need for belonging can be a powerful factor in joining and remaining a member of groups.

Obviously, group members are most attracted to group meetings when friendly, pleasant interactions take place. Besides feeling relaxed, members are more apt to share their ideas and relate to others within the group. Initially, icebreaker exercises can help members become more comfortable, and goals can be set that incorporate the personal goals of members (see Chapter 4). The more members feel involved in making decisions, the more they will feel that their views are respected.

Highly cohesive groups have low rates of absenteeism and low turnover in membership. In addition, members are generally motivated to complete assigned tasks, and they are apt to conform to group norms. They are more willing to listen, accept suggestions, and defend the group against external criticism. Because a group provides a source of security, it often rewards members by becoming a support system that reduces anxiety, heightens self-esteem, adds meaning to living, and often helps members resolve personal problems. Therefore, membership in a cohesive group enhances a member's psychological health by transmitting feelings of being valued, accepted, and liked.

Members should be rewarded for jobs well done rather than coerced or manipulated to help create a cooperative atmosphere, not a competitive one. Again, pleasing interactions, rather than a constant war of words or negative banter, increase a group's cohesion. If a difficult situation arises, a problem-solving approach should be used. A win–lose approach usually decreases cohesion (see Chapter 6).

Trust among group members is another necessary condition for effective communication, cooperation, and cohesion. When distrust exists, individuals will not disclose sensitive

EXERCISE 1.4   Variables that Affect Group Cohesion

GOAL: This exercise is designed to help you understand the variables that contribute to group cohesion.

1. Describe a highly cohesive group (perhaps a sports team, a group at school, or a church group) that you participated in. Identify the variables that contributed to group cohesion.

2. Describe a group that you have participated in that has very little cohesion. Identify the variables that led this group to have very little cohesion.

personal information or commit their resources to accomplishing group goals. Even though some groups have "built-in" prestige, being a member of certain groups can potentially damage a member's reputation (for example, a member of a board of directors of a nursing home beset by a well-publicized scandal involving extensive patient abuse).

A group's cohesion will generally decrease when there is a long-term disagreement on how to define or resolve a major problem. Unreasonable or excessive demands on members, such as forcing a shy person to give a speech, will also sharply reduce the group's attractiveness. Dominating members and those who engage in repulsive behavior are certainly not large drawing cards. Scapegoats who are blamed for difficult situations may react aggressively or drop out. Finally, cohesion can be decreased if outside activities of the members are curtailed because of the group. For example, a student group that meets 2 or 3 nights a week may interfere with study time, exercising, and socializing.

LO 4 Describe the Differences Between Reference Groups and Membership Groups

MEMBERSHIP AND REFERENCE GROUPS

A **membership group** is a group in which a person belongs or does not belong. However, some people are marginal members of a group. For example, everyone enrolled at a college campus is a member of the student body, but some students are only marginal members because they are not involved in any campus activities. Carol works nearly full-time in the evening and does not live on campus, but she does attend classes. She identifies primarily with the people she works with, and other students influence her very little. Carol, then, has limited psychological membership in the student body and only minor identification with the campus. Full psychological membership in a group occurs only when a person is positively attracted to the group and accepted as a member. The more fully a person is a member of a group, the greater will be that person's commitment to accomplishing group goals.

Individuals who aspire to membership in a group will act as the members act. Students who want to be admitted to a fraternity or sorority, for example, will act like members to increase their chances of being admitted. Aspiring members are psychologically identifying with the group, even though they are not members.

Voluntary membership is freely chosen, whereas **involuntary membership** is required. Social workers often work with involuntary groups in prison settings, mental hospitals, residential treatment facilities, and schools, where members are often uninterested, hostile, or disruptive.

Practically all of us are members of a variety of groups. Jim, for example, is a family member, a Roman Catholic, a PTA member, a forward on a basketball team, a member of the National Association of Social Workers, and a member of the local board of Planned Parenthood. Occasionally there are conflicts because the groups may schedule meetings at the same time and have different norms and values. Planned Parenthood's views on birth control and abortion, for example, differ from those espoused by the Catholic Church. To resolve this dilemma, Jim can compartmentalize his values by accepting Planned Parenthood's views on abortion and birth control and most of the Catholic doctrine except the Church's views on abortion and birth control. The resolution of conflicts resulting from multiple memberships is often attained through much anxiety and great personal cost.

Reference groups are groups whose influence we accept and identify with. In the example given earlier, Carol is a member of a student body and a work group. Because she primarily identifies with her work group, it serves as a reference group for her, but the student body does not. Reference groups have two distinct functions: (1) normative, for members who seek to conform to their positions and standards for behavior; and (2) decision making, for members who use group standards, or norms, as the basis for making and evaluating decisions.

Some members of a group are referents who influence and are influenced by other members. In a large group, only a small subgroup of members are referents. These referents "make sense" to other members (who identify with them), as they are viewed as experts or authorities, or have most of the power. Occasionally, people select a reference group in terms of an issue. For example, Jim uses Planned Parenthood as a reference group to express his feelings on birth control and abortion, whereas he uses the Catholic Church as a reference group for his views on suicide, euthanasia, life after death, and morality.

BREAKING THE ICE

In most newly formed groups, the leader has the initial responsibility of seeking to create an atmosphere in which members feel comfortable. Members of a new group are apt to have a number of concerns: "Will I be respected and accepted?" "Will this group be worth my time and effort?" "Will I feel embarrassed or inferior?" "Will I be able to form new friendships?" "Are the other members the kind of people I will like?" "What will my roles and responsibilities be—and will I like them?" "Will I have a leadership role?" "Will others expect more of me than I am capable of giving?" "Will my personal goals or expectations be realized?" "If I find I do not like or enjoy this group, is there a nice way to get out?"

To help members become comfortable, the leader might use an ice-breaker exercise. (Several such exercises are described at the end of this chapter.) Such exercises are designed to help members become acquainted with one another, introduce themselves, reduce anxieties, and facilitate communication. Each group has a unique personality. In most social work groups, the leader attempts to create an atmosphere in which the members trust one another and want to share their thoughts and ideas. Ice breakers are an important step in establishing such an atmosphere.

As a student, you have probably observed that each class has a unique personality. Norms are established in their first few sessions, for example, as to whether students will share and discuss their opinions and beliefs. If a norm of "silence" is established, the instructor generally ends up doing practically all the talking. Such a class becomes a "chore"

EXERCISE 1.5   Understanding Membership and Reference Groups

GOAL: This exercise is designed to help you understand the concepts of reference groups and membership groups.

1. Identify a group that you are a member of that is not a reference group for you. Why is it not a reference group for you?

2. Identify a group that you are a member of that is a reference group for you. Describe why you identify with this reference group.

for the instructor and for the students. Many of the ingredients that go into determining whether a class will establish a norm of "talking" or of "silence" are unknown. Certainly, a norm of talking is facilitated by ice breakers.

Ice-breaking exercises can also accomplish specific objectives, such as obtaining information on the members' expectations for the group. One such ice breaker is described at the end of this chapter. Before we consider ice-breaker exercises, the pitfalls, ethics, and guidelines on conducting classroom exercises will be summarized.

EXPERIENTIAL LEARNING

It is important that social work students receive experiential training in classes to prepare them for the realities of social work practice. Social workers encounter many sensitive situations in the course of their work: divorce, suicide, child abuse and neglect, incest, and death. In a classroom, a qualified instructor observes the level of psychological stress in participants, provides feedback on how to better handle sensitive situations, and intervenes if necessary. After students graduate and begin working with clients, such guidance is seldom available. Therefore, it is vital that they develop their skills through practical classroom applications before they venture into real group counseling situations.

Classroom exercises offer a variety of payoffs. They can illustrate key theoretical concepts, clarify values, or help students develop skills such as assessment and intervention. They are generally fun and often teach students more effectively than other mechanisms. Exercises also help students get acquainted, build group cohesion, and increase group morale.

LO 5   Comprehend Guidelines on How to Conduct Classroom Exercises

EP1a

Ethics and Guidelines for Conducting Exercises

1. The leader has the tasks of explaining the objectives, describing the steps, beginning the exercise, keeping the members on task and on time, modeling appropriate values and skills, leading the members in discussing and evaluating the exercise after it is conducted, and being alert to the emotional reactions of the members to the exercise.
2. Generally, the more enthusiasm the instructor displays for class exercises, the more enthusiasm the students will display.
3. Students learn in different ways. Some will be more responsive and learn more from exercises than others.
4. The learning needs of the students should determine the kinds of exercises used. Leaders may want to modify the exercises in this text to meet special learning needs. In designing or modifying an exercise, leaders should consider the following questions: Is this the best exercise to accomplish the learning objectives? Should the exercise be modified to better fit the characteristics of the group? How can processing of the exercise be best accomplished? Is there sufficient class time to conduct the exercise? Is the group too large or too small for the exercise? Are the required materials available? What problems may arise? Is there sufficient time to process problems?
5. To allot enough time, the leaders should estimate how much time each step in the exercise will take.
6. When an exercise is introduced, group members should be informed of the objectives, given an overview of what will occur, and encouraged to ask questions. Members have a right to expect clear information before beginning the exercise. To build trust, the leader should not give false information or incorrect answers to questions. If an accurate answer to a question raised before the exercise is conducted will reveal information the exercise is designed to convey, the leader may say, "It is best to delay answering this question, as the exercise is designed to reveal the answer."
7. The instructor should always be present when an exercise is being conducted.

8. The leader should have specific educational objectives for each exercise and be able to articulate these objectives. Students have the right to know what the objectives are. (If stating the objectives at the beginning will "give away" a point hidden in the exercise, the objectives should be carefully explained at the end.)

9. The leader should carefully plan each exercise and be qualified to conduct it. The exercises in this text are explained in considerable detail. The leader should prepare for each exercise by reading and visualizing the steps and by thinking about how this specific class might respond.

10. A few exercises may arouse strong emotions because they may touch an area in which a student is struggling. The instructor should thus observe students closely, be prepared to talk privately with such students after class, and be aware of appropriate counseling resources for students whose psychological stress is severe.

11. The instructor should seek to establish a supportive, caring, and respectful atmosphere among the students.

12. The class should understand the importance of keeping sensitive personal information confidential.

13. Once the objectives and format of an exercise are explained, student participation should be voluntary. Students who do not wish to participate should be excused with the understanding that every student is expected to participate in most of the exercises.

14. No exercise should be so secretive or sensitive that other faculty could not be invited to observe.

15. It is generally better to use one or two exercises to demonstrate a point than to use several.

16. If numerous exercises are conducted during a term, the instructor should seek to have each student take an active role in at least some of them. Special efforts should be made to involve those students who are quiet and nonassertive.

17. The instructor should critique student skills or behavior in a positive way. The student should not be made to feel inferior, incompetent, or inadequate. When a shortcoming is pointed out, the student should also be praised for what she or he did well. The feedback should focus on behavior rather than on the person, on observations rather than on judgments. A problem-solving approach in which shortcomings are identified and alternatives for improvement provided works well. The feedback should focus on sharing ideas and information rather than on giving advice. The instructor should never embarrass a student in front of classmates, and sensitive subjects should be covered in a private meeting with that student.

18. The instructor should provide encouragement by being positive and by praising, at one time or another, each student for such actions as making positive contributions, putting forth effort, displaying progress, showing unique skills, or being perceptive and respectful of others.

19. After completion, each exercise should be discussed and evaluated in an open, relaxed atmosphere. Students must feel free to raise questions, express thoughts and concerns, and discuss the merits and shortcomings of the exercise. Such an evaluation brings about closure, which is important, and helps the leader improve the exercise for future use.

20. Even the most carefully designed exercises sometimes fail. An important instruction may have been left out. The students may be distracted by other concerns and fail to give the exercise their undivided attention. The exercise may be poorly designed. When an exercise flops, it is generally best to acknowledge that things did not go as planned. Attempting to cover up an obvious flop will only cause students to question the honesty and effectiveness of the leader. Humor can "take the edge off," and the leader may be able to achieve the learning objectives by using another closely related exercise. At times, an exercise may be a complete loss. How the instructor reacts will be a factor in determining the students' confidence in the instructor. In addition, an appropriate reaction will help students learn how to respond to failures in groups they lead. Because humans are fallible by nature, some exercises will not achieve the desired objectives, and instructors should learn from such mistakes.

Pitfalls to Avoid in Conducting Class Exercises

1. Class exercises are not designed to solve emotional problems. Certainly the leader should not seek to meet his or her emotional needs through such exercises.
2. Class exercises should not be used simply to fill class time. They should have legitimate teaching objectives and value.
3. An exercise should not be used if there is insufficient time to discuss or process the activity.
4. Exercises should not replace other forms of instruction, such as lectures.
5. Although some students enroll in social work and psychology courses to solve their own personal problems, experiential exercises should *not* encourage students to disclose material they will later regret having divulged. If extremely personal information is revealed, the class atmosphere must be supportive. Subsequent discussion should be more generalized and objective.

Summary

The following summarizes the chapter's content in terms of the learning objectives presented at the beginning of the chapter.

1. Understand the history of social group work.
   The roots of group social work began in the settlement houses and the YMCAs and YWCAs in the 1800s.

2. Identity the primary types of groups in social work.
   The following types of groups are described: social conversation, recreation/skill building, education, task, problem solving and decision making, focus, self-help and mutual aid, socialization, treatment, and sensitivity and encounter training.

3. Understand the four models of group development over time.
   Four models of group development over time are presented: Garland, Jones, and Kolodny Model; Tuckman Model; Northen and Kurland Model; and Bales Model.

4. Describe the differences between reference groups and membership groups.
   A membership is a group in which a person belongs or does not belong. A reference group is a group that a person identifies with.

5. Comprehend guidelines on how to conduct classroom exercises.
   A number of guidelines are presented on how to ethically conduct group exercises.

Group Exercises

GOAL: The following exercises are designed to help break the ice in new groups and are just a sample of the many ice-breaker exercises available. The group leader should select exercises appropriate to specific groups and modify them as needed.

EXERCISE A: Getting Acquainted

The leader asks the members to sit in a circle and explains that the goal is to get acquainted. The group members are asked to make a list of what they would like to know about each other, such as name, year in school, major, and reason for taking the course. An interesting item the leader may decide to add is "most embarrassing moment" or "tell us something about you that would surprise us." The list should be written on a blackboard or flip chart. One by one the members, including the leader, respond to the listed items. The leader should then ask if there is additional information the members want to know about him or her, including training and professional experience, and should answer all questions except those considered too personal.

EXERCISE B: Introducing to a Partner

Follow the same format as in Exercise A. The only variant is that after the items are listed, the members pair off and gather the information from their partners. If there is an uneven number of members, form one subgroup of three. Allow 5 minutes for information gathering. Partners then introduce each other to the group.

EXERCISE C: Personal Expectations for the Group

The leader asks the members to introduce themselves. Possible items that might be covered are the following:

> Name
> Year in school
> Major
> Paid experience in social work
> Volunteer experience in social work
> Most embarrassing experience (for humor)
> Reason for taking course
> Personal expectations for the class or group
> Something about you that would surprise us

This ice breaker is useful as a first step in seeking to identify the personal goals of members. The leader's goals and objectives for the group should then be given. A discussion may well ensue, and it might focus on setting group goals. The leader should be flexible, seeking to set goals that meet the legitimate expectations of the members. If one or more expectations are beyond the objectives of the group, the leader should tactfully indicate this and explain why.

EXERCISE D: Searching for Descriptors

The leader passes out a list of descriptors designed for a specific group. (A *descriptor* is a word or phrase that identifies an item.) Some possibilities are given here. Each group member then finds three others who say "yes" to specific descriptors. (The number "three" may be increased or decreased.) Each member should then give a completed list to the leader. The exercise may be ended by asking the members what items of interest they learned about others.

SAMPLE DESCRIPTORS

Likes professional football
Is a Leo
Plays golf
Likes classical music
Has had a paid or volunteer job in social work
Is dating somewhat steadily or is married
Has received a speeding ticket
Owns a car
Has water-skied
Has traveled in Mexico
Has meditated
Likes to jog

Enjoys riding horses
Has flown airplanes
Attends church regularly

EXERCISE E: Why I Decided to Be a Social Worker

Each member writes down on a sheet of paper the reasons that she or he decided to become a social worker. These reasons may include specific incidents or events. Each member then states his or her name and shares with the group the reasons he or she has decided to pursue a career in social work.

Competency Notes

EP 6a   Apply knowledge of human behavior and the social environment, person-in-environment, and other multidisciplinary theoretical frameworks to engage with clients and constituencies.

EP 7b   Apply knowledge of human behavior and the social environment, person-in-environment, and other multidisciplinary theoretical frameworks in the analysis of assessment data from clients and constituencies. (pp. 18–23)

Four models of group development are presented that social workers use to engage with and assess groups.

EP 1a   Make ethical decisions by applying the standards of the NASW Code of Ethics, relevant laws and regulations, models for ethical decision-making, ethical conduct of research, and additional codes of ethics as appropriate to context. (pp. 27–29)

Ethical guidelines are presented that allow social workers to lead group exercises in an ethical manner.

Key Terms and Concepts

Ad Hoc Committee	Descriptive Factors	Power and Control	Skill-Building Recreational
Behavioral Attributes	Differentiation	Preaffiliation	Groups
Board of Directors	Informal Recreational Groups	Reference Groups	Struggles
Change	Intimacy	Refreezing	Task Force
Closed-Ended Group	Involuntary Membership	Representative Group	Unfreezing
Cohesion	Membership Group	Separation	Voluntary Membership
Committee	Open-Ended Groups		

2

Social Group Work and Social Work Practice

W hat do social workers do? How is social work different from psychology, psychiatry, guidance and counseling, and other helping professions? What is the relationship between social work and social welfare? What knowledge, skills, and values do social workers need to be effective? This chapter will seek to address these questions. There have been a number of other efforts to address these same issues.[1] This chapter is largely an effort to integrate these prior conceptualizations. The purpose of this chapter is to describe social work as a profession and thereby assist social workers and other interested persons in understanding and articulating what social work is and what is unique about the social work profession.

LO 1   Conceptualize Social Work Practice

DEFINITION OF SOCIAL WORK

Social work has been defined by the National Association of Social Workers (NASW) as follows:

> Social work is the professional activity of helping individuals, groups, or communities to enhance or restore their capacity for social functioning and to create societal conditions favorable to their goals.

> Social work practice consists of the professional application of social work values, principles, and techniques to one or more of the following ends: helping people obtain tangible services; providing counseling and psychotherapy for individuals, families, and groups; helping communities or groups provide or improve social and health services; and participating in relevant legislative processes.

> The practice of social work requires knowledge of human development and behavior; of social, economic, and cultural institutions; and of the interaction of all these factors.[2]

The term **social worker** is generally applied to graduates (with bachelor's or master's degrees) of educational programs in social work who are employed in the field of social welfare. A social worker is a *change agent*, a helper who is specifically employed for the purpose of creating planned change.[3] As a change agent, a social worker is expected to be skilled at working with individuals, groups, families, and organizations and in bringing about community changes.

LEARNING OBJECTIVES

This chapter will help prepare students to:

LO 1
Conceptualize social work practice.

LO 2
Understand the medical model approach and the ecological approach to assessing and changing human behavior.

LO 3
Specify the goals of social work practice.

LO 4
Understand the strengths perspective in working with clients.

LO 5
Understand the conceptualization of social work practice that is presented in the Educational Policy Statement of the Council on Social Work Education for baccalaureate degree programs and master's degree programs in social work.

RELATIONSHIP BETWEEN SOCIAL WORK AND SOCIAL WELFARE

The goal of social welfare is to fulfill the social, financial, health, and recreational requirements of all individuals in a society. Social welfare seeks to enhance the social functioning of all age groups, both rich and poor. When other institutions in our society (such as the market economy and the family) fail at times to meet the basic needs of individuals or groups of people, then social services are needed and demanded. "Social welfare is about how people, communities and institutions in a society take action to provide certain minimum standards and certain opportunities."[4]

Examples of social welfare programs and services are foster care, adoption, day care, Head Start, probation and parole, public assistance programs (such as food stamps), public health nursing, sex therapy, suicide counseling, recreational services (Boy Scouts and YWCA programs), services to populations at risk (such as older persons), school social services, medical and legal services to the poor, family planning services, Meals on Wheels, nursing home services, shelters for battered spouses, services to persons with acquired immunodeficiency syndrome (AIDS), protective services for victims of child abuse and neglect, assertiveness training, encounter groups and sensitivity training, public housing projects, family counseling, Alcoholics Anonymous, runaway services, services to people with developmental disabilities, and rehabilitation services.

Almost all social workers are employed in the field of social welfare. There are, however, many other professional and occupational groups working in the field of social welfare, as illustrated in Figure 2.1.

FIGURE 2.1   Examples of Professional Groups Within the Field of Social Welfare

Professional people staffing social welfare services include attorneys providing legal services to the poor; urban planners in social planning agencies; physicians in public health agencies; teachers in residential treatment facilities for the emotionally disturbed; psychologists, nurses, and recreational therapists in mental hospitals; and psychiatrists in mental health clinics.

WHAT IS THE PROFESSION OF SOCIAL WORK?

The NASW defines the social work profession as follows:

> The social work profession exists to provide humane and effective social services to individuals, families, groups, communities, and society so that social functioning may be enhanced and the quality of life improved. . . .

> The profession of social work by both traditional and practical definition, is the profession that provides the formal knowledge base, theoretical concepts, specific functional skills, and essential social values which are used to implement society's mandate to provide safe, effective, and constructive social services.[5]

Social work is thus distinct from other professions (such as psychology and psychiatry) as it is the profession that has the responsibility and mandate to provide social services.

A social worker needs training and expertise in a wide range of areas to be able to effectively handle problems faced by individuals, groups, families, organizations, and the larger community. Although most professions are becoming more specialized (for example, most medical doctors now specialize in one or two areas), social work continues to emphasize a generic (broad-based) approach. The practice of social work is analogous to the old general practice of medicine. A general practitioner in medicine (or family practice) has training to handle a wide range of common medical problems faced by people, and a social worker has training to handle a wide range of common social and personal problems faced by people.

GENERALIST SOCIAL WORK PRACTICE

There used to be an erroneous belief that a social worker was a caseworker, a group worker, or a community organizer. Practicing social workers know that such a belief is faulty because every social worker is involved as a change agent in working with individuals, groups, families, organizations, and the larger community. The amount of time spent at each level varies from worker to worker, but every worker will, at times, be assigned and expected to work at these five levels and therefore needs training in all of them. A generalist social worker has the skills, and utilizes those skills, to work with the following five client systems: individuals, groups, families, organizations, and communities.

A generalist social worker is trained to use the problem-solving process to assess and intervene with the problems confronting individuals, families, groups, organizations, and communities.

The Baccalaureate Program Directors (BPD) organization defined **generalist practice** as follows:

> Generalist social work practitioners work with individuals, families, groups, communities, and organizations in a variety of social work and host settings. Generalist practitioners view clients and client systems from a strengths perspective in order to recognize, support, and build upon the innate capabilities of all human beings. They use a professional problem-solving process to engage, assess, broker services, advocate, counsel, educate, and organize with and on behalf of the client and client systems. In addition, generalist practitioners engage in community and organizational development. Finally, generalist practitioners evaluate service outcomes in order to continually improve the provision and quality of services most appropriate to client needs.

> Generalist social work practice is guided by the NASW Code of Ethics and is committed to improving the well-being of individuals, families, groups, communities, and organizations and furthering the goals of social justice.[6]

The Council on Social Work Education (2015) in *Educational Policy and Accreditation Standards* also defined *generalist practice*:

> Generalist practice is grounded in the liberal arts and the person-in-environment framework. To promote human and social well-being, generalist practitioners use a range of

EXERCISE 2.1   Your Areas of Interest in Social Work

GOAL: This exercise is designed to help you identify the social work areas that you desire to work in.

1. Rank the following five client systems in the order that you prefer to work with them (with 1 indicating your first choice).

_____ Individuals
_____ Families
_____ Groups
_____ Organizations
_____ The larger community

2. Describe the reasons for your ranking order.

3. Describe the areas of social work (such as services to battered spouses) that you prefer to work in. Also specify your reasons for your selected areas.

prevention and intervention methods in their practice with diverse individuals, families, groups, organizations, and communities based on scientific inquiry and best practices. The generalist practitioner identifies with the social work profession and applies ethical principles and critical thinking in practice at the micro, mezzo, and macro levels. Generalist practitioners engage diversity in their practice and advocate for human rights and social and economic justice. They recognize, support, and build on the strengths and resiliency of all human beings. They engage in research-informed practice and are proactive in responding to the impact of context on professional practice.[7]

The crux of generalist practice involves a view of the situation in terms of the person-in-environment conceptualization (described under "Ecological Model," p. 40 in this chapter) and the capacity and willingness to intervene at several different levels, if necessary, while assuming any number of roles. The case example in the box "Generalist Practice Involves Options Planning" illustrates the approach of responding at several different levels in a variety of roles.

This text should facilitate readers' learning of a generalist practice approach in social work by describing a variety of assessment and intervention strategies. Through learning these strategies, readers can then select those approaches that hold the most promise in facilitating positive changes in clients (who may be individuals, groups, families, organizations, or communities).

Generalist Practice Involves Options Planning

Jack Dawson is a social worker at a high school in a Midwestern state. Four teenagers have been expelled (consistent with school board policy) for drinking alcoholic beverages at the school during school hours. Mr. Dawson assesses the situation and identifies the following potential courses of action. He can serve as an advocate for the youths by urging the school board and the administration to reinstate the youths. Mr. Dawson is aware that the expulsions are upsetting not only to the youths and their parents, but also to the police department and the business community (because expelled youths tend to spend the day on city streets). He can involve the four teenagers in one-to-one counseling about their expulsion and their drinking patterns. He can involve these youths (along with others having drinking problems) in group counseling at the school. He can function as a broker to have the youths receive individual or group counseling from a counseling center outside the school system. He can

ascertain the willingness of the parents to become involved in family therapy and serve as a broker to link the interested families with a counseling center that offers this service. He can raise the issue to parents, to the business community, to the police department, to the school administration, and to the school board of whether expulsion from school for drinking alcoholic beverages is a desirable policy. (Perhaps a better school system policy in cases like this is to place the youths on "in-school suspension," where they are required to stay in a study room for a few days.) Expulsion is a drastic measure that may adversely affect the futures of these youths. Mr. Dawson can serve as an organizer and a catalyst to encourage interested parents and school staff to use the incident as a rationale for incorporating educational material on alcohol and other drugs into the curriculum. (The selected courses of action will depend on a variety of factors, including a cost-benefit analysis of each course.)

EP 8a

A VARIETY OF ROLES

In working with individuals, groups, families, organizations, and communities, a social worker is expected to be knowledgeable and skillful in filling a variety of roles. The particular role selected should (ideally) be determined by what will be most effective, given the circumstances. The following material identifies some, but certainly not all, of the roles assumed by social workers.

Enabler

In this role, a worker *helps* individuals or groups articulate their needs, clarify and identify their problems, explore resolution strategies, select and apply a strategy, and develop their capacities to deal with problems more effectively. This role model is perhaps the most frequently used approach in counseling individuals, groups, and families and is used in community practice—primarily when the objective is to help people organize to help themselves.

(It should be noted that this definition of the term **enabler** is very different from the definition used in reference to chemical dependency. There the term refers to a family member or friend who facilitates the substance abuser in persisting in the use and abuse of drugs.)

Broker

A broker links individuals and groups who need help and do not know where to find it with community services. For example, a wife who is physically abused by her husband might be referred to a shelter for battered women. Nowadays even moderate-sized communities have 200 to 300 social service agencies and organizations. Even human services professionals are often only partially aware of the total service network in their community.

Advocate

The role of advocate has been borrowed from the law profession. It is an active, directive role in which the social worker represents a client or a citizens' group. When a client or a citizens' group needs help and existing institutions are uninterested (or openly negative and hostile), the advocate's role may be appropriate. The advocate provides leadership in collecting information, arguing for the validity of the client's need and request, and challenging the institution's decision not to provide services. The purpose is not to ridicule or censure a particular institution, but to modify or change one or more of its service policies. In this role, the advocate is a partisan who is exclusively serving the interests of a client or a citizens' group.

Empowerer

A key goal of social work practice is **empowerment**, the process of helping individuals, families, groups, organizations, and communities increase their personal, interpersonal, socioeconomic, and political strength and influence. Social workers who engage in empowerment-focused practice seek to develop the capacity of clients to understand their environment, make choices, take responsibility for those choices, and influence their life situations through organization and advocacy. Empowerment-focused social workers also seek a more equitable distribution of resources and power among different groups in society. This focus on equity and social justice has been a hallmark of the social work profession as practiced by Jane Addams and other early settlement workers.

Activist

An activist seeks basic institutional change; often the objective involves a shift in power and resources to a disadvantaged group. An activist is concerned about social injustice, inequity, and deprivation. Tactics involve conflict, confrontation, and negotiation. Social action is concerned with changing the social environment in order to better meet the recognized needs of individuals. The methods used are assertive and action oriented (for example, organizing welfare recipients to work toward improvements in services and increases in money payments). Activities of social action include fact finding, analysis of community needs, research, dissemination and interpretation of information, organizing activities with people, and other efforts to mobilize public understanding and support on behalf of some existing or proposed social program. Social action activity can be geared toward a problem that is local, statewide, or national in scope.

Mediator

The mediator role involves intervention in disputes between parties to help them find compromises, reconcile differences, or reach mutually satisfactory agreements. Social workers have used their value orientations and unique skills in many forms of mediation (for example, divorcing spouses, neighbors in conflict, landlords and tenants, labor and management, and contenders for child custody). A mediator remains neutral, not siding with either party in the dispute. Mediators make sure they understand the positions of both parties. They may help clarify positions, identify miscommunication about differences, and help both parties present their cases clearly.

Negotiator

A negotiator brings together people in conflict and seeks to bargain and compromise to find mutually acceptable agreements. Somewhat like mediation, negotiation involves finding a middle ground that all sides can live with. However, unlike a mediator (who maintains a neutral position), a negotiator is usually allied with one side or the other.

Educator

The educator gives information to clients and teaches them adaptive skills. To be an effective educator, the worker must first be knowledgeable. Additionally, the worker must be a good communicator so information is conveyed clearly and is readily understood by the receiver. An educator can teach parenting skills to young parents, instruct teenagers in job-hunting strategies, and teach anger-control techniques to individuals with aggressive tendencies.

Initiator

An initiator calls attention to a problem or to a potential problem. It is important to recognize that sometimes a potential problem requires attention. For example, if a proposal is made to renovate a low-income neighborhood by building middle-income housing units, the initiator will be concerned that low-income residents could become homeless if the proposal is approved, because these current residents may not be able to afford middle-income units. However, calling attention to problems usually does not resolve them, so the initiator role must often be followed by other kinds of work.

Coordinator

Coordination involves bringing components together in an organized manner. For example, a multiproblem family may need help from several agencies to meet its complicated financial, emotional, legal, health, social, educational, recreational, and interactional needs. Frequently, someone at an agency must assume the role of case manager to coordinate services from different agencies and avoid both duplication of services and conflict among the services.

Researcher

At times every worker is a researcher. Research in social work practice can involve reading literature on topics of interest, evaluating the outcomes of one's practice, assessing the merits and shortcomings of programs, and studying community needs.

Group Facilitator

A group facilitator serves as a leader for a group discussion in a therapy group, an educational group, a self-help group, a sensitivity group, a family therapy group, or a group with some other focus.

Public Speaker

Social workers occasionally talk to a variety of groups (for example, high school classes, public service organizations such as Kiwanis, police officers, staff at other agencies) to inform them of available services or to argue the need for new services. In recent years, various new services have been identified (for example, family preservation programs and services for people with AIDS). Social workers who have public speaking skills are better able to explain services to groups of potential clients and funding sources and are apt to be rewarded (including financially) by their employers for these skills.

A SYSTEMS PERSPECTIVE

Social workers are trained to take a systems perspective on their work with individuals, groups, families, organizations, and communities. A systems perspective emphasizes looking beyond the presenting problems of clients in order to assess the complexities and interrelationships of their problems. A systems perspective is based on systems theory. Key concepts of general systems theory are *wholeness*, *relationship*, and *homeostasis*.

The concept of **wholeness** means that the objects or elements within a system produce an entity greater than the additive sums of the separate parts. Systems theory is antireductionistic, asserting that no system can be adequately understood or totally explained once it has been broken down into its component parts. (For example, the central nervous system is able to carry out thought processes that would not be revealed if only the parts were observed.)

The concept of **relationship** asserts that the pattern and structure of the elements in a system are as important as the elements themselves. For example, Masters and Johnson have found that sexual dysfunctions primarily occur due to the nature of the relationship between husband and wife, rather than the psychological makeup of the partners in a marriage system.[8]

Systems theory opposes simple cause-and-effect explanations. For example, whether a child will be abused in a family is determined by a variety of variables and the patterns of these variables, such as the parents' capacity to control their anger, relationships between the child and parents, relationships between the parents, degree of psychological stress, characteristics of the child, and opportunities for socially acceptable ways for the parents to ventilate anger.

EXERCISE 2.2   Your Interest in Various Social Work Roles

EP 8a

GOAL: This exercise is designed to help you identify the social work roles in which you would like to become involved.

1. Check one of the following for each of the indicated roles.

	I Desire to Become Involved in This Role	Uncertain	I Do Not Want to Become Involved in This Role
Enabler			
Broker			
Advocate			
Empowerer			
Activist			
Mediator			
Negotiator			
Educator			
Initiator			
Coordinator			
Researcher			
Group Facilitator			
Public Speaker			

2. Describe your reasons for selecting the particular roles in which you desire to become involved.

3. Describe your reasons for selecting the particular roles in which you do not want to become involved.

The concept of **homeostasis** suggests that living systems seek a balance to maintain and preserve the system. Jackson, for example, has noted that families tend to establish a behavioral balance or stability and to resist any change from that predetermined level of stability.[9] Emergence of the state of imbalance (generated either within or outside the marriage) ultimately acts to restore the homeostatic balance of the family. If one child in a family is abused, that abuse often serves a function—as indicated by the fact that if that that child is removed, a second child is often abused. Or if one family member improves through seeking counseling, that improvement will generally upset the balance within the family, and other family members will have to make changes (such changes may be adaptive or maladaptive) to adjust to the new behavior of the improved family member.

Ecological theory is a subcategory of systems theory and has become prominent in social work practice, as discussed in the next section.

LO 2   Understand the Medical Model Approach and the Ecological Approach to Assessing and Changing Human Behavior

EP 7b

MEDICAL MODEL VERSUS ECOLOGICAL MODEL

From the 1920s to the 1960s, most social workers used a medical model approach to assessing and changing human behavior. This approach, initiated primarily by Sigmund Freud, views clients as **patients**. The task of the provider of services is first to diagnose the causes of a patient's problems and then to provide treatment. The patient's problems are viewed as being inside the patient.

Medical Model

In regard to emotional and behavioral problems of people, the medical model conceptualizes these problems as **mental illnesses**. People with emotional or behavioral problems are then given medical labels such as schizophrenia, paranoia, psychosis, and insanity. Adherents of the medical approach believe the disturbed person's mind is affected by some generally unknown internal condition that is thought to result from a variety of possible causative factors: genetic endowment, metabolic disorders, infectious diseases, internal conflicts, unconscious uses of defense mechanisms, and traumatic early experiences that cause emotional fixations and prevent future psychological growth.

The medical model has a lengthy classification of mental disorders defined by the American Psychiatric Association (APA). The major categories of mental disorders are listed in Table 2.1.

The medical model approach arose in reaction to the historical notion that the emotionally disturbed were possessed by demons, were mad, and were to be blamed for their disturbances. These people were "treated" by being beaten, locked up, or killed. The medical model led to viewing the disturbed as in need of help, stimulated research into the nature of emotional problems, and promoted the development of therapeutic approaches.

The major evidence for the validity of the medical model approach comes from studies suggesting that some mental disorders, such as schizophrenia, may be influenced by genetics (heredity). The bulk of the evidence for the significance of heredity comes from studies of twins. For example, in some studies identical twins have been found to have a concordance rate (that is, if one has it, both have it) for schizophrenia of about 50%.[10]

Keep in mind that the rate of schizophrenia in the general population is about 1%.[11] When one identical twin is schizophrenic, the other is 50 times more likely than the average to be schizophrenic. This suggests a causal influence of genes, but not genetic determination, as concordance for identical twins is only 50%, not 100%.

EXERCISE 2.3   Understanding the Major Mental Disorders

GOAL: This exercise is designed to assist you in understanding the major mental disorders. Briefly describe several people you know who have the mental disorders identified in Table 2.1. For confidentiality reasons, do not use the real names of the people.

The following is an example of a desired brief description. Fred, age 67, was diagnosed with Alzheimer's disease 5 years ago. He is now in an assisted-living facility. His wife visits him nearly every day.

Ecological Model

In the 1960s, social work began questioning the usefulness of the medical model. Environmental factors were shown to be at least as important in causing a client's problems as internal factors. Research also was demonstrating that psychoanalysis was probably ineffective in treating clients' problems.[12]

Then social work shifted at least some of its emphasis to a **reform approach** that seeks to change systems to benefit clients. The enactment of the antipoverty programs, such as Head Start, is an example of a successful reform approach.

In the past several years, social work has focused on using an **ecological approach**. This approach integrates both treatment and reform by conceptualizing and emphasizing the dysfunctional transactions between people and their physical and social environments. Human beings are known to develop and adapt through transactions with all elements of their environments. An ecological model gives attention to both internal and external factors. It does not view people as passive reactors to their environments, but rather as active participants in dynamic and reciprocal interactions.

It tries to improve the coping patterns of people in their environments to obtain a better match between an individual's needs and the characteristics of his or her environment. One emphasis of an ecological model is on the person-in-environment, which is conceptualized in Figure 2.2.

Figure 2.2 suggests that people interact with many systems. With this conceptualization, social work can focus on three separate areas. First, it can focus on the person and seek to develop problem-solving, coping, and developmental capacities. Second, it can focus on the relationship between a person and the systems he or she interacts with and link the person with needed resources, services, and opportunities. Third, it can focus on the systems and seek to reform them to meet the needs of the individual more effectively.

The ecological model views individuals, families, and small groups as having transitional problems and needs as they move from one life stage to another. Individuals face many transitional changes as they grow older, such as learning to walk, entering first grade, adjusting to puberty, graduating from school, finding a job, getting married, having children, children leaving home, and retiring.

TABLE 2.1   Major Mental Disorders According to the American Psychiatric Association

NEURODEVELOPMENTAL DISORDERS include, but are not limited to, intellectual disabilities (sometimes called cognitive disabilities), communication disorders (such as language disorder), autism spectrum disorder, attention-deficit/hyperactivity disorder, specific learning disorder (such as impairment in reading), and motor disorders (such as developmental coordination disorder, stereotypic movement disorder, and Tourette's disorder).

SCHIZOPHRENIA SPECTRUM AND OTHER PSYCHOTIC DISORDERS include, but are not limited to, schizotypal (personality) disorder, delusional disorder, schizophrenia, schizoaffective disorder, and catatonic disorder.

BIPOLAR AND RELATED DISORDERS include, but are not limited to, bipolar I disorder, bipolar II disorder, and cyclothymic disorder.

DEPRESSIVE DISORDERS include, but are not limited to, disruptive mood dysregulation disorder (such as major depressive disorder), persistent depressive disorder, and premenstrual dysphoric disorder.

ANXIETY DISORDERS include separation anxiety disorder, specific phobia (such as fear of injections and transfusions), social anxiety disorder, panic disorder, and agoraphobia.

OBSESSIVE-COMPULSIVE AND RELATED DISORDERS include obsessive-compulsive disorder, hoarding disorder, trichotillomania (hair-pulling disorder), and excoriation (skin-picking) disorder.

TRAUMA- AND STRESSOR-RELATED DISORDERS include reactive attachment disorder, posttraumatic stress disorder, and acute stress disorder.

DISSOCIATIVE DISORDERS include dissociative identity disorder and dissociative amnesia.

SOMATIC SYMPTOM AND RELATED DISORDERS include somatic symptom disorder, illness anxiety disorder, and factitious disorder (includes factitious disorder imposed on self and factitious disorder imposed on another).

FEEDING AND EATING DISORDERS include pica, rumination disorder, avoidant/restrictive food intake disorder, anorexia nervosa, bulimia nervosa, and binge-eating disorder.

ELIMINATION DISORDERS include enuresis and encopresis.

SLEEP-WAKE DISORDERS include insomnia disorder, hypersomnolence disorder, narcolepsy, breathing-related sleep disorders (such as central sleep apnea), and parasomnias (such as sleepwalking type, sleep terror type, nightmare disorder, rapid eye movement sleep behavior disorder, restless legs syndrome, and substance/medication-induced sleep disorder).

SEXUAL DYSFUNCTIONS include delayed ejaculation, erectile disorder, female orgasmic disorder, female sexual interest/ arousal disorder, genitopelvic pain/penetration disorder, male hypoactive sexual desire disorder, and premature (early) ejaculation.

GENDER DYSPHORIA includes gender dysphoria.

DISRUPTIVE, IMPULSE-CONTROL, AND CONDUCT DISORDERS include oppositional defiant disorder, intermittent explosive disorder, conduct disorder, antisocial personality disorder, pyromania, and kleptomania.

SUBSTANCE-RELATED AND ADDICTIVE DISORDERS include alcohol-related disorders (such as alcohol use disorder and alcohol intoxication); caffeine-related disorders (such as caffeine intoxication); cannabis-related disorder (such as cannabis use disorder and cannabis intoxication); hallucinogen-related disorders; inhalant-related disorders; opioid-related disorders; sedative-, hypnotic-, or anxiolytic-related disorders; stimulant-related disorders (such as cocaine abuse); tobacco-related disorders; and non-substance-related disorders (such as gambling disorders).

NEUROCOGNITIVE DISORDERS include delirium and major and mild neurocognitive disorders (such as Alzheimer's disease, vascular disease, traumatic brain injury, substance/medication use, HIV infection, Parkinson's disease, and Huntington's disease).

PERSONALITY DISORDERS include paranoid personality disorder, schizoid personality disorder, schizotypal personality disorder, antisocial personality disorder, borderline personality disorder, histrionic personality disorder, narcissistic personality disorder, avoidant personality disorder, dependent personality disorder, and obsessive-compulsive personality disorder.

PARAPHILIC DISORDERS include voyeuristic disorder, exhibitionistic disorder, frotteuristic disorder (such as recurrent sexual arousal from touching or rubbing against a nonconsenting person), sexual masochism disorder, sexual sadism disorder, fetishistic disorder, and transvestic disorder.

OTHER MENTAL DISORDERS include mental disorders due to another medical condition.

MEDICATION-INDUCED MOVEMENT DISORDERS AND OTHER ADVERSE EFFECTS OF MEDICATION include neuroleptic-induced parkinsonism and medication-induced acute dystonia.

OTHER CONDITIONS THAT MAY BE A FOCUS OF CLINICAL ATTENTION include relational problems (such as parent-child relational problems), abuse and neglect (such as child abuse and neglect, child sexual abuse, child psychological abuse, spouse or partner violence or neglect, and adult abuse by nonspouse), educational and occupational problems, housing and economic problems (such as homelessness), problems related to crime or interaction with the legal system, religious or spiritual problems, victim of terrorism or torture, personal history of military deployment, and overweight or obesity.

SOURCE: *Diagnostic and Statistical Manual of Mental Disorders*, Fifth Edition by the American Psychiatric Association, 2013, Washington, DC: American Psychiatric Association.

FIGURE 2.2   **Person-in-Environment Conceptualization**

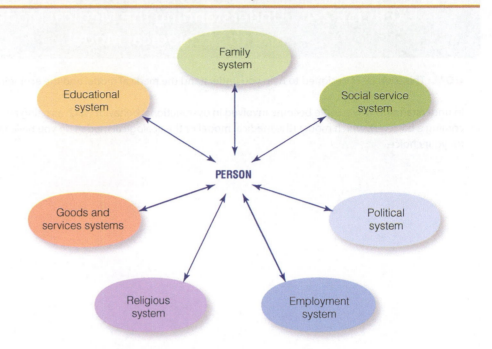

People in society continually interact with many systems, some of which are shown in this figure.

Families have a life cycle of events that also require adjustment, including engagement, marriage, birth of children, parenting, children going to school, children leaving home, and loss of a parent (perhaps through death or divorce).

In addition, small groups have transitional phases of development. Members of small groups spend time getting acquainted, gradually learn to trust each other, begin to self-disclose more, learn to work together on tasks, develop approaches to handle interpersonal conflict, and face adjustments to the group's eventual termination or the departure of some members.

A central concern of an ecological model is to articulate the transitional problems and needs of individuals, families, and small groups. Once these problems and needs are identified, intervention approaches are then selected and applied to help individuals, families, and small groups resolve the transitional problems and meet their needs.

An ecological model can also focus on the maladaptive interpersonal problems and needs in families and groups. It can seek to articulate the maladaptive communication processes and dysfunctional relationship patterns of families and small groups. These difficulties cover an array of areas, including interpersonal conflicts, power struggles, double binds, distortions in communicating, scapegoating, and discrimination. The consequences of such difficulties are usually maladaptive for some members. An ecological model seeks to identify such interpersonal obstacles and then apply appropriate intervention strategies. For example, parents may set the price for honesty too high for their children. In such families, children gradually learn to hide certain behaviors and thoughts, and even learn to lie. If the parents discover such dishonesty, an uproar usually occurs. An appropriate intervention in such a family is to open up communication patterns and help the parents understand that if they really want honesty from their children, they need to learn to be more accepting of their children's thoughts and actions.

EXERCISE 2.4   Understanding the Medical Model and the Ecological Model

GOAL: This exercise is designed to help you understand the medical model and the ecological model.

In understanding why people become involved in dysfunctional behavior (such as being anorexic, committing a crime, or becoming a batterer), which model (the medical model or the ecological model) do you believe is more useful? State the reasons for your choice.

Two centuries ago, people interacted primarily within the family system. Families were nearly self-sufficient. In those days, the **person-in-family** was a way of conceptualizing the main system for individuals to interact. Our society has become much more complex. Today, a person's life and quality of life are interwoven and interdependent upon many systems, as shown in Figure 2.2.

LO 3   Specify the Goals of Social Work Practice

GOALS OF SOCIAL WORK PRACTICE

The NASW has conceptualized social work practice as having four major goals.[13]

Goal 1: Enhance the Clients' Problem-Solving, Coping, and Developmental Capacities

Using the person-in-environment concept, the focus of social work practice at this level is on the "person." With this focus, a social worker serves primarily as an *enabler*. In the role of an enabler, the worker may take on activities of a counselor, teacher, caregiver (that is, providing supportive services to those who cannot fully solve their problems and meet their own needs), and behavior changer (that is, changing specific parts of a client's behavior).

Goal 2: Link Clients with Systems that Provide Resources, Services, and Opportunities

Using the person-in-environment concept, the focus of social work practice at this level is on the relationships between persons and the systems with which they interact. With this focus, a social worker serves primarily as a **broker**.

Goal 3: Promote the Effective and Humane Operation of Systems that Provide Resources and Services

Using the person-in-environment concept, the focus of social work practice at this level is on the systems people interact with. One role a worker may fill at this level is that of an **advocate**. Additional roles at this level are the following:

A **program developer** seeks to promote or design programs or technologies to meet social needs.

A **supervisor** seeks to increase the effectiveness and efficiency of the delivery of services through supervising other staff.

A **coordinator** seeks to improve a delivery system through increasing communications and coordination among human service resources.

A **consultant** seeks to provide guidance to agencies and organizations through suggesting ways to increase the effectiveness and efficiency of services.

Goal 4: Develop and Improve Social Policy

The focus of Goal 4 is on the statutes and broader social policies that underlie available resources. Major roles of social workers at this level are **planner** and **policy developer**. In these roles, workers develop and seek adoption of new statutes or policies and propose elimination of ineffective or inappropriate statutes and policies. In these planning and policy development processes, social workers may take on an advocate role and, in some instances, an activist role.

The Council on Social Work Education (CSWE) is the national accrediting body for social work education in the United States. It describes the purpose of social work as follows (CSWE, 2015):

> The purpose of the social work profession is to promote human and community well-being. Guided by a person-in-environment framework, a global perspective, respect for human diversity, and knowledge based on scientific inquiry, the purpose of social work is actualized through its quest for social and economic justice, the prevention of conditions that limit human rights, the elimination of poverty, and the enhancement of the quality of life for all persons, locally and globally.[14]

This description of the purpose of social work is consistent with the four goals of social work mentioned earlier. However, it adds one more goal, as follows.

Goal 5: Promote Human and Community Well-Being

The social work profession is committed to enhancing the well-being of all human beings and to promoting community well-being. It is particularly committed to alleviating poverty, oppression, and other forms of social injustice. About 15% of the U.S. population has an income below the poverty line. Social work has always advocated for developing programs to alleviate poverty, and many practitioners focus on providing services to the poor.

Poverty is global; every society has members who are poor. In some societies, as much as 95% of the population lives in poverty. Social workers are committed to alleviating poverty not only in the United States but also worldwide. Alleviating poverty is obviously complex and difficult. Social work professionals work with a variety of systems to make progress in alleviating poverty, including educational systems, healthcare systems, political systems, business and employment systems, religious systems, and human services systems.

Oppression is the unjust or cruel exercise of authority or power. In our society, numerous groups have been oppressed—including African Americans, Latinos, Chinese Americans, Native Americans, women, persons with disabilities, gays and lesbians, various religious groups, and people living in poverty. (The listing of these groups is only illustrative and certainly not exhaustive.) Social injustice occurs when some members of a society have less protection, fewer basic rights and opportunities, or fewer social benefits than other members of that society. Social work is a profession that is committed not only to alleviating poverty but also to combating oppression and other forms of social injustice.

Social justice is an ideal condition in which all members of a society have the same basic rights, protection, opportunities, obligations, and social benefits. Economic justice is also an ideal condition in which all members of a society have the same opportunities to attain material goods, income, and wealth. Social workers have an obligation to help groups at risk increase their personal, interpersonal, socioeconomic, and political strength and influence through improving their circumstances. Empowerment-focused social workers seek a more equitable distribution of resources and power among the various groups in society. Diverse groups that may be at risk include those distinguished by "age, class, color, culture, disability and ability, ethnicity, gender, gender identity and expression, immigration status, marital status, political ideology, race, religion/spirituality, sex, sexual orientation, and tribal sovereign status."[15]

EXERCISE 2.5   Your Interest in Achieving the Goals of Social Work

GOAL: This exercise is designed to help you identify your interest in the activities associated with the five goals of social work.

1. Check the boxes that identify your interest level in each of the five goals of social work.

	Highly Interested	Somewhat Interested	Uncertain	Somewhat Disinterested	Not Interested
Goal 1					
Goal 2					
Goal 3					
Goal 4					
Goal 5					

2. For goals in which you are "Highly interested," state the reasons for your decisions.

3. For goals in which you are "Somewhat disinterested" or "Not interested," state the reasons for your decisions.

EXERCISE 2.6   Applying the Problem-Solving Approach

GOAL: This exercise is designed to assist you in applying the problem-solving approach.

Describe a dilemma that you faced (or are currently facing) in which you used the six stages of the problem-solving approach. In your description, describe what you did for each of the six stages.

EP 7b
EP 8b
EP 9b

A PROBLEM-SOLVING APPROACH

In working with individuals, families, groups, organizations, and communities, social workers use a problem-solving approach. Steps in the problem-solving process can be stated in a variety of ways. The following is a simple statement of this process:

1. Identify as precisely as possible the problem or problems.
2. Generate possible alternative solutions.
3. Evaluate the alternative solutions.
4. Select a solution or solutions, and set goals.
5. Implement the solution(s).
6. Follow up to evaluate how the solution(s) worked.

LO 4   Understanding the Strengths Perspective in Working with Clients

STRENGTHS PERSPECTIVE

The strengths perspective seeks to identify, use, build on, and reinforce the abilities and strengths that people have, in contrast to the pathological perspective, which focuses on their deficiencies. It emphasizes people's abilities, interests, aspirations, resources, beliefs, and accomplishments. For example, strengths of African Americans in the United States are found in more than 100 predominantly African American colleges and universities; fraternal and women's organizations; and social, political, and professional organizations. Many of the schools, businesses, churches, and organizations that are predominantly African American have developed social service programs, such as family support services, mentoring programs, food and shelter services, transportation services, and educational and scholarship programs. Through individual and organized efforts, self-help approaches and mutual aid traditions continue among African Americans. African Americans tend to have strong ties to immediate, extended family. They tend to have a strong religious orientation, a strong work and achievement orientation, and a belief in egalitarian role sharing.[16]

According to Saleebey,[17] five principles underlie the guiding assumptions of the strengths perspective:

1. *Every individual, group, family, and community has strengths.* The strengths perspective is about discerning these resources. Saleebey notes:

   > In the end, clients want to know that you actually care about them, that how they fare makes a difference to you, that you will listen to them, that you will respect them no matter what their history, and that you believe that they can build something of value with the resources within and around them. But most of all, clients want to know that you believe they can surmount adversity and begin the climb toward transformation and growth (p. 12).[18]

2. *Trauma, abuse, illness, and struggle may be injurious, but they may also be sources of challenge and opportunity.* Clients who have been victimized are seen as active and developing individuals who, through their traumas, learn skills and develop personal attributes that assist them in coping with future struggles. There is dignity to be found in having prevailed over obstacles. We often grow more from crises that we find ways to handle effectively than from periods of time in our lives when we are content and comfortable.

3. *Assume that you do not know the upper limits of the capacity to grow and change, and take individual, group, and community aspirations seriously.* This principle means workers need to hold high their expectations of clients and form alliances with their visions, hopes, and values. Individuals, families, and communities have the capacity for restoration and rebounding. When workers connect with the hopes and dreams of clients, clients are apt to have greater faith in themselves. Then they are able to put forth the effort needed for their hopes and dreams to become self-fulfilling prophecies.

4. *We best serve clients by collaborating with them.* A worker is more effective when seen by the client as a collaborator or consultant rather than as an expert or a professional. A collaborative stance by a worker makes her or him less vulnerable to many of the adverse effects of an expert-inferior relationship, including paternalism, victim blaming, and preemption of client views.

5. *Every environment is full of resources.* In every environment (no matter how harsh), there are individuals, groups, associations, and institutions with something to give, and with something that others may desperately need. The strengths perspective seeks to identify these resources and make them available to benefit individuals, families, and groups in a community.

Most social workers now recognize the importance of the strengths perspective in working with clients. If workers only focus on the shortcomings, weaknesses, deficiencies, and problems of clients, those clients are apt to lose their self-esteem and sense of worth. They are apt to view themselves as "losers" and give up trying to improve their lives. Once they give up trying, it will be a self-fulfilling prophecy that they will have no chance of becoming self-sufficient. They will live a life of being dependent on society for "handouts."

On the other hand, if workers treat clients as "equals" and work with them to help them identify their strengths and resources, these clients will more readily realize they have self-worth and that they have the capacities to improve their lives and to improve the lives of their family members. The old adage of the "fish story" is important to remember. If we give a hungry family fish, we feed them for a day. If we teach them how to fish, we feed them for a lifetime!

Expanding on this analogy, if a worker is assigned to work with a family who is in extreme poverty and the worker only arranges to have that family receive a monthly check to meet subsistence needs, those family members are apt to view themselves as "losers" and become chronically dependent on the government. On the other hand, if the worker helps these family members identify their strengths (such as helping them to recognize their aptitudes for certain jobs and links them to job training programs), the family members are apt to have an improving sense of worth and gradually obtain gainful employment and become productive members in society. (It should be noted that the worker involved with this family also needs to help the family deal with other barriers that the family may face, such as issues with child care, access to quality healthcare, alcohol or other drug abuse issues, anger management issues, and transportation issues.)

A few additional case examples of the powerful impacts of the strengths perspective will be mentioned. Several years ago I was the faculty supervisor for an intern in a child protective services unit at a human services agency. The field supervisor recommended a final grade of "A+", praising the following skills of the intern: building a relationship with clients, problem solving, writing case reports, empathy, and testifying in court. Later that day I met with the intern on a one-to-one basis. I praised the intern for excelling and asked her what led to her doing so well, as she averaged "B" grades in her social work courses and in her general education courses. Her answer brought tears to my eyes and underscored the importance of the strengths perspective. Her response was as follows. "I never told you this, as I don't want anyone to feel sorry for me. I have a learning disability known as dyslexia. (Dyslexia is a reading disorder, which also affects writing, spelling, and sometimes speaking. people with dyslexia include Steven Spielberg and Whoopi Goldberg.) I had major trouble in learning to read; when I was in the third grade, I was reading only at a first grade level. I was sent to the school social worker for an evaluation. The social worker noted I had the strengths of being highly motivated to learn to read and that I was working very hard to learn to do so in school and at home. This social worker referred me to the school psychologist, who tested me and discovered I was dyslexic. In this third grade some teachers were advocating that I be placed in Special Ed courses. I did not want the stigma that is attached to being a Special Ed child. This social worker made a major difference in my life. She arranged for me to have a tutor who was skilled in working with children with a learning disability. The worker also met with my parents who were very supportive of me and instructed them in how they could help me better learn to read. This social worker made a major difference in my life; she is the reason I chose to major in social work and become a social worker: In my classes in elementary school, middle school, high school, and college, I have always had to work harder than most other students. At this college I have also received services from the students with a Disability unit. I think my experience with overcoming dyslexia has facilitated me in empathizing and working with the clients that were assigned to me in field placement."

The following is another example. Stevie Wonder has been among the most influential Black music artists over the past five decades.[19] He is a songwriter, producer, singer, and musician. He was inducted into the Rock and Roll Hall of Fame in 1989. He was born Steveland Judkins on May 13, 1950, in Saginaw, Michigan. When born, he was suffering from retinopathy of prematurity, which eventually caused his retina to detach, resulting in his blindness. With the support and encouragement of his parents, he learned to play the piano at the age of 7. By the age of 9, he had also mastered playing drums and harmonica. After his family moved to Detroit in 1954, he joined a church choir and began to develop his singing potential. In 1961, at the age of 11, Stevie was discovered by Ronnie White of the group The Miracles, who arranged an audition at Motown Records. Almost immediately he was signed by Berry Gordy to Motown Records. Clarence Paul came up with the "Wonder" surname, as Stevie at the time was being introduced as the "8th Wonder of the World." Clarence Paul also supervised his early recordings and helped him develop his singing talents and his talents as a multi-instrumentalist. Why did Stevie Wonder become one of our country's greatest entertainers? He certainly was born with immense musical potential. But he also had supportive parents and a number of mentors and advisers who recognized this potential and who helped him develop it.

Another person who excelled because of the strengths perspective is Temple Grandin.[20] She was born August 29, 1947. She did not begin to speak until she was nearly 4 years old.

Instead, she communicated her frustrations by screaming. At 3 years old she was labeled autistic, and doctors told her parents that she should be institutionalized.

Grandin's mother spoke to a doctor who suggested speech therapy. The mother hired a nanny who spent hours playing games with Grandin and her sister. At age 4, Grandin began talking and making developmental progress. Grandin considers herself lucky to have had a supportive mother and supportive mentors from primary school onwards.

Temple Grandin graduated from Hampshire Country School, a boarding school in New Hampshire, in 1966. She earned her bachelor's degree in psychology from Franklin Pierce College in 1970, she received her master's degree in animal science from Arizona State University in 1975, and she received her doctoral degree in animal science in 1989 from the University of Illinois at Urbana-Champaign. She is a professor at Colorado State University.

She is a philosophical leader of both animal welfare and autism advocacy movements. Grandin advocates early interventions to address autism, as well as supportive teachers who can direct the fixations of autistic children in fruitful directions.

She is a best-selling author on animal welfare and autism. She is an inventor of a number of livestock-handling facilities that keep cattle calm and prevent them from getting hurt.

Temple Grandin's life story illustrates that no one should be stereotyped as having "no hope for the future" because of receiving a physical/mental disability diagnosis, such as that of autism. She had supportive people in her early years (mother, teachers, mentors) who helped her focus on her strengths, rather than her limitations.

EXERCISE 2.7   The Strengths Perspective Applied to a Homeless Family

GOAL: This exercise is designed to assist you in applying the strengths perspective to a case.

1. Read the following case scenario:

Ms. Hull was recently evicted from her two-bedroom apartment. She had been working at a small business that did not offer health insurance coverage to her. She is a single mother with three children, ages 7, 9, and 10. She developed pneumonia that hung on because she could not pay to see a physician. The small business experienced financial problems, and her employment was terminated. She has been seeking another job but has not found one. She wants a job that has health benefits. Unable to pay rent, she was evicted from her apartment. She cares a lot for her children, and they display respect for her. The children are all doing well in school. Ms. Hull and her children lived on the street for 3 days and nights but then located a homeless shelter at the Salvation Army. They have been at the homeless shelter for the past 2½ weeks. The children are fairly healthy and are respectful of the services they are receiving from the shelter. Ms. Hull has largely recovered from her pneumonia, partly because of the physician's visit she asked the Salvation Army to arrange for her.

2. List the strengths that you identify in this family.

EP 8b

MICRO, MEZZO, AND MACRO PRACTICE

Social workers practice at three levels: (1) **micro**—working on a one-to-one basis with an individual, (2) **mezzo**—working with families and other small groups, and (3) **macro**—working with organizations and communities or seeking changes in statutes and social policies.

The specific activities performed by workers include, but are not limited to, the following.

Social Casework

Aimed at helping individuals on a one-to-one basis meet personal and social problems, casework may be geared to helping the client adjust to his or her environment or to changing certain social and economic pressures that adversely affect an individual. Social casework services are provided by nearly every social welfare agency that provides direct services to people. Social casework encompasses a wide variety of activities, such as counseling runaway youths, helping unemployed people secure training or employment, counseling someone who is suicidal, placing a homeless child in an adoptive or foster home, providing protective services to abused children and their families, finding nursing homes for stroke victims who no longer need to be confined to a hospital, counseling individuals with sexual dysfunctions, helping alcoholics acknowledge they have a drinking problem, counseling those with a terminal illness, being a probation and parole officer, providing services to single parents, and working in medical and mental hospitals as a member of a rehabilitation team.

Case Management

Recently, some social service agencies have labeled their social workers **case managers**. The tasks performed by case managers are similar to those of caseworkers. The job descriptions of case managers vary from service area to service area. For example, case managers in a juvenile probation setting are highly involved in supervising clients, providing some counseling, monitoring clients to make certain they are following the rules of probation,

You Can't Be an Effective Direct Practice Worker without Being a Competent Group Worker

I have been mentoring adjunct faculty for the past three decades. I have informed the adjunct faculty that they need to hone their teaching skills by valuing and utilizing a wide variety of group work skills. I firmly believe that an effective instructor in social work education (BSW programs, MSW programs, and doctoral programs) needs to be a skilled group worker. An effective instructor has to be skilled at effectively using the following group work skills: establishing professional relationships; being a servant leader (see Chapter 3); respect for diversity; problem solving; inspiring members to be all that they can be; the strengths perspective; facilitating discussions; being culturally competent; having skills at conflict resolution and handling disruptive members; setting group norms; creating a cooperative atmosphere; setting relevant objectives and assessing the extent to which members are attaining these objectives; adhering to social work ethics, including confidentiality and professional boundaries; being empathic; being perceptive; and setting realistic goals with members.

As you reflect on these skills, is it not accurate that your most effective and popular social work instructors were those who were highly effective group work leaders?

As I reflect on the importance of an effective social work instructor having a wide variety of group work skills, the following corollary appears evident. An effective direct practice worker (including one who works on a one-to-one basis with clients) needs to have command of a variety of group work skills. An effective direct practice worker has to be skilled at using the following group work skills: establishing professional relationships; being a servant leader; respect for diversity; problem solving; inspiring individuals to be all that they can be; the strengths perspective; facilitating discussions; being culturally competent; having skills at conflict resolution and handling disgruntled individuals; setting norms for proceeding; creating a cooperative atmosphere; setting relevant goals and assessing the extent to which clients are attaining these goals; adhering to social work ethics, including confidentiality and professional boundaries; being empathic; and being perceptive.

linking clients and their families with needed services, preparing court reports, and testifying in court. On the other hand, case managers at a rehabilitation center for people with a cognitive disability are apt to be involved in providing job training to clients, counseling clients, arranging transportation, disciplining clients for unacceptable behavior, acting as an advocate for clients, and acting as liaison with the people who supervise clients during their nonwork hours (at a group home, foster home, residential treatment facility, or their parents' home). Hepworth and Larsen describe the role of a case manager as follows:

> Case managers link clients to needed resources that exist in complex service delivery networks and orchestrate the delivery of services in a timely fashion. Case managers function as brokers, facilitators, linkers, mediators, and advocates. A case manager must have extensive knowledge of community resources, rights of clients, and policies and procedures of various agencies, and must be skillful in mediation and advocacy.[21]

Group Work

The intellectual, emotional, and social development of individuals may be furthered through group activities. In contrast to casework or group therapy, it is not primarily therapeutic, except in a broad sense. Different groups have different objectives, such as socialization, information exchange, curbing delinquency, recreation, changing socially unacceptable

A Social Worker as a Dream Manager

Some clients do not want anything to do with a social worker, psychologist, psychiatrist, or other similar professional because they do not want to listen to the "psycho-babble." They view themselves as above going to a "shrink." Is there a way for a counselor to break through this "resistance"? Mathew Kelly suggests there may be a way, by being a "dream manager." The following is a brief description of this approach.

Matthew Kelly, an internationally known speaker and author, wrote the book *The Dream Manager*.[a] The essence of *The Dream Manager* is that a company can achieve remarkable results by helping its employees fulfill their dreams. Kelly believes each person has a dream. He believes that it is the dream that defines a person's frame of mind. (I will use "her" for the pronoun in this context.) Her dream, or dreams, defines her attitude toward life, her personality, her future aspirations, and her goals. We, hopefully, become our dreams. If we do not attain our dreams, we feel unfulfilled, empty, frustrated, and depressed. Helping people chase and fulfill their dreams should be the primary focus of all relationships—whether that relationship is between husband and wife, employer and employee, salesperson and customer, real estate agent and potential buyer, parent and child, or social worker and client.

In the book, Kelly asserts we can reach our dreams if we help other people reach theirs. (Is that not the essence of why people pursue a career in social work?) Our dreams tell us not only what sort of person we are today, but also what sort of person we aspire to be in the tomorrows of our lives. Is not the link between the private dreams of a person who is working for an employer closely linked to the satisfaction level of working for that employer? The more that a person believes

she is achieving her dreams in working with an agency/company, the greater the satisfaction level she will have with working for that agency/company. And this analogy applies for all relationships. The more that a partner in a romantic relationship feels she is attaining her dreams in that relationship, the more she will be committed to improving that relationship. The more a client feels that she is identifying and attaining her dreams with her social worker, the more she will be committed to working with that social worker.

We need all kinds of help and encouragement to remain connected to our dreams; otherwise, we lose the motivation to work on making progress. Kelly asserts that companies with high levels of worker satisfaction are those in which the management focuses on helping employees identify and realize their dreams within that company. A high degree of employee satisfaction is a major factor in a company advancing.

Applying this analogy to the relationship between a social worker and a client, is it not accurate that for a resistant client, the more a social worker can help that client identify her dreams, and then attain her dreams, the greater the likelihood that that client will form a constructive relationship with her social worker, and the more motivated she will be to work on improving her life—as she simultaneously works on attaining her dreams?

With, a number of clients who are resistant to working with a "shrink" (and in fact for any client), might it not be valuable to reframe the description of the role of a social worker to the client as being that of "a dream manager"?

---

a. Matthew Kelly, *The Dream Manager* (New York: Beacon Publishing, 2007).

values, and helping achieve better relations between cultural and racial groups. For example, a group worker at a neighborhood center may, through group activities, seek to curb delinquency patterns and change socially unacceptable values; or a worker at an adoption agency may meet with a group of applicants to explain adoption procedures and help applicants prepare to become adoptive parents. Activities and focuses of groups vary: arts and crafts; dancing; games; dramatics; music; photography; sports; nature study; woodwork; first aid; home management; information exchange; and discussion of such topics as politics, sex, marriage, religion, and career selection.

Group Treatment

Group treatment is aimed at facilitating the social, behavioral, and emotional adjustment of individuals through the group process. Participants in group treatment usually have emotional, interactional, or behavioral difficulties. Group treatment has several advantages over one-to-one counseling, such as the operation of the **helper therapy** principle, which maintains it is therapeutic for the helper (who can be any member of a group) to feel he or she has been helpful to others.[22] In contrast to one-to-one counseling, group pressure is often more effective in changing maladaptive behavior of individuals, and group treatment is a time saver as it enables the therapist to treat several people at the same time. A few examples in which group treatment might be used are for individuals who are severely depressed, have drinking problems, are victims of a rape, are psychologically addicted to drugs, have a relative who is terminally ill, are single and pregnant, are recently divorced, or have an eating disorder.

Additional advantages of group treatment over one-to-one treatment include:

- Feedback—A member with a personal challenge receives multiple types of feedback from a variety of perspectives from other members.
- Vicarious learning—Each member learns by hearing about other members' coping strategies.
- Social support—Members receive support from one another.
- Resources—A wide pool of knowledge about services and resources is shared among members involving their concerns.
- Practice of new behaviors—Other members provide opportunities to try out new behaviors in the safe environment of the group. For example, a member who is shy can try out more assertive responses.
- Hope—A member with current challenges is inspired with hope by hearing how other members have coped effectively with similar situations.

Family Treatment

A type of group treatment aimed at helping families with interactional, behavioral, and emotional problems, family treatment can be used with parent-child interaction problems, marital conflicts, and conflicts with grandparents. Widely varying problems are dealt with in family treatment or family counseling, such as disagreements between parents and youths on choice of friends and dates, drinking and other drug use, domestic tasks, curfew hours, communication problems, sexual values and behavior, study habits, and grades received.

Community Organization

The aim of community organization is to stimulate and assist the local community to evaluate, plan, and coordinate efforts to provide for the community's health, welfare, and recreation needs. It is perhaps not possible to define precisely the activities of a community organizer, but such activities are apt to include encouraging and fostering citizen participation, coordinating efforts between agencies or between groups, public relations and public education, research, planning, and resource management. A community organizer acts as a catalyst in stimulating and encouraging community action. Agency settings where such specialists are apt to be employed include community welfare councils, social planning agencies, health planning councils, and community action agencies. The term **community organization** is now being replaced in some settings by such labels as **planning, social planning, program development, policy development**, and **macro practice.**

Barker defines community organization as:

An intervention process used by social workers and other professionals to help individuals, groups, and collectives of people with common interests or from the same geographic areas to deal with social problems and to enhance social well-being through planned collective action. Methods include identifying problem areas, analyzing causes, formulating plans, developing strategies, mobilizing necessary resources, identifying and recruiting community leaders, and encouraging interrelationships between them to facilitate their effors.[23]

Policy Analysis

Policy analysis involves the systematic evaluation of a policy and the process by which it was formulated. Those who conduct such an analysis consider whether the process and the result are clear, equitable, legal, rational, compatible with social values, superior to the

---

EXERCISE 2.8   Identifying Your Interest in Various Social Work Activities

GOAL: This exercise is designed to assist you in identifying the types of social work responsibilities that you want to pursue.

1. For each of the following activities, check the box that indicates your level of interest in engaging in it.

	Highly Interested	Somewhat Interested	Uncertain	Somewhat Disinterested	Not Interested
1. Social casework					
2. Case management					
3. Group work					
4. Group treatment					
5. Family treatment					
6. Community organization					
7. Policy analysis					
8. Administration					

2. For the activities that you checked "Highly interested," state the reasons for your selections.

3. For the activities that you checked "Somewhat disinterested" or "Not interested," state the reasons for your selections.

alternatives, cost effective, and explicit. Frequently such an analysis identifies certain shortcomings in the policy, and those conducting the policy analysis then usually recommend modifications designed to alleviate these shortcomings.

Administration

Administration is the activity that involves directing the overall program of a social service agency. Administrative functions include setting agency and program objectives, analyzing social conditions in the community, making decisions relating to what services will be provided, employing and supervising staff members, setting up an organizational structure, administering financial affairs, and securing funds for the agency's operations. Administration also involves setting organizational goals, coordinating activities toward the achievement of selected goals, and making and monitoring necessary changes in processes and structure to improve effectiveness and efficiency. In social work, the term **administration** is often used synonymously with **management**. In a small agency, administrative functions may be carried out by one person, whereas in a larger agency several people may be involved in administrative affairs.

Other areas of professional activity in social work include research, consulting, supervision, planning, program development, and teaching (primarily at the college level). The ability to study and evaluate one's own practice and to evaluate programs is an important skill for a social worker. Skills essential for social work practice are described further in the next section. Generalist social workers are expected to have an extensive knowledge base, to possess numerous skills, and to adhere to a well-defined set of professional social work values.

LO 5   Understand the Conceptualization of Social Work Practice that Is Presented in the Educational Policy Statement of the Council on Social Work Education for Baccalaureate Degree Programs and Master's Degree Programs in Social Work

EP 1a through EP 9d

KNOWLEDGE, SKILLS, AND VALUES NEEDED FOR SOCIAL WORK PRACTICE

In *Educational Policy and Accreditation Standards (EPAS)*, the Council on Social Work Education (2015) identified knowledge, skills, values, and cognitive and affective processes that accredited baccalaureate and master's degree programs are mandated to convey to social work students. *EPAS* is based on a competency approach. The following material is reprinted with permission from *Educational Policy and Accreditation Standards*.[24]

The mandated content that BSW and MSW programs are required to provide to students are summarized in the following nine competencies.

Social Work Competencies

The nine social work competencies are listed in the following sections. Programs may add competencies that are consistent with their mission and goals and that respond to their context. Each competency describes the knowledge, values, skills, and cognitive and affective processes that comprise the competency at the generalist level of practice, followed by a set of behaviors that integrate these components. These behaviors represent observable components of the competencies, and the preceding statements represent the underlying content and processes that inform the behaviors.

Competency 1–Demonstrate Ethical and Professional Behavior   Social workers understand the value base of the profession and its ethical standards, as well as relevant laws and regulations that may affect practice at the micro, mezzo, and macro levels. Social workers understand frameworks of ethical decision making and how to apply principles of critical thinking to those frameworks in practice, research, and policy arenas. Social workers recognize personal values and the distinction between personal and professional values. They also understand how their personal experiences and affective reactions influence their professional judgment and behavior. Social workers understand the profession's history, its mission, and the roles and responsibilities of the profession. Social workers also understand the role of other professions when engaged in interprofessional teams. Social workers recognize the importance of lifelong learning and are committed to continually updating their skills to ensure they are relevant and effective. Social workers also understand emerging forms of technology and the ethical use of technology in social work practice. Social workers:

- make ethical decisions by applying the standards of the NASW Code of Ethics, relevant laws and regulations, models for ethical decision making, ethical conduct of research, and additional codes of ethics as appropriate to context;
- use reflection and self-regulation to manage personal values and maintain professionalism in practice situations;
- demonstrate professional demeanor in behavior; appearance; and oral, written, and electronic communication;
- use technology ethically and appropriately to facilitate practice outcomes; and
- use supervision and consultation to guide professional judgment and behavior.

Competency 2–Engage Diversity and Difference in Practice   Social workers understand how diversity and difference characterize and shape the human experience and are critical to the formation of identity. The dimensions of diversity are understood as the intersectionality of multiple factors, including but not limited to, age, class, color, culture, disability and ability, ethnicity, gender, gender identity and expression, immigration status, marital status, political ideology, race, religion/spirituality, sex, sexual orientation, and tribal sovereign status. Social workers understand that, as a consequence of difference, a person's life experiences may include oppression, poverty, marginalization, and alienation, as well as privilege, power, and acclaim. Social workers also understand the forms and mechanisms of oppression and discrimination and recognize the extent to which a culture's structures and values, including social, economic, political, and cultural exclusions, may oppress, marginalize, alienate, or create privilege and power. Social workers:

- apply and communicate understanding of the importance of diversity and difference in shaping life experiences in practice at the micro, mezzo, and macro levels;
- present themselves as learners and engage clients and constituencies as experts of their own experiences; and
- apply self-awareness and self-regulation to manage the influence of personal biases and values in working with diverse clients and constituencies.

Competency 3–Advance Human Rights and Social, Economic, and Environmental Justice   Social workers understand that every person, regardless of position in society, has fundamental human rights such as freedom, safety, privacy, an adequate standard of living, healthcare, and education. Social workers understand the global interconnections of oppression and human rights violations, and are knowledgeable about theories of human need and social justice and strategies to promote social and economic justice and human rights. Social workers understand strategies designed to eliminate oppressive structural barriers to ensure that social goods, rights, and responsibilities are distributed equitably and that civil, political, environmental, economic, social, and cultural human rights are protected. Social workers:

- apply their understanding of social, economic, and environmental justice to advocate for human rights at the individual and system levels; and
- engage in practices that advance social, economic, and environmental justice.

Competency 4–Engage in Practice-informed Research and Research-informed Practice   Social workers understand quantitative and qualitative research methods and their respective roles in advancing a science of social work and in evaluating their practice. Social workers know the principles of logic, scientific inquiry, and culturally informed and ethical approaches to building knowledge. Social workers understand that evidence that informs practice derives from multidisciplinary sources and multiple ways of knowing. They also understand the processes for translating research findings into effective practice. Social workers:

- use practice experience and theory to inform scientific inquiry and research;
- apply critical thinking to engage in analysis of quantitative and qualitative research methods and research findings; and
- use and translate research evidence to inform and improve practice, policy, and service delivery.

Competency 5–Engage in Policy Practice   Social workers understand that human rights and social justice, as well as social welfare and services, are mediated by policy and its implementation at the federal, state, and local levels. Social workers understand the history and current structures of social policies and services, the role of policy in service delivery, and the role of practice in policy development. Social workers understand their role in policy development and implementation within their practice settings at the micro, mezzo, and macro levels, and they actively engage in policy practice to effect change within those settings. Social workers recognize and understand the historical, social, cultural, economic, organizational, environmental, and global influences that affect social policy. They are also knowledgeable about policy formulation, analysis, implementation, and evaluation. Social workers:

- identify social policy at the local, state, and federal level that affects well-being, service delivery, and access to social services;
- assess how social welfare and economic policies affect the delivery of and access to social services;
- apply critical thinking to analyze, formulate, and advocate for policies that advance human rights and social, economic, and environmental justice.

Competency 6–Engage with Individuals, Families, Groups, Organizations, and Communities   Social workers understand that engagement is an ongoing component of the dynamic and interactive process of social work practice with, and on behalf of, diverse individuals, families, groups, organizations, and communities. Social workers value the importance of human relationships. Social workers understand theories of human behavior and the social environment and critically evaluate and apply this knowledge to facilitate engagement with clients and constituencies, including individuals, families, groups, organizations, and communities. Social workers understand strategies to engage diverse clients and constituencies to advance practice effectiveness. Social workers understand how their personal experiences and affective reactions may affect their ability to effectively engage with diverse clients and constituencies. Social workers value principles of relationship building and interprofessional collaboration to facilitate engagement with clients, constituencies, and other professionals as appropriate. Social workers:

- apply knowledge of human behavior and the social environment, person-in-environment, and other multidisciplinary theoretical frameworks to engage with clients and constituencies; and
- use empathy, reflection, and interpersonal skills to effectively engage diverse clients and constituencies.

Competency 7–Assess Individuals, Families, Groups, Organizations, and Communities   Social workers understand that assessment is an ongoing component of the dynamic and interactive process of social work practice with, and on behalf of, diverse individuals, families, groups, organizations, and communities. Social workers understand theories of human behavior and the social environment and critically evaluate and apply this knowledge in the assessment of diverse clients and constituencies, including individuals, families, groups, organizations, and communities. Social workers understand methods of assessment with diverse clients and constituencies to advance practice effectiveness. Social workers recognize the implications of the larger practice context in the assessment process and value the importance of interprofessional collaboration in this process. Social workers understand how their personal experiences and affective reactions may affect their assessment and decision making. Social workers:

- collect and organize data and apply critical thinking to interpret information from clients and constituencies;
- apply knowledge of human behavior and the social environment, person-in-environment, and other multidisciplinary theoretical frameworks in the analysis of assessment data from clients and constituencies;
- develop mutually agreed-on intervention goals and objectives based on the critical assessment of strengths, needs, and challenges within clients and constituencies; and
- select appropriate intervention strategies based on the assessment, research knowledge, and values and preferences of clients and constituencies.

Competency 8–Intervene with Individuals, Families, Groups, Organizations, and Communities   Social workers understand that intervention is an ongoing component of the dynamic and interactive process of social work practice with, and on behalf of, diverse individuals, families, groups, organizations, and communities. Social workers are knowledgeable about evidence-informed interventions to achieve the goals of clients and constituencies, including individuals, families, groups, organizations, and communities. Social workers understand theories of human behavior and the social environment, and critically evaluate and apply this knowledge to effectively intervene with clients and constituencies. Social workers understand methods of identifying, analyzing, and implementing evidence-informed interventions to achieve client and constituency goals. Social workers value the importance of interprofessional teamwork and communication in interventions, recognizing that beneficial outcomes may require interdisciplinary, interprofessional, and interorganizational collaboration. Social workers:

- critically choose and implement interventions to achieve practice goals and enhance capacities of clients and constituencies;
- apply knowledge of human behavior and the social environment, person-in-environment, and other multidisciplinary theoretical frameworks in interventions with clients and constituencies;
- use interprofessional collaboration as appropriate to achieve beneficial practice outcomes;
- negotiate, mediate, and advocate with and on behalf of diverse clients and constituencies; and
- facilitate effective transitions and endings that advance mutually agreed-on goals.

Competency 9–Evaluate Practice with Individuals, Families, Groups, Organizations, and Communities   Social workers understand that evaluation is an ongoing component of the dynamic and interactive process of social work practice with, and on behalf of, diverse individuals, families, groups, organizations, and communities. Social workers recognize the importance of evaluating processes and outcomes to advance practice, policy, and service delivery effectiveness. Social workers understand theories of human behavior and the social environment and critically evaluate and apply this knowledge in evaluating outcomes. Social workers understand qualitative and quantitative methods for evaluating outcomes and practice effectiveness. Social workers:

- select and use appropriate methods for evaluation of outcomes;
- apply knowledge of human behavior and the social environment, person-in-environment, and other multidisciplinary theoretical frameworks in the evaluation of outcomes;
- critically analyze, monitor, and evaluate intervention and program processes and outcomes; and
- apply evaluation findings to improve practice effectiveness at the micro, mezzo, and macro levels.

SOCIAL GROUP WORK AS A COMPONENT OF SOCIAL WORK PRACTICE

Social work practice involves providing humane and effective social services to individuals, families, groups, organizations, and communities. Social work with groups has considerable overlap in providing social services to individuals, families, organizations, and communities. The skills, knowledge, and values needed for effective social work practice with groups are similar to the skills, knowledge, and values needed for effective social work practice with individuals, families, organizations, and communities.

The material in this text on verbal communication, nonverbal communication, problem solving, interviewing, counseling, and contracting is applicable to social work practice with both individuals and groups. A family, as described in Chapter 9, is a subtype of a group. The close relationships between a group and an organization are described in Chapter 10, as are the close relationships between a group and a community. Acquiring the skills, values, and knowledge needed for effective practice with groups will simultaneously increase a social worker's ability to work effectively with individuals, families, organizations, and communities.

Summary

The following summarizes the chapter's content in terms of the learning objectives presented at the beginning of the chapter.

1. Conceptualize social work practice.

This chapter conceptualizes social work practice. Social work with groups is an integral component of social work practice. Social work is defined. The relationship between social work and social welfare is described. Almost all social workers are employed in the field of social welfare. The Council on Social Work Education in EPAS (2015) has defined generalist social work practice:

Generalist practice is grounded in the liberal arts and the person-in-environment framework. To promote human and social well-being, generalist practitioners use a range of prevention and intervention methods in their practice with diverse individuals, families, groups, organizations, and communities based on scientific inquiry and best practices. The generalist practitioner identifies with the social work profession and applies ethical principles and critical thinking in practice at the micro, mezzo, and macro levels. Generalist practitioners engage diversity in their practice and advocate for human rights and social and economic justice. They recognize, support, and build on the strengths and resiliency of all human beings. They engage in research-informed practice and are proactive in responding to the impact of context on professional practice.

A social worker is expected to be knowledgeable and skillful in filling a variety of roles, including enabler, broker, advocate, empowerer, activist, mediator, negotiator, educator, initiator, coordinator, researcher, group facilitator, and public speaker.

2. **Understand the medical model approach and the ecological approach to assessing and changing human behavior.**

    In regard to emotional and behavioral problems of people, the medical model conceptualizes these problems as mental illnesses. The ecological approach to emotional and behavioral problems integrates both treatment and reform of systems by conceptualizing and emphasizing the dysfunctional transactions between people and their physical and social environments.

3. **Specify the goals of social work practice.**

    The following goals of social work practice are described:
    1. *Enhance the clients' problem-solving, coping, and developmental capacities.*
    2. *Link clients with systems that provide resources, services, and opportunities.*
    3. *Promote the effective and humane operation of systems that provide resources and services.*
    4. *Develop and improve social policy.*
    5. *Promote human and community well-being.*

4. **Understand the strengths perspective in working with clients.**

    The strengths perspective seeks to identify, use, build on, and reinforce the abilities and strengths that people have, in contrast to the pathological perspective, which focuses on their deficiencies. It emphasizes people's abilities, interests, aspirations, resources, beliefs, and accomplishments.

5. **Understand the conceptualization of social work practice that is presented in the Educational Policy Statement of the Council on Social Work Education for baccalaureate degree programs and master's degree programs in social work.**

    In EPAS (2015), the CSWE has identified the knowledge, skills, values, and cognitive and affective processes that accredited baccalaureate and master's degree programs are mandated to convey to social work students. This EPAS material is presented.

Group Exercises

EXERCISE A: Options Planning

EP 7b
EP 8b

GOAL: This exercise is designed to help students gain an awareness of how generalist social workers generate options for combating social problems.

The leader briefly describes generalist social work practice and indicates that options planning is one important aspect. The leader should state the purpose of this exercise, ask students to form subgroups of about five students, and then read the first vignette to the subgroup. Give them about 10 minutes to arrive at their options. Then ask the subgroups to share their options with the class. Seek to stimulate class discussion of various options. Proceed with the remaining vignettes in the same manner.

VIGNETTE #1

Blackhawk High School has recently had significant increases in the number of female students who have become pregnant. Many of these students become single mothers who face a number of obstacles in providing quality child care while trying to continue their education. The community is becoming increasingly concerned about the rising pregnancy rate and the difficulties these young mothers are encountering. The principal of the school requests that the school social worker, Ms. Gomez, do something to "fix" these problems. What are realistic options that she might initiate and pursue?

VIGNETTE #2

A Midwest medium-sized city has agreed to take up to 1,000 refugees at the federal government's request from a Middle Eastern country to relocate in this city. The mayor of this city appoints a task force to provide recommendations on what actions the city should take to assist these residents to assimilate to this city. Dr. Conley, a social work professor in the city, is appointed to this task force. Many of the refugees do not speak English. The recommendations for actions that the city should take involve (among other things) recommendations for what services should be offered to the refugees. What realistic options should this task force recommend?

VIGNETTE #3

Mr. Komarek is a social worker for a human services department in a small rural community that has no shelter for homeless individuals or families. Community leaders have asked the county public welfare department to do something about the increasing number of homeless in the community. The director of the agency, responding to community pressure, assigns Mr. Komarek to head up a task force (that is, a committee) to combat the homeless problem. What realistic options could be pursued by Mr. Komarek and this task force?

VIGNETTE #4

The mayor of a large city has appointed a task force to develop recommendations for improving living conditions in the inner city. The inner city has high rates of unemployment, crime, drug and alcohol abuse, births outside of marriage, substandard housing, high school dropouts, homeless individuals and families, gang activity, and homicides. A great many people are receiving public assistance. Ms. Taylor, a social worker and social planner employed by United Way, is appointed to this task force. What realistic recommendations for improving living conditions should be advanced by this task force?

EXERCISE B: Social Work with Groups and Generalist Practice

GOAL: This exercise is designed to help students acquire a working knowledge of key terms used in social work.

Step 1. The leader states the purpose of this exercise. Indicate that social workers must be able to describe to others what the profession of social work is and how it is distinct from other professions. Students form subgroups of about five students each. The leader asks each subgroup to discuss answers to the first of the following four questions. Give the subgroups about 10 minutes to arrive at their answers. Then ask them to share their answers with the class. After this process is completed, the leader may summarize the answer to this question given in this chapter and may compare it with the answers arrived at by the subgroups. The answers from the class may be better than the answers in the text.

Step 2. Proceed with the remaining three questions in a similar manner.

QUESTIONS

1. Define social work and social welfare, and describe the relationship between the two.
2. Define the profession of social work and describe how it is distinct from such other helping professions as psychology and psychiatry.
3. Define the terms "social worker" and "generalist social worker."
4. Describe how social work practice with groups is distinct from, but similar to, social work practice with other client systems—that is, individuals, families, organizations, and communities.

EXERCISE C: Assessing Social Work Competencies and Behaviors in Field Placement

EP 1a
through
EP 9d

GOAL: This exercise is designed to facilitate students and the social work program in assessing the extent to which students have acquired the competencies and behaviors for social work practice while the students are in field placement.

Step 1: This field instrument may be used by agency field supervisors to evaluate the performance of the interns they are supervising. One way of using the instrument is to evaluate the intern at the end of field placement. The instrument is completed by the field instructor and reviewed with the student intern and faculty liaison for the dual purposes of providing a grade for the field placement and assessing the individual student's attainment of social work behaviors and competencies. Another approach is for field instructors to complete the evaluation midway through the length of the field placement (that is, midsemester for a one-semester field placement or midyear for a two-term field placement), then again at termination of the field placement. With either approach, benchmarks (as specified in 2015 *EPAS*) need to be established.

Rating Scale for Evaluation of Field Placement Performance	
Midterm ☐	Final ☐
Name of Intern	
Date	

INSTRUCTIONS FOR RATING INTERNS ON THE NINE COMPETENCIES IN THE FIRST PART OF THE EVALUATION:

The standard by which an intern is to be compared is that of a new beginning-level social worker. The nine competencies that are specified in this evaluation form are those established in 2015 by our national accrediting organization (the Council on Social Work Education). Under each competency statement are several items that we ask that you rate according to the following criteria.

1	The intern has excelled in this area
2	The intern is functioning above expectations for interns in this area
3	The intern has met the expectations for interns in this area
4	The intern has not as yet met the expectations in this area, but there is hope that the intern will meet the expectations in the near future
5	The intern has not met the expectations in this area, and there is not much hope that the intern will meet the expectations in this area in the near future
n/a	Not applicable, as the intern has not had the opportunity to demonstrate competence in this area

Comments may be made under any competency statement, if desired. Please be sure to indicate those areas in which you think the intern is particularly strong and those areas that need improvement.

This evaluation is intended to give the intern feedback about her or his performance. The agency supervisor's rating of these items will not directly be used to calculate the grade that is given to the intern. The faculty supervisor has the responsibility of assigning the grade for the course. The grade that is assigned will be based on **the faculty supervisor's overall evaluation of the student's performance in placement in conjunction with the agency supervisor's evaluation, intern logs, seminar participation, and assigned papers**.

If you prefer to use another evaluation system **in addition** to this form to evaluate a student's performance, please discuss this with the faculty supervisor.

Competency 1: Demonstrate Ethical and Professional Behavior						
Makes ethical decisions by applying the standards of the NASW Code of Ethics, relevant laws and regulations, models for ethical decision making, ethical conduct of research, and additional codes of ethics as appropriate to context	1	2	3	4	5	na
Uses reflection and self-regulation to manage personal values and maintain professionalism in practice situations	1	2	3	4	5	na
Demonstrates professional demeanor in behavior; appearance; and oral, written, and electronic communication	1	2	3	4	5	na
Uses technology ethically and appropriately to facilitate practice outcomes	1	2	3	4	5	na
Uses supervision and consultation to guide professional judgment and behavior	1	2	3	4	5	na

Comments:

Competency 2: Engage Diversity and Difference in Practice						
Applies and communicates understanding of the importance of diversity and difference in shaping life experiences in practice at the micro, mezzo, and macro levels	1	2	3	4	5	na
Presents herself/himself as a learner and engages clients and constituencies as experts of their own experiences	1	2	3	4	5	na
Applies self-awareness and self-regulation to manage the influence of personal biases and values in working with diverse clients and constituencies	1	2	3	4	5	na

Comments:

Competency 3: Advance Human Rights and Social, Economic, and Environmental Justice						
Applies her/his understanding of social, economic, and environmental justice to advocate for human rights at the individual and system levels	1	2	3	4	5	na
Engages in practices that advance social, economic, and environmental justice	1	2	3	4	5	na

Comments:

Competency 4: Engage in Practice-informed Research and Research-informed Practice						
Uses practice experience and theory to inform scientific inquiry and research	1	2	3	4	5	na
Applies critical thinking to engage in analysis of quantitative and qualitative research methods and research findings	1	2	3	4	5	na
Uses and translates research evidence to inform and improve practice, policy, and service delivery	1	2	3	4	5	na

Comments:

Competency 5: Engage in Policy Practice						
Identifies social policy at the local, state, and federal level that affects well-being, service delivery, and access to social services	1	2	3	4	5	na
Assesses how social welfare and economic policies affect the delivery of and access to social services	1	2	3	4	5	na
Applies critical thinking to analyze, formulate, and advocate for policies that advance human rights and social, economic, and environmental justice	1	2	3	4	5	na

Comments:

Competency 6: Engage with Individuals, Families, Groups, Organizations, and Communities						
Applies knowledge of human behavior and the social environment, person-in-environment, and other multidisciplinary theoretical frameworks to engage with clients and constituencies	1	2	3	4	5	na
Uses empathy, reflection, and interpersonal skills to effectively engage diverse clients and constituencies	1	2	3	4		na

Comments:

Competency 7: Assess Individuals, Families, Groups, Organizations, and Communities						
Collects and organizes data and applies critical thinking to interpret information from clients and constituencies	1	2	3	4	5	na
Applies knowledge of human behavior and the social environment, person-in-environment, and other multidisciplinary theoretical frameworks in the analysis of assessment data from clients and constituencies	1	2	3	4	5	na
Develops mutually agreed-on intervention goals and objectives based on the critical assessment of strengths, needs, and challenges within clients and constituencies	1	2	3	4	5	na
Selects appropriate intervention strategies based on the assessment, research knowledge, and values and preferences of clients and constituencies	1	3	3	4	5	na

Comments:

Competency 8: Intervene with Individuals, Families, Groups, Organizations, and Communities						
Critically chooses and implements interventions to achieve practice goals and enhance capacities of clients and constituencies	1	2	3	4	5	na
Applies knowledge of human behavior and the social environment, person-in-environment, and other multidisciplinary theoretical frameworks in interventions with clients and constituencies	1	2	3	4	5	na
Uses interprofessional collaboration as appropriate to achieve beneficial practice outcomes	1	2	3	4	5	na
Negotiates, mediates, and advocates with and on behalf of diverse clients and constituencies	1	2	3	4	5	na
Facilitates effective transitions and endings that advance mutually agreed-on goals	1	2	3	4	5	na

Comments:

Competency 9: Evaluate Practice with Individuals, Families, Groups, Organizations, and Communities						
Selects and uses appropriate methods for evaluation of outcomes	1	2	3	4	5	na
Applies knowledge of human behavior and the social environment, person-in-environment, and other multidisciplinary theoretical frameworks in the evaluation of outcomes	1	2	3	4	5	na
Critically analyzes, monitors, and evaluates intervention and program processes and outcomes	1	2	3	4	5	na
Applies evaluation findings to improve practice effectiveness at the micro, mezzo, and macro levels	1	2	3	4	5	na

Comments:

Overall Evaluation at __MIDTERM:__
Please check one of the following at the midterm evaluation. At the final evaluation do __NOT__ complete this section.
☐   This intern is excelling in field placement by performing above expectations for interns.
☐   This intern is meeting the expectations of a field placement intern.
☐   This intern is functioning somewhat below the expectations of a field placement intern. There is a question whether this intern will be ready for beginning-level social work practice by the end of placement.
☐   This intern is functioning below the expectations of a field placement intern. There is considerable concern that this intern will not be ready for beginning-level social work practice by the end of placement. This intern should perhaps be encouraged to pursue another major.

Comments/elaboration:

FINAL OVERALL EVALUATION:
Please check one of the following at the final evaluation. At the midterm evaluation do <u>NOT</u> complete this section.
☐ This intern has excelled in field placement by performing above expectations for interns. If an appropriate position were open at this agency for a beginning-level social worker, this intern would be considered among the top candidates for this position.
☐ This intern has met the expectations of the field placement. This intern is ready for beginning-level social work practice.
☐ This intern is not yet ready for beginning-level social work practice.
☐ This intern is not yet ready for beginning-level social work practice, has demonstrated serious problems in performance, and perhaps should be encouraged to pursue another major.

Comments/elaboration:

Signature of Agency Field Instructor	
Agency	Date

The following section should be completed by the intern:
My agency supervisor and faculty supervisor have discussed this evaluation with me, and I have received a copy. My agreement or disagreement follows:
☐ I agree with the evaluation
☐ I do not agree with the evaluation
Intern's Signature
Date
☐ If the intern disagrees with the evaluation, she/he should state that disagreement in writing and submit a copy to both the agency supervisor and the faculty supervisor. The disagreement should be specific and should relate to the items in the evaluation.

NOTE TO FACULTY

This exercise may be very valuable in obtaining assessment information for reaffirmation of accreditation by the Commission on Accreditation of the CSWE.

EXERCISE D: Social Work Value Issues

EP 1b

GOAL: To clarify your values in regard to a number of prominent issues in social work.

Step 1. The leader explains the purpose of this exercise, indicating that social workers need to be aware of their personal and professional values so that they know when they should take a neutral position in working with clients and when they should sell or enforce a particular set of values for clients.

Step 2. The leader distributes the following questionnaire to students and indicates that *their responses will remain anonymous*. The questionnaire uses the following scale: (1) Definitely not, (2) Probably not, (3) Probably yes, and (4) Definitely yes.

VALUES QUESTIONNAIRE

1. Would you marry someone of a different race?

    1   2   3   4

2. If you were going to adopt a child, would you adopt a child of a different race?

    1   2   3   4

3. Are you in favor of a woman becoming president of the United States?
   1   2   3   4

4. Do you believe busing should be used to attempt to achieve racial integration in schools?
   1   2   3   4

5. Do you support affirmative action programs that assert that certain minority groups and women should be given preference in hiring over white males?
   1   2   3   4

6. Do you believe a father who commits incest with his 10-year-old daughter should be placed in jail?
   1   2   3   4

7. Do you believe prostitution should be legalized?
   1   2   3   4

8. If you or your partner were pregnant and in a situation where it would be very difficult to raise a child, would you seriously consider an abortion?
   1   2   3   4

9. Do you support a constitutional amendment to make abortions illegal?
   1   2   3   4

10. If you are a female, would you be willing to be a surrogate mother? If you are male, would you be willing to have your wife or future wife become a surrogate mother?
    1   2   3   4

11. Do you believe the death penalty should be used for certain crimes?
    1   2   3   4

12. Do you believe the United States should support an extensive program to develop the capacity to clone human beings?
    1   2   3   4

13. Do you support artificial insemination for humans?
    1   2   3   4

14. Do you believe people should retain their virginity until they marry?
    1   2   3   4

15. If a candidate for president of the United States were a Buddhist, would you be less apt to vote for him or her?
    1   2   3   4

16. If you are married, would you seriously consider having an extramarital affair?
    1   2   3   4

17. Do you believe persons with a profound intellectual disability who will never be able to function enough to sit up should be kept alive indefinitely at taxpayers' expense?
    1   2   3   4

18. Do you believe marijuana should be legalized?
    1   2   3   4

19. Would you be upset if a son or daughter of yours were gay/lesbian?
    1   2   3   4

20. Do you believe you could objectively counsel someone who had brutally raped four women?
    1   2   3   4

21. Do you think people should limit the size of their families to two children?
    1   2   3   4

22. Do you favor a law to limit families to two children?
    1   2   3   4

23. Do you think a person who is gay should be allowed to teach in elementary and secondary schools?
    1   2   3   4

24. Do you approve of a young couple trying out marriage by living together before actually getting married?

  1   2   3   4

25. Would you be in favor of a group home for drug addicts in your neighborhood?

  1   2   3   4

26. Do you think the government should help support day care centers for working mothers?

  1   2   3   4

27. In case of war, do you think women in the military service should take part in active combat?

  1   2   3   4

28. Do you think the United States should build more nuclear power plants to generate electricity?

  1   2   3   4

29. Would you encourage your son to have premarital sex?

  1   2   3   4

30. Would you encourage your daughter to have premarital sex?

  1   2   3   4

31. When you become an older person and unable to care for your needs, would you be willing to be placed in a nursing home?

  1   2   3   4

32. Do you support physician-assisted suicide when the victim is terminally ill and in intense pain?

  1   2   3   4

33. Would you consider marrying someone who is divorced and has two children? (Assume you are single in answering this question.)

  1   2   3   4

34. Do you believe you would enjoy being a social worker at a group home for persons with an intellectual disability?

  1   2   3   4

35. Do you believe the legal drinking age should be less than 21 years?

  1   2   3   4

36. Would you marry someone who is of a different religion than you?

  1   2   3   4

37. Do you believe there are circumstances that justify a person taking his or her own life?

  1   2   3   4

38. Would you divorce your spouse if you found out he or she had an extramarital affair?

  1   2   3   4

39. Would you allow a child of yours to play frequently with a child who has AIDS?

  1   2   3   4

40. Do you believe most welfare recipients are able-bodied loafers?

  1   2   3   4

41. Do you believe you would be comfortable in hugging a person who has AIDS?

  1   2   3   4

42. Do you believe you would be comfortable rooming with a person who has AIDS?

  1   2   3   4

43. Do you think social workers should inform a client's current sexual partners that the client is HIV positive if the client refuses to do so?

  1   2   3   4

Step 3. The leader collects the questionnaires so that anonymity is assured and lists the question numbers on the blackboard. After tallying the results (with the help of volunteers), the leader seeks to open a discussion. For example, if most of the students indicate that they would not marry someone of a different race, the leader asks, "Does this suggest that most of you may have some racial prejudices?"

EXERCISE E: Olga and Igor

GOALS: To identify some of your values, to see that your values often differ markedly from those held by others, and to see that it is often difficult to accept someone else's values.

Step 1. The leader explains the goals of the exercise. The class forms into subgroups of four or five persons. Each subgroup rates the five characters in the following story. A number 1 rating is given to the "best" character, that person who displays the most desirable behaviors in this situation. A number 5 rating is given to the person who displays the most objectionable behaviors. The story is read aloud two times.

> Two primitive societies are separated by a turbulent river full of people-eating piranhas. An earlier civilized society (which left the area decades ago) built a bridge connecting the societies. Olga lives in Caribou Society and is very much in love with, and engaged to, Igor, who lives in Moose Society. Both societies are highly opposed to premarital sex. Both Olga and Igor are still virgins. Six days before the wedding a monsoon destroys the bridge. Olga and Igor are on separate sides. Both believe there is no way for them to get across or to ever see each other again. Both are distraught.
>
> The night before the scheduled wedding, Blackbeard the sailor visits Caribou Society. Olga asks Blackbeard to give her a ride across. Blackbeard says OK, on the condition that Olga goes to bed with him in his boat as they are crossing. Olga definitely doesn't want to do this. But she fears she'll never marry Igor, or even see him again. Olga deliberates about it for 4½ hours. She asks a long-time friend, Solomon, for advice. Solomon says, "It's your problem. You have to decide. There is nothing I can do to help. I don't like the idea of your marrying anyone in Moose Society anyway."
>
> Olga finally says "yes" to Blackbeard. When they get across, Igor is in ecstasy over seeing Olga. Olga kisses and hugs him and then starts to cry. Burdened with guilt, she confesses that she had to go to bed with Blackbeard as the price for getting across. Igor is outraged. He feels Olga has been tainted. He tells Olga he cannot marry her and that he never wants to see her again. Olga runs to Samson, a mutual friend. Olga tells her story to Samson, and Samson rushes to find Igor. Upon finding Igor, Samson punches him out and knocks him silly. Olga looks on and laughs during the fight.

Step 2. The subgroups arrive at a consensus for rating the characters from one to five.

Step 3. The names of the characters are written on the blackboard (Olga, Igor, Solomon, Samson, and Blackbeard) and a representative from each subgroup writes the subgroup's ranking next to each name.

Step 4. Someone from each subgroup describes the reasons for their rankings. The differences in rankings are then discussed, especially how the values expressed for the rankings differed substantially among the subgroups. The leader might conclude by stating that it is important to identify our values in order to keep our personal value judgments in check when we deal with clients.

EXERCISE F: Genie and the Magic Lantern

GOAL: To identify what you really want at the present time.

Step 1. The leader explains the purpose of the exercise and asks the students to imagine the following: "Let's assume when you go home tonight there will be a magic lantern. After you rub the lantern, a genie will appear and will give you the three things you want most in life now. These things can be anything you want, tangible or intangible. Please list these three things on a sheet of paper."

Step 2. The group forms a circle, and volunteers share what they wrote.

Step 3. After a number of examples, the leader summarizes what appear to be trends in what respondents want most in life at the present time. The class discusses how the respondents' lives would change if their wishes were fulfilled. The exercise ends with students discussing what they learned.

EXERCISE G: Pregnancy and Tragedy

EP 1b

GOAL: To examine a number of values through making decisions about a value vignette.

Step 1. The leader explains the goal of the exercise and asks students to form subgroups of five persons. The subgroups are informed that their task is to rank the following characters as to who is most and least responsible for Lucy's death. The rankings are 1, most responsible, to 6, least responsible. The following story should be read twice.

Lucy is 18 years old, white, and an attractive college freshman. She believes strongly in racial equality, even though her parents have told her on several occasions that they are opposed to interracial dating and marriage. In her courses, Lucy meets Kent, an African American and a college sophomore, and they begin dating.

Lucy becomes pregnant. After a long, agonizing view of the alternatives, both Lucy and Kent decide it would be best to seek an abortion. Neither Lucy nor Kent has the money to obtain an abortion from an abortion clinic or from a hospital.

Lucy goes home with the hope of asking her parents for the necessary funds. She begins by telling her mother that she is dating Kent, that Kent is African American, and that they have become sexually involved. Her mother immediately becomes upset and calls in Lucy's father. Both parents angrily tell Lucy she must stop seeing Kent or they will no longer pay her college bills. Lucy is not able to inform her parents she is pregnant.

Lucy is distraught. She returns to college. The next day Lucy hears of a person who will perform the abortion at half price. Kent goes along with her to the abortionist who, it turns out, is quite unskilled and unsanitary. Lucy begins hemorrhaging on the table; Kent rushes her to the hospital, but it is too late, and Lucy dies. The hospital administrator tells Kent that Lucy is the third person who has been admitted to this hospital for hemorrhaging after being treated by this abortionist (the other two lived). The hospital administrator adds that it's about time someone informs the police.

Step 2. The subgroups arrive at a ranking for who is most to least responsible for Lucy's death:

_____ Lucy

_____ Kent

_____ Lucy's father

_____ Lucy's mother

_____ The abortionist

_____ The hospital administrator

Step 3. The names of the characters are written on the blackboard, and a representative from each subgroup writes the subgroup's ranking on the blackboard. Each subgroup then provides the reasons for its ranking. A discussion of the values underlying the rankings by these subgroups follows.

Competency Notes

EP 8a   Critically choose and implement interventions to achieve practice goals and enhance capacities of clients and constituencies. (pp. 36–39)

Roles assumed by social workers include enabler, broker, advocate, empowerer, activist, mediator, negotiator, educator, initiator, coordinator, researcher, group facilitator, and public speaker. Exercise 2.2 allows students to examine their interest in becoming involved in these various social work roles.

EP 7b   Apply knowledge of human behavior and the social environment, person-in-environment, and other multidisciplinary theoretical frameworks in the analysis of assessment data from clients and constituencies. (pp. 40–44)

The medical model and the ecological model are two contrasting models in conceptualizing the problems and challenges faced by clients. Exercise 2.3 gives students an introduction to using the medical model.

| **EP 7b** | Apply knowledge of human behavior and the social environment, person-in-environment, and other multidisciplinary theoretical frameworks in the analysis of assessment data from clients and constituencies; |

EP 8b Apply knowledge of human behavior and the social environment, person-in-environment, and other multidisciplinary theoretical frameworks in interventions with clients and constituencies.

EP 9b Apply knowledge of human behavior and the social environment, person-in-environment, and other multidisciplinary theoretical frameworks in the evaluation of outcomes. (p. 47)

The problem-solving approach provides a framework for analyzing challenges faced by clients and then intervening and evaluating interventions with clients. Exercise 2.6 allows students to apply the problem-solving approach. The systems perspective is an essential perspective for intervening with clients.

EP 8b Apply knowledge of human behavior and the social environment, person-in-environment, and other multidisciplinary theoretical frameworks in interventions with clients and constituencies. (pp. 51–55)

This material conceptualizes the activities performed by social workers as social casework, case management, group work, group treatment, family treatment, community organization, policy analysis, and administration.

EP 1a through EP 9d All the competencies and behaviors of 2015 *EPAS*. (pp. 55–59) This section reprints the knowledge, skills, values, and cognitive and affective processes needed for social work practice, as stated in 2015 *EPAS*.

EP 7b Apply knowledge of human behavior and the social environment, person-in-environment, and other multidisciplinary theoretical frameworks in the analysis of assessment data from clients and constituencies.

EP 8b Apply knowledge of human behavior and the social environment, person-in-environment, and other multidisciplinary theoretical frameworks in interventions with clients and constituencies. (pp. 60–61)

This exercise is designed to assist students in being creative in developing options to improve services to vulnerable populations.

EP 1a through EP 9d All the competencies and behaviors of 2015 *EPAS*. (pp. 62–66) This exercise is designed to have field supervisors assess the extent to which their students have attained the knowledge, skills, and values for social work practice, as stated in 2015 *EPAS*.

EP 1b Use reflection and self-regulation to manage personal values and maintain professionalism in practice situations. (pp. 66–68)

This exercise is designed to help students clarify their values in regard to a number of prominent issues in social work.

EP 1b Use reflection and self-regulation to manage personal values and maintain professionalism in practice situations. (p. 70)

This exercise is designed to have students examine a number of their personal values.

Key Terms and Concepts

Administration	Enabler	Micro	Reform Approach
Advocate	Generalist Practice	Patients	Relationship
Broker	Helper Therapy	Person-in-Family	Social Planning
Case Managers	Homeostasis	Planner	Social Worker
Community Organization	Macro	Planning	Supervisor
Consultant	Macro Practice	Policy Developer	Wholeness
Coordinator	Management	Policy Development	
Ecological Approach	Mental Illnesses	Program Developer	
Empowerment	Mezzo	Program Development	

3

Group Dynamics: Leadership

Leadership occurs whenever one person in a group influences other members to help the group reach its goals. Because all group members influence each other at various times, each individual exerts leadership. However, a difference exists between being a designated leader—a president or chairperson—and engaging in leadership behavior. A **designated leader** has certain responsibilities, such as calling meetings and leading discussions, whereas **leadership** refers to influential behavior in general.

LO 1   Describe Five Major Approaches to Leadership

EP 7b
EP 8b

APPROACHES TO LEADERSHIP

Five major approaches to leadership theory—trait, position, leadership style, distributed functions, and servant leadership—are summarized in the following sections.

The Trait Approach

Aristotle observed: "From the hour of their birth some are marked for subjugation, and others for command." This trait approach to leadership, which has existed for centuries, assumes that leaders have inherent personal characteristics, or traits, that distinguish them from followers. This approach asserts that leaders are born, not made, and emerge naturally instead of being trained. It has also been called the "great man" or "great woman" theory of leadership. According to Krech, Crutchfield, and Ballachey, who reviewed research studies on leadership traits, a leader needs to be perceived as (1) a member of the group he or she is attempting to lead, (2) embodying to a special degree the norms and values central to the group, (3) the most qualified group member to accomplish the task at hand, and (4) fitting members' expectations about how he or she should behave and what functions he or she should serve.[1]

Some research on personality traits indicates that leaders tend to be better adjusted and more dominant, extroverted, "masculine," and interpersonally sensitive than their followers. Other traits, such as intelligence, enthusiasm, dominance, self-confidence, and egalitarianism, have also been found to characterize leaders.[2] Although potential leaders tend to have more positive attributes than other group members, they cannot be so successful that members perceive them as "different." For example, Davis and Hare found that "B" students were the campus leaders, whereas the more intelligent "A" students were considered "grinds" who occasionally were treated as outcasts for being "curve wreckers."[3] Also, the member who talks most has been found to win most decisions and so becomes the leader, unless he or she talks too much and antagonizes other group members.[4]

LEARNING OBJECTIVES

Is the statement "He's a born leader" valid, or is leadership a learned characteristic rather than an inherited trait? This chapter will help prepare students to:

LO 1
Describe five major approaches to leadership.

LO 2
Identify effective group leadership functions, roles, and techniques.

LO 3
Understand that the use of power is a necessary component of group functioning.

LO 4
Describe five bases of power in groups, and identify the different consequences of using these bases.

LO 5
Understand the effects of unequal power in groups.

LO 6
Comprehend how to start and lead a group.

LO 7
Understand strengths-based leadership.

Two postulated leadership traits that have received considerable attention are charisma and Machiavellianism. We will take a brief look at each of these traits.

Charisma   Charisma has been defined as "an extraordinary power, as of working miracles."[5] Johnson and Johnson give the following definition of a charismatic leader:

> The charismatic leader must have a sense of mission, a belief in the social-change movement he or she leads, and confidence in oneself as the chosen instrument to lead the movement to its destination. The leader must appear extremely self-confident in order to inspire others with the faith that the movement he or she leads will, without fail, prevail and ultimately reduce their distress.[6]

Some charismatic leaders appear to inspire their followers to love and be fully committed to them. Other charismatic leaders offer their followers the hope and promise of deliverance from distress.

Charisma has not been precisely defined, and its components have not been fully identified. The qualities and characteristics that each charismatic leader has will differ somewhat from those of other charismatic leaders. The following leaders all have been referred to as charismatic, yet they differed substantially in personality characteristics: John F. Kennedy, Martin Luther King Jr., Julius Caesar, General George Patton, Confucius, Gandhi, and Winston Churchill.

One flaw with the charisma approach to leadership is that people who are viewed as having charisma tend to express this quality in a variety of ways. A second flaw is that many people do well as leaders without being viewed as having charisma. For example, many group therapists are effective in leading groups even though they are not viewed as charismatic.

Machiavellianism   Niccolò Machiavelli (1469–1527) was an Italian statesman who advocated cunning, deceit, and duplicity as political methods rulers should use for increasing their power and control. Machiavelli was not the originator of such an approach; earlier theorists conceptualized leadership in terms of manipulation for self-enhancement. However, the term **Machiavellianism** has become associated with the notion that politics is amoral and that any means should be used to achieve political power. Machiavellian leadership is based on the concepts that people (1) are basically fallible, gullible, untrustworthy, and weak; (2) are impersonal objects; and (3) should be manipulated so that the leader can achieve his goals.

Christie and Geis conclude that Machiavellian leaders have four characteristics:

1. They have little emotional involvement in interpersonal relationships—it is easier to manipulate others if "followers" are viewed as impersonal objects.
2. They are not concerned about conventional morality; they take a utilitarian view (what they can get out of it) rather than a moral view of their interactions with others.
3. They have a fairly accurate perception of the needs of their followers, which facilitates their capacity to manipulate them.
4. They have a low degree of ideological commitment; they focus on manipulating others for personal benefit, rather than on achieving long-term ideological goals.[7]

It should be noted that some Machiavellian leaders have considerable charisma, but they use their charisma to manipulate their followers.

Although a few leaders may have Machiavellian characteristics, most do not. Today very few groups would function effectively or efficiently with Machiavellian leaders.

In recent years the trait theory of leadership has declined in popularity, partly because research results have raised questions about its validity. For example, different leadership positions often require different leadership traits. The characteristics of a good leader in the military differ markedly from those of a good group therapy leader. Moreover, traits found in leaders have also been found in followers. Although qualities such as high intelligence and a well-adjusted personality may have some correlation with leadership, many highly

EXERCISE 3.1   The Charismatic Leader

GOAL: This exercise is designed to assist you in identifying charismatic people and understanding the various characteristics that lead a person to be charismatic.

1. Write the names of three people you identify as being charismatic. These may be presidents, political leaders, religious leaders, teachers, acquaintances, and so on. For each person you identify, list the characteristics that cause this person (in your view) to be charismatic.

2. For the three people you wrote about, identify the charismatic characteristics that all three individuals appear to have in common.

3. Do any of these people have unique charismatic characteristics (that is, characteristics that are not held by the other two)? If "yes," identify the person and describe his or her unique characteristics.

intelligent people never get top leadership positions, and some highly intelligent leaders (Adolf Hitler, for example) have been emotionally unstable. The best rule for leader selection involves choosing individuals with the necessary skills, qualities, and motivation to help a group accomplish its goals.

The Position Approach

In most large organizations, there are several levels of leadership, such as president, vice president, manager, supervisor, and foreman. The position approach defines leadership in terms of the authority of a particular position. It focuses on studying the behavior, training, and personal background of leaders in high-level positions.

Studies using the position approach, however, have revealed little consistency in how people assume leadership positions. Obviously, some individuals may become leaders with little related training (in family businesses, for example), whereas others spend years developing their skills. Also, individuals in different leadership positions have been found to display a variety of appropriate behaviors. For example, a drill sergeant in basic military training is not expected to be empathetic, but a sensitivity group leader is. It is difficult to compile a list of leadership traits by using this approach. Not surprisingly, the position approach has shown that what constitutes leadership behavior depends upon the particular requirements of the position.

Another problem with the position approach is that it is difficult to define which behavior of a designated leader is leadership behavior and which is not. Certainly not all of the behavior of a designated authority figure is leadership behavior. For instance, an inexperienced individual in a position of authority can mask incompetence with an authoritarian attitude. Also, the leadership behavior among group members who are not designated leaders is difficult for the position approach to explain because this approach focuses its attention on designated leaders.

The Leadership-Style Approach

Because researchers on the trait and the position approaches were turning out contradictory results, Lewin, Lippitt, and White focused on examining leadership styles. Their research uncovered three: authoritarian, democratic, and laissez-faire.[8]

Authoritarian Leaders   These types of leaders, who have more absolute power than democratic leaders, set goals and policies, dictate the activities of the members, and develop major plans. The leader alone is the purveyor of rewards and punishments and knows the succession of future steps in the group's activities. Authoritarian leadership is generally efficient and decisive. One of the hazards, however, is that group members may respond out of necessity and not because of commitment to group goals. The authoritarian leader who anticipates approval from subordinates may be surprised to find that backbiting and bickering are common in the group. Unsuccessful authoritarian leadership is apt to generate factionalism, behind-the-scenes jockeying for position among members, and a decline in morale.

EXERCISE 3.2   Machiavellian Leaders

GOAL: This exercise is designed to assist you in understanding the characteristics of Machiavellian leaders.

Some authorities view Joseph Stalin, Adolf Hitler, and Saddam Hussein as Machiavellian leaders. Identify three people you view as Machiavellian leaders. (These people may include one or more of the leaders just mentioned.) For each person you list, write the characteristics he or she had (or has) that are Machiavellian in nature.

Democratic Leaders   In contrast, democratic leaders seek the maximum involvement and participation of every member in all decisions affecting the group and attempt to spread responsibility rather than concentrate it. Democratic leadership can lead to slow decision making and confusion, but it is frequently more effective because of the strong cooperation that emerges from group participation. Interpersonal hostilities between members, dissatisfactions with the leader, and concern for personal advancement all become issues that are discussed and acted upon. With democratic leadership, the private complaining that is kept behind the scenes in the authoritarian approach usually becomes public. When this occurs, such conflicts can be more openly and readily confronted and dealt with. Once this public conflict has been resolved in a democratic group, however, a strong personal commitment usually develops, which motivates members to implement group decisions rather than to subvert them. The potential for sabotage in an authoritarian group is high, and therein lies the major advantage of the democratic style. The democratic leader knows that mistakes are inevitable and the group will suffer from them, but he or she must learn to stand back and allow the democratic process to continue without interference.

Depending on the situation, authoritarian or democratic leadership may be more effective, assuming members' expectations about appropriate behavior for each situation are met.[9] When group members anticipate a democratic style, as they do in educational settings or discussion groups, the democratic style is utilized well. When members anticipate forceful leadership from their superiors, as in industry or the military, individuals accept a more authoritarian form of leadership.

Laissez-Faire Leaders   These leaders participate very little, and group members are generally left to function (or flounder) with little input. Group members seldom function well under a laissez-faire style, which may be effective *only* when the members are committed to a course of action, have the resources to implement it, and need minimal leadership to reach their goals. For example, laissez-faire leadership may work well in a college department in which the faculty members are competent, conscientious, and responsible and have the resources to meet their objectives.

The Distributed-Functions Approach

Because different leadership styles are required in different situations (even within the same group), research in recent years has focused more on how leadership functions are distributed. The distributed-functions approach disagrees with the "great person," or trait, theory of leadership and asserts that every member of a group will be a leader at times by taking actions that serve group functions. Leadership is defined as the performance of acts that help the group maintain itself and reach its goals. Leadership functions include setting goals, selecting and implementing tasks, and providing resources to accomplish group goals while maintaining the group's cohesion and satisfying the needs of individual members. The functional approach involves determining what tasks, or functions, are essential to achieve group goals and how different group members should participate.

With this approach, the demands of leadership are viewed as being specific to a particular group in a particular situation. For example, cracking a joke may be a useful leadership tactic in certain situations if it relieves tension. But when other members are revealing intense personal information in therapy, humor may be a counterproductive and therefore inappropriate leadership behavior.

Many individuals who fear taking a leadership role are uncertain about leadership functions and feel they lack the proper qualities of a leader. Amazingly, even the most fearful and anxious students have already taken on many leadership roles, and nearly everyone has assumed leadership responsibilities by adolescence. Functional leadership involves a learned set of skills that anyone with certain minimal capabilities can acquire. Responsible membership is the same thing as responsible leadership because both maintain the group's cohesion and accomplish its goals. Because people can be taught

EXERCISE 3.3   Authoritarian, Democratic, and Laissez-Faire Leaders

GOAL: This exercise is designed to help you understand these three types of leadership styles.

1. Identify someone who used an authoritarian style in leading a group. State what the leader did that led you to conclude his or her style was authoritarian. Also state what the reactions of the other group members were to this authoritarian style.

2. Identify someone who used a democratic style in leading a group. State what the leader did that led you to conclude his or her style was democratic. Also state what the reactions of the other group members were to this democratic style.

3. Identify someone who used a laissez-faire style in leading a group. State what the leader did that led you to conclude his or her style was laissez-faire. Also state what the reactions of the other group members were to this laissez-faire style.

leadership skills and behaviors, the implication of this theory is that nearly everyone can be taught to be an effective leader.

Servant Leadership Approach

Servant leadership is an approach to leadership that was initially developed by Robert K. Greenleaf.[10] A servant leader is someone who looks to the needs of the group. The servant leader is working with the members to solve problems and asks himself or herself how he or she can help and promote their personal development. The servant leader places the main focus on the members, as he or she believes that content and motivated members are best able to reach their goals. In contrast to an autocratic style of leadership, in which the autocratic leader makes most of the decisions, decision-making responsibilities are shared with the members in the servant leadership style. The highest

EXERCISE 3.4   Applying the Distributed-Functions Approach

GOAL: This exercise is designed to show you that you have already taken on leadership functions in a group.

The distributed-functions approach asserts that every member of a group will be a leader at times by taking actions that serve group functions. Identify a group that you are currently in or that you were a member of in the past. Describe the actions you took that were useful to the group. (When you made positive contributions to this group, you were taking on leadership responsibilities.)

priority of a servant leader is to support, encourage, and enable members to unfold their full potential and abilities. (A highly competent teacher probably uses many of the concepts of a servant leader.)

Larry C. Spears has identified the following 10 concepts that characterize a servant leader:

- Listening: A servant leader is motivated to listen to members, is supportive of their opinions, and validates their concerns. The servant leader not only attends to verbalized concerns, but also to what is "unspoken."
- Empathy: A servant leader seeks to understand and empathize with the members. The members are viewed as people who need respect and appreciation in order to facilitate personal development; and the more that members develop, the more successful and productive they are apt to become.
- Healing: A servant leader seeks to help members solve their issues and conflicts in relationships, as he or she wants to encourage and support the personal development of each member. Such "healing" is postulated to lead to a working environment in the group that is dynamic, fun, and free of the fear of failure.
- Awareness: A servant leader seeks to have a high level of self-awareness and to be perceptive of what the members are thinking and feeling. He or she also seeks to be aware of the interpersonal relationships in the group.
- Persuasion: A servant leader does not try to coerce members into compliance with what he or she wants, but instead seeks to convince members to share decision-making responsibilities.
- Conceptualization: A servant leader thinks beyond day-to-day realities by conceptualizing long-term goals and strategies for reaching those goals. He or she has a personal vision that incorporates what is in the best interests of all members of the group.
- Foresight: A servant leader has the capacity to foresee the likely outcome of possible implementation strategies. (This characteristic is closely related to conceptualization.)
- Stewardship: A servant leader not only seeks to facilitate the personal development and productivity of the group, but also realizes that he or she has an obligation to

do what is best for the greater society. Openness and persuasion are more important than control.

- Commitment to the growth of people: A servant leader focuses on nurturing the professional, personal, and spiritual growth of members. He or she seeks to validate the ideas of all the members and involves them in decision making.
- Building community: A servant leader not only seeks to develop a productive and contented group, but also seeks to build a strong community. It is postulated that members will have considerable growth with this style of leadership, which will lead these members to add to the development of the communities in which they live.[11]

Servant leadership is a lifelong journey that includes self-discovery, a desire to serve others, and a commitment to developing the group members that one works with. Servant leaders are humble, caring, visionary, empowering, relational, competent, good stewards, and community builders. They put others first, are skilled communicators, are compassionate collaborators, are systems thinkers, and are ethical. Instead of a top-down hierarchical style, servant leaders emphasize trust, collaboration, empathy, and ethical use of power. Servant leaders do not seek to increase their own power, but seek to lead by better serving others.

Servant leadership not only facilitates the personal development of group members, but has the potential to influence the broader society in a positive way. Group members tend to be attracted to this style of leadership and tend to be happier and more productive. (Servant leadership is not only an effective approach to leading a group, but is also an effective management style for a supervisor to use in supervising employees. Managers who empower and respect their staff tend to get better performance in return.)

Will servant leadership work well in all groups? Undoubtedly not! Certain settings probably require a more forceful form of leadership—such as in the military or in a prison setting.

EXERCISE 3.5   Servant Leaders

GOAL: This exercise is designed to help you understand the servant leadership approach. Identify someone who used the servant leadership approach in leading a group. Perhaps the person was a teacher or a member of the clergy. State what the leader did that led you to conclude his or her style was servant leadership. Also state what the reactions of the other group members were to this style.

LO 2   Identify Effective Group Leadership Functions, Roles, and Techniques

EP 8b

LEADERSHIP ROLES

Task and Maintenance Roles

Through considerable research on problem-solving groups, Bales has identified two specific leadership functions: the task specialist and the social/emotional, or group maintenance, specialist.[12] All groups, whether organized for therapeutic reasons, problem solving, or other purposes, rely on members performing task roles and group maintenance roles satisfactorily. **Task roles** are those needed to accomplish specific goals set by the group.

Task roles refer to the actions of individuals that help move the project, discussion, decision, or task along. These roles include:

Initiating: Proposing tasks of goals, defining a group problem, suggesting a procedure of ideas for getting the task accomplished, defining the task, and seeking to provide a structure for the meeting.

Information of Opinion Seeking: Requesting facts, seeking relevant information about a question or concern, asking for suggestions or ideas or opinions, and collecting data.

Clarifying: Interpreting or reflecting ideas and suggestions, clarifying conclusions, indicating alternatives and issues to be considered by the group, giving examples, defining terms, asking for clarification or an example, building on the ideas of others, and developing half-stated ideas into fully developed possibilities.

Summarizing: Pulling together related ideas, restating suggestions after the group has discussed them, offering a decision or conclusion for the group to accept or reject, and restating the decisions or action plans of the discussion.

Consensus Testing: Checking with the group to see how much agreement has been reached and how ready the group members are to consider a decision or plan of action.

Maintenance roles refer to the actions of individuals which preserve or strengthen social/emotional bonds with the group. These roles include:

Encouraging: Being friendly and warm and responsive to others, accepting others and their contributions, encouraging others to contribute, praising others for their contributions, and pointing out the progress and accomplishments of the group.

Harmonizing: Attempting to reconcile disagreements, reducing tension, and getting members to explore their differences and find common ground in their opinions.

Expressing Group Feelings: Sensing and verbalizing feelings, mood, and tensions in the group and sharing one's own feelings with other group members.

Fostering Communication: Helping to keep communication open, facilitating the participation of others, suggesting procedures that permit sharing remarks, asking others for their opinion, being sensitive and perceptive of the nonverbal signals of members who want to participate, and asking others for their input when one member is monopolizing the conversation.

Compromising: When someone is disagreeing with you, seek to find a compromise that will "work" for you and the other member; when the group is stuck, offer suggestions for getting unstuck; encourage the group to figure out a compromise when disagreement arise; and help the group define its ground rules that will facilitate handling disagreements. [13]

Each of the foregoing task and maintenance functions may be required periodically within a group, and effective group members (and leaders) are sensitive to these needs.

A task leader emerges in many groups because he or she has the best ideas and does the most to guide discussions. Because this person concentrates on a task and generally plays an aggressive role in moving the group toward the goal, hostility is apt to arise and the task leader may be disliked. Concurrently, a second leader may emerge: a social/emotional specialist who concentrates on group harmony and resolves tensions and conflicts within the group. In groups with an official leader, the leader is expected to be both the task specialist and the social/emotional specialist. In groups without an official leader, these two functions are generally assumed by two different emergent leaders. When social/emotional group maintenance needs are met, a group will continually improve its task effectiveness. However, when maintenance needs are ignored, a group's task effectiveness deteriorates.

Hersey and Blanchard have developed a situational theory of leadership that points out when leaders should focus on task behaviors, on maintenance behaviors, or on both.[14] In essence, the theory asserts that when members have low maturity in terms of accomplishing a specific task, the leader should engage in high-task behaviors and low-maintenance behaviors. Hersey and Blanchard refer to this situation as **telling**—the leader's behavior is most effective when the leader defines the roles of members and *tells* them how, when, and where to do needed tasks. The task maturity of members increases as their experience and understanding of the task increase. For moderately mature members, the leader should engage in high-task behaviors and high-maintenance behaviors. This combination of behaviors is referred to as **selling**. The leader should not only provide clear directions about role and task responsibilities, but also use maintenance behaviors to get the members to "buy into" the decisions that have to be made.

Hersey and Blanchard also assert that when the group members' commitment to the task increases, so does their maturity. When members are committed to accomplishing the task and have the ability and knowledge to complete the task, the leader should engage in low-task behaviors and high-maintenance behaviors. This is referred to as **participating**. Finally, for groups in which members are both willing and able to take responsibility for directing their own task behavior, the leader should engage in low-task and low-maintenance behaviors; this is referred to as **delegating**. Delegating allows members considerable autonomy in completing the task.

Other Roles

The designated group leader has a special obligation to assume, or to assist others in assuming, timely and appropriate task and maintenance roles. Each leader is also responsible for a variety of functions, which range from setting initial policies to planning for termination. To meet the needs and particular developmental stage of a group, a leader may be required to assume any of the previously described roles in addition to these:

Executive: Coordinates the activities of a group.

Policy Maker: Establishes group goals and policies.

Planner: Decides the means by which the group shall achieve its goals.

Expert: Offers a ready source of information and skills.

External Group Representative: Serves as official spokesperson.

Controller of Internal Relations: Controls the group structure and in-group relations.

Purveyor of Rewards and Punishments: Promotes, demotes, and assigns pleasant or unpleasant tasks.

Arbitrator and Mediator: Acts as both judge and conciliator and has the power to reduce or increase factionalism within the group.

Exemplar: Serves as a model of behavior for other members.

Ideologist: Serves as the source of group beliefs and values.

Scapegoat: Serves as the target for members' frustrations and disappointments.

EXERCISE 3.6   Your Task and Maintenance Contributions to a Group

GOAL: This exercise is designed to assist you in understanding your task and maintenance contributions to a group.

1. Identify a group you are currently participating in or have participated with in the past. Briefly describe this group, including its goals.

2. Review the list of task roles and then describe your task contributions to this group.

3. Review the list of maintenance roles and then describe your maintenance contributions to this group.

LO 3   Understand that the Use of Power Is a Necessary Component of Group Functioning

POWER AND INFLUENCE IN GROUPS

Although the use of power in human interactions is often viewed negatively, it is, in fact, a normal part of relationships because people are frequently influencing and being influenced by one another. The terms **power** and **influence** will be used interchangeably in this chapter. Both terms refer to the capacity of an individual to motivate others to carry out certain actions or to behave in a particular way. Earlier in this chapter, leadership was defined as one member of a group influencing other members to achieve group goals and promote group maintenance. In an effective group, each member at times takes a leadership role by performing task and maintenance functions. Task functions move the group forward; maintenance functions improve the social/emotional atmosphere of the group.

In making decisions, group members present their views and opinions in an effort to influence group members. For example, some members attempt to incorporate their personal goals into the group's goals or to promote the strategies for action they want implemented. Members influence each other to commit their time and resources to the group.

Controversies are usually settled through mutual influence, as members seek acceptable compromises or solutions. The use of power is indeed a necessary component of effective group functioning, and it is natural and generally desirable for every member to influence other members in the pursuit of both personal and group goals.

Every group member has a need to control what happens in a group because people join groups to attain personal goals they cannot achieve individually. If members do not exert power, their chances of achieving their personal goals are small, and they are apt to become apathetic and disengage themselves from the group.

When group members are cooperating, power is asserted in the same direction, and members encourage each other to put forth greater effort, as they would on a sports team. However, when members are competitive or have incompatible goals, their assertions of power conflict. Republican and Democratic congressional representatives, for example, are constantly competing with each other, and their efforts to influence frequently clash.

Group members in conflict sometimes resort to manipulation; that is, they influence others for their own purpose or profit. Often, this manipulation is dishonest or unfair, for it involves the use of power for one's own benefit at the expense of other members. When people say they do not want to have power over others, they usually mean they do not want to manipulate others. If group members feel coerced by threats or discover they are manipulated in other ways, they usually react with anger, distrust, resentment, and retaliation. Manipulation, then, is a destructive kind of power because it decreases cooperation and can cause serious maintenance problems. "Influencing with integrity" is in contrast to manipulation. In a group, influencing with integrity involves seeking to influence the group in a direction that is in the group's best interests.

An effective group member is skillful in influencing others in a positive way. The amount of power a member has depends on how valuable his or her resources are. If a member has vital resources that are also available to others, that member will have less power. Interestingly, it is *not* a person's *actual* resources that determine power; instead, it is the *perception* of the other group members as to the value of a member's resources. It is possible to have vital resources but little power if these resources are ignored or unknown. It is also possible to have great power but few vital resources if members exaggerate the importance of such resources.

LO 4   Describe Five Bases of Power in Groups, and Identify the Different Consequences of Using These Bases

EP 7b
EP 8b

POWER BASES IN GROUPS

French and Raven have developed a framework for understanding the extent to which one group member influences another by identifying five bases of power: reward, coercive, legitimate, referent, and expert.[15] This framework allows group members to analyze the source of their power and offers suggestions on when, and when not, to use their power to influence others.

Reward Power

Rewards include such things as promotions, pay increases, days off, and praise. Reward power is based on B's (one member's) perception that A (another member or the entire group) has the capacity to dispense rewards or remove negative consequences in response to B's behavior. This power will be greater if the group members value the reward and believe they cannot get it from anyone else. Group members will usually work hard for someone who has high reward power and will communicate effectively with him or her. Reward power can backfire, however, if group members feel they are being conned or bribed. If reward power is used by A in a conflict situation with B, B is apt to feel he is being bribed and controlled, and may eventually refuse to cooperate.

Coercive Power

The ability to fire a worker who falls below a given level of production is a common example of coercive power, which is based on B's perceptions that A can dispense punishments or remove positive consequences. Coercive power stems from the expectation on the part of B that he will be punished by A if he fails to conform to the required standards set by A. The distinction between reward and coercive power is important. French and Raven note that reward power will tend to increase the attraction of B toward A, whereas coercive power will decrease this attraction. If coercive power is used by A to attempt to settle a conflict, it often increases B's hostility, resentment, and anger. Threats often lead to aggression and counterthreats; for example, military threats often increase conflict between rival countries. Coercive power may exacerbate conflict by leading both A and B to distrust each other and to retaliate against each other. Therefore, whenever possible, coercive power should not be used to settle conflicts.

Legitimate Power

Legitimate power is directly related to an internalized value or norm and is probably the most complex of the five power bases. Legitimate power is based on the perception by B that A has a legitimate right to prescribe what constitutes proper behavior for him or her and that B has an obligation to accept this influence. Cultural values constitute one common basis for legitimate power and include intelligence, age, caste, and physical characteristics as factors determining power. For example, in some cultures the aged are highly respected and are granted the right to prescribe behavior for others. The legitimate power inherent in a formal organization is generally determined by a relationship between positions rather than between people. A supervisor in a factory, for instance, has the inherent right to assign work. A third basis for legitimate power is a legitimizing agent, for example, an election. The election process legitimizes a person's right to a position that already had a legitimate range of power associated with it.

The limits of legitimate power are generally specified at the time that power is assigned (for example, in a job description). The attempted use of power outside of this range will decrease the legitimate power of the authority figure and decrease his or her attractiveness and influence.

Referent Power

Referent power occurs when one individual, A, influences another, B, as a result of identification. Identification in this context means either a feeling of oneness with A or a desire for an identity such as A's. The stronger the identification of B with A, the greater the attraction to A and the greater the referent power of A. Verbalization of referent power is "I am like A, and therefore I will believe or behave as A does," or "I want to be like A, and I will be more like A if I believe or behave as A does." In ambiguous situations (that is, situations where there are no objective right or wrong beliefs or opinions), B will seek to evaluate his or her thoughts, beliefs, and values in terms of what A thinks, believes, and values. In ambiguous situations, B is apt to adopt the thoughts, beliefs, and values of the individual or group with which B identifies. French and Raven note that B is often not consciously aware of the referent power that A exerts.

Expert Power

Accepting a physician's advice in medical matters is a common example of expert influence, which is based on the perception that a person has knowledge or expertise that is the source of power. Another example would be accepting a counselor's suggestions. Experts can influence B (the responder) only if B thinks that A (the expert) has the right answer and B trusts A. The range of expert power is more limited than that of referent power because the expert is seen as having superior knowledge or ability only in specific areas. French and Raven note that the attempted exertion of expert power outside the perceived range will reduce that power because confidence in the expert seems to be undermined.

French and Raven theorize that for all five types, the stronger the basis of power, the greater the power. Referent power is thought to have the broadest range. Any attempt to use power outside the prescribed range is hypothesized to reduce the power.

EXERCISE 3.7   The Power Bases in This Class

GOAL: This exercise is designed to assist you in understanding and applying the power bases that were developed by French and Raven.

This class can be reviewed as being a group. For each of the listed power bases, answer the following: Who in this class has this power base? Have these people engaged in actions that demonstrated this power base? If "yes," write down these actions.

Reward Power:

Coercive Power:

Legitimate Power:

Referent Power:

Expert Power:

LO 5   Understand the Effects of Unequal Power in Groups

EFFECTS OF UNEQUAL POWER

The effectiveness of a group is improved when power is based upon expertise and competence and is relatively equal among members. Members are more committed to implementing decisions when they feel they have had a fair say in making a decision. If a group is dominated by a few powerful members, the low-power members are likely to feel less committed to carrying out the decisions they perceive as being made by the powerful members. When power is relatively balanced, however, the members are generally more cooperative with each other.

Unequal power often leads to distrust between the high- and low-power members. The low-power members fear they will be manipulated and are reluctant to share their thoughts completely with the high-power members because they believe that if they express views in opposition to the views of the high-power members, they are apt to receive fewer rewards and may be coerced. High-power members avoid revealing weaknesses because they fear the low-power members may come to think they are undeserving of their power and seek to grasp it. The problem-solving capacity of groups is generally increased when members have fairly equal power or when the group has flexible and gradually changing power patterns that tend to equalize influence among group members.

Power based on authority or popularity can dramatically reduce the problem-solving capacities of groups when the tasks require expertise and competence. High-power people generally believe that low-power people really do like them because they see themselves as benevolent. They generally believe that low-power people communicate honestly with them and do not hide valuable information from them. When low-power members express dissatisfaction, however, high-power people frequently are not benevolent. Instead, they perceive that the low-power people are "making waves" and "not appreciating what is being done for them." In such situations high-power people may withhold rewards and use threats and coercion. These reactions usually intensify the conflict and polarize the two sides.

When threatened, high-power people may maintain power by instituting rules or norms that legitimize their power and make it illegal to change the status quo.[16] After the South lost the Civil War, for example, the White power structure in the South sought to maintain its power by keeping schools, restaurants, and public restrooms segregated. Processes were established that prevented many Black people from voting, and few were hired for high-status positions. Numerous state and local laws were enacted to legitimize this segregation.

High-power people may also maintain their position by creating severe penalties for attempting to change the status quo. Blacks in the South were lynched for such offenses as seeking to be served in White restaurants. In addition, high-power members may seek to deter low-power members from rebelling by dispensing a variety of rewards to those low-power members who support the status quo.

Halle has observed that the greater a person's power becomes, the less sufficient it seems because the requests and claims upon it increase faster than the capacity to fulfill them.[17] For example, although the United States has become very powerful in the past 50 years, requests for domestic and military help from other countries have increased more rapidly than the country's ability to fulfill them. The power of the United States thus seems insufficient.

How do low-power people relate to high-power people? There are a variety of strategies. One is to emphasize and exaggerate the degree to which high-power people like them, overestimating their goodwill.[18] Low-power people using this strategy direct much of their attention and communication to high-power people, seeking to remain on good terms with them.

A second strategy for low-power people is to become apathetic and submissive. Authoritarian leadership often breeds this reaction. A third strategy is to become angry and rebel; rebellion sometimes leads to destructive violence.

Low-power people can use a variety of strategies to change the distribution of power.[19] One is to endear themselves by frequently complimenting high-power people and agreeing with them. The hope is that high-power people will come to depend on them and reward them with more power. A second strategy is to develop personal resources and organizations so that they are less vulnerable to exploitation and less dependent upon high-power people. This strategy builds a separate power structure. A third strategy is to build coalitions with other parties. Right-to-life groups, for example, have formed a coalition with leaders in the Roman Catholic Church in an attempt to make abortions illegal. A fourth strategy is to use existing legal procedures to bring pressures for change. The civil rights movement has used the court system extensively to force the power structure to make changes. A fifth strategy involves low-power members organizing and using confrontation techniques to force the power structure to change.

Perhaps the best known authority on using power confrontation techniques is Saul Alinsky.[20] Alinsky and his associates organized many citizens' groups to confront established power structures. For example, in the 1960s Alinsky was working with a citizens' group known as the Woodlawn Organization in the inner city of Chicago. City authorities had made commitments to this organization to improve several conditions in the neighborhood. When it became clear the commitments would not be honored, however, the Woodlawn Organization sought ways to pressure the city into meeting its commitments. The proposed solution was to embarrass city officials by tying up all the lavatories at O'Hare, one of the world's busiest airports. Alinsky describes this effort as follows:

> An intelligence study was launched to learn how many sit-down toilets for both men and women, as well as stand-up urinals, there were in the entire O'Hare airport complex and how many men and women would be necessary for the nation's first "shit-in."

> The consequences of this kind of action would be catastrophic in many ways. People would be desperate for a place to relieve themselves. One can see children yelling at their parents, "Mommy, I've got to go," and desperate mothers surrendering, "All right—well, do it. Do it right here." O'Hare would soon become a shambles. The whole scene would become unbelievable and the laughter and ridicule would be nationwide, it would probably get a front page story in the *London Times*. It would be a source of great mortification and embarrassment to the city administration. It might even create the kind of emergency in which planes would have to be held up while passengers got back aboard to use the plane's toilet facilities.

> The threat of this tactic was leaked (. . . there may be a Freudian slip here . . . so what?) back to the administration, and within 48 hours the Woodlawn Organization found itself in conference with the authorities who said they were certainly going to live up to their commitments and they could never understand where anyone got the idea that a promise made by Chicago's City Hall would not be observed.[21]

Community change efforts through group projects are often enjoyable!

COLEADERSHIP OF A GROUP

Advantages

Coleadership has both advantages and disadvantages. The advantages (and benefits) will first be described. During meetings of the group, coleaders can help each other in doing the tasks (described earlier) associated with leading a group. Between meetings, the coleaders can meet to discuss what went well at the last meeting and what needs to be improved; they then can discuss what may be done to make the next meeting even more constructive and effective. Such sharing will not only be beneficial to the group, but also is apt to facilitate the professional growth of both coleaders.

If an effective coleader is paired with an inexperienced leader who has leadership potential, the effective leader can mentor the inexperienced leader.

Coleadership provides two people to observe and attend to the dynamics taking place in a group. As a result, the nonverbal communication of the other group members is more apt to be accurately identified. (As an aside, it is best for coleaders to sit across from one another so that they can more closely observe the nonverbal communication of all the group members; if the coleaders sit next to each other, it is difficult to observe what is going on with group members to their immediate left and right.)

EXERCISE 3.8   Groups of Equal Power and Unequal Power

GOAL: This exercise is designed to help you understand the effects of equal power and unequal power among members in a group.

1. Describe a group that you participated in where group members had approximately the same amount of power.

2. Describe a group that you participated in where a few group members had most of the power and the rest of the members had very little power.

3. Which group were you most attracted to? What were the reasons for this attraction?

4. Review the section on the effects of unequal power. Describe how these research results are consistent or inconsistent with your experiences of being in a group of equal power and then in a group of unequal power.

Coleaders are also apt to be a source of support for one another. (We all know that in a group setting when we feel confident and supported, we are apt to be more effective in communicating and also in problem solving.) In addition, coleaders in group treatment settings can assist one another in role-plays, simulations, and solving the challenges being faced by the other group members. Also, if one leader becomes uncertain as to what to say or do about a particular issue that is being discussed, the other coleader is available to step in.

Disadvantages

There are a few potential drawbacks to coleadership. Leadership of the group may financially be more expensive—perhaps twice as expensive—as there may be two leaders who have to be paid by someone. Communication time between meetings between the two leaders may also incur a financial cost.

Conflict and tension between the coleaders, if it occurs, is apt to be detrimental to achieving the goals of the group, as well as to achieving the individual goals of the members. When the coleaders consistently pursue differing strategies or courses of action, the group will be dramatically delayed in achieving tasks, group goals, and individual goals.

Toseland and Rivas note:

> Experience has shown that it is worse to have a coleader with whom one does not agree than to lead a group alone. Therefore, group workers should be cautious in choosing a coleader. Difficulties may arise when workers agree to colead a group without carefully considering whether they can work together effectively. Potential coleaders may want to examine each other's styles while leading a group or during team meetings before agreeing to colead a group.[22]

Wright asserts that the decision to have coleaders should be based on the needs of the group members rather than on group facilitators' preferences for individual or dual leadership.[23] There are certainly situations that call for coleadership—for example, in a group of couples that have marital issues, it is often highly advantageous to have both a male and female leader in order to be representative of both male and female points of view.

LO 6   Comprehend How to Start and Lead a Group

EP 8b

GUIDELINES FOR FORMING AND LEADING A GROUP

The theory of leadership emphasized in this chapter is the distributed-functions approach, which asserts that every group member takes on leadership responsibilities at various times, and every effective action by a member is simultaneously an effective leadership action. Being a designated leader is not that different from taking on leadership roles. This section will summarize a number of suggestions for how to form and lead a group effectively.

Homework

The key to successful group leadership is extensive preparation. Even experienced leaders carefully prepare for each group and for each group session.

In planning for a new group, the following questions must be answered: What is the purpose or general goals of the group? How can these goals be achieved? What are the characteristics of the members? Do some members have unique individual goals or needs? What resources are needed to accomplish group goals? What is the agenda for the first meeting? What is the best way for members to suggest and decide on the specific goals of the group? Should an ice-breaker exercise be used? Which one? Should refreshments be provided? How should the chairs be arranged? What type of group atmosphere will best help the group accomplish its tasks? What is the best available meeting place? Why has the leader been selected? What do the members expect from the leader?

To plan the first meeting, a leader should view the group as a new member would view it. Here are a few questions a new member might have: What will be the goals of this group? Why am I joining? Will my personal goals be met? Will I feel comfortable? Will I be accepted? Will the other members be radically different in terms of backgrounds and interests? If I do not like this group, can I leave gracefully? Will other members respect what I have to say, or will they laugh and make fun of me? By considering such concerns, the leader can plan the first meeting to help other members feel comfortable and to clarify the goals and activities of the group.

Before the first meeting, it is *absolutely essential* that a leader identify the group's needs and expectations as precisely as possible. A group whose leader and members disagree on goals cannot succeed.

There are a variety of ways to identify what the members want. The leader may have an opportunity to ask them before the first meeting. If that is not possible, the leader can at least talk to the organizer of the meeting about the group's expectations.

The first meeting is always a good time to clarify the group's goals. The leader also needs the answers to the following questions:

1. How many members are expected?
2. What are their characteristics: age, socioeconomic status, racial and ethnic background, gender, and educational/professional background?
3. How knowledgeable are the members about the topics the group will be dealing with?
4. What are the likely personal goals of the various members?
5. How motivated are the members to accomplish the purposes for which the group is being formed? Voluntary membership usually indicates greater motivation. Individuals who have been ordered by a court to participate in an alcohol rehabilitation program, for example, have little motivation and may even be hostile.
6. What values are the members likely to have? While being careful to avoid stereotyping, a leader must understand, for example, that teenagers on juvenile probation will differ significantly from retired priests.

In planning a meeting, it is helpful for a leader to visualize how the meeting will go. For example, a leader may want to visualize the following first meeting:

The members will arrive at various times. I will be there early to greet them, introduce myself, assist them in feeling comfortable, and engage in small talk. Possible topics that are apt to be of interest to these new members are _____, _____, and _____.

I will begin the meeting by introducing myself and the overall purpose of the group. I will use the following ice-breaker exercises for members to introduce themselves and get acquainted. 1 will ask the group to give me a list of four or five items they would like to know about the other members. Then the members will introduce themselves and respond to the items. I will also respond to the items and encourage the members to ask questions about me and the group.

After the ice-breaker exercise, I will briefly state the overall purpose of the group and ask for questions. Possible questions are _____. My answers will be _____.

We will proceed to the agenda, which has been mailed to the members. During the discussion of each agenda point, the following questions may arise: _____. My answers are _____.

The kind of group atmosphere I will seek to create is democratic and egalitarian. Such an atmosphere is best suited for encouraging members to become committed to the group goals and to contribute their time and resources. I will create this atmosphere by arranging the chairs in a circle, by drawing out through questions those who are silent, by using humor, and by making sure I do not dominate the conversation.

I will end the meeting by summarizing what has been covered and the decisions that have been made. We will set a time for the next meeting. I will finally ask if anyone has any additional comments or questions. Throughout the meeting I will seek to establish a positive atmosphere, partly by complimenting the members on the contributions they make.

If a group has met more than once, the leader needs to review the following kinds of questions: Have the overall goals been decided upon and clarified? If not, what needs to be done in this clarification process? Is the group making adequate progress in accomplishing its goals? If not, what are the obstacles that must be overcome? Is the group taking the most effective course of action to reach its goals? What is the agenda for the next meeting? What activities should be planned? Will successful completion of these activities move the group toward accomplishing its overall goals? If not, which other activities will? Is each member sufficiently motivated to help the group accomplish its goals? If not, why? What might be done to stimulate their interest?

Planning a Session

In planning a session, the leader must keep the group's overall goals—as well as those for that session—in mind. (For material on how to set group goals, see Chapter 4.) To be effective, the leader must know exactly what should be accomplished in each session and make sure that all the items on the agenda contribute to the goals. Here is a checklist that may help leaders plan successful group sessions. An effective leader will do the following:

1. Select relevant content. The material should not only be relevant to the specific goals for the session but also to the backgrounds and interests of the participants. Time-management advice for college students, for example, probably will be different from that for business executives. Time-saving tips for students will likely focus on improving study habits; business executives will be more interested in how to manage time in an office setting. An excellent way to evaluate possible material is to define precisely how it will be valuable to members of the group. The leader should ask: "If a group member wants to know why he or she should know this, can I give a valid reason?" If that question cannot be answered precisely, the material should be discarded and replaced with more relevant material.

2. Use examples. Examples help illustrate key concepts and stimulate the participants. People tend to remember examples more readily than statistics or concepts. Vivid case histories that illustrate the drastic effects of spouse abuse, for instance, will be remembered much longer than statistics on the extent of spouse abuse.

3. Present materials in a logical order. It is generally desirable to begin by summarizing the agenda items for the session. Ideally, one topic should blend into the next. Group exercises should be used in conjunction with related theoretical material.

4. Plan the time. Once the content of a session is selected and organized, the time each segment requires should be estimated. Accurate estimates will help determine whether planned material and activities are appropriate for the allotted time. A good leader also knows what material can be deleted if time is running short and what can be added if the session progresses more rapidly than planned. Substitute activities must also be available to replace speakers who fail to appear or films that fail to arrive.

5. Be flexible. A variety of unexpected events may make it desirable to change the agenda during a session. Interpersonal conflict between members may take considerable time, or it may become clear that subjects related to the group's overall purpose are more valuable for the group to focus on than the prepared agenda.

6. Change the pace. People pay attention longer if there is an occasional change of pace. Long lectures or discussions can become boring. Group exercises, films, guest speakers, breaks, debates, and other activities will help vary the tempo of a meeting or session. In group therapy, one way to change the pace is to move from one member's problems to those of another. Lectures can be more stimulating if the instructor:

   - speaks extemporaneously instead of reading material
   - walks around the room occasionally, rather than standing or sitting in one place
   - draws out participants by asking questions

An excellent way to learn how to give more stimulating presentations is to observe the non-verbal and verbal communication patterns of dynamic speakers. It is critical to use appropriate transitions so that the topics blend into one another smoothly.

Relaxing Before You Start a Meeting

Before beginning a meeting, the leader is likely to be nervous about how the session may go. Some anxiety, in fact, is helpful because it increases alertness, and that will make the leader more attentive, producing a better meeting. Too much anxiety, however, reduces effectiveness. Relaxation techniques that can alleviate excessive anxiety are described in Chapter 11. They are highly recommended and include walking, jogging, listening to music, meditating, and being alone to clear the mind. Effective group leaders generally learn they can reduce their level of anxiety through using one or more relaxation techniques. Practice in leading groups also builds confidence and reduces anxiety.

Cues upon Entering the Meeting Room

It is essential that a leader be on time, but arriving early is better because it allows the leader to see that materials, seating arrangements, refreshments, and any other needs are in place as planned. The leader will also have an opportunity to observe the members before the group begins. He or she can gain information about the interests of the participants from their age, gender, clothes and personal appearance, conversation, and interaction with one another. An effective leader observes such cues and uses them to create an initial bond with the participants. For example, this author was asked to give a workshop on suicide prevention to a high school class. Upon arriving, I was informed by the teacher that one of the students in the class had recently committed suicide. Instead of beginning with my planned presentation, I asked each student to write down, anonymously, one or two concerns or questions that they had about suicide. We then had a lively discussion based on their questions and concerns. Such a discussion was probably more valuable than the formal presentation (which I never gave) because it focused on their specific questions and concerns.

Seating Arrangements

Seating is important for several reasons. It can affect who talks to whom and influence leadership roles and, as a result, affect group cohesion and morale. In most groups members should have eye contact with one another. The group leader must be able to make eye contact with everyone to obtain nonverbal feedback on what the members are thinking and feeling.

A circle is ideal for generating discussion, encouraging a sense of equal status for each member, and promoting group openness and cohesion. The traditional classroom arrangement, on the other hand, has the effect of placing the leader in a position of authority. It also tends to inhibit communication because members can easily make eye contact only with other members seated nearby.

Tables have advantages and disadvantages. They provide a place to write and to put work materials, and some members feel more comfortable at a table because they can lean on it. But tables restrict movement and may serve as barriers between people.

The leader should thus carefully consider the use of tables. In business meetings or other "working" sessions, for example, tables are necessary. In therapy groups, however, tables are seldom used. When work surfaces and written communication are required, small tables in a circle can be an effective arrangement.

The shape of the tables can also influence the way group members interact. If the table is rectangular, the leader traditionally sits at one end, becomes the head of the table and the "authority," tends to do more talking, and has a greater influence on the discussion than other group members. A round or square table, however, establishes a more egalitarian atmosphere. The "head of the table" effect can also be reduced by placing two rectangular tables together to make a square.

In new groups, or even established ones, members are likely to sit next to friends. If it is important for everyone in the group to interact, the leader may want to ask people to sit next to individuals they do not know. People are most apt to talk to others sitting at right angles to them and then to those next to them. Those sitting directly across receive less communication, and those sitting anywhere else are even less likely to be addressed.

Introductions

The leader's credentials should be summarized at the first meeting to give the group a sense of confidence that the leader can fulfill the expectations of the members. If the leader is being introduced, a concise summary of the leader's credentials *for the expected role* is desirable. If the leader is introducing himself or herself, the important credentials should be summarized in an informative but modest way. The summary should be made in a way that helps create the desired atmosphere—whether it be formal or informal, fun or serious, or whatever. An excellent way to handle the introductions in many groups is to use an ice-breaker exercise, as described in Chapter 1.

It is highly desirable for the leader to learn the names of all group members as quickly as possible. This requires extra attention, and name tags can help everyone be more comfortable sooner. Members appreciate being called by name because it affirms their importance.

If the group is small, the members can introduce themselves individually, perhaps using an ice breaker. In addition to the usual personal information, it is helpful for members to state their expectations for the group as they introduce themselves. This helps uncover hidden agendas that are incompatible with the goals of the group. If a stated expectation is beyond the scope of the group, the leader should tactfully point this out to avoid later frustration or dissatisfaction.

Clarifying Roles

The leader of a group should be clear as to his or her roles and responsibilities. If they are unclear, the leader may want to discuss them with the group. One way of doing this is for the group to select goals and then make decisions about the tasks and responsibilities that *each* member will have in working toward the goals of the group. In most situations it is clearly a mistake for the leader to do the bulk of the work. Generally, the group will be most productive if all members make substantial contributions. The more members contribute to a group, the more likely they are to feel a part of the group. Such positive feelings will benefit everyone.

Even if the leader is certain of the appropriate roles, others may be confused or may have different expectations. If there is any doubt, the leader should explain the roles clearly. If group members indicate different expectations, the group should then make decisions about who will do what.

In explaining his or her role, the leader should be modest about personal skills and resources, attempting to come across as a knowledgeable person rather than as an authority figure who has all the answers. The leader must also be prepared to explain the reasoning behind exercises and other actions or activities. The leader's role will vary from group to group and from situation to situation.

Agenda

Most meetings are more effective if the leader provides an agenda several days beforehand. Ideally, all members of the group should have an opportunity to suggest items for the agenda. The agenda should be briefly reviewed at the start of the meeting to give each member a chance to suggest additions, deletions, or other changes. In some meetings it may be appropriate for the group to discuss, and perhaps vote on, the suggested changes in the agenda.

Additional Guidelines for Leading a Group

This section briefly summarizes additional suggestions for effectively leading a group. Future chapters will expand on the following guidelines:

1. Understand that leadership is a shared responsibility. Every member will take on leadership roles at times. Designated leaders should not seek to dominate a group or believe they are responsible for directing the group in all of its task and maintenance functions. In fact, productivity and group cohesion are substantially increased when everyone contributes.
2. Use decision-making procedures best suited for the issues facing a particular group. (See Chapter 6 for a discussion of a variety of decision-making procedures and their consequences.)

3. Use a problem-solving approach to handle the issues and problems facing the group. (See Chapter 6 for a summary of how to use the problem-solving approach.)
4. Create a cooperative atmosphere rather than a competitive one. (See Chapter 4.)
5. View controversy and conflict as natural and desirable for resolving issues and arriving at good decisions. In resolving conflicts, seek to use a no-lose, problem-solving approach rather than a win–lose approach. (See Chapter 6.)
6. Generally, seek to confront members who are hostile or disruptive (Chapter 4).
7. Use appropriate self-disclosure (Chapter 5).
8. Seek to create an atmosphere of open and honest communication. (See Chapter 5 for ways to improve verbal communication and be an active listener and for ways to improve nonverbal communication.)
9. Provide stimulating, relevant content and exercises that illustrate the concepts and help members try out suggested new behaviors. In an assertiveness group, for example, theoretical material on how to be more assertive should be followed by practice in being more assertive. (The chapters in this text use this format.)
10. Give attention to how to end a session. A few minutes before the session is scheduled to conclude, or when the group has exhausted the subject, a brief summary emphasizing the major points to be remembered leaves the group with a sense of achievement and signals the end of the session. Additional ways to end a session are described in Chapter 14.

Leaders are not born. They are made—through training, practice, and experience. By learning how to lead groups effectively, individuals become more aware of themselves, grow as people, become more self-confident, feel good about themselves, develop highly marketable skills, learn to improve interpersonal relationships, and help themselves and others accomplish important tasks. Everyone reading this text has the potential to become an effective group leader. This chapter has sought to demystify leadership by describing what an effective leader does and is. It is now up to you to further develop your capacities in being a leader. You can do it!

EP 8b

STANDARDS FOR SOCIAL WORK PRACTICE WITH GROUPS

As the name suggests, the Association for the Advancement of Social Work with Groups, Inc. (AASWG) is an international professional organization that seeks to promote and advance social work practice with groups. Its offices are incorporated in New York. This organization has formulated the standards for social work practice with groups presented in Figure 3.1.

FIGURE 3.1   Standards for Social Work Practice with Groups (formulated by the Association for the Advancement of Social Work with Groups)

Purpose

These standards represent the perspective of the Association for the Advancement of Social Work with Groups, Inc. on the value and knowledge and skill essential for professionally sound and effective social work practice with groups and are intended to serve as a guide to social work practice with groups.

Introduction

The Standards focus on central distinguishing concepts of social work with groups and highlight the unique perspective that social group workers bring to practice. By design, the standards are general rather than specific and descriptive rather than prescriptive. They are applicable to a wide range of groups encountered by social group workers in a variety of practice settings. These groups include, among others, treatment, support, psychoeducational, task, and community-action groups. The Standards draw heavily on the *Code of Ethics* from the National Association of Social Work (the United States), group theory from the social sciences, knowledge of individuals and the environment, the historical roots of social group work practice, current practice with groups, and practice research. Thus, they are based on practice wisdom, theories of group work practice, and empirical evidence. They emphasize the understanding and use of group processes and the ways members help one another to accomplish the purposes of the group. The role of the worker, as articulated in the standards, reflects the values of the social work profession generally, as well as the unique features associated with social work with groups.

Section I: Core Values and Knowledge

The group worker should understand the history of group work and the evolving visions of group workers as they faced the challenges posed by each historical era. During this evolution, the following values emerged as the ones that are essential to the practice of group work.

A. Core Values

1. Respect for persons and their autonomy

   In view of the quality of persons, people are to be treated with respect and dignity. In group deliberations no one person should be more privileged in a group than other persons, not a worker, a group member, nor the agency director; in a group this occurs when a worker helps each member to appreciate the contributions of the other members so that everyone's ideas are heard and considered. This principle is stated while recognizing that the worker, by virtue of his or her position in the agency and his or her expertise, is likely to have a great deal of influence. This requires the worker to use his or her influence prudently and transparently.

   A major implication of this principle is a respect for and a high value placed on diversity in all of its dimensions, such as culture, ethnicity, gender, sexual orientation, physical and mental abilities, and age.

2. The creation of a socially just society

   The group offers an opportunity to live and practice the democratic principles of equality and autonomy, and the worker should use his or her knowledge and skills to further this. The worker should be mindful of the quest for a society that is just and democratically organized, one that ensures that the basic human needs of all its members are met. This value is presented to the group whenever this is appropriate and reinforced when members articulate it.

B. Core Knowledge

There are special areas of knowledge that enable group workers to more ably serve the group. This includes knowledge of the history and mission of our profession as it impacts group work with poor people, minorities, and other disenfranchised people. Understanding when group work is the practice of choice is important. The skills needed to carry out the professional mission emerge from our values and knowledge that requires specialized education.

1. Knowledge of individuals
   a. The nature of individual human growth and behavior, emphasizing a biopsychosocial perspective and a "person-in-environment" view. The forces impacting the person and the group are important factors in group work assessment and intervention. This includes viewing the members in the context of the group and of the community.
   b. The familial, social, political, and cultural contexts that influence members' social identities, interactional styles, concerns, opportunities, and the attainment of their potentials.
   c. The capacity of members to help one another and to change.
   d. The capacity of members to contribute to social change in the community and beyond the group.
   e. Competency-based assessment.
   f. The group worker places an emphasis on members' strengths, in addition to their concerns. The worker also must understand protective and risk factors that affect individuals' need for services and their ability to act.
   g. The worker has an appreciation and understanding of such differences as those due to culture, ethnicity, gender, age, physical and mental abilities, and sexual orientation among members and between members and himself or herself that may influence practice.
2. Knowledge of groups and small group behavior
   a. The worker understands that the group is an entity separate from the individual members. The group has its own dynamics, culture, and other social conditions.
   b. The worker understands that the group consists of multiple helping relationships so that members can help one another to achieve individual goals and pursue group goals. This is often referred to as "mutual aid."
   c. The democratic process in groups occurs as the members evolve a sense of "ownership" of the group in which each member's contribution to the group is solicited and valued.
   d. The group can develop in such a way that members, individually and collectively, are empowered to act on their own behalf as well as on behalf of the group.

(continued)

FIGURE 3.1 (continued)

    e. Groups can develop goals that members are committed to pursuing. These goals may be for either individual member growth, group development, and/or social change.

    f. Group members as well as the group as a whole can seek changes in the social environment.

    g. The phases of group development influence change throughout the life of the group.

    h. Group processes and structures encompass all transactions that occur within the group and give meaningfulness to the life of the group. These consist of such conditions as roles, norms, communications, the expression of affect, and the nature of interaction patterns. These shape and influence individual member behavior as well as the development of the group and also determine whether and how the group will accomplish its purposes. The members can come to understand how group processes and structures shape and influence both individual member behavior as well as the development of the group.

    i. Groups are formed for different purposes and goals (for example, education, problem solving, task accomplishment, personal change, social action), and this influences what the worker does and how the group accomplishes its goals, as well as the nature of the contract between the worker and members, among the members, and between the group and the sponsoring organization.

3. Knowledge of the function of the group worker

    a. The worker promotes individual and group autonomy.

    b. The worker helps the group members to select means of achieving individual and group purposes.

    c. The worker's assessments and interventions are characterized by flexibility, sensitivity, and creativity.

    d. The worker should have a clear understanding of the stages of group development and the related group character, members' behaviors and tasks, and worker tasks and skills that are specific to each stage.

    e. Practice should be based on currently available knowledge and research and represent contemporary practice principles.

    f. The worker has responsibility for ongoing monitoring and evaluation of the success of the group in accomplishing its objectives through personal observation, as well as collecting information in order to assess outcomes and processes. The worker seeks the involvement of its members in the process of evaluation. Specifically, this means that members should be involved in evaluation of outcomes throughout the life of the group. Workers should systematically evaluate the achievement of goals. The worker should be knowledgeable about methods of evaluation of group work and ways of measuring or otherwise determining accomplishment of group and individual goals. The worker should use all available evidence regarding effectiveness of particular interventions for different kinds of groups.

    g. The worker should maintain appropriate records of group processes and outcomes and ensure the confidentiality of these.

    h. The worker should have commitment to supporting research on group work and to disseminating knowledge about effective practice through professional meetings, education, and scholarship.

    i. The worker adheres to professional, ethical, and legal requirements generally associated with social work practice as well as those specifically associated with social work with groups. The worker seeks to prevent any action in the group that may harm any member.

    j. Workers should have a commitment to engage in reflective practice in which they assess their own practice and seek supervision and/or consultation in order to enhance their practice.

Section II: Pregroup Phase: Planning, Recruitment, and New Group Formation

A. Tasks and Skills

1. The worker should identify aspirations and needs of potential group members as perceived by members, workers, and the agency.

2. The worker should obtain organizational support for and affirmation of the group.

3. The worker should select the group type, structure, processes, and size that will be appropriate for attaining the purposes of the group.

4. The worker should reach out to and recruit potential group members.

5. The worker should obtain consent from potential members and relevant others as required by ethical guidelines and organizational requirements.

6. The worker should clarify potential group members' goals and expectations of the group work service and use this information to assess prospective members' potential investments in the pursuit of group goals. The worker should help members specify these goals in terms that can lead to the determination of their attainment.

7. The worker should establish an appropriate meeting place and meeting time that will be conducive to members' comfort, safety, and access to the group.

8. The worker should prepare members for the group in ways that are appropriate. This will differ depending on the extent to which the group is intended to attain individual goals or to accomplish task purposes in the agency and community. The worker should be empathic in identifying members' feelings and reactions to joining the group.

9. The worker should know how to select members for the group in relationship to principles of group composition, although this principle may not apply to some task groups in which other bodies determine the group's membership.

10. The worker should develop a clear statement of group purpose that reflects member needs and agency mission and goals. This is often done cooperatively with the group members.

11. The worker should consider potential contextual, environmental, and societal impacts on the group.

12. The worker, as appropriate, should explain group purposes and processes to nonmembers such as other agency personnel, relevant community entities, and parents or referring agencies in the case of groups promoting individual change.

13. The worker should determine issues of group content (what will go on during sessions) as well as the use of activities, supplies needed, and resources.

14. The worker should identify methods that will be used to track group progress (for example, group progress notes, formal and informal evaluations).

15. After each session, the worker should debrief and plan with the co-facilitator (if there is one) and arrange for consultation and/or supervision on a regular basis. If there is a co-facilitator, they should consider together the implications of their similarities and differences with respect to such issues as approaches, styles, and communication.

B. Required Knowledge

1. Organizational mission and function and how these influence the nature and development of the group work service.
2. Social and institutional barriers that may impact on the development of group work service.
3. How to assess the impact on the group in the community and agency context.
4. Issues associated with group composition (for example, gender, education, socioeconomic status, previous group experience, occupation, race, ethnicity, age, and presenting problems).
5. The influence of cultural factors on potential members' lives and their ways of engaging in group interactions and relationships with others, the agency, and the worker.
6. The importance of diversity in relationship to how a group attains its goals.
7. The theoretical approaches utilized by group workers and how to select the ones most appropriate and effective for the proposed group.
8. Issues associated with group structure (for example, group size, length of sessions, duration of group, meeting place, open or closed to new members, resources and supplies, and transportation).
9. The impact of human development/life-cycle factors on potential members' needs and abilities and group goals.
10. Types of groups, such as task groups, treatment groups, psychoeducational groups, and sociorecreational groups, and their applicability to individual, organizational, and community needs.
11. Issues related to group content such as discussion processes and purposeful use of activities and simulations. Such issues include how these kinds of content are affected by stage of group development, capacities of members, and the purposes of the group.
12. Contracting procedures, including the identification and clarification of group purpose, behavioral standards, and norms needed to actualize group goals as determined by potential members, the worker, and the agency.
13. Recruitment procedures such as community outreach and referral processes.
14. How to identify and develop resources required for group functioning.
15. Group monitoring and evaluation procedures (for example, group progress notes, pretest and posttest measures, and questionnaires) to track worker interventions, group progress, and the group work service.
16. The importance of consultation and supervision in enhancing the quality of group work service.

Section III: Group Work in the Beginning Phase

A. Tasks and Skills

1. Task: Establishing a Beginning Contract
   The worker and members collaboratively develop a beginning contract for work that identifies tasks to be accomplished, goals to be achieved, and the process by which the work is to occur. The worker identifies the community's and/or agency's stake in the group, the group purpose and process, and clarifies worker and member roles. Confidentiality and limits thereof are clearly identified. The worker assists members in identifying and clarifying individual goals and group goals. The worker helps the members link individual goals with group purposes. The worker invites full participation of all members and solicits member feedback on the progress of the group. The worker employs special skills in working with mandated members and understands the impact on group dynamics of members' mandated status.

(continued)

FIGURE 3.1 (continued)

2. Task: Cultivating Group Cohesion
   The worker establishes rapport with individual members and the group as a whole. The worker also aids the group members in establishing relationships with one another so as to promote group cohesion. The worker highlights member commonalities, links members to one another, and encourages direct member-to-member communication.
3. Task: Shaping Norms of Participation
   The worker seeks to aid the group in establishing norms for participation that promote safety and trust, facilitate a culture of work, and cultivate mutual aid. The worker is active in modeling these norms and instructing members when needed about productive group participation. The worker appreciates the impact of various psychological, sociocultural, and environmental forces on these norms. The worker promotes group exploration of nonproductive norms when these arise. The worker demonstrates respect for sociocultural differences, promotes autonomy and self-determination, and encourages member empowerment.

B. Required Knowledge

1. An understanding of the dynamic interaction between the community, agency, group, and individual members of the group with which he or she is working.
2. The relevant theories and evidence-based practices regarding the developmental, psychosocial, and clinical needs of the group members and how this informs beginnings.
3. The group type and technology being employed and the ways such may impact group functioning in the beginning stage.
4. The characteristics and needs of the beginning stage of group development and the related skills. Knowledge is needed regarding such variations as working with mandated members, replacing a previous worker, and receiving new members into an ongoing group.

Section IV: Group Work in the Middle Phase

A. Group Tasks and Worker Skills/Action:

1. Task: Assist group to make progress on individual and group goals. When group goals are a major focus, as in task and community groups, the worker encourages individual members to use their skills in pursuit of group goals.

   Skills/actions:
   a. Reinforce connections between individual concerns/needs and group goals.
   b. Offer programmatic ideas and activities that support group purpose and assist in helping members achieve individual and group goals.
   c. Assess progress toward individual and group goals.
   d. Identify difficulties and obstacles that interfere with the group and its members' abilities to reach their goals.
   e. If obstacles are related to the specific needs of an individual member, when appropriate, offer individual time outside of group.
   f. Ensure that group has attended to any special needs of individual members (for example, physical, cognitive, language, or cultural needs).
   g. Assist members to engage in problem solving, in making choices and decisions, and in evaluating potential outcomes of decisions.
   h. Summarize sessions with the group.
   i. Plan next steps with the group.
   j. Recontract with members, if needed, to assist in achieving individual and group goals.

2. Task: Attend to group dynamics/processes.

   Skills/actions
   a. Support members to develop a system of mutual aid.
   b. Clarify and interpret communication patterns among members, between members and workers, and between the group systems and systems outside the group.
   c. Model and encourage honest communication and feedback among members and between members and workers.
   d. Review group values and norms.
   e. Assist members to identify and articulate feelings.
   f. Assist members to perceive verbal and nonverbal communication.
   g. Help members mediate conflict within the group.
   h. Assist members to make connections with other group members that may continue after the group ends, if this is appropriate.
   i. Use tools of empowerment to assist members to develop "ownership" of the group.

Task:

1. Assist members to identify and access resources from inside and outside the group.
2. Include knowledge, skills, and other resources of group worker, group members, and sources outside the group.
3. Ensure that workers are using the best possible practice techniques in facilitating the group.

Skills/actions:

1. Use group approaches appropriate to the populations served and the tasks undertaken as demonstrated in the literature, worker and agency experience, and other sources of professional knowledge.
2. Use record-keeping techniques to monitor leadership skills and group process.
3. Access and use supervision.

B. Required Knowledge

1. Group dynamics.
2. Role theory and its application to members' relationships with one another and the worker.
3. Communication theory and its application to verbal and nonverbal interactions within the group and between the group and others external to the group.
4. Problem-solving processes in groups.
5. Conflict resolution in groups.
6. Organizational theories.
7. Community theories.
8. Developmental theories.
9. Evaluation theories and methods.
10. The impact of diversity, class, race, gender, sexual orientation, and ability status.
11. Knowledge about the group's relations with its environment.
12. Specific knowledge of issues being addressed in the group.
13. Awareness of self.

Section V: Group Work in the Ending Phase

A. Tasks and Skills

1. Prepare members for the group's ending in advance.
2. In a direct practice group, help members identify gains they have made and changes that have resulted from their participation in the group. In a task group, members may discuss what they have learned from this experience that will be useful to them in other task groups. This involves a consideration of how achieving group goals will contribute to the functioning of the organization and/or community.
3. Discuss the impact of the group on systems outside of the group (for example, family, organization, community).
4. Discuss the movement the group has made over time.
5. Identify and discuss direct and indirect signs of members' reactions to ending.
6. Share worker's feelings about ending the group.
7. Assist members in sharing their feelings about ending with one another and with the worker.
8. Systematically evaluate the achievement of individual and group goals. Routine and systematic evaluation of the group experience could/should occur over time rather than in the ending stage alone.
9. Help members make connections with other agencies and programs as appropriate.
10. Assist members in applying new knowledge and skills to their daily lives.
11. Encourage members to give feedback to the worker on the worker's role and actions in the group.
12. Help members apply new knowledge and skills to their activities outside of the group.
13. Prepare record material about the group for the agency, for individual members, and for referrals as needed.

B. Required Knowledge

1. Group dynamics related to endings. These will be different depending on the type of group (for example, long-term, short-term, open-ended, single session). There are also special issues when a member or worker leaves the group but parts of the group continue or there is a new worker.
2. Formal and informal resources that maintain and enhance members' growth.

(continued)

FIGURE 3.1 (continued)

3. Influence of past losses and separation in lives of members and the worker on endings.
4. Agency policies related to the worker maintaining connections following the ending of a group or member service.
5. Various forms of evaluation, formal and informal, and of evaluation measures, both qualitative and quantitative.

Section VI: Ethical Considerations

National and/or regional social work organizations typically have codes of ethics to which social workers must adhere. For example, social group workers in the United States are expected to be knowledgeable about and responsive to the ethical mandates of the social work profession, as explicated in the National Association of Social Workers (NASW) *Code of Ethics*. Although the entire code is important, there are items with particular relevance to social group work.

Similarly, Canadian social workers must follow the Canadian Association of Social Workers *Code of Ethics* (2005). The expectation of AASWG is that social workers will respect the code of ethics relevant to their locations of practice wherever in the world that may be, as long as it is respectful of all persons.

Other social work ethical guides exist and may be more relevant for specific countries. Each needs to be considered in the context of work with groups and may call for some modifications or additions that reflect the unique situations of group work.

A. Elements of Ethical Practice in Social Group Work

1. Knowledge and use of best practices that reflect the state of the art and knowledge and research evidence regarding social work with groups.
2. A basic discussion with prospective members of informed consent and an explanation of what group work offers and requires of the members individually and as a group.
3. Maximizing member choice and minimizing coercive processes by members or workers to the extent possible. Emphasizing member self-determination and empowerment of the group.
4. Discussion of the importance, limits, and implications of privacy and confidentiality with the members.
5. Helping the group maintain the purposes for which it was formed, allowing for changes as mutually agreed upon.
6. Each member is given the help he or she requires within the parameters of the group's purpose, including individual meetings when appropriate.
7. Clarifying the decision-making process.
8. Clarifying how members may be chosen for or excluded from the group.
9. Maintaining group records and storing them in a secure location.

B. Ethical Issues in the Use of New Techniques

As new techniques are used, such as those based on electronic communications, workers should pay attention to ethical issues, practice skills, and knowledge and evaluation of these techniques. The following is a general statement with reference to electronic communications:

Increasingly, practice with groups of all kinds is being done by utilizing technologies such as computer and telephone facilities, and professional associations are assessing both effectiveness and ethical issues.

Issues such as member interaction, decision making, group structure, mutual aid, and particularly confidentiality are of vital concern.

Worker competency may require new skills and knowledge not only in technology but also in communication techniques.

Clearly these technologies are likely to be extremely valuable for all persons seeking resources, as well as for the profession's ability to share information about practice, including emerging approaches. In the meantime, workers contemplating their use should consider the appropriate codes of ethics as guides and document all of their processes related to such work.

References

National Association of Social Workers. (approved, 1996, revised 1999). *Code of Ethics for Social Workers*. Washington, DC: NASW.

Canadian Association of Social Workers/Association Canadienne des Travailleuses Sociaux. (2005). *Code of Ethics*. Ottawa, Canada: CASW/ACTS.

SOURCE: Reprinted with permission from The Association for the Advancement of Social Work with Groups, Inc. (AASWG, Inc.) (2nd edition, 2006).

LO 7　Understand Strengths-Based Leadership

STRENGTHS-BASED LEADERSHIP

For more than 30 years, Gallup scientists have been examining decades of data on the topic of leadership. They have studied more than 1 million work teams, conducted over 20,000 in-depth interviews with leaders, and interviewed more than 10,000 followers around the world to ask precisely why they followed the most important leader in their life.

In the text, *Strengths Based Leadership*, authors Tom Rath and Barry Conchie reveal the results of this research.[24] The findings demonstrate that leaders get more out of their workers in the workplace if they emphasize that the workers should focus on doing what they are already good at. Efforts to correct shortcomings of the workers rarely pay off. Leaders also need to amplify their own strengths, rather than seek to correct their shortcomings. The findings further indicate that to be an effective leader, the leader needs to know his or her strengths and to get the people with the right strengths on his or her team. It is a mistake for a leader to seek to convey to the workers that she or he has all the desirable characteristics that workers admire, as no one can possibly have all those qualities.

When followers were asked what qualities they most admired in leaders, a large number of qualities were identified. These include the following: building trust, showing compassion, creating hope for success, making things happen by turning thoughts into action, being adaptable, having the ability to identify all the factors that might affect a situation, having good organizational skills, being ethical, having a "presence" by being able to take control of a situation and making good decisions, being a good conversationalist and presenter, being good at anticipating the obstacles to succeeding, being good at recognizing and cultivating the potential in others, having and conveying empathy for others, being good at making corrections to stay on track, being able to inspire others with their visions of a better future, being good at building consensus, being accepting of others, having a gift for figuring out how people who are different can work together productively, appreciating intellectual discussions, having a great desire to learn and wanting to continuously improve, being upbeat and having an enthusiasm that is contagious, having deep satisfaction in working with others to achieve desirable goals, being committed to stable values such as honesty and loyalty, being good at figuring out what is wrong and resolving it, having self-confidence that their decisions are right, and loving the challenge of meeting new people and winning them over.

Given this laundry list of desired qualities in a leader, it is clear that no one can possibly have all these qualities. Leaders need to identify their own strengths and then amplify these strengths. Also, they need to get the right people on their team with the strengths they are lacking in.

Summary

The following summarizes the chapter's content in terms of the learning objectives presented at the beginning of the chapter.

1. **Describe five major approaches to leadership.**
   Five approaches to leadership theory are summarized: trait approach, leadership-style approach, position approach, distributed-functions approach, and servant leadership approach. The preferred approach in this text is the distributed-functions approach, which asserts that every member of a group will be a leader at times by taking actions that serve group functions.

2. **Identify effective group leadership functions, roles, and techniques.**
   There are two specific leadership functions: the task specialist and the social/emotional (or group maintenance) specialist. Task roles for each of these functions are identified.

3. **Understand that the use of power is a necessary component of group functioning.**
   The terms "power" and "influence" are used interchangeably in this chapter. Both terms refer to the capacity of an individual to motivate others to carry out certain

actions or to behave in a particular way. Motivating others is a necessary component of group functioning.

4. Describe five bases of power in groups, and identify the different consequences of using these bases.
The following power bases in groups are described: reward, coercive, legitimate, referent, and expert. Referent power is thought to have the broadest range.

5. Understand the effects of unequal power in groups.
Unequal power between group members often leads to distrust between the high-power and low power members.

6. Comprehend how to start and lead a group.
The chapter summarizes a number of guidelines for forming and leading a group. The Association for the Advancement of Social Work with Groups has formulated standards for social work practice with groups, which are presented in this chapter.

7. Understand strengths-based leadership
Strengths-based leadership has found that leaders get more out of their workers in the workplace if they emphasize that the workers should focus on doing what they are already good at. Efforts to correct shortcomings of the workers rarely pay off. Leaders also need to amplify their own strengths, rather than seek to correct their shortcomings. The findings further indicate that to be an effective leader, the leader needs to know his or her strengths and to get the people with the right strengths on his or her team.

Group Exercises

EP 1b

GOAL: To identify the specific fears about being a designated leader for a group and to provide information to reduce those fears.

Step 1. The group leader should state the purpose of this exercise. Each student should then be handed a sheet of paper and instructed to complete anonymously the sentence "My specific fears about being a designated leader of a group are . . ." The leader should emphasize that the completed statements will be collected and discussed.

Step 2. The responses should be collected in a way that ensures anonymity and then read aloud. After a concern is read, the students should suggest ways of reducing the concern. If a concern involves handling hostile members, for example, the class, with help from the instructor, may suggest strategies for coping with them. If a member fears that he or she does not have the traits needed to lead a group, it may be pointed out that research has found that no specific traits distinguish leaders from followers and that the distributed-functions theory of leadership asserts that practically anyone can be trained to be a leader.

Step 3. After Step 2 is completed the group leader or the instructor may want to summarize key points on how to lead a group and explain that future sessions will explore these points in greater depth.

EXERCISE B: Task Functions and Group Maintenance Functions

GOAL: To show that at times nearly everyone takes a leadership role in groups that involves performing task and group maintenance functions.

Step 1. The group leader should indicate that this exercise will elicit the class's thoughts on what criteria should be used for admitting students into the social work program at this campus. The leader should then explain that the Council on Social Work Education (the national organization that accredits social work programs) requires every program to have criteria for admitting students. There is considerable variation in criteria among the programs in this country. Common criteria include a minimum grade point average and a vaguely defined "aptitude for social work."

Step 2. The class then forms subgroups of five or six students and each selects an observer. The observers then form a group in another room or hallway. The subgroups should not begin discussing their primary task until the observers return.

Step 3. The observers are told that their task is to record *significant* task and group maintenance functions performed by each member of their subgroups. The leader may need to explain that task functions are statements designed to help the subgroup accomplish its task and that group maintenance functions are statements made to strengthen the social/emotional aspects of group life. Observers should be given a handout that summarizes the task roles and group maintenance roles developed by Johnson and Johnson, which appear in this chapter. The observers will be asked after the exercise is over to summarize to their subgroups how each member contributed through certain task and group maintenance functions.

Step 4. The leader and observers return to the subgroups. The subgroups are informed that their task is to develop criteria for admitting students to the social work program at this campus. The subgroup is free to suggest various criteria, but should probably begin by discussing:

1. whether a grade point average should be used for admission and what it should be, and
2. how "aptitude for social work" should be defined and measured.

Step 5. The subgroups should work for 20 to 30 minutes, and each should then state and explain its proposed criteria. Time should then be called, and each subgroup should be asked to indicate to the class what criteria were arrived at.

Step 6. The group leader should indicate that one of the purposes of this exercise is to demonstrate that most members in a group assume leadership roles by carrying out task and group maintenance functions. The leader should then define task and group maintenance functions.

Step 7. Each observer summarizes to his or her subgroup, but *not* to the whole class, the significant task and group maintenance functions performed by each member.

Step 8. End the exercise by asking members if they have any thoughts or comments.

EXERCISE C: Power Bases

GOAL: To practice analyzing influence attempts in terms of power bases.

Step 1. The group leader explains the purpose of the exercise, describes the five bases of power developed by French and Raven, and briefly discusses the effects of using each base.

Step 2. The class divides into subgroups of three members each and answers the following questions:

1. What bases of power does the instructor of this course have?
2. What bases of power does a student in this class have?
3. What is the primary power base the instructor has?
4. What is the primary power base a student has?

Step 3. The subgroups share their answers to these questions by having one member from each subgroup write the answers on the blackboard. The class then discusses the reasons for the similarities and differences between the answers arrived at by the subgroups.

Step 4. In all likelihood the instructor will be seen as having much more power than the students. The group leader should summarize the effects of unequal power on communication and on relationships within a group (as described in this chapter). Students then discuss how they feel when an instructor attempts to present himself or herself on a level equal or superior to students. Further, what are the positive and negative aspects of each relationship?

EXERCISE D: Leading a Group

EP 8b

GOAL: This exercise is designed to facilitate the development of group leadership skills.

Step 1. The instructor explains the purpose of the exercise. Students form subgroups of two or three students. They are instructed to prepare a presentation in a future class. Each subgroup is told its presentation needs to do the following: (1) State the goal or goals of the presentation, (2) present to the rest of the class certain theoretical material that provides information on how the goals can be achieved, and (3) lead the class in one or more group exercises—exercises that illustrate key concepts and give participants practice in acquiring the skills that are described in the theoretical material. For topic suggestions, the students may want to look at the text.

Step 2. In future classes, the subgroups present. Each presentation is graded by the instructor on (a) the quality and relevancy of the material, (b) the extent to which the subgroup got the participants involved and interested in the material, and (c) the extent to which the presentation was consistent with the requirements for the assignment.

Competency Notes

EP 7b   Apply knowledge of human behavior and the social environment, person-in-environment, and other multidisciplinary theoretical frameworks in the analysis of assessment data from clients and constituencies.

EP 8b   Apply knowledge of human behavior and the social environment, person-in-environment, and other multidisciplinary theoretical frameworks in interventions with clients and constituencies. (pp. 72–79)

The following approaches to leadership assist students in assessing group leadership and how to be an effective group leader: trait, position, leadership style, distributed functions, and servant leadership.

EP 8b   Apply knowledge of human behavior and the social environment, person-in-environment, and other multidisciplinary theoretical frameworks in interventions with clients and constituencies. (pp. 80–82)

The material on task roles and maintenance roles in groups assists students in understanding the roles that need to be fulfilled in order for a group to be effective.

EP 7b   Apply knowledge of human behavior and the social environment, person-in-environment, and other multidisciplinary theoretical frameworks in the analysis of assessment data from clients and constituencies.

EP 8b   Apply knowledge of human behavior and the social environment, person-in-environment, and other multidisciplinary theoretical frameworks in interventions with clients and constituencies. (pp. 83–86)

The power bases in groups include reward, coercive, legitimate, referent, and expert. Students need to understand power bases to assess these bases in groups, and to use these bases to improve their interventions in groups.

EP 8b   Apply knowledge of human behavior and the social environment, person-in-environment, and other multidisciplinary theoretical frameworks in interventions with clients and constituencies. (pp. 89–94)

Guidelines are presented on how to effectively form and lead groups. The Association for the Advancement of Social Work with Groups has formulated standards for social work practice with groups.

EP 8b   Apply knowledge of human behavior and the social environment, person-in-environment, and other multidisciplinary theoretical frameworks in interventions with clients and constituencies (pp. 94–100)

The Association for the Advancement of Social Work with Groups has formulated standards for social work practice with groups.

EP 1b   Use reflection and self-regulation to manage personal values and maintain professionalism in practice situations. (p. 102)

This exercise assists students in identifying their fears about leading a group, and suggestions are generated for overcoming these fears.

EP 8b   Apply knowledge of human behavior and the social environment, person-in-environment, and other multidisciplinary theoretical frameworks in interventions with clients and constituencies. (p. 104)

This exercise is designed to facilitate the development of group leadership skills in students.

Key Terms and Concepts

Delegating	Leadership	Power	Task Roles
Designated Leader	Machiavellianism	Selling	Telling
Influence	Participating		

4

Group Dynamics: Goals and Norms

LO 1 Set Personal and Group Goals in Groups

SETTING PERSONAL AND GROUP GOALS

A goal is an end toward which an individual or group of people is working. It is an ideal or a desired achievement that people value. A personal goal is a goal held by a member of a group. A group goal is a goal held by enough members of a group that the group can be said to be working toward achieving it.

All groups have goals, and every individual who joins a group has personal goals. Groups generally have both short-range and long-range goals. The short-range goals should be stepping-stones to the long-range goals. Group goals are important for several reasons. The effectiveness and efficiency of the group and its procedures can be measured by the extent to which goals are achieved. Goals guide groups and their members by giving the group's programs and efforts direction. Conflicts between group members are often resolved according to which position is most helpful in achieving group goals. Group goals are also a strong motivating force that stimulates members to work together. Once members make a commitment to achieve a certain goal, they will feel an obligation to put forth their abilities, efforts, and resources to achieve it.

A member's commitment to a group goal will depend on (1) how attracted this member is to the group; (2) how attractive the goal appears; (3) how likely it appears the group can accomplish the goal; (4) the ability to measure progress toward achieving the goal and the ability to measure when the goal is attained; (5) the rewards the group and the member will receive when the goal is attained; (6) the challenge presented by the goal, as a moderate risk of failure is usually more challenging than a high or low risk of failure[1]; and (7) the types of interactions the member will have with other group members in working toward the goal (some ways of interacting are more enjoyable and rewarding than others).

Setting group goals is the first step in measuring the effectiveness of a group. Once goals are set, the tasks necessary to accomplish the goals must be determined. Next, responsibilities for carrying out the tasks must be agreed upon or assigned and deadlines for completing those tasks set. As the process proceeds, the extent to which deadlines have been met and tasks achieved must be evaluated. The final measurement is whether the group has achieved its goals. An effective group is one that has considerable success in achieving its goals. (The processes of setting group goals, determining the tasks for accomplishing the goals, assigning tasks to each member, and setting deadlines for accomplishing the tasks are, in reality, also the components of forming contracts with group members about expectations. Contracts and group goals should be reviewed periodically as the group progresses and revised if necessary.)

LEARNING OBJECTIVES

Just as a baseball team has a short-term goal of winning a game and a long-term goal of clinching a pennant, individuals and groups must identify short-term and long-term goals to function effectively. This chapter will help prepare students to:

LO 1
Set personal and group goals in groups.

LO 2
Understand and identify hidden agendas.

LO 3
Comprehend the differences between competitive groups and cooperative groups.

LO 4
Apply the nominal group approach.

LO 5
Understand the importance of group norms, and comprehend how norms are formed.

LO 6
Identify group pressures to conform.

LO 7
Identify various types of hostile or disruptive group members, and comprehend how to handle disruptive group members.

Group members will be more motivated to achieve group goals if they are involved in setting those goals. Through involvement, members will be (1) more likely to have their personal goals become a component of the group goals, (2) more aware of the importance of choosing these goals, and (3) more committed to providing their resources to achieve the goals.

Personal Goals

The personal goals of members may be *very* diverse. In a stress management group, for example, some members may join because they want to learn how to relax, others because they are lonely and want companionship, and still others because their spouses urged them. Some may join because they have heard good things about the group leader and want to "check it out." A few may join because they do not believe stress is destructive and want to convince others of this belief.

Although some members are acutely aware of their personal goals, others may not be. For example, freshman social work majors sometimes attend a meeting of the Student Social Work Club at the urging of a faculty member without having given much thought to their personal goals and objectives.

The more similarity there is between the personal goals of members and the goals of the group, the more attracted to the group the members are likely to be and the more willing to provide their resources and energies to the group. If the personal goals of the group are homogeneous (alike), members are more apt to agree on group goals, to work together toward achieving those goals, and to be happier with the group. Heterogeneous personal goals do not necessarily spell failure for a group, but they do require special attention.

EXERCISE 4.1   Identifying Your Personal Goals

GOAL: We need to identify our personal goals in every group we participate in so that we then can select the kinds of group activities that will allow us to achieve our personal goals, and thereby result in the group being personally useful to us. This exercise is designed to assist you in setting personal goals.

Specify the personal goals that you have in this class. Your personal goals should include a summary of the knowledge, skills, and values you want to acquire and perhaps also the grade you hope to attain.

LO 2   Understand and Identify Hidden Agendas

HIDDEN AGENDAS

When members have heterogeneous personal goals, hidden agendas are more likely to develop. (If members have homogeneous personal goals, these goals are apt to become group goals, and hidden agendas are less likely to arise.) A **hidden agenda** is a personal goal

---

EXERCISE 4.2   Hidden Agendas and Their Effects

GOAL: This exercise is designed to help you understand hidden agendas, their effects, and how you can more effectively respond to someone who has a hidden agenda in a group.

1. Describe a group that you participated in where one of the other members had a hidden agenda that was eventually revealed. What was the hidden agenda? How did this hidden agenda adversely affect the group?

2. How effective were the other group members in handling this hidden agenda?

3. As you reflect on how the other group members handled this hidden agenda, is there a course of action that could have been taken that would have dealt with this hidden agenda more effectively? If "yes," describe this course of action.

4. Describe a hidden agenda that you had when participating in a group. How did your hidden agenda affect the group?

held by a member but unknown to other group members, which interferes with the group's efforts. At times, hidden agendas can be very destructive. For example, I have participated in groups where an individual observed the comments and actions of others to obtain evidence to bring legal harassment charges. Usually, however, hidden agendas are less destructive than this and may consist of little more than a lonely person's wish to monopolize the group's "air time" with insignificant small talk. Because this type of behavior can slow progress severely, a group's goals should incorporate to some extent the personal goals of its members. Leaders can also minimize the effects of hidden agendas by making the group's goals clear at the outset.

Certain signals suggest hidden agendas. A member may fail to contribute or may say and do things that impede group activities. When hidden agendas appear to exist, the consequences of confronting a member about disruptive behavior must be evaluated. If the consequences appear beneficial, then the member should be confronted, either openly or privately. Whatever method of confrontation appears to be most beneficial should be used. Sometimes, however, hidden agendas are best left undisturbed. For example, a group member who has recently experienced the death of a spouse may use a nontherapy group to ventilate pain. In this situation, it may or may not be constructive to confront the person.

When confronting a member about a hidden agenda, avoid blaming or criticizing. The confrontation should lead to a trusting, open discussion of the issue. If the hidden agenda is rational and legitimate, extensive efforts should be made to help the member. Alternatives for resolving the concern could be explored and one or more implemented to resolve the problem. (Later in this chapter, additional suggestions are given on how to confront someone.) Perhaps the goals of the group can even be revised to incorporate the more personal issue, or perhaps the member can be helped to achieve the personal goal outside the group. A group member grieving over the death of a spouse, for example, may be referred to a counselor or to a survivors' group where the grief can be expressed and worked out more effectively.

ESTABLISHING GROUP GOALS

Although group goals can be developed in a variety of ways, the procedures in the following sections are recommended because they involve group members in the decision-making process. After the leader shares his or her views on the goals of the group, members are asked to explain their own reasons for joining—that is, their personal goals. Working together, the leader and group members discuss the merits of the goals presented and discuss additional goals, refining and rewording them until a final list is developed. Decision-making procedures, as outlined in Chapter 6, may be used to resolve conflicts and attain agreement. The final list should be typed and distributed to each member for reference.

Alternatively, the group leader may interview each member before the first meeting about personal and group goals and then develop a composite list to present at the first meeting of the group. This list is then discussed and amended until most members are satisfied. A less effective way to determine group goals is for the leader to attempt to "sell" the group a set of goals he or she believes is preferable. If group goals are prescribed in this manner or by the constitution of the group, they should still be fully discussed by members, who may refine and reword them.

Effective groups usually follow a variation of the following format. Long-range goals are set first, and efforts are made to state these goals in operational and measurable terms. Short-range goals are then established and prioritized as to their importance in achieving the long-range goals. Tasks are also identified to achieve short-range goals and then ranked according to their importance. For high-priority tasks, specific responsibilities are assigned to group members and deadlines are set for completion. Future evaluations then identify the progress being made in achieving the tasks and goals.

EP 7b
EP 9b

Operational and Measurable Goals

An **operational goal** is one that can be directly translated into courses of action to achieve the goal. A goal such as "Each member of this class will be able to describe the difference between personal and group goals" is operational. Students could put this goal into action by studying the first part of this chapter and then taking a test that asks them to define both terms. The test scores measure whether the class reached the goal.

A **nonoperational goal** is one that cannot be achieved through specific actions. "Everyone in this class will learn how to cure all emotional and behavioral problems," for example, is nonoperational because treatment approaches have not been developed to treat successfully all people who have emotional and behavioral problems. A goal that is nonoperational is *much* harder to achieve. For instance, it may be centuries before we know whether it is possible to treat all emotional and behavioral problems successfully.

In practice, groups should strive to develop operational goals so that a course of action can be developed and the goal more readily achieved. "Helping students to better manage stress in their lives through instructing them in meditation," for example, is much more operational than "Seeking ways to help students better manage stress."

Group goals should also be measurable. For example, the goal "Having everyone in this class become a great group leader" is very difficult to measure *without* criteria to use in judging what constitutes a great leader. In contrast, the following goal is more measurable: "By the end of this semester, every student in this class will have demonstrated that she or he can lead a group at a level that the instructor deems *satisfactory*." One way to make this goal operational is by having the students take turns being a group leader. For each session the instructor then rates the student who leads the group as doing a "satisfactory" or "less than satisfactory" job. Students who receive a "less than satisfactory" rating can be given additional opportunities to lead the class and have their performance rated again. Progress toward this goal is simply measured by counting the number of students who receive an overall "satisfactory" rating.

Operational, measurable goals are valuable for a variety of reasons. They help guide the members and the group in planning and working on tasks. A group that is unclear as to what its goals are will be even more confused as to what specific tasks are needed to reach those goals. Operational and measurable goals also measure the effectiveness of the leader because the leader's actions can be judged in terms of movement toward group goals. Clear goals, in fact, often make leadership easier because the group knows what it is trying to achieve and is less likely to question a leader's actions that move the group toward its goals.

In addition, operational and measurable goals make it easier to communicate the purpose of the group to other groups and to nonmembers. Such goals also help evaluate progress. Each course of action can be assessed to determine its payoffs in attaining goals. The group can easily determine whether a course of action should be continued or abandoned. Clear goals and documented progress toward those goals are especially valuable when accountability is required by funding sources or others. A final advantage is that conflicts between members can often be resolved by determining which position appears to best help the group reach its goals. When conflicts arise in groups that do not have measurable and operational goals, there is no logical way to determine whose view has higher payoffs. As a result, the conflict is not apt to be resolved and may force the group to spend more time maintaining harmony than completing its work.

Forming clear goals that are operational and measurable is a lengthy, time-consuming process. The goal-setting stage is often when a group flounders the most. It occurs early in the life of a group, when members are also testing their interest and commitment and when interpersonal relationships are being formed. Arriving at goals the members can support often takes much longer than anticipated. The value of setting clear goals, however, far outweighs the time and effort saved by accepting goals that are vague and that may later be seriously challenged. Johnson and Johnson note, "The more time a group spends establishing agreement on clear goals, the less time it needs in achieving them—and the more likely it will be that the members will work effectively for the common outcome."[2]

EXERCISE 4.3   Group Goals and Personal Goals in This Class

GOAL: This exercise is designed to assist you in understanding the dynamics between group goals and personal goals.

1. Specify the group goals that the instructor wants for this class. (Usually, the "Course Objectives" section of the syllabus will specify the group goals desired by the instructor. In his or her lectures, the instructor may have identified additional desired group goals.)

2. Have all the students in the class "accepted" the desired group goals? If "no," describe why you believe some students have not accepted the instructor's group goals.

3. Did the instructor ask the students for additional group goals that they desired for the class? If "yes," did the students suggest additional group goals? If "yes," what were the additional group goals that were suggested, and were they adopted for this class?

4. Do you believe some members of the class have personal goals or hidden agendas that are inconsistent with the group goals? (These personal goals or hidden agendas may include "not wanting to study very much" or "wanting help in resolving a personal dilemma.") If "yes," specify these inconsistent personal goals or hidden agendas.

5. Earlier in Exercise 4.1 you identified your personal goals for this class. Are your personal goals consistent with the group goals? If some are inconsistent, please specify these inconsistent personal goals.

Research has found that groups have a better chance to be effective when the following are met:

1. The goals are clear, operationally defined, and measurable.
2. The members see the goals as being relevant, attainable, meaningful, and acceptable.
3. Both personal and group goals can be attained by the same activities and tasks.
4. The goals are viewed as challenging and have a moderate risk of failure.
5. The resources needed to accomplish the tasks are available.
6. There is high coordination among group members.
7. The group members maintain a cooperative rather than a competitive atmosphere.[3]

LO 3 Comprehend the Differences Between Competitive Groups and Cooperative Groups

EP 7b

COMPETITION VERSUS COOPERATION

Groups tend to have either a cooperative or a competitive atmosphere. A cooperative group is marked by open and honest communication, trust, pooling of resources, and cohesion. Research into problem-solving groups has found a number of positive consequences of a cooperative group atmosphere. Cooperation among members increases creativity, coordination of effort, division of labor, emotional involvement in group accomplishment, helping and sharing, interpersonal skills, cooperative attitudes and values, positive self-attitudes, congeniality among group members, positive attitudes toward the group and tasks, divergent thinking, acceptance of individual and cultural differences, and problem-solving skills.[4]

A cooperative group atmosphere results when the personal goals of group members are perceived to be compatible, identical, or complementary. An example of a highly cooperative group is a football team where the main goal of each member is to win, and the main goal of the team is to win. In a cooperative group, each member seeks to coordinate his or her efforts with those of other group members to achieve the goals of the group. In establishing a cooperative atmosphere, rewards to members must be based on the quantity and quality of group performance, rather than on individual performance.

In contrast, a competitive atmosphere is usually destructive. Competition exists when the members perceive their personal goals to be incompatible, different, conflicting, or mutually exclusive. In a highly competitive group, a member can achieve a goal only if the other group members fail to obtain their goals.[5] A group interview of several applicants for a job vacancy, such as an audition for a play, for example, is intentionally competitive. Each member seeks to accomplish personal goals while seeking to block other group members from accomplishing theirs. The negative consequences of competition in problem-solving groups are numerous. Competition decreases creativity, coordination of effort, division of

EXERCISE 4.4   The Effects of a Competitive Group Member

GOAL: This exercise is designed to help you understand the effects of a competitive group member and to then reflect upon what a group might constructively do to minimize the adverse effects of a competitive member.

1. Describe the behavior of a competitive person in a group in which you participated. Did the competitive behavior adversely affect the group? If "yes," please specify the adverse effects.

2. When a competitive person adversely affects a group, what constructive course of action might the other group members take in order to minimize the adverse effects?

labor, helping and sharing, and cohesion. Competition promotes ineffective communication, suspicion and mistrust, high anxiety about goal accomplishment, competitive values and attitudes, negative self-attitudes, animosity between group members, and negative attitudes toward the group and its tasks. Competition also encourages the rejection of differences of opinion, divergent thinking, and cultural and individual differences. A competitive atmosphere leads to low effectiveness in solving complex problems.[6]

Are there any situations in which competition is beneficial? There are a few. For example, in team sports coaches have discovered it is beneficial to have highly talented athletes compete for starting positions. Such competition generally encourages athletes to work harder. But even in team sports, successful coaches know that a key to winning is instilling a sense of team effort (that is, cooperative atmosphere) so that each player focuses not on individual recognition but on helping the team win by playing the role he or she has been assigned.

Kelly and Stahelski examined the question of what happens when a competitive person joins a group that has a cooperative atmosphere.[7] Because cooperative groups are much more effective in solving problems than competitive groups, the question is significant. Three consequences were found to occur. The competitive behavior of the new member leads the other members to behave competitively. The competitive person views the former cooperative members as having always been competitive. The former cooperative members are generally aware that their competitive behavior is largely a consequence of the new member's competitiveness. Thus, it appears that one competitive person can change a cooperative group into a competitive group.

The positive characteristics of a cooperative group are readily destroyed by a competitive person. All of the following decrease when a competitive person joins a formerly cooperative group: trust, congeniality among members, openness of communication, and problem-solving orientation.[8] Why does a competitive person have such a strong, destructive effect? Apparently, the cooperative members realize the competitive person will, if given a chance, take advantage of their cooperativeness and use it to his or her personal advantage. In many situations, their only recourse to prevent exploitation is to become competitive. Thus, even though cooperation is by far the most effective atmosphere in problem-solving groups, it takes only one competitive person to change the atmosphere to a destructive, competitive one. If a cooperative group is to survive, the members must work together to reduce feelings of competitiveness among the members.

LO 4   Apply the Nominal Group Approach

THE NOMINAL GROUP APPROACH

EP 7b

The nominal group approach, developed by Delbecq and Van de Ven, can be used as an aid in formulating group goals.[9] This approach is a problem-identification technique for designing or modifying programs and involves meeting with potential users to assess their needs. A nominal group is "a group in which individuals work in the presence of others but do not verbally interact."[10] By simply allowing group members to list their needs on paper *without group discussion*, each member's personal views can be ascertained. Too often in the past, new programs have been developed by "experts" who lacked a clear picture of the needs of their consumers, with the result being the creation of programs that ineffectively serve consumers. So the prime objective of the nominal group approach is to identify the needs of the consumer group (that is, the potential users of a new service) in order to develop a program that effectively serves them.[11]

A nominal group meeting can be conducted within a half-hour or an hour; it has often been used by university faculty to identify topics students wish to have covered in classes. For example, the nominal group approach was used by the social work department at the author's university in connection with an elective workshop in grief management.[12] Enrollment was limited to 30 students. At the first class meeting, the students were asked, using a nominal group approach, "What specific topics do you want covered in this course?" The specific steps in conducting a nominal group are described in Exercise C at the end of this chapter. (The responses given in the grief management class appear in Table 4.1.)

TABLE 4.1	Highest-Ranking Topics for Grief Management Course	
Topics		**Number of Votes**
1. Suicide		13
2. Getting over the loss and loneliness that result from the death of someone else		9
3. The terminally ill and how to relate to them		9
4. Funeral director—guest speaker		9
5. AIDS		8
6. Getting over the loss of a close relationship		8
7. Coping skills for myself and others		8
8. Hospice movement—guest speaker		8
9. How to come to terms with your own death		7
10. Should one be permitted to take one's own life?		7
11. How to change fears and negative attitudes about death		6
12. Communication with survivors (that is, people who have had someone close to them die)		6
13. Sudden infant death syndrome (SIDS)		6
14. Life after death		5
15. How to help others (parents) deal with the death of someone close (children)		4

When a nominal group is used with a subgroup of a consumer group, care should be taken to obtain a representative cross-section of the consumer group. Before using the nominal group approach, the subgroup should be informed of the purpose of the study. However, the researchers should generally *not* provide any information on what they think should be the results of using the nominal group approach so as not to bias the participants.

Research on the merits of the nominal group approach suggests that it is superior to brainstorming and to other types of group interaction for generating information relevant to a problem situation. It elicits more suggestions and covers more areas of interest.[13] (Brainstorming has the shortcoming that the items first suggested tend to set the direction for future items that are generated.) The nominal group is designed to receive input from all group members rather than just the more vocal or aggressive ones, as often happens in conventional group discussions. Evaluation of items is avoided, which substantially reduces the pressure against expressing minority opinions or unconventional ideas. Conflicting, incompatible ideas are tolerated. Furthermore, the approach appears to save time, as it can be conducted faster than interacting group processes.[14] The nominal group approach has a gamelike quality, as the group generates creative tension, which appears to stimulate individuals to do their best in suggesting items.

LO 5 Understand the Importance of Group Norms, and Comprehend How Norms Are Formed

GROUP NORMS

Group norms are rules that specify proper group behavior. To be a norm, a rule must be accepted by a majority of the group. If a person recognizes a norm and believes the benefits of conforming outweigh the consequences of deviating, the norm can influence that person's behavior. At first, members may conform because of pressures from the group. As time passes, though, members generally internalize norms and conform automatically. Norms provide one of the most important mechanisms of social control over members of groups and over society as a whole.

Every group has norms. If you frequently socialize with a certain group of students, for example, your group will gradually set norms as to what is acceptable and unacceptable behavior at gatherings. Your classes will have certain norms as well, covering smoking, chewing bubble gum, arriving late, absences, meeting deadlines, raising a hand before speaking, and cheating on exams.

Some norms are set formally—bylaws and constitutions of organizations, for instance, specify responsibilities for the officers. Other norms are set informally. During a department meeting, the department chair may frown at a faculty member who is reading her mail. If that faculty member responds to the nonverbal communication and puts aside her mail, other faculty members may observe the nonverbal interaction and decide never to read their mail during meetings. Through this process a norm against reading mail has informally been established.

Norms have an "ought to" or "must" quality, and they vary in importance. There are strong pressures to obey and, in some cases, severe penalties for violating *important* norms—confidentiality in therapy groups, for example. If a member violates confidentiality by revealing personal information about another member to others outside the group, he or she may be penalized by expulsion from the group. Failure to obey less important norms, such as not belching at meetings, generates only mild disapproval and little or no penalty.

Members are often only subconsciously aware of many of the norms that are guiding their behavior. If one were to ask a group member to define the group's norms, he or she would probably be able to list only a few because many norms are taken for granted. Norms relating to dress, promptness, or foul language are often given little thought by group members.

When people enter a new group, they generally feel strange and uncomfortable because they are unaware of the norms. So they search for clues to norms, asking themselves such questions as these: What is appropriate to disclose, and what is not? Who is in the "in" group, and who is left out? Is smoking permissible? Can I tell a joke? Do members raise their hands before speaking? What role does each member play? Is the group competitive or cooperative? Are there hidden agendas? Are there coalitions? Which members are more powerful?

How Norms Are Learned and Developed

Some group norms are fairly universal, so new members who have worked in groups before will be aware of many norms that are likely to be operating. For example, an individual who joins a therapy group will expect other members to be honest, open, and self-disclosing. Many groups have norms such as reciprocity (if someone, does something kind or helpful for you, you should do something kind or helpful in return), fair play (don't lie or cheat to get what you want), social responsibility (you should help those who need it), and shared air time (everyone should have a chance to talk and no one should monopolize the conversation).

New members learn norms by talking privately with a group member they trust. They may ask questions like this: Who has the power? Is it acceptable to say or do such and such? Are there coalitions in the group? Do some members have hidden agendas? Are there personal matters that some members are sensitive about? Someone who is overweight, for example, may express discomfort with comments on dieting, and other members may individually decide not to mention dieting when the overweight person is present.

Although norms are learned in a variety of ways, the most common way is through positive and negative reinforcement. Through a process of trial and error, members identify which of their behaviors are accepted and rewarded by the group and which are judged inappropriate or destructive. Another way members identify norms is through "modeling," which involves learning through observing another member's behavior.

Some norms are in the bylaws, constitution, minutes, and/or other documents of a group or organization. For example, there may be guidelines for placing an item on the agenda, the duties and responsibilities of the officers, and the decision-making procedures for resolving crucial issues. Furthermore, norms can take the form of role expectations that can be official or unofficial. Officially, the chair of a group is expected to call and run meetings; the secretary keeps minutes. Unofficially, a wealthy member is expected to make donations when the group needs funds. Likewise, a member who is skilled at reducing tension is expected to ease the tension level when it gets too high.

Some norms develop less formally through nonverbal communication. For example, the leader of a therapy group may shake her head in disapproval of one member mimicking another. The other members note the gesture and then individually (without discussion) decide not to mimic anyone in the group in the future.

Some norms become known only after they are violated. Napier and Gershenfeld give an example:

> A minister may preach about justice and racial equality and may urge his congregation to live according to these principles, all of which they accept from him. However, when he marches in a picket line, the congregation may rebuke him for transcending his position.

EXERCISE 4.5   Group Norms in This Class

GOAL: This exercise is designed to assist you in identifying group norms and understanding the processes that led to their development.

1. Specify the group norms that exist for proper behavior in this class.

2. Identify the processes that occurred that led to these group norms. (For example, the department may have standards for acceptable behavior in a class; the *Code of Ethics* of the National Association of Social Workers has statements on confidentiality, honesty, and opposition to making racist and sexist remarks. The *Educational Policy and Accreditation Standards* of the Council on Social Work Education has statements on diversity, promoting social and economic justice, and advancing human rights. The instructor may have made statements about proper behavior in this class. Some students may have made statements about what they view as offensive remarks and behaviors.)

He may be sanctioned with a statement to the effect that ministers may preach about justice and equality, but action on social issues is for others. In this situation, neither the minister nor the congregation knew the norm existed until an action took place that was contrary to the norm; the congregation then made known the violation by the threat of sanctions.[15]

New norms may develop from suggestions on group policy or procedures made by group members. For example, a member may suggest, "In order for an item to be placed on the agenda, the members must be informed of it at least 48 hours prior to the meeting to give them an opportunity to think about it." If the group approves of the suggestion, it becomes a policy and a norm.

LO 6   Identify Group Pressures to Conform

CONFORMITY

Conformity means yielding to group pressure. To conform, a group member must experience conflict between the influences exerted by the group (group norms) and his or her personal values. A member experiencing this type of conflict has two options: announce an independent position or conform by agreeing with the group's position in either an expedient or a true manner. The **expedient conformer** can outwardly agree but inwardly disagree, whereas a **true conformer** agrees both outwardly and inwardly.

There have been a number of classic studies of conforming behavior. Sherif examined what has been called the "autokinetic effect" of conformity.[16] In his experiment, subjects in a darkened room were asked to judge how far a dot of light moved. Although the light *appeared* to move, it actually did not (the autokinetic effect). Each subject saw the dot of light and made a series of individual judgments as to how far it moved. The subjects were then brought together in groups of three to judge how far the light moved. Their judgments tended to converge into a group standard. Later, when they again viewed the light by themselves, they tended to retain the group standard as their answer. The essential finding was that when a situation is ambiguous and there is no objective way of determining the "right" answer, members rely on the group to help define reality. In real life, this finding means that membership in a group determines much of what individuals will see, learn, think about, and do.

Asch also examined conforming behavior and investigated what happens when an individual's judgment conflicts with that of other group members.[17] The experiments involved two sets of cards, as shown in Figure 4.1.

Subjects from psychology classes who volunteered for the experiment were arranged in groups of seven to nine. They were seated at a table and asked to state in turn which line was closest in size to the standard. In the control groups, practically all subjects chose Line 2. The responses in the experimental groups, however, were of greater interest. In the experimental groups all of the group members except for *one subject* were accomplices of the experimenter. The *subject* was always seated so that he would give his opinion last. All of

FIGURE 4.1   **Cards in Asch Conformity Studies**

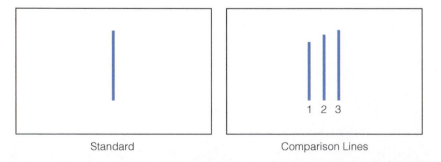

Standard   Comparison Lines

the accomplices chose the same wrong line. When it came to the subject's turn, he was faced with relying on his own judgment or conforming to the group's judgment, even though he probably perceived it as wrong. In a variety of similar studies, Asch found that more than one-third of the subjects conformed to the group judgment. Such a high level of conformity is amazing considering there was no overt group pressure to conform, the situation was not ambiguous, and the subjects did not know each other.

According to Schachter, everyone has a need to evaluate the "rightness" of feelings, opinions, values, and attitudes, as well as the extent of abilities. He conducted studies to demonstrate that in the absence of objective, nonsocial means of evaluation, a person will rely on other people as comparative points of reference. He called this the theory of social comparison. Studies by Schachter and Singer provide support for this theory.[18] Subjects were aroused by an injection of adrenaline and then exposed to the actions of a peer. In some cases, the peer (actually the experimenter's confederate) behaved in a highly euphoric manner, whereas for other subjects he acted as if he were angry. The experimenters predicted that those subjects who did not have an appropriate explanation for the physiological sensations aroused by the drug (because they had been uninformed or misinformed about the drug and its effects) would imitate the inappropriate behavior of the confederate and interpret their feelings in a manner consistent with the confederate's behavior. The predictions were confirmed. Furthermore, the control subjects, who were either informed of the effects of adrenaline or did not receive the injection, displayed few imitative responses of the confederate. To a large extent, then, the peer defined social reality for the experimental subjects (that is, those subjects injected with adrenaline who did not receive an explanation of the physiological sensations aroused by the drug).

Numerous conclusions have been drawn from conformity research and are summarized as follows[19]:

1. Group pressure influences behavior, even when the bogus group consensus is obviously wrong. In one study, for example, 50 military officers were asked to indicate which of two figures shown side by side, a star and a circle, was larger in area. The circle was clearly about one-third larger, but under group pressure, 46% of the officers agreed with the bogus group consensus that the star was larger.
2. Many people can be pressured into yielding on attitudes and opinions even on personally significant matters. For example, the same 50 military officers were asked, first privately and then later under group consensus conditions, to consider the statement: "I doubt whether I would make a good leader." In private, none of the officers expressed agreement, but under unanimous group pressure, 37% expressed agreement.
3. Although yielding occurs more often on difficult, subjective items than on easy, objective ones, there are extremely large individual differences. A few people yield on almost all items, a few on none. Most yield on some and not on others.
4. When people are retested privately on the same items some time later, a major part of the yielding effect disappears because the person tends to rely on personal judgment. Yet a small part of the yielding effect remains, indicating group pressure can change attitudes.
5. As a group increases in size, the pressure to yield increases and more yielding occurs. When a person is opposed by only one other person, there is very little yielding. Yielding is markedly reduced when a person has the *support* of one other person (a partner) in the group.

Apparently, a dissident opinion has a tremendous effect in strengthening the independence of like-minded people.

In a dramatic study involving conformity, Milgram demonstrated that subjects in an experimental situation would administer electric shocks of dangerous strength to another person when instructed to do so by the experimenter.[20] (The other person, unknown to the subject, did not actually receive the electrical shocks.) Even when they were instructed to give increasingly strong shocks and the victim protested in anguish, most subjects followed the experimenter's orders. This series of studies on obedience demonstrated that people will yield to "authoritative" commands even when the behavior is incompatible with their own normal moral standards of conduct. Milgram suggested that his studies help us understand why the German people complied with the unethical commands of Hitler. Group pressures, especially when viewed as authoritative, have a tremendous effect on a person's actions, attitudes, and beliefs.

Idiosyncrasy Credits   Every member of a group gains credits (and increased status) by exhibiting competence and conforming to the expectations applicable at a given time. Eventually, these credits allow a person to break the norms and rules of the group without being chastised. To some extent, after credits have been accumulated, nonconformity to general procedures or expectations serves as a confirming feature of one's status and further enhances one's position. Yet there is a limit to the number of idiosyncrasy credits awarded. Nonconformity beyond this limit will result in a dramatic decrease in status and perhaps even in rejection by the other group members.[21] For example, a star basketball player at a college may eventually be kicked off the team if he or she continues to be arrested for criminal activity.

EXERCISE 4.6   Your Yielding to Group Pressure

EP 1b

GOAL: This exercise is designed to help you understand that all of us have yielded at one time or another to group pressure. The exercise also helps you understand your feelings about yielding.

1. Describe a group that you participated in, in which you yielded to group pressure. Specify the issue or action that you yielded to. (If you have difficulty in identifying a time when you yielded, feel free to identify an issue in which you yielded to pressure from your parents.)

2. Specify your thoughts and feelings during the time when you yielded. Also specify your thoughts and feelings after you yielded.

3. If you had to do it over, would you still yield? Why or why not?

Do's and Don'ts of Norms

Norms should be established that will improve the group's capacity to function effectively, such as starting meetings on time or cooperating rather than competing. Because norms exist only to allow the group to function effectively, nonfunctional norms should be identified and then either discarded or replaced with more appropriate standards. In some settings, it is desirable to write down crucial norms. In group homes for delinquent youths, for example, all the rules about smoking, drinking, curfew hours, attending school, and domestic duties should be posted so that the residents are fully aware of them. The consequences of violating these norms should also be clearly written out.

Important norms should be enforced immediately after a violation and as consistently as possible. If norms are not enforced, they will lose their effectiveness, and a new norm (that it is OK to break such a rule) may begin to emerge. In most social service settings, social workers *must* follow through on consequences when clients violate important norms. Social workers lose their credibility with clients when consequences do not follow violations. Most centers serving runaways, for example, clearly spell out that residents cannot use alcohol or drugs while at the center. Residents who do are asked to leave. In one center, workers failed to expel a resident caught using alcohol, and the next day most of the residents were drinking beer.

EXERCISE 4.7   Understanding Idiosyncrasy Credits

GOAL: This exercise is designed to show you the effects of idiosyncrasy credits.

1. Describe someone's behavior that violated the norms of a group to which you belong or belonged. (Perhaps it was during a time when you went out for a night on the town with a group of friends.)

2. Was this norm-violating behavior tolerated by the other group members, or did the group reject this person? If the behavior was tolerated or excused by the other group members, was it because this person had idiosyncrasy credits? If "yes," what were the bases of these credits (such as "he or she does many positive things for the group")?

Group leaders should personally attempt to model the norms they believe are important. At a group home, for example, residents will not keep their rooms clean if the group leader's office is a mess.

Problems of Conformity

Hostile or disruptive members who fail to conform to group norms may be present in any group, even in those where membership is voluntary. However, they are more likely to be found in involuntary groups. Involuntary members often (at least at initial group meetings) wish they were a thousand other places than at the meeting. They may be angry and believe the time spent in the group will be completely wasted.

An involuntary client is one who is compelled to be a recipient of a social worker's (or another professional person's) services. For example, an individual may be required to be a recipient by a court order, by incarceration, or by family or employer pressure.

The following are a variety of settings in which social workers encounter involuntary clients: correctional institutions, protective services, mental health facilities, certain public schools, group homes, residential treatment facilities, nursing homes, and hospitals. In each of these settings, social workers may be expected to lead groups of unwilling clients.

LO 7   Identify Various Types of Hostile or Disruptive Group Members, and Comprehend How to Handle Disruptive Group Members

EP 7b
EP 8b

TYPES OF DISRUPTIVE BEHAVIOR

Unwilling group members can display counterproductive behavior. To more vividly describe some of these disruptive behaviors, we will look at the behaviors as if they were characters or personalities.

The Bear

This person openly expresses anger, rage, frustration, resentment, and hostility. The bear may be unhappy as a member of the group or with what is happening in the group. Discontent can be expressed in a variety of ways: verbally, by attacking other members of the group; nonverbally, by facial expressions; or physically, by aggressively pushing and shoving another member.

The bear who directly expresses unhappiness in an active fashion can also express unhappiness in passive-aggressive ways through indirect aggression. Bach and Wyden have called indirect aggression "crazy-making."[22] Indirect aggressors maintain a front of kindness but find subtle, indirect ways of expressing their anger, rage, or frustrations. Bach and Wyden label direct aggression "clean fighting" because feelings are expressed openly and can be identified and resolved. "Dirty fighters" use indirect tricks and never clearly express their feelings, which often causes a great deal of pain and can destroy effective communication in a group. Most disruptive behaviors involve an element of indirect aggression.

If you have a relationship with a "dirty fighter," he or she will identify what will "press your buttons" (that is, "get your goat"). When the "dirty fighter" is angry or frustrated with you, he or she will casually and subtly "press these buttons" to get you going.

The Eager Beaver

This person volunteers to do crucial tasks but has little intention of completing them and is simply seducing other members into believing he or she is a willing contributor. The eager beaver may partially perform some of the tasks to show good faith, but then employ a variety of excuses to explain why the tasks cannot be completed on time.

The Clown

This disrupter is rarely serious. He or she is always joking and clowning around, even when the other members want to be serious. A clown inhibits other members from expressing their thoughts and feelings because they fear they may be ridiculed.

The Psychoanalyzer

Continual analysis of what other members are doing and saying is the psychoanalyzer's forte. He or she often uses psychological terms and delights in analyzing what others really mean and what is wrong with them. The psychoanalyzer often slows down a group by getting members to engage in mind reading rather than task completion. Other members are inhibited from expressing their thoughts and feelings; they fear they may be analyzed as having psychological problems.

The Withholder

A withholder has important information or resources that would help the group accomplish its task but intentionally withholds assistance. He or she is more interested in watching the group struggle and spin its wheels.

The Conformity Power of Groups

The power of groups over individuals is great, as shown by the following examples.

On February 4, 1974, Patty Hearst, a college student and daughter of a wealthy publishing magnate, was kidnapped by the Symbionese Liberation Army, an ultraradical group. She was forcibly dragged from her home in Berkeley, California, taken to a house by her abductors, and placed in a closet. For several days, she remained in this closet with no lights. She was blindfolded, her hands were bound, and she was given food but was unable to dispose of her body wastes. Besides making constant threats against her life, her captors told her that her family had abandoned her by not complying with the kidnap demands. She was informed that her parents said it was all right with them if she was put to death. At times, Patty was also sexually assaulted by her captors. After a number of weeks passed, she was released from the closet. A few days later she was taken to a bank where (according to Ms. Hearst) her captors forced her to participate in a bank robbery. She was given a gun to use during the robbery, and one of her captors (armed with a gun) kept an eye on her. After this robbery, she was taken back to her place of captivity and informed that she was now guilty of bank robbery and murder, and that the Federal Bureau of Investigation (FBI) would shoot her on sight. For the next several months, Ms. Hearst conformed because of this pressure and joined her captors in committing additional crimes and in trying to avoid apprehension by the police. After her apprehension, 19 months later, she claimed that she had committed bank robbery and other crimes because she was brainwashed by her captors. She was given a light prison sentence for her role in the robberies.

In the 1960s, Jim Jones, a minister, started a religious commune called the People's Temple Movement in San Francisco, California. Gradually, the members were asked to give all their personal property to the People's Temple. In return, the Temple provided food, shelter, social services, and social and spiritual programs. Jones had considerable charisma and was successful in seducing the members to center their whole lives around the Temple and its activities. To gain further control over his followers, Jim Jones took them to an isolated area in the jungles of Guyana, South America. Rumors that the members were being sexually and physically abused and were being treated as slaves filtered back to California. In response to these complaints, Congressman Leo Ryan and a small staff went to Guyana to investigate the People's Temple Movement. Jim Jones ordered Ryan killed so that he could not report on the abuses he saw. Ryan was shot to death. Jim Jones then concluded that the United States would take strong retaliatory action and urged his followers to take their own lives en masse so they could be reunited in paradise. More than 900 men, women, and children committed mass suicide by drinking a fruit punch containing cyanide.

The power of conformity is also exhibited in religious cults such as Hari Krishna, ISIS, and Scientology, whose members are able to convince middle-class youths to join and forgo their education, career goals, families, and material possessions.

SOURCE: Adapted from "Patty's Own Story," *Wisconsin State Journal* (September . 24, 1975): 1–2.

The Beltliner

Everyone has a psychological "beltline" under which are subjects that he or she is extremely sensitive about. Beltline items may include physical characteristics, intelligence, past behavior, past unhappy events, or personality characteristics. An overweight person, for example, may be highly sensitive about comments related to obesity. Members who make subtle negative comments about the sensitive areas of other members threaten group cohesion and morale. A beltliner is a dirty fighter.

The Guiltmaker

A group member may attempt to control others by making them feel guilty. The guiltmaker traps the group into helping him or her with personal needs and goals, rather than working toward group goals. The guiltmaker uses such common expressions as "Yon never do anything for me" and "All I've done for you and this is the thanks I get" to trigger the guilt response.

The Catastrophe Crier

By exaggerating the seriousness of a problem, a catastrophe crier would have group members believe that consequences will be not minor, but disastrous. Because the catastrophe crier focuses only on examining the severity of the problem and not on developing and implementing problem-solving approaches, he or she intensifies a problem rather than solving it.

The Subject Changer

This person does not want a group to deal with crucial issues or with controversy and conflict. When difficult situations arise, he or she tries to change the subject. If successful, a subject changer prevents the group from dealing with crucial topics. There are a variety of reasons for seeking to change a subject. For example, the changer may detest heated debates or may fear the debate will reveal something he or she wishes to keep hidden.

The Whiner

A whiner continually complains about one thing or another without taking action to resolve the problem. Because the whiner seeks attention and sympathy from other members, he or she slows down a group in accomplishing its tasks.

The Benedict Arnold

If a group is competing with another group, a betrayer, or "Benedict Arnold," supplies confidential information to the other group. This person may encourage people outside the group to ridicule or disregard it or slyly have the group's funding cut back. Inside the group this member may attempt to prevent the group from accomplishing its goals. People appointed to head departments at state and federal levels, for example, are expected by the public to be voices for the growth and progress of those departments. But some appointees have betrayed this trust by a hidden agreement with the appointers to be a "hatchet man" and cut the services and funding requests of their departments.

The Trivial Tyrannizer

Instead of honestly sharing concerns, frustrations, and discontent, this member annoys a group with constant interruptions and digressions. He or she may arrive late for meetings and leave early, fail to show up for crucial meetings requiring everyone's attendance, or bring up concerns that the group has already acted on. Besides raising trivial questions about the wording of the minutes, for instance, this person may yawn or read something when other members are speaking.

The Shirker

A group member may be disruptive simply by failing to do anything for the group. When assigned certain tasks, the shirker will evade these responsibilities by using a variety of excuses.

The Power Grabber

A power grabber may attempt to become the group leader or the power source behind the group leader by convincing other members that he or she has more expertise than anyone else in the group or by buying the support of others with money, favors, or promises. A power grabber may create conflicts that make the leader look bad and sabotage the efforts of the leader, even though he or she may not assume leadership power.

The Paranoiac

Because he or she is excessively or irrationally suspicious and distrustful of others in the group, the paranoiac always feels picked on. Much of this person's time is spent defending himself or herself and finding fault with other group members. Paranoiac individuals often feel that other members must be discredited before they can amass enough evidence to discredit the paranoiacs.

It should be noted that some disrupters are intentionally aware of the effects of their behavior. Most of the previous examples are of this type. On the other hand, some disrupters are acting out of unconscious personal needs and therefore may not be aware their behavior is having a disruptive effect. The following suggestions on handling disruptive behavior apply whether the disrupter is aware or unaware of the effects of his or her behavior.

HANDLING DISRUPTIVE BEHAVIOR

Hostile and disruptive behavior can be handled in three basic ways: (1) members can be allowed to continue to be disruptive and the effects can be ignored or minimized; (2) the leader can confront members about their disruptive behavior; and (3) other group members can confront the disruptive behavior. The approach chosen should be based on what method will be most helpful to the group.

Minimizing Disruptiveness

If a disruptive group member is allowed to express discontent to the group, he or she may become less disruptive as time goes on through a ventilating process. When a member is disruptive, it is often helpful for the leader to ask the person tactfully to express his or her concerns. The group may then decide to deal with the concerns, especially those that are legitimate. With some concerns resolved, the disruptive group member may become more satisfied with the group and begin to feel the group has something to offer.

Let us assume, for example, that a man is angry and embarrassed about being sent to "Group Dynamics," a group consisting of people found guilty of driving while intoxicated. This man may be angry that he got a ticket, whereas others who drink and drive have not been caught and "sentenced" to the group by a judge. At the initial meetings, he may aggressively ask a litany of questions: "What is the purpose of the group?" "What evidence is there that the group will do any good?" "What does one have to do in the group to pass?" "What qualifications does the group leader have for leading this group?" "Has the group leader ever been intoxicated while driving?" "If not, how can the leader understand what the members are thinking and feeling?" "If so, how can the leader be hypocritical by attempting to 'play therapist' when he or she has similar problems?" "Will members be forced to reveal personal things?" "What is the purpose of each of the group exercises?" "Does the leader believe the people in this group are drunks?"

The leader can handle these concerns by allowing this man to air his views and by providing honest answers. Furthermore, the group leader may acknowledge that he or she would also be angry if placed in that member's position. This approach seeks to allow members to ventilate their concerns, to answer their questions, and to convey understanding of their unhappiness. The goal is to create an atmosphere in which the group will be receptive to the content and exercises that will make the group effective.

Most of the time, my first strategy in responding to a disgruntled group member when he or she voices a concern is to "kill that person with kindness." I seek to convey that the disgruntled person has a legitimate concern (or at least a partially legitimate concern), which often leads that person to feel validated. Usually, once the disgruntled person feels validated, she or he will "buy into" what the group is trying to accomplish and then make positive contributions.

Leader Confrontation

The group leader can confront the member about his or her disruptive behavior, either with other group members present or at a private meeting. The choice of private or group confrontation should be based on which will be most beneficial. If other members are present, they may be able to elaborate on the ways in which the member's behavior is disrupting the group and emphasize the seriousness of the problem. A disadvantage of group confrontation is that a hostile member may feel he or she is being "ganged up on."

During a confrontation, the group leader should seek to fully and assertively express concerns in a nonblaming way by using I-messages (see Chapter 5 for I-messages and Appendix 1: Module 2 for assertiveness).[23] Some confronters make the mistake of primarily using the two types of you-messages: solution and put-down messages. Solution messages order, direct, command, warn, threaten, preach, moralize, or advise. Put-down messages blame, judge, criticize, ridicule, or name call.

I-messages consist of a nonblaming description of the effects of the disruptive member's behavior on the group or on the leader. The group leader simply tells the member which behavior is disruptive and then leaves it up to that member to take responsibility for changing it. I-messages generally lead to honesty and openness in a relationship, whereas you-messages usually reduce communication and polarize relationships.

Sometimes simply confronting a member with the disruptive behavior will lead to a change because he or she may not be aware of the behavior's negative effects. Once informed, the member may alter the behavior or reveal reasons for being disruptive. For example, the disruptive member may be resentful because he or she has not been assigned more responsibilities in the group. Assigning that person more tasks may lead not only to a cessation of the disruptive behavior, but also to him or her becoming a contented, productive member. When concerns underlying the disruptive behavior are resolved, it often ceases. In such a confrontation, the leader must tactfully ask questions to identify the reasons for the disruptive behavior.

However, confrontation may not always stop the behavior, for the disrupter may either continue along the same line or switch to another method of disruption. A "clown," for example, may become a "subject changer" or a "betrayer." If the disruptive behavior continues after a confrontation, the group leader can either ignore the disruptive behavior as much as possible and minimize its effects or confront the member again. In choosing the second alternative, the group leader must clearly inform the member that adverse consequences will result, explain those consequences, and follow through on implementing them if disruptive behavior continues.

For example, a group leader may inform a disruptive member in a court-imposed Group Dynamics class that he has four choices: (1) to participate in meetings and get as much out of them as possible; (2) not to participate but to attend in order to meet the court's requirement; (3) to attend and continue disrupting the class, with the court then being informed of his disruptive behavior; or (4) not to come to class, in which case the lack of attendance will be documented, the court notified, and that person's driver's license possibly suspended.

Some students tend to monopolize a class by rambling on about topics only remotely connected to what is being discussed. Usually, simply informing them privately about the rambling and the need to share "air time" solves the problem. However, a few students continue rambling even after the first confrontation. They are then informed privately that they must raise their hands before talking and will be called on only once or twice each session, depending on the class. Furthermore, indicate that if they try to talk before raising their hands, the class members will be asked if they believe some people are using up too much class time. If the answer is "yes," the class will then be asked to set rules for sharing class time. The second confrontation has always resulted in less rambling.

Group Confrontation

The third approach is to have another group member, rather than the leader, confront the disruptive member; the same guidelines apply here that were described earlier for such a confrontation. There are certain situations in which the confrontation is best handled by someone other than the leader. For example, several years ago a social work department at a large eastern university recruited someone from another university to chair the department.

A faculty member in that department had wanted the position and felt cheated. When the new chair came, this faculty member refused to do any departmental tasks and was at times verbally disruptive during faculty meetings. Two other faculty members in this department met with the disgruntled party to explain the reasons he was not selected, to allow him to express his resentment, and to politely request that he seek to be more cooperative because it was in everyone's best interests. This confrontation was quite successful and changed the disgruntled faculty member's attitude.

If confrontation is necessary, a decision has to be made by the group leader and by other concerned members about who should do it. Generally, the decision should be based on who appears to have the best chances of influencing the disruptive member.

REDUCING THE LIKELIHOOD OF DISRUPTIVE BEHAVIOR

Group members are less apt to be disruptive when their personal goals are identified and incorporated into the group goals. By involving all group members in setting goals and making decisions, the group's communication, cohesion, and problem-solving effectiveness are likely to increase. An autocratic leadership style discourages commitment, whereas a democratic style promotes it. Moreover, autocratic leadership is less satisfying to members and may lead to disruptive behavior. Group goals that are clear, operational, and measurable also tend to increase members' satisfaction and commitment to the group and reduce frustrations, as discussed earlier in this chapter.

A cooperative atmosphere leads to higher morale, open and honest communication, more effective problem solving, and increased group cohesion and satisfaction. As discussed earlier in this chapter, a competitive atmosphere is more apt to lead to disruptive behavior.

If some members are disruptive in similar ways, the group can discuss the effects of the disruptions in a nonblaming way and set "house rules" for handling disconcerting behavior. For example, three or four people who are smoking may be irritating the nonsmokers. House rules may be established as to when and where smoking may take place. Or some members may be habitually late. This problem can be discussed, and the group can agree on some rules regarding meeting times and tardiness.

Disruptive behavior usually decreases if the group leader is well organized, covers relevant and interesting material, and effectively helps the members reach decisions and accomplish goals. A group leader should also pay attention to meeting the social/emotional needs of members and actively strive to have all members participate in making decisions. He or she cannot play favorites and must follow through on what is initiated. If the group leader has serious problems in one or more of these areas, discontent and disruptive behavior will probably increase.

The more assertively and competently the leader presents himself or herself, the more trust and confidence the group members will display. If the leader is aggressive, the members will usually feel angry or intimidated and respond either aggressively or passive-aggressively. If the leader is nonassertive, the members will tend to have a low level of confidence in the leader and may begin asking whether a new leader should be selected.

If a group is not functioning well, the leader should confront the group with his or her concerns and ask the group to help identify the reasons so that changes can be made. Depending on the circumstances, these can be identified at a group meeting or through written reports that ensure anonymity. Using this confrontational approach, the leader commits himself or herself to working with the group to make changes. For example, I taught a practice course in which hardly anyone was asking questions or making comments. During the fifth week of the class, I confronted the class in the following manner: "I think we've got a problem. This is the fifth week of this practice class, and no one is saying anything. To make this class go, we need to start talking. One of the first skills that social workers need is the ability to talk. I'm not convinced that people in this class can talk. So far, it's been mainly me that's been talking. Now, I'm going to shut up and let you talk. I want you to tell me why you're not talking. I'm a big boy. 1 can take whatever you have to say." After a few minutes of silence, some students began talking, and we ended up having a lively discussion. Basically,

EXERCISE 4.8   Handling Disruptive Behavior of a Group Member

GOAL: This exercise is designed to help you better handle the disruptive behavior of a group member.

1. Describe the disruptive behavior of someone who was also a member of a group in which you were involved.

2. How did the disruptive behavior affect the group?

3. What actions (if any) did the other group members take to attempt to minimize the effects of the disruptive behavior? Were these actions effective?

4. If the actions were not effective, review the material in this text on handling disruptive behavior. What actions might have been taken by you (or by other group members) to more effectively handle the disruptive behavior?

the students said I was primarily lecturing, which led them to be passive, and they requested exercises to try out the theories and principles I was presenting. In future classes, I adjusted my teaching approach to include exercises. After this confrontation, the students became more verbal in future sessions (though still not as verbal as I desired).

When members are forced to attend a group they do not want to attend, as in the case of involuntary clients, the group leader may begin by saying something like, "I know most of you really don't want to be here, and I wouldn't either if I were forced to come. I wonder if we might begin by talking about your anger and unhappiness about being here?" Then the group leader should attempt to convey the purposes of the group, what is going to happen, and how the members can satisfy the minimal requirements for "passing." The group leader can mention that members can (1) choose to actively participate and get as much out of the group as possible; (2) remain silent and listen to what others have to say; (3) vent their anger and unhappiness in disruptive ways (which will probably anger and alienate others in the group); or (4) refuse to come, which will have certain consequences. The group leader can then indicate that he or she cannot control their behavior, so the choice among these alternatives is up to each member. Such an approach almost always leads the involuntary clients to choose either the first or second alternative, perhaps because such an approach leads these clients to conclude that the leader is understanding of their anger—and they then focus on making the best choices in this predicament.

Sometime during the life of the group, one or more members may struggle with the leader for control. There are a variety of ways to handle a power struggle. (1) The person (or persons) may be given limited leadership responsibilities. This "second-in-command" approach may satisfy the member, who may become very helpful. He or she may accomplish important group tasks or, in therapy groups, prove to be a useful "co-counselor." (2) The group leader and the member desiring to be the leader can meet privately and work out a shared leadership arrangement to present to the group or identify the changes that the member would like to see made. (3) The leader may display in a tactful manner (through words and actions) that he or she is the person best qualified to lead the group. (Following this strategy, a political campaign-like atmosphere sometimes occurs, with the leader and the aspiring leader acting as competing candidates, both seeking to impress other group members with their leadership qualifications.) (4) The group leader can resign, ask the members whom they wish to have as their leader, and indicate that he or she would again take the position if the group so desired. (5) Another strategy is to ask for a vote of confidence. If a majority vote of support is not received, the group leader promises to step down. By rallying resources and supporters in a display of strength, a group leader can usually show the aspiring leader that a takeover attempt is futile. (6) Finally, the group leader can threaten the aspiring leader with certain adverse consequences. Sometimes these threats boomerang and motivate the aspiring leader to work harder or are used to convince other group members that the present group leader lacks moral integrity.

Summary

The following summarizes the chapter's content in terms of the learning objectives presented at the beginning of the chapter.

1. **Set personal and group goals in groups.**
   All groups have goals, and every individual who joins a group has personal goals. Procedures for setting group goals were described.

2. **Understand and identify hidden agendas.**
   Some members may have a hidden agenda, which is a personal goal held by a member (which is unknown to other group members) that interferes with the group's efforts.

3. Comprehend the differences between competitive groups and cooperative groups.
   Groups tend to have either a cooperative or a competitive atmosphere. There are a number of positive consequences of a cooperative group atmosphere. A competitive atmosphere is usually destructive. The positive characteristics of a cooperative group are readily destroyed by a competitive person.

4. Apply the nominal group approach.
   A nominal group is a group in which members work in the presence of others, but do not verbally interact. This approach is a problem-identification technique for designing or modifying programs and involves meeting with potential users to assess their needs.

5. Understand the importance of group norms, and comprehend how norms are formed.
   Group norms are rules that specify proper group behavior. The processes through which norms are learned and developed are described.

6. Identify group pressures to conform.
   Conformity means yielding to group pressure. To conform, a group member must experience conflict between the influences exerted by the group (group norms) and his or her personal values. Because group members have a tendency to want to be accepted and liked by others, there is considerable group pressure to conform.

7. Identify various types of hostile or disruptive group members, and comprehend how to handle disruptive group members.
   Types of disruptive behaviors of group members are identified. Strategies for handling disruptive behaviors of members in a group are presented, which include minimizing disruptiveness, leader confrontation of the member engaging in disruptive behavior, and other group members confronting the disruptive member.

Group Exercises

EXERCISE A: Setting Personal and Group Goals

GOAL: To identify personal goals for this class and to set group goals.

Step 1. The group leader begins by explaining the purpose of the exercise. Then the group leader should explain what operational and measurable goals are and summarize their importance.

Step 2. Each member makes a list of personal and group goals for the class on a sheet of paper. The instructor should also prepare a list of group goals for the class.

Step 3. A listing should be made on the blackboard of the personal and group goals suggested by each student (inform students that they have a right to privacy and do not need to identify their personal goals). The instructor's list of group goals should also be put on the blackboard.

Step 4. The class should then discuss the personal and group goals listed on the blackboard and decide what the goals for the class will be. (The group leader should have previously read the material in Chapter 6 on procedures for decision making.) In arriving at class goals, it should be made clear that because the instructor is responsible for the course, he or she may exclude or add any group goal.

Step 5. After group goals are established, the following questions should be discussed with the group:

1. Are all of these goals operational and measurable? If not, how can they be improved?
2. What difficulties were encountered in setting group goals?

3. Did it take longer than expected?
4. Did anyone become frustrated at some point? Why?
5. How satisfied is the group with the goals that were set?
6. How does the group feel about the instructor having a greater say as to what the group's goals should be?
7. Are these goals realistically attainable?
8. Are these group goals compatible with personal goals?
9. Are individuals committed to work toward attaining these group goals?

EXERCISE B: A Sphinx Foundation Grant

GOAL: To observe what happens when some members are cooperative and others are competitive.

Step 1. The group leader explains that the exercise involves setting goals. Students are to assume that the Sphinx Foundation has awarded $100,000 to the students and faculty in this social work program to improve the program and/or social services in the community surrounding the campus. The task of the class is to arrive at recommendations as to how these funds should be used. The class is divided into three equal subgroups.

Step 2. Each subgroup meets for 15 minutes to develop proposals. A representative then presents the proposals to representatives of the other two subgroups.

Step 3. The three representatives meet in the center of the room for 15 minutes to present the proposals to each other and work toward a decision for the class. The three subgroups observe the negotiations. A subgroup cannot meet with the other subgroups, but members in a subgroup may talk among themselves. The subgroups may not talk with their representatives, but they may send written messages.

Step 4. The representatives should next confer with their subgroups for 5 minutes.

Step 5. The representatives then meet in the center of the room for 5 minutes to attempt to reach an agreement. Next, they meet with their subgroups for 5 minutes. And, finally, they meet again in the center of the room to seek to reach a final agreement.

Step 6. Discuss the following questions:

1. Was an agreement reached? Why or why not?
2. Did the representatives and the subgroups attempt to be cooperative or competitive? Why? What were the results of being primarily either cooperative or competitive?
3. Were the proposals primarily designed to benefit students, the department, or social services in the community? Why was this particular focus the major emphasis?
4. What are the representatives' feelings about this exercise? Did the representatives feel pressure from their subgroup? If so, what type of pressure?
5. How were decisions made within each subgroup, and how did the representatives make decisions?

EXERCISE C: The Nominal Group Approach

GOAL: Demonstrate how to conduct a nominal group.

Step 1. The leader begins by describing what a nominal group is and how it can be used. The leader then explains that the goal of the exercise is to identify shortcomings in the college's social work program by obtaining the views of the participants as to their wants and needs. In a classroom setting, it is not necessary to obtain a representative cross-section of the group because the students compose the total population of potential users.

Step 2. The participants are randomly divided into small groups of five to eight students. Each group should be seated around a separate table. (When tables are not available, classroom desks can be arranged in groups of five to eight with only limited inconvenience.)

Step 3. The leader distributes a sheet of paper containing a question participants must answer in writing. (An alternative to distributing a sheet of paper is to write the question on the blackboard.) One question that might be used is the following:

> Without mentioning names, what do you see as the shortcomings of our social work program?
>
> Please—No talking

Step 4. For 15 to 20 minutes, the participants privately list their responses to the question. No talking is permitted during this time.

Step 5. One member of each group is designated as recorder. The recorder asks each group member to state a shortcoming and lists each response on flip-chart sheets with a magic marker in full view of other members. This process continues until each member has given all of his or her responses. Listing is done separately for each group. Each response is recorded exactly as each member states it, and there is no discussion.

Step 6. The flip-chart sheets are then posted on the wall with masking tape near the group involved. A brief, informal discussion follows and focuses on clarifying what the ideas mean. There are two different approaches to reviewing the items: (1) all items are made known to the whole class or (2) each group briefly reviews only the items recorded for its group. Both approaches appear to work. For smaller groups, the first is usually used. When the total number of listed items becomes very large, the second approach is generally more effective.

Step 7. Once the participants are familiar with the items on the flip-chart sheets, each is asked to list on index cards the five items he or she feels are most important.

Step 8. These items are handed in anonymously and then tabulated on the flip-chart sheets, or each student can simply check five items on the flip-chart sheets with a magic marker. These results are then briefly discussed with the students. (The instructor may well find it desirable to share the results with the other faculty in the department, and a faculty meeting may be arranged to discuss and take action on the highly rated items.)

EXERCISE D: Identifying and Changing Group Norms

GOAL: To give practice in identifying norms that exist in a group and to assess whether some of these norms should be changed.

Step 1. The group leader explains what group norms are and states the purpose of this exercise. The class then forms subgroups of three or four students. Each subgroup makes a list of norms that exist in the class.

Step 2. From this list, the subgroups identify a few of the norms that they would like to see altered and propose changes.

Step 3. A representative from each subgroup writes its list of norms on the blackboard, circling the norms the subgroup wants changed.

Step 4. A class discussion follows. Are the subgroups generally in agreement or disagreement as to the norms that exist in the class? For the norms that are circled, a representative from each subgroup should state why the subgroup would like to see these norms changed and present the subgroup's suggestions for replacing these norms. The class should then discuss whether the changes are desirable. (Because the instructor has primary responsibility for how the class is conducted, the instructor has the right to veto any suggested change.)

EXERCISE E: An Ornery Instructor

GOAL: To help develop an awareness of norms that exist in the group and to look at what happens in a group when the leader acts under a new set of norms.

Step 1. This exercise is perhaps best done by the instructor. The instructor begins the class in a fashion very different from what he or she generally does. For example, the instructor may dress much more, or much less, formally. If chairs are generally in a circle, they should be put in rows. If the instructor generally engages in small talk before starting the class, this should be avoided. If the instructor comes across as a warm person, he or she should attempt to come across as a cold person. The instructor may take roll, for instance, and announce that from this point forward a student's grade will be dropped one full grade for each missed class period. The instructor may openly criticize students who arrive late or who otherwise disrupt the class in minor ways. The instructor may indicate he or she is unhappy with the way the class is going, and therefore new rules will be implemented: roll call will be taken each day; there will be a quiz every week; each student's attitude and participation in the class will now count as 30% of the final grade; any student who fails to take an exam at the scheduled time or who does not get a paper in on time will receive no higher than a D in the course; and the students will be graded down severely if they do not participate in class.

Step 2. After 10 or 15 minutes of this uncharacteristic behavior, the instructor should explain the real purpose of the exercise, which involved the intentional violation of existing norms. The instructor then asks what the class was thinking and feeling when he or she applied a new set of norms in the class. The instructor may conclude by stating that norms are very important in guiding the direction of a group and that significant changes in norms often lead to confusion and resistance.

EXERCISE F: How Group Decisions Affect Values

GOAL: To show how group decisions affect individual values.

Step 1. The group leader explains that the purpose of this exercise is to help students assess their values. The leader then distributes the following questionnaire, explains that the results will be anonymous, and instructs students not to talk while filling it out. The class then forms subgroups of five or six members. The questions are as follows:

1. Do you believe gay and lesbian teachers should be allowed to teach young children?
   a. Definitely
   b. Probably
   c. Undecided
   d. Probably not
   e. Definitely not
2. Do you believe individuals who have such a profound intellectual disability that they will never function beyond a 6-month mental age level should be kept alive at taxpayers' expense?
   a. Definitely
   b. Probably
   c. Undecided
   d. Probably not
   e. Definitely not
3. Do you believe people have a right to take their own lives?
   a. Definitely
   b. Probably
   c. Undecided
   d. Probably not
   e. Definitely not
4. Should teenage females be allowed to have an abortion on demand without the consent of a parent?
   a. Definitely
   b. Probably
   c. Undecided

d. Probably not

e. Definitely not

5. Would you allow your child to attend classes at a school that a child with AIDS is also attending?

a. Definitely

b. Probably

c. Undecided

d. Probably not

e. Definitely not

Step 2. The questionnaires are collected and kept separate for each subgroup. The subgroups are then asked to discuss each topic and arrive at a single answer for each question. Each subgroup should be given an additional questionnaire on which to record its answers.

Step 3. After the subgroups have completed Step 2, each member should again fill out the questionnaire anonymously. Again, the questionnaires for each subgroup should be kept separate.

Step 4. Prior to conducting this exercise, the group leader should arrange to have the instructor tabulate the results. The results should be recorded according to the following format:

SUBGROUP A

		Number of students selecting this alternative		
		Prediscussion Replies	Group Decision Replies	Postdiscussion Replies
Question 1	a.			
	b.			
	c.			
	d.			
	e.			
Question 2	a.			
	b.			
	c.			
	d.			
	e.			
Question 3	a.			
	b.			
	c.			
	d.			
	e.			
Question 4	a.			
	b.			
	c.			
	d.			
	e.			
Question 5	a.			
	b.			
	c.			
	d.			
	e.			

Step 5. During a break, the responses for all the subgroups are put on the blackboard or entered on a transparency according to the format listed in Step 4. The following questions should then be discussed: Do the prediscussion replies differ from the postdiscussion replies? If "yes," what are the reasons some members changed their views? Do group discussions and group decisions appear to influence value judgments by students? When students answered the individual questionnaire after the group decision, did they feel a conflict between the group view and their personal values? If "yes," how did they feel about this conflict, and how did they attempt to resolve it?

EXERCISE G: Confrontation and I-Messages

GOAL: To practice confrontation and using I-messages.

Step 1. The group leader begins by explaining the goals of the exercise. Then I-messages should be described. I-messages are a nonblaming description of the effects of another's behavior on you. In using I-messages, the sender does not necessarily have to use the term "I"; the key is to describe the effects of another's behavior on you in a nonblaming way, without being critical or suggesting solutions. (See Chapter 5 for a more detailed description of I-messages.)

Step 2. The following situations involve confrontation using role-playing, and the "confronter" is urged to use I-messages. Two different students should be asked to volunteer for each role-play and are given the following instructions:

Role-play 1. You're a group leader, and a member of your group has been 10 to 15 minutes late for every meeting. His habitual tardiness has been disruptive, and you fear that other members may follow this person's example and also arrive late. Your task is to confront this member about being late.

Role-play 2. You're a group leader, and there has been interpersonal conflict in the group that is not being dealt with because each time efforts are made to deal with the conflict, Jim (or Jill) either makes a joke of it or changes the subject. Your task is to confront Jim (or Jill) about this.

Role-play 3. You're a nonsmoker, along with most other group members. Jean (or John) usually sits next to you and frequently smokes a cigarette, which you find increasingly irritating. Your task is to confront Jean (or John) about this.

Role-play 4. You're a group member, and the group has been going nowhere because goals have not been established. The leader appears confused and uncertain about group procedures. The group is composed of students who are supposed to advise the social work faculty on curriculum and departmental policies. You are aware that this is the first group the leader has led. Your task is to confront the leader and explain that you and other members feel confused and frustrated because it appears that the group has been floundering.

Step 3. After each role-play, discuss how well each confronter (1) assertively expressed his or her concerns and (2) used I-messages to express the concerns.

EXERCISE H: Confronting and Being Confronted by Others

EP 1b
EP 1c
EP 1e

GOAL: To practice tactfully confronting a partner about his or her group performance and to receive feedback on group performance.

NOTE: The instructor should lead this exercise because it may generate strong emotions in the participants.

Step 1. The group leader explains the purposes of the exercise. Before beginning, the group leader indicates that some members need to work on controlling their disruptive behavior. The group leader should also explain that other issues may be brought up in the confrontation.

The group leader briefly summarizes the following ways in which members are disruptive to suggest areas that the confronting student may want to mention tactfully to his or her partner.

The Bear	The Eager Beaver
The Psychoanalyzer	The Beltliner
The Guiltmaker	The Withholder
The Clown	The Catastrophe Crier
The Subject Changer	The Whiner
The Benedict Arnold	The Trivial Tyrannizer
The Shirker	The Power Grabber
The Paranoiac	

Step 2. Next, each member pairs up with another. The instructor explains that the task of each student is to confront his or her partner tactfully about behavior related to group performance that he or she might work on. First, one student is the confronter and the other the listener; then roles are reversed. The group leader should emphasize the importance of (1) first complimenting the partner on demonstrated strengths to balance out the negative feelings that may result from the confrontation, (2) using I-messages, and (3) being tactful and making the confrontation as positive as possible.

Step 3. After the confrontations, the instructor asks the students how they felt about the experience and encourages discussion of the positive and negative aspects of the exercise.

Competency Notes

EP 7b Apply knowledge of human behavior and the social environment, person-in-environment, and other multidisciplinary theoretical frameworks in the analysis of assessment data from clients and constituencies.

EP 9b Apply knowledge of human behavior and the social environment, person-in-environment, and other multidisciplinary theoretical frameworks in the evaluation of outcomes. (pp. 110–112)

The concepts of operational goals and measurable goals allow social workers to assess the quality of goal statements.

EP 7b Apply knowledge of human behavior and the social environment, person-in-environment, and other multidisciplinary theoretical frameworks in the analysis of assessment data from clients and constituencies. (pp. 112–114)

The concepts of cooperative atmosphere and competitive atmosphere allow social workers to assess an important group dynamic.

EP 7b Apply knowledge of human behavior and the social environment, person-in-environment, and other multidisciplinary theoretical frameworks in the analysis of assessment data from clients and constituencies. (pp. 114–115)

The nominal group approach is an important problem-identification technique.

EP 1b Use reflection and self-regulation to manage personal values and maintain professionalism in practice situations. (p. 120)

This exercise assists students in reflecting about their yielding to group pressure.

EP 7b Apply knowledge of human behavior and the social environment, person-in-environment, and other multidisciplinary theoretical frameworks in the analysis of assessment data from clients and constituencies.

EP 8b   Apply knowledge of human behavior and the social environment, person-in-environment, and other multidisciplinary theoretical frameworks in interventions with clients and constituencies. (pp. 122–129)

This conceptualization of disruptive group behaviors allows social workers to assess disruptive behaviors in groups and provides suggestions for handling disruptive behaviors in groups.

EP 1b   Use reflections and self-regulation to manage personal values and maintain professionalism in practice situations.

EP 1c   Demonstrate professional demeanor in behavior; appearance; and oral, written, and electronic communication.

EP 1e   Use supervision and consultation to guide professional judgment and behavior. (pp. 135–136)

This exercise allows students to practice tactfully confronting a partner on his or her group performance and to receive feedback on group performance.

Key Terms and Concepts

Expedient Conformer   Nonoperational Goal   True Conformer
Hidden Agenda   Operational Goal

5

Verbal and Nonverbal Communication

All cooperative group interaction, whether verbal or nonverbal, depends upon effective communication. Through communication, members argue, trade insults, debate issues, arrive at group goals, assume tasks and responsibilities, laugh, and work out differences. Effective communication occurs between two or more people when the receiver interprets the sender's message in the way the sender intended. The meaning of a communication is the response it elicits in the receiver, regardless of the intent of the sender.

Strong communication skills are also important for social workers as a way of supporting self-care. Social workers who use effective communication skills in expressing their own needs, asking for help, clarifying their roles in the workplace, interacting effectively and differently with clients, and giving/receiving support in the workplace report lower levels of burnout.[2]

LO 1   Understand a Model of Communication

EP 1b
EP 1c
EP 6a
EP 6b

A MODEL OF COMMUNICATION

Although most people think they understand what communication is all about, they are not fully aware of the process that goes on whenever people share ideas. This section will briefly summarize the process. We will begin by assuming that you, a sender, want to express a thought or a feeling.

The first thing you do is translate your thoughts and feelings into symbols (usually spoken words, but also nonverbal signals) that others can understand. This process is called **encoding**. Finding the precise symbols to express what you think or feel can be difficult. The next step is to *send the message.* There are a number of ways of sending a message: by letter, e-mail, telephone, note, spoken word, touch, posture, gestures, and facial expressions. When your message reaches a receiver, the receiver **decodes** the message by interpreting it in terms of thoughts or feelings that mean something to the receiver. The completed process is shown in Figure 5.1.

This process is one-way communication, in which a sender directs a message to a receiver. Most communication is a two-way process, however, as the initial sender directs a message to a receiver and the receiver responds. Two-way communication is diagrammed in Figure 5.2.

With effective communication, what the receiver decodes is what the sender sends, However, frequently something goes wrong. A friendly joke is taken as an insult. A subtle request is missed. A constructive suggestion is taken as a put down.

LEARNING OBJECTIVES

Sigmund Freud noted, "He that has eyes to see and ears to hear may convince himself that no mortal can keep a secret. If his lips are silent, he chatters with his fingertips; betrayal oozes out of him at every pore"[1] To be effective, group members and social workers must be able to communicate their thoughts and feelings accurately. This chapter will help prepare students to:

LO 1
Understand a model of communication.

LO 2
Identify factors that interfere with the communication process.

LO 3
Communicate more effectively.

LO 4
Have an increased understanding of nonverbal communication.

FIGURE 5.1   **A Model of Communication**

Our model identifies the areas in which misinterpretations may occur. First, the sender may have difficulty putting into symbolic form the thoughts and feelings he or she wishes to express. Second, the message may not be sent effectively. There may be too much noise for the sender to be fully heard, or the sender may not speak loudly enough. Although nonverbal cues tend to be ambiguous, words also have a variety of meanings and may connote something different from what the sender intends. Third, during the decoding process, the receiver may misunderstand the sender's message as a result of several factors, including physiological factors; individual attitudes, values, beliefs, defense mechanisms, and stereotypes; and perceptual factors, such as not listening. Later in this chapter, we will take a closer look at how each of these factors influences communication.

One-Way Communication

Some groups and many corporations use one-way communication. The boss or group leader gives instructions and orders or makes announcements to the other group members, who are not allowed to respond with their thoughts, feelings, and ideas. In one-way communication, the listener's role is only to receive the sender's messages and to carry out instructions and orders. The advantages of one-way communication are that messages and instructions are given quickly, and the boss does not have to deal with the questions and concerns of the listeners. In authority hierarchies, messages are often passed down through several levels.

Some studies have examined what happens when information is passed through several people using one-way communication.[3] As the message is passed along, it tends to become more simplified and distorted because of the three psychological processes of leveling, sharpening, and assimilation. First, receivers reduce, or **level**, the amount of information because they recall less information than they receive. In successive messages, fewer details are mentioned and fewer words are used. Second, a few high points become dominant and readily remembered, or *sharpened,* whereas much of the remainder is forgotten. Third, the receivers interpret, or **assimilate**, much of the message in terms of their own unique personalities and reference frames. This process involves changing the unfamiliar to some known context, leaving out material that seems irrelevant, and substituting material that gives meaning in terms of the receiver's frame of reference.

FIGURE 5.2   **A Model of Two-Way Communication**

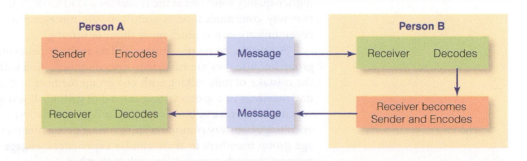

Directive or Coercive Communication   A variation of one-way communication involves feedback, which McGregor has labeled **directive** or **coercive** communication.[4] With this approach, a chairperson delivers a message, and group members have an opportunity to seek clarification. The feedback is limited to determining how well the members understand the message. When the chair determines that the members understand the message, communication ceases. This type of communication is based on the premise that the chair's view on an issue is in the best interest of the group or organization. Directive or coercive communication has an advantage over simple one-way communication because a process is in place to determine whether members understand the message.

Problems with One-Way Communication   Some serious drawbacks exist to one-way and directive communication. The members may have valuable information that could improve the group's productivity, but because it is not communicated to the chair, it is never considered. In addition, the details of the original message are lost, and the original message is distorted as it is passed from one level to another. These distortions will reduce the coordination between hierarchy levels and sometimes result in ineffective implementation of the chair's directives. In addition, the morale of the group and the commitment of members to carry out the directives are substantially reduced when the members have no input into the decision-making process. A major defect of U.S. corporations in the past has been that communication was usually a one-way process. Japanese corporations tended to produce higher-quality products at lower cost, partially as a result of the positive two-way communication between workers and management. In Japanese companies, workers identify their concerns and offer suggestions for improving productivity in periodic meetings with management. (Many U.S. corporations have now moved toward implementing two-way communication between workers and management.)

Communication Breakdown   In one Wisconsin county, two deaf parents whose children were placed in foster care almost lost their children permanently due to communication breakdown. In a one-year period, there were four out of eight courtroom hearings in which interpreters were not in attendance. When interpreters were present, the judges failed to ask them of their qualifications to ensure the parents could understand them. The parents were also sent letters informing them to contact case managers via voice telephone or e-mail; however, "neither parent was given a computer or devices" that could have allowed them to be able to contact the case manager. When an appropriate interpreter was located, it was also found that both parents read at or below the second-grade level. Once all aspects of communication were addressed, the parents were more successful in their ability to get their children back.[5]

Two-Way Communication

Some groups use two-way communication, which allows all members to participate fully. There are numerous benefits to be gained through this type of interaction. Because minority opinions are encouraged and often expressed, two-way communication improves cohesion, group morale, trust, and openness. Conflicts and controversies are resolved through higher-quality solutions as the resources and ideas of all the members are pooled. Although two-way communication is almost always more productive and effective than one-way communication, it is much more time consuming.

A mistake some new group leaders make is believing they are running an effective group because they are using two-way communication with members; however, they make the mistake of only talking with one group member at a time. They tend to have one-on-one meetings in a group setting instead of getting all group members engaged in the conversation. In order to build cohesion and group relationships, it is important for leaders to encourage two-way communication among group members. The group leader can encourage group members to share similar experiences, engage in problem solving, or provide support through conversation with each other.

EXERCISE 5.1   The Emotional Effects of One-Way Communication

GOAL: This exercise is designed to assist you in understanding the emotional impact of one-way communication.

1. Describe a situation where someone (perhaps an employer, a parent, or a teacher) used one-way communication with you.

2. How did you feel when you were not allowed to voice your opinion, were not allowed to share your thoughts, and were not allowed to ask a question?

3. Were you motivated to do what the person who used one-way communication wanted you to do?

Problems with Two-Way Communication   The authority hierarchy also affects two-way communication because high-status people tend to talk more, and most messages are directed to high-status members. Often members with little power take few risks and avoid frank remarks because they fear the consequences. High-authority members are often reluctant to reveal their limitations and vulnerabilities for fear of appearing weak and undeserving of their status. This tendency of high-authority members also reduces honest and open communication.

When there are sharp differences in status and authority among members, a cooperative atmosphere should be established to encourage the full participation of all members. Also, if the group is to be effective, group norms must indicate that the ideas and opinions of all group members are valuable and essential.

Culture and Communication

Social workers are increasingly finding themselves working with more diverse cultures, with diverse language and communication styles. Intercultural communication is the "exchange of information or engagement in dialogue among people of different cultures"[6] Miscommunication can occur when group members from different cultures have different expectations for the group process. For example, for some cultures it may be inappropriate to display emotions in groups. Group leaders who encourage a display of emotions from these group members may lose respect among these members. Group leaders, especially those from dominant cultures, need to be willing to educate themselves about cultural differences among group members.

LO 2   Identify Factors That Interfere with the Communication Process

PERCEPTION

Let us go back to the model of communication presented at the beginning of the chapter. Among the areas in which communication can go awry is the receiver's perception of the sender's message. The message perceived by the receiver depends not only on the encoding processes of the sender, but also on the receiver's decoding, or interpretation. For example, the receiver may *add* to the sender's message. If a student of the opposite sex tells you, "You really look nice today," you may perceive that the sender is really saying, "I'd like to be romantically involved with you." A receiver also may *not fully comprehend* everything the sender is saying, just as an undergraduate may not fully grasp all the details of a sophisticated, abstract lecture given by a senior faculty member. Finally, a receiver may *distort* portions of the message because, for example, it cannot be heard clearly.

What a receiver perceives, then, *becomes the message*. This message may be fully accurate, partially accurate, or completely inaccurate. An ink blot test demonstrates that there are huge variations in what individuals perceive in an ill-defined or nebulous communication. The perception of any sender's message is based on the receiver's experiences, the receiver's needs, and the sender's actual message. Because a receiver's response is always a combination of what is seen, heard, *and* happening within the receiver at that moment, it is unlikely that two people will ever perceive the same thing in exactly the same way.

The Perceptual Process

Because receivers are exposed to much more input than they can possibly handle, perceptions are organized to attach meaning to individual experiences. The first step of this process is to *select* data considered important enough to interpret.

Several factors cause receivers to select certain messages and ignore others. For example, stimuli that are *intense* (loud, large, or bright) stand, out; someone who laughs loudly at a party will attract more attention than people who are quiet. *Repetitious* stimuli also attract attention and are widely used by advertisers. For example, Smokey the Bear—who reminds people to be careful to avoid starting forest fires—has become a symbol through repetitive advertising. Because a *change in stimuli* attracts attention, the constant noise level of cars going by will be tuned out, but any unusual sound will get our attention. **Motives** often determine the information selected from an environment.

If an individual is hungry while traveling, he or she is much more apt to notice billboards advertising food and restaurants. If a person has a hobby or becomes an expert in some area, relevant information is also more likely to be observed. A group member sensitive about a certain subject is much more likely to pay attention to a comment even remotely related to his or her sensitive area.

The second step of the perceptual process is to **organize** data in some meaningful way. To make sense of human behavior, for example, people will interpret a specific behavior in terms of their favorite theories. If we believe in psychoanalytic theory, we will attempt to understand or interpret behavior according to a psychoanalytic model. If we believe in the principles of cognitive–behavioral theory, our interpretation of the same behavior will be very different. A psychoanalyst would say that a single woman who becomes pregnant has an unconscious desire (such as wanting to hurt her father or mother) that leads her to become pregnant. In contrast, a cognitive–behavioral specialist would say that she decided to have intercourse because she believed that the anticipated rewards outweighed the potential consequences.

Group members constantly select what is important to remember and respond to and organize messages in order to interpret and react to them. In the organizational process, past experiences, knowledge of human behavior, beliefs, values, attitudes, stereotypes, and defense mechanisms lead individuals to hear and see what they want; information that supports a person's views is remembered, whereas information that forces individuals to question their firm beliefs and attitudes is often ignored or forgotten.

Physiological Influences

Each individual perceives the world in a unique way because of a number of physiological factors. Although only one world exists "out there," each person perceives a somewhat different world because of his or her own perceptual hardware.

Taste   There are fairly wide variations in the ways people experience taste. Although there are four basic types of taste—sweet, sour, salty, and bitter—individual taste buds permit considerable variation. Experiments have shown that litmus paper treated with PTC (phenylthiocarbamide) will taste salty, bitter, sweet, or sour, or have no taste at all, depending on who tastes it.[7] Arguments and discussions concerning the palatability of food often center on which food tastes better, but the simple fact is that the same food tastes different to different people.

Smell   There are also wide variations in the sense of smell. Odors pleasing to one person are repulsive to others. Such variations in perception thus affect communication.

Temperature   Sensitivity to temperature also varies greatly. Some people may be perspiring at 70° F, whereas others may be shivering. When a person has a fever, his or her perception of the "ideal" temperature changes, for example, and disagreements over appropriate temperatures in offices and houses are frequent.

Hearing   Noisy environments (factories, rock clubs, airports) have contributed to hearing loss, and people with significant uncorrected hearing losses are apt to miss parts of communications in a group. Often, they are forced to "fill in" by guessing the sounds they cannot hear, reading lips, and observing nonverbal communication.

Vision   People who are color blind, farsighted, nearsighted, or otherwise visually impaired perceive objects differently from people who have good vision. Sherri Adler briefly describes how her poor vision affected communication with her husband, Ron:

Since I've known Ron we've had some experiences that have caused communication problems because of our differences in vision: He has perfect eyesight, and even when I'm wearing contacts he can see better than I can.

A few summers ago we drove to Colorado. I would get angry (and frightened) when he continuously passed cars on narrow two-lane roads, and he would get mad at me for following slow-moving cars for thirty minutes without passing. When I explained that I just couldn't see as far up the road as he could, we realized that we didn't see things the same way and that our safety would be threatened if I was to drive the way he wanted me to.[8]

Other Physiological Factors   Other physiological factors also influence our perception. If we are relaxed and well rested, we are apt to perceive a joke played on us by a friend as being humorous, and we are likely to laugh heartily. However, if we are in ill health, under high stress, fatigued, tired, hungry, thirsty, or nearly asleep, that same joke may not seem funny. All of these physiological factors have a substantial effect on our perceptions and the way we relate to people. For some women, the menstrual cycle plays a role in shaping moods and perceptions, and thus it may affect communication. There is some evidence that men may also have a 4- to 6-week physiological cycle of high periods and low periods.[9] Both males and females have a daily cycle in which a number of changes occur in sexual drive, body temperature, alertness, tolerance to stress, and mood, largely due to hormonal cycles.[10] Because of these daily changes, the prime time for productive work varies with individuals.

Sociopsychological Influences

Sociopsychological factors, including defense mechanisms, beliefs, attitudes, values, and stereotypes, influence what we perceive.

Defense Mechanisms   A defense mechanism is a psychological attempt to avoid or escape from painful conditions such as anxiety, frustration, hurt, and guilt. An individual's defense mechanisms are usually activated when he or she faces information that conflicts with his or her self-image. Defense mechanisms preserve self-concept and self-esteem and soften the blows of failure, deprivation, or guilt. Common defense mechanisms are briefly summarized in Figure 5.3.

Although everyone uses defense mechanisms to cope with unpleasant situations, defense mechanisms can become destructive when a person's perception of reality becomes seriously distorted. The following example illustrates how defense mechanisms can severely distort a message. (Names have been changed in this example.)

Dr. Nystrom was recruited from a different university to chair the social work department at a medium-sized Midwestern university. Three weeks after the start of the first semester, four students came to Dr. Nystrom's office to complain about the teaching of Dr. Weller, a new faculty member. Dr. Nystrom asked the students to present their concerns to Dr. Weller, but the students wanted to remain anonymous. Dr. Nystrom then asked the students to specify their concerns. Next, he informed Dr. Weller of the concerns. Dr. Weller appeared stunned and said little.

The next day Dr. Weller barged into Dr. Nystrom's office. "I know my teaching is good," she declared. "I spent most of last night trying to figure out what's happening. It is clear to me there is nothing wrong with my teaching. I've concluded that you are turning students against me." (This is rationalization and projection.) Dr. Nystrom was unable to convince Dr. Weller that he was not turning students against her, and their relationship deteriorated, Ever since then, Dr. Weller has been convinced that Dr. Nystrom is seeking to have her contract terminated. Dr. Weller has continued to receive low student evaluations but has rationalized them with excuses, such as ill health and claiming that faculty in the department are turning students against her. This paranoia has had a destructive effect on departmental morale.

FIGURE 5.3   Common Defense Mechanisms

Rationalization: One of the most common defense mechanisms is rationalization, the development of a logical but false explanation that protects a person's self-concept. Group members who use this mechanism actually believe the excuses they have dreamed up. For example, a student who fails an exam may blame it on poor teaching or having to work outside of classes rather than acknowledging the real reasons, such as not studying.

Projection: By using this defense mechanism, group members can unconsciously attribute their unacceptable ideas and impulses to others. An example would be a person who wanted to make himself look good by making others look bad. Psychologically, this person does not want to admit to himself that he has such selfish motives. So he projects the selfishness onto others by believing they are trying to make him look bad, which then justifies his own negative behavior.

Denial: An individual can escape psychic pain by rejecting or denying reality. When people are confronted with a serious loss, they are likely to initially deny it. For example, a person can deny that a loved one has died. Many alcoholics deny they have a drinking problem.

Reaction Formation: Group members can avoid facing an unpleasant truth by acting opposite to the way they feel. Individuals who are angry and cannot admit it to others or themselves often act as if there is nothing wrong. By using the reaction-formation defense mechanism, sad and lonely individuals can act as if they are the life of the party, laughing and telling jokes. Also, people at funerals who are grieving deeply may behave as if everything is fine. The defense mechanism of denial is generally involved in reaction formation, as the individual seeks to deny painful facts, events, or feelings.

Compensation: This mechanism involves offsetting a real or fancied defect of inferiority by creating a real or fancied achievement or superiority. A recently divorced father may attempt to soften his children's pain by buying them expensive toys. Also, just as unhappily married college students can avoid dealing with their marriage by putting all their energies into their studies, people who have "failed" in their careers and personal life can compensate for their failure by getting "high" on alcohol and drugs.

Identification: When you were 7 or 8 you had heroes or heroines who you idealized and imitated. Some adults hide their real feelings in certain situations and instead of being themselves imitate someone they admire. The problem with this mechanism is that people "hooked" on identification cannot respond to a situation genuinely. They deny their real feelings and instead act as their hero would.

Fantasy: This mechanism involves using fantasy to dull the pain of reality. It is not uncommon, for example, for an unhappy adopted child to fantasize that her natural parents are exalted, loving people who will one day rescue her. Everyone daydreams, but most people soon return to reality. Some fantasies, however, endure and have destructive effects. For example, a former client of mine thought he could bring his deceased mother back to life by bringing female corpses to his home. After digging up several graves, he was arrested.

Regression: Some adults regress to an infantile or childlike state when ill or in trouble, with the subconscious goal of receiving more care and attention. When certain group members are confronted about their failings, they shed tears in an attempt to be excused for not fulfilling crucial commitments.

Isolation: The separation of an object (idea, experience, or memory) from the emotions associated with it results in the person showing no emotion to the object. This mechanism makes it possible for an individual to avoid the pain of anxiety, shame, or guilt. For example, a person uses this mechanism when discussing a violent act he or she has committed and shows no emotion.

Displacement: This mechanism occurs when hostile or aggressive feelings are vented against safer objects or people rather than against those who caused the feelings. A husband who has had a frustrating day at work, for example, may verbally or physically abuse his wife, children, or family pets.

Undoing: When a person feels guilty about some act or wish, she can undo her guilt by acting in a manner that reflects the reverse of this act or wish. The classic example is an unfaithful spouse who lavishes attention on his or her mate.

Communication That Fosters Defensiveness   Gibb has found that we are more likely to respond defensively to certain types of communication and that defensiveness is **reciprocal**.[11] If a sender begins to respond defensively, the receiver will react by putting up defenses, which will then increase the sender's defensiveness. Gibb has identified six types of messages that increase a receiver's defensiveness: evaluative, controlling, manipulative, indifference, superiority, and certainty.

Any message perceived as **evaluative** or *judgmental* increases the receiver's defensiveness. When an individual is being evaluated or rated, he or she is more on guard. In contrast, nonblaming communication reduces defensiveness.

Communication meant to *control* behavior or thoughts also increases defensiveness. For example, when a salesperson aggressively attempts to sell a product, many customers react defensively. Gibb indicates that defensiveness is decreased when the sender projects

EXERCISE 5.2   Using Defense Mechanisms

GOAL: This exercise is designed to assist you in better understanding defense mechanisms.

1. Reread the list of defense mechanisms discussed in this section. List the ones that you remember someone else using. Indicate for each whom the user was (first name only), and describe how this person used the defense mechanism.

2. List the defense mechanisms that you remember using yourself. Describe how you used each of these mechanisms.

a willingness to share in the solution of a problem, for example, "Let's find a solution that works for both of us."

Defensiveness also increases when people discover that someone is trying to **manipulate** them. Because people would rather be asked to do something directly than be tricked into doing it, manipulative communication leads to distrust and defensiveness. An honest request may not always produce an immediate positive response, but it will lead to more open and honest communication and support in crucial situations.

Indifference to another person's feelings and thoughts increases defensiveness by conveying a lack of concern and implying that the person involved is not important. Defense mechanisms then allow the receiver to maintain a sense of value to offset the indifference. Gibb has found that empathy reduces defensiveness and is much more beneficial to relationships than indifference.

When someone relates to us in a **superior** way, we often become angry, tune that person out, or use defense mechanisms to maintain our self-respect. Some individuals go to great lengths to cut the superior person "down to size." Relating on an **equal basis** is much more conducive to openness, sharing, and reducing defensiveness. Instructors who relate to students as equals, for example, are using better educational and communication methods than instructors who attempt to impress students with their superior position and knowledge.

The final type of communication that, as Gibb notes, increases defensiveness is **certainty**. This type involves messages from people who steadfastly assert that their way of doing things is the *only* way or who act as if they have all the answers. Gibb notes that people who work hard at demonstrating certainty usually feel insecure and inferior; their certainty is a reaction formation. In this case, defensiveness can be reduced when openness to new information and ideas is communicated.

Defensiveness is probably the greatest barrier to effective communication and should be avoided. Messages should be sent in ways that do not make either senders or receivers defensive.

Beliefs, Values, and Attitudes   Individuals use their beliefs, values, and attitudes to select, interpret, and organize information. If a member in a group is liked, her comments receive more attention and support. Dislike sparks disagreement or strenuous opposition. Sometimes a group member will dislike another so intensely that he automatically votes against every motion that person makes, even those to his direct benefit.

The importance of beliefs and values in communication can be illustrated with a few examples. If parents are conservative and strongly opposed to interracial marriages, they will probably be opposed to interracial dating. A Roman Catholic who strongly opposes abortions will feel close to a speaker who supports that belief and be repelled by someone who favors choice. Deeply religious individuals often become threatened when someone professes that some other religion than theirs is the one, true religion. Finally, people with different sexual values will usually avoid discussing sexuality with each other.

Beliefs have a major impact on perception and sometimes lead to inaccurate interpretations of a message. For example, some people incorrectly believe that others are generally attempting to control them or put them down. Under this system of belief, they are apt to misinterpret general statements, jump to conclusions, and become defensive. Open and honest communication is unlikely to occur. This type of misinterpretation of messages has also been called the tendency to *personalize* messages.

EXERCISE 5.3   Defensive Communication

GOAL: This exercise is designed to assist you in understanding the types of communication that foster defensiveness.

For each of the following types of communication, describe a time when someone used this type of communication with you and describe your emotional reactions in each situation.

a. Evaluative or judgmental communication:

b. Communication to control you:

c. Communication to manipulate you:

d. Indifferent communication:

e. Superior communication, which suggested you were inferior:

f. Certainty communication:

Stereotypes   Stereotypes are fixed mental images of a group that are applied to all of its members. Stereotypes may be partially accurate or completely erroneous. You can discover some of the stereotypes you hold by considering the mental images you get in response to the following phrases: "a macho male," "a Republican," "a welfare mother," "a policeman," "a person who is gay," "a handicapped person," "an ex-con." For most of these phrases, you probably were able to get a mental picture of such people, and you probably have beliefs about their lifestyles, values, interests, and attitudes. During your first interaction with someone who fits into one of these categories, you are apt to respond in terms of your preconceived expectations. For example, if you distrust and fear police officers, you will probably be guarded in what you say and do if you meet an officer, and you will be apt to end the interaction as rapidly as possible.

SELF-DISCLOSURE

One of the main reasons we are not fully understood when we communicate is that we do not fully express what we are thinking and feeling. We often ponder how much we should share about our thoughts and feelings. What are the costs and benefits of self-disclosure?

Self-disclosure has been defined as "the process of deliberately revealing information about ourselves that is significant and that would not normally be known by others."[12] Some people are *over*disclosers in that they either talk too much about themselves or they talk revealingly about themselves at inappropriate times. If a student social work club is discussing a proposal for a new course on aging, for example, it would be inappropriate for a student to indicate that she has periodically thought about suicide. *Under*disclosers do not want others to know them intimately and speak very little about themselves even when the situation calls for it. An underdiscloser may encourage friends to share their personal concerns but then refuse to talk personally about herself. Appropriate self-disclosure can be defined as the right amount of self-revelation at the right time.

The risks of self-disclosure have been described by Jourard: "When you permit yourself to be known, you expose yourself not only to a lover's balm, but also to a hater's bombs. When he knows you, he knows just where to plant them for maximum effect."[13] The risks of self-disclosure include subsequent criticism, laughter, disapproval, or rejection, as well as a danger that the information may be used against the individual involved. If a student discloses to a class that he has a drinking problem, there is always the danger that someone in the class may inform a potential employer.

People fail to disclose appropriately for many reasons. Some may fear closeness, rejection, and criticism, or they may be ashamed of their thoughts, feelings, or past actions. In certain instances, disclosure will put pressure on a group member to change; for example, a person may be reluctant to acknowledge that he has a drinking problem because he knows that if he acknowledges the problem, pressure will be put on him to give up drinking (which he does not want to do). Jourard asserts that self-disclosure is necessary for psychological health and growth because people cannot be themselves unless they know themselves.[14] Through self-disclosure people can know themselves better; nonetheless, many cannot or will not face troubled parts of themselves and so resist self-disclosure.

If thoughts and feelings are not shared, an individual is not accurately communicating what he or she is really thinking and feeling and will not be fully understood. Honest and open relationships that are meaningful are based on self-disclosure with people accepting individuals as they are. A close, meaningful relationship is most likely possible with mutual self-disclosure.

The question of whether to disclose can be answered by following a simple guideline. Individuals should self-disclose when the potential benefits outweigh the potential risks; making realistic judgments about the potential benefits and risks is the hard part. A leader of a therapy group usually should self-disclose if the information will be therapeutic for group members. For example, if members have drinking problems, a leader who shares her personal experiences with drinking could provide useful information and increase rapport with those members who are struggling with their drinking problems. On the other hand, a leader who is still emotionally involved with a problem usually *should not* self-disclose, or group members may view her as a client rather than a therapist. If a leader of a group of battered women tearfully relates a sexual assault, members may feel that she cannot be objective in dealing with their situations.

It is also important to remember that there are degrees of self-disclosure; you do not have to tell everything. It is possible to share some opinions, feelings, thoughts, or experiences while reserving riskier information. By observing the reactions of the receivers, senders can better determine whether it is in their best interests to reveal more.

What is disclosed should be relevant to the present relationship with the receivers. For example, a romantic relationship could disintegrate if past sexual relationships were disclosed. Most people know their partners have had previous sexual experiences, but few want to hear the intimate details.

The Johari Window

Luft and Ingram developed a graphic model of self-disclosure in groups known as the **Johari** (taken from the authors' first names, Joe and Harry) **Window**.[15] Diagram A in Figure 5.4 represents everything there is to know about you—your needs, dislikes, past experiences, goals, desires, secrets, beliefs, values, and attitudes. However, you do not know everything about yourself. You are aware of some things and unaware of other things, as diagrammed in Figure 5.4(B). In addition, the frame can be divided to show what others know about you and what others do not know about you, as shown in Figure 5.4(C).

By combining parts B and C of Figure 5.4, we get a Johari Window, as illustrated in Figure. 5.4(D). A Johari Window divides everything about you into four parts. Quadrant 1 of part D is the *open* area of yourself—the part of which both you and others are aware. This area has been referred to as the "public self," as it represents how one knowingly presents himself or herself. Quadrant 2 is your *blind* area, which represents the part of yourself that

---

EXERCISE 5.4   Feeling Good After Self-Disclosure

GOAL: This exercise is designed to assist you in understanding that self-disclosure is beneficial at times.

1. Describe something personal that you self-disclosed and afterward were glad that you did. Further describe why you were glad you self-disclosed.

2. Not all self-disclosure is beneficial. Describe your thoughts as to when you should and should not self-disclose.

FIGURE 5.4 **A Johari Window**

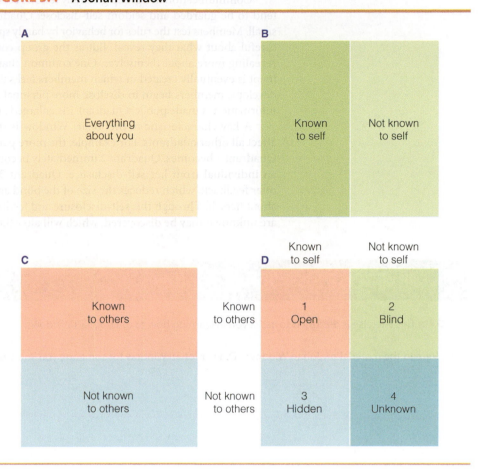

others are aware of but that you are not. It has been called the "bad breath" area because although others may know you have bad breath, you do not. Quadrant 3 is the *hidden* area, the part you are aware of but others are not. This part has been called the "secret" area, as you know all kinds of things about yourself that you are not telling the group. Quadrant 4 is your *unknown* area, which represents that part of you of which neither you nor others are aware. A Johari Window can be individualized by moving the boundaries into the position that best describes a single personality. For example, the Johari Window in Figure 5.5 describes a man who is very aware of himself but who tends to hide much of himself from others.

FIGURE 5.5 **A Johari Window Showing a Hidden Personality Type**

Communication in a group generally follows certain principles. Initially, group members tend to be guarded and seldom self-disclose; Quadrant 1 of their Johari Windows will be small. Members test the rules for behavior by barely speaking, giving short answers, and being careful about what they reveal. But as the group continues, group members usually begin revealing more about themselves. One common characteristic of groups is that an environment is eventually created in which members feel safe and protected. After a feeling of trust develops, members begin to disclose more personal aspects of their lives. As secret, private information is made public, Quadrant 1 is enlarged and Quadrant 3 becomes smaller.

A key characteristic of the Johari Window is that a change in any one quadrant will affect all other quadrants. For example, the more personal information is shared, the larger Quadrant 1 becomes. Quadrant 2 immediately becomes smaller as others know more about an individual from her self-disclosure. Quadrant 3 may become smaller because others offer feedback, which reduces the size of the blind area as the individual gets to know more about herself. Through this self-disclosure and feedback process, parts of an individual that are unknown may be discovered, which will alter the size of Quadrant 4.

EXERCISE 5.5   Johari Windows

GOAL: This exercise is designed to assist you in learning how to draw Johari Windows.

1. Reread the material on Johari Windows. Draw a Johari Window for someone you know quite well.

2. Draw a Johari Window that represents you.

3. Summarize what each of these windows depicts.

The implications of the Johari Window are that the more information is shared, the more others know and the greater the feedback. This feedback often leads to greater self-awareness, more sharing about ourselves, and more sharing on the part of others.

It should be cautioned, however, that self-disclosure is usually best done gradually. If the first bits of self-disclosure are well received and accepted, the individuals can feel that it is safe to reveal more. It is generally a mistake to try to build a relationship by immediately divulging all the secrets and private details about oneself. Besides the risk of the divulged information being used against the self-discloser, there is also the danger that hasty "undressing" of oneself may scare others away.

LO 3   Communicate More Effectively

HOW TO COMMUNICATE EFFECTIVELY

Given all the factors that can lead to garbled messages, it is important that everyone attempt to send messages effectively. Numerous suggestions are given in the following sections for improving communication for both a sender and a receiver.

Sender

If nonverbal and verbal messages match, a receiver can better interpret the information. Double and often contradictory messages are sent when nonverbal and verbal messages do not agree. Messages should be complete and specific. If you have to request a special favor of someone, it is usually desirable to explain why. Also, it is important to specify your request. Vague or incomplete messages are often misinterpreted.

"Own" your messages by using personal pronouns such as "I" to show that you are clearly taking responsibility for your thoughts and feelings. When group members "disown" messages by saying "someone said" or "most people would feel," it is difficult to determine whether *they* think and feel this way or whether they are simply repeating the thoughts and feelings of others.

Each message should be phrased in a way that is appropriate to the receiver's frame of reference. The words you use in explaining the Johari Window to a child should be quite different from those you use with classmates. Also, supporting verbal messages with handouts, pictures, and written messages will help the receiver understand them. Always ask for feedback when you are unsure whether the receiver has accurately perceived the message.

Express your concerns to others in nonblaming rather than judgmental or evaluative terms. Judgmental or evaluative words make others defensive. Note the immense difference between "I feel put down by what you just said" and "I'm really getting tired of your running me into the ground—watch it." The first is apt to foster communication, the second defensiveness.

Physical factors that interfere with effective communication include chairs in a row rather than in a circle, poor acoustics, loud outside noises, an unacceptable room temperature, ineffective lighting, uncomfortable chairs, and too little time allotted to discuss issues. Reducing the effects of these barriers to communication generally increases the accuracy of the communication between senders and receivers.

Receiver

Communication is often halted when the receiver takes a message personally. Instead of jumping to the wrong conclusions, a receiver should ask questions that will clarify the sender's intentions and reasoning. Clarification can be ascertained by paraphrasing the sender's message in a question: "Are you saying . . . ?" or "Are you feeling . . . ?" If the receiver immediately disagrees, then the sender may become cautious and defensive, which will interfere with open and honest communication. It is important to remember that communication is fostered if you speak up for yourself *only after* you are accurately aware of the sender's message. In resolving an argument, a group leader can use the principle of *role reversal*.

The receiver restates the ideas and feelings of the sender accurately and to the sender's satisfaction before proceeding to present his or her own views. The receiver should express the sender's feelings and ideas in his or her own words rather than parroting or mimicking the words of the sender. Before indicating approval or disapproval, a receiver should place himself or herself in the sender's shoes in order to understand what the sender is thinking and feeling.

Social workers should be aware that a sender may not have communicated his or her feelings or meaning accurately or fully. The sender may have chosen the wrong words or used words that were ambiguous. For example, the phrase "I care about you" has meanings ranging from "I care about you as much as I care about any human being" to "I'm in love with you." In such situations, it is extremely important to seek clarification by asking questions in a nonblaming, nonevaluative fashion.

Listening Skills

To communicate effectively, it is essential to develop good listening skills. Unfortunately, many people are caught up in their own interests and concerns, and they are distracted by those thoughts when someone is speaking to them. Kadushin explains why it is difficult for an interviewer to develop good listening skills:

> The nature of spoken communication presents a special hazard, seducing the interviewer into an easy nonlistening. The hazard lies in the great discrepancy between the number of words that are normally spoken in one minute and the number of words that can be absorbed in that time. Thought is much more rapid than speech. The average rate of spoken speech is about 125 words per minute. We can read and understand an average of 300–500 words per minute. There is, then, a considerable amount of dead time in spoken communication, during which the listener's mind can easily become distracted. The listener starts talking to herself to take up the slack in time. Listening to the internal monologue may go on side by side with listening to the external dialogue. More often, however, it goes on at the expense of listening to the external dialogue. The interviewer becomes lost in some private reverie—planning, musing, dreaimng.[16]

Kadushin gives the following suggestions on how to listen effectively:

> Rather than becoming preoccupied as a consequence of the availability of the spare time between the slow spoken words, the good interviewer exploits this time in the service of more effective listening. The listener keeps focused on the interviewee but uses the time made available to the mind by slowness of speech to move rapidly back and forth along the path of the interview, testing, connecting, questioning: How does what I am hearing now relate to what I heard before? How does it modify what I heard before? How does it conflict with it, support it, make it more understandable? What can I anticipate hearing next? What do I miss hearing that needs asking about? What is he trying to tell me? What other meanings can the message have? What are his motives in telling me this?[17]

Active Listening

Thomas Gordon has developed four techniques that are designed to improve communication: active listening, I-messages, collisions of values, and no-lose problem solving.[18] No-lose problem solving is described in Chapter 6.

Active listening is recommended when listening to a problem. For example, a member in a therapy group says, "I'm fat and ugly—all my friends have boyfriends and not me." For such situations Gordon recommends that the group leader (or another member) use active listening. The steps involved in active listening are the receiver of a message tries to understand what the sender's message means or what the sender is feeling, and then the receiver puts this understanding into his or her own words and restates it for the sender's verification. An active listening response to the previous statement might be, "You want very much to have a boyfriend and think the reason you don't is related to your physical appearance." An active listening response involves either *reflecting feelings* or *restating content*.

Gordon lists a number of advantages of active listening. It facilitates problem solving by the person with the problem, which fosters the development of responsibility. By talking a problem through instead of only thinking about it, a person is more apt to identify the root and arrive at a solution. When a person feels that others are listening, he or she will be more likely to listen to them in the future. In addition, the relationships between group members will probably improve, because when individuals feel they are heard and understood, positive emotions toward others increase. Finally, active listening helps a person with a problem to explore, recognize, and express feelings.

When first using the technique, receivers may make some mistakes. One is to use the technique to guide the person with the problem to a solution preferred by the receiver. The sender will usually then feel manipulated, and the approach may be counterproductive. A second mistake is to parrot back the words rather than paraphrase the intended meanings or feelings. For instance, if a member shouts at a group leader, "You stupid jerk," an appropriate response would be "You're angry with me," not "You think I'm a jerk."

I-Messages

Active listening is used when someone else has a problem. Many occasions arise when another group member causes a problem for you. For example, another group member may irritate or criticize you. You may remain silent and irritated or send a "you-message." There are two types of you-messages: a *solution* message and a *put-down* message. A solution message orders, directs, commands, warns, threatens, preaches, moralizes, or advises. A put-down message blames, judges, criticizes, ridicules, or name-calls. Examples of you-messages include, "You stop that," "Don't do that," "Why don't you be good," "I hate you," and "You should know better."

Gordon asserts that I-messages are better. For example, if a member is loudly tapping a pencil on a table, an I-message might be, "The tapping of the pencil is irritating to me." This example also shows that it is possible to send an I-message without using the word "I."

I-messages, in essence, are nonblaming messages that simply communicate how the sender of the message believes the receiver is affecting the sender. I-messages do not provide a solution, and they do not criticize. The following simple format illustrates how to phrase an I-message: The sender says to the receiver, "When_____ you (sender identifies the irritating behavior), I feel_____ (sender describes his or her feelings)." When first practicing I-messages, a group member might give a put-down, such as "When you act stupid, I feel hurt." It is important to redirect this into a nonblaming, nonjudgmental message such as, "When you interrupt me when I am talking, I feel hurt." The use of I-statements may take practice and should be monitored by the group leader to ensure proper use.

Active Listening Example in a Group Session at a Runaway Center

Sixteen-year-old youth: I hate school. I'm no longer going to go.

Counselor: You're so unhappy with what's happening at school that you're thinking about dropping out.

Youth: Yes, my home life is a shambles, and school isn't going well either.

Counselor: It's really depressing to have both your home life and school not going well.

Youth: Sometimes, like now, I feel like giving up. I've tried pretty hard to make things better at home and at school.

Counselor: You're feeling bad because the things you've done haven't worked out the way you'd like.

Youth: Yes, I got an F on the English paper I got back yesterday.

Counselor: You're feeling especially bad because of the grade you got on your English paper.

Youth: Since the commotion at home, my grades have started to fall.

Counselor: You're thinking that your problems at home may be affecting your schoolwork.

Youth: I don't really want to admit it to myself, but I guess it's true. For the last several weeks it's been harder for me to concentrate on school.

Counselor: You feel your grades are slipping because you haven't been able to concentrate because of what is happening at home.

Youth: I guess when I'm at school I have to focus more on my schoolwork. Maybe if I talked to some of my teachers and let them know what I'm going through, they might be more understanding. I guess I really don't want to drop out of school.

EXERCISE 5.6   Learning to Use I-Messages

GOAL: This exercise is designed to assist you in learning to phrase I-messages. (Note: For this exercise it is highly desirable to later discuss in class whether your attempts at phrasing I-messages meet the guidelines for stating an I-message.)

Describe an I-message you would use when someone does the following:

a. You are in a car driving with someone who lights up a cigarette. You do not like to be exposed to secondhand smoke for health reasons.

b. You are riding in a car with someone who is speeding and driving recklessly. You fear an accident may occur.

c. You are trying to sleep. It is 3:00 A.M. and you have two exams in the morning. In a neighboring apartment someone turns on his or her stereo loudly.

You-messages, such as "you do everything wrong" or "you messed up" are generally counterproductive because people do not like to be ordered or criticized. You-messages frequently result in an ongoing struggle between the two people involved.

In contrast, I-messages communicate the effect of behavior much more honestly. I-messages tend to be more effective because they help the other group member assume responsibility for his or her behavior. An I-message says that you trust the group member to respect your needs and to handle the situation constructively. I-messages are much less likely to produce an argument. They tend to facilitate honesty, openness, and more cordial relationships within the group.

It should be noted that I-messages will work only if the receiver does not want his or her actions to adversely affect the sender of the message. If the receiver does not want to cause discomfort to the sender, the receiver is apt to seek to change his or her adversive behavior when informed by an I-message of how it is adversely affecting the sender. However, if the receiver enjoys causing discomfort to the sender, then the use of an I-message by the sender is apt to result in an *increase* in the receiver's adversive behavior, as the receiver is now more fully aware of how to create discomfort in the sender. (An I-message is an invitation by the sender to the receiver for a dialogue.)

Collisions of Values

Collisions of values between group members are common. Likely areas of conflict include values about abortion, sexual behavior, clothing, religion, use of drugs, hairstyles, and conscientiousness in carrying out assigned group tasks.

Gordon asserts that there are three constructive ways to resolve value conflicts. The first is to model the values you hold as important. If you value honesty, be honest. If you value openness, be open. If you are not living according to the values you profess, then you need to change either your values or your behavior. Congruence between behavior and values is important if you want to be an effective role model.

The second way is to attempt to be a consultant to the members with whom you are in conflict. There are some do's and don'ts for a good consultant. First of all, a good consultant inquires whether the other person would like to hear his or her views. If the answer is no, then do not proceed to consult because the other group member will react negatively. If the answer is yes, be sure you have all the pertinent facts. Then share these facts once so the other person understands them. Let the other group member have the responsibility of deciding whether to follow the suggestions. To continue consulting, a person must be neither uninformed nor a nag.

The third way to reduce tensions over a values issue is to modify your values. By examining the values held by the other group member, you may realize they have merit, and you may move toward those values or increase your understanding of why the person holds his or her values.

EP 1d

Technology and Groups

For many individuals, their main form of communication is done through technology, whether it be e-mails, text messaging, social media, chat rooms, online classrooms, or another form. Technology allows individuals from different regions, different time zones, those who may be homebound or who lack adequate transportation, or many other factors to be able to communicate through one platform. Individuals in social work have entered the technology world through providing offline individual/group counseling, telephone counseling, cyber therapy, self-guided web-based interventions, social networking sites, e-mails, and text messageing.[19] Due to the increasing nature of the use of technology in social work, the National Association of Social Workers (NASW) set guidelines for those engaging in these technologies. Group leaders need to be aware of how technology can affect communication and take necessary steps to prevent any disruptions or miscommunications that could occur.

EXERCISE 5.7   Resolving Collisions of Values

GOAL: This exercise is designed to assist you in learning to identify and resolve collisions of values.

1. Describe a situation in your life where you had a serious collision of values with someone.

2. Describe how this situation was resolved. (If it has not been resolved, describe the issues that still need to be resolved.)

3. Review the material on collision of values in this text. Does this material suggest a better way of resolving the collision of values that you experienced? If it does, please indicate which approach you believe would have been more beneficial for you to use.

LO 4   Have an Increased Understanding of Nonverbal Communication

NONVERBAL COMMUNICATION

It is impossible not to communicate. No matter what we do, we transmit information about ourselves. Even an expressionless face at a funeral communicates something. As you are reading this, stop for a minute and analyze what nonverbal messages you would be sending if someone were observing you. Are your eyes wide open or are they half closed? Is your posture relaxed or tense? What are your facial expressions communicating? Are you occasionally gesturing? What would an observer deduce you are feeling from these nonverbal cues?

Nonverbal cues often reveal feelings a person is intentionally trying to hide. Bodily reactions such as sweating, stammering, blushing, and frowning often reveal the presence of emotions—fear, embarrassment, or discomfort—that people would rather hide from others. By developing skills in reading nonverbal cues, group leaders can become more aware of what others are feeling and how to interact with them more effectively. Because feelings stem from thoughts, nonverbal cues that reveal what people are feeling also transmit information about what people are thinking.

In literature, perhaps the greatest reader of nonverbal cues was Sherlock Holmes. In this exchange Holmes deduces the following about his friend Watson:

> "How do I know that you have been getting yourself very wet lately, and that you have a most clumsy and careless servant girl?" . . .

> "It is simplicity itself," said he; "my eyes tell me that on the inside of your left shoe, just where the firelight strikes it, the leather is scored by six almost parallel cuts. Obviously they have been caused by someone who has very carelessly scraped round the edges of the sole in order to remove crusted mud from it. Hence, you see, my double deduction that you had been out in vile weather, and that you had a particularly malignant boot-slitting specimen of the London slavey."[20]

Functions of Nonverbal Communication

Nonverbal communication interacts with verbal communication and can repeat, substitute for, accent, regulate, or contradict what is spoken.

Repetition   Nonverbal messages may **repeat** verbal messages. A husband may say he is really looking forward to becoming a father and repeat this happy anticipation with glowing facial expressions.

Substitution   Nonverbal messages may **substitute** for verbal messages. If you know a close friend has just failed an important exam, even though she may not talk about it, you can get a fairly good idea of what she is thinking and feeling by watching her.

Accentuation   Nonverbal messages may **accent** verbal messages. If someone you are dating says she is angry and upset with something you did, she may emphasize the depth of these feelings by pounding a fist and pointing an accusing finger. (Accentuation and repetition are closely related, although accentuation usually involves greater emphasis.)

Regulation   Nonverbal messages may serve to **regulate** verbal behavior. Looking away from someone who is talking to you indicates that you are not interested in talking.

Contradiction   Nonverbal messages may **contradict** verbal messages. An example is someone with a red face, bulging veins, and a frown yelling, "Angry! Hell no, what makes you think I'm angry?" When nonverbal messages contradict verbal messages, the nonverbal messages are often more accurate. When receivers perceive a contradiction between nonverbal and verbal messages, they usually believe the nonverbal.[21]

EXERCISE 5.8   Interpreting Nonverbal Cues

GOAL: This exercise demonstrates that nonverbal cues may be correctly interpreted as well as misinterpreted.

1. Describe a situation where you correctly interpreted the nonverbal cues of someone.

2. Describe a situation where you misinterpreted the nonverbal cues of someone.

3. When nonverbal cues contradict the verbal message of someone, which message (the verbal or the nonverbal) are you more apt to believe?

The Risk of Misinterpretation   Although nonverbal messages can be revealing, they can also be unintentionally misleading. Think of the times when people have misinterpreted your nonverbal messages. Perhaps you tend to say little when you first wake up, and others have interpreted this as meaning that you are angry or troubled. Perhaps you have been quiet on a date because you were tired or because you were thinking about something that happened recently—has your date at times misinterpreted your behavior to mean you are bored or unhappy with the relationship? While deep in thought have you had an expression on your face that others have interpreted as a frown? Nonverbal behavior is often ambiguous. A frown, for example, may represent a variety of emotions: anger, rejection, confusion, unhappiness, fatigue, or boredom. *Nonverbal messages should be interpreted not as facts but as clues to be checked out verbally to determine what the sender is thinking and feeling.*

Forms of Nonverbal Communication

Nonverbal communication may take many forms. We communicate by the way we move, the expressions we make, the clothes we wear, even by the way we arrange our homes and offices. The following discussion examines the different avenues of nonverbal expression, including posture and body orientation, gesture, touch, choice of clothing, control of personal space and setting of boundaries, facial expression, voice tone and level, personal appearance, and design of personal environments.

Posture   An indication of how much posture can communicate is the large number of phrases that have posture as a metaphor:

> "He can stand on his own two feet."
> "I've got a heavy burden to carry."
> "She's got a lot of backbone."
> "Stand tall."

In picking up nonverbal cues from posture, it is important to note both the overall posture of a person and changes in posture. People tend to be relaxed in nonthreatening situations and to tighten up when under stress. Some people never relax, and their rigid posture shows it.

The degree of physical tenseness can reveal status differences. In interactions between a higher- and a lower-status person, the higher-status person is usually more relaxed, the lower-status person more rigid and tense.[22] For example, note the positions that are usually assumed when a faculty member and a student are conversing in the faculty member's office.

Teachers and public speakers often watch the posture of students or people in the audience to gauge how a presentation is being received. If people in the audience are leaning forward in their chairs, it is a sign the presentation is going well. If the audience members are slumping in their chairs, the presentation is probably beginning to bomb.

Body Orientation   Body orientation is the extent to which we face toward or away from someone with the head, body, and feet. Facing someone signals an interest in starting or continuing a conversation, whereas facing away signals a desire to end or avoid conversation. The phrase "turning your back" concisely summarizes the message that is sent when you turn away from someone. Can you remember the last time someone signaled a wish to end a conversation with you by turning away?

Facial Expressions   The face and eyes are generally selected as the primary source of nonverbal communication because facial expressions often are mirrors that reflect thoughts and feelings. Ekman and Friesen have identified six basic emotions that facial expressions reflect: fear, surprise, anger, happiness, disgust, and sadness.[23] These expressions appear to be recognizable in all cultures; people seeing photos of such expressions are quite accurate in identifying the emotions behind them.

Nonverbal Behavior Among Poker Players

Oswald Jacoby has noted that poker players use nonverbal messages extensively and has divided poker players into three classes: naive players, tricky players, and unreadable players.

Naive players are usually beginning players who possess few skills. When they look worried, they probably are. When they have a mediocre hand, they take a long time to bet. They bet quickly on a good hand but frown and scowl and look like bad luck has bitten them if they are dealt poor cards. A bluff is accompanied by a guilty look; when they raise a bet, everyone else folds. Naive players reveal their hands by body language that is seldom apparent in veteran poker buffs. Players of this type usually quit poker at an early stage because of their "bad luck."

Most poker players are "tricky" players and act exactly the opposite of the way they really feel. When they have a poor hand, they exude confidence, and when they have a good hand, they tremble a little and look nervous as they bet. Sometimes they do a triple cross by acting the way they really feel.

Unreadable players show no consistency in their behavior. They will randomly exude confidence or look nervous, and these nonverbal messages will give no clue as to the nature of their hand. Unreadable players are the most successful.

SOURCE: Adapted from Jacoby, O. (1974). *Oswald Jacoby on Poker*. New York: Doubleday.

Yet facial expressions are a complex source of information. They can change rapidly; slow-motion films have found that a fleeting expression can come and go in a fifth of a second. In addition, there are at least eight distinguishable positions of the eyes and lids, at least 8 positions for the eyebrows and forehead, and at least 10 for the lower face.[24] Multiplying these different combinations leads to several hundred possible combinations. Therefore, it is almost impossible to compile a directory of facial expressions and their corresponding emotions.

Because people are generally aware that their facial expressions reflect what they are feeling and thinking, they may mask them. For example, a person who is angry and does not want others to see the anger may hide this feeling by smiling. In using facial expressions to interpret feelings, social workers must be aware that the sender may be concealing his or her real thoughts and feelings.

Eye Contact   When you want to end a conversation, or avoid a conversation, you look away from the other person's eyes. If you want to start a conversation, you often seek out the receiver's eyes. You may wait until the receiver looks at you: when he does, it is a signal that he is ready to begin talking.

The eyes can also communicate dominance or submission. When a high-status person and a low-status person are looking at each other, the low-status person tends to look away first. Downcast eyes often signal submission or giving in. Of course, downcast eyes may also signal sadness, boredom, fatigue, remorse, or disgust.

Good salespeople are aware that eye contact is a sign of involvement and often manage to catch our eyes. Then they begin their pitch and maintain "courteous" eye contact. They know social norms require a receiver to hear what a person has to say once the person is allowed to begin speaking. These social norms trap us into listening to the sales pitch once eye contact has been made. Salespeople in stores utilize eye contact in another way. They determine which items a customer is looking at most and then emphasize these items in their sales pitch.

The importance of eyes in communication is reflected in these common phrases:

"He could look right through you."
"She has an icy stare."
"He's got shifty eyes."
"Did you see the gleam in her eye?"

Eye expressions suggest a wide range of human feelings. Wide-open eyes imply wonder, terror, frankness, or naiveté. Lowered eyelids may mean displeasure. A constant stare connotes coldness; eyes rolled upward suggest the person believes another's behavior is strange or unusual.

When we become emotionally aroused or interested in something, the pupils of our eyes dilate. Some counselors are sufficiently skilled in reading pupil dilation to tell when they touch a sensitive area by watching a client's eyes. Hess and Polt measured the amount of pupil dilation while showing men and women various kinds of pictures.[25] The greater the subject's interest in the pictures, the more the eyes dilated. Women's eyes dilated an average of 20% when looking at pictures of nude men. Men's eyes dilated an average of 18% when looking at pictures of nude women. Surprisingly, the greatest increase in pupil size occurred when women looked at a picture of an infant and mother.

Gestures   Most of us are aware that our facial expressions convey our feelings. When we want to hide our true feelings, we concentrate on controlling our facial expressions. We are less aware that our gestures also reveal our feelings, however, and as a result, gestures are sometimes better indicators of feelings.

People who are nervous tend to fidget. They may bite their fingernails, tap their fingers, rub their eyes or other parts of their body, bend paper clips, or tap a pencil. They may cross and uncross their legs, rhythmically swing a crossed leg back and forth, or rhythmically move a foot up and down.

Many other gestures provide clues to a person's thoughts and feelings. Clenched fists, whitened knuckles, and pointing fingers signal anger. When people want to express friendship or attraction, they tend to move closer to each other. Hugs can represent a variety of feelings: physical attraction, "good to see you," "best wishes in the future," and friendship. Shaking hands is a signal of friendship and a way of saying hello or goodbye.

Scheflen notes that a person's sexual feelings can be signaled through gestures. He describes "preening behavior," which sends a message that the sender is attracted to the receiver. Preening includes rearranging one's clothing, combing or stroking one's hair, and glancing in a minor. Scheflen cites a number of invitational preening gestures that he asserts are specific to women: exposing a thigh, protruding a breast, placing a hand on a hip, exhibiting a wrist or palm, or stroking a thigh.[26] Naturally, these gestures do not always suggest sexual interest.

There are also invitational preening gestures for men. As a woman talks, a man may gaze into her eyes intently. As conversation continues, he may lean in farther and farther toward the woman until he starts to close the gap between them. A man may stand with his pelvis thrust forward or sit or stand with legs wide apart. He may also stick his thumbs in his belt loops, with his fingers aiming at his pelvic region, or thrust his hands in his pocket, thumbs pointing toward his pelvis. Male preening behaviors may include straightening his jacket or tie, rolling up sleeves or cuffs, or smoothing his hair. He also may tend to mimic the woman's gesture.[27]

Gestures are used in relation to verbal messages to repeat, substitute, accent, contradict, and regulate. Some people literally speak with their hands, arms, and head movements. Their gestures may be so automatic that they are surprised when they see themselves on videotape and observe the number of gestures they use.

Psychologists Michael Kraus and Dacher Keltner found that people of higher socioeconomic status (SES) are ruder when conversing with others.[28] Their study showed that body language can signal a person's SES. The researchers videotaped pairs of undergraduate students who were strangers to one another during one-on-one interviews. The researchers then observed certain gestures that indicate level of interest in the other person during one-minute slices of each conversation. They found that students whose parents were from higher SES backgrounds engaged in more "impolite" gestures, such as doodling, grooming, and fidgeting. Lower SES students engaged in more "I'm interested" gestures, such as laughter and raising of the eyebrows. Like a peacock's tail, the seemingly snooty gestures of higher SES students indicate modern society's version of "I don't need you." Lower SES individuals cannot afford to brush off others. They have fewer resources and tend to be more dependent on others.

Touching   Spitz has demonstrated that young children need direct physical contact, such as being cuddled, held, and soothed. Without direct physical contact, the emotional, social, intellectual, and physical development of children will be severely stunted.[29] Spitz observed that in the 19th century, high proportions of children died in orphanages and other childcare institutions. The deaths were not found to be caused by poor nutrition or inadequate medical care but by lack of physical contact with parents or nurses. From this research came the practice of "nurturing" children in institutions—picking babies up, holding them close, playing with them, and carrying them around several times a day. With this practice, the infant mortality rate in institutions dropped sharply. Montagu describes research findings that suggest that eczema, allergies, and certain other medical problems are in part caused by a person's lack of physical contact with a parent during infancy.[30]

Adults also need physical contact. People need to know that they are loved, recognized, and appreciated. Touching (through holding hands, hugging, pats on the back) is a way of communicating warmth and caring. Unfortunately, most American men and some American women have been socialized to refrain from touching, except in sexual contexts. Sidney Simon has noted:

> In our now more than slightly cockeyed world, there seems to be little provision for someone to get touched without having to go to bed with whoever does the touching. And that's something to think about. We have mixed up simple, healing, warm touching with sexual advances. So much so, that it often seems as if there is no middle way between "Don't you dare touch me!" and "Okay, you touched me, so now we should make love!"[31]

Our language is a mirror of our culture. Common phrases suggest that more importance is placed on the senses of sight and hearing than on touch:

"Seeing is believing."
"It's good to see you again."
"It's really good to hear from you."
"I've got my eye on you."

We have coined few phrases that include words for touch. For example, when leaving someone we say, "See you again soon," rather than "Touch you again soon." If we should say the latter, it would be apt to be interpreted as having sexual connotations.

But touching someone is in fact an excellent way of conveying a variety of messages, depending on the context. A hug at a funeral will connote sympathy, whereas a hug when meeting someone says, "It's good to see you." A hug between parent and child means, "I love you," whereas a hug on a date may have sexual meanings. Numerous therapists have noted that *communication and human relationships would be vastly improved if people reached out and touched others more—with hugs, squeezes of the hand, kisses, and pats on the back.* Touch is crucial for the survival and development of children, and touch is just as crucial for adults to assure them that they are worthwhile and loved.

There is a danger that a hug by someone who wants to send a message of nonsexual love and support may be misinterpreted by the receiver as being an incident of sexual harassment. One way of avoiding this predicament is for the person who wants to give a hug to ask the receiver: "Would you like a hug?"

Clothing   Clothes keep us warm, protect us from illness, and cover certain areas of our body so we are not arrested for indecency. But clothes have many other functions. Uniforms such as those worn by police officers or firefighters tell us what a person does and what services he or she can render. People intentionally and unintentionally send messages about themselves by what they wear. Clothes give messages about occupations, personalities, interests, group norms, social philosophies, religious beliefs, status, values, mood, age, nationality, and personal attitudes. There are numerous "wardrobe engineers" (tailors, manufacturers, sellers of clothes) who assert that people can obtain what they want by improving their wardrobes, and there is some truth to the phrase "clothes make the person."

The importance of clothes in determining judgments that people make about strangers was demonstrated in a study by Hoult. Hoult began by having 254 female students rate the photos of male models on qualities such as "best looking," "most likely to succeed," "most intelligent," "most likely to date or double-date with," and "best personality." For these photos, Hoult obtained independent ratings of clothes and models' heads. Hoult then placed higher-ranked outfits on models with lower-ranked heads. Lower-ranked clothing was placed on models with higher-ranked heads. He found that, regardless of how the model's head was ranked, higher-ranked clothing was associated with an increase in rank and lower-ranked clothing was associated with loss of rank.[32]

Adler and Towne have described an experiment in which a student spent a week hitchhiking back and forth from Los Angeles to Santa Barbara, a distance of 100 miles. On Tuesday, Thursday, and Saturday, the student wore stay-pressed slacks, well-shined leather shoes, and an ironed shirt; on Monday, Wednesday, and Friday, he wore old blue jeans, sandals, and a tie-dyed sweatshirt. Other than the clothes, the student kept other factors constant, such as where he stood and at what time of day. The student described the results:

> It was incredible! On my three grubby days I got rides from people who looked just like I did. Two of them drove old VW buses, and the third had a '55 Ford pickup truck. They all wore Levis, boots, et cetera, and all had pretty much the same life style. On the days when I dressed up, I got rides in shiny new Oldsmobiles and Cadillacs from people who were completely opposite from the ones I'd driven with the day before.[33]

Any given item of clothing can convey several different meanings. For example, the tie a person selects to wear may reflect "sophistication" or "nonconformity." In addition, the way the tie is worn (loosened, tightly knotted, thrown over one's shoulder, soiled and wrinkled) may provide additional information.

Clothes also affect our self-image. If a person feels appropriately dressed, he or she is usually more self-confident, assertive, and outgoing. If not, he or she becomes more reserved, less confident, and less assertive.

With clothes (as with other forms of nonverbal communication), there is a real danger of misreading nonverbal messages. We often judge others on the basis of skimpy information, and frequently these interpretations are in error. Sometimes we get "burned" by our misinterpretations. Several years ago I had a client who for the previous 10 years had lived elegantly, traveling all over Europe and North America, staying in the finest hotels. He financed his lifestyle by writing bad checks. When he needed money he would dress in an expensive suit because, he explained, people took his check much more readily when he was well dressed.

Personal Boundaries

Each of us wears a kind of invisible "bubble" of personal space wherever we go. The area inside this bubble is strictly private; only people who are emotionally close to us are allowed inside. You can sometimes tell how people are feeling toward each other by noting the physical distance between them. In fact, Hall has identified four distinct distances, or zones, in people's daily interactions that guide their relations with others. These zones are intimate, personal, social, and public.[34] The particular zone chosen depends upon the context of the interaction, feelings toward the person, and interpersonal goals. Boundary behavior, like other nonverbal signals, provides group leaders with important information. For example, the distance maintained by group members should indicate to the group leader the members' personal preferences in individual interactions. These preferences, which may change considerably as the group progresses toward its goals, should be respected; otherwise, leaders are likely to encounter problems, such as resistance or distrust.

Intimate Zone   This zone begins with skin contact and extends out about 18 inches. Only people who are very close emotionally enter this zone, primarily in private situations—comforting, conveying caring, making love, and showing love and affection. When a person voluntarily allows someone to enter this distance, it is a sign of trust because defenses are lowered. On the other hand, if a person maintains a "safe" distance of 2 or more feet, it probably means that the person is still sorting out the relationship.

When an uninvited intruder moves into this intimate zone, people usually feel invaded and threatened. Their posture becomes more upright, their muscles tense, and they may move back and avoid eye contact as a way of signaling they want a less intimate relationship. When people are forced to stand close to strangers on crowded buses and elevators, they generally avoid eye contact and try not to rub against others, probably to say, "I'm sorry I'm forced to invade your territory—I'll try not to bother you."

Personal Zone   This zone, which ranges from approximately 18 inches to 4 feet, is the distance at which a couple stands apart from each other in public. Interestingly, if someone of the opposite sex stands close to someone we are dating or married to, we tend to wonder whether this person is trying to "move in" on us. If we see our spouse or date move close to someone of the opposite sex, we may become suspicious and jealous.

The far range of the personal zone (from about 2½ to 4 feet) is a distance at "arm's length," just beyond the other person's reach. Interactions occurring at this distance may still be reasonably close, but they are much less personal than those at the near range of the personal zone. Sometimes, communication at "arm's length" represents a test by people to determine whether they want the relationship to become emotionally closer.

Social Zone   This zone, which ranges from about 4 to 12 feet, usually encompasses business communications. The nearer part of this zone (from about 4 to 7 feet) is the distance at which coworkers usually converse and at which salespeople and customers usually interact. Hall indicates that the 7- to 12-foot range is used for more impersonal and formal situations. For example, this is the distance at which your boss talks to you when seated behind a desk. If you were to pull your chair around to the side of the boss's desk, a different kind of relationship would be signaled. The way furniture is arranged and the plants and wall hangings that people have in an office also convey signals about their values and interests and the type of relationship they want to establish. If the desk is placed between the office owner and the customer, client, or student, the desk acts as a barrier and suggests that the office owner wants formal and impersonal interaction. An office in which a desk is not used as a barrier and that has plants suggests the office owner wants warmer, less formal interactions.

Public Zone   This zone extends outward from 12 feet. Teachers and public speakers generally use the nearer range of public distance. In the farther range (beyond 25 feet), two-way communication is very difficult. Any speaker who voluntarily places considerable distance between himself or herself and the audience is not interested in having a dialogue.

Territoriality

Territoriality is behavior characterized by identification with an area in a way that indicates ownership and a willingness to defend it against those who may invade it.[35] Many birds and small animals (including dogs, geese, snakes, and skunks) will strike out at much larger animals if they feel their territory is being invaded.

Territoriality also exists in human interactions. Traditionally, Dad and Mom have their chairs, and each child has a separate bedroom. The feeling of territorial ownership is sometimes extended to objects that are not really owned. Students in a class tend to select a certain seat to sit in. If someone else should happen to sit in that seat, the first student may feel that ownership rights are being violated, even though clearly the school campus owns the chairs.

Acquired properties—cars, homes, leisure-time equipment, plants, and clothes—are strong indicators of interests and values and often become topics of conversation. Material objects also communicate status messages, as wealthy people own more property than the poor. Generally, more personal space and greater privacy are granted to people of higher status. Before entering your boss's office, for example, you knock and then wait for an invitation. With people of an equal or lower status, you frequently walk right in.

Voice

Depending on emphasis, a word or phrase may carry many meanings. For example, look at how the meanings of the following sentences are changed by changing the word that is emphasized:

He's giving this money to Herbie.
(HE is the one giving the money; no one else.)
He's *giving* this money to Herbie.
(He is GIVING, not lending, the money.)
He's giving *this* money to Herbie.
(The money being exchanged is not from any other source; it is THIS money.)
He's giving this *money* to Herbie.
(MONEY is the unit of exchange, not a check.)
He's giving this money to *Herbie*.
(The recipient is HERBIE, not Eric or Bill or Rod.)[36]

Usually people raise their voice at the end of a question and lower it at the end of a declarative statement. Sometimes people intentionally manipulate their voice to contradict the verbal message.

In addition to emphasizing particular words, our voices communicate in other ways. These include length of pauses, tone, pitch, speed, volume, and disfluencies (such as stammering or saying "uh," "um," and "er"). Taken together, these factors have been called paralanguage, which deals with *how* something is said and not with what is said.[37]

By using paralanguage, group members can contradict their verbal messages. For example, by simply changing the tone or inflection in his or her voice, a person can convey the following messages literally or sarcastically:

"I really like you."
"I'm having a perfectly wonderful time."
"You're really terrific."
"There's nothing that I like better than liver sausage."

Mehrabian has found that when the paralanguage and the verbal message are contradictory, the paralanguage carries more meaning.[38] When there is a contradiction between words and the way something is said, receivers usually interpret the message by the way it was said.

An excellent way to learn more about how a group uses paralanguage is to videotape a meeting and then watch the replay. This process also provides valuable feedback about group members' use of other forms of nonverbal communication.

Physical Appearance

Although it is common to hear people say that it is only inner beauty that really counts, research shows that outer beauty (physical attractiveness) influences responses for a broad range of interpersonal interactions. Singer found that male college professors tended to give higher grades to female students who were physically attractive than to those who were less attractive.[39] According to Mills and Aronson, attractive females could modify attitudes of male students more than less attractive females could.[40] Widgery and Webster have determined that attractive people, regardless of sex, will be rated high on credibility, which greatly increases their ultimate persuasiveness in a variety of areas—sales, public speaking, changing attitudes, being recognized as a credible counselor, and so on.[41] An attractive applicant for a position is much more apt to receive an employment offer than an unattractive applicant.

Unattractive defendants are more likely to be judged guilty in courtrooms and to receive longer sentences.[42] The evidence is clear that *initially* we respond much more favorably to physically attractive people. Attractiveness serves to open doors and create greater opportunities.

EXERCISE 5.9 Reading Nonverbal Cues

GOAL: This exercise is designed to help you apply the material in this chapter on nonverbal cues to a real-life situation.

1. Go to a restaurant (a dining hall on campus is fine) and observe two strangers who are dining. For about 10 to 15 minutes record information about the nonverbal communication cues of both individuals.

	Person A	Person B
Posture		
Body Orientation		
Facial Expressions		
Eye Contact		
Gestures		
Touching		
Clothing		
Personal Boundaries		
Physical Appearance		

2. Review the material you wrote down. Speculate about the following for each of these people: What is the socioeconomic status of each? Is either one stressed, happy, upset, and so on? What appears to be the nature of the relationship between these two individuals?

Physically attractive people outstrip less attractive people on a wide range of socially desirable evaluations, including personality, popularity, success, sociability, persuasiveness, sexuality, and often happiness.[43] Attractive women, for example, are more apt to be helped and less likely to be the objects of aggressive acts.[44] Less attractive people are at a disadvantage from early childhood. Teachers, for example, interact less (and less positively) with unattractive children.[45] Physical attractiveness is also a crucial factor in determining the number of personal interactions. Practically everyone prefers the most attractive date, regardless of his or her own attractiveness and regardless of rejection by the most attractive date.[46]

Interestingly, unattractive men seen with attractive women are judged higher in a number of areas than attractive men seen with attractive women.[47] They are considered to make more money, be more successful, and have more intelligence. Apparently, the evaluators reasoned that unattractive males must compensate for their appearance in other areas to obtain dates with attractive women.

Our weight suggests certain stereotypes, which may or may not be accurate. People who are overweight are judged to be older, more old-fashioned, less strong physically, more talkative, less good-looking, more agreeable and good-natured, more sympathetic, more trusting, more dependent, and more warmhearted. Muscular individuals are rated as being stronger, better looking, younger, more adventurous, more self-reliant, more mature in behavior, and more masculine. A person with a thin physique is rated as younger, more suspicious of others, more tense and nervous, less masculine, more pessimistic, quieter, more stubborn, and more inclined to be difficult.[48] Overweight and very thin people have been discriminated against when attempting to obtain jobs, purchase life insurance, adopt children, or enter college.[49] There are stereotypes (which may be erroneous) people who are severely overweight or underweight have a low self-image. The important point here is that even our body weight communicates messages.

Being physically attractive does not mean that a person will be more intelligent, more successful, better adjusted, and happier than less attractive people. Attractiveness initially opens more doors to success, but after a door is opened, it is performance that determines outcome. It should also be noted that everyone has the ability to improve his or her physical appearance. Dieting, exercising, managing stress, learning to be assertive, adequate sleep, and good grooming habits will substantially improve a person's physical appearance.

Environment

Perhaps all of us have been in immaculate homes that have "unliving rooms" with furniture coverings, plastic lamp coverings, and spotless ashtrays that send nonverbal messages of "Do not get me dirty," "Do not touch," "Do not put your feet up," and "Stay alert to avoid a mistake." Owners of these homes wonder why guests cannot relax and have a good time. They are unaware that the environment is communicating messages that lead guests to feel uncomfortable.

A study by Maslow and Mintz found that the attractiveness of a room shapes the kind of communication that takes place and influences the happiness and energy of people working in it.[50] The researchers used an "ugly" room, which looked like a janitor's closet, and a "beautiful" room, which was furnished with drapes, carpeting, and comfortable furniture. To gauge the subjects' energy levels and feelings of well-being, researchers asked them to rate a series of pictures of models' faces. When subjects were in the ugly room, they became tired and bored sooner, taking longer to complete their task. They described the room as producing fatigue, headaches, monotony, and irritability. When the subjects moved to the beautiful room, they displayed a greater desire to work. They also rated the faces they were judging higher and communicated many more feelings of comfort, importance, and enjoyment. This experiment provides evidence supporting the commonsense notion that workers do a better job and generally feel better when they are in an attractive environment.

Wall decorations, types of furniture, and placement of furniture in a meeting area convey messages as to whether the group leader wants informal, relaxed communications or formal, to-the-point communications. A round table, for example, suggests egalitarian communication, whereas a rectangular table suggests status and power differences. At a rectangular table, high-status people generally sit at one end of the table and low-status individuals sit at the other. If sides of equal strength hold a meeting around a rectangular table, each side sits at opposite ends, rather than intermingling. A classroom in which the chairs are in a circle suggests the instructor wants to create an informal atmosphere. A classroom with the chairs in rows suggests the instructor wants to create a formal atmosphere.

When clients come into the offices of helping professionals, the offices communicate messages. A clean, neat waiting room with comfortable chairs, plants, and soft background music communicates warmth, caring, and a professional approach. Negative messages are sent by an unclean room, hard chairs, few wall decorations, and loose paint on walls. A messy office may suggest to a client that the worker is overwhelmed, perhaps burning out, and therefore is unlikely to be of much help. Workers can *tell* their clients that they want them to feel comfortable by providing comfortable padded chairs instead of hard wooden ones, by providing tissues, by having plants and wall decorations that suggest the workers really like their jobs, and by arranging the furniture to facilitate communication.

Other Nonverbal Cues

Social workers need to be aware of other nonverbal cues. When people become anxious, angry, embarrassed, or otherwise emotionally excited, they have a pronounced facial blush or extensive reddening of the chest and neck. In therapy, such a cue may signal that the client is focusing on emotionally charged material, which often needs to be explored.

The breathing pattern of a group member is another cue. When a member is anxious or emotionally excited, breathing rate increases, which can be observed by watching the person's chest.

Another nonverbal cue commonly observed by psychotherapists, educators, and others is a change in muscle tension. When you become acquainted with someone, a common cue that you often use (and frequently are not aware of) to tell whether that person is relaxed or tense (or emotionally excited) is the degree of tenseness of muscles in that person's face, neck, and arms.

When a person is relaxed, the temperature on the surface of his or her hands is normally 10 to 15 degrees warmer than when the person is tense. As part of the reaction to stress, blood flows inward. When a person is relaxed, blood flows outward and warms the hands and skin. When you shake hands with someone, you are apt to receive information about whether that person is relaxed or under stress. (It should be noted that variables other than stress may cause a person's hand to feel colder. For example, the person may have been outside in cold weather or recently held a cold drink.)

Summary

The following summarizes the chapter's content in terms of the learning objectives presented at the beginning of the chapter.

1. Understand a mode of communication.
A model of communication is presented. One-way communication is compared and contrasted with two-way communication. Some serious drawbacks exist with one-way communication.

2. Identify factors that interfere with the communication process.
What a receiver of a message perceives the message to be *becomes the message*.
The perception may be fully accurate, partially accurate, or completely inaccurate.
A number of variables can affect the accuracy of the perception, including defense mechanisms.

3. Communicate more effectively.
Guidelines are presented for both senders and receivers for improving communication. Guidelines for when, where, and what members should self-disclose in groups are discussed. Members should self-disclose when the potential benefits outweigh the potential risks. The Johari Window (a graphic model of self-disclosure) is presented.

4. Have an increased understanding of nonverbal communication.
The following forms of nonverbal communication are described: posture, body orientation, facial expressions, eye contact, gestures, touching, clothing, personal boundaries, territoriality, voice, physical appearance, environment, breathing patterns, change in muscle tension, and hand temperature. The more competence that group leaders and group members develop in perceiving nonverbal and verbal communications accurately, the more effectively they are apt to function in a group.

Group Exercises

EXERCISE A: The Johari Window

GOAL: To introduce the Johari Window and demonstrate how it can be used to further self-awareness.

Note: The instructor should lead this exercise, and students should be told **not to disclose personal information.**

Step 1. The group leader describes what the Johari Window is and how increased self-disclosure generally leads to greater self-awareness and more meaningful relationships. The group leader may also describe why group members are initially reluctant to self-disclose but gradually begin to do so. With appropriate self-disclosure in groups, cohesion and group morale generally increase. The group leader should note that personal information should *not be* disclosed during this exercise.

Step 2. The members pair up into subgroups. Each member draws a Johari Window representing himself or herself and then his or her partner. These drawings should be made privately.

Step 3. The partners share their drawings with each other. Each describes the reasons for drawing the window in the form that is displayed. The two partners discuss the similarities and differences in their drawings; for example, why did A draw himself or herself as not being very open, whereas B drew A as being a very open person?

Step 4. The class discusses thoughts about the merits and shortcomings of the Johari Window and what they learned from the exercise.

EXERCISE B: Defense Mechanisms

GOAL: To become more aware of the use of defense mechanisms.

Step 1. The group leader begins by stating the purpose of the exercise and giving brief descriptions of common defense mechanisms (see the relevant section in this chapter).

Step 2. Each member lists on a sheet of paper the three defense mechanisms a *friend* uses most often and then describes one or two examples of each. The leader explains that students will be asked to share what they write with two other students.

Step 3. After Step 2 is completed, the class forms subgroups of three students, and each member is asked to share what he or she wrote. The two listeners should provide feedback on whether the defense mechanisms have desirable or undesirable consequences. For the undesirable, the members discuss more effective approaches.

Step 4. The class discusses what they learned from the exercise and how they feel about it.

EXERCISE C: Distortions in Transmitting Information

GOAL: To demonstrate the effects of transmitting information through a series of one-way and two-way communications among group members.

Step 1. The leader explains the purpose of the exercise, asks 10 students to step outside, and informs them that their task will be to repeat to someone else what they hear. The remaining students are observers. The first five students will use one-way communication, and the second five will use two-way communication. A copy of the following story is distributed to the observers, who are asked to record what each participant adds to the communication and what each participant leaves out of the communication.

Step 2. The first participant returns, and the leader slowly reads the following story to him.

> A farmer in western Kansas put a tin roof on his barn. Then a small tornado blew the roof off, and when the farmer found it two counties away, it was twisted and mangled beyond repair.
>
> A friend and lawyer advised him that the Ford Motor Company would pay him a good price for the scrap tin, and the farmer decided he would ship the roof up to the company to see how much he could get for it. He crated it up in a very big wooden box and sent it off to Dearborn, Michigan, marking it plainly with his return address so that the Ford Company would know where to send the check.
>
> Twelve weeks passed, and the farmer didn't hear from the Ford Company. Finally, he was just on the verge of writing to find out what was the matter, when he received an envelope from Ford. It said, "We don't know what hit your car, mister, but we'll have it fixed for you by the 15th of next month."[51]

The story is read once, and no questions are allowed. The second participant enters, the first repeats the story to the second, and so on. The fifth participant should repeat the story to the observers, and this fifth repetition should be tape-recorded to play back later.

Step 3. The sixth participant enters and is told that he or she may ask questions about the story he or she is about to hear. The story is read and questions answered. The process is repeated until the 10th participant repeats the story to the observers. The 10th repetition should be tape-recorded to play back later.

Step 4. The group leader explains the effects of leveling, sharpening, and assimilation on the transmission of information. Some observers summarize verbally what each participant added to and left out of the story.

Step 5. The group leader describes why two-way communication is generally superior to one-way communication. The group leader should then play back the 5th and 10th participants' descriptions of the story. A discussion should then follow as to which version was closer to the original story.

EXERCISE D: The Intruder

GOAL: To present a model for communication and to demonstrate that there are fairly wide variations in what students perceive.

Step 1. Prior to the meeting, the group leader arranges for a friend or acquaintance to barge into the class and create a scene. This accomplice should not be known to anyone in class.

Step 2. The group is informed that the purpose of this exercise is to become aware of factors that reduce or prevent effective communication. The group leader describes the communication model presented at the beginning of this chapter. When the group leader is nearly finished, the leader should *unobtrusively* signal the accomplice to enter. The accomplice should barge in, create a ruckus, say some disparaging things about the group leader, threaten the group leader, and then leave angrily.

Step 3. The leader explains that the purpose of this exercise is to see how closely the students' perceptions match. Ask each student to write down on a sheet of paper the following information:

1. The intruder's height and weight
2. What the intruder was wearing
3. What the intruder looked like
4. What the intruder said and did

Step 4. Several descriptions are read aloud and differences discussed. If there are sharp differences, why did they occur? The leader explains that perceptual differences between people are a major barrier to effective communication.

EXERCISE E: Active Listening

GOAL: To develop active-listening skills.

Step 1. The leader explains the purpose of the exercise and describes what active listening is and what it is designed to accomplish. The leader indicates that active listening involves using two types of statements: reflecting feelings and restating content.

Step 2. Students pair off. (If there is someone without a partner, the leader should participate.) One member of each pair selects a topic to discuss for about 10 minutes. The topic may involve (1) a philosophical or moral issue such as abortion, (2) a problem with a friend or a relative, or (3) a problem at school.

Step 3. The member who selects a topic discusses the issue for about 10 minutes. The listener should try to respond solely with active-listening statements.

Step 4. After the discussion, the presenter should discuss with the listener the quality of the active-listening statements. Did the listener make the mistake of making suggestions, asking questions, or beginning to talk about personal experiences? Did active listening motivate the presenter to continue talking? Did the presenter perceive the active-listening statements to be primarily "natural" or "artificial"?

The listener should then discuss with the presenter his or her thoughts and feelings about using active-listening statements. Did the listener want to make other types of statements? If so, what?

Step 5. The roles should then be reversed and the process repeated.

Step 6. Students form a circle and discuss the merits and shortcomings of active listening. Did any unique or unusual events occur?

EXERCISE F: My Nonverbal Communication

GOAL: To identify and observe nonverbal messages that people respond to and to give feedback on the ways in which nonverbal messages are used constructively.

Step 1. The leader describes the purpose of the exercise. She asks the class to identify various types of nonverbal behaviors on the blackboard. A partial list would include:

Muscle tension	Breathing patterns
Eye contact	Clothes
Smiles	Distance between people
Eyebrow movements	communicating
Gestures	Touch
Voice tone	Silence and pauses
Facial color	Facial expressions

Step 2. The class forms groups of three students each. Each subgroup member is asked to select his or her all-time favorite movie.

Step 3. Each group member talks for a minute and a half to his or her small group on the selected topic. The two who are observing in each group should note the speaker's nonverbal signals. The leader should inform the subgroups when it is time for each member to start and to stop talking.

Step 4. After all three group members have spoken, group members share what they liked about the way each communicated nonverbally.

Step 5. Group members are then asked to think about their nonverbal communication *privately* and about what they could change to communicate more effectively nonverbally.

EXERCISE G: Nonverbal Cues

GOAL: To learn the kinds of nonverbal cues that should be used to obtain social work employment and establish a relaxed, nonthreatening atmosphere for clients.

Step 1. The group leader states the goals of the exercise. The first task for each member of the class is to assume that he or she is a director of a social service agency interviewing applicants for a social work position. As director, which nonverbal cues might enter into the decision as to which applicant to hire? (Responses should be listed on the blackboard.)

Step 2. The second task for each student is to assume the role of a client who is emotionally upset and has painful decisions to make, such as whether to get a divorce. As a client, which nonverbal cues by a counselor would establish a relaxed, nonthreatening atmosphere that would increase the chances of the client fully sharing concerns? As responses are given, they are also listed on the blackboard.

Step 3. The similarities and differences between the two lists are discussed. For the differences, the possible reasons for these discrepancies are also discussed.

EXERCISE H: A Popular Faculty Member

GOAL: To become more aware of using nonverbal communication in assessing human behavior.

Step 1. The group leader selects a popular faculty member with whom the students are familiar. The class indicates the specific nonverbal cues used by this instructor to increase his or her effectiveness. The following clues should be considered: clothing, eyes, facial expressions, posture, physical appearance, gestures and other body movements, and paralanguage.

Step 2. With this same instructor in mind, the class focuses on the appearance of this faculty member's office and imagines that this is the only information they have about the instructor. The class then discusses the nonverbal messages sent by the types of objects, arrangement of objects, and general conditions of the office. Next, the class discusses which of these nonverbal messages give an impression different from what the instructor is like. Which are consistent? Finally, the class discusses the types of interaction the office atmosphere suggests should take place—for example, whether the communication is expected to be formal and businesslike or relaxed and informal.

EXERCISE I: Double Messages

GOAL: To understand how verbal messages can contradict nonverbal messages.

Step 1. The class divides into two groups of equal size and is informed that this is an exercise in keeping conversations going. One group leaves for a separate room or the hallway.

Step 2. The remaining, or first, group is told that this is really an exercise in learning more about how people react when someone seems to be saying one thing verbally and another nonverbally. Each member's task is to pick a topic to discuss with another person in the other group for 10 minutes. The topic maybe anything, such as politics, movies, or sports. While discussing the topic, each person should periodically *nonverbally* contradict his or her verbal message by using facial expressions, gestures, laughter, and voice fluctuations. Furthermore, each person should note and observe the partner's nonverbal reactions to these double messages.

Step 3. The second group is told that each person will be paired with someone in the first group. The partner in the first group will start a conversation on a topic. The task of each person in this second group is to keep the discussion going and to inject controversial topics into the conversation.

Step 4. The room should be large enough to allow individuals to spread out and carry on conversations. Perhaps two rooms can be used. Individuals from both groups pair off and discuss the topic for approximately 10 minutes.

Step 5. The real purpose of the exercise is now explained to the second group. The first group discusses the following questions with the second group listening. What nonverbal cues did they use to contradict their verbal messages? Was sending a double message hard to do? What were the reactions to these double messages?

Then the second group discusses the following: How did they feel about their partners during this exercise? Did they believe what their partners were saying verbally? How did they cope with the double messages they were receiving? When nonverbal messages conflicted with verbal messages, which were they more likely to believe?

EXERCISE J: The Flat Tire

GOAL: To become more aware of individual differences and skills in using nonverbal cues to relay messages.

Step 1. The leader explains that the exercise involves students relaying messages nonverbally. Four students volunteer to leave the room. Then the following is read to a fifth volunteer who must try to remember and communicate it nonverbally to the first student who returns. That student will then nonverbally communicate it to the second student, and so on.

> You are driving a car and your right front tire goes flat. You get out and kick the tire. You go to the trunk, open it, and there's no spare. You angrily slam the trunk shut. You then attempt to hitchhike to a gas station you recently passed. A motorcyclist stops to give you a ride to the gas station.

The volunteers receiving the message may ask questions, but the senders must communicate their answers nonverbally.

While these five volunteers are acting out this exercise, the remainder of the class responds to the following questions on paper each time the message is relayed: What did the relayer add to or delete from the message? If there was a communication breakdown as a result of a weakness in a nonverbal cue, how could this have been avoided by using a better one?

Step 2. The person who receives the final message states it verbally. This message is compared to the original, and the whole class discusses the two questions in Step 1.

EXERCISE K: Communicating While Blindfolded

GOAL: To better understand, how communication is affected when the sense of sight is not used.

Step 1. The leader explains that nonverbal communication is heavily dependent on the sense of sight. We watch other people's facial expressions, eyes, posture, hand gestures, and body movements. The leader describes the goal of the exercise and asks for five or six volunteers. These volunteers sit in a circle in the middle of the class. The volunteers are given a controversial topic to discuss (for example, whether the elderly who have a terminal illness and are in severe pain have a right to take their own lives). All volunteers are either blindfolded or asked to keep their eyes tightly shut while discussing the topic. The topic is discussed for 10 to 15 minutes.

Step 2. At the end of 10 or 15 minutes, the discussion ends. The volunteers remove their blindfolds or open their eyes, and discuss the following questions:

1. How did it feel to be blindfolded?
2. How did not being able to see affect the communications?
3. Did having a blindfold on interfere with being able to concentrate on what was said?
4. Was it difficult to hear?
5. Do they think they gestured more or less than they usually do?

6. During this exercise, did they become aware of anything they had not noticed before?

7. Does not being able to see the people you are talking to substantially hamper communication? If yes, in what ways?

Step 3. As an additional optional step, this exercise may be repeated with a new group of volunteers.

EXERCISE L: Giving and Receiving Feedback About Nonverbal Communication

GOAL: To observe nonverbal communication in others and receive feedback about nonverbal communication.

Step 1. The group leader states the purpose of the exercise and divides the class into two groups of equal size; if there is an uneven number, the group leader can participate. Each member in one group should pair up with someone in the other group.

Step 2. One group sits in an inner circle, and the other group members sit in an outer circle to observe the nonverbal communication of their partners. The inner circle discusses a controversial topic that will arouse strong emotions. The topic can be abortion or whether a male and female who both have a severe intellectual disability should legally be permitted to marry and have children. The discussion should continue for 10 to 20 minutes. People in the outer circle observe the nonverbal communication of their partners—gestures, body movements, eye behavior, paralanguage, facial expressions, and so on.

Step 3. After the discussion, the observing partner informs his or her partner as to what nonverbal cues were used and what messages were communicated. After the observing partner is finished, the partner who was observed should have an opportunity to discuss his or her degree of agreement with the observer's interpretations.

Step 4. The roles of the partners are reversed and Steps 2 and 3 repeated.

Step 5. The class discusses what they learned from this exercise.

EXERCISE M: Zones of Personal Space

GOAL: To observe how the distance between communicators affects what people are thinking and feeling.

Step 1. The leader explains the purpose of the exercise. Two people volunteer for an exercise to illustrate these effects.

Step 2. The volunteers stand at the farthest corners of the room, away from each other. Their task is to slowly, very slowly, move toward each other. As they are slowly moving toward each other, they engage in small talk about topics of their choosing. They should continue slowly walking and conversing until they touch. When they touch they should slowly start moving away from each other but continue to converse. At the point when they are most comfortable in conversing, they should stop.

Step 3: Other volunteers may be selected to repeat the exercise until interest wanes.

Step 4. The volunteers involved in this exercise should then determine the distances between partners that were most comfortable and least comfortable for conversing. The leader of the exercise should note the points at which the various pairs were most comfortable in conversing and then make some statements about the extent of the congruence between these "most comfortable points" and the theoretical material in the chapter as to the "most comfortable point" for conversing in this type of situation.

Competency Notes

EP 1b Use reflection and self-regulation to manage personal values and maintain professionalism in practice situations.

EP 1c Demonstrate professional demeanor in behavior; appearance; and oral, written, and electronic communication.

EP 6a Apply knowledge of human behavior and the social environment, person-in-environment, and other multidisciplinary theoretical frameworks to engage with clients and constituencies.

EP 6b Use empathy, reflection, and interpersonal skills to effectively engage diverse clients and constituencies.

The content of the chapter and the exercises within the chapter are focused on students better understanding verbal communication and nonverbal communication. The content and the exercises are also designed to help students learn to communicate more effectively.

EP 1d Use technology ethically and appropriately to facilitate practice outcomes.

This section summarizes aspects of technology in social work with groups (p. 157).

Key Terms and Concepts

Accent	Directive or Coercive	Johari Window	Reciprocal
Assimilate	Encoding	Level	Regulate
Certainty	Equal Basis	Manipulate	Repeat
Contradict	Evaluative	Motives	Substitute
Decodes	Indifference	Organize	Superior

6

Task Groups*

LO 1   Identify a Variety of Task Groups

EP 1c
EP 6a

A VARIETY OF TASK GROUPS

Task groups are used to generate new ideas, to make decisions, and to find solutions to organizational problems. Task groups have three primary purposes: (1) meeting client needs, (2) meeting organizational needs, and (3) meeting community needs.

Task groups to meet client needs include treatment teams. A few examples will illustrate treatment teams. A group of professionals who deliver home-based hospice care may meet weekly to review the services being provided to patients. Professionals at a county mental health center may meet weekly to review the services being provided to clients who are living in the community. Professionals at a rehabilitation center may meet weekly to review services to clients at that facility. Often, at such meetings a second focus is on **team building**; time is devoted to improving how members function as a group. At times, treatment teams meet for the purpose of developing, monitoring, and coordinating treatment plans for a particular client—for example, professionals at a mental health center may meet to develop a treatment plan for a depressed elderly man whose wife has recently died.

Task groups to meet organizational needs include committees and boards of directors. The most common type of task group is the committee. Members of a committee may be appointed or elected. A committee is "charged" with completing one or more tasks. Committees may be temporary creations (ad hoc committees) or be more permanent parts of the structure of an organization (standing committees). A board of directors is a governing board charged with responsibility for setting the policies governing the agency. Members of the board provide guidance to the management of an organization.

There are a variety of task groups to meet community needs. Social action groups empower members to engage in collective, planned change efforts to improve some aspect of the community's social or physical environment. For example, nontraditional students at a campus may organize and advocate for a childcare center being established at the campus. **Coalitions** (sometimes called alliances) are groups of organizations or social-action groups that come together to exert influence by sharing expertise and resources. Coalition members believe their common goals have a greater chance of being achieved by united action than by members acting alone. For example, several organizations, local government leaders, and civil leaders may form a coalition to

*   Sarah Hessenauer, MSW, PhD (chair of the Social Works Department, University of Wisconsin–Whitewater; Associate Professor) assisted in revising this chapter.

LEARNING OBJECTIVES

Social workers and other helping professionals are often called upon to chair committees, focus groups, teams, and other task groups. This chapter will help prepare students to:

LO 1
Identify a variety of task groups.

LO 2
Comprehend how to lead task groups.

LO 3
Understand that one of the major functions of task groups is problem solving.

LO 4
Utilize the brainstorming technique.

LO 5
More effectively resolve interpersonal conflicts.

LO 6
Understand that a second major function of task groups is decision making.

LO 7
More effectively handle groupthink.

explore ways to reduce racial tensions in a community. **Delegate councils** are formed for the purpose of facilitating interagency cooperation and communication and studying community-wide social issues. Members of delegate councils are elected or appointed by a variety of sponsoring units. For example, representatives from each of the human service agencies in a community may have monthly meetings to share information, discuss ways to improve interagency communication, and study emerging issues (such as increases in family violence).

LO 2   Comprehend How to Lead Task Groups

GUIDELINES FOR LEADING TASK GROUPS

A number of guidelines will be given. These guidelines are not mandates, as some circumstances will result in the desirability of deviating from these guidelines.

Establishing the Group's Purpose

The first and critically important question is "What is the group's purpose?" Toseland and Rivas state: "A statement of purpose should be broad enough to encompass different goals, yet specific enough to define the common nature of the group's purpose. A clear statement of purpose helps members answer the question 'What are we doing together?'"[1]

A variety of sources may generate the group's purpose. A social worker may seek to form a task group to study an emerging social issue. An agency director, or agency staff, may identify the need for the establishment of an ad hoc committee. Recipients of services may request that a task force be established to advocate against government-proposed cuts in services. A group of ministers may advocate for the establishment of a delegate council of community agencies and civic leaders to study the need for an expansion of church-affiliated childcare centers.

Potential Sponsorship of the Task Group

In assessing an organization as sponsor for the proposed group, the organizer(s) of the group should pay careful attention to the purpose of the group and the organization's policies and goals. A delegate council of ministers, rabbis, and priests may be a good fit for sponsoring a task force to study the need for an expansion of church-affiliated childcare centers in a community. On the other hand, the local Hooters restaurant may not be a good fit for sponsoring a task force to study the sociopolitical environment for women in the community.

Selecting Potential Members

Potential members should be selected for their expertise, their interest in the task, and their position and power (including their political influence) to help the group accomplish its purpose. It is also important to seek diversity in membership (including ethnicity, gender, age, and sociocultural factors). Representation of consumers and potential consumers of services under review should also be included.

Recruiting Members

Recruiting can be accomplished in a variety of ways. Directors of organizations and agencies may be asked (by phone, e-mail, or direct contact) to appoint a representative. If an organizer of a group has a list of potential members, announcements can be mailed directly to them. Announcements may be posted in public places. There may be television, newspaper, and radio announcements.

For ad hoc committees and standing committees within agencies, membership is usually determined by the director, by an executive committee of the agency, or in staff meetings. For many task groups, direct contact with desired group members is often the most effective recruitment approach.

Size of the Group

The organizer needs to make decisions regarding how many members are needed to accomplish the tasks effectively and efficiently. There is no optimal size for task groups.

Larger groups are better for accomplishing complex tasks, partly because of the increase in expertise and resources of a larger membership. In larger groups, fewer difficulties arise when one or more members are absent. Larger groups also have disadvantages. Each member has less of an opportunity to speak, and each member will receive less individualized attention. There is also a greater danger of competing alliances being formed. Larger groups are also more difficult for the leader to manage. They frequently require more formalized procedures (such as parliamentary procedures) to accomplish their meeting agendas. They also have greater difficulty achieving cohesiveness and reaching consensus.

Orienting Members to the Group

The purpose needs to be carefully explained. Members' views about the importance of the purpose need to be attended to. Members may be oriented by the organizer of the group prior to the first meeting. During the first meeting, the purpose of the group should again be reviewed, and perhaps attention should be given to establishing more specific goals for the group. Individual goals of members may need to be discussed. Prior to the first meeting, it may be desirable to send background material to the members. At the first meeting, if questions arise about how the group will conduct its business, discussions should occur, leading to the establishing of routine procedures. Task groups often adopt the following routine procedure: reviewing and approving the minutes from the previous meeting, making announcements, discussing old business, and bringing up and discussing new business.

Meeting Place and Room

The setting for the group has a profound effect on the conduct of group meetings and on the behavior of group members. Room size, chair comfort, acoustics, seating arrangements, furnishings, refreshments, and atmosphere should all be considered. Too large a room can put too much distance between members and result in some members tuning out. Too small a room can lead to discomfort and is especially challenging for anyone who tends to be claustrophobic. People in wheelchairs will need wheelchair access. Carpeting, lighting, work tables, and other furnishings need to be considered in order to create an informal, comfortable atmosphere. Some people physically react to lighting that is too bright. Overly dim lighting is annoying to many people.

First Meeting

If the members are not already familiar with one another, introduction of members by the leader needs to be facilitated. For example, the leader may first introduce himself or herself and give a brief description of his or her background experiences that are related to the group's purpose. Group members may then be asked to do the same, often in round-robin fashion. Usually it is advantageous to then use an appropriate ice breaker, such as "Tell me something personal about you that we would find surprising."

The purpose and function of the group need to be discussed as they are perceived by the leader, other members, and the sponsoring organization(s). The task and socioemotional aspects of the group need to be attended to and balanced by the leader. Group goals need to be set. The leader should attend to facilitating the members' motivation to work in the group. Perhaps obstacles to achieving individual and group goals may need to be discussed.

It is helpful to have an agenda for the first, and future, meetings. Often, it is desirable to send the agenda to members prior to the first meeting.

Working with Resistive and Disruptive Members

Resistance is to be expected. Ambivalent feelings about change are common, as it is rare for changes to be proposed and worked on without ambivalent feelings. Acknowledging members' ambivalence is a helpful way to get members to recognize their reactions to change. An open discussion of members' ambivalence issues and their questions about the capacity of a group to achieve a goal helps all members problem-solve and arrive at creative approaches for achieving desired changes and goals. Leaders should treat members' suggestions and ideas about how to proceed with respect. (Additional material on working with disruptive members is presented in Chapter 4.)

Although task groups are usually successful and useful, they can be a source of frustration for members when they function ineffectively. This writer remembers a college promotions committee meeting he attended that lasted for 8 hours (from 4 P.M. to midnight), dragging along simply because some committee members must "not have had a life," as they enjoyed the opportunity to talk about topics unrelated to promotions. Meetings that are not run well are boring and unsatisfying. The leader has an obligation to keep the members focused on the task and to move the meeting along to progress in completing the agenda items. Toseland and Rivas state:

> . . . well-run meetings can be a positive experience. They have drawn people together by creating effective teamwork in which ideas are shared, feelings are expressed, and support is developed for group members and for the decisions made by the group. There are few experiences in the workplace to equal the sense of cohesion, commitment, and satisfaction that members feel when their ideas have been heard, appreciated, and used in resolving a difficult issue and arriving at a decision.[2]

The Middle Stages

The primary purpose of task groups are problem solving and decision making. Members, including the leader, often need to complete a number of tasks related to accomplishing group goals prior to meetings. (Some members are conscientious about doing this, whereas some drive a group "crazy" by promising to do certain tasks and never completing them.) When the latter happens and such people are identified, the group is probably better off not assigning essential tasks to such members. In certain task groups parliamentary procedures are used to conduct business. Most people learn parliamentary procedures through "modeling." They observe a group using parliamentary procedures and learn to use such procedures themselves (including making motions, seconding motions, having a discussion, amending the motion, calling the questions, and voting on the motion or on the amended motion.)

Adjourning a Meeting

When a meeting is near the ending time, it is often desirable for the leader to summarize what has been accomplished during the meeting. It may be constructive to praise members for their work. Future agenda items should be specified and recorded. Perhaps a statement needs to be made about the progress that has been achieved in terms of the overall schedule. It is also often desirable to summarize as clearly as possible the tasks that members agreed to accomplish before the next meeting. The date, time, and place of the next meeting should be established.

Evaluating and Terminating

It is essential for a group to evaluate the extent to which it has accomplished its goals during the middle phases and when the group is nearing the time when it plans to terminate. Evaluation methods and approaches are described at some length in Chapter 14.

The ending of a group is often a bittersweet experience for members. They are pleased about their accomplishments (which may be celebrated with a get-together, perhaps at a restaurant). The ending of a group may also have unpleasant aspects. Members may be somewhat sad if the goals that were set have not been fully accomplished. (This writer remembers a committee he worked on that involved writing a great proposal; the members looked forward to doing the project if the grant was approved. Sadly, it was not.) Some members may also experience sadness, as they have enjoyed the camaraderie of working with others and realize it is ending. Some members may have enjoyed the excitement that is generated when a group continues to creatively problem-solve. Considerable material is provided on the process of terminating a task group in Chapter 13.

EXERCISE 6.1   Successful and Unsuccessful Group Experiences

GOAL: This exercise is designed to have you reflect about how you felt when you participated in a successful group and when you participated in an unsuccessful group.

1. Describe a successful group in which you participated. Indicate why you deemed this group as successful— perhaps the goals were accomplished or perhaps you enjoyed the camaraderie, and so on.

2. What were the feelings you experienced about participating in this group?

3. Describe an unsuccessful group in which you participated. Indicate why you defined this group as unsuccessful—perhaps the goals were not accomplished, you disliked certain members, or you were asked to leave, and so on.

4. What were the feelings you experienced about participating in this group?

LO 3   Understand That One of the Major Functions of Task Groups Is Problem Solving

PROBLEM-SOLVING APPROACH

In a nutshell, practically all of the work done by social work practitioners involves problem solving. Social workers use a problem-solving approach extensively to help individuals, families, small groups, organizations, and community groups. Problem solving has been defined by Johnson and Johnson as follows:

> *Problem solving* is the process of resolving the unsettled matters of finding an answer to a difficulty; it is a process that results in a solution to a problem, and it involves changing the actual state of affairs until it is identical with the desired state of affairs.[3]

Problem solving can be broken down into six steps: (1) identifying and defining the problem, (2) assessing the size and causes of the problem, (3) developing alternative strategies or plans for solving it, (4) assessing the merits and shortcomings of these alternative strategies, (5) selecting and implementing the most desirable strategy or strategies, and (6) evaluating the success of the strategies used.

Identification and Definition

The more precisely and accurately a problem is defined, the easier it is to solve. Contrast the following two statements describing problems: "Fifty-seven young children in a six-block-square area of this city are in need of care during the daytime because their parents are working." Here the terms of the problem are defined concretely. Because the problem group, its locale, and a time period are specified, the problem can be easily addressed. Now consider another example: "Some children in some school systems in this city seem to be becoming more apathetic about the way their lives are going, and something should be done about it." Because no particular group and no clear symptoms have been identified, there is no way to determine a solution.

When using the problem-solving approach, a group should initially (1) determine the actual or current state of affairs and (2) specify the desired state of affairs. The differences between the actual and desired state of affairs should be thoroughly discussed and agreed upon. If the group concludes that serious negative consequences are associated with the actual state of affairs, then members' commitment to reach the desired state of affairs is apt to be high.

Arriving at a group definition of a workable problem can be difficult. Brainstorming, which is described in this chapter, can help develop descriptions of the problem. These descriptions are then rephrased until an agreed-upon definition, including a precise statement of both the actual and the desired state of affairs, is reached.

Assessment of Size and Causes

Once the workable problem is defined, the group next gathers information to help it assess the magnitude and causes of the problem. In assessing the magnitude, the following questions arise: Who is affected? How many people are affected? How seriously? Where are they located?

Often, identifying the causes of a problem will suggest strategies for resolving it. If high unemployment is a problem in a state and most of the unemployed are untrained for available jobs, this suggests that programs to train the unemployed for available jobs will help alleviate unemployment. Only rarely is it possible to resolve a problem without knowing its causes. For example, some urban renewal projects have rebuilt blighted areas without knowing all the causes that led to the deterioration of housing and living conditions.

Development of Alternative Strategies

The third problem-solving step is to formulate alternative ways to solve the problem. Brainstorming is a useful technique for generating a wide range of strategies. Sometimes, the wildest suggestions may stimulate other members to come up with one or more pragmatic alternatives. If group members cannot produce workable strategies, outside experts may be consulted as an alternative to brainstorming.

Assessment of Strategies

Next, the merits and shortcomings of each strategy must be assessed, and often a cost–benefit analysis of each strategy is done. Costs include time, material resources, and professional fees. Although the actual costs and benefits of each strategy are often difficult to assess objectively, reasoned assessments must be made as to what resources will be needed and what the outcomes of applying these resources will be. For example, if racial segregation is a problem in a large city, judgments must be made as to whether the costs of school busing to achieve school integration (such as transportation costs and movement away from the benefits of the neighborhood school concept) justify this type of busing.

Selection and Implementation

The fifth step involves two separate processes. The first is *decision making,* in which the group selects one of the proposed alternatives. (Decision making in a group can be done in a variety of ways. Many of these approaches are described later in this chapter.) After a strategy is selected, the group must *implement* the strategy. Generally, the more solid the group support for the selected strategy, the greater are the chances for its successful implementation. Required tasks must be identified, jobs assigned, and deadlines set for starting and completing each task.

Evaluation

Once implementation is complete, evaluating the strategy's success in two areas is necessary: Was the strategy fully implemented, and what were its effects? The main criterion is the extent to which the strategy has narrowed the discrepancy between the actual and the desired state of affairs. This is why precise descriptions of each problem are necessary.

If the strategy was not fully implemented, then additional efforts may be required. If the strategy has been fully implemented without achieving the desired state of affairs, perhaps new strategies are in order. In addition, implementation of a strategy may expose other problems. For example, the 1960s civil rights movement focused on reducing racial discrimination. But it also generated awareness that many other groups are discriminated against, including women, gays, lesbians, and people with a disability.

The evaluation phase should demonstrate the extent to which the problem has been resolved, what remains to be resolved, and what new problems have been identified. Not surprisingly, the evaluation phase often leads to another problem-solving effort. The old problem is redefined or another problem is identified. The steps of the problem-solving approach are then repeated.

BARRIERS TO EFFECTIVE PROBLEM SOLVING

There are several barriers to effective problem solving: inadequate definitions; invalid hypotheses; poor communication; and lack of skills, resources, and motivation within the group.

Inadequate Definitions

If a problem is stated imprecisely, individual group members are apt to vary in their interpretations of the problem. For example, take the following problem statement: "Children are under too much pressure in our school systems." Possible interpretations of "too much pressure" include academic pressure, pressure to use alcohol and drugs, religious pressure, pressure from teachers and parents, pressure resulting from racial tensions, pressure to have sexual experiences, and pressure to break the law. Unless the problem is defined more precisely, group members will probably disagree on how to solve it.

Invalid Hypotheses

Closely related to inadequate definitions, invalid hypotheses and theories about the causes of a problem also erect a formidable barrier. Emotionally disturbed people were once thought to be possessed by demons, for example, and in the early 1900s, criminals were considered to be mentally retarded.[4] Two hundred years ago, physicians thought that bloodletting (through using leeches) would help heal people who were physically ill. If a group has faulty theories about the causes of a problem, the members are apt to develop ineffective strategies to solve it. For example, we know today that seeking to drive demons out of someone who has emotional problems will not alleviate emotional trauma, and bloodletting does not heal.

Poor Communication

Poor communication in the group may exist for a variety of reasons. Group members may not possess well-developed communication skills, or some may withhold information in an attempt to manipulate others in the group. Interpersonal conflict between group members may inhibit them from participating effectively. With poor communication, a group will generate fewer alternative strategies and inadequately assess their potential consequences. In addition, enthusiasm and commitment to implement the proposed group strategy will be diminished.

Lack of Skills

A group may lack the skills to define and solve a problem. A group may not have the expertise to design and conduct a necessary research study, for instance, or the skills to write a grant proposal to obtain needed resources. When the group lacks an essential skill, the group must acquire the skill by recruiting appropriate new members or retaining an outside consultant.

Lack of Resources

There never seems to be sufficient financial resources to accomplish everything that is desired. A planning group to combat the homeless problem, for example, may be partially stifled by lack of funds to build a sufficient number of low-cost housing units for the homeless.

Lack of Motivation

Some groups fail to solve problems because their members are not motivated to do so. By creating a supportive, trusting, cooperative atmosphere, a leader can encourage unmotivated members to participate. Unmotivated members can be asked to share their reasons for not participating, and perhaps changes can be made to encourage their input. The motivated members can also carry the group to some initial successes in the hope that the unmotivated members would be inspired to participate more. Relatively easy tasks could be delegated to these individuals, who should be complimented for their efforts.

Personality Differences

Whenever you join a group of people together, personality differences may appear. These differences may encourage a wide range of thinking; however, it may also lead to conflict. When the conflict occurs early in a task, it may affect later tasks.[5] Conflict can occur when a group member takes things personally, feels left out, does not get the attention he or she wants, or was not allowed to take on a desired role in the group. Personality differences need to be acknowledged early and group conflict strategies need to be addressed to ensure task completion is not held up.

LO 4   Utilize the Brainstorming Technique

BRAINSTORMING

Brainstorming is a procedure designed to generate ideas in quantity through the full participation of all group members. The procedure helps individuals share their ideas without the interruption of discussion or evaluation. By allowing members to present any idea that comes to mind, more and often better ideas are generated than if the same people had worked independently. Brainstorming was developed by Osborn, who outlined the following ground rules nearly half a century ago.[6] Brainstorming can last anywhere from 1 minute to half an hour. The session continues as long as ideas are being generated. Each session is to be freewheeling and open. The wilder and more absurd the ideas, the better, as these ideas may lead to a breakthrough or a new course of action. Criticism or evaluation of any idea is not allowed. The ideas are simply listed for the group as rapidly as possible without comment, discussion, or clarification.

In this case the quantity of ideas counts, not quality. A greater number of ideas will increase the likelihood of usable ideas. Members are encouraged to build on the ideas of other group members whenever possible so that thoughts are expanded and new combinations of ideas are formulated. The focus is always on a single issue or problem. Members should not skip from problem to problem or try to brainstorm a multiproblem situation.

A relaxed, congenial, cooperative atmosphere should be promoted, and all members, no matter how shy and reluctant to participate, should be encouraged to contribute. It is often advisable to limit members to one idea at a time so that less vocal individuals will feel encouraged to express their ideas. For new members unfamiliar with brainstorming, the rationale and rules should be explained. If groups are being formed specifically for brainstorming, the membership should include a diversity of opinions and backgrounds. After the brainstorming session is over, the group selects the best ideas (or a synthesis of these ideas) related to the issue or problem.

Brainstorming has a number of advantages because it increases involvement of all members, reduces a group's dependency upon a single authority figure, and provides a procedure for obtaining a large number of ideas in a relatively short period. The pressure to say the "right things" to impress others in the group is reduced, and the process is interesting, fun, and stimulating. An open sharing of ideas within a nonevaluative climate allows each group member to build upon the ideas of others to create unique combinations.

If group members find brainstorming a strange experience, however, it can lead initially to a sense of discomfort.[7] In a restricted, self-conscious group, brainstorming may actually hinder participation, because it forces members into patterns of behavior that are felt to be "uncomfortable."[8]

In other situations, brainstorming may be effective as an ice breaker to open up a stuffy and inhibited group.[9] What effect brainstorming will have on the group depends partially on the group leader's skills and timing in using the approach.

LO 5   More Effectively Resolve Interpersonal Conflicts

CONFLICT

Conflict is an antagonistic state of action involving divergent ideas or interests and is inevitable in groups. Johnson and Johnson summarize the potential merits and dangers of a conflict in a group:

> A conflict among group members is a moment of truth in group effectiveness, a test of the group's health, a crisis that can weaken or strengthen the group, a critical event that may bring creative insight and closer relationships among members—or lasting resentment, smoldering hostility, and psychological scars. Conflicts can push members away from one another or pull them into closer and more cooperative relationships. Conflicts may contain the seeds of group destruction or the seeds of a more unified and cooperative unit . . . They have the potential for producing both highly constructive and highly destructive consequences for group functioning.[10]

Many people in our society erroneously believe that conflicts only produce negative results and should be avoided. Conflict is seen as a cause of divorce, low work morale, deterioration of friendships, psychological trauma, violence, and social disorder. In reality, the cause of these destructive events is the ineffective and harmful management of conflicts. Because people have divergent interests, beliefs, values, and goals, it is inevitable that conflicts will occur in interpersonal relationships.

Conflicts are not only a natural part of any relationship within a group; they are also desirable because when handled effectively, they have a number of payoffs. Without conflict, members may become bored, and disagreements often spark the interest and curiosity of group members and produce lively discussions. Conflicts motivate members to define issues more sharply, search harder for resolution strategies, and work harder in implementing solutions. Conflicts can also lead to greater commitment, cohesion, communication, and cooperation and can revitalize stagnant groups. By expressing and working out their dissatisfactions, group members can assess their beliefs, values, and opinions. Therefore, verbal conflicts can also lead to personal growth and encourage innovation and creativity.

TECHNIQUES FOR RESOLVING CONFLICTS

There are a variety of strategies for resolving conflicts. These strategies will be summarized in the following sections.

Win-Lose Approach

In ineffective groups, resolutions of conflict between opposing positions become win-lose situations. In many competitive fields, such as sports, business, and politics, individuals or teams are pitted against each other. In groups, conflicts are often cast in the same competitive mold. Because each side denies the legitimacy of the other's interests and concerns, members attempt to sell their position without really listening to the other side. Power blocs are formed to support one position against another. The original goals and objectives of the group may fade into the background as a "win" on issues becomes the only objective of the warring sides.

In win-lose situations, the group as a whole loses because it fails to achieve its long-range goals and objectives. The losing side is not motivated to carry out the winning decision. The losers resent the winners and may attempt to reverse the decision or impede its implementation. In such an atmosphere, distrust increases between opposing sides, communication becomes more limited and inaccurate, and group cohesion decreases. Members' unresolved feelings often result in biased judgments and actions; members will frequently refuse to vote for a good idea simply because they dislike the person who suggested it.

Obviously, communication is severely hampered in groups that handle conflict in a win-lose fashion. Conflict in win-lose situations leads to the denial or distortion of unpleasant facts and information, as each side is apt to deny, hide, or distort information inconsistent with its position in an effort to win.[11] Members misinterpret the ideas and actions of those

EXERCISE 6.2   My Tolerance for Conflicts

GOAL: This exercise is designed to assist you in assessing whether you need to become more assertive in confronting interpersonal conflicts.

1. Do you shy away (by usually giving in) from interpersonal conflicts? If "yes," explain your reasons.

2. If you shy away from interpersonal conflicts, do you feel when you give in that the other person is "trodding" on your personal rights?

3. Do you believe that you need to more assertively confront your interpersonal conflicts? If "yes," what do you intend to do in order to become more assertive in confronting conflicts?

perceived as opponents, causing "blind spots" in communication. A win-lose approach leads to deceitful expression of ideas and feelings because winning sometimes receives higher priority than honesty. Disagreement tends to be interpreted as personal rejection on the part of opposing group members, and the group's future decisions are generally poor.

No-Lose Problem Solving

The no-lose problem-solving approach asserts that it is almost always possible for both sides to have their needs met in a conflict situation. This approach, which is a variation of the problem-solving approach described earlier in this chapter, was developed by Gordon and is based on two basic premises: (1) all people have the right to have their needs met and (2) what is in conflict between the two sides is almost never their *needs,* but their *solutions* to those needs.[12]

The distinction between needs and solutions is all-important. For example, assume that a student social work club is arguing over whether to fund a graduation party for seniors or a campus day care center in danger of being closed. An analysis of needs and solutions in this discussion would reveal that the club is arguing over solutions rather than needs. There is a need to honor the graduating seniors and a need for the day care center to receive operating funds. However, there are a variety of ways of meeting both needs. The club may spend its current funds on a graduation party and then hold a fundraiser for the day care center; or they may fund the center and hold a graduation party by having members donate food, refreshments, and a few dollars at the party. Half of the club's funds could go to the center and the remainder to a reduced-cost graduation party. In addition, many other solutions could be generated to meet these needs.

The six steps to the **no-lose problem-solving approach** are:

1. Identify and define the needs of each opposing side.
2. Generate possible alternative solutions.
3. Evaluate the alternative solutions.
4. Decide on the best acceptable solution.
5. Work out ways of implementing the solution.
6. Evaluate how it worked.[13]

The first step is by far the most difficult because group members often view conflicts in terms of win-lose and attempt to identify and meet primarily their own needs. When each side's needs in a conflict are identified, however, what usually are in conflict are not the *needs* of each side but their *solutions*. No-lose problem solving will generally lead to creative solutions after *all six steps* are followed. (Readers will note the "no-lose problem-solving process" is identical to the "problem-solving process" described earlier in this chapter.)

The advantages of this no-lose approach are that both sides fulfill their needs, and group harmony and cohesion are increased. The resentment, hostility, and subversive actions of a win-lose situation are also eliminated. Actually, it is in each group member's best interest to resolve conflicts in a way that will help all members achieve their short-term goals and needs and increase the long-term effectiveness of the group, so that the long-term goals and needs of *all* members have a better chance of being achieved. Frequently, with groups that function in terms of win-lose, the winning side may win some battles, but the effectiveness of the group may diminish. All members may thus fail to accomplish their long-term goals and satisfy their needs.

With a problem-solving approach, members tend to listen to one another, recognize the legitimacy of another's interests, and influence one another with rational arguments. Instead of a competitive environment, problem solving encourages an atmosphere of cooperation.

The differences between a win-lose strategy and a problem-solving strategy are summarized in Figure 6.1. A cooperative problem-solving approach in a group also promotes **creativity**. Creativity is a process of bringing something new into existence; it results from productive controversy. Because a problem is viewed from new perspectives, new alternatives can be suggested and formulated for resolving the problem.

Deutsch has identified three means of fostering creativity in a group[14]: (1) an appropriate level of motivation for finding a viable solution must be aroused, (2) there must be a

FIGURE 6.1 Win-Lose Strategy Versus Problem-Solving Strategy

WIN-LOSE STRATEGY	PROBLEM-SOLVING STRATEGY
The conflict is defined as a win-lose situation.	The conflict is viewed as a problem.
Each side seeks solutions to meet only its need.	Each person seeks to find solutions to meet the needs of all members.
Each side attempts to force the other side into submission.	Each person cooperates with others to find mutually acceptable compromises.
Each side increases its power by emphasizing its independence from the other and the other's dependence upon itself.	Each person equalizes power by emphasizing interdependence.
Each side inaccurately, deceitfully, and misleadingly communicates its goals, needs, and ideas; information inconsistent or harmful to one's position is not shared.	Each person honestly and openly communicates goals, needs, and ideas.
No expression of empathy or understanding is made of the views, values, and opinions of the other side.	Efforts are made to convey empathy and understanding of the views, values, and opinions of others.
Threats are used to attempt to force the other side into submission.	Threats are avoided to reduce the defensiveness of others.
Rigid adherence to one's position is expressed.	A willingness to be flexible is expressed.
Changes in position are made very slowly in an effort to force concessions from the other side.	Positions are changed readily to help in problem solving.
No suggestions are sought from third parties, as the focus is on forcing the other side to give in.	Third parties are sought to help in problem solving.

cooperative problem-solving atmosphere in the group that allows members to reformulate the problem once an impasse has been reached, and (3) diverse ideas must be suggested or available that can be flexibly put together into new and varied solutions.

Groups are most creative when the motivational level is high enough for members to maintain problem-solving efforts despite frustrations and dead ends. However, this level should not be so high that it overwhelms the group by causing members to become too tense to concentrate. Excessive tension leads to defensiveness and reduces receptiveness to innovative approaches. Too much anxiety inhibits members from fully expressing their views, interferes with their listening to the views of others, and often leads to closed-mindedness.

Creative group members seek out different ways of looking at the problem and innovative ways of resolving it in an open-minded way. That is, a member assesses relevant information based on its *own* merits, not on how it resembles or differs from his or her own ideas, opinions, and assumptions. When conflict occurs between two members, each can listen to the other's criticisms, judge their validity fairly, and suggest new strategies that take into account both members' concerns. This leads to a creative solution to the problem.

In contrast, a closed-minded person views relevant information from his or her own assumptions, beliefs, and frame of reference.[15] Closed-minded members emphasize the differences between what they believe and do not believe, ignoring or denying information contrary to their value system. They tend to have contradictory beliefs that they fail to question, and in their efforts to defend these beliefs, they stifle creativity.

Role Reversal

A useful strategy in resolving both intragroup and intergroup conflict is role reversal. The basic rule for role reversal is this: *Each person expresses his or her opinions or views only after restating the ideas and feelings of the opposing person.* These ideas and feelings should be restated in one's own words rather than parroted or mimicked in the exact words of the other person. It is advisable to begin the restatement with words such as "Your position is . . . ," "You seem to be saying . . . ," or "You apparently feel . . ." Approval or disapproval, blaming, giving advice, interpreting, or persuading should be avoided.

EXERCISE 6.3   Creativity Inspired by Conflict

GOAL: This exercise is designed to help you understand how conflict often inspires creativity.

Describe a conflict that you had with someone that inspired a creative solution that was satisfying to you and to the other person.

In addition, nonverbal messages should be consistent with the verbal paraphrasing and convey interest, openness, and attentiveness to the opposition's ideas and feelings. Above all, role reversal should be the expression of a sincere interest in understanding the other person's feelings, ideas, and position.

Role reversal can result in a reevaluation and a change of attitude concerning the issue by both parties because the group members involved are apt to be perceived as people who are understanding, willing to compromise, cooperative, and trustworthy.[16] The approach has also been found to increase cooperative behavior between role reversers, to clarify misunderstandings, to change win-lose situations into problem-solving situations, and, most important, to allow the issue to be perceived from the opponent's frame of reference.

A shortcoming of this approach is that some people do not like being forced to repeat the words spoken by the person they are in conflict with. Other people do not like hearing the words they have just spoken repeated. For both of these types of people, the following technique is often more acceptable and more effective.

Empathy

A technique closely related to role reversal is the expression of empathy. Empathy involves putting yourself in the shoes of the person you are in conflict with and expressing your understanding of what she is thinking and saying. Some examples of phrases that are useful in helping you express empathy are:

"What you seem to be saying is . . ."
"I take it that you think . . ."
"I sense that you feel _____ about this issue."

When expressing empathy, it is essential to mirror what was said in a nonjudgmental way that will help you grasp the essence of what the other person is thinking or feeling.

Similar to role reversal, empathy is used to facilitate open communication, assist in clarifying misunderstandings, increase cooperative behavior, and facilitate the process of no-lose problem solving.

Inquiry

If you are in conflict with someone and you are confused regarding his or her thoughts and feelings, the inquiry technique may be useful. This technique involves using gentle, probing questions to learn more about what the other person is thinking and feeling. Tone of voice is crucial in inquiry because asking a question sarcastically or defensively is apt to draw defensive responses from the person you are in conflict with.

I-Messages

As described in Chapter 5, the technique of using I-messages also facilitates more open and honest communication between parties in conflict. In contrast, you-messages tend to increase defensiveness between parties in conflict.

Disarming

When you are in conflict with someone, using the disarming technique is frequently an effective strategy in resolving the conflict. The disarming technique involves finding some truth in what the other person (or side) is saying and then expressing your "agreement"—even if you feel that the other person is largely wrong, unreasonable, irrational, or unfair. There is always a grain of truth in what the other person says, even if it sounds obnoxious and insulting. When you disarm the other person with this technique, the individual will recognize that you respect him or her. Once disarmed, the other person will not feel so dogmatic and will be less likely to insist that he or she is entirely right and you are entirely wrong. As a result, the individual is apt to be more willing to examine the merits of your point of view. If you want respect, *give* respect first. If you want to be listened to, disarming helps you listen to the other person first and facilitates open (rather than defensive) communication. Friendly responses facilitate open communication, whereas hostile responses usually produce defensive communication.

In using the disarming technique, it is important to be genuine in what you say and to express your agreement sincerely.

Stroking

Closely related to disarming, stroking is saying something genuinely positive to the person (or side) you are in conflict with, even in the heat of battle. Stroking tells the other person that you respect him or her, even though both of you may be angry. During an argument or conflict, you are apt to feel the need to reject the other person before you get rejected (to "save face"). Often, people overreact and differences of opinion are blown out of proportion. To prevent this rejection, simply let the other person know that, although you are at odds, you still think highly of him or her. This makes it easier for the other person to open up and to listen because he or she will feel less threatened.

Letting Go or Forgiving

If we hold a long-term grudge against someone, we are primarily hurting (both emotionally and healthwise) ourselves. Emotionally we hurt ourselves by being in a state of periodic anger (which occurs when we think about the perceived "wrong"). By holding a grudge, we also raise our level of stress, which, as described in Chapter 11, often leads to a variety of stress-related illnesses. Mentally nursing a grudge puts your body through the same strains as a major stressful event—muscles tense, blood pressure rises, and sweating increases.

Two strategies to get rid of holding a long-term grudge are "letting go" and forgiving. With the "letting go" strategy, we reframe our thinking so that we no longer dwell on the perceived wrong. One way of reframing our thinking is to do a rational self-analysis (described in Module 1). If there is no way to change a perceived "wrong," the best thing we can do for our mental and physical well-being is to "let go" of it.

Forgiveness is actually another strategy for "letting go." When you forgive someone who has hurt you, you make yourself—rather than the person who hurt you—responsible for your happiness.

Mediation

In the past two decades, mediation has increasingly been used to resolve conflicts between disputing groups. The federal government established federal mediators way back in 1913 to help resolve issues between employers and employees.[17] It was expected that mediated

EXERCISE 6.4 Disarming and Stroking

GOAL: This exercise is designed to assist you in understanding and applying disarming and stroking to resolve conflict.

1. Describe an experience where two people were having a conflict (one of those people may have been you) and the conflict was resolved (at least partially) by one of the people using disarming or stroking.

2. Summarize your thoughts on the merits and shortcomings of disarming and stroking in resolving conflict.

settlements would prevent costly strikes or lockouts for workers and employers alike and that the welfare and safety of Americans would be protected. Federal use of mediation in labor disputes set a precedent for many states to pass laws and train a cadre of mediators to handle intrastate labor conflicts.

The Civil Rights Act of 1964 created the Community Relations Service of the U.S. Department of Justice to use mediation to resolve disputes relating to discriminatory practices based on race, color, or national origin.[18] Diverse private agencies, civil rights commissions, and state agencies now use mediation to handle charges of sex, race, and ethnic discrimination. The federal government funds neighborhood justice centers that provide free or low-cost mediation services to the public to resolve disputes informally, inexpensively, and efficiently.[19] Disputes settled through mediation are resolved much more efficiently and creatively than those resolved in court. Mediation is also used in schools and colleges to settle disputes between students, between students and faculty, between faculty members, and between faculty and administration. The criminal justice system uses mediation to resolve disputes in correctional facilities, for example, prison riots, hostage negotiations, and institutionalized grievance procedures.

Mediation is also used extensively in family disputes involving child custody and divorce proceedings, disputes between parents and children, conflicts involving adoption and the termination of parental rights, and domestic violence situations.

Moore states, "In family disputes, mediated and consensual settlements are often more appropriate and satisfying than litigated or imposed court outcomes."[20]

Mediation is used to settle disputes between business partners, private individuals, governmental agencies and individuals, landlords and tenants, businesses and customers, and in personal injury cases.

Many professionals now occasionally act as mediators to help people or groups in conflict resolve their concerns. Such professionals include attorneys, social workers, psychologists, and guidance counselors. A few social workers, attorneys, and other professionals are working full time as mediators—often in public or private mediation agencies.

Moore defines mediation as follows:

> Mediation involves the intervention of an acceptable, impartial, and neutral third party who has no authoritative decision-making power to assist contending parties in voluntarily reaching their own mutually acceptable settlement of issues in dispute . . . Mediation leaves the decision-making power in the hands of the people in conflict. Mediation is a voluntary process in that the participants must be willing to accept the assistance of the intervener if the dispute is to be resolved. Mediation is usually initiated when the partners no longer believe that they can handle the conflict on their own and when the only means of resolution appears to involve impartial third-party assistance.[21]

There are various models of the mediation process.[22] As an illustration, the model developed by Blades will be summarized.[23] According to Blades, the mediation process involves five stages:

1. *Introduction/Commitment:* This first stage usually is accomplished in a 1- to 2-hour session. The mediator sets ground rules, describes mediation, answers questions, discusses fees, and seeks to gain a commitment to the process from the two parties. The mediator also seeks to develop an understanding of the more pressing issues, gains a sense of the personal dynamics of the two parties, and tries to ascertain whether they are ready and willing to mediate. If one or both of the parties are not willing to mediate, then the mediation probably should not proceed. If one or both of the parties are hesitant to proceed, the mediator usually describes the alternatives to mediation— such as a lengthy and expensive court battle.

2. *Definition:* The two parties, with the mediator's assistance, define the areas in which they already agree and disagree. Certain disputes, such as division of property issues in divorce mediation, are apt at this stage to require a considerable amount of information.

3. *Negotiation:* Once the two parties agree on the issues in conflict and relevant factual information on these issues is obtained, the two parties are ready to begin negotiating. At this stage the mediator seeks to have the parties focus on one issue at a time. A problem-solving approach is used in which the needs of each party are first identified and alternatives are generated. The mediator recedes into the background when discussions are proceeding well and steps in when emotions intensify or when the two parties are overlooking creative solutions that will meet their needs.

4. *Agreement:* Once alternatives are generated and related facts are evaluated, the two parties are ready to begin making agreements on the issues. The role of the mediator is to maintain a cooperative atmosphere and to keep the two parties focused on a manageable number of issues. The mediator summarizes areas of agreement and provides legal or other information necessary to a discussion. The mediator helps the two parties examine the merits and shortcomings of the options. During this stage the mediator praises the parties for the progress they are making and gets them to praise themselves for progress made. A mediator seeks to create a positive atmosphere.

5. *Contracting:* In this final stage of mediation, the two parties review the agreements and clarify any ambiguities. The agreements are almost always written in the form of a contract, which is available for future reference. Either party, the mediator, or everyone together may do the actual writing of the contract. The contract expresses what each party agrees to do and may set deadlines for the diverse tasks to be completed. It also specifies consequences if either party fails to meet the terms of the contract. Mediators seek to have specific agreements stated in concrete form to prevent future controversies. The ultimate goal of mediation is a contract in which no one is a loser and that both parties willingly abide by.

One of the major techniques a mediator uses is a caucus.[24] At times a mediator or either party may stop the mediation and request a caucus. In a caucus the two parties are physically separated from each other, and there is no direct communication between them. The mediator meets with one of the parties or with both parties individually. There are a wide variety of reasons for calling a caucus. A caucus may be used to vent intense emotions privately, to clarify misperceptions, to reduce unproductive or repetitive negative behavior, to seek clarification of a party's interests, to provide a pause for each party to consider an alternative, to convince an uncompromising party that the mediation process is better than going to court, to uncover confidential information, to educate an inexperienced disputant about the processes of mediation, or to design alternatives that will later be brought to a joint session.

Some parties are willing in a caucus to privately express possible concessions. Usually such concessions are conditional upon the other party making certain concessions. By the use of caucuses, a mediator can go back and forth, relaying information from one party to the other and seek to develop a consensus.

What If These Strategies Do Not Work?

If used appropriately, these strategies will help resolve interpersonal conflicts in the vast majority of cases. When these strategies fail to work, you can probably correctly conclude that the person you are in conflict with does not really want to resolve the conflict. Perhaps the other person is a hostile person who wants to generate conflicts to meet his or her personal needs in order to vent his or her anger and hostility. Or perhaps the other person really wants to be in conflict with you in order to make your life uncomfortable.

What can you do when you become aware that the other person really wants to sustain the conflict with you? Using the Law of Requisite Variety is an option. This law states that if you continue to creatively come up with new ways of responding to the daggers being thrown at you, eventually the other person will grow tired of the turmoil and will finally decide to bury the hatchet. Two examples are presented in Figure 6.2.

FIGURE 6.2   Two Examples of Using the Law of Requisite Variety

Janice and Pete Palmer were married about a year ago. Unknown to Janice, Pete was having lunch about once a month with a former partner (Paula) whom he dated over a 3-year period. Seven months ago Janice walked into a restaurant at noon and saw her husband with Paula. In a fit of rage, Janice stomped out. That evening she and Pete had a major uproar about this. Pete claimed Paula was just a friend and that nothing romantic was occurring. Janice yelled and screamed. Pete indicated he would stop having lunch with Paula. But he did not keep his promise. About once a month he continued to see Paula, and when Janice found out, there was a major argument. Janice suggested a number of resolution options, including marriage counseling. Pete refused to go to counseling and indicated he had decided (the win-lose approach) that he was going to continue having lunch with Paula. Then one day Janice ran into one of her former partners—Dave. Dave invited Janice for lunch or dinner. A light bulb went on for Janice—she accepted the invitation and made plans for dinner. She went home and gleefully told Pete she ran into Dave (who Pete knew had dated Janice in the past). Pete became jealous and tried to talk Janice out of having dinner with Dave. Janice said "No way. If it's OK for you to see Paula, then it follows that it's OK for me to see Dave." Pete was in anguish during the time Janice and Dave were having dinner. When Janice came home, Pete politely said he had called Paula that evening to inform her he was canceling their next scheduled lunch and that he felt it was best that they no longer meet for lunch. Pete then asked Janice if she also would no longer get together with Dave. She said, "Yes." Through this experience, Pete and Janice learned to respect and appreciate each other to a greater extent.

Vicki Stewart was a secretary for an attorney, Randy Fuller, who frequently criticized her and never complimented her. The harder she sought to perform well, the more, it seemed she was criticized. She tried a variety of resolution strategies—discussing the conflict with him, discussing it with his supervisor, and making a point of complimenting him to set a good example. Nothing worked. Finally, she decided upon a new approach. Mr. Fuller's grammar and spelling were atrocious. Ms. Stewart always improved the spelling and grammar when given rough drafts from Mr. Fuller and the other attorneys in the office. When Mr. Fuller gave her a rough draft of a legal brief to the state supreme court, Ms. Stewart typed it as is and sent it after Mr. Fuller signed it (he frequently signed such documents without proofreading them). When Mr. Fuller finally read the brief 3 weeks later, he was first angry and then discussed the matter with his supervisor. His supervisor at first laughed and then informed Mr. Fuller that in order to avoid a similar situation in the future, he needed to show appreciation to Ms. Stewart. After a few more days of reflecting about it, Mr. Fuller decided it was in his personal interest to display more respect and appreciation to Ms. Stewart.

INTERGROUP CONFLICT

Just as there is conflict within groups, conflicts often arise *between* groups. Within a single organization, various groups are often forced to vie for funding, human resources, and power. For example, in a university, members of different department faculties (for example, sociology, psychology, social work) may have conflicts over which department will receive authorization to add a new course (such as human sexuality), which department will be given a new faculty position, what the budget allocation for each department will be, and which department will use what human service agencies for field placements for students.

As with intragroup conflict, the sides involved in intergroup (or between-group) conflict can use either a win-lose approach or a no-lose problem-solving approach to attempt to resolve the conflict. The same advantages and disadvantages described for intragroup conflicts hold true for intergroup conflicts.

When the conflicts are formulated in terms of win-lose situations, the results are both predictable and destructive.[25] Each group becomes much more cohesive as members join together to defend their group against attack; members will close ranks and frequently put aside intragroup conflicts. Group members become more willing to accept autocratic leadership because rapid, consistent decisions must be made and "a solid front" presented. The groups in conflict tend to become more polarized as each perceives its position as right and moral, and the opposing groups are belittled and devalued. Members' satisfaction with the group increases because they feel an increased sense of identity with their group and an increased sense of belonging.

Hostility increases between the two groups. Distortions in perceptions increase as each group highlights the best parts of itself and the worst parts of the other group. Communication and interaction between the groups decrease as each group assigns inaccurate and uncomplimentary stereotypes to the opposing group and views it as distinctly inferior.

EXERCISE 6.5　Resolving Your Conflicts Effectively

GOAL: This exercise is designed to assist you in learning how to resolve interpersonal conflicts more effectively.

1. Describe a serious interpersonal conflict that you had with someone who was important to you.

2. What conflict resolution strategies did you use to attempt to resolve the conflict?

3. What conflict resolution strategies did the other person seek to use?

4. Has the conflict been successfully resolved? If "yes," describe what led to the resolution. If "no," specify why it has not been resolved.

5. Review the conflict resolution techniques described in this chapter. Specify those that you believe might have been effective in more rapidly resolving the conflict. Provide an explanation for your views.

6. Which conflict resolution techniques do you intend to use in the future?

Because group members often misinterpret the other side's position, distrust is heightened, and negotiators are often selected from each group to work out differences. These negotiators tend to be the most militant leaders of each group and tend to assert only their group's position rather than work toward a creative agreement that will meet the needs of all sides. They want at any cost to avoid giving in so that they are not branded as losers or traitors. If a third party is brought in to decide the dispute, the winning side will view the third party as fair and objective, whereas the losing side will view the third party as biased, thoughtless, and irrational.

There are two usual outcomes when intergroup conflict is cast in a win-lose mold. One outcome is a stalemate, in which the opposing groups continue battling and remain deadlocked, perhaps for years. In the other outcome, one side wins and the other side loses.

The side that loses initially loses cohesiveness and may even disband. Members analyze the reasons for losing, often place blame, and then quarrel among themselves. Previous unresolved conflicts surface and tension increases. The group often finds a scapegoat, such as the leader, the third-party negotiator, or the least conforming members of the group. If an "ineffective" leader is blamed for the defeat, he or she may be replaced. Through a reassessment of the loss, the group reshapes some of its goals and reexamines its positive stereotypes of itself and its negative stereotypes of the opposing groups. This, in effect, may lead to a more realistic assessment of itself and of the opposing groups. Once a loss has been accepted, a losing group that sees hope of victories in the future may reorganize and again become effective. If future victories appear impossible, members may become so demoralized, depressed, and apathetic that they drift away from the group or become uninvolved and nonproductive.

The group that wins generally celebrates and feels a strong sense of cohesion. It becomes self-satisfied, loses its fighting spirit, and members tend to relax, perhaps even becoming playful, while putting forth little effort for group work. Consequently, the winning group makes few changes—it is content.

In contrast to the win-lose approach, a problem-solving strategy can be used to resolve intergroup conflict through a variety of structural arrangements. One arrangement is for the leaders or representatives of each group to meet, or, if the groups are small enough, a meeting of *all* the members involved can be scheduled. If necessary, a mediator can be chosen to call a meeting of representatives from the groups, or an ongoing committee of representatives from each group can be selected to work on present conflicts and new issues.

Calling a meeting is the easy part; the hard part is to convince each side that it is in the best interest of everyone to use a problem-solving approach. The benefits of using a problem-solving approach for intergroup conflict are the same as those described for intragroup conflict in this chapter. One way of pointing the conflicting groups in this direction is to (1) briefly summarize the disadvantages and likely future problems in using a win-lose approach, (2) indicate the potential benefits to all sides in using a problem-solving approach, and (3) ask the groups in conflict to try the problem-solving approach.

The most important point about intergroup conflict is that it is much better if each side uses a cooperative, problem-solving approach rather than a win-lose approach. Group leaders must be aware that it is very difficult to undo the negative feelings and resentments that result from a competitive win-lose situation. If need be, third-party mediators or arbitrators should be brought in early in a win-lose conflict to turn the situation around.

The win-lose strategy and the no-lose problem-solving strategy are frequently mutually exclusive. If two groups are in conflict, negotiators for each side cannot be both honest and deceitful. They cannot simultaneously convey and withhold empathy and understanding or use threats to win and avoid threats in order to reduce defensiveness. Moreover, these negotiators cannot simultaneously be flexible and rigid.

Although the problem-solving approach is by far the most desirable, a win-lose approach may be necessary when an opposing side refuses to use a problem-solving strategy. Being open, flexible, and willing to make concessions to a group using a win-lose strategy may increase the chances of being exploited and of losing.

LO 6   Understand That a Second Major Function of Task Groups Is Decision Making

DECISION MAKING

The effectiveness of a group largely depends on its ability to make good, sound decisions on such issues as when to meet, how meetings will be conducted, why the group is meeting, and what it will do. Decisions almost always involve choosing among several different options and reaching a consensus. Members of some groups are only vaguely aware of how decisions are made, whereas others spend hours debating how decisions will be made. Seldom is the same procedure used for arriving at all decisions in a group, as different circumstances warrant varied decision-making processes. In our society, important decisions are usually made by groups rather than individuals. If a problem or issue is complex, a group usually makes a better decision than an individual.[26]

The Bases of Decisions

Most people tend to believe that decisions are made primarily on the basis of objective facts and figures. In fact, values and assumptions form the bases of most decisions, and facts and figures are used only in relation to these subjective, learned experiences. Consider the following list of questions. What do they indicate about how we make our most important decisions?

1. Should abortions be permitted or prohibited during the first weeks following conception?
2. Should homosexuality be viewed as a natural expression of sexuality?
3. When does harsh disciplining of a child become child abuse?
4. When should confidentiality be violated?
5. Should the primary objective of imprisonment be rehabilitation or retribution?

Answers to these questions are not usually based on data uncovered after careful research; they are based on individual beliefs about the value of life, personal freedom, and protective social standards. Even everyday decisions are based largely on values.

Practically every decision is also based on certain **assumptions**. Without assumptions, nothing can be proven. Assumptions are made in every research study to test any hypothesis. In a market survey, for example, analysts assume that the instruments they use (such as a questionnaire) will be valid and reliable. It cannot even be proven the sun will rise in the east tomorrow without assuming that its history provides that proof. The same holds true for groups involved in decision making. For example, if a local group decides that busing should be used to facilitate racial integration, it probably assumes busing will have certain benefits. On the other hand, if a group decides not to use school busing, it is assuming the probable costs will outweigh the predicted benefits. In either case, the assumption cannot be proven beforehand. Proof comes only when the decision is implemented and its effects are evaluated.

The purpose of statistical information and research studies is to test assumptions, hypotheses, and beliefs. All of the following are beliefs held by many Americans:

- The death penalty has a deterrent effect on people who are considering committing serious crimes such as homicide.
- Most welfare recipients are able to work but would rather live it up on welfare.
- Patients with mental illness are more likely to commit a crime than other people.
- Gay men are apt to display effeminate mannerisms.
- Crimes committed by the lower class are the most costly in our society.

That each of these beliefs has been invalidated by research shows the importance of scientifically testing beliefs. Research demonstrates that a country's adoption of a death penalty generally does not result in a decrease in homicide rates or in rates of other serious crimes.[27] Only a small fraction of welfare recipients are able to work—the vast majority cannot work because they are children, are beyond the age of retirement, have a disability, or are homebound mothers with young children.[28] People labeled as mentally ill are no more likely to commit crimes than people considered sane.[29] Gay males are no more apt to be effeminate than male heterosexuals,[30] and white-collar crime appears to be the most costly in our society.[31]

APPROACHES TO DECISION MAKING

Before discussing an issue leading to a decision, a group must know what decision-making approach it will use because different approaches lead to diverse consequences for the future operation of the group. An effective group is aware of these consequences and must choose the best approach considering the amount of time available, the nature of the decision to be made, and the kind of atmosphere the group wants to create. The nature of the task, the history of the group, and the kind of setting in which the group is working must also be considered. Six decision-making approaches will be discussed:

1. Consensus of the group
2. Simple majority vote
3. Two-thirds or three-fourths majority vote
4. Delegated decisions
5. Multiple voting
6. Averaging individual opinions

Consensus

This approach is the most effective for motivating all group members to support and work for the decision because everyone comes to agree with the final decision. This approach is also the most time consuming, as the concerns of each member have to be recognized. Johnson and Johnson describe consensus as follows:

> Consensus is more commonly defined as a collective opinion arrived at by a group of people working together under conditions that permit communications to be sufficiently open— and the group climate to be sufficiently supportive—so that everyone in the group feels he has had his fair chance to influence the decision. When a decision is made by consensus, all members understand the decision and are prepared to support it. Operationally, consensus means that all members can rephrase the decision to show that they understand it, that all members have had a chance to tell how they feel about the decision, and that those members who continue to disagree or have doubts will, nevertheless, say publicly that they are willing to give the decision an experimental try for a period of time.[32]

To use consensus effectively, the group must have a trusting, cooperative atmosphere. Members must feel free to present their views but must do so as clearly and logically as possible. They must refrain from blindly arguing their own individual views and listen to and respect the views of other members. Members should also *avoid* going along with the group if they believe the majority opinion is a mistake. It is dangerous to yield to the majority if the only reason is to avoid conflict and to appear united. This type of conforming can lead to dangerous groupthink, described later in this chapter. Members, however, should yield to the majority opinion if that position appears to have merit and has a fair chance for positive outcomes.

Differences of opinion should be sought and dealt with respectfully. Divergent views increase the chances of reviewing all crucial aspects of an issue, building upon the views of others, and making viable decisions.

The participation of all members is encouraged, with emphasis placed on finding the best solution that everyone can agree on and support. If a group becomes stalemated over two alternatives, a third alternative is often sought to incorporate the major desires of both subgroups. In this way, the group avoids the kind of divisiveness that can occur with other types of decision making, such as voting.

Consensus is difficult to achieve because it requires that members be flexible. They must also understand that the thorough discussion of divergent points of view should lead to a synthesis of ideas, resulting in an innovative, creative, and high-quality decision. Active participation, equally distributed power, and a substantial amount of time are necessary to analyze divergent views and cooperatively synthesize ideas that will be agreeable to everyone.

Because consensus resolves controversies and conflicts, it increases the group's ability to make high-quality decisions in the future. Other forms of decision making do not resolve conflicts and controversies. When group members feel they have participated in the decision and support it, they may contribute more of their resources to implement the decision. Consensus is useful in making important, serious, and complex decisions in which the success of the decision depends upon all members being committed to it.

Simple Majority Vote

Most groups use a simple majority vote approach. Issues are discussed until they are clarified and a vote is then taken.

There are several advantages to this type of decision making. Decisions are arrived at much faster. Most decisions do not warrant the full support of all members. Even groups in which members have little trust in one another can become operational by using a simple majority vote approach. This approach will also work in groups in which communication among members lacks openness and in groups in which some members are unwilling to give up their favorite positions.

However, shortcomings of the simple majority vote approach are numerous. Minority opinions are not always safeguarded. Racial groups, women, certain ethnic groups, lesbian, gay, bisexual and transgender (LGBTQ) groups, and people with a disability have received the brunt of many adverse decisions made by simple majority voting. Majority voting frequently splits a group into winners and losers, and sometimes the number of losers is nearly as great as the number of winners, who can represent as much as 49% of the vote. These losers may feel their concerns are not receiving attention, refuse to support group efforts, and work to subvert or overturn the decision. Obviously, if voting alienates a minority, the future effectiveness of the group is diminished. There is a danger that a majority rule may be interpreted by a minority as being an unfair means of control and manipulation. Therefore, to maintain its effectiveness, groups that use majority voting should create a climate in which members feel they have had their day in court and feel an obligation to support the final group decision.

Two-Thirds or Three-Fourths Majority Vote

A high-percentage majority vote, such as two-thirds or three-fourths, is used primarily for decisions of substantial consequence, such as enacting amendments to the U.S. Constitution or changing the bylaws and constitution of an organization. A high-percentage majority vote is also often used by governmental decision-making units to pass emergency requests for special funds.

This type of vote is a compromise between the consensus and simple majority approaches. A high-percentage majority vote takes more time than a simple majority because more votes are needed, but less time than consensus because not everyone must agree. A strong minority can block a decision, so a small majority cannot force its views on that minority. However, a small minority may still feel controlled and manipulated by a majority rule. A high-percentage majority vote will generally draw stronger support from group members than a simple majority, but it will not generate as much support as consensus. Psychologically, the losing side on a 76% to 24% vote under a three-fourths majority system is more apt to go along with the winning side than if the winning side won by 51% under a simple majority system.

For crucial decisions that require the support of practically all members, it is advisable to reach as strong a majority agreement as possible. A decision not to grant a faculty member tenure, for example, is less likely to be appealed if the vote in a department is 20 to 1 rather than 11 to 10.

Delegated Decisions

Because large groups cannot carefully debate and make all daily decisions, many groups delegate less important decisions to an expert, the group leader, or a subgroup. Subgroups include executive, temporary, and standing committees. However, the types of decisions to be delegated must be well defined to avoid potential conflicts and to limit the authority of group members selected to make less important decisions. In many groups, conflicts and disagreements arise when these limits are not clarified. It is common for group members and leaders to differ on which decisions should be made by the leader and which should be made by the group as a whole. When a leader's decision-making authority is in doubt, the group as a whole should deal with the question. Otherwise, the leader may be criticized for overextending his or her authority.

Expert   Authority can be delegated to the person in the group with the most expertise in a particular area. The expert can review the issues and inform the group of the decision. A major problem is that it is often difficult to determine which member has the most expertise. Personal popularity and power often interfere with the accurate selection of the most expert member. Because the group is leaving the decision to a single member, there is often little or no discussion of options. This may limit the number of viable options that the expert considers. Finally, a decision made by one person may not receive the support of other members to implement it.

Group Leader   A group may allow the leader to make certain decisions. Before making some of these decisions, however, the leader may call a meeting of the group, describe the issues, and use the discussion to arrive at a decision. A chancellor or president of a university often uses this approach by seeking the advice and suggestions of various subgroups. The most time-efficient method is when the leader makes a decision without any group discussion. This procedure works best for uncomplicated, less important issues. Although efficient, it may not be effective. Because the group may not understand the issues, members may disagree with the decision and withhold resources to implement it. If members feel that the leader is overstepping his or her authority, they may retaliate by limiting that authority or by replacing the leader. In addition, without input from the group, a leader is less likely to be fully aware of all the viable courses of action. By involving the group, the leader will hear a variety of options and give group members an opportunity to express their views. Still, if the leader's decision is unpopular, support for implementation will be limited.

Subgroup   Another approach to delegating decisions is to allow a subgroup, such as an executive committee or a temporary committee, to make certain decisions. When a subgroup makes a decision, it should consider the views of the larger group because unpopular decisions are generally not supported. If the subgroup continually makes unpopular decisions, the larger group can retaliate by reviewing the decisions, changing the membership of the subgroup, reducing the subgroup's decision-making powers, or disbanding the subgroup. Subgroups are especially effective when a group has a large number of minor decisions to make and limited time.

Multiple Voting

If an organization has a number of alternatives before it, a series of ballots may be taken until one alternative receives the required number of winning votes. Multiple voting may be done in a variety of ways. In selecting a presidential candidate, both the Republican and Democratic conventions ballot until one candidate receives a majority. Another approach is to keep narrowing the number of choices. For example, if there are 50 options, each member may first vote for five options. The 10 options receiving the most votes are considered in the second round, with members voting for three options. In the third round, the top four options are considered, with members voting for two options each. In the fourth and final round, the top two options are considered, and members vote for one option. With this type of multiple voting, it is essential that the members agree on the voting rules prior to voting. Otherwise, those who want a choice that is not selected may charge, *after* reviewing the results of the voting, that the group leader is arbitrarily and capriciously excluding their favorite choices.

Averaging Individual Opinions

In an emergency, it may not be possible to assemble the members for a meeting. In this situation, the group leader may contact each individual member to obtain his or her vote. The alternative chosen is the one receiving the most votes. Fewer than 50% of the votes could pass the motion, as the other votes may be spread over a variety of options. This approach may also be used for making decisions the leader does not believe are important enough for a group meeting.

However, there are a number of disadvantages to this approach. Without group discussion, many of the members may not be fully aware of all the issues, alternatives, or consequences of the proposal. A poor decision may result because the votes of the least informed members may cancel out the votes of the most knowledgeable. With little involvement, members are unlikely to have much commitment toward implementing the decision. There is also a danger that a subgroup opposed to the decision may feel it has been left out and may work hard to overturn the decision or impede its implementation. Another danger is that the person conducting the vote may influence the members to vote for his or her position.

GROUP VERSUS INDIVIDUAL DECISION MAKING

In theory, the task of making a decision within a group should follow a rational problem-solving process—identify the problem, generate proposed solutions, weigh the merits and shortcomings of proposed solutions, and select the alternative with the fewest risks and the greatest chance of success. In practice, however, subjective influences can impede this process.

We have all heard our share of amusing yet halfway serious anecdotes about "run-around meetings," "inconclusive conclusions," and "slower-than-snails committees." Although group-made decisions have the advantage of being based on a wider variety of information and a greater variety of expertise, they are also susceptible to subjective influences in the group. Without awareness of these subjective obstacles, groups will not necessarily make better decisions than individuals.

Each group member brings not only his or her objective knowledge and expertise to the decision-making process but also his or her subjective experience: unique attitudes, feelings, biases, and vested interests. These will probably not be expressed at the start of a meeting but will be triggered in the course of the ensuing discussion. As the decision-making process continues, there is an increasing tendency for individuals to allow their reactions to one another to interfere with objective thought.

Is group decision making inferior or superior to individual decision making? Individual decision making occurs when decisions are made without group interaction. A leader, an expert, or a poll of individuals makes a decision that must be implemented by the group. There is overwhelming evidence that group decision making is usually superior.[33] This conclusion applies even when the individual decision is made by an expert.

There appear to be several reasons why group decision making is usually superior.[34] Through group interaction, the knowledge, abilities, and resources of each member are pooled. An individual acting alone often lacks the information, skills, or resources needed to arrive at the best decision. Also, working in the presence of others motivates a person to put forth more effort, be more careful, and increase the quality of his or her work. Having more people working on a problem increases the probability that someone in the group will suggest a viable solution. Through group interaction, the members can build on each other's ideas, develop a decision based on this building-block approach, and identify the positive and negative consequences of each alternative. Because it is always easier to identify other people's mistakes than our own, the problem areas in the favorite alternatives of others can be identified and analyzed. In addition, different ways of looking at problems and tasks are more likely to result when different individuals are contributing. Also, when group members have participated in making a decision, they will be more likely to accept and support it.

Although groups are better than the average individual, they may not be better than an outstanding expert. Therefore, a group of novices is apt to perform worse than an expert.

It should be noted, however, that subjective influences can substantially reduce the quality of group decision making. Some group members may alter their actual opinions or hold back relevant information because they do not want to displease others in the group. One or several members may begin to contribute so much to the discussion or state their opinions so forcefully that others begin to resign themselves to being inactive. Arguments that are not pertinent to the issue at hand may take on major significance. For some group members, winning such arguments becomes more important than reaching a decision. Interpersonal attractions and repulsions among group members also influence decision making; some members are inclined to support alternatives of lower quality that are advocated by members they are attracted to, and they are inclined to reject higher-quality alternatives advocated by group members whom they dislike. Sometimes a combination of subjective influences results in the development of *groupthink*.

LO 7   More Effectively Handle Groupthink

GROUPTHINK

Janis first identified groupthink as a result of a study done on groups of U.S. presidential advisors.[35] During this study, he found that powerful social pressures were often exerted when a dissident began to voice objections to what otherwise appeared to be a group consensus. Groupthink is a problem-solving process in which proposals are accepted without a critical, careful review of the pros and cons of the alternatives and in which considerable social pressure is brought to bear against those expressing opposing points of view. Groupthink occurs partially because the norms of the group hold that it is more important to bolster group morale than to evaluate all alternatives critically. Another group norm that increases groupthink is that members should remain loyal by sticking with the policies to which the group is already committed, even when those policies are not working.

Janis has listed a number of factors that promote groupthink:

1. Members have an illusion of being invulnerable, which leads them to become overly optimistic about their selected courses of action. This illusion also leads them to take extraordinary risks and causes them to fail to respond to clear warnings of danger.
2. Members have an unquestioning belief in the moral lightness of their group, which leads them to ignore the ethical consequences of their decisions.
3. The group applies social pressures to display disapproval toward any member who momentarily questions the basic policies of the group or who raises questions about a policy alternative favored by the majority.
4. The group constructs rationalizations to discount warnings and other forms of negative feedback that would, if taken seriously, lead the members to rethink basic assumptions about policies that are not working.
5. Group members hold stereotyped views of the leaders of opposing groups. Opposing group leaders are viewed either as so evil that it would be a mistake to try to negotiate differences or as so stupid or so weak that they will not be able to prevent this group from attaining its objectives.

EXERCISE 6.6   My Groupthink Experience

GOAL: This exercise is designed to assist you in understanding and applying the theoretical material on groupthink.

1. Describe a group experience that you had where you believed the group was going in the wrong direction and you failed to express your thoughts or opinions.

2. Specify why you failed to express your thoughts or opinions.

3. Do you believe your reasons for not expressing your thoughts or opinions are consistent or inconsistent with groupthink? Explain your views.

6. Members sometimes assume "mind guard" roles in which they attempt to protect their leader and the group from negative information that might lead them to question the morality and effectiveness of past decisions.

7. Members keep quiet about their misgivings and even minimize to themselves the importance of these misgivings. Through self-censorship, members avoid deviating from what appears to be group consensus.

8. The members believe practically everyone in the group fully agrees on the policies and programs of the group.

Groupthink spawns a number of poor decision-making practices. The group limits its discussion to those courses of action consistent with past decisions and policies; as a result, more divergent strategies (some of which are viable) are not considered. The group fails to reexamine a selected course of action, even when risks, drawbacks, and unintended consequences become clear. The group makes little effort to get cost–benefit information on possible strategies from appropriate experts. Members seek primarily to obtain facts and listen to opinions that support their preferred policy and tend to ignore facts and opinions that do not. The group fails to work out contingency plans to cope with foreseeable setbacks, and it spends little time considering how the chosen strategy might be sabotaged by political opponents or hampered by bureaucratic red tape.

To prevent the development of groupthink, a group has to be "on guard" about its dangers. Members must realize their selected courses of action may fail and be aware of the ethical consequences of their decisions. The group should welcome the questioning of basic policies by members and realistically assess the merits and shortcomings of the views being expressed by opposing groups. Members should feel free to express their misgivings about the basic policies and strategies of their group. The group should welcome the advancement of new and novel strategies for resolving the problems that it is combating. Finally, the group needs to consistently apply the problem-solving approach in assessing problems, in generating alternatives, in evaluating these alternatives, and in selecting and implementing strategies.

A concept similar to group think is hyperbonding.[36] This occurs when group members became overly connected with one another and may develop unhealthy norms, which are accepted by the majority. The group members have a tendency to want to be overly social instead of focusing on the task assigned to the group. There may be group pressure for all members, including the leader, to conform to these norms. Some of these disruptive behaviors include excessive talking, bringing outside problems of group members into the group setting, and side talk. It is important to recognize this dynamic and call attention to it when it is occurring. The group may need to be reminded of the goals of the group and to refocus on the group task.

Summary

The following summarizes the chapter's content in terms of the learning objectives presented at the beginning of the chapter.

1. Identify a variety of task groups.
   Task groups are used to generate new ideas, to make decisions, and to find solutions to organizational problems. Task groups have three primary purposes: (1) meeting clients' needs, (2) meeting organizational needs, and (3) meeting community needs.

2. Comprehend how to lead task groups.
   Guidelines are presented for effectively leading task groups.

3. Understand that one of the major functions of task groups is problem solving.
   A key strategy that successful task groups generally use is the problem-solving approach. The following barriers to effective problem solving are discussed: inadequate definitions of the problems, invalid hypotheses, poor communication, lack of skills, lack of resources, and lack of motivation.

4. Utilize the brainstorming technique.
   Brainstorming is described, which is a procedure designed to generate ideas in quantity through the full participation of all group members.

5. More effectively resolve interpersonal conflicts.
   Conflicts between members in groups are discussed. Conflicts are an inevitable part of human interactions. Conflicts are only destructive when they are not adequately resolved. The following conflict resolution strategies are presented: win-lose approach, no-lose problem solving, role reversal, empathy, inquiry, I-messages, disarming, stroking, mediation, and the Law of Requisite Variety.

6. Understand that a second major function of task groups is decision making.
   The following approaches to decision making are presented: consensus, simple majority vote, two-thirds or three-fourths majority vote, delegated decisions, multiple voting, and averaging individual opinions. Although group decision making usually leads to higher-quality decisions than those made by the average individual, group decisions (especially when arrived at by a group of novices) may not be better than decisions made by an outstanding expert.

7. More effectively handle groupthink.
   Groupthink is a problem-solving process in which proposals are accepted without a critical, careful review of the pros and cons of the alternatives and in which considerable social pressure is brought to bear against those opposing points of view. Groupthink leads to a number of poor decision-making practices.

Group Exercises

EXERCISE A: Suspended from High School

GOAL: To learn how to use the problem-solving approach in a group.

Step 1. The group leader describes the stages of the problem-solving approach:

1. Identify and define the problem.
2. Assess the size and causes of the problem.
3. Develop alternative strategies or plans for solving it.
4. Assess the merits and shortcomings of these alternative strategies.
5. Select and implement the most desirable strategy or strategies.
6. Evaluate the success of the strategy or strategies used.

Step 2. The class divides into subgroups of four or five students each. Each subgroup is to apply the problem-solving approach to the following situation:

Five students have been suspended for a 4-day period for drinking alcoholic beverages at their high school, which is located in a small city of 5,400. It has been the policy of the school board to suspend any student caught drinking at school. In the past 5 months six students have been suspended. The police department is unhappy with the suspensions because when the students are suspended, they usually loiter on the city streets during school hours. The school social worker contacted the parents of the five suspended students, and only one couple indicated an interest in receiving counseling for their daughter. The other parents stated they were not sufficiently concerned to talk further about the suspensions.

The task of each subgroup is to arrive at answers (and reasons for their answers) to each of the following five questions:

1. What do you see as the most serious problem to deal with?
2. What do you believe are the causes of this problem?
3. What possible strategies could combat this problem?
4. What do you see as the merits and shortcomings of each of these strategies?
5. Which of these strategies would you select to combat the problem you have identified?

Step 3. Each subgroup shares its answers and reasoning with the class. After all of the subgroups have presented their answers, the class discusses why different problems and strategies were defined and selected by the subgroups.

EXERCISE B: Brainstorming

GOAL: To show how to use brainstorming.

Step 1. The leader describes the purpose of brainstorming and its ground rules, as explained in this chapter.

Step 2. The leader gives the class an issue or problem to brainstorm. If the class is very large, subgroups of 10 to 15 students may be formed. The issue or problem should be one that the class has some awareness of and background on. One possible topic: "What do you see as the major problem (without naming any person) in our social work program?"

Step 3. The most important problem should be singled out after the brainstorming is completed. For example, each class member could list his or her choices for the five most serious problems on a note card. A tally could then be made, and the problem receiving the most votes would then be declared the most serious problem.

Step 4. After the most serious problem is determined, a second brainstorming exercise is conducted to generate a list of strategies to resolve it. Following this brainstorming, the most viable strategies should be identified.

Step 5. A discussion elicits the view of the class as to the strengths and shortcomings of brainstorming.

EXERCISE C: Busing to Achieve Racial Integration

GOAL: To observe and negotiate intergroup conflict.

Step 1. The group leader provides the following background information:

All of you live in a middle-class suburb of Middletown, which has had no racial problems. Your suburb is located next to the big city of Skyscraper. A recent study by the federal government has found that four public schools in the inner city of Skyscraper are racially segregated, as 98% of the students are African American. This inner-city school district is spending only half as much money per child on education as is your suburb of Middletown. The dropout rate in these inner-city schools is 55% compared to 10% in Middletown. Only 15% of the graduates from the inner-city schools in Skyscraper go on to college, whereas 65% of the graduates from Middletown go on to college. The federal government has ruled that the school districts in Middletown and Skyscraper must become racially integrated through busing between the systems. Three groups—concerned parents, civil rights activists, and school staff—have been asked by the Middletown School Board to arrive at some recommendations to present to the school board on how to integrate the school districts. The school board of Middletown will act on these recommendations and then propose them to the Skyscraper School Board as a way of implementing the federal government's declaration that the school districts in the two communities must become racially integrated.

Step 2. The class is randomly divided into the three groups. Each group receives a handout that describes the group's views and tasks. (No group should be informed of the views of the other two groups.) The views and tasks are further described in the following material:

Concerned parents: You want what is best for your child. You do not want your child to associate with children from inner-city areas. You are vehemently opposed to a busing system that would send your children to an inner-city school. You are less opposed to students being bused from Skyscraper to Middletown, but you want to keep the number of children who are bused to Middletown as small as possible. You are also concerned that your taxes will increase because of busing. Your group tasks are (1) to develop two to four proposals for possible presentation to the Middletown School Board that will get the federal government off your back while minimizing any possible changes in your child's education and (2) to select a person who will represent your group in negotiations with the other two groups in arriving at a set of proposals to present to the school board.

School staff: Your group is composed of teachers, school administrators, and school social workers. Value-wise, you are in favor of racial integration. You are also in favor of the neighborhood school concept in which the school is a center that serves students and parents in the neighborhood. Therefore, you are unsure whether to support school busing. Some of your staff members fear that juvenile crime, vandalism, and racial clashes will increase if busing occurs. Your tasks are (1) to develop two to four proposals for possible presentation to the Middletown School Board that will creatively further racial integration while interfering very little with the neighborhood school concept in Middletown and (2) to select a person who will represent your group in negotiations with the other two groups in arriving at a set of proposals to present to the school board.

Civil rights activists: Your group is delighted that the federal government has declared that the school districts in Skyscraper and Middletown must become racially integrated. You believe such integration will be highly valuable in reducing racial prejudice and racial discrimination in the future. You are ambivalent about using school busing, but you are unaware of other strategies to integrate schools. Your group is composed of a number of community leaders, generally with a liberal orientation. Members of your group include clergy, social workers, directors of social service agencies, and concerned business leaders. You fear that members of the other two groups may seek to minimize efforts to integrate the school systems. Your tasks are (1) to develop two to four proposals that will fully integrate the school systems and (2) to select a person who will represent your group in negotiations with the other two groups in arriving at a set of proposals to present to the school board.

Step 3. After each group has prepared a set of proposals, the negotiators for the three groups meet to arrive at a consistent set of proposals to present to the Middletown School Board. The other class members observe the negotiations.

Step 4. The group leader defines the win-lose and problem-solving strategies and describes the following techniques that are useful in resolving conflicts: role reversal, stroking, disarming, empathy, I-messages, and inquiry. The class then discusses the following five questions:

1. Did the negotiators arrive at a consistent set of proposals? Why or why not?
2. Did the negotiators use primarily a win-lose or a problem-solving strategy?
3. Did any of the negotiators use the techniques of role reversal, stroking, empathy, I-messages, disarming, or inquiry?
4. How creative were the proposals arrived at by the three groups and the three negotiators?
5. What did the students learn from this exercise?

EXERCISE D: Creative Thinking

GOAL: To gain experience in coming up with answers that require creative thinking.

Note: In doing these exercises on creativity, the group leader is encouraged to add or substitute exercises of his or her own.

Step 1. The group leader explains that questions will be asked that require innovative thinking. The leader may want to create a competition and a game-like atmosphere by dividing the class into two or more subgroups and recording a tally mark on the blackboard when a subgroup shouts out the correct response. (The correct answers are given in Appendix 2.)

1. In counting from 0 to 100, how many 9's do you come across?
2. Two women are playing checkers. They play five games, and each woman wins the same number of games. How come?
3. You are told to take five pills, one every half-hour. How many hours will they last?
4. A yacht in the harbor has a 10-foot ladder hanging over the side. If the tide rises 2 feet an hour, how many hours will it take for the water to reach the top of the ladder?
5. Do they have a Fourth of July in England?
6. Why can't someone living in Washington, DC, be buried west of the Mississippi River?
7. How many outs are there in a baseball inning?
8. A man builds a rectangular house with all four exposures facing south. Then he goes outside and kills a bear. What color is the bear? Where is the house located? (Award a correct response for each answer.)
9. If it takes 3 minutes to boil an egg, how long will it take to boil seven eggs?
10. Assume two cars start to travel toward each other from a distance of 2,000 miles. If car A travels at a rate of 150 mph and car B at 100 mph, how far will each car be from its origin when they meet?
11. A farmer had 3 two-thirds-size haystacks in one field and 6 three-fifths-size haystacks in another field. He put them all together. How many did he have then?
12. "Jill is my niece," said Paul to his sister Karen. "She is not my niece," said Karen," Explain this.
13. If you had 12 dollars and spent all but 4 dollars, how much would you have left?

EXERCISE E: The Manhattan Glass

GOAL: To interact in small groups to solve problems that require creativity.

Step 1. The class divides into subgroups of three students each and receives the necessary materials (such as matches and handouts) for solving the problems. After one subgroup completes the problem, it is declared a winner and all subgroups receive another problem. A tally of which subgroup arrives at the correct answer first for each problem is kept on the blackboard.

Task 1. These 12 matches are positioned to form one large square and four small squares. By changing the position of exactly three matches, reduce the number of squares to three small squares.

Task 2. These four full-sized matches form a Manhattan glass. The half-match is a cherry. By moving just two matches, make another Manhattan glass of the same shape and size with the cherry on the outside. Do not move the cherry.

Task 3. Connect all nine dots with only four straight lines without lifting your pencil from the paper.

Task 4. By drawing only two straight lines, divide this shape into four equal parts with two dots in each part.

Task 5. Place the numbers 1 through 11 in the 11 circles shown so that every 3 numbers in a straight line add up to 18.

EXERCISE F: Brainteasers

GOAL: To creatively arrive at answers to 25 brainteasers.

Step 1. The group leader gives the following 25 brainteasers to each student. The class divides into subgroups of about five people. The groups have 20 minutes to arrive at answers. The leader starts by indicating that the first answer is "sandbox" and instructs each subgroup to write its answers on a sheet of paper.

Step 2. The subgroups exchange papers for grading. The leader reads the right answers and then asks each subgroup how many correct answers it produced.

1 [SAND]	**2** MAN ——— BOARD	**3** STAND ——— I	**4** R /E/A/D/I/N/G	**5** WEAR ——— LONG
6 R ROADS A D S	**7** T O W N	**8** CYCLE CYCLE CYCLE	**9** LE VEL	**10** 0 ——— M.D. Ph.D. B.S.
11 KNEE ——— LIGHTS	**12** II III ——— OO	**13** CHAIR	**14** DICE DICE	**15** T O U C H
16 GROUND ——— feet feet feet feet feet feet	**17** MIND ——— MATTER	**18** He's/Himself	**19** ECNALG	**20** DEATH/LIFE
21 G.I. ——— CCC CC	**22** ——— Program	**23** B L O **C** U S E	**24** J YouUMe S T	**25** mt

---

EXERCISE G: Resolving Conflicts

GOAL: To practice using techniques to resolve conflicts in real-life situations.

Step 1. The leader describes each of the following techniques that are useful in resolving conflicts: role reversal, stroking, no-lose problem solving, disarming, empathy, I-messages, inquiry, and the Law of Requisite Variety. The students are then instructed to try to use one or more of these techniques to resolve interpersonal conflicts that arise in their daily lives during the next seven days. (To facilitate remembering details of their efforts to use these techniques in conflict situations, students are instructed to record the details of the incidents in a journal.)

Step 2. After a week or so, the leader asks in class for volunteers to (1) describe which techniques they used, (2) briefly summarize the details of the conflict they encountered, and (3) reveal the extent to which the techniques were useful in resolving the conflict. (If no one volunteers, the leader should cite one or two examples of how he or she used these techniques to resolve interpersonal conflicts in the recent past. Such sharing by the leader may lead others to share their experiences.)

EXERCISE H: Funding Social Programs Involves Hard Choices

GOAL: To analyze how decisions are made, to understand that most decisions are based on values and assumptions, and to realize that setting budgets for social programs involves hard choices because of scarce resources.

Step 1. The group leader states that funding sources (such as the federal, state, and local governments or United Way) have to make difficult choices about how much money to allocate to diverse social programs. Financial resources to fund all social programs are simply unavailable, and some people suffer greatly because they do not receive the needed services and funds.

Step 2. The group divides into subgroups of five or six students. A person from each subgroup volunteers to be an observer for that group. The observer's role is to record information during the exercise related to the following four questions:

1. Which decision-making procedures were used by the group? Possible procedures include consensus, simple majority voting, two-thirds or three-fourths majority voting, and multiple voting. (These procedures should be briefly defined for the observers; the definitions may be given on a handout.)
2. What values and assumptions were expressed as reasons for the decision the subgroup made?
3. Which members appeared to have the most influence in arriving at a decision?
4. What did the influential members say or do to influence the subgroup?

After the exercise is over, the observers will be asked to share this information with the class. The observers should not vote or participate in the discussion of the subgroup.

Step 3. Each subgroup is informed that it is the funding source for a local community and that it has $10 million to allocate for the following social programs, which need a total of $15 million. Each subgroup has the task of deciding how much money to allocate to each agency. No subgroup can go over the $10 million limit. (The group leader should distribute the following information on a handout.)

The Center for Developmental Disabilities needs $1.5 million to care for individuals who have severe cognitive disabilities. All of these individuals are so intellectually affected that they are unable to walk. It costs $220,000 a year to care for each individual. If the center does not receive its requested funds, there is a danger that some of these clients may not receive the necessary medical care and may die.

The Anti-Poverty Agency needs $3.5 million to maintain families at an income level of only 80% of that defined as the poverty line. It costs $18,500 per year to maintain a family of three (generally a single parent with two children). If the agency does not receive its requested funds, there is a danger that many of these families will go hungry, have inadequate shelter, and lack essential clothing for winter.

Protective Services needs $1 million to combat abuse, neglect, and incest. If the agency does not receive all of its needed funds, there is the danger that a number of children will continue to be exposed to abuse, neglect, or incest, which could severely affect them for the rest of their lives.

The Mental Health Center needs $2.5 million to help clients with severe emotional problems, some of whom are so depressed they are suicidal. If the center does not receive all of its needed funds, inadequate services will be provided to clients, and there is a danger that the problems of many clients will intensify. A few may even take their own lives.

The Alcohol and Drug Abuse Treatment Center needs $2 million to help chemically dependent clients and their families. If the center does not receive all of its needed funds, inadequate services will mean the problems experienced by the clients and their families are apt to intensify. Because alcohol and drug abuse are contributing factors to many other problems (such as poverty, mental illness, and family violence), there is a danger these problems will also intensify.

The Shelter for Battered Women, which is located in a house in a residential area, is requesting $500,000. If funds are cut back, the shelter staff assert they will have to turn away some of the battered women and their children who need shelter and other services.

Group Homes for Youths runs four group homes—two for young women and two for young men. It needs $500,000. If needed funds are cut back, this agency will have to reduce the number of youths it is serving. Some will be transferred to more expensive residential treatment programs, some returned to unhealthy home environments, and some will simply run away.

The Red Cross needs $1 million for its blood bank and for disaster relief. If funds are cut back, there is a danger there will be an insufficient supply of blood available for transfusions, and many of the families who are hit by disasters (such as tornadoes and floods) will not be served.

The Rehabilitation Center provides work training and sheltered work to clients with a variety of physical or mental disabilities. It needs $2 million, or it will be forced to turn away clients. If clients are turned away, they will lose hope of becoming productive and perhaps self-supporting and will end up requesting assistance from the Mental Health Center and the Anti-Poverty Agency.

Equal Rights is an agency providing a wide range of services to racial minorities in the area—work training, job placement, and housing location. It also investigates and takes legal action against employers and landlords charged with racial discrimination. The agency needs $500,000. If funds are cut back, there is a danger that discrimination against racial minorities will increase.

Step 4. Each subgroup shares with the class its decisions for allocating funds and the reasons behind them. (The cuts that are made can be summarized on the blackboard by having the leader list the names of the agencies and then having a representative from each subgroup list the amount of money that was cut—totaling $5 million—from the requested allocations.) Ask the subgroup members to share their feelings about the exercise. After each subgroup finishes, the observer for that subgroup should inform the class of the answers to the four questions listed in Step 2. The leader should ask if anyone noted that the Shelter for Battered Women, which has one house, was requesting the same amount of money as Group Homes for Adolescent Youth, which runs four group homes.

EXERCISE I: Consensus

GOAL: To learn about the complexities of arriving at a consensus on an issue when people hold strongly divergent views.

Step 1. The group leader defines a consensus and describes the group atmosphere necessary to reach a consensus.

Step 2. The class is given a controversial issue to discuss and bring to a consensus. For example, the class may be asked whether it supports physician-assisted suicide for persons who are terminally ill who are expected to live less than six months.

Step 3. After the exercise is over, the students discuss their feelings about the pressure to arrive at a consensus in the face of strongly divergent views and why the class was, or was not, able to arrive at a consensus.

EXERCISE J: Subjective Influences on Merit Raises

GOAL: To demonstrate that group decisions are often substantially affected by subjective influences.

Step 1. Six students volunteer to play the roles of social work faculty members on a merit committee at a university. The department has 18 faculty members, and six of these members have applied for "superior" merit increases. The committee has a total of $12,000, all of which must be distributed to these six applicants. The three areas of recognizing merit increases are teaching excellence, research and publishing, and services to the campus and the community.

The decision on how much money to distribute to each applicant rests entirely with this committee. The committee may recommend that all, or nearly all, of the $12,000 be distributed to one or two applicants, with the others receiving little or none, or the committee may distribute the money fairly evenly among the applicants. The committee is provided with the information in Table 6.1 about the meritorious activities of the applicants. (This information may be displayed on the chalkboard or on individual sheets distributed to the class.).

Step 2. The leader hands out an individual "additional information card" to each role-player. Each card has a one-sentence description of one of the applicants. The other role-players are not allowed to see the information on the card. (These cards should be prepared in advance.) Each card provides information likely to foster a strong personal reaction toward the respective faculty member. The role-players are told they are free to bring up the information on their cards during the role-playing or to disregard the information. The leader is free to be creative in writing the additional information on the cards. The following are some appropriate examples:

"Garcia is planning to retire next year, so a significant merit increase would not only recognize his years of public service to the community, but would also substantially increase the pension he will receive after retirement because monthly payments from the pension plan are based on a teacher's last three earning years."

"Pagel, a single mother with three young children, is working on her doctorate and is by far the lowest-paid member of the department; in fact, she's barely able to financially provide for her family."

"Riesen is married but is also secretly dating one of the female students in the social work program; he refuses to advise students or to serve on departmental committees."

TABLE 6.1

Faculty Member	Summary and Meritorious Activities	Teacher Rating[1]
Juan Garcia	Served on university budget committee. Is president of the board of directors of the United Way in the community.	4.1
Karen Pagel	Attended two professional conferences. Is the faculty advisor to the Student Social Work Club.	4.2
Dale Riesen	Published a social work textbook and two articles in professional journals.	3.5
Jean Duvey	Is chair of the department and did the bulk of the work needed to achieve reaccreditation of the social work program by the Council on Social Work Education.	4.0
Kevin Aaron	Wrote and received a grant on "Long Instance Social Work Education" that brought $150,000 to the program for using communication technology to provide social work education classes to other communities in the state.	3.9
Joyce Jackson	Presented three papers on child abuse intervention at national conferences.	4.3

[1] Based on student course evaluations. (5 = highest, 1 = lowest)

"Duvey works many more hours for the department than any other faculty member, but much of the work that she does (paperwork and advising of prospective students) goes unnoticed by the other faculty members."

"Aaron is addicted to alcohol (he was recently involved in a drunk-driving accident and left the scene of the accident in which someone was injured); he refuses to acknowledge his alcohol abuse and has hidden the drunk-driving incident from the other social work faculty members and the university administration."

"Jackson has been extremely helpful to you and the other young instructors in the department, but her mentoring of young faculty members has not been recognized financially by the campus."

Step 3. The role-players discuss the applicants for merit awards. The role-players are given an opportunity to share their additional information about one faculty member. Also, if they desire, they can fabricate and share additional information (which may be positive or negative in nature) about the faculty member listed on their cards. The role-players then end up making decisions about how much money to assign to each of the six applicants.

Step 4. The role-players and the class then process the decisions that were arrived at by discussing the following kinds of questions:

1. Did the additional information—and/or any other subjective information that was fabricated—play an important role in determining the amount of the merit raises assigned to the six applicants?
2. Did the role-players reveal the additional information on their cards in the group discussions? Why or why not?
3. What were the key values (such as quality teaching or family values) that contributed to the decisions that were made?
4. In making group decisions such as this one which tends to have greater weight—objective information or subjective information?

Competency Notes

EP 1c   Demonstrate professional demeanor in behavior; appearance; and oral, written, and electronic communication.

EP 6a   Apply knowledge of human behavior and the social environment, person-in-environment, and other *multidisciplinary theoretical frameworks* to engage with clients and constituencies

The content and exercises in this chapter are designed to enhance the capacities of students to participate in and lead task groups.

Key Terms and Concepts

Assumptions	Creativity	No-Lose Problem-Solving
Coalitions	Delegate Councils	Approach
Conflict		Team Building

Working with Diverse Groups

The profession of social work has had a long tradition of seeking to protect the rights of vulnerable populations and advocating equal opportunities for their members. For example, the *Code of Ethics* of the National Association of Social Workers (NASW) states:

> Social workers should act to prevent and eliminate domination, exploitation, and discrimination against any person, group, or class on the basis of race, ethnicity, national origin, color, age, religion, sex, sexual orientation, marital status, political belief, mental or physical disability, or any other preference, personal characteristic, or status.[1]

The *Code* also states:

> Social workers should act to expand choice and opportunity for all persons, with special regard for vulnerable, disadvantaged, oppressed, and exploited persons and groups.

> Social workers should promote conditions that encourage respect for the diversity of cultures and social diversity within the United States and globally.[2]

LO 1 Define Key Terms Involving Diversity

EP 2a
EP 2b
EP 2c
EP 3a
EP 3b

DEFINITIONS OF KEY TERMS

Unfortunately, there has been a long history of prejudice, discrimination, and oppression against vulnerable populations in our culture. Some definitions may be useful.

Prejudice means prejudging, making a judgment in advance of due examination. Prejudice is a combination of stereotyped beliefs and negative attitudes, so that prejudiced individuals think about members of a minority group in a predetermined, usually negative, categorical way.

Discrimination involves taking action against people because they belong to a category. Discriminatory behavior often derives from prejudiced attitudes.

Merton, however, notes that prejudice and discrimination can occur independently of each other. Merton describes four different "types" of people:

1. The *unprejudiced nondiscriminator*, in both belief and practice, upholds American ideals of freedom and equality. This person is not prejudiced against other groups and, on principle, will not discriminate against them.
2. The *unprejudiced discriminator* is not personally prejudiced but may sometimes, reluctantly, discriminate against other groups because it seems socially or financially convenient to do so.
3. The *prejudiced nondiscriminator* feels hostile to other groups but recognizes that law and social pressures are opposed to overt discrimination. This person does not translate prejudice into action.

4. The *prejudiced discriminator* does not believe in the values of freedom and equality and consistently discriminates against other groups in both word and deed.[3]

An example of an unprejudiced discriminator is the owner of a condominium complex in an all-white, middle-class suburb who refuses to sell a condominium to an African American family because he fears that doing so will reduce the value of the remaining units. An example of a prejudiced nondiscriminator is a personnel director of a fire department who believes Hispanics are unreliable and poor firefighters yet complies with affirmative action efforts to hire and train Hispanic firefighters.

It should be noted that it is difficult to keep personal prejudices from eventually leading to some form of discrimination. Strong laws and firm informal social norms are necessary to break the causal relationship between prejudice and discrimination.

Two types of discrimination exist—**de jure** and **de facto**. De jure discrimination is legal discrimination. The so-called Jim Crow laws in the South in the last century gave force of law to many discriminatory practices against blacks, including denial of the right to trial, prohibition against voting, and prohibition against interracial marriage. Today, in the United States, there is practically no de jure discrimination, as these laws have been declared unconstitutional and have been removed.

De facto discrimination refers to discrimination that actually exists, whether legal or not. Housing patterns in many cities are an example of de facto discrimination. Wealthy whites tend to live in affluent suburbs, nonwhites in inner-city areas. The effects of such segregation tend to carry over to other arenas—for example, clear discrepancies in the quality of educational systems between affluent suburbs and inner-city areas.

Oppression is the unjust or cruel exercise of authority or power. Members of vulnerable populations in our society are frequently victimized by oppression from segments of the white power structure. Oppression and discrimination are closely related, as all acts of oppression are also acts of discrimination.

Stereotypes are fixed mental images of a group that are applied to all its members. Stereotyping is the attribution of a fixed and usually inaccurate and unfavorable conception to a category of people.

Social workers must also be aware of micro-aggressions in groups. Micro-aggressions are subtle, offensive attacks on a minority individual or group. A Hispanic female may be told she has "good English" although she was born and raised in the United States. An older male could be told he "probably can't remember anything anyways," referencing memory loss that can come with age. Micro-aggressions are damaging as they lead group members, especially minorities, to not feel validated or safe in a group.

A **minority group** is a group that has a subordinate status and is subjected to discrimination. It is not size that is critical in defining a group as a minority, but rather lack of power. Women comprise the majority in our society but are a minority according to this definition.

There are also other important terms to be aware of when working with diverse groups.

Racism is when an individual or group members are stereotyped or face discrimination based on their ethnic or cultural backgrounds. An example would be African American group members not talking to a fair-skinned African American/Hispanic biracial female in a group due to not believing she should identify as an African American.

Unconscious racism occurs when individuals are not aware of their own unconscious racist attitudes. It is important for group leaders to work hard to become aware of all of their biases and prejudices and the biases and prejudices of group members in order to create a safe environment for all group members.

Color blindness is a form of racism that occurs when there is total disregard for another person's race, ethnicity, or age, believing that these factors do not matter. Group leaders need to be able to recognize differences in race, ethnicity, and gender to ensure all group members' individual needs are addressed and to validate differences that each individual brings to the group experience.

Some individuals take racism to a higher level and engage in "othering" in which they believe all other ethnic groups are "not like us" and are outside the "norm" of their identified

EXERCISE 7.1   Some of My Stereotypes

GOAL: This exercise is designed to identify some of your personal stereotypes that you need to be aware of in order to develop an objective approach to social work practice with diverse groups.

1. Assume that you are single. Place an X by the description of anyone you would be hesitant to marry.

_____ Person who is bisexual
_____ Person who is blind
_____ Person who is deaf
_____ Person who has cerebral palsy
_____ Person who is an elder
_____ Person who has genital herpes
_____ Person who has a mild cognitive disability
_____ Person who has been hospitalized for an emotional problem
_____ A Native American
_____ A Puerto Rican
_____ An Italian
_____ A German
_____ A Yugoslav
_____ A Norwegian
_____ A Samoan
_____ An Arab
_____ An Israeli
_____ A Chinese
_____ A Russian
_____ An American
_____ A Cuban
_____ A French person
_____ A Mexican
_____ A white Protestant
_____ A Roman Catholic
_____ A Jew
_____ A Muslim
_____ An African American
_____ A Japanese
_____ A Filipino
_____ An Eskimo
_____ A Brazilian
_____ A Hungarian
_____ A Vietnamese
_____ A Pakistani
_____ A Korean
_____ A white American

2. As specifically as possible, state (next to each group that you checked) the reasons for the groups you checked.

3. Do you hold stereotypes about the individuals you checked?

race. This can lead to a "they are not like us therefore they are not with us" mentality. Othering can be disruptive in a group and needs to be addressed.

Another concept, white privilege, includes benefits, advantages, or access to power typically bestowed on those identified as white. Some of these privileges include not ever having to face job discrimination, reading books in which their race is the predominant race talked about, or being afforded financial loans at a lower interest rate. It is important for white social workers to recognize the concept of white privilege and become more self-aware in order to provide culturally competent services. Social workers should aim to engage in cultural humility (see content later) in which they recognize their own privileges and biases while also being committed to learning about another individual's experiences.

Lastly, ageism is when an individual or group of people face racism, stereotypes, and discrimination based on their age. An example is an older aged adult not being invited to attend a group due to a concern that the older aged adult will not be able to relate to younger group members. Group leaders need to find opportunities for all age groups to benefit from group experiences and aim to find similarities among group members when appropriate.

Diverse groups are groups with characteristics that are distinct from the dominant group in a society. Many diverse groups in our society are also vulnerable populations.

The Council on Social Work Education (2015) states social work educational programs need to "provide a learning environment in which respect for all persons and understanding of diversity and difference are practiced."[4]

In *Educational Policy and Accreditation Standards* the Council on Social work Education (2015) states that social work educational programs are mandated to have a commitment to diversity, "including but not limited to age, class, color, culture, disability and ability, ethnicity, gender, gender identity and expression, immigration status, marital status, political ideology, race, religion/spirituality, sex, sexual orientation, and tribal sovereign status."[5]

Tribal sovereignty refers to the right of Native American tribes to govern themselves, define their own membership, manage tribal property, and regulate tribal business and domestic relations. It further recognizes the existence of a government-to-government relationship between such tribes and the federal government. There are more than 500 federally recognized Native American tribes in the United States.

Social justice is an ideal condition in which all members of a society have the same basic rights, protection, opportunities, obligations, and social benefits.[6] Economic justice is also an ideal condition in which all members of a society have the same opportunities for attaining material goods, income, and wealth.

In working with diverse groups, a social worker needs (1) to be aware of personal stereotypes and preconceptions about diverse groups, (2) to have knowledge about the diverse groups that he or she is working with and the special needs of those groups, and (3) to be aware of which intervention techniques are apt to be effective with those groups and which are not.

LO 2 Understand Stereotyping and Multiculturalism

STEREOTYPING AND MULTICULTURALISM: A PERSPECTIVE

As with most other social work texts, this text presents descriptive information on many of the groups identified in the Educational Policy and Accreditation Standards (EPAS). The client groups identified in EPAS include, but are not limited to, "age, class, color, culture, disability and ability, ethnicity, gender, gender identity and expression, immigration status, marital status, political ideology, race, religion/spirituality, sex, sexual orientation, and tribal sovereign status."[7]

Traditionally, such descriptive information has been thought to increase social workers' capacities to be culturally competent with these groups. However, some social work authorities are now raising questions as to whether presenting descriptive information about specific groups leads to stereotypes and prejudices against these groups.[8] For example, if we describe women as being more emotional than men and men as being more rational than women, such a perception and categorization can steer expectations for an individual or a group. Such perceptions and categorizations are often inaccurate when applied to an individual member of a group, as well as to the group as a whole.

Another example may help further clarify this perspective. There is a perception that Asian Americans are a "model minority," as they are viewed as an "over-achieving, supersuccessful ethnic group without significant problems."[9] However, perceiving Asian Americans as overachieving and supersuccessful raises a number of questions that may negatively affect those labeled as Asian Americans, such as: Will such a perception lead Asian American children to feel undue pressure to be supersuccessful? Will it lead those Asian Americans who are not supersuccessful to view themselves as "failures"? Will social service agencies and policy makers tend to ignore developing human service programs for Asian Americans, as they are already perceived to be "supersuccessful"? Will providers of services (such as dentists, car dealers, plumbers, electricians) tend to charge Asian Americans more, as they are apt to be perceived to be "wealthy"?

It should be noted that the stereotyping of Asian Americans as being overachieving and supersuccessful misrepresents the diverse experiences of Asian Americans by glossing over huge differences within a group of people who come from more than two dozen countries, most of which have their own distinct language and culture. In this regard, Ziauddlin Sardar notes:

> White people . . . look at me and exclaim: "Surely, you're Asian." However, there is no such thing as an Asian. Asia is not a race or identity: it is a continent. Even in Asia, where more than half of the world's population lives, no one calls him or herself "Asian." . . . In the U.S., the Asian label is attached to Koreans, Filipinos, and Chinese. In Britain, we do not use the term Asian to describe our substantial communities of Turks, Iranians, or Indonesians, even though these countries are in Asia.[10]

Presenting descriptive information about a group may also lead to negative stereotyping and then to overt discrimination. For example, there is descriptive information that indicates African Americans tend to have higher rates (compared to whites) of poverty, homelessness, births outside of marriage, school dropouts, criminal arrests, and criminal convictions.[11] Does such information lead to the expectation by non–African Americans that African American individuals they meet are apt to "fit" such descriptive information? For example, the poverty rate for African Americans is about 27%, whereas for whites it is 10%.[12] Will this information lead a non–African American to expect that African American individuals they encounter are apt to be "poor"? What may be ignored by the non–African American is that most African Americans (73%) are not living in poverty.

This text will continue to use the traditional approach of presenting descriptive information about the diverse categories identified in the EPAS for two reasons. First, most social work educators deduce that the EPAS was written with the expectation that descriptive information will be presented in the social work curriculum on these categories. Second, the social work authorities who are concerned about descriptive information being presented have not yet arrived at a new definition of diversity that enables us to develop a knowledge base of information about the diverse groups identified in the EPAS who have been and still are victimized by discrimination. This author urges readers to be aware of the dangers of stereotypes being generated by descriptive information about the diverse groups identified in this text.

An additional caveat about diversity will be mentioned. Everyone has multicultural diversity. We differ from one another in terms of such variables as age, economic status, education, family type, gender, personality type, ethnicity, religion, geographic origin, sexual orientation, communication types, attire, language, political views, physical abilities, lifestyle, and so forth. Therefore, when we meet someone who, for example, is Japanese American, it is essential to recognize that there are many other facets of that individual in addition to just his or her ethnicity.

The EPAS (CSWE 2015) states,

> "The dimensions of diversity are understood as the intersectionality of multiple factors including but not limited to age, class, color, culture, disability and ability, ethnicity, gender, gender identity and expression, immigration status, marital status, political ideology, race, religion/spirituality, sex, sexual orientation, and tribal sovereign status."[13]

Intersectionality is the consideration of the simultaneous operation and/or effects of two or more categories of inequality.[14]

LO 3   Identify Stereotypes and Preconceptions

YOUR STEREOTYPES AND PRECONCEPTIONS

Our society has had a long history of discriminating against vulnerable populations. The extent of the discrimination has changed with time for some diverse groups. Italian Americans and Chinese Americans, for example, were victimized by discrimination to a greater extent during the last century than now.

All of us have some prejudices against vulnerable populations because we were socialized where prejudices abound. Abraham Lincoln is recognized as the person who was most responsible in our society for ending slavery. But Lincoln had prejudices against African Americans, as illustrated in the following statement:

> I will say, then, that I am not, nor ever have been, in favor of bringing about in any way the social and political equality of the white and black races; that I am not, nor ever have been, in favor of making voters or jurors of Negroes, nor of qualifying them to hold office, nor to intermarry with White people . . . and in as much as they cannot so live, while they do remain together there must be the position of superior and inferior, and I as much as any other man am in favor of having the superior position assigned to the White race.[15]

As social workers, it is critically important for each of us to recognize our personal prejudices and stereotypes against vulnerable populations. Social workers have taken a professional value position to combat discrimination as stated in the NASW *Code of Ethics*. In working with vulnerable populations, it is important to be aware of our stereotypes and prejudices so that we do not subtly discriminate against such populations. By being aware of our prejudices and stereotypes, we can work on reducing and eliminating them.

Currently there are a number of commonly accepted myths and stereotypes about gays and lesbians. Some of these myths will be summarized and then followed with factual information. As you read these myths, consider whether or not you believe any of them.

Myth 1—Appearance and Mannerisms   All gay men are effeminate; they have a "swishy" walk, talk with a lisp, and are limp-wristed. Correspondingly, all lesbians are masculine; they have short hair, dress mainly in men's clothes, and appear manly.

Fact   Because of these stereotypes, many people erroneously believe it is easy to identify gays and lesbians. The fact is that most gays and lesbians dress, look, and behave just like everyone else. Except for a small percentage of individuals, it is impossible to recognize a gay or lesbian simply by his or her appearance or mannerisms.[16]

EXERCISE 7.2   Questionnaire about Gays and Lesbians

GOAL: This exercise is designed to assess your views about gays and lesbians.

1. Answer the following questionnaire in terms of your current views.

1. Gay men are effeminate; they have a "swishy" walk, talk with a lisp, and are limp-wristed.

    a. True   b. False

2. Most lesbians are masculine; they have short hair, dress mainly in men's clothes, and appear manly.

    a. True   b. False

3. Gay men desire to be women.

    a. True   b. False

4. Lesbians desire to be men.

    a. True   b. False

5. In a gay or lesbian couple, one partner will assume the dominant (sometimes called masculine) role and the other will assume the submissive (sometimes called feminine) role.

    a. True   b. False

6. Most gay men are child molesters.

    a. True   b. False

7. People are either gay/lesbian or heterosexual.

    a. True   b. False

8. Most gays and lesbians are mentally ill.

     a. True   b. False

9. Gays and lesbians are to blame for the AIDS epidemic.

    a. True   b. False

10. People choose to be gay or lesbian

    a. True   b. False

2. Read the material in this chapter on myths and facts about gays and lesbians. Did this material lead you to want to change any of your answers to these questions? If yes, specify which answers you would change.

Myth 2—Gender Identity   Gay men desire to be women, and lesbians desire to be men.

Fact   This myth confuses gender identity (masculine or feminine) with choice of sexual partner (same sex or heterosexual). The fact is that although gays and lesbians generally choose a sexual partner of the same sex, their gender identity is identical to that of heterosexuals. A gay man views himself as male and does not desire to be female. A lesbian views herself as female and does not desire to be male.[17]

Myth 3—Sexual Roles In a gay or lesbian couple, one partner will assume the dominant (sometimes called masculine) role and the other will assume the submissive (sometimes called feminine) role.

Fact Such role-playing occurs infrequently, as most gays and lesbians engage in many forms of behavior and do not restrict themselves to one or another role. Gay or lesbian partners often switch roles during the sexual act or engage in mutual oral-genital stimulation. In regard to role-playing outside the sexual act itself, the vast majority of gay men do not attempt to play the female role, and the vast majority of lesbians reject the entire practice of male–female role playing.[18]

Myth 4—Child Molesters Gay men are child molesters.

Fact The vast majority of child molesting is done by heterosexual men to young girls.[19] Parents should be more fearful that heterosexual male teachers will try to seduce their young daughters than that the gay male teachers will molest their young sons. There is no reason to assume that a person who is gay/lesbian is more apt to be a child molester than is a heterosexual.

Myth 5—Gay/Lesbian or Heterosexual People are either gay/lesbian or heterosexual.

Fact Kinsey and his colleagues demonstrated that it is a mistake to conceptualize gay/lesbian and heterosexuality as comprising two separate categories. Instead, these researchers found that many people have had some heterosexual and some same-sex experiences to varying degrees.[20] Their seven-point continuum is shown in Figure 7.1. Probably a majority of adults either have had a gay or lesbian experience or have fantasized about having one.

Myth 6—Mental Illness Gay and lesbians are mentally ill.

Fact Research has found no evidence that gays/lesbians are less well adjusted than heterosexuals. Personality tests reveal no differences (except for sexual orientations) between gays and lesbians and heterosexuals.[21] In 1973, the American Psychiatric Association voted to remove homosexuality from its list of mental disorders, and thus homosexuality is no longer officially classified as a psychiatric disorder.

Myth 7—AIDS Gays and lesbians are to blame for the AIDS epidemic.

Fact Although gay men are a high-risk group for the AIDS virus in our society, very few cases have been reported among lesbians. (Gay men are at high risk for acquiring AIDS due to the transfer of bodily fluids that occurs during anal intercourse.) AIDS is a life-threatening disease for anyone (gay/lesbian or heterosexual) who is HIV infected. In many African countries, the majority of people afflicted with AIDS are heterosexuals.

FIGURE 7.1 **Sexual Orientation**

1	2	3	4	5	6	7
Exclusively heterosexual	Mostly heterosexual with incidental homosexual experience	Heterosexual with substantial homosexual experience	Equal heterosexual and and homosexual experience	Homosexual with substantial heterosexual experience	Homosexual with incidental heterosexual experience	Exclusively homosexual

Gay men are not the cause of AIDS. Blaming a deadly disease on the group that, in the United States, has suffered and died disproportionately from AIDS is a classic case of blaming the victim. Although it is true that the largest single risk group of persons with AIDS is gay men, it is ludicrous to conclude that this group caused this health crisis. AIDS is caused by a virus. It is also ludicrous to assert that gay men want to deliver the disease to the world after first delivering it to themselves. Quite the contrary, the gay male community in the United States has been in the forefront of educating people about behavior that minimizes the transmission of the disease. Gay men have radically altered their sexual behavior patterns, as evidenced by a substantial drop in the rate of transmission of the disease among this group in the past few years.

Myth 8—Sexual Preference   People choose to be gay or lesbian.

Fact   Research shows that sexual orientation is established early in life, perhaps long before adolescence.[22] Although every person has the potential to behave sexually in the manner he or she may choose, one's true sexual orientation may be set before birth or at a very early age and then no longer influenced by the environment. Many same-sex–oriented persons behave as if they are heterosexual in this society because there are so many sanctions against same-sex behavior. However, their true sexual orientation and preferred sexual partner, in the absence of these negative sanctions, would be someone of the same gender. Human beings certainly have the ability to respond sexually to people who are not their preferred sexual partners, but to do so requires going against the current of their innermost inclinations. The question of what causes a person's sexual orientation to be set (either as same sex or heterosexual) has not as yet been answered. It appears that some people are naturally heterosexual in orientation and others are naturally same-sex, just as some people are naturally left-handed and others are naturally right-handed.

LO 4   Recognize the Importance of Social Workers Having In-Depth Knowledge of the Diverse Groups They Work With

KNOWLEDGE ABOUT DIVERSE GROUPS

Social workers sometimes make the mistake of using their own social, cultural, or economic values as the norm. See, for example, Figure 7.2. If a social worker has experienced the prejudices that a client is exposed to and was raised in an environment similar to a client's, that worker may be more perceptive about and empathetic to that client. An African American social worker, for example, may better understand what African American clients are saying and experiencing than a white social worker would. Similarly, a worker with a disability may be more perceptive to what a client with a disability is thinking and feeling. Conversely, clients who are members of a vulnerable population may initially feel they are being better understood when the worker is a member of the same group.

On the other hand, a social worker does not need to be a member of the client's minority group in order to work effectively with that client. The problematic nature of cross-cultural social work does not preclude its effectiveness. Mizio has noted, for example, that effective white workers can establish viable working relationships with nonwhite clients and that some nonwhite workers are less effective with others of the same race or culture than white workers.[23] The following example illustrates this point:

> In answering the question of whether a white middle-class psychiatrist can treat a black family, I cannot help but think back over my own experiences. When I first came to New York and decided to go into psychotherapy I had two main thoughts: (1) that my problems were culturally determined, and (2) that they were related to my Catholic upbringing. I had grown up in an environment in which the Catholic Church had tremendous influence.

FIGURE 7.2   Case Example of a Social Worker Mistakenly Viewing a Client from the Worker's Values

Bill Ridder, an adult services worker at a human services agency, received an anonymous call that a 79-year-old male, Vern Broad-cort, was living in abysmal conditions. Ridder made a home visit. Vern Broadcort lived alone in a rural area in northern Minnesota. The house was a mess. There was nearly an inch of dirt and newspapers on the floor. The house had no running water or toilet facilities, and Broadcort's clothes were filthy. He had not taken a bath for over a year. The house was heated, even in winter, by only a small wood stove in the kitchen. The refrigerator had a rancid odor because some of the food had spoiled. There were no clean dishes; a green mold was growing on some that had been used but not washed. Broadcort mentioned he occasionally washed his dishes in rainwater. The dishwater that was in a large bowl had a muddy dark brown color to it.

Ridder also visited some of Broadcort's neighbors, who expected the house to catch fire one of these days. They said Broadcort frequently drank himself into a stupor and then would smoke cigarettes. When he coughed, which he often did (according to the neighbors), hot ashes from the cigarette would be blown several feet away. Broadcort did appear mentally alert, however, and he stated his doctor felt he was in fair health. He did suffer from emphysema, arthritis, and an occasional occurrence of gout.

Ridder decided that the best place for Broadcort to live was in a nursing home and found one with an available bed. He then asked Broadcort if he would be interested in moving there. The reply from Broadcort shocked Kidder. "No way am I moving to a nursing home," he said. "This is my home. I was born and raised here, and I intend to die here. If you should get a court order to send me to a nursing home, I'll give up the will to live and soon die there. I personally don't believe you can get a court order to make me move out of here. I own this place, and, I'm mentally alert and not hurting anyone. Who do you think you are that you can come in here and tell me where to live?"

Ridder went back to his supervisor to discuss the case. The supervisor informed Ridder that Broadcort, if mentally competent, had the right, to live where he chose, as long as he was not hurting anyone else in the process. The supervisor then tactfully asked Ridder to think about whether he was seeking to force his values onto Broadcort, who obviously was content with his living environment. Ridder thought a while and agreed that he probably was.

With these factors in mind, I began to think in terms of the kind of therapist I could best relate to. In addition to being warm and sensitive, he had to be black and Catholic. Needless to say, that was like looking for a needle in a haystack. But after inquiring around, I was finally referred to a black Catholic psychiatrist.

Without going into too much detail, let me say that he turned out to be not so sensitive and not so warm. I terminated my treatment with him and began to see another therapist who was warm, friendly, sensitive, understanding and very much involved with me. Interestingly enough, he was neither black nor Catholic. As a result of that personal experience, I have come to believe that it is not so much a question of whether the therapist is black or white but whether he is competent, warm and understanding. Feelings, after all, are neither black nor white.[24]

Perhaps it is helpful to state the obvious. We are all human, and we all have some uniquenesses and differences. But being human, we also have a lot in common. As with any client, the social worker who is working with a client who is a member of a vulnerable population needs the skills that will lead to positive changes. Such skills include listening, relationship building, competence, empathy, and problem solving. A worker's effectiveness is also increased substantially by knowledge of a client's minority group and its unique characteristics.

There are an immense number of different minority groups in our society—several racial groups, numerous ethnic groups, women, gays and lesbians, many religious groups, people with mental or physical disabilities, older persons, and others. It is beyond the scope of this chapter to describe the unique characteristics of these diverse groups. Instead, a few characteristics of some minority groups will be summarized to illustrate the importance of learning about the minority group of a client.

When working with Native Americans (American Indians) it is considered rude—an attempt to intimidate, in fact—to maintain direct eye contact.[25] Social workers and other professionals need to respect this cultural pattern by seeking to substantially reduce direct eye contact with Native Americans.

If a male client begins talking about his partner, it is a mistake to assume the partner is a woman and refer to the person as "she" or "her."[26] The client may be gay. Such an erroneous assumption could lead the client to terminate the interview and further contact. Obviously, this caution applies to female clients as well. Most helping professionals have also come to realize that attempts to change a client's sexual orientation are usually unsuccessful. In the past, some heterosexual therapists attempted to change homosexual orientation, with poor results. As explained previously, sexual orientation appears to be established early in life.

Chicano men, in contrast to Anglo men, have been described as exhibiting greater pride in their maleness.[27] Machismo—a male's sense of personal virility—is highly valued among Chicano men and is displayed by males to portray dominance and superiority. Machismo is demonstrated differently by different people. Some may seek to be irresistible to women and to have a number of sexual partners. Some resort to weapons or fighting. Others boast of their achievements, even those that never occurred. Recent writers have noted that the feminist movement, urbanization, upward mobility, and acculturation are contributing to the decline of machismo.[28] Chicanos also tend to be more familistic than Anglos. Familism is the belief that the family takes precedence over the individual. Schaefer notes:

> Familism is generally regarded as good because an extended family provides emotional strength at times of family crisis . . . The many significant aspects of familism include: (1) importance of the *compadrazo* (godparent-godchild relationship); (2) benefits of financial dependency of kin; (3) availability of relatives as a source of advice; and (4) active involvement of the elderly within the family.[29]

On the negative side, familism may discourage youth from pursuing opportunities that will take them away from the family. It should be noted that the differences between Chicanos and Anglos with regard to machismo and familism are differences of degree, not of kind. Later in this chapter we will examine how the concept of familism can be utilized in providing services to Chicanos.

Our culture places a high value on physical beauty. Americans spend large proportions of their budgets on clothes, cosmetics, exercise programs, and special diets to look more attractive. Beauty is identified with goodness and ugliness with evil. Movies, television, and books portray heroes and heroines as physically attractive and villains as ugly. Snow White, for example, was beautiful, whereas the evil witch was ugly. Unfortunately, this emphasis on the body beautiful has caused those with a disability to be the object of cruel jokes and has occasionally resulted in people with a disability being shunned or treated as inferior. Wright has noted that the emphasis on the body beautiful has also led society to believe that those with a disability "ought" to feel inferior.[30] Wright has coined the term *the requirement of mourning* for this expectation of society.[31] An able-bodied person who spends a great deal of time, money, and effort to be physically attractive psychologically wants a person with a disability to mourn the absence of physical perfection. The able-bodied person needs feedback that it is worthwhile and important to strive to have an attractive physique.

Another consequence of the body-beautiful cult is that people with a disability are sometimes pitied. Most resent such pity and the accompanying condescension. They want to be treated as equals. Our society also tends to equate a specific disability with general incompetence. Weinberg has noted that people talk louder in the presence of someone who is blind, assuming that people who cannot see cannot hear either.[32] People with a physical disability at times are assumed to be mentally and socially challenged.[33]

In seeking to participate fully in our society, people with a disability must face not only the obstacles created by their disabilities but also the additional obstacles created by society's reaction to disability. When working with people with a disability, helping professionals need to provide assistance in both areas. Social workers also need to advocate for eradicating prejudices and discrimination against people with a disability to ensure equal rights and opportunities for them.

There are many ways for social workers to learn about the values, beliefs, and culture of diverse individuals and groups. The approaches include reading books and articles, watching videos and films, joining clubs and organizations that have numerous diverse members, socializing with people of diverse backgrounds, taking courses in diversity, attending workshops on diversity, living in communities with diversity, and so on.

LO 5   Work More Effectively with the LGBTIQQ Population in Groups

WORKING WITH THE LGBTIQQ POPULATION IN GROUPS*

The LGBTIQQ population represents a unique group of individuals that may benefit from some specific considerations. Social workers should be mindful of specific challenges that may present themselves in a group context and sensitive to situations that may affect members of this population. The use of language is the most important issue that group leaders should be mindful of. Here we are going to use the term LGBTIQQ (or LGBT for short), which stands for lesbian, gay, bisexual, transgender, intersex, questioning, and queer. As we have just learned, this community has historically been misrepresented by numerous stereotypes and myths. The LGBT community itself is substantially more diverse than many people realize and includes a vast array of individuals with varying appearances, mannerisms, values, norms, and cultures that cannot be homogenized. Even within the LGBT community, there has been considerable debate and a limited consensus as to the necessity and appropriateness of labeling the community as a whole and/or what that label should be. This continued debate is influenced by the fact that language and labels have been historically used to aid prejudice, discrimination, and marginalization of the community, just as we have learned that people cannot be neatly labeled heterosexual or homosexual, how people are labeled within the gay community also defies simple definitions. This has been particularly relevant to those in the transgender and intersex community, who struggle not only with a sexual orientation identifier but also a gender identity that may not conform to simple explanation. Some choose to identify as simply "gay" or "queer" or "rainbow" regardless of their gender status. The word **queer** has been reclaimed from its prior use as a prejudicial label by some in the community as an all-encompassing word that captures the diversity within people that identify as LGBT. At its root, *queer* represents someone who is odd or different from the rest of the heterosexual community, which seems rather apt to many people in the LGBT community.

Social workers should be mindful that the general consensus is that anywhere between 3% and 10% of the population as a whole identifies as LGBT. Therefore, in any given group context, 3% to 10% of the participants could potentially be members of that community, whether they publically identify themselves as such or not. Social workers should defer to individual group participants as to whether or not they wish to identify themselves as LGBT and which label they prefer. Unfortunately, substantial prejudice still exists within our culture, and as a result, some group participants may choose not to be open about their sexuality. Significant numbers of individuals in our society feel homosexuality is a moral or religious issue and may hold prejudicial views as a result. Group participants that identify as LGBT may feel hesitant to discuss their sexuality or identify as LGBT for fear of a potential negative response or discrimination from other group members. Although sexuality may be an irrelevant issue in many group contexts, other groups include significant personal disclosure and processing of private matters and struggles, such as in therapeutic or self-help groups. It's also important to remember that group participants who identify as LGBT have the same right to be open about their personal lives as those who identify as heterosexuals. Group members often share personal stories or examples and discuss spouses, families, or children as appropriate.

Some individual group members may at times express prejudicial views, stereotypes, or pejorative comments related to the LGBT community. Social workers must balance a respect for individual values and opinions with our effort to combat prejudice and discrimination. As group facilitators and leaders, social workers need to take a strong lead in combating language and behavior that is prejudicial, regardless of their own personal views. LGBT group members have a right to a comfortable and inclusive environment, just as all other group members. This leadership should always first begin with setting a good example for group participants. In some groups social workers may need to take a more

---

*   This section was written by Craig Mead, MSW, LSW, Licensed social worker at Presence St. Mary and Elizabeth Medical Center, Chicago, IL.

proactive role and set firm boundaries and expectations to address such conduct. Although an overly confrontational approach may be counterproductive, such instances present a valuable teaching moment to combat prejudice and discrimination. It is often preferable and beneficial to use the group process to address this type of an issue. Such situations present an opportunity to discuss and reach a group consensus as to what type of conduct and language is appropriate and acceptable within the parameters decided by participants. As group facilitators, it is not our job to suppress ideas and opinions. However, it is our job to create a safe, supportive, and inclusive environment based upon mutual respect, honesty, and genuine care and concern for one another.

POSTURE OF RECIPROCITY

Kalyanpur and Harry assert that a key approach for a social worker in providing culturally responsive services is a "posture of reciprocity."[34] With the posture of reciprocity, a worker establishes a relationship with diverse clients in which both the worker and the clients not only feel free but also are expected to share their relevant beliefs and values about key service issues.

To illustrate the importance of the posture of reciprocity, Kalyanpur and Harry describe a court case involving white social workers and a Hmong family—a court case in which the social workers failed to take a posture-of-reciprocity approach. While the social workers were providing services to this Hmong family, they knew that one of the children (7-year-old Kou) had two club feet and wanted Kou to have corrective surgery. The social workers were aware that in the United States a club foot is considered a deformity and therefore a stigmatizing condition. When Kou's parents refused surgery, the social workers did not ask the parents for an explanation. Inquiring and explaining their own views on this situation would have been consistent with the posture of reciprocity. Instead of taking this approach, the social workers petitioned a court to order the surgery to be performed.

In court, Kou's parents stated that Kou's club feet were "a sign of good luck" and that Kou was born with club feet so that a "warrior ancestor whose own feet were wounded in battle could be released from a sort of spiritual entrapment."[35] They opposed the operation because they believed a superior being had made it possible for the warrior ancestor to escape his spiritual entrapment by Kou's being created with two club feet. To defy the superior being by having the surgery, the Hmong family argued, would result in the superior being's taking out wrath on this Hmong family, and probably on the larger Hmong community. The judge ruled in favor of the parents and did not order surgery.

Some important questions arise from this case. Does the Hmong family's refusal of surgery for their son's club feet because of a belief that the condition is a blessing to the family constitute abuse? Whose views are best for the child—the parents' or the social workers'? Is the child better off living his life with two club feet, which are seen as a blessing in the Hmong community, or having corrective surgery, which is viewed in the Hmong community as defying the superior being? In any case, would not a frank and open sharing of beliefs and values between the social workers and the Hmong family have been a better approach? Perhaps such an approach would have prevented the development of an adversarial relationship as a result of the social workers' charging the parents with abuse when they refused surgery.

WHICH INTERVENTION TECHNIQUES WORK?

The feelings you stated in Exercise 7.3 are similar to those of many members of racial and ethnic groups when they seek help from a social service agency in this country. They probably have been victimized by Anglo prejudice and discrimination in the past. Perhaps they have even been victimized by entire systems—education, law enforcement, and healthcare, for example. When they seek help, they may display their fears and concerns through anxiety, fear, and visible stress. Some may appear depressed, nonassertive, and passive because they feel overwhelmed and seek to be compliant. Others may be extremely sensitive to the slightest evidence of unjust treatment and may respond aggressively to such normal procedures as waiting or filling out forms.

EXERCISE 7.3   Victimized in Iran

GOAL: This exercise is designed to assist you in understanding the fears and trepidations of certain ethnic and racial groups when they seek help from a social service agency in this country.

1. Imagine that you and a friend are traveling in Iran. In a medium-size city in central Iran, your knapsacks are stolen, and they contain your passports, other forms of identification, travelers checks, and money. What are your fears and trepidations?

2. If you decide to go to a social service agency for help, would you be wary of how you will be treated? Would you be worried the agency may not believe your story and perhaps will turn you over to the police—who may throw you in jail?

3. Because you do not speak the national language, would you be worried about how you will communicate your predicament?

White workers with nonwhite clients need to be aware that the emotional reactions displayed by clients will probably be a combination of their reactions to their problems and to their distrust of agencies they view as part of the white power structure. If clients are highly anxious and fearful, workers need initially to focus on putting them at ease by conveying warmth, competence, calmness, and interest. They need to listen carefully to clients, convey understanding, and identify specific fears so those fears can be alleviated.

Anger Management

Social workers should generally not personalize the outbursts of anger from clients. Clients may display anger for a variety of reasons over which the individual worker has little or no control. The venting of feelings can sometimes reduce anger, and the worker can be available for that process. Often it is helpful for the worker to identify the source of the anger and attempt to deal with that. Sometimes anger can be dissipated simply by conveying warmth and understanding and helping the client solve a problem. If a worker believes the client may become violent, he or she should invite one or more coworkers to participate in the sessions. If a worker is making a home visit and senses danger, it may be advisable to say something such as, "I think we need some time to cool off in order to take a more objective look at this. I'll be back tomorrow at this same time." If the visit involves investigation of child abuse or some other potentially volatile situation, a police officer might be asked along for the return visit.

There is a limit to the verbal abuse that a worker should take from a client. To maintain credibility, the worker must have the respect of the client, and that means limiting verbal abuse. A variety of statements can be used. For example: "I realize you are angry. But I've reached the limit of listening to your verbal abuse. Either we are going to discuss this calmly, or I'm going to have to ask you to leave. Which do you prefer?"

Cultural Communication

In working with adult clients who are not fluent in English, it is better to avoid using the client's bilingual children as interpreters.[36] Using the children as interpreters embarrasses parents because it makes them partially dependent on their children and suggests they are ignorant of essential communication skills. In addition, children probably will not communicate well because of their limited vocabulary and experience. When an interpreter is used, another important guideline is that the worker should talk to the client, not to the interpreter. Talking to the translator places the client in the position of bystander rather than central figure in the relationship.

Workers should always use their own patterns of communication and avoid the temptation to adopt the client's accent, vocabulary, or speech.[37] Mistakes in pronunciation or usage may be offensive or make the worker appear insincere.

Space limitations here do not permit a complete listing of which intervention techniques work with specific minority groups. The following examples, however, demonstrate the need for a worker to learn the techniques appropriate to a particular client or group.

As mentioned earlier, Chicanos tend to have a strong sense of familism. Delgado and Humm-Delgado suggest that natural support systems are a useful resource in providing assistance to Chicanos.[38] These support systems include extended family, folk healers, religious institutions, and merchant and social clubs. The extended family includes the family of origin, nuclear family members, other relatives, godparents, and those considered to be like family. Folk healers are prominent in Chicano communities. Some use treatments that blend natural healing methods with religious or spiritual beliefs. Religious institutions (especially the Roman Catholic Church) provide such services as pastoral counseling, emergency money, locating jobs, housing assistance, and some specialized programs, such as drug abuse treatment and prevention. Merchant and social clubs can provide items such as native foods, herbs, referral to other resources, credit and information, prayer books, recreation, and the services of healers. The reluctance of Chicano clients to seek help from a social welfare agency can be reduced by greater use of these natural support systems. Outreach can be done through churches and community groups.

If a social welfare agency gains a reputation for utilizing such natural support systems in the intervention process, Chicanos will have greater trust in the agency and be much more apt to seek help. Utilizing such natural support systems also increases the effectiveness of the intervention process.

Religious organizations that are predominantly African American usually have a social and spiritual mission. They are apt to be highly active in efforts to combat racial discrimination. Many prominent African American leaders, such as the late Martin Luther King, Jr., and Jesse Jackson, have been members of the clergy. African American churches have served to develop leadership skills. They have also served as social welfare organizations to meet such basic needs as food, clothing, and shelter. African American churches are natural support systems that workers need to utilize to serve troubled African American individuals and families.

A worker with an urban background employed in a small rural community needs to live a life consistent with community values and standards. Someone who violates community norms will not be effective in a small community because he or she will not have the necessary credibility. A worker in a small community needs to identify community values regarding religious beliefs and patterns of expression, dating and marriage patterns, values related to domestic and wild animals (for example, opposing deer hunting in rural communities may run counter to strong local values), drug usage, political beliefs and values, and sexual mores. Once such values are identified, the worker should attempt to achieve a balance between the kind of lifestyle he or she wants and the kind of lifestyle the community expects.

Kadushin recommends that workers in initial meetings with adult clients of diverse racial and ethnic groups should observe all formalities.[39] Such usage would include a formal title (Mr., Miss, Mrs., Ms.), the client's proper full name, greeting with a handshake, and other common courtesies. In initial contacts, workers should also show their agency identification and state the reasons for the meeting. In addition, agencies and workers should establish working hours that coincide with the needs of the groups being served. Doing so might mean evening and weekend hours to accommodate working clients.

In the area of group services to racially diverse clients, Davis recommends that membership be selected in such a manner that no one race vastly outnumbers the others.[40] Sometimes it is necessary to educate clients about the processes of individual or group counseling. Using words common to general conversation is much better than using sophisticated technical jargon that clients are not likely to comprehend.

Native Americans place a high value on the principle of self-determitiation.[41] This sometimes presents a perplexing dilemma for a worker who wonders "How can I help if I can't intervene?" Native Americans will request intervention infrequently, and the worker needs to have the patience to wait for the request. How long this will take varies. During the waiting period, the non–Native American worker should be available and may offer assistance as long as there is no hint of coercion. One help is accepted, the worker will be tested. If the client believes the worker has been helpful, the word will spread and the worker is likely to have more requests for help. If the worker is not helpful, this assessment will also spread and the worker will face increased difficulties.

To establish rapport with African Americans, Hispanics, Native Americans, or clients of other groups that have suffered from racial oppression, a peer relationship should be sought in which there is mutual respect and mutual sharing of information. An attitude of superiority is offensive and should be avoided.

When working with gays or lesbians, it is not uncommon for workers to experience homophobia—the irrational fear of homosexuality—because same-sex orientation has traditionally been viewed negatively as an illness, an emotional disturbance, a deviance, a criminal act, a sin. Personal homophobia must be confronted and resolved, however. One way is to apply social work values to gay clients. It is a serious mistake for a worker to convey a negative evaluation of a client's same-sex orientation because it contradicts the basic social work value of the client's right to self-determination. Another suggestion is for a worker to become familiar with the gay lifestyle and gay community. Such knowledge is essential in helping gay clients identify and evaluate the various alternatives available.[42] Knowing resource people within the gay community will also enable a worker to be more aware of available services, activities, and events. Many services that focus on specific aspects of gay life are needed by gays and lesbians. These include support groups for gay men who are in the process of recognizing their same-sex orientation, legal advice for gay parents seeking child custody, counseling for gay couples, information on safer sex practices to avoid acquiring AIDS, and lesbian support groups.

Social workers have an obligation to help protect the civil rights of gays and lesbians through education and advocacy. Sexual orientation should be respected instead of criticized. Political candidates who are advocates of gay rights should be supported. Agencies that discriminate against gays and lesbians need to be confronted and educated to provide their services in a fair and just manner. Social workers should encourage the development of local support groups, if such groups have not been developed in the community. Gramick has suggested that social workers need to refuse to accept homophobic behavior from colleagues and states that such actions should be pointed out as a violation of the NASW *Code of Ethics.*[43] As stated earlier, social workers have an obligation to advance social and economic justice for all vulnerable populations. The social work concept of ethnic-sensitive practice highlights the major emphases in this section.

LO 6 Apply the Concepts of Ethnic-Sensitive Practice, Empowerment, and the Strengths Perspective

ETHNIC-SENSITIVE PRACTICE

Traditionally, professional social work practice has used the medical model for the delivery of services. The medical model is a deficit model that focuses on identifying problems or deficits within a person (see Chapter 2). The medical model largely ignores environmental factors that affect the person-in-situation. A major shortcoming of a deficit model is that it focuses on the deficits of a person or a group while ignoring strengths and resources. (When one emphasizes only the shortcomings of a person, that person's self-esteem is apt to be severely affected negatively; that person may define himself or herself in terms of shortcomings and, in the process, overlook strengths and resources.)

Ethnic-sensitive practice seeks to incorporate understanding of diverse ethnic, cultural, and minority groups into the theories and principles that guide social work practice.[44] Ethnic-sensitive practice is based on the view that practice must be attuned to the values and dispositions related to clients' ethnic group membership and social-class position. Ethnic-sensitive practice requires that social workers have an in-depth understanding of the effects of oppression on racial and ethnic groups.

Another important segment of the conceptual framework is the concept of the "dual perspective."[45] This concept is derived from the view that all people are a part of two systems: (1) the dominant or sustaining system (the society that one lives in), which is the source of power and economic resources, and (2) the nurturing system, composed of the physical and social environment of family and community. The dual-perspective concept asserts that the adverse consequences of an oppressive society on the self-concept of a person of color or of any minority group can be partially offset by the nurturing system.

Ethnic-sensitive practice requires that social workers have a special obligation to be aware of and seek to redress the oppression experienced by ethnic groups. Ethnic-sensitive practice assumes that each ethnic group's members have a history that has a bearing on the members' perceptions of current problems. For example, the individual and collective history of many African Americans leads to the expectation that family resources will be available in times of trouble.[46] Ethnic-sensitive practice, however, assumes that the present is most important. For example, many Mexican American and Puerto Rican women currently feel tension as they attempt to move beyond traditionally defined gender roles into the mainstream as students and paid employees.[47]

Ethnic-sensitive practice does not introduce new practice principles or approaches. Instead, it urges the adaptation of prevailing therapies, social work principles, and skills to take account of ethnic reality. Regardless of which practice approach is used, two concepts and perspectives that are emphasized are empowerment and the strengths perspective.

Empowerment

Empowerment has been defined as "the process of helping individuals, families, groups, and communities increase their personal, interpersonal, socioeconomic, and political strength and influence toward improving their circumstances."[48]

In working with a vulnerable group, empowerment counters the negative image or stereotype of the group (which has been established through a long history of discrimination) with a positive value or image and an emphasis on the ability of each group member to influence the conditions of his or her life. Empowerment counters hopelessness and powerlessness with an emphasis on the ability of each person to address problems competently, beginning with a positive view of the self. Empowerment counters oppression and poverty by helping vulnerable groups and their members to increase their ability to make and implement basic life decisions.

Strengths Perspective

The strengths perspective is closely related to empowerment. The strengths perspective seeks to identify, use, build on, and reinforce the abilities and strengths that people have, in contrast to the pathological perspective, which focuses on their deficiencies. It emphasizes people's abilities, interests, aspirations, resources, beliefs, and accomplishments. The strengths perspective is described at some length in Chapter 2.

LO 7   Engage in Culturally Competent Practice

CULTURALLY COMPETENT PRACTICE*

Projections indicate that by the middle of the 21st century, nearly half the population of the United States will be people of color.[49] Social workers will be dealing with people who are increasingly diverse, politically more active, and more aware of their rights. It is therefore incumbent upon social workers to become increasingly culturally competent. To become culturally competent, social workers need to (1) become aware of culture and its pervasive influence, (2) learn about their own cultures, (3) recognize their own ethnocentricity, (4) learn about other cultures, (5) acquire cultural knowledge about their clients, and (6) adapt social work skills and intervention approaches accordingly.[50]

The major professional social work organizations have in the past few decades taken strong positions to work toward ending discrimination and oppression of vulnerable groups. The NASW, for example, has lobbied for the passage of civil rights legislation. The NASW *Code of Ethics* has an explicit statement that:

> Social workers should act to prevent and eliminate domination, exploitation, and discrimination against any person, group or class on the basis of race, ethnicity, national origin, color, age, religion, sex, sexual orientation, marital status, political belief, mental or physical disability, or any other preference, personal characteristic, or status.[51]

The EPAS of the CSWE requires that baccalaureate and master's programs in social work include content on diversity, human rights, and the promotion of social and economic justice.[52] Professional social work education is committed to preparing social work students to understand and appreciate cultural and social diversity. Students are taught to understand the dynamics and consequences of oppression, and they learn to use intervention

---

* Material in this section is adapted from *Introduction to Social Work and Social Welfare*, 8th ed. by Zastrow. ©2004. Reprinted with permission of Brooks/Cole.

strategies to combat social injustice, oppression, and their effects. The Association of Black Social Workers also has been very active in combating racial prejudice and discrimination.

Social workers have an obligation to work vigorously toward ending discrimination against vulnerable groups and advancing social justice. The social work professional needs to recognize the reality of practice in a culturally diverse environment. Social workers do have many of the prejudices and misperceptions of the general society, and the tendency to use one's own prejudices and stereotypes poses dangers for the well-meaning practitioner.

A number of guidelines/principles compose cultural competence in social work practice.[53] These guidelines/principles are "ideal" standards. It should be noted most social workers are working towards meeting these standards; many social workers have some limitations in meeting some of these standards.

Social workers need to:

A. Be aware of culture and its pervasive influence
B. Learn about their own culture
C. Learn about other cultures, particularly of the major client groups they serve
D. Need to adapt social work skills and intervention approaches to best serve clients of diverse groups
E. Function in accordance with the ethics, values, and standards of the profession
F. Be knowledgeable about community resources and services, and make appropriate referrals for their diverse clients
G. Be aware of the impacts of social policies and programs on diverse client populations, and advocate for improvements in these programs
H. Advocate for personnel practices (in hiring, admissions, and retention) in social work agencies and educational programs that facilitate diversity within the social work profession
I. Participate in training and educational programs that advance cultural competence in social work practice
J. Provide or advocate for the conveying of information and services (including using interpreters) in language that clients comprehend

EXERCISE 7.4   Cultural Competence in Social Work Practice

GOAL: This exercise is designed to assist you in assessing standards of cultural competence that you need to work on.

Step 1: Review the standards for cultural competence that are listed in this chapter.

Step 2: List the standards (using the letters A, B, C, etc.) that you believe you have significant competence in.

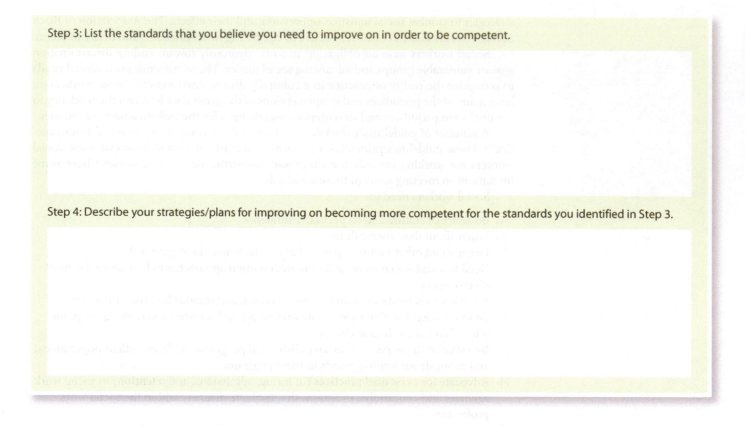

Step 3: List the standards that you believe you need to improve on in order to be competent.

Step 4: Describe your strategies/plans for improving on becoming more competent for the standards you identified in Step 3.

CULTURAL HUMILITY

In recent years the social work profession has been advocating the adoption of the construct of "cultural humility" into social work practice. Cultural humility is somewhat related to cultural competence. The two will be contrasted. The goal of cultural competence is to build an understanding of diverse cultures in order to better and more appropriately provide services. The goal of cultural humility is to encourage personal reflection and growth around culture in order to increase the cultural awareness of service providers.

Three factors are involved in a worker progressing toward cultural humility. The first factor is a lifelong commitment to self-evaluation and self-critique. This factor encourages lifelong learning with no end goal, but with an appreciation of the journey of growth and understanding. We never arrive at a point where we are done learning!

The second factor of cultural humility is a commitment to fixing power imbalances where no power imbalance ought to exist. This factor encourages social workers to realize their own power, prejudices, and privilege and to be willing to accept that acquired credentials and educational degrees alone are insufficient to address social inequality. This factor encourages workers to embrace the idea of learning with and from clients.

The third factor of cultural humility is a commitment to develop partnerships with people and groups who advocate for advancing the human rights of members of diverse groups. Advocacy groups can often have more of an impact on changing oppressive policies, practices, and systems than individuals acting alone. This factor of cultural humility offers clients a mechanism by which they can be seen and heard.

Cultural humility is a tool (a mind-set) that should be used by social workers to gain more insight into their personal biases and to better connect with members of diverse groups. Social workers need to be aware that they can never be truly "competent" about any culture that differs from their own culture.

Advance Human Rights   In recent years, the CSWE has placed increased emphasis on human rights. For example 2015 EPAS states,

> Social workers understand that every person regardless of position in society has fundamental human rights such as freedom, safety, privacy, an adequate standard of living, health care, and education. Social workers understand the global interconnections of oppression and human rights violations, and are knowledgeable about theories of human need and social justice and strategies to promote social and economic justice and human rights.[54]

Reichert, however, has noted that "human rights" has received very limited attention in social work curricula and in social work course materials and lectures.[55] Often, a human rights focus is "invisible" in social work curricula. Social work literature continually prefers the term *social justice* in analyzing core values relevant to the social work profession. Social justice is an ideal condition in which all members of a society have the same basic rights, protection, opportunities, obligations, and social benefits.

Human rights are conceived to be fundamental rights to which a person is inherently entitled simply because she or he is a human being. Human rights are thus universal (applicable everywhere) and egalitarian (the same for everyone).

Reichert compares the concept of "human rights" to the concept of "social justice":

> Human rights provide the social work profession with a global and contemporary set of guidelines, whereas social justice tends to be defined in vague terminology such as fairness versus unfairness or equality versus inequality . . . This distinction gives human rights an authority that social justice lacks. Human rights can elicit discussion of common issues by people from all walks of life and every corner of the world.[56]

What are basic "human rights"? A clear specification of basic human rights has not been agreed upon. A key starting point in articulating such rights is the *Universal Declaration of Human Rights* of the United Nations (UN).[57] The following rights are identified in this document:

> All humans are born free and equal in dignity and rights.
> Everyone is entitled to all of the rights in the UNDR regardless of any distinction.
> The right to life, liberty, and the security of the person.
> Prohibition of slavery.
> Prohibition of torture.
> Right to recognition as a person before the law.
> All must be treated equally under the law.
> Right to a remedy of any violation of these rights.
> Prohibition of arbitrary arrest, detention, or exile.
> Right to a fair trial.
> People shall be presumed innocent until proven guilty.
> Right to freedom from arbitrary interference with private life.
> Right to freedom of movement.
> Right to seek asylum.
> Right to a nationality.
> Right to marry; marriage must be consented to by both parties; the family is entitled to protection from the state.
> Right to property.
> Right to freedom of thought, conscience, and religion.
> Right to freedom of opinion and expression.
> Right to freedom of assembly and association.
> Right to participate in the government of one's country.
> Right to economic, social, and cultural rights necessary for dignity and free development of personality.
> Right to work and equitable compensation.
> Right to rest and leisure from work.

Right to an adequate standard of living, including food, clothing, housing, and medical care.

Right to education.

Right to participate in cultural activities and to share in scientific achievements.

Right to a world order in which these rights can be realized.

Each has duties to their community; rights shall be limited only in regards to respecting the rights of others.

None of the rights may be interpreted as allowing any action to destroy these rights.

Every member nation of the United Nations has approved the *Universal Declaration*, but it is not legally binding on any nation. Because it articulates human rights in somewhat vague terms, determining when (or if) a country/government is violating basic human rights is sometimes difficult. Most countries recognize that the safeguarding of human rights has evolved into a major worldwide goal. Yet identifying violations is currently an imprecise science. It is common for a government to accuse other governments of violating human rights while at the same time "overlooking" its own violations. Reichert states:

The United States; compared to many other countries, fails to fulfill its obligation to promote human rights for all . . . For instance, our failure to provide adequate health care for children and all expectant mothers violates the same Universal Declaration of Human Rights that U.S. political leaders continually call upon to denigrate China, Cuba, and Iraq, among other countries. The infant mortality rate is higher in the United States than in any other industrialized nation . . . and, within the U.S. itself, infant mortality rates are disparate among racial groups, with African-American infants suffering a mortality rate more than twice that of non-Hispanic whites.[58]

It is hoped that greater attention to articulating basic human rights will lead countries to initiate programs that safeguard such rights for all citizens. Increased attention to articulating and protecting basic human rights has promise of being a key countervailing force to facilitate curbing discrimination against people of color, women, persons with disability, gays and lesbians, and other groups currently victimized by discrimination.

LO 8   Understand the RAP Framework for Leading Multiracial Groups

THE RAP FRAMEWORK FOB LEADING MULTIRACIAL GROUPS

Whenever people of different races interact in a group, the leader should assume that race is an issue but not necessarily a problem. Race is an issue in a multiracial group because it is an apparent difference among participants and one that is laden with considerable social meaning. The leader of a multiracial group should not attempt to be color-blind because being color-blind leads to ignoring important dynamics related to race.

In leading a multiracial group, Davis, Galinsky, and Schopler urge that the leader use the RAP framework.[59] RAP stands for: *recognize, anticipate,* and *problem-solve.* Each element will be briefly described in the sections that follow.

Recognize

Recognizing crucial ethnic, cultural, and racial differences in any group requires the leader to be both self-aware and aware of the racial dynamics of the group. A leader of a multiracial group needs to

- Be aware of personal values and stereotypes.
- Recognize racial, ethnic, and cultural differences among the members.
- Respect the norms, customs, and cultures of the populations represented in the group.
- Become familiar with resources (community leaders, professionals, agencies) in the community that are responsive to the needs of the racial components of the group.

These resources can be used as consultants by the leader when racial issues arise and may also be used as referral resources for special needs of particular members.

- Be aware of various forms of institutional discrimination in the community and of their impact on various population groups.
- Be aware of racial tensions in the community that may concern members of the group. Such tensions may directly affect interactions among members of different races in the group.

Anticipate

Anticipating how individual members will be affected by racial issues prepares the leader to respond preventively and interventively when racial issues arise. The leader should anticipate potential sources of racial tension in the group when the members formulate their group goals and when the leader structures the group's work. Because relationships between members and race-laden outside issues (that is, outside of the group) change over time, anticipating racial tensions is an ongoing leadership responsibility. To anticipate tensions and help members deal effectively with them, the leader should

- Seek to include more than one member of any given race. If the group has a solo member, the leader should acknowledge the difficulty of this situation for that member and should make it clear that that member is not expected to serve as the representative of his or her race.
- Develop a leadership style that is culturally appropriate to the group's specific racial configuration. This requires that the leader become knowledgeable about the beliefs, values, and cultures of the various racial components of the group.
- Treat all members with respect and equality in both verbal and nonverbal communications.
- Help the group formulate goals responsive to the concerns and needs expressed by all the members.
- Seek to empower members to obtain their rights, particularly if they are being victimized by institutional discrimination or other forms of racism in the community.
- Acknowledge in initial contacts with members and in initial sessions that racial and ethnic differences do exist in the group and that any issues that arise in the group regarding race must be openly discussed—even if discussing such issues and differences is uncomfortable.
- Encourage the development of norms of mutual respect and appreciation of diversity.
- Announce in initial sessions that at times people do and say things that are racially inappropriate. When this occurs, these comments and actions will be thoroughly discussed in order to resolve the issues and to work toward appreciation of differences.

Problem-Solve

When incidents related to racial issues do arise, the leader must intervene to resolve the issues. The leader should:

- Use a problem-solving approach (described in Chapter 6). Briefly, this approach involves identifying the issues and needs of each party, generating alternatives to meet those needs, evaluating the merits of each of these alternatives, and selecting and implementing the most promising alternative.
- Use conflict resolution approaches (described in Chapter 6). These approaches include role reversal, empathy, inquiry, I-messages, disarming, stroking, and mediation.
- Use interventions and goals that are culturally acceptable and appropriate for all members of the group.
- Provide some rules when involving members in problem solving and conflict resolution (for example, no name calling).
- Assist members in being assertive in confronting and dealing with problems related to race.
- Be prepared to advocate outside the group on a member's behalf when that member is being victimized by discrimination and oppression in the community.

LO 9   Apply Principles of Feminist Intervention in Social Work Practice

FEMINIST INTERVENTION*

The feminist perspective on social work intervention has been developed by a number of authors; no one is specifically recognized as its founder.

Feminism is a multifaceted concept that is difficult to define accurately. In *The Social Work Dictionary*, Barker defines *feminism* as "the social movement and doctrine advocating legal and socioeconomic equality for women. The movement originated in Great Britain in the eighteenth century."[60] Barker then defines *feminist social work* as "the integration of the *values*, skills, and knowledge of social work with a feminist orientation to help individuals and society overcome the emotional and social problems that result from *sex discrimination*" [61] [italics added].

Feminist therapy contends that women are in a disadvantaged position in the world due to gender, sex, race, ethnicity, sexuality, religion, and other categories. Feminist therapy believes that many problems that arise in therapy are due to disempowering social forces; thus, the goal of therapy is to help clients (mostly women) recognize these forces and empower themselves.

Kirst-Ashman and Hull define *feminism* as

> the *philosophy of equality* between women and men that involves both *attitudes* and *actions*, which infiltrates virtually *all aspects of life*, which often necessitates providing *education and advocacy* on the behalf of women, and which appreciates the existence of *individual differences* and personal accomplishments regardless of gender [original emphasis].[62]

Let us examine the five emphasized components of this definition. The **philosophy of equality** between men and women does not mean that women should adopt behaviors that are typically masculine. It means that women and men should have equal or identical rights to opportunities and choices and that neither women nor men should be discriminated against on the basis of gender.

The second component embodies *both attitudes and actions*. In regard to attitudes, feminism emphasizes the importance of viewing other people in a fair, objective perspective and of avoiding stereotyping. In regard to actions, feminism involves a commitment to act on one's beliefs involving gender equality. For example, a supervisor (male or female) who asserts that he or she believes in feminism has an obligation to confront a male supervisee who tells sexist jokes or who treats women according to traditional gender-based stereotypes (for example, making demeaning comments about female social workers being too emotionally involved with their clients).

In the third component, *all aspects of life*, equality does not apply just to equal opportunity to attain a specific job or promotion, it involves many other aspects of life, such as freedom to have opinions on political, social, and religious issues; freedom to ask another person out for a date; freedom to decide what to do with leisure time; freedom to attend, or not to attend, college; freedom to choose to become involved in competitive sports; and freedom to choose to have a sexual encounter.

The fourth component is the frequent need to *provide education and advocacy* on behalf of women. Feminism involves valuing equal opportunities for women as well as for men. Because women have been subjected to sex-role stereotyping and gender-based discrimination, a person who values feminism has an obligation to provide education and advocacy on behalf of women. For example, the male employee who is telling sexist jokes at work needs to be educated about sexual harassment. He also needs to be informed about the negative impact such jokes have on women and that adverse consequences will result if he continues to make sexist remarks. Feminist advocacy involves speaking out for

---

*   Material in this section is adapted from *The Practice of Social Work*, 7th ed., by Zastrow. © 2003. Reprinted with permission of Brooks/Cole.

(or championing the rights of) those women who need help. These women are usually in positions of lesser power and opportunity.

The fifth component is the appreciation of *individual differences*. The feminist perspective places a high value on empowering women by emphasizing individual qualities and strengths.

Principles of Feminist Therapy

Nine principles of feminist intervention have been identified[63]:

1. A client's problems should be viewed "within a sociopolitical framework."[64] Feminist intervention is concerned with the inequitable power relationship between women and men and is opposed to all "power-over" relationships, regardless of gender, race, class, age, and so on. Such relationships lead to oppression and domination. Feminism is concerned with changing all social, economic, and political structures based on the relationships between the haves and the have-nots. The problems of the have-nots are often rooted in a sexist social and political structure. Another way of stating this principle is that "personal is political." According to Van Den Bergh:

   > This principle maintains that what a woman experiences in her personal life is directly related to societal dynamics that affect other women. In other words, an individual woman's experiences of pejorative comments based on sex are directly related to societal sexism. For ethnic minority women, racism and classism also are factors that affect well-being.[65]

   A primary distinguishing characteristic of feminist treatment is to help the client analyze how her problems are related to systematic difficulties experienced by women in a sexist, classist, and racist society.

2. Traditional sex roles are pathological, and clients need encouragement to free themselves from traditional gender-role bonds. Women are put in a double bind due to **femininity achievement incompatibility**. There is a traditional view in our society that a woman cannot be both feminine and an achiever. Achievement, erroneously, is thought to reduce a woman's femininity, and the truly feminine woman is thought to be someone who does not seek to be an achiever. Traditionally, women have been socialized to fill a "learned helplessness" role. Van Den Bergh describes the effects of such sex-role stereotyping:

   > Sex-role stereotypes suggest that women should be submissive, docile, receptive, and dependent. The message is one of helplessness; that women cannot take care of themselves and are dependent upon others for their well-being. This sets up a dynamic in which a woman's locus of control is external to herself, preventing her from believing that she can acquire what she needs on her own in order to develop and self-actualize. In other words, oversubscription to sex-role stereotypes engenders a state of powerless-ness in which a woman is likely to become involved in situations where she becomes victimized . . . For example, because young girls are socialized to be helpless, when they become women they tend to have a limited repertoire of responses when under stress; e.g., they respond passively.[66]

   In feminist treatment, clients are helped to see how their difficulties may be related to oversubscription to traditional sex-role stereotypes. They are shown that by internalizing traditional sex roles, women are inevitably set up to play passive, submissive roles and experience low self-esteem and self-hatred. The feminist approach asserts that clients need encouragement to make their own choices and pursue the tasks and achievements they desire, rather than be constrained by traditional sex roles.

3. Intervention should focus on client empowerment. Van Den Bergh describes the empowerment process:

   > Helping women to acquire a sense of power, or the ability to affect outcome in their lives, is a crucial component of feminist practice. Empowerment means acquiring knowledge, skills, and resources that enhance an individual's ability to control her own life and to influence others. Traditionally women have used indirect, covert techniques to get what they want, such as helplessness, dependency, coyness, and demureness.[67]

Empowerment is fostered in a variety of ways: (1) by helping the client define her own needs and clarify her personal goals so she can derive a sense of purposefulness; (2) by providing the client with education and access to resources; (3) by helping the client see that the direction and ability to change lie within herself (that is, alterations in her life will result only from her own undertakings); and (4) by focusing on the identification and enhancement of the client's strengths rather than on her pathologies. Women need to be empowered so they can increase their ability to control their environments in order to get what they need.

4. Clients' self-esteem should be enhanced. Self-esteem and self-confidence are essential for empowerment. Self-esteem can be enhanced in a variety of ways. The worker should try to be an encouraging person. The worker should help clients identify and recognize their unique qualities and strengths. Many clients with low self-esteem tend to blame themselves for everything that is wrong. For example, a battered woman typically tends to blame herself for being battered. These clients need to look more realistically at those areas in which they are blaming themselves and feeling guilt. They need to distinguish where their responsibility for dysfunctional interactions ends and other individuals' responsibility begins.

5. Clients should be encouraged to develop their identity (sense of self) on the basis of their own strengths, attributes, qualities, and achievements. It is a serious mistake for a woman to develop her identity in terms of her spouse or dating partner. Women need to develop an independent identity that is not based on their relationships with others.

6. Clients need to value and develop social support systems with other women. In a society that devalues women, it is all too easy for some women to view other women as insignificant. With social support systems, women can ventilate their concerns and share their experiences and the solutions they have found to similar problems. They can serve as brokers in identifying resources and can provide emotional support and nurturance to one another.

7. Clients need to find an effective balance between work and personal relationships. Feminist intervention encourages both women and men to share in the nurturant aspects of their lives and in providing economic resources.

8. The nature of the relationship between practitioner and client should approach equality as much as possible. Feminist practitioners do not view themselves as experts in resolving clients' problems, but as catalysts whose role is helping clients empower themselves. Feminist practitioners try to eliminate dominant/submissive relationships. In regard to an egalitarian relationship, Van Den Bergh notes:

> Obviously, there is an innate power differential between practitioner and client because the former has expertise and training as an "authority." However, the feminist admonition is to avoid abusing that status; "abuse" in this sense might be, for example, taking all credit for client change, or using terminology and nomenclature that are difficult for the client to understand.[68]

9. Many clients can benefit from learning to express themselves assertively. The steps in assertiveness training are described in Appendix 1: Module 2. As indicated earlier, many women are socialized to be passive and nonassertive, and as a result, they have difficulty expressing themselves assertively. Clients can be helped through individual and group counseling.

Clients who learn to express themselves assertively will experience increased self-confidence and self-esteem. They will be better able to communicate their thoughts, feelings, and opinions. Also, learning to express oneself assertively is an important component of empowerment.

Many women feel considerable anger over being victimized by sex discrimination and gender stereotyping. Some of these women turn these feelings inward, resulting in depression. Assertiveness training can help women recognize their right to be angry and also help them identify and practice constructive ways to express their anger assertively, rather than aggressively.

EXERCISE 7.5   Feminist Intervention

GOAL: This exercise is designed to further your understanding of feminist issues and feminist intervention.

1. Describe the plight of a female who you know would benefit from feminist intervention. Do not give identifying information (such as last name) of this person in your description.

2. Speculate how a social worker could use the principles of feminist therapy to counsel this person.

Using Feminist Intervention in Groups

The feminist perspective on therapy can be, and usually is, used in conjunction with other theoretical approaches. Group therapists who have a feminist perspective almost always have training in and use other psychotherapeutic approaches—such as behavior therapy, reality therapy, rational therapy, and transactional analysis. They also often use a number of specific treatment approaches—such as assertiveness training, parent effectiveness training, mediation, meditation, sex therapy, and relaxation techniques.

Feminist intervention is particularly applicable in group therapy with women who have been victimized by sex discrimination and sex-role stereotyping. By sharing their experiences, such women can help each other identify the problems encountered in inequitable power relationships between women and men. Such sharing facilitates their recognizing that many of their blocked opportunities are directly related to societal sexism. Such sharing also helps them recognize how their difficulties may be related to traditional sex-role stereotypes. The group approach facilitates members to pursue the tasks and achievements they desire, rather than be constrained by traditional sex roles.

The group setting also is conducive to empowering members to increase their capacities to control their environment in order to get what they want. Members in such a setting are also encouraged to develop an independent identity. Social support systems for women are almost always developed in such a setting, as women are encouraged to share their experiences and the solutions they have found to similar problems. These women often serve as brokers to one another in identifying resources. In addition, the group setting is conducive to members' learning to express themselves assertively, including learning ways to express their anger assertively.

A case example of feminist intervention follows:

Marcia is the mother of three children and has lived with her abusive husband, Dennis, for years. The abuse was particularly violent when Dennis was intoxicated—which he was several times a month. Over the years, Dennis had succeeded in isolating Marcia from her family and friends, in lowering her self-esteem, and in making Marcia financially dependent on him (that is, he prevented her from working outside the home).

One evening while intoxicated, Dennis smashed Marcia in the face and chest with his fists, breaking her nose and three ribs. The oldest child called 911 and an ambulance came, along with two police officers. Dennis was jailed for the evening for domestic abuse, and Marcia received emergency care at a hospital. The hospital social worker persuaded Marcia to take her children with her to a battered women's shelter, where they stayed for 44 days.

During this time she had daily group counseling with other battered women. The group was led by a social worker with a feminist perspective, who applied many of the principles of that perspective. Marcia came to realize that she and many of the other women in the group were being victimized by men who held traditional gender-role stereotypes. The women were given educational material and were led in exercises that helped Marcia become more assertive, express her anger about being dominated by her husband, recognize that she had a right to end an abusive relationship, and realize she was a person worthy of respect. She received help from the shelter's staff in applying and being accepted for public assistance, receiving job training as a dental technician, obtaining a job in this field, finding an apartment for herself and her children, filing for divorce, and obtaining a restraining order against her soon-to-be-ex-husband who had continued to harass her.

Now, 2 years later, caring for her three children (both financially and emotionally) continues to be a challenge. But she is much happier with her life and with the kind of person she is becoming. She also is pleased that her children are slowly but surely gaining pride in her and respect for her.

Evaluation of Feminist Therapy

Because the feminist perspective is almost always used in conjunction with other therapeutic approaches, it is extremely difficult to conduct evaluative studies that test its effectiveness.

Van Den Bergh and Cooper emphasize that the feminist perspective is consistent with the core values of social work practice, including equality, respect for individuals, and promotion of social and economic justice for populations at risk.[69] They conclude that "a feminist social work practice is a viable way to accomplish the unique mission of social work, to improve the quality of life by facilitating social change."[70]

Although most contemporary approaches to psychotherapy look for the causes of a client's problems inside the client (for example, internal conflicts, repressed feelings, and early childhood traumas), the feminist perspective emphasizes viewing a client's problems in terms of the social, political, and economic systems that affect the client. This perspective is consistent with social work's emphasis on the person-in-environment, a systems approach, and an ecological approach.

The feminist perspective has also been helpful in identifying and conceptualizing numerous structural problems in our society. For example, feminists who practiced in the mental health field in the early 1970s began to view traditional psychotherapy as an agent of social control that maintained traditional sex roles by encouraging women to "adapt."[71] Feminists have asserted that women need to be recognized as having the right to their reproductive capacities (including the right to choose to terminate a pregnancy); otherwise, their lives would be largely controlled by the men who impregnate them, as raising a child requires a commitment of at least two decades. Feminists have also drawn attention to the sociopolitical forces that have led to an increase in the feminization of poverty in our society.

An extremely positive aspect of the feminist perspective is the view that all social workers have an obligation to identify inequalities in our social, economic, and political systems and then use macropractice techniques to confront these inequalities. Sometimes feminist social workers may involve clients in changing systems. Van Den Bergh notes:

> The social worker should model her concern for changed societal conditions that eliminate institutionalized inequalities by working on some social change projects, such as abortion rights, comparable worth, anti-apartheid activism, or environmental protection. Clients can be encouraged to engage in social activism themselves, as the experience of collective action can help to validate one's sense of self, personal worth, and power to change. However, judgment will have to be used as to whether this is appropriate, based on the client's current level of functioning and willingness to take risks.[72]

Feminism is concerned with ending oppression and discrimination in our society and throughout the world.

The women's movement is bringing about a gender-role revolution in our society. Men and women are becoming aware of the negative effects of gender-role distinctions. More and more women are entering the labor force. Women are becoming more involved in athletics and pursuing a number of professions and careers that previously were all male. Changes are also occurring in human interactions; more women are being assertive and seeking out egalitarian relationships with men. To some extent, men are (more slowly) beginning to realize the negative effects of gender-role distinctions. They are gradually realizing that the stereotypical male role limits their opportunities in terms of emotional expression, interpersonal relationships, occupations, and domestic activities.

One limitation of the feminist perspective is that a number of uninformed people reject feminism in reaction to stereotypes. Apparently feminism has had some difficulties in informing segments of the general public about its basic tenets and principles. In this regard, Kirst-Ashman and Hull state:

> Some people have extremely negative reactions to the word "feminism." The emotional barriers they forge and the resulting resistance they foster makes it very difficult even to approach the concept with them. Others consider feminism a radical ideology which emphasizes separatism and fanaticism. In other words, they think feminism involves the philosophy adopted by women who spurn men, resent past iniquities, and strive violently to overthrow male supremacists. Still others think of feminism as an outmoded tradition that is no longer relevant.[73]

GROUP DEVELOPMENT STAGES IN WOMEN'S GROUPS*

Schiller believes that groups go through distinctive developmental stages. (See, for example, the models described in Chapter 1.) However, she proposes a modified version of developmental stages in women's groups.[74] This model is based on a feminist perspective of women's psychological development and the relational model, with particular emphasis placed on issues of status, power, and conflict. The differences between women and men in groups regarding these issues are reflected in the developmental stages identified for women's groups. Schiller's perspective is significant to social workers leading women's groups because it states the need for group leaders to have an understanding of the

---

*   The description of this model was written by Michael Wallace, MSW, instructor (retired) at the University of Wisconsin-Whitewater.

"particular and unique patterns of growth and development" so they can "intervene more effectively and in a style that best meets the differential needs of the group and its members."[75]

The relational model proposed for women in groups is structured much like the five-stage model presented by Garland, Jones, and Kolodny (described in Chapter 1). In fact, Schiller concurs with them regarding preaffiliation (stage 1) and termination (stage 5) and views these two stages as universal to all groups. The difference is in the middle three stages of development in women's groups:

2. Establishing a relational base
3. Mutuality and interpersonal empathy
4. Challenge and change[76]

Second Stage—Establishing a Relational Base

The second stage of Schiller's model differs significantly from most models of group development. The emphasis here is not on power and control. Rather, focus is on "establishing a common ground and a sense of connection with each other and with the facilitator."[77] In women's groups at this stage, members find similarities in their experiences and seek approval from one another and the group leaders. The relational base is the establishment of a sense of safety within the group.

Third Stage—Mutuality and Interpersonal Empathy

The third stage corresponds with what other theorists have termed the work stage.[78] At this stage of development in women's groups, members move beyond making connections and recognize their similarities. They are now at a place of increased trust and self-disclosure. This allows group members to respect differences without losing their connection with one another. If the group has been able to successfully negotiate the second stage, then the relational base will allow for both respect for differences and empathetic connection.

Fourth Stage—Challenge and Change

In order for growth and change to happen, group members must be able to challenge themselves and each other. This can be accomplished by confronting issues of how individuals view themselves, their world, and/or their interpersonal relationships. How this occurs in women's groups is uniquely different compared to men's groups. This is because of the different values placed on power by women as opposed to men. For example, power in men's groups seems to come from their individual power. Power in women's groups seems to evolve from a sense of community. Therefore, in order for this stage to develop, women must "have sufficiently experienced connection, empathic attunement, and respect for differences "Then women are "free to challenge themselves, each other, and the facilitators."[79] If this can be established, it allows members of women's groups to challenge one another, take risks, and express disagreements without fearing the loss of valued connections made with one another.

Summary

The following summarizes the chapter's content in terms of the learning objectives presented at the beginning of the chapter.

1. Define key terms involving diversity.
   The following terms are defined: *prejudice, discrimination, oppression, minority group, diverse groups, social justice,* and *human rights.*

2. Understand stereotyping and multiculturalism.
Stereotypes are fixed mental images of a group that are applied to all its members. Stereotyping is the attribution of a fixed and usually inaccurate and unfavorable conception to a category of people.

Everyone has multicultural diversity. We differ from one another in terms of such variables as age, economic status, education, family type, gender, personality type, ethnicity, religion, geographic origin, sexual orientation, communication types, attire, language, political views, physical abilities, lifestyle, and so forth. Therefore, when we meet someone who, for example, is Japanese American, it is essential to recognize that there are many other facets of that individual in addition to just his or her ethnicity.

3. Identify stereotypes and preconceptions.
All of us have some prejudices and stereotypes against vulnerable populations where prejudices abound. As social workers, it is important to be aware of our stereotypes and prejudices so that we do not subtly discriminate against vulnerable populations.

4. Recognize the importance of social workers having in-depth knowledge of the diverse groups they work with.
Social workers sometimes make the mistake of using their own social, cultural, or economic values as the norm. There are many ways for social workers to learn about the values, beliefs, and culture of diverse individuals and groups. The approaches include reading books and articles, watching videos and films, joining clubs and organizations that have numerous diverse members, socializing with people of diverse backgrounds, taking courses in diversity, attending workshops on diversity, living in communities with diversity, and so on.

5. Work more effectively with the LBTIQQ population in groups.
Guidelines are presented for working with the LBTIQQ population in groups.

6. Apply the concepts of ethnic sensitive practice, empowerment, and the strengths perspective.
Ethnic-sensitive practice, empowerment, and the strengths perspective are described. The importance of social workers is described. The importance of social workers using these concepts in social work practice with diverse groups is emphasized.

7. Engage in culturally competent practice.
The social work professional needs to recognize the reality of practice in a culturally diverse environment. Social workers do have many of the prejudices and misperceptions of the general society, and the tendency to use one's own prejudices and stereotypes poses dangers for the well-meaning practitioner. The NASW standards for cultural competence in social work practice are presented.

8. Understand the RAP framework for leading multiracial groups.
The RAP framework (recognize, anticipate, and problem-solve) for leading groups is presented.

9. Apply principles of feminist intervention in social work practice.
The feminist perspective on social work intervention is presented. Although most contemporary approaches to psychotherapy look for the causes of a client's problems inside the client (for example, internal conflicts, repressed feelings, and early childhood traumas), the feminist perspective emphasizes viewing a client's problems in terms of the social, political, and economic systems that affect the client. This perspective is consistent with social work's emphasis on the person-in-environment, a systems approach, and an ecological approach.

Group Exercises

EXERCISE A: Coming Out of the Closet

GOAL: To identify stereotypes and myths that you may hold about gays and lesbians.

Step 1. The students assume they have a gay or lesbian orientation, which they have been hiding. Each student then writes a letter to his or her parents revealing this sexual orientation and asking for acceptance and support.

Step 2. As the students are writing their letters, the leader observes their verbal and nonverbal communication and makes notes on apparent stereotypes. (Students are apt to express stereotypes in conversations with students seated next to them.) A few volunteers are asked to read their letters to the class.

Step 3. After a few letters are read, the leader summarizes apparent stereotypes he or she observed.

Step 4. As an optional step, the myths and facts about homosexuality may be summarized. A summary of this material appears earlier in the chapter.

Step 5. If negative stereotypes are expressed, the leader should seek to initiate a discussion of how a heterosexual worker who has negative stereotypes about homosexuality can seek to be objective in working with clients who are homosexual.

EXERCISE B: Spaceship to Futura

GOAL: To clarify your feelings about groups that have been discriminated against.

Step 1. The group leader indicates that one purpose of this exercise is to help students clarify their values related to the continuation of the human race after a nuclear war. The class forms subgroups of five or six, and the following vignette is read to the students:

The United States has discovered a planet, Futura, in another galaxy whose environment is very similar to Earth's. There is every indication that the planet will be able to support human life, although no human life has been detected on Futura. The United States has just completed a spaceship that will be able to travel to Futura. The spaceship is being built on a remote island in the Pacific Ocean and will hold only seven people. Your subgroup has been appointed by the government to select the first seven people to go to Futura. Your subgroup is in frequent contact with the chief scientist for this project. The spaceship is remarkable in that it has a new computer system that has already been programmed to automatically guide the spaceship to Futura without requiring a pilot.

Suddenly, a nuclear war breaks out between the world powers. It is New Year's Eve. Russia, China, the United States, and Israel are already launching their nuclear warheads. It looks like the nuclear destruction may eliminate human civilization on this planet. The chief scientist frantically calls. The spaceship must take off in 15 minutes to Futura, or it will be destroyed. She and your subgroup believe that the seven people who go may be the only people left to start the human race again.

There are 13 people at the spaceship. Your subgroup must decide who will be selected. (If the 13 people themselves decide, they are likely to become irrational and begin fighting.) Your subgroup has only 15 minutes to make a decision. If a decision is not made in 15 minutes, a nuclear warhead is apt to hit the island and destroy the spaceship. All you know about the 13 people is the following:

1. The chief scientist, female, 47 years old
2. A Hispanic peasant, female, 4 months pregnant

3. An African American male, third-year medical student
4. A white female, prostitute, 27 years old, a Communist
5. A white male, gay, Olympic athlete, 24 years old
6. A white biology professor, 67 years old
7. A rabbi, 27 years old
8. A white female on public assistance, 28 years old, has been arrested for several felonies, has never been employed
9. A female home economist, 24 years old, white, has cerebral palsy
10. A Korean child, male, 8 years old
11. A white male with a moderate cognitive disability due to a lack of oxygen at birth, 33 years old
12. A white female elementary schoolteacher, 27 years old, has genital herpes
13. A 28-year-old white farmer, has had a vasectomy

Step 2. The group leader distributes copies of this list to the students, and the subgroups begin their discussions. The group leader informs the subgroups when 10, 5, 3, and 1 minute remain. At the end of 15 minutes, the discussions end.

Step 3. Each subgroup shares its selections and reasoning. The leader then conducts a discussion that explores what values underlie the selections, why certain individuals were rejected, how a social worker can be objective when faced with personal prejudice or stereotypes, and what students think they have learned.

EXERCISE C: Feminist Intervention in Counseling

GOAL: Assist students in applying the feminist perspective to counseling.

Step 1. Either describe the principles of the feminist perspective to therapy or have the students read the material in this chapter.

Step 2. Ask for a volunteer to role-play being a counselor who uses the feminist perspective in a simulated counseling situation. Ask for a second volunteer (probably a female) to role-play a situation in which the feminist perspective might be useful. Possible examples include:

1. A woman discovers her partner has had three affairs since they began dating 4 years ago.
2. A woman is frequently verbally abused by her partner.
3. A woman is physically abused by an alcoholic husband; she feels she cannot leave him because she has three young children and is not employed outside the home.
4. A female employee is being sexually harassed by her male employer; for financial reasons, she needs to continue working.

Step 3. Instruct the two volunteers to role-play this simulated counseling situation. After the role-playing, ask the class to discuss (1) what the "counselor" did well in applying the feminist perspective to counseling and (2) what else the "counselor" might have done to apply the feminist perspective to this counseling situation.

Step 4. If time permits, repeat Steps 2 and 3 with a different client problem.

EXERCISE D: Are You a Feminist?

GOAL: Help students assess the extent to which they have a feminist perspective and identify some key tenets of the feminist perspective.

Step 1. Instruct the students to answer "true" or "false" to each of the following statements on a sheet of paper. Inform them that their responses will remain anonymous and that they should not write their name on the paper. Read each statement slowly, giving the students an opportunity to answer.

STATEMENTS

1. Men make better supervisors than women.
2. Men make better leaders than women.
3. A woman would not do as good a job as a man in being president of this country.
4. Women should have the primary responsibility for raising children in our society.
5. In a heterosexual couple, the man should be the head of the household.
6. A male and a female living together should share the housework equally (for example, cleaning the bathroom, washing dishes, cooking, doing the laundry, vacuuming, grocery shopping, taking out the garbage).
7. Women and men living together tend to share housework equally in our society.
8. Women should have the same access to jobs and social status as men.
9. A man who frequently relates jokes that are degrading to women in a work setting where women are present is guilty of sexual harassment.
10. I am willing to advocate on behalf of women (for instance, poor women or women who have been sexually assaulted).
11. Our society is generally structured politically, socially, and economically by and for men.
12. In heterosexual couples, the male has the obligation to be the primary breadwinner.
13. It is generally inappropriate for a woman to ask a man out on a date.
14. A male has a right to expect sexual gratification after dating a woman several times.

Step 2. Write the numbers of the statements on the blackboard. Ask the students to hand in their responses. Ask for volunteers to tally the responses on the board.

Step 3. After the responses are tallied, reread each statement. Discuss the results, encouraging students to make comments or raise questions about the issues.

Step 4. End the exercise by indicating that those students who answered true to statements 6, 8, 9, 10, 11 and false to statements 1, 2, 3, 4, 5, 7, 12, 13, 14 probably have a belief system that is consistent with the feminist perspective.

EXERCISE E: Double Standards

GOAL: Help students identify and examine double standards for male and female interactions.

Step 1. Ask the males to form subgroups of four or five people and the females to form subgroups of four or five people. Ask each subgroup to identify double standards in dating relationships, marital relationships, and sexual behaviors between males and females. For example, society generally allows males to be more aggressive and to use more vulgar language, and males are expected to ask females for dates, but females traditionally have been raised to believe they should not ask males for dates. For each double standard, the subgroup should decide whether the double standard is desirable or undesirable. (Males are separated from females in this exercise because they may have differing views about the desirability of the double standards that are identified.)

Step 2. After the subgroups have completed their work, ask a representative from each subgroup to summarize the double standards the group identified and its views on the desirability of these double standards. Class discussion may well ensue. End the exercise by summarizing the items identified and the differences between males and females regarding the desirability of such double standards.

EXERCISE F: Understanding Stereotypes

GOAL: To increase understasnding of the origins and effects of stereotypes and to explore ways to change negative stereotypes.

Step 1. In subgroups of three or four students, make a list of common stereotypes about people who are:

On public assistance	Jewish
Gay	Native American
Elders	Hispanic
Asian	Black
Arab	White

Step 2. Each subgroup lists its stereotypes on aboard that displays the stereotypes to the whole class.

Step 3. A class discussion then is held on the following questions:

1. Are the stereotypes largely negative or positive?
2. Are the stereotypes accurate or erroneous?
3. What are the probable origins of these stereotypes?
4. What can be done to change the negative stereotypes in a more positive direction?

Competency Notes

EP 2a	Apply and communicate understanding of the importance of diversity and difference in shaping life experiences in practice at the micro, mezzo, and macro levels.
EP 2b	Present themselves as learners and engage clients and constituencies as experts of their own experiences.
EP 2c	Apply self-awareness and self-regulation to manage the influence of personal biases and values in working with diverse clients and constituencies.
EP 3a	Apply their understanding of social, economic, and environmental justice to advocate for human rights at the individual and system levels.
EP 3b	Engage in practices that advance social, economic, and environmental justice (all of this chapter).
	The content of the chapter and the exercises within the chapter are focused on students acquiring all of these behaviors.

Key Terms and Concepts

Color Blindness	Femininity Achievement	Philosophy of Equality	Stereotypes
De Facto	Incompatibility	Prejudice	Unconscious Racism
De Jure	Intersectionality	Queer	
Discrimination	Minority Group	Racism	
Diverse Groups	Oppression	Social Justice	

8

Self-Help Groups

Self-help groups are voluntary associations in which members provide each other with various types of help, usually nonmaterial and nonprofessional, for a particular shared, usually challenging, characteristic. The help may take the form of providing and evaluating relevant information, listening to and accepting others' experiences, sharing personal experiences, providing sympathetic understanding, and establishing social networks. A self-help group may also seek to better inform the public about an issue and perhaps engage in advocacy.

MENDED HEARTS: AN EXAMPLE

Founded by four patients recovering from heart surgery in a Boston hospital in 1951, Mended Hearts is now a national organization for heart surgery patients and their families.[1] The four patients shared their concerns about their uncertain future and the pain and changes in lifestyle they faced. They also focused on the positives—new feelings of well-being, their plans and hopes for the future, and the happiness they experienced from having "mended hearts." From these experiences, they concluded such conversations would be immensely helpful to others facing heart surgery. With the assistance of a heart surgeon, Dr. Dwight Harken, they formed the first Mended Hearts group. They adopted the slogan, "It's great to be alive and to help others." Mended Hearts was formally incorporated in 1955, and a constitution and bylaws were adopted. As hospitals began performing heart surgeries in other regions in the country in the 1960s, chapters of Mended Hearts were formed in these regions. With the number of heart surgeries sharply increasing since the 1960s, the number of chapters and members has grown dramatically.

Meetings are typically held in the hospitals where heart surgeries are performed. At a typical meeting, a physician or medical expert will speak on an aspect of heart disease, surgery, and the recovery process. Other meetings will feature other topics and speakers on exercise, Social Security, nutrition, insurance, employment, or related topics. A question-and-answer period usually follows. The meetings are open to heart patients, their spouses, and professionals.

Local chapters generally have a monthly newsletter with a variety of information on advances in heart surgery, inspirational material, anniversaries of members' heart surgeries, and announcements of the activities of the local and national organizations.

An important service provided by Mended Hearts is accredited visitors who visit heart patients before and after surgery to offer support, information, and encouragement. To become accredited, the visitors, who have all had heart surgery, attend a series of seminars (8 to 10 hours of training) that consist of lectures, role-plays, and discussions of visitor guidelines. They are

LEARNING OBJECTIVES

Self-help groups constitute one alternative to coping alone by assisting members to meet their specific needs through the understanding and help of others who have had similar experiences. This chapter will help prepare students to:

LO 1
Define self-help groups.

LO 2
Understand two classifications of self-help groups.

LO 3
Describe the benefits of self-help groups.

LO 4
Comprehend how to start a self-help group and the roles that social workers may play within self-help groups.

LO 5
Access online self-help groups.

then tested on their knowledge of functions of the heart, various heart problems, and the corresponding treatment approaches. Before making visits by themselves, prospective visitors accompany accredited visitors on their hospital rounds. This process screens potential visitors to ensure an effective, high-quality program.

Mended Hearts volunteers also provide online visiting to patients, family members, and caregivers through e-mail check-ins and by providing materials electronically. Such volunteers also provide telephone visiting to offer words of hope to patients, family members, and caregivers.

In a study of the impact of Mended Hearts, Borman and Lieberman conclude:

> Our findings with Mended Hearts . . . indicate that those patients who are forced into early retirement seem to benefit the most from their service responsibilities as Mended Hearts visitors. At the same time, from the perspective of those about to undergo heart surgery, such visits from those who have had the experience seem to be most welcome.[2]

LO 1   Define Self-Help Groups

DEFINITION AND CHARACTERISTICS

Self-help groups are diverse. Some are small, grassroots affiliations unrelated to external structures. Others are part of large, well-organized, national organizations. The diversity of self-help groups has been summarized by Lieberman and Borman:

> Self-help groups have been seen as support systems; as social movements; as spiritual movements and secular religions; as systems of consumer participation; as alternative care-giving systems adjunct to professional helping systems; as intentional communities; as subcultural entities that represent a way of life; as supplementary communities; as expressive-social influence groups; and as organizations of the deviant and stigmatized.[3]

Hepworth, Rooney, Rooney, and Strom-Gottfried and Larsen define self-help groups this way:

> In self-help groups, members have central shared concerns, such as coping with addiction, cancer, or obesity. These groups are distinguished from treatment and task groups by the fact that the self-help group is led by nonprofessionals who are managing the same issues as members of the group, even though a social worker or other professional may have aided in the development or sponsorship of the group. Self-help groups emphasize interpersonal support and the creation of an environment in which individuals may retake charge of their lives. Such groups offer resources and support for such shared problems as addictions, aggressive behavior, mental illness, disabilities, the death of a child, gambling, weight control, family violence, sexual orientation, and AIDS, among others. It is the social worker's task to offer support and consultation to such groups without taking them over.[4]

Self-help groups emphasize peer solidarity rather than hierarchical governance. They tend to disregard in their organizational structure the usual institutional distinctions between board of directors, professionals, and consumers, as members (at various times) give and receive help and share responsibility for performing leadership tasks and for accomplishing the goals of the group. Self-help groups tend to be self-supporting and thrive largely on donations from friends and relatives rather than on government funds, foundation grants, or fees from the public.

Riessman summarizes the distinctive characteristics of self-help groups as follows:

- Noncompetitive, cooperative orientation
- Anti-elite, antibureaucratic focus
- Emphasis on the indigenous—people who have the problem and know a lot about it from the inside, from experiencing it
- Attitude of do what you can, one day at a time. You can't solve everything at once.

- Shared, often revolving, leadership
- Attitude of being helped through helping (the helper-therapy principle) . . .
- Understanding that helping is not a commodity to be bought and sold
- Strong optimism regarding the ability to change
- Understanding that although small may not necessarily be beautiful, it is the place to begin and the unit to build on
- Critical stance toward professionalism, which is often seen as pretentious, purist, distant, and mystifying. Self-helpers like simplicity and informality.
- Emphasis on the consumer, or, in Alvin Toffler's term, the "prosumer." The consumer is a producer of help and services.
- Understanding that helping is at the center—knowing how to receive help, give help, and help yourself . . .
- Emphasis on empowerment[5]

When people help each other in self-help groups, they tend to feel empowered, as they are able to control important aspects of their lives. When help is given from the outside (from an expert or a professional), there is a danger that dependency may develop, which is the opposite effect of empowerment. Empowerment increases motivation, energy, personal growth, and an ability to help that goes beyond helping oneself or receiving help.

LO 2   Understand Two Classifications of Self-Help Groups

EP 7b

CLASSIFICATION OF SELF-HELP GROUPS

Two different classifications of self-help groups will be summarized in order to convey the varieties and focuses of self-help groups that now exist. The first classification is by Katz and Bender, and the second is by Powell.

Katz and Bender Classification

Katz and Bender have formulated the following classification of self-help groups [6]:

1. Groups that focus on self-fulfillment or personal growth; examples are Alcoholics Anonymous, Recovery, Inc. (for former mental patients); Gamblers Anonymous; and Weight Watchers.
2. Groups that focus on social advocacy; examples are welfare rights organizations, MADD (Mothers Against Drunk Drivers), and the Committee for the Rights of the Disabled. Katz and Bender note that the advocacy "can be both on behalf of broad issues, such as legislation, the creation of new services, change in the policies of existing institutions and so on; or it can be on behalf of individuals, families, or other small groups."[7]
3. Groups whose focus is to create alternative patterns for living; examples are gay liberation and certain religious cults, such as the Moonies.
4. "Outcast haven" or "rock-bottom" groups. Katz and Bender define this type as follows:

   These groups provide a refuge for the desperate, who are attempting to secure personal protection from the pressures of life and society, or to save themselves from mental or physical decline. This type of group usually involves a total commitment, a living-in arrangement or sheltered environment, with close supervision by peers or persons who have successfully grappled with similar problems of their own.[8]

   Ex-drug addict organizations are one example.

5. Groups of mixed types that have characteristics of two or more categories; an example is Parents Without Partners, which focuses on personal growth, advocacy, and providing social events.

Powell Classification

Powell classifies self-help groups into the following five categories[9]:

1. *Habit-disturbance organizations:* These organizations focus on a specific and concrete problem. Examples of this category include Alcoholics Anonymous, SmokeStoppers, Overeaters Anonymous, Gamblers Anonymous, Take Off Pounds Sensibly (TOPS), Women for Sobriety, Narcotics Anonymous, and Weight Watchers.

2. *General-purpose organizations:* In contrast to habit-disturbance organizations, general-purpose organizations address a wider range of problems and predicaments. Examples of this category are Parents Anonymous (for parents of abused children), Emotions Anonymous (for people with emotional problems), the Compassionate Friends (for people who have experienced a loss through death), and GROW, an organization that works to prevent the hospitalization of mental patients through a comprehensive program of mutual aid.

3. *Lifestyle organizations:* These organizations seek to provide support for, and advocate for, the lifestyles of people whose members are viewed by society as being different (the dominant groups in society are generally indifferent or hostile to that difference). Examples of this category include Widow-to-Widow Programs, Parents Without Partners, ALMA (Adoptees' Liberty Movement Association), Parents/FLAG (Parents and Friends of Lesbians and Gays), the National Gay and Lesbian Task Force, and the Gray Panthers, an intergenerational group that advocates for the elderly.

4. *Physical handicap organizations:* These organizations focus on major chronic diseases and conditions. Some are for people with conditions that are relatively stable, some for conditions that are likely to get worse, and some for terminal illnesses. Examples of this category include Make Today Count (for the terminally ill and their families), Emphysema Anonymous, Lost Chord clubs (for those who have had laryngectomies), stroke clubs, Mended Hearts, the Spina Bifida Association, and Self-Help for Hard of Hearing People.

5. *Significant-other organizations:* The members of these organizations are parents, spouses, and close relatives of troubled and troubling people. Very often, members of significant-other groups are last-resort caregivers. Significant others contend with dysfunctional behavior. Through sharing their feelings, they obtain a measure of relief. In the course of sharing, they may also learn about new resources or new approaches. Examples of such organizations include Al-Anon, Gam-Anon, Toughlove, and the National Alliance for the Mentally Ill.

LO 3   Describe the Benefits of Self-Help Groups

BENEFITS OF SELF-HELP GROUPS

Many direct-service self-help groups emphasize the following for their members: (1) a confession to the group that they have a problem; (2) a testimony to the group recounting their past experiences with the problem and their plans for handling the problem in the future; (3) the requirement that when a member feels an intense urge of a recurrence (such as to drink or abuse a child), the member calls another member of the group who comes over to stay with the person until the urge subsides.

There appear to be several reasons self-help groups are successful. The members have an internal understanding of the problem, which helps them to help others. Having experienced the misery and consequences of the problem, they are highly motivated and dedicated to finding ways to help themselves and their fellow sufferers. The participants also benefit from the helper-therapy principle; that is, the helper gains psychological rewards by helping others.[10] Helping others makes a person feel "good" and worthwhile and enables the helper to put his or her own problems into perspective. Other members have problems that may be as serious or more serious.

Some self-help groups (such as parents of children and adults with a cognitive disability) raise funds and operate community programs. Many people with a personal problem use self-help groups in the same way that others use social agencies. An additional advantage of self-help groups is that they generally operate with a minimal budget. As discussed earlier, self-help groups often empower their members. Over 1,200 self-help groups are now in existence.

Many people who have problematic behaviors (such as abusing their children) have few friends and relatives they can turn to for help and are thus socially isolated. Those who join a self-help group soon become aware that associating with caring others who have experienced similar problems is a source of immense support. Hepworth and Larsen summarize some of the benefits of a self-help group for members:

1. Having a reference group wherein one shares common problems or concerns with others and is accepted by them.
2. Gaining hope based on the knowledge that other members have experienced similar difficulties and are coping (or have coped) successfully with them.
3. Confronting problems head-on and accepting responsibility for them as a result of confrontations by other members.
4. Putting their problems in perspective and applying knowledge and skill derived from the experiences shared by others.[11]

Borman found five therapeutic factors of direct service self-help groups:

1. *Cognitive restructuring:* Members develop a new perspective on themselves and their problems.
2. *Hope:* Members develop hope that their lives will get better as they see the lives of others with similar problems improve.
3. *Altruism:* Members feel good about themselves for helping others.
4. *Acceptance:* Members feel they will not be rejected or blamed for their problems.
5. *Universality:* Members become aware that they are not alone in having the problems they face.[12]

Kurtz summarizes the results of some of the findings of outcome research on self-help groups:

> Useful outcomes of self-help participation included reduced psychiatric symptomatology, reduced use of professional services, increased coping skills, increased life satisfaction, and shorter hospital stays. Members of health-related groups reported better adjustment, better coping, higher self-esteem, and improved acceptance of the illness.[13]

LINKAGE WITH SOCIAL WORKERS

Because self-help groups are often more effective than one-to-one counseling or group therapy in treating problematic behaviors, it is vitally important that social workers relate to them constructively. Social workers need to be aware of the self-help groups available in their community so they can function as brokers or case managers in making appropriate referrals for clients. Social workers also need to be knowledgeable about how self-help groups function so that they work in synergy, rather than in competition, with such programs.

Another major function that social workers can perform with self-help groups is to work as consultants. There is a myth that self-help groups are antiprofessional. In reality, many were started with the help of one or more professionals, and most continue to receive professional consultation. Professionals can provide support and consultation on organizational issues, resources for members in unique circumstances, fundraising activities, efforts to enact or change legislation, and social advocacy efforts to change the service policies of one or more agencies. Maguire has provided a partial list of the ways in which a professional can assist a self-help group:

1. Help arrange a meeting place.
2. Help locate funds.

EXERCISE 8.1   Merits and Shortcomings of a Self-Help Group

GOAL: This exercise is designed to assist you in having a better understanding of the merits and shortcomings of self-help groups.

Describe an I-message you would use when someone does the following:

1. Interview someone who has participated in a self-help group. (If you have participated yourself, you may answer the questions in this exercise by sharing your personal experiences.) Most campuses have several self-help groups, such as an eating disorder group, a gay/lesbian group, and groups combating substance abuse. The student counseling center is usually a good resource for identifying contact people for the available self-help groups. Describe the goals of the self-help group that you investigate.

2. Describe the activities of this self-help group.

3. Ask the person you interview to summarize the merits and shortcomings of this self-help group and then record this information here.

3. Refer members to the group.
4. Arrange or provide training of members and leaders.
5. Accept referrals from the group.
6. Help provide credibility of the group within the professional community and within the community.[14]

Another important function that social workers can serve is to help form needed self-help groups in a community. Hepworth and Larsen note:

> Practitioners can also serve as organizers where resources are sparse and appropriate self-help groups do not exist. By working with clients who demonstrate leadership potential, a practitioner may stimulate them, assisting them as needed, to contact a national or regional self-help organization for the purpose of establishing a local chapter. If a national organization does not exist, the practitioner may serve as a catalyst and consultant in organizing a local group, which necessitates working with selected lay leaders in recruiting members, developing objectives and bylaws (if needed), arranging facilities, planning refreshments, and developing an organizational meeting.[15]

LO 4 Comprehend How to Start a Self-Help Group and the Roles That Social Workers May Play within Self-Help Groups

STARTING A SELF-HELP GROUP

Starting a self-help group is similar to starting any group. If there is a national organization, it is essential to contact this organization to get material on guidelines for establishing a local chapter. If a national organization does not exist, then it may be necessary to start from "scratch." The following kinds of questions need to be answered:

1. What are the goals of the group?
2. What kinds of services should be provided to meet the goals?
3. What are the criteria for membership?
4. What are the costs; for example, will dues be charged?
5. Where will the group meet?
6. How will potential members be contacted?
7. What are the procedures for joining and leaving the group?
8. What kind of organizational structure should the group have?

These questions should not be answered by the professional alone. Self-help groups tend to work best when concerned and motivated individuals who are facing a problem meet and arrive at answers to these questions. Most self-help groups have evolved as circumstances warrant rather than being carefully planned from the start.

A few comments will be made about some of these questions. Usually the nature of the problem will determine how to contact potential members. For example, if former heart surgery patients want to start a Mended Hearts chapter, they should first contact heart surgeons to explain the group and to determine if the surgeons would like a local chapter of Mended Hearts at the hospital. The surgeons can be a valuable resource by providing access to new patients facing heart surgery. For other groups, prospective members may be contacted in a variety of ways: radio and television announcements, notices in church buildings and social service agencies, flyers to service providers, door-to-door solicitation, flyers mailed to target groups, and notices in local newspapers.

Generally, it is best to hold meetings at a public agency, business, church, or private agency. If meetings are held in the home of a member, that member may eventually decide that regular meetings are too much of an inconvenience. Rotating meetings in the homes of individual members is generally not a good idea either because members may find it

Examples of Self-Help Groups

Organization	Service Focus
Abused Parents of America	For parents who are abused by their adult children
Adoptees' Liberty Movement Association	For adoptees searching for their natural parents
Alcoholics Anonymous	For adult alcoholics
American Diabetes Association	Clubs for diabetics, their families, and friends
American Sleep Apnea Association	For persons with sleep apnea and their families
Burns United Support Group	For burn victims
Candlelighters Childhood Cancer Foundation	For parents of young children with cancer
Concerned United Birthparents (CUB)	For parents who have surrendered children for adoption
Conjoined Twins International	For families of conjoined twins
CROHNS	For persons with Crohn's disease and their families
Depressed Anonymous	For depressed persons
Divorce Care	For divorced persons
Emotions Anonymous	For persons with emotional problems
Encephalitis Support Group	For those with encephalitis and their families
Families Anonymous	For relatives and friends of drug abusers
Fortune Society	For ex-offenders and their families
Gam-Anon	For families of gamblers
Gray Panthers	An intergenerational group
Herpes Anonymous	For persons with herpes and their families and friends
High Risk Moms, Inc.	For women experiencing a high-risk or problem pregnancy
Impotents World Association	For impotent men and their partners
Make Today Count	For persons with cancer and their families
Molesters Anonymous	For men who molest children
National Organization for Women	For women's rights
Overeaters Anonymous	For overweight persons
Parents Anonymous	For parents of abused children
Sexaholics Anonymous	For those with sexually self-destructive behavior
WINGS Foundation, Inc.	For men and women traumatized by incest

frustrating to continually locate new places. New members may get so discouraged with changes in the meeting place that they drop out.

In the process of starting a self-help group, Lieberman and Borman note:

> There is an early zig-zag process of groping, trying out various approaches, dropping some, and developing new ones. Changes occur on a number of fronts . . . : (1) organizational size; (2) organizational structure; (3) program focus; (4) nature of membership; (5) nature of leadership; (6) articulation with professionals and agencies; and (7) sources of financial support.[16]

The American Self-Help Group Clearinghouse is a web-based database of over 1,100 national and international self-help support groups for health, mental health, addictions, abuse, disabilities, parenting, caregiver concerns, and other stressful life situations. It is compiled and edited by Barbara J. White and Edward J. Madara, with the web version updated by Anita M. Broderick and Paul Riddleberger, PhD. Any self-help group contained in the database can be accessed by typing a keyword on the website. The website can be easily accessed by going to the Internet and typing in "American Self-Help Group Clearinghouse."

LO 5   Access Online Self-Help Groups

ONLINE SELF-HELP GROUPS

The personal computer is a tool for overcoming some of the traditional barriers to group participation. Such barriers include no local self-help group available, lack of time or transportation for travel, limitations of a severe physical disability, and rarity of the condition. Over 1,200 self-help groups now connect people with one another through e-mail, chat rooms, and websites on the Internet.[17] The personal computer can be a source of education about disabilities by providing information to both sufferers and interested professionals. For example, the frequently forgotten population of homebound caregivers can use a computer to find specific information and prompt support.

Online self-help groups readily can be accessed with a personal computer. If you don't know the exact address for an online self-help group that you want, simply go to the Internet and type in "American Self-Help Group Clearinghouse." When the website is accessed, type in a keyword of the online support group that you want on the website.

Some self-help groups (such as the Alzheimer's Association) offer home pages that provide hypertext links to an immense variety of literature. (**Hypertext** refers to highlighted words or images that, when selected by mouse click or keyboard arrow, connect directly with another resource without the necessity of typing or even knowing its web address.)

There are four primary forms of online self-help support networks: (1) chat rooms, (2) bulletin boards, (3) e-mail, and (4) listservs. Chat rooms are virtual spaces where individuals can post messages and receive feedback interactively in a short time frame. In contrast, bulletin boards are usually open 24 hours a day. They enable individuals to post messages that can be answered at any time. E-mail allows an individual to write messages to particular individuals who can respond at any time. Listservs allow large groups of individuals to present and receive information and news. Thus, some computer-assisted group meetings occur in real time; that is, everyone participates at a specific time and the discussion is interactive. Other group meetings require members to post messages to which other members can respond at any time.

Alcoholics Anonymous: A Self-Help Group

In 1929, Bill Wilson was a stock analyst. When the stock market crashed, he lost most of his money and took to the bottle: A few years later his doctor warned him that his continual drinking was jeopardizing his health and his life. Bill W. underwent what he perceived was a spiritual experience, and he made a commitment to stop drinking. He had discovered that discussing his drinking problem with other alcoholics helped him to remain sober. One of the people he discussed his problem with was Robert Smith, an Ohio doctor and an alcoholic. Together they formed Alcoholics Anonymous (AA), a self-help group composed of recovering alcoholics.

AA stresses (1) an admission to the group that the member has a drinking problem, (2) a testimony to the group, recounting past experiences with the drinking problem and plans for handling the problem in the future, and (3) support from another member of the group, who will even stay with a person who feels an intense urge to drink until the urge subsides. Today, AA has chapters in over 100 countries.

The term "recovering" is used because AA believes there is no such thing as a permanently recovered alcoholic. The local chapters (usually from 10 to 30 persons per chapter) meet once or twice a week for discussion sessions. These groups resemble traditional group therapy meetings without the presence of a trained professional leader.

Bill W. and Dr. Bob, as they are known within AA, remained anonymous until their deaths; local chapters still follow the treatment procedures they initiated: the sharing of similar experiences in order to abstain from the first drink that is too many and the thousand drinks that are not enough.

AA is still widely regarded as the treatment approach that has the best chance of helping an alcoholic. In testimony to its value are hundreds of other self-help groups with treatment programs based on the AA model—Weight Watchers, Prison Families Anonymous, Parents Without Partners, Debtors Anonymous, Gamblers Anonymous, Emotions Anonymous, Emphysema Anonymous, and many more.

SOURCE: Gartner, A., & Wessman, F. (1980). *Help: A working guide to self-help groups* (p. 8). New York: Franklin-Watts.

EXERCISE 8.2   Checking Out Outline Self-Help Groups

GOAL: This exercise is designed to familiarize you with online self-help groups.

Using the Internet, check out the web pages of three online self-help groups. Some suggested websites are the following:

Alcoholics Anonymous: www.alcoholicsanonymous.org
Adult Children of Alcoholics: www.adultchildren.org
American Foundation for Suicide Prevention: www.afsp.org
Gamblers Anonymous: www.gamblersanonymous.org
Overeaters Anonymous: www.overeatersanonymous.org
Sexaholics Anonymous: www.sa.org

Summarize the information you found for the three online self-help groups

An AA Meeting

Alcoholics Anonymous (AA) is a remarkable human organization. Its chapters now cover every part of the United States and most of the world. There is more caring and concern among the members for one another than in most other organizations. Group members work together to save each other's lives and restore self-respect and sense of worth. AA has helped more people overcome their drinking problems than all other therapies and methods combined.

AA is supported entirely by voluntary donations from the members at meetings. There are no dues or fees. Each chapter is autonomous, free of any outside control by the AA headquarters in New York City or by any other body. There is no hierarchy in the chapters. The only office is that of group secretary. This person chooses a chairperson for each meeting, makes the arrangements for meetings, and sees that the building is opened, the chairs set up, and the tea and coffee put on. The group secretary holds office for only a limited time period; after a month or two the secretary's responsibilities are transferred to another member.

The only requirement for membership in AA is a desire to stop drinking. All other variables (such as economic status, social status, race, religion) do not count. Members can even attend meetings while drunk, as long as they do not disturb the meeting.

AA meetings are held in a variety of physical locations—churches, temples, private homes, business offices, schools,

libraries, or banquet rooms of restaurants. The physical location is unimportant.

When a newcomer first arrives, he or she will usually find people setting up chairs, placing ashtrays, putting free literature on a table, and making coffee. Other members will be socializing in small groups. Someone is apt to introduce himself or herself and other members to the newcomer. If someone is shy about attending the first meeting alone, he or she can call AA and someone will take the person to the meeting and introduce him or her to the other members.

When the meeting starts, everyone sits down around tables or in rows of chairs. The secretary and/or chairperson and one or more speakers sit at the head of a table or on a platform if the meeting is in a hall.

The chairperson opens with a moment of silence, which is followed by a group recitation of a prayer that is nondenominational. The chairperson then reads or gives a brief description of Alcoholics Anonymous and may read or refer to a section of the book *Alcoholics Anonymous* (a book that describes the principles of AA and gives a number of case examples).

Then the chairperson usually asks if anyone is attending for the first, second, or third time. The new people are asked to introduce themselves according to the following: "Hello, my name is (first name), and this is my first (second, third)

(continued)

An AA Meeting (*continued*)

meeting." Those who do not want to introduce themselves are not pressured to do so. New members are the lifeblood of AA and the most important people at the meeting in the members' eyes. (All the longer-term members remember their first meeting and how frightened and inhibited they felt.)

If the group is small, the chairperson usually then asks the longer-term members to introduce themselves and say a few words. If the group is large, the chairperson asks volunteers among the longer-term members to introduce themselves by saying a few words. Each member usually begins by saying, "My name is (first name), I am an alcoholic" and then discloses a few thoughts or feelings. (The members do not have to say they are alcoholics unless they choose to do so.) All members sooner or later generally choose to say this, to remind themselves that they are addictive drinkers who are recovering and that alcoholism is a lifelong disease, which they must battle daily. Those who introduce themselves usually say whatever they feel will be most helpful to the newcomers. They may talk about their first meeting, or their first week without drinking, or something designed to make the newcomers more comfortable. Common advice for the newcomers is to get the phone numbers of other members after the meeting so that they can call them when they feel a strong urge to drink. AA considers such help as vital in recovering. The organization believes members can remain sober only through receiving the help of people who care about them and who understand what they are struggling with.

AA members want newcomers to call when they have the urge to drink, at any time, day or night. The members sincerely believe that by helping others they are helping themselves to stay sober and grow. Members indicate such calling is the newcomer's ace in the hole against the first drink, if everything else fails. They also inform newcomers that it is good to call others when lonely just to chat.

In his own words, a newcomer explains how AA began to help him:

> Here's what happened to me. When I finally hit bottom and called AA for help, a U.S. Air Force officer came to tell me about AA. For the first time in my life, I was talking to someone who obviously really understood my problem, as four psychiatrists had not, and he took me to my first meeting, sober but none too steady. It was amazing. I went home afterward and didn't have a drink. I went again the next night, still dry, and the miracle happened a second time. The third morning my wife went off to work, my boys to school, and I was alone. Suddenly I wanted a drink more than I had ever wanted one in my life. I tried walking for a while. No good. The feeling was getting worse. I tried reading. Couldn't concentrate. Then I became really desperate, and although I wasn't used to calling strangers for help,

I called Fred, an AA-er who had said that he was retired and would welcome a call at any time. We talked a bit; he could see that talking on the phone wasn't going to be enough. He said, "Look, I've got an idea. Let me make a phone call, and I'll call you back in ten minutes. Can you hold on that long?" I said I could. He called back in eight, asking me to come over to his house. We talked endlessly, went out for a sandwich together, and finally my craving for a drink went away. We went to a meeting. Next morning I was fine again, and now I had gone four days without a drink.[1]

After such discussion, speakers may describe their lives of drinking, how drinking almost destroyed their lives, how they were introduced to AA, their struggles to remain sober one day at a time, how AA has helped them, and what their lives are now like.

At the end of a meeting the chairperson may ask the newcomers if they wish to say anything. If they do not wish to say much, that is okay. No one is pressured to self-disclose what they do not want to reveal.

Meetings usually end after the chairperson makes announcements. (The collection basket for donations is also passed around. New members are not expected, and frequently not allowed, to donate any money until after their third meeting. If someone cannot afford to make a donation, none is expected.) The group then stands, usually holding hands, and repeats in unison the Lord's Prayer. Those who do not want to join in this prayer are not pressured to do so. After a meeting the members socialize. This is a time for newcomers to meet new friends and to get phone numbers.

AA is a cross-section of people from all walks of life. Anonymity is emphasized. It is the duty of every member to respect the anonymity of every person who attends. Concern for anonymity is a major reason for two kinds of meetings in AA, open and closed. Anyone is welcome at open meetings. Only people with drinking problems are allowed at closed meetings. Therefore, if a person feels uncomfortable going to an open meeting and has a drinking problem, closed meetings are an alternative.

Members do not have to believe in God to get help from AA. Many members have lost, or never had, a faith in God. AA does, however, assert that faith in some higher power is a tremendous help in recovery because such a belief offers a source of limitless power, hope, and support whenever one feels he or she has come to the end of his or her resources.

How does AA help? New members, after years of deteriorating feelings of rejection, loneliness, misunderstanding, guilt, and embarrassment, find they are not alone. They feel understood by others who are in similar predicaments. Instead of being rejected,

---

[1]   Vaughan, C. (1984). *Addictive drinking* (pp. 75–76). New York: Penguin Books.

(continued)

they are welcomed. They see that others who had serious drinking problems are now sober, apparently happy that way, and are in the process of recovering. It gives them hope that they do not need alcohol to get through the day and that they can learn to enjoy life without alcohol. They find that others sincerely care about them, want to help them, and have the knowledge to do so.

At meetings they see every sort of personal problem brought up and discussed openly, with suggestions for solutions being offered by others who have encountered similar problems. They can observe that group members bring up "unspeakable" problems without apparent embarrassment and that others listen and treat them with respect and consideration. Such acceptance gradually leads newcomers to share their personal problems and to receive constructive suggestions for solutions. Such disclosure leads individuals to look more deeply into themselves and to ventilate deep personal feelings. With the support of other members, newcomers gradually learn how to counter strong desires to drink through such processes as calling other members.

Newcomers learn that AA is the means of staying away from that first drink. AA also serves to reduce the stress that compels people to drink by (1) providing a comfortable and relaxed environment and (2) having members help each other to find ways to reduce the stresses encountered in daily living. AA meetings and members become a safe port that is always there when storms start raging. AA helps members to be programmed from negative thinking to positive thinking. The more positive a member's thinking becomes and the more stress is relieved, the better he or she begins to feel about himself or herself, the more the compulsion to drink decreases, and the more often and more effectively the person begins to take positive actions to solve his or her problems.

Computer-mediated services have a number of advantages. They offer a variety and diversity of support. They can provide services to homebound people for whom transportation to the offices of professionals is a major challenge. They can provide services to individuals in geographic areas that have few, or almost no, human services. They also offer anonymity to those who do not like to share the details of their concerns in face-to-face settings. Online services, after the initial purchase of a computer, are relatively inexpensive.

EXERCISE 8.3   Using the American Self-Help Group Clearinghouse

EP 8a

GOAL: This exercise is designed to show you how to access the website for the American Self-Help Group Clearinghouse.

1. Identify a problem (such as a health problem or a personal problem) that a friend or relative has. Go to the Internet and type in "American Self-Help Group Clearinghouse." Then type in the name of the problem. If no self-help group is available, then select another problem that a friend or relative has, and type in that problem.

2. Summarize the information you found for self-help groups that focus on this problem.

Computer-mediated services also have some shortcomings. Computer-mediated services often lack clear and accountable leadership—which can lead to misinformation or even potentially harmful interactions; for example, some vulnerable people have been victimized by sexual predators whom they met over the Internet.

Over 1,200 additional self-help groups can be located by typing in "American Self-Help Group Clearinghouse" on the Internet. When this website is accessed, type in a keyword of the support group that you want.

Summary

The following summarizes the chapter's content in terms of the learning objectives presented at the beginning of the chapter.

1. **Define self-help groups.**
   Self-help groups are voluntary associations in which members provide each other with various types of help, usually nonmaterial and nonprofessional, for a particular shared, usually challenging, characteristic. Self-help groups have been seen as social movements, support systems, spiritual movements and secular religions, systems of consumer participation, alternative care-giving systems adjunct to professional helping systems, intentional communities, subcultural entities that represent a way of life, supplementary communities, and organizations of the deviant and stigmatized. There is immense diversity among various self-help groups.

2. **Understand two classifications of self-help groups.**
   Katz and Bender classify self-help groups as:
   1. Groups that focus on self-fulfillment or personal growth
   2. Groups that focus on social advocacy
   3. Groups whose focus is to create alternative patterns for living
   4. "Outcast haven" or "rock-bottom" groups"
   5. Groups of mixed types that have characteristics of two or more categories

   Powell classifies self-help groups as:

   1. Habit disturbance organizations
   2. General-purpose organizations
   3. Lifestyle organizations
   4. Physical handicap organizations
   5. Significant-other organizations

3. **Describe the benefits of self-help groups.**
   Self-help groups have an impressive track record in being successful. Because self-help groups are often more effective than one-to-one counseling or group therapy in treating problematic behaviors, it is very important that social workers relate to them constructively.

4. **Comprehend how to start a self-help group and the roles that social workers may play within self-help groups.**
   Starting a self-help group is similar to starting any group. Guidelines are presented on how a social worker should start a self-help group and the roles that social workers may play within the self-help groups.

5. **Access online self-help groups.**
   More than 1,200 self-help groups can be located by typing in "American Self-Help Group Clearinghouse" on the Internet. When this website is accessed, type in a keyword of the self-help group that you want.

Group Exercises

EXERCISE A: Alcoholics Anonymous

GOAL: To increase awareness of how a self-help group functions.

Step 1. Local chapters of Alcoholics Anonymous usually hold some open meetings that anyone may attend. The leader contacts a local chapter, inquires whether the class may attend, and makes the necessary arrangements—including time, date, and place. If these arrangements cannot be made with AA, the leader contacts other self-help groups in the community.

Step 2. At the class period following the meeting of the self-help group, the leader leads a discussion of the students' thoughts about the meeting they attended. The class also discusses the merits and shortcomings of this self-help group.

EXERCISE B: Combating Terrorism

GOAL: To increase awareness of how a social action self-help group functions.

Step 1. The leader explains the purpose of the exercise and indicates that terrorism is one of the most serious problems currently faced by all nations. The students are told that their function is to serve as a social action self-help group. The class forms subgroups of five or six people. Each subgroup has the task of developing recommendations that this self-help group will then advocate to confront worldwide terrorism. (If the leader thinks it advisable, some other topic may be chosen.)

Step 2. Each subgroup selects its top three recommendations for confronting worldwide terrorism.

Step 3. The class reassembles. Each subgroup presents its three recommendations and lists them on the blackboard; the students then select the top five recommendations their self-help group ought to advocate for. A discussion should then follow on how this self-help group can realistically seek to implement these recommendations.

Competency Notes

EP 7b   Apply knowledge of human behavior and the social environment, person-in-environment, and other multidisciplinary theoretical frameworks in the analysis of assessment data from clients and constituencies (pp. 254–255).

The Katz and Bender classification and the Powell classification of self-help groups provide conceptual frameworks for students to assess and better understand the diversity of self-help groups.

EP 8a   Critically choose and implement interventions to achieve practice goals and enhance capacities of clients and constituencies (p. 263).

This exercise introduces students to the American Self-Help Clearinghouse, which has information on more than 1,200 self-help groups. Social workers are apt to find this clearinghouse a valuable resource to refer clients to who could benefit from a self-help group.

Key Term and Concept

Hypertext

9

Social Work with Families

The focus of social work services is often the family, an interacting, interdependent system. The problems faced by people are usually influenced by the dynamics within the family, and dynamics within the family are, in turn, influenced by the wider social and cultural environment. Because a family is an interacting system, change in any member will affect all others. Tensions between a husband and wife, for example, will be felt by their children, who may then respond with disturbed behavior. Treating the children's behavior alone will not get to the root of the family problem.[1]

Another reason for the focus on the family rather than the individual is that other family members are often needed in the treatment process. They can help identify family patterns. In addition, the whole family, once members perceive the relationships among their various behaviors, can form a powerful team in reestablishing healthier patterns. For example, family members can pressure their alcoholic mother to acknowledge her problem. They may provide important emotional support for her efforts to stop drinking. They may also need counseling themselves (or support from a self-help group) to assist in coping with them when she is drinking.

LO 1   Describe the Diversity of Family Forms

DIVERSITY OF FAMILY FORMS

The family is a social institution that is found in every culture. The U.S. Census defines **family** as a group of two or more persons related by blood, marriage, or adoption.[2] It should be noted that such a definition does not cover a number of living arrangements in which the members consider themselves to be a family, such as:

- A husband and wife raising two foster children who have been in the household for several years
- Two lesbians in a loving relationship, who are raising children born to one of the partners in a previous heterosexual marriage
- A man and a woman who have been living together for years in a loving relationship but have never legally married

A broader definition of *family* that encompasses all of the above is as follows: a family is a kinship system of all relatives living together or recognized as a social unit.[3] Such a definition recognizes unmarried same-sex and opposite-sex couples and families, foster families, children being raised by grandparents, and any relationship that functions or feels like a family.

LEARNING OBJECTIVES

A family is one category out of a number of categories of small groups. This chapter will help prepare students to:

LO 1
Describe the diversity of family forms

LO 2
Describe the societal functions of families

LO 3
Understand how to use two family assessment techniques

LO 4
Comprehend aspects of families for workers to focus on

LO 5
Describe family problems and the social work services available to families

A wide diversity of family patterns exists in the world. Families in different cultures take a variety of forms. In some societies, the husband and wife live in separate buildings. In others, they live apart for several years after the birth of a child. In some societies, husbands are permitted to have more than one wife. In a few countries, wives are allowed to have more than one husband. Some cultures permit (and a few encourage) premarital and extramarital intercourse.

Some societies have large communes where adults and children live together. There are communes in which the children are raised separately from adults. In some cultures, surrogate parents (rather than the natural parents) raise the children. Some societies encourage certain types of gay/lesbian relationships, and a few recognize gay/lesbian, as well as heterosexual, marriages.

In many cultures, marriages are still arranged by the parents. In a few societies, an infant may be "married" before birth (if the baby is of the wrong sex, the marriage is dissolved). Some societies do not recognize romantic love. Some cultures expect older men to marry young girls. Others expect older women to marry young boys. Most societies prohibit the marriage of close relatives, but a few subcultures encourage marriage between brothers and sisters or between first cousins. Some expect a man to marry his father's brother's daughter, whereas others insist that he marry his mother's sister's daughter. In some societies, a man, on marrying, makes a substantial gift to the bride's father, whereas in others the bride's father gives a substantial gift to the new husband.

These are indeed substantial variations in family patterns. People in each of these societies feel strongly that their particular pattern is normal and proper, and many feel the pattern is divinely ordained. Suggested changes in their particular form are viewed with suspicion and defensiveness and are often sharply criticized as being unnatural, immoral, and a threat to the survival of the family.

In spite of these variations, sociologists note that most family systems can be classified into two basic forms: The extended family and the nuclear family. An **extended family** consists of a number of relatives living together, such as parents, children, grandparents, great-grandparents, aunts, uncles, in-laws, and cousins. The extended family is the predominant pattern in preindustrial societies. The members divide various agricultural, domestic, and other duties among themselves.

A **nuclear family** consists of a married couple and their children living together. The nuclear family type emerged from the extended family. Extended families tend to be more functional in agricultural societies where many "hands" are needed; the nuclear family is more suited to the demands of complex, industrialized societies, as its smaller size and potential geographic mobility enable it to adapt more easily to changing conditions—such as the need to relocate to obtain a better job.

Although the nuclear family is still the predominant family form in the United States, Canada, and many other industrialized countries, it is a serious mistake for social workers and other helping professionals to use the nuclear family as the ideal model that individuals in our society should strive to form. Many other family forms are functioning in our society, such as the following:

- A married couple without children who are the primary caregivers for the wife's mother, who has Alzheimer's disease and resides with the couple
- Two gay men in a committed relationship, each of whom has joint custody of two children with his former wife
- A childless married couple who have decided not to conceive children
- A single parent with three young children
- A blended family in which the husband and wife have children in the current marriage, plus children from earlier marriages, all of whom live in the household
- An unmarried young couple living together in what amounts to a trial marriage

In the past few decades, there has been a trend in the United States for greater diversity in marital arrangements and family forms. There are increasing numbers of transracial marriages, marriages between spouses of diverse ages and cultural backgrounds, transracial adoptions, single-parent families, and blended families. Although some social workers may personally judge a few of these types to be "wrong," it is essential that they not allow their personal beliefs to reduce the quality or quantity of professional services that are provided to these family units. It is also essential that social workers who work with families of diverse cultural backgrounds learn about those backgrounds and understand the customary norms for family functioning.

Some family forms have been discriminated against, such as a single-parent household and a gay or lesbian couple with children. Recognizing this discrimination, the Council on Social Work in Education's *Educational Policy and Accreditation Standards* (2015) identified "marital status" as a population at risk and thereby a group that social workers are obligated to work with to end discrimination.[4]

EXERCISE 9.1   Composition and Strengths of My Family

EP 1b

GOAL: This exercise is designed to assist you in identifying your "core" family members and the strengths of your family.

1. Specify the names and approximate ages of your "core" family members. (These may, or may not, include aunts, uncles, grandparents, foster children, etc.) Also, briefly describe each member. (Example: Jim Ryberg is my dad. He is 47, a truck driver, and a devout Catholic.)

2. Specify the strengths of your family. (Do not identify current family challenges, which will be focused on in a later exercise.) Consider such strengths as reputation in the community, health of members, exercise patterns, caring for one another, educational levels, financial resources, support from others, religious values, fun activities the family does together, rituals for family holidays, and so on.

LO 2   Describe the Societal Functions of Families

SOCIETAL FUNCTIONS OF FAMILIES

Families in modern industrial societies perform the following essential functions that help maintain the continuity and stability of society:

1. *Replacement of the population.* Every society has some system for replacing its members. Practically all societies consider the family the unit in which children are to be produced. Societies define the rights and responsibilities of the reproductive partners within the family unit. These rights and responsibilities help maintain the stability of society, although they are defined differently from one society to another.

2. *Care of the young.* Children require care and protection until at least the age of puberty. The family is a primary institution for the rearing of children. Modern societies have generally developed supportive institutions to help in caring for the young—for example, medical services, day care centers, parent training programs, and residential treatment centers.

3. *Socialization of new members.* To become productive members of society, children have to be socialized into the culture. Children are expected to acquire a language, learn social values and mores, and dress and behave within the norms of society. The family plays a major role in this socialization process. In modern societies, numerous other groups and resources are also involved in this socialization process. Schools, the mass media, peer groups, the police, movies, and books and other written material are important influences. (Sometimes these different influences clash by advocating opposing values and attitudes.)

4. *Regulation of sexual behavior.* Failure to regulate sexual behavior results in clashes between individuals because of jealousy and exploitation. Every society has rules that regulate sexual behavior within family units. Most societies, for example, have incest taboos, and most disapprove of extramarital sex.

5. *Source of affection.* Humans need affection, emotional support, and positive recognition from others (including approval, smiles, encouragement, and reinforcement for accomplishments). Without such affection and recognition, our emotional, intellectual, physical, and social growth would be stunted. The family is an important source for obtaining affection and recognition because family members generally regard each other as among the most important people in their lives and gain emotional and social satisfaction from family relationships.

LO 3   Understand How to Use Two Family Assessment Techniques

EP 7b

FAMILY ASSESSMENT

There are a variety of ways to assess families. Conducting a social history of a family and its members is a widely used approach. With regard to family assessment, however, two techniques have received considerable discussion in recent years: eco-maps and genograms.

The Eco-Map

The eco-map (see Figure 9.1) is a paper-and-pencil assessment tool used to assess specific troubles and plan interventions for clients. The eco-map, a drawing of the client family in its social environment, is usually drawn jointly by the social worker and the client. It helps both parties achieve a holistic or ecological view of the client's family life and the nature of the family's relationships with groups, associations, organizations, and other families and individuals. The eco-map has been used in a variety of situations, including marriage and family counseling and adoption and foster care home studies. It has also been used to supplement traditional social histories and case records. The eco-map is a shorthand method for recording basic social information. The technique helps clients and workers gain insight into the clients' problems by providing a "snapshot view" of important interactions at a particular point in time. Ann Hartman is the primary developer of this tool.[5]

A typical eco-map consists of a family diagram surrounded by a set of circles and lines used to describe the family within an environmental context. Eco-map users can create their own abbreviations and symbols, but the most commonly used symbols are shown in Figure 9.1.

First, a circle (representing the client's family) is drawn in the center of a large blank sheet of paper (see Figure 9.2). The composition of the family is indicated in the circle.

FIGURE 9.1 **Commonly Used Symbols in an Eco-Map**

40	Female, 40 years old
38	Male, 38 years old
▲	Person, sex and age unknown
62	Deceased female, died at age 62
++++++++	A stressful, conflict-laden relationship
– – – – – –	A tenuous, uncertain relationship
———	A positive relationship or resource (the thicker the line, the stronger or more positive the relationship or resource)
——→	The direction of the giving and receiving exchanges of a relationship or resource (in some relationships, the client may primarily receive or give)

FIGURE 9.2 **Setting Up an Eco-Map**

Social Environment

FIGURE 9.3   **Sample Eco-Map: The Wilbur Family**

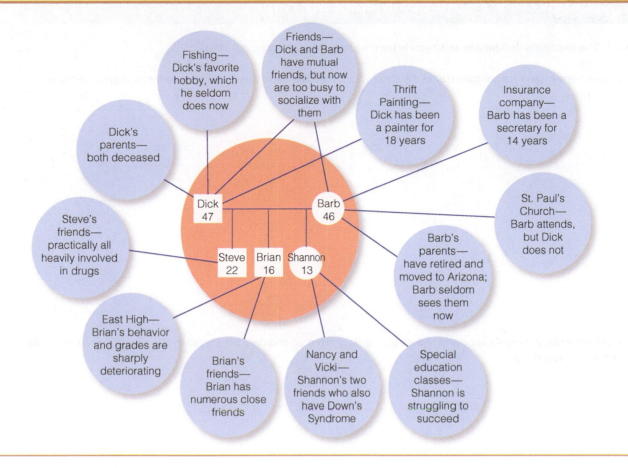

Other circles are then drawn around the family circle. These circles represent other systems—that is, the groups, other families, individuals, and organizations—with which the family ordinarily interacts.

Lines are drawn to describe the relationships that members of the client family have with these systems. Arrows show the flow of energy (giving or receiving resources, and communication between family members and significant systems). Figure 9.3 shows the eco-map for the Wilbur family case example (see box on p. 273)

A major value of an eco-map is that it helps both worker and client view the client's family from a system and ecological perspective. Sometimes, as happened in the Wilbur case example, clients and workers gain greater insight into the social dynamics of a problematic situation.

In summary, eco-maps are useful to both workers and clients. For the workers, a completed eco-map graphically displays important interactions of a client family with other systems (that is, the groups, other families, individuals, and organizations) that the family ordinarily interacts with at a particular point in time. Such a diagram allows the worker to better understand the environmental factors affecting the family. It then helps the worker generate hypotheses of problematic dynamics in the family-environmental system, which the worker can then further explore by questioning the family members. Once problematic dynamics are identified, the worker can focus attention on helping family members generate strategies to resolve the problematic dynamics.

Similarly, for the client family members, an eco-map helps them identify and understand problematic dynamics in their family-environmental system. Once identified, family

EXERCISE 9.2   An Eco-Map of My Family

GOAL: This exercise is designed to assist you in learning how to construct an eco-map.

1. Draw an eco-map of a significant day in the life of your family. The event may be a happy event (perhaps a wedding) or a crisis.

2. Briefly describe the significant event represented in your eco-map and the roles played by the people and other significant factors you identified.

members are then in a position to generate strategies (together with their worker) to resolve the dynamics.

The Genogram

The genogram is a graphic way of investigating the origins of a client's or client family's presenting problem by diagramming the family over at least three generations. The client and worker usually jointly construct the family genogram, which is essentially a family tree. Bowen is the primary developer of this technique.[6] The genogram helps the worker and family members examine problematic emotional and behavioral patterns in an inter-generational context. Patterns tend to repeat themselves; what happens in one generation often occurs in the next. Genograms help family members identify and understand family relationship patterns.

Case Example of Using an Eco-Map: The Wilbur Family

Barb and Dick Wilbur are contacted by Mary Timm, school social worker at East High School. The Wilburs' second-oldest' son, Brian (age 16), had a knife in his jacket at school and liquor on his breath. The Wilburs are shocked. They agree to meet with Ms. Timm the next day to discuss these incidents. Brian will also be present.

At the meeting Ms. Timm asks Brian why he brought a knife to school. At first, he refuses to respond. Ms. Timm also notes that records show he used to receive mainly B's, but now his grades are primarily D's and F's. Mr. and Mrs. Wilbur also sternly ask Brian what is happening. They add that the school system has informed them that he apparently has been drinking during school hours. Gradually tears come to Brian's eyes. He says no one cares about him. He asserts his parents are too busy at work and too busy looking after his older brother, Steve, and his younger sister, Shannon.

At first, Mr. and Mrs. Wilbur are surprised. They indicate they love Brian very much. Gradually they disclose they have been so involved with the demands of their other two children that they may have been "shortchanging" Brian in recent months. Shannon, age 13, has Down's syndrome and requires considerable individual attention, especially with her coursework (Shannon is enrolled in special education courses.)

Brian is asked where he obtained the knife. He hesitantly indicates his older brother, Steve, gave it to him for "protection." Brian adds that he sees nothing wrong with carrying a knife. Steve frequently carries a pistol. In addition, Brian says Steve urged him to take the knife to school because some people who are unhappy with Steve have said they may come after Brian. Ms. Timm asks Mr. and Mrs. Wilbur if they know anything about this. Barb and Dick suggest it may be best if Brian is excused at this point. Ms. Timm sets up a later meeting with Brian, and he leaves.

Both Barb and Dick then become teary-eyed. They indicate they are nearing their wit's end. Both work full time, and in recent years Steve and Shannon have required so much of their attention that they now no longer are able to spend any time with their former friends. In addition, they have been arguing more and more. They feel that their family is disintegrating and that they are "failing" as parents. They also disclose that Steve is addicted to both alcohol and cocaine and has been for several years. He has been in for inpatient treatment three times but always goes back to using soon after leaving treatment. They don't know where Steve is getting the money for his cocaine habit. They fear he may be dealing. He hasn't been able to hold a full-time job. He is usually terminated because he shows up for work while under the influence. Currently, he is working part-time as a bartender.

Mr. and Mrs. Wilbur fear that unless something is done soon, Brian may follow in Steve's footsteps. They add they have contemplated asking Steve to leave but are reluctant to do so because they feel it is their parental obligation to provide a house for their children as long as the children want to stay.

At this point Ms. Timm suggests it may be helpful to diagram their present dilemma. Together the Wilburs and Ms. Timm draw the eco-map shown in Figure 9.3 (see p. 271)

While drawing the map, Ms. Timm asks whether providing housing for Steve is helping him or whether it may be a factor in enabling him to continue his drug use and his irresponsible behavior. The eco-map helps the Wilburs see that as a result of working full time and spending the remainder of their working hours caring for Shannon, Steve, and Brian, they are gradually becoming too emotionally and physically exhausted to cope. During the past few years, they have stopped socializing. The Wilburs ask Ms. Timm to explain what she means by "enabling" Steve to continue his drug use and his irresponsible behavior. Ms. Timm explains enabling and indicates that a "tough love" approach may be an option. (In this case, a tough love approach would involve the Wilburs' demanding that Steve live elsewhere if he continues to abuse alcohol and cocaine.) Ms. Timm also gives them pamphlets that describe enabling and tough love. They make an appointment for the next week.

For the next several weeks Ms. Timm continues to meet weekly with the Wilburs and individually with Brian. The Wilburs eventually decide to use a tough love approach with Steve. Steve leaves but continues to use alcohol and cocaine. However, living on his own does appear to be somewhat beneficial, as he now works full time at a maintenance job to pay his bills. With Steve out of the house, Barb and Dick are able to spend more time with Brian and Shannon, and they begin to socialize again with some of their former friends.

Commonly used genogram symbols are shown in Figure 9.4. Together, the symbols provide a visual picture of a family tree for at least three generations, including the following: who the members are; their names, ages, and gender; marital status; sibling positions; and so on. When relevant, additional items of information are included, such as emotional difficulties, behavioral problems, religious affiliation, ethnic origins, geographic

FIGURE 9.4   **Commonly Used Genogram Symbols**

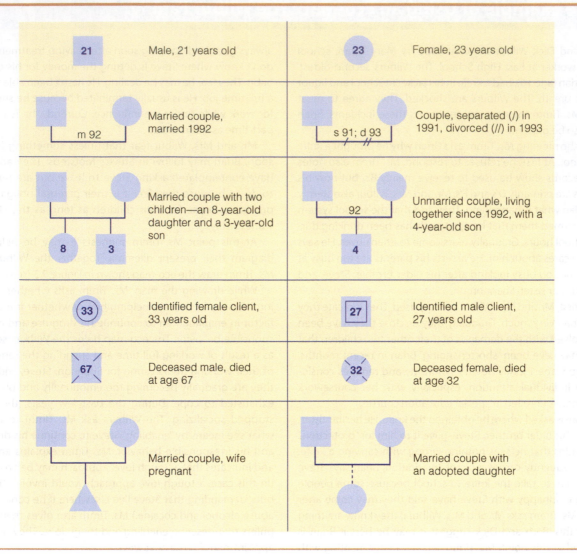

Male, 21 years old	Female, 23 years old
Married couple, married 1992	Couple, separated (/) in 1991, divorced (//) in 1993
Married couple with two children—an 8-year-old daughter and a 3-year-old son	Unmarried couple, living together since 1992, with a 4-year-old son
Identified female client, 33 years old	Identified male client, 27 years old
Deceased male, died at age 67	Deceased female, died at age 32
Married couple, wife pregnant	Married couple with an adopted daughter

locations, occupations, socioeconomic status, and significant life events. The use of the genogram is illustrated in the Kull family case example in Figure 9.5. (For the full case example, see p. 277.)

In summary, genograms are useful to both worker and clients. For the worker, a completed genogram graphically points out intergenerational family dynamics. Such a diagram allows the worker to better understand the intergenerational patterns affecting a client family. It then helps the worker generate hypotheses of problematic patterns from prior generations, which the worker can further explore by questioning family members. Once problematic dynamics are identified, the worker can then focus attention on helping family members generate strategies to resolve the patterns. A strengths perspective should also be used by workers—that is, they should also focus on helping family members identify intergenerational patterns that are *resources* that will help the family confront challenges. (Such resources include longevity, high educational achievement levels, valuing and practicing good health patterns, low rates of divorce, and high levels of constructive community participation.)

EXERCISE 9.3   A Genogram of My Family

GOAL: This exercise is designed to assist you in learning how to construct a genogram.

1. Draw a genogram of your family.

2. Specify significant patterns that tend to repeat themselves in your family.

3. Identify any dysfunctional patterns in your family that tend to be repeated. For each identified dysfunctional pattern, seek to specify courses of action that may stop these patterns from being repeated.

FIGURE 9.5   Sample Genogram: The Jim and Diane Kull Family

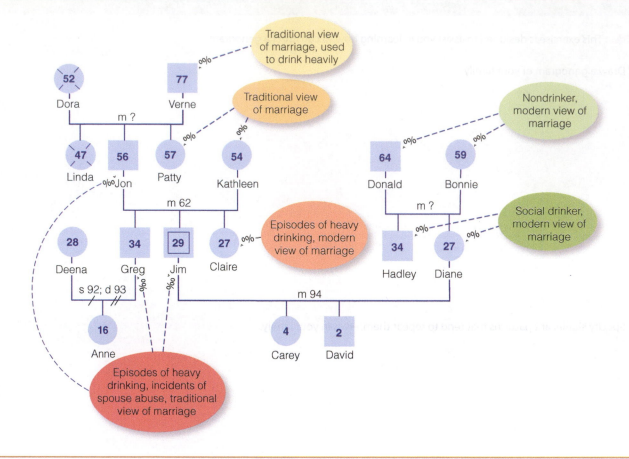

Similarly, for the client family, a genogram helps them identify and understand problematic intergenerational patterns and resources. Once such patterns are identified, family members can begin to generate strategies (together with their worker) to break these patterns.

The eco-map and the genogram have a number of similarities. With both techniques, users gain insight into family dynamics. Some of the symbols used in the two approaches are identical. There are differences, however. The eco-map focuses attention on the family's interactions with groups, resources, organizations, associations, other families, and other individuals. The genogram focuses attention on intergenerational patterns, particularly those that are problematic or dysfunctional.

LO 4   Comprehend Aspects of Families for Workers to Focus On

ASPECTS OF FAMILIES FOR WORKERS TO FOCUS ON

In assessing families and providing services to families, there are certain aspects that provide significant information about their challenges and about their strengths. Frequently, the strengths (assets and resources) can be utilized to resolve their challenges and to enhance their overall functioning. Aspects that social workers should attend to are verbal communication patterns, nonverbal communication patterns, family roles of members, personal goals and family goals, norms and cultural values, and culturagrams.

Case Example of Using a Genogram: The Kull Family

Jim Kull is referred by Rock County District Attorney's Office to the Rock County Domestic Violence Program. He was arrested two nights ago for an incident in which his wife, Diane, received several severe bruises on her body and her face. Kris Koeffler, a social worker, has an intake interview with Mr. Kull. Mr. Kull is an involuntary client and is reluctant to discuss the incident. Ms. Koeffler informs Mr. Kull he has a right not to discuss it, but if he chooses not to, she is obligated to inform the district attorney that he refused services. She adds that in such cases the district attorney usually files a battery charge with the court, which may lead to jail time.

Mr. Kull reluctantly states he and his wife had a disagreement, which ended with her slapping him and him defending himself by throwing a few punches. He adds that yesterday, when he was in jail, he was informed she left home with the children and is now staying at a women's shelter. He is further worried she may contact an attorney and seek a divorce.

Ms. Koeffler inquires about the specifics of the "disagreement." Mr. Kull indicates he came home after having a few beers, his dinner was cold, and he "got on" Mrs. Kull for not cleaning the house. He adds that Mrs. Kull then started "mouthing off," which eventually escalated into them pushing and hitting each other. Ms. Koeffler then inquires whether such incidents had occurred in the past. Mr. Kull indicates "a few times," and then adds that getting physical with his wife is the only way for him to "make her shape up." He indicates he works all day long as a carpenter while his wife sits home watching soap operas. He feels she is not doing her "fair share"; he states the house usually looks like a "pigpen."

Ms. Koeffler asks Mr. Kull if he feels getting physical with his wife is justifiable. He responds with "sure," and adds that his dad frequently told him "spare the rod and spoil both the wife and the kids." Ms. Koeffler asks if his father was at times abusive to him when he was a child. He indicates that he was and adds that to this day he detests his dad for being abusive to him and to his mother.

Ms. Koeffler then suggests that together they draw a "family tree," focusing on three areas: episodes of heavy drinking, episodes of physical abuse, and traditional versus modern gender stereotypes. Ms. Koeffler explains that a traditional gender stereotype includes the husband as the primary decision maker and the wife as submissive to him and primarily responsible for domestic tasks. The modern gender stereotype involves an equalitarian relationship between husband and wife. After an initial reluctance (related to his expressing confusion as to how such a "tree" would help get his wife back), Mr. Kull agrees to cooperate in drawing such a "tree." The resulting genogram is presented in Figure 9.5.

The genogram helps Mr. Kull see that he and his wife are products of family systems that have strikingly different values and customs. In his family the males drink heavily, have a traditional view of marriage, and use physical force in interactions with their spouse. Mr. Kull further adds his father also physically abused his brother and sister when they were younger. On questioning, Mr. Kull mentions he frequently spanks his children and has struck them "once or twice." Ms. Koeffler asks Mr. Kull how he feels about repeating the same patterns of abuse with his wife and children that he despises his father for using. Tears come to his eyes, and he says "not good."

Ms. Koeffler and Mr. Kull then discuss courses of action that he might take to change his family interactions and how he might best approach his wife in requesting that she and the children return. Mr. Kull agrees to attend Alcoholics Anonymous (AA) meetings as well as a therapy group for batterers. After a month of attending these weekly meetings, he contacts his wife and asks her to return. Mrs. Kull agrees to return *if* he stops drinking (because most of the abuse occurred when he was intoxicated), *if* he agrees to continue to attend group therapy and AA meetings, and *if* he agrees to go to counseling with her. Mr. Kull readily agrees (Mrs. Kull's parents, who have never liked her husband, express their disapproval.)

For the first few months, Mr. Kull is on his best behavior and there is considerable harmony in the family. Then one day, on his birthday, he decides to stop for a few beers after work. He drinks until he is intoxicated. When he finally arrives home, he starts to verbally and physically abuse Mrs. Kull and the children. For Mrs. Kull, this is the last straw. She takes the children to her parents' house, where they stay for several days until they are able to find and move into an apartment. She also files for divorce and follows through in obtaining one.

At first glance, this case is not a "success." In reality, many social work cases are not successful. However, Mr. Kull now realizes that he has acquired, and acts out, certain dysfunctional family patterns. Unfortunately, he is not ready to make lasting changes. Perhaps in the future he will be more committed. At the present time he has returned to drinking heavily. Mrs. Kull and the children are safer and can now start to break the cycle of abuse.

Verbal Communication Patterns

All cooperative family interaction, whether verbal or nonverbal, depends upon effective communication. Through communication, members argue, trade insults, debate issues, arrive at goals, assume tasks and responsibilities, laugh, and work out differences. Effective communication occurs between two or more people when the receiver interprets the sender's message in the way the sender intended. The meaning of a communication is the response it elicits in the receiver, regardless of the intent of the sender.

Verbal communication, including one-way communication and two-way communication, is described in Chapter 5.

In most families the members communicate with a pattern of two-way communication. One-way communication, however is apt to occur with an autocratic head (which is apt to be the father or mother) of the family. With an autocratic head, the other family members are apt to feel constrained in expressing their thoughts and feelings. Some serious drawbacks exist with one-way communication. Those who feel constrained to express themselves may feel they are being related to as being "second-class citizens." In addition, they may have valuable information that could improve the family's functioning, but because it is not communicated, it is never considered. The adage "Children should be seen, but not heard," fosters one-way communication.

There are numerous benefits to be gained through two-way communication. It improves family morale, trust, and openness. Conflicts and controversies are more readily resolved, as the resources and ideas of all the family members are pooled.

With communication, sociopsychological factors (including defense mechanisms, beliefs, attitudes, values, and stereotypes) influence what we perceive. Chapter 5 describes the impact of defense mechanisms, beliefs, values, and stereotypes on what we perceive.

EXERCISE 9.4   Analyzing Verbal Communication Patterns in Families

EP 1b

GOAL: This exercise is designed to assist you in analyzing constructive and problematic verbal communication patterns in families.

Step 1: Specify the constructive verbal communication patterns in your family.

Step 2: Specify the problematic verbal communication patterns in your family.

Step 3: Summarize your thoughts on how the problematic verbal communication patterns in your family could be improved.

In families, double-blind communication sometimes occurs. In double-blind communication, the sender of a message places the receiver in a situation where, no matter how he or she responds, the sender will criticize. This situation can occur when Father says, on the one hand, that all good children pick up their toys, yet on the other hand tells his son that all "real" boys are messy. The boy who receives these two messages will be unable to please his father whether he keeps his toys neat or messy. He may solve the problem by refusing to listen at all. At the extreme, he may pull away from reality to such a degree that he develops a severe emotional disturbance.

Nonverbal Communication Patterns

Nonverbal communication may take many forms. We communicate by the way we move, the expressions we make, the clothes we wear, even by the way we arrange our homes. We communicate by our posture, gestures, the way we touch others, choice of clothing, facial expressions, rings, tattoos, eye contact with others, and our personal appearance. Nonverbal communication patterns are described in Chapter 5.

Nonverbal communication interacts with verbal communication and can repeat, substitute for, accent, regulate, or contradict what is spoken. When receivers perceive a contradiction between nonverbal and verbal messages, they usually believe the nonverbal.

EXERCISE 9.5   Analyzing Nonverbal Communication Patterns in Families

EP 1b

GOAL: This exercise is designed to assist you in analyzing constructive and problematic nonverbal communication patterns in families.

Step 1: Specify the constructive nonverbal communication patterns in your family.

Step 2: Specify the problematic nonverbal communication patterns in your family.

Step 3: Summarize your thoughts on how the problematic nonverbal communication patterns in your family could be improved.

Family Roles of Members

A family role is a culturally determined pattern of behavior that is prescribed for a person who occupies a specific status or rank in relation to other family members. There are an infinite number of roles that different family members may play. Some roles are quite common for family members. Parents have the roles of guiding, directing, and raising the children. Parents also generally have the role of earning financial support for the family. Children are generally assigned the role of "student" and "helper" with household tasks. The "helper" role may be further divided among the children, with one being the "dish washer," another being the one who "takes out the garbage," and so on. There are many other possible roles for both the children and the parents. Examples for children include "princess," "trouble maker," "star athlete," "pianist," "bully," and "clown." Mom or dad may have the roles of "family protector," "primary decision maker," "cook," "grocery shopper," "coach for a sport," and "alcoholic."

Sharon Wegscheider indicates that members of alcoholic families tend to assume roles that both protect the chemically dependent person from taking responsibility for his or her behavior and actually serve to maintain the drinking problem.[7] She identifies several roles that are typically played by family members in addition to the chemically dependent person: the chief enabler, the family hero, the scapegoat, the lost child, and the mascot.

The chief enabler's main purpose is to assume the primary responsibility for the family functioning. The abuser typically continues to lose control and relinquishes responsibility. The chief enabler, on the other hand, takes on more and more responsibility and begins making more and more family decisions. A chief enabler is often the parent or spouse of the chemically dependent person.

Conditions in families of chemically dependent people often continue to deteriorate as the dependent person loses control. A positive influence is needed to offset the negative. The family hero fulfills this role. The family hero often is the "perfect" person who does well at everything he or she tries. The hero works very hard at making the family appear to be functioning better than it is. In this way, the family hero provides the family with self-worth.

Another typical role played by someone in the chemically dependent family is the scapegoat. Although the alcohol abuse is the real problem, a family rule may mandate that this fact be denied and the blame be placed elsewhere. Frequently, another family member is targeted with the blame. The scapegoat often behaves in negative ways (for example, gets caught for stealing, runs away, becomes extremely withdrawn), which draws the spotlight to him or her. The scapegoat's role is to distract attention away from the dependent person and onto something else. This role helps the family avoid addressing the problem of chemical dependency.

Often there is also a lost child in the family. This is the person who seems rather uninvolved with the rest of the members yet never causes any trouble. The lost child's purpose is to provide relief to the family from some of the pain it is suffering. At least there is someone in the home who neither requires much attention nor causes any stress. The lost child is simply there.

Finally, chemically dependent families often have someone playing the role of mascot. The mascot is the person who probably has a good sense of humor and appears not to take anything seriously. Despite how much the mascot might be suffering inside, he or she provides a little fun for the family.

In working with a family, it is important for a social worker to identify the specific roles that each family member is filling and to determine which roles are functional for a family and which are dysfunctional. For the dysfunctional roles, the worker needs to make a decision whether seeking to change some of these roles would be beneficial.

Personal Goals and Family Goals

Chapter 4 described "personal goals and group goals." As a reader, it may be useful for you to review this material. Because a family is a group, it is important for a worker to recognize

EXERCISE 9.6   Functional Roles and Problematic Roles in Families

EP 1b

GOAL: This exercise is designed to assist you in identifying functional and problematic roles in families.

Step 1: Specify the functional roles that members of your family play.

Step 2: Specify the problematic roles that some members of your family may play.

Step 3: Speculate how these problematic roles can realistically be changed in a constructive direction.

that each family member has personal goals and the family has family goals. The personal goals of family members may be supportive of the family goals. For example, a family may have a goal of having each family member living a happy and productive life. If each of the children has a personal goal of doing well academically in school, such a goal is supportive of the family goal. On the other hand, if one of the family members has a goal of seeking to be "high" daily on a chemical substance, such a goal is in conflict with the family goal of each member living a productive life.

Sometimes a family member may have a hidden agenda. A hidden agenda is a personal goal held by a member that is unknown to the other family members and that interferes with the family goals. Assume, again, that a family has a goal of each family member living a happy and productive life. If a family member thinks he or she can get rich quickly by gambling in casinos and seeks to do so weekly without the other members being aware of the activity, such an activity is probably a hidden agenda.

Often, in working with a family, it is important for a worker to: identify the personal goals of each family member, determine the family goals, identify any hidden agendas, and work toward the personal goals becoming more consistent with constructive family goals.

EXERCISE 9.7   Personal Goals, Family Goals, and Hidden Agendas

EP 1b

GOAL: This exercise is designed to assist you in identifying personal goals, family goals, and hidden agendas in families.

Step 1: Specify the personal goals for each member of your family.

Step 2: Specify the family's goals.

Step 3: Specify any hidden agendas that you have that your family is unaware of.

Norms and Cultural Values

Norms are rules that specify proper behavior in a group. Family norms are rules that specify proper behavior in a family. Family norms ideally should allow the entire family and each individual member to function effectively and productively. There is considerable variation between families in their set of norms or rules for the family. It should be noted that not all family norms are considered constructive; for example, most Americans view the practice of female circumcision in some Middle Eastern countries to be highly dysfunctional and destructive.

A cultural value is a culture's idea about what is good, fair, right, and just. A family tends to take on the values of its culture and make those values part of its family norms. But there are exceptions. For example, many Roman Catholics do not adhere to the church's prohibitions against premarital intimacy and prohibitions against using most forms of contraceptives.

In families with problematic family norms, the family rules do not allow the family or individual members to function effectively and productively. In many families, the parents may set rules that the children do not agree with (and which the children may actively violate). Common areas of disagreement are when to go to bed, study habits, keeping one's bedroom neat and tidy, smoking, choice of friends, use of alcohol selection, what to spend money on, etc.

A social worker needs to attend to family norms and seek to do what is reasonable to make the rules more beneficial for constructive family functioning. Social workers also need to comprehend the cultural values of the clients they are working with. Clients are apt to adopt their cultural norms as family norms (but there are a number of exceptions). As a start in learning cultural values of clients of ethnic groups that they are unfamiliar with, workers can discover information by Googling the cultural values of the ethnic group of the client. For example, by Googling the following ethnic groups, I received the following cultural values:

Hmong in America: Family is very important. They often have large networks of cousins and other relatives working together. Extended families are a base part of Hmong life. There is a tendency for Hmong girls in their teen years to marry older men.

Mexican Americans: Place high value on family over individualism. Have numerous extended family get-togethers. They tend to value traditions, including celebrations. Many adhere to the Catholic religion.

Chinese Americans: High value placed on group cooperation and individual modesty. Tend to have a small number of close lifelong friends who feel obligated to give each other whatever help might seem required. Tend to avoid direct confrontation.

Swedish Americans: Culture in Sweden values "socialism" (for example, Swedes have five weeks of paid vacation each year, free schooling for children from preschool through college, and a year of paid maternity leave for each child). Swedish Americans are apt to place a higher value on socialism than most other Americans.

Japanese Americans: Place a high value on education. A substantial percentage of Japanese Americans attain college degrees.

Arab Americans: Family is very important. Believe that men and women are different and complementary. The husband is often the primary decision maker. Older persons are valued for their wisdom. Tend to believe that dignity, honor, and reputation are more valuable than material success. Tend to believe that much of one's fate in life is dependent on God's will.

Culturagrams   A culturagram is a family assessment instrument developed by Congress to help social workers better understand culturally diverse clients and their families.[8] It identifies 10 areas of culturally diverse families that social workers are urged to attend to. These 10 areas will be specified and briefly discussed.

EXERCISE 9.8   Norms and Cultural Values in Families

EP 1b

GOAL: This exercise is designed to assist you in understanding the significance of norms and cultural values in families.

Step 1: Specify the functional norms in your family.

Step 2: Specify the problematic norms in your family, and briefly indicate why they are problematic.

Step 3: Specify norms in your family that are also cultural values of your ethnic group.

• Reasons for Relocation: The reasons for relocating vary among families. Some come to the United States because of economic opportunities. Some relocate because of religious or political discrimination in their country of origin. Some revisit their country of origin on a regular schedule. Some never go home again. Some have fond memories of their country of origin, and some never want to return due to an array of adverse circumstances. Social workers need an awareness of this area in order to better understand the stresses and attractions affecting families. (In asking questions to gather information in this area, as well as in the nine other areas, the social worker needs to tactfully phrase his or her questions so as to not offend the family members. For example, the family may have lived a long time in the community and may be offended if they believe the worker is stereotyping them as being "recent arrivals.")

- Legal Status: If a family is undocumented and fears deportation, the members are apt to become more secretive and socially isolated. They may fear the social worker may report their undocumented status to officials who may arrest them. Undocumented family members may not be eligible for certain services. For undocumented clients it is particularly important for the social worker to establish trust and assure the family members about the confidentiality of contact.

- Length of Time in the Community: Family members who have arrived a fairly long time ago are apt to be more acculturated than recent arrivals. The ages of family members when they arrived are also of significance. Children, because of attending school and thereby developing peer relationships, often become more rapidly assimilated than their parents.

- Language: Often families who have a native language other than English use their native language at home and then begin to speak English with the outside community. Children are apt, because of school, to more rapidly learn English than their parents. Conflicts sometimes arise in families in which the parents speak little English and therefore use their native language, whereas the children may see the value of speaking in English.

- Health Beliefs: Families from different cultures may have a wide range of health beliefs. Some may only believe in "spiritual healing" or seek the preferred treatment when they are ill from a person in their culture, who may have very little professional medical training. Some may believe the only treatment that should be used is prayer or some other spiritual ritual that is unique to their culture. Some immigrants may choose to use a combination of Western medicine and traditional folk beliefs.

- Crisis Events: Every family, and every family member, has crises. A social worker needs to be aware of the crises that families have experienced, as well as the interpretations that are assigned to the crises. For example, in a culture in which the father is expected to be the primary financial provider and then develops a disability that prevents him from working, what meaning is assigned to the disability by each of the family members? Also, if a family highly values virginity prior to marriage, what meaning is attached to the rape of a teenage daughter?

- Holidays and Special Events: Every culture has holidays (some of which are unique) and special events. Some events celebrate transitions from one developmental stage to another—such as a bar mitzvah, wedding, christening, or funeral. It is important for a social worker to learn the significance of important holidays and events and to show respect for them.

- Contact with Cultural and Religious Institutions: There are hundreds of religions in the world, with varying beliefs. Some religions believe in reincarnation. Some believe in sacrificing animals. Some believe in such practices as female circumcision. Some terrorist groups value a "holy war." It is essential for a social worker to have knowledge of the cultural and religious practices of their clients.

- Values About Education and Work: Some families believe it is more important for young adults to remain at home than seek a college education away from home. Some families have beliefs that members of their family can only obtain jobs that pay minimum wage (or slightly above). Some families believe the mother's place is at home rather than having a job outside the home.

- Values About Family—Structure, Power, Myths, and Rules: Some families desire an extended family structure, and others place a higher value on a nuclear family structure. Some families value a patriarchal structure, some a matriarchal structure, and some an egalitarian structure. In a few families, one (or more) child may control what happens in a family. Who does what domestic tasks in a family varies substantially between families. Child-rearing practices vary substantially—with the mother, or father, or older child, or grandparent being the primary person in charge of young children.

LO 5   Describe Family Problems and the Social Work Services Available to Families

FAMILY PROBLEMS AND SOCIAL WORK SERVICES

Family Problems

An infinite number of problems occur in families. Exhibit 9.1 lists a few of them. Thorman indicates that problems within families tend to be clustered in the following four categories:

1. Marital problems: These include communication difficulties, disagreements over children, conflicts over finances, sexual difficulties, infidelity, and conflicts over recreational time. Marital counseling is one of the social services that may be useful in resolving some of these issues.

2. Parent/child relationship difficulties: Parents and children may have many disagreements over a wide range of areas, including choice of friends, assigned tasks and responsibilities, study habits, grades in school, when to start dating, use of alcohol and other drugs, smoking, choice of clothes, how to spend leisure time, and choice of career. Social services available include family counseling, parent effectiveness training (see Module 4), and use of behavior therapy (see Module 2).

3. Personal problems of individual family members: An immense array of personal challenges may develop, including health issues, being depressed or anxious, a learning disability, shyness, low self-esteem, an addiction (such as alcohol or gambling), and being a single parent. The social services that are available are numerous, and most of them are problem specific. For example, rational therapy (see Module 1) might be used for someone who is depressed, assertiveness training (see Module 2) may be used for someone who is shy or who has anger management issues, medical care should probably be sought for someone who has heart issues, etc.

Exhibit 9.1   A Sampling of Family Problems

Divorce	Money management difficulties
Alcohol or drug abuse	Injury from serious automobile accident involving one or more members
Unwanted pregnancy	
Bankruptcy	A child with a severe cognitive disability
Poverty	Incarceration or institutionalization of one or more members
Terminal illness	
Chronic illness	Compulsive gambling by one or more members
Death	Victim of a crime
Desertion	Forced retirement of a wage earner
"Empty-shell" marriage	Caregiver for an elderly relative
Emotional problems of one or more members	Involvement of a child in delinquent and criminal activities
Behavioral problems of one or more members	
Child abuse	Illness of a member who acquires AIDS
Child neglect	A runaway teenager
Sexual abuse	Sexual dysfunctions of one or more members
Spouse abuse	Infidelity
Elder abuse	Infertility
Unemployment of wage earners	

4. Stresses imposed on the family by the external environment: Such stresses may include loss of a job, inadequate income, being homeless, inadequate access to transportation, inadequate schools, living in a dangerous neighborhood, car accident, and house damaged by a tornado. Social services that are available again are problem specific. Red Cross services may assist for a weather disaster, job training may be useful for someone who is unemployed, homeless shelters are sometimes available for the homeless, etc.[9]

EXERCISE 9.9   Challenges Faced by My Family

EP 1b

GOAL: This exercise is designed to assist you in identifying challenges your family is currently facing and to begin problem-solving these challenges.

1. Specify the challenges/difficulties that one or more members of your family are currently facing. (You have the right to not reveal challenges you do not wish to reveal.)

2. For each of these challenges, what actions are being taken to confront them?

3. If one or more challenges are currently not being effectively confronted, specify other options for each that might be tried. (Feel free to consult with others about identifying other options.)

Social Work Services

When problems arise in a family, social services are often needed. The types and forms of services that social workers provide to troubled families are extremely varied. We can group them into two major categories: in-home services and out-of-home services.

In-home services are preventive. Although not all are offered literally within the home itself, they are specifically designed to help families stay together. They include financial aid, protective services (services to safeguard children or frail older adults from abuse and neglect), family preservation services (intensive crisis intervention within the home setting where children are so seriously at risk that removal to foster care would otherwise be required), family therapy (intensive counseling to improve family relationships), day care (caretaking services for children or older adults to provide respite for caregivers who might otherwise be overwhelmed or to permit them to work outside the home), homemaker services (for the same purpose), and family-life education (classes, often offered at traditional family service agencies, that cover such topics as child development, parenting skills, and communication issues). Not all of these services can be provided by social workers, but workers must know where to find them and how to help the family obtain them when needed.[10]

Out-of-home services are services that must be operationalized when the family can no longer remain intact. They are a manifestation that something has gone seriously wrong, because the breakup of any family amounts to a tragedy that will have ramifications beyond family boundaries. Although family members usually receive the blame, the larger system (social environment and the level of support it provides to troubled families) may be called into question. Out-of-home services include foster care, adoption, group homes, institutional care (for example, residential treatment centers), and the judicial system (which provides a different kind of institutional care, prison, or jail, for family members who have run into difficulty with the law).

To perform these services, social workers engage in a variety of roles (for example, broker, educator, advocate, supporter, mediator). The following examples illustrate many common services and important roles:

- Mark Schwanke, age 32, has AIDS. Ms. Seely, a social worker with the AIDS Support Network in the community, serves as a case manager in providing a variety of services to Mark, his wife (who is HIV positive), and their two children. These services include medical information and care, housing, counseling, emotional support services, and financial assistance. Because of frequent discrimination against persons with AIDS and persons with HIV, Ms. Seely often must advocate on the family's behalf to ensure that they receive the services they need.

- Beth Roessler, age 15, has been convicted of committing six burglaries. Steve Padek, a juvenile probation officer and social worker, is her juvenile probation officer. Mr. Padek provides the following services to Beth and her mother, who is divorced: he holds weekly supervision meetings with Beth to monitor her school performance and leisure activities, links Beth's mother with a Parents Without Partners group, and conducts several counseling sessions with Beth and her mother to mediate conflicts in their relationship.

- The aunt of Amy Sund, a 3-year-old child, has contacted Protective Services about Amy's mother (Pat) and her lover's physical abuse of Amy. Investigators confirm the abuse; Amy has bruises and rope burns on her body. Instead of referring the case to court, Protective Services refers the case to Family Preservation for services. Maria Gomez, social worker at Family Preservation, meets with Pat Sund and Amy a total of 37 times over the next 90 days. Pat Sund terminates her relationship with her abusive lover, is accepted into a financial assistance program through the Social Services Department for a two-year period, and enrolls in a job training program. Ms. Gomez arranges for childcare for Amy when Ms. Sund is attending the job training program. Ms. Gomez also arranges for a temporary housekeeper who provides training in cleaning the apartment and in making meals. Ms. Gomez encourages Ms. Sund to join the local chapter of Parents Anonymous, which she does. (Parents Anonymous is described in Chapter 1.) Had family preservation services been unavailable or unsuccessful, Amy would have had to be placed in a foster home.

- Cindy Rogerson, age 27, has three young children. She is badly battered by her husband and contacts the House of Hope, a shelter for battered women and their children. Sue Frank, a social worker at the shelter, makes arrangements for shelter for Mrs. Rogerson and her children. The oldest child is attending school, so Ms. Frank arranges for him to continue attending school. Ms. Frank provides one-to-one counseling to Mrs. Rogerson at the shelter to help her explore her options and to inform her of potential resources that she may not be aware of. Ms. Frank also leads groups at the shelter for residents and nonresidents, which Mrs. Rogerson is required to attend while at the shelter. After two and a half weeks, Mrs. Rogerson decides she wants to return to her husband. Ms. Frank convinces Mrs. Rogerson to give her husband an ultimatum prior to returning—he must receive family counseling together with her from the Family Service agency in the community and must attend a group for batterers in the community. Mr. Rogerson reluctantly agrees. Mrs. Rogerson, at the urging of Ms. Frank, only then returns to live with her husband, with the understanding that she will leave immediately if he hits her again or if he drops out of either family counseling or the group for batterers.

- Katy Hynek, age 76, has Alzheimer's disease. She has been living alone in her house since her husband died three years ago. Her physician contacts Adult Services of the Department of Social Services and requests that an assessment of living arrangements be conducted. Linda Sutton, social worker, does an assessment and determines that Katy Hynek can no longer live alone. Katy's son Mark and his wife Annette agree to have Katy move in with them. During the next 19 months, Ms. Sutton has periodic contact with the Hyneks. As is common with this disease, Katy Hynek's physical and mental condition continues to deteriorate. Ms. Sutton listens to Mark and Annette's concerns and seeks to answer their questions about the disease. She also provides suggestions to help them cope with the changes in Katy's condition. As Katy's condition deteriorates, Ms. Sutton makes arrangements for Katy to attend an adult day care center during the daytime, partly for respite care for Mark and Annette. At the end of 19 months, Mark and Annette request a meeting with Ms. Sutton to discuss the possibility of placing Katy in a nursing home as her condition has so deteriorated that she now needs 24-hour care. (For example, she gets up in the middle of the night and gets lost in closets; she is also now incontinent.) The pros and cons of placing Katy in a nursing home are identified and discussed. Making the decision is exceedingly emotional and agonizing for Mark and Annette. With a careful discussion of the entire situation with Ms. Sutton, Mark and Annette decide they have no choice but to seek a nursing home placement. Ms. Sutton gives them the names of three nursing homes, which they visit, and then they select one.

- Mr. and Mrs. Logan have been married for seven years and have been trying to have one or more children for the past five years. They eventually go to a fertility clinic and discover that Mrs. Logan has endometriosis, which prevents her from conceiving. The Logans are distraught. Three months later, they decide to adopt. Being Catholic, they contact Catholic Social Services. Rhonda Lopez, a social worker, is assigned to work with them. The Logans undergo a three-month home study to determine their eligibility to adopt. They meet the eligibility requirements. They anxiously wait 8 months, and two older children (Jessica, age 7, and her brother Mark, age 5) become available. A trial placement is arranged. The Logans and the two children experience some adjustments, which Ms. Gomez assists them with. After seven months, the adoption is finalized.

Multifamily Groups*

MULTIFAMILY GROUP EXPERIENCES

The concept of multifamily groups has been around since the early 1960s.[a] In comparison to working with one single family, multifamily groups gather two or more families together in a variety of social work settings, including schools, hospitals, and inpatient/outpatient counseling settings. Multifamily groups serve many purposes, some of which include educating all the families about a topic of similar interest, providing a socialization opportunity for the families, and/or providing an opportunity for families to be able to share stories and obtain mutual aid from each other. Families learn that they are not alone in the situations they are facing and learn about how others have dealt with a similar situation while increasing their knowledge about resources to help them deal with current issues. These groups can consist of adults, children, and the targeted client, all of whom are dealing with a similar issue but who may be in different stages of awareness and knowledge about the primary topic of the group. In addition, groups range in size from 2 to 4 families to upwards of 10 families or more. In these cases, the size of the room and the number of facilitators are important factors to consider. Examples of these types of multifamily groups include providing education to families regarding medication adherence in a medical setting, providing resources for families with an autistic child, and providing education on positive parenting techniques.

The skills utilized in running multifamily groups are similar to those of running any other type of group. Families should be assessed to ensure they meet the goals of the group and to ensure they can participate effectively in the group process. Group goals and norms should be established in the beginning stages of the formation of the group. During the middle phases, the families should be encouraged to provide support and share with the other members. In the end phases, the families should be encouraged to share their feelings about termination, to summarize what they have learned, and to provide feedback about the group to the facilitator(s).

One major difference in multifamily groups is that the group leaders should try to encourage both intrafamily (asking each family to clarify family concerns) and interfamily (asking members from different families to provide feedback) communication.[b] As the group progresses, the family members themselves should be encouraged to be more active in the group process, both as individuals and as part of a family.

MULTIFAMILY GROUP THERAPY

The more advanced types of multifamily group experiences are multifamily group therapy (MFGT) or multigroup family counseling (MFCG). MFGT was developed in the 1960s by Laquer as a means of working with families of schizophrenics in a therapeutic hospital setting.[c] The goal of MFGT is that sessions are structured by master's-level therapists who employ specific systemic techniques to facilitate change.[d] These types of multifamily therapy groups include families who have experienced the loss of a family member, families struggling with an adolescent with an eating disorder, and families struggling with alcohol or drug use in the family.

ADVANTAGES OF MULTIFAMILY GROUPS

Nahum and Brewer identify multiple advantages of multifamily group work compared to individual family work.[e] Some of these advantages include: it is more economical, provides for family-to-family transfer of knowledge, builds community-based resourcefulness, assists in catalyzing emotions, and provides family-to-family modeling and mentoring. One example of a successful model for a multifamily group is the following description of FAST.

FAMILIES AND SCHOOL TOGETHER: A MULTIFAMILY APPROACH TO STRENGTHENING FAMILIES

Families and Schools Together, Inc. (FAST) was founded in 1988 by Dr. Lynn McDonald, a professor in social work in Madison, Wisconsin.[f] FAST is an evidence-based program in which students and families participate in an experiential after-school program in order to engage parents and strengthen families. The program is aimed at assisting at-risk students through early intervention, family empowerment, and community involvement. In order to enhance the program, school personnel and community members (including a parent advocate, social workers, and counselors) are involved to provide support to the families involved. Currently, FAST is being implemented in 46 states and 13 countries.[g]

FAST has several versions, including programs for babies through teenagers. Once the FAST leaders are identified, they participate in up to six days of training. Participants are educated on the FAST curriculum, develop goals for their program, and participate in team-building activities.

The FAST program can consist of home visits, multifamily group sessions, and follow-up sessions. During the program, all of the families involved participate in activities, such as opening and closing ceremonies, creating family flags, eating meals together, structured play and communication time, and

(continued)

graduation ceremonies. In addition, childcare is provided on site while family members participate in multifamily groups, one for the youth and one for the adults.

A social worker who is a part of FAST provides support throughout the program, from helping with meals to providing education on communication. In addition, the social worker plays a facilitative role in the parent or student groups. The social worker also acts as a mentor and support person to all involved.

During the multifamily sessions, family members are encouraged to participate in activities that support their family units, such as introduction of family members, creating family flags, and preparing a meal for the other families. In the parent-only multifamily groups, parents are encouraged to share difficulties they face in their families, learn parenting techniques, receive education on alcohol/drug and mental health issues, and share experiences and resources with other parents.

Research indicates that students who participate in FAST show increased academic performance in schools and higher levels of family involvement in schools. In addition, families who have been FAST participants reported reduced aggression in the home, increased family communication, improved parent and school communication, decreased isolation, and improved coping skills. In addition, the parents reported increased involvement in the community.[h]

Two examples of family exercises that can be used with students in social work classes and with older children in multifamily groups follow.

EXERCISE B: Definition of Family

GOAL: To help students identify what is meant by the word family.

Step 1: Break students up into groups of three in order to create their own family unit. As part of this family, they need to come up with their own definition of the word *family* to present to the rest of the class. (Examples of possible responses are "two adults with a child living together"; "a group of people living together"; or "people who provide emotional support to one another.")

Step 2: Have each "family" share their definition with the rest of the class.

Step 3: After listening to all of the separate definitions, have the families discuss which definition they liked the most and least and why.

Step 4: Ask all members to discuss any strengths or obstacles associated with coming up with their "family" definition.

Step 5: Ask the class as a group to discuss their thoughts about this exercise and what they learned from it.

EXERCISE A: Family Picture

GOAL: To assist students in increasing their awareness of their identity as part of a family "unit."

Step 1: Ask students to draw a picture that represents their family. Encourage the students to contact each of their family members to ask what they would want to be in the picture. If possible, have students meet one on one with each of their family members to have them add their own art work to the picture.

Step 2: Ask each student to explain his or her picture. Have students identify what each of their family members contributed to the picture.

Step 3: Ask the class as a group to discuss their thoughts about this exercise and what they learned from it.

* This material was written by Katherine Drechsler and Dr. Sarah Hessenauer. Ms. Drechsler is a lecturer at the University of Wisconsin–Whitewater and is a doctoral student in social work at George Williams College. Dr. Hessenauer is an associate professor and chair of the Social Work Department at the University of Wisconsin–Whitewater.

a   Cassano, D. (1989). Multi-family group therapy in social work practice I. *Social Work with Groups: A Journal of Community and Clinical Practice 12*(1), 3–14. doi: 10.1300/J009v12n0I_02.

b   Cassano, D. (1989). The multi-family therapy group: Research on pattern of interaction II. *Social Work with Groups: A Journal of Community and Clinical Practice 12*(1), 15–39.

c   Clemency, C., & Rayle, A. (2006). Hitting closer to home: A multiple family prevention group for adolescent disordered eating. *Journal for Specialist in Group Work, 31*(3), 219–245.

d   Asen, E., & Schuff, H. (2006). Psychosis and multiple family group therapy. *Journal of Family Therapy, 28*(1), 58–72. doi: 10.1111/j.1467-6427.2006.00337.x

e   Nahum, D., & Brewer, M. (2004). Multi-family group therapy for sexually abusive youth. *Journal of Child Sexual Abuse 13*(3–4), 215–243.

f   Families and Schools Together, Inc. (2012). Retrieved from http://www.familiesandschools.org/

g   Ibid.

h   Ibid.

SUMMARY

The following summarizes the chapter's content in terms of the learning objectives presented at the beginning of the chapter.

1. **Describe the diversity of family forms.**
    A wide diversity of family patterns exists in the world. Although the nuclear family is still the predominant family form in our society, it is a serious mistake for social workers to use the nuclear family as the ideal model that individuals should strive to form. Many other family forms also function well and deserve respect.

2. **Describe the societal functions of families.**
    Family patterns and forms are substantially affected by the culture (larger system) in which they are located. Families in our society perform the following functions that help maintain continuity and stability in society: replacement of the population, care of the young, socialization of new members, regulation of sexual behavior, and provision of affection.

3. **Understand how to use two family assessment techniques.**
    Two assessment techniques are described: eco-maps and genograms. An eco-map provides a snapshot view of important family interactions at a particular point in time. A genogram, essentially a family tree, is a graphic way of investigating the origins of family problems over at least three generations.

4. **Comprehend aspects of families for workers to focus on.**
    In assessing families, and providing services to families, certain aspects provide significant information about their challenges and about their strengths. Frequently, the strengths (assets and resources) can be utilized to resolve their challenges and to enhance their overall functioning. Aspects that social workers should attend to are verbal communication patterns, nonverbal communication patterns, family roles, personal goals and family goals, norms and cultural values, and culturagrams.

5. **Describe family problems and the social work services available to families.**
    An infinite number of problems can occur in families. Problems within families tend to be clustered in four categories: marital problems, parent/child relationship difficulties, personal problems of individual family members, and stresses imposed on the family by the external environment. When there are problems in a family, social services are often needed. There is extensive variation in the types and forms of services that social workers provide to troubled families.

Group Exercises

EXERCISE A: Family Counseling

EP 8b

GOAL: To demonstrate the dynamics taking place in family counseling.

Step 1: The instructor states the purpose of the exercise. Four students are asked to volunteer to role-play the following roles.

Keith is the father and husband in the family. The family bought a house three years ago and struggles financially to make the monthly mortgage payments. Keith is 44 years old and was a salesman for a new car dealership in the community. The community has encountered serious economic challenges, as a General Motors (GM) plant closed its doors about six months ago; the GM plant was the financial "lifeline" for the community. Sales of new cars for Keith's dealership have plummeted in recent months, and Keith's job has been terminated. The family is now struggling to pay their bills.

Monica is the mother and wife in the family. She is 39 years old and has been a dental assistant for the past 13 years. Monica has a sister, Cheri, who has recently approached Monica, asking her if she would be willing to be a surrogate mother for her and her husband, Karl. Cheri and Karl have been trying to have a child for the past six years and now have been medically found to be infertile. Cheri and Karl live in a neighboring state and are financially secure; Cheri is a real estate agent and Karl is an attorney. The proposed surrogacy would be a gestational surrogacy, in which a transfer of a previously created embryo from Cheri and Karl would be transferred to Monica in a medical setting. Cheri and Karl state they will pay for all the medical expenses and give Keith and Monica $20,000.

Kimberly is the daughter and is 16 years old. Academically she is doing well in high school. She wants to go to college, but is worried about how to pay for it. She has been dating Richard for the past five months and is now worried she may be pregnant. She has not told her parents about this concern, but is hoping to subtly reveal this concern in family counseling.

Jason is the son and is 15 years old. He is a good athlete in both basketball and baseball. He was on the junior varsity basketball team, but was recently suspended because of his low grades. He has not informed his family as yet of his suspension. Academically he was doing okay a year ago, but with his father losing his job, he questions whether working hard in school really pays off. Also, he is at an age where he is often embarrassed at being seen with his parents or his sister—he thinks they are "not cool."

Monica states to the family that she would like to be a surrogate mother for Cheri and Karl; she adds this may be an answer to the family's financial crisis. Keith, Kimberly, and Jason are shocked that Monica wants to be a surrogate mother. Each has a number of questions as to what it would mean to each of them and to the family. Heated arguments occur, and the family decides to seek family counseling.

Step 2: The instructor asks for two volunteers to be the family counselors. This family counseling situation is then role-played.

Step 3: The instructor than asks the class' reactions to the role-play. In addition, the instructor asks the class to state what the "family counselors" did well and what they might have done differently.

EXERCISE B: You and Your Family

GOAL: To identify and relate some basic group concepts to dynamics occurring in your own family. The group concepts include verbal and nonverbal communication and family group norms.

Note: *Students should be urged not to divulge sensitive personal information.*

Step 1. Using the information presented in this chapter and in Chapters 7 and 8, the leader asks students to identify the verbal and nonverbal communication patterns operating within their own families and to write down their ideas. Writing down thoughts helps make students think more deeply about their own families and commit themselves to an opinion.

Step 2. The students divide into groups of four to six people to discuss the following questions among themselves:

1. What are the verbal and nonverbal communication patterns in your family?
2. What are the similarities among the group's families in their verbal and nonverbal communication patterns?
3. What are the differences among the families in their verbal and nonverbal communication patterns?

Step 3. One student from each group summarizes the group's conclusions for the entire class.

Step 4. The leader directs the group's attention to the concept of group norms, and each individual writes down a summary of the norms operating in his or her own family.

EP 7b

GOAL: To analyze your family in terms of the group concepts described in this text. It is expected students will gain a better understanding of how their family is structured and how it functions from this exercise.

Step 1. The leader explains the purpose of the exercise, indicates it is a visualization exercise, and states the following, pausing briefly after each question.

I want you to get in a comfortable position, and close your eyes. Take a couple of deep breaths, and relax. Keep your eyes closed during this exercise. I want you to think of your family as I ask you a number of questions. Who is the primary leader in your family? Who makes most of the major decisions in your family? Is the primary leader autocratic, democratic, or laissez faire? Is leadership distributed among different family members in different areas as suggested by the distributed functions theory? Who is generally the task specialist? Who is generally the social-emotional specialist? Who has the most power in your family? For this power person, what is the basis of this power? Is it reward power, coercive power, legitimate power, expert power, or referent power?

What are the rules or norms that exist in your family about dating, drug and alcohol use, acceptable sexual behaviors, the way you dress, religious expectations, expectations about going to college? Who set these rules or norms, and how were they set? What is your role in your family?

How are disputes usually settled in your family? Is a win-lose approach used or is a problem-solving approach generally used? Are major decisions made by consensus, by simple majority voting, or autocratically? Do members use active listening to further communications? Is the role reversal technique used to foster communication and to settle disputes? When your father is angry, how does he communicate his anger nonverbally? When your mother is angry, how does she communicate her anger nonverbally? Do members seek to express their irritation to others, or do members seek to hide their irritation in order to attempt to avoid conflict? Does your family have a cooperative atmosphere or a competitive atmosphere? One person can destroy the morale in a family— has this occurred in your family? Think about each family member—who is generally nonassertive, who is usually aggressive, and who is generally assertive?

What are the major sources of stress in your family at the present time? What different stress management techniques are used in your family—such as meditation, positive thinking, exercising, taking vacations, rewarding yourself with personal goodies, taking mental health days, using support groups, talking problems out with others, seeking to change distressing events, or seeking to challenge and change negative and irrational thinking? Do certain members of your family tend to procrastinate? For those who procrastinate, what do you think would help them stop procrastinating? How well do members of your family manage time?

Probably every person is grieving about something; what are the members of your family grieving about? What are the usual ways of handling grief in your family?

Are some members of your family presently chemically dependent? If so, how are other members of your family reacting to the dependency—for example, are they enablers, are they trying to ignore the problem, are they fighting about it? What can realistically be done to help reduce problems in this area?

Do the different members of your family have a fairly well-thought-out sense of who they are? Do the different members have generally a positive sense of self? For those who have a low self-concept, what might realistically be done to improve their sense of self?

      What are the family values about religion, sexual behavior, chemical use, going to college, smoking, whom you associate with, racial integration, politics, majoring in social work?

      Do members of your family generally communicate openly with each other? Do some members send vague, indirect messages? Do some members send double-blind messages? Are some members afraid to express their needs and desires? How can communication be improved in your family? My questions have ended. Take a minute or two to relax, and then open your eyes.

Step 2. The students discuss whether such concepts are useful in helping them to analyze and better understand their families. Students are invited to share a family situation—such as seeking ideas on how to deal with parents who are autocratic, or how to handle the problems created by someone who is chemically dependent. The students discuss the merits of this exercise.

Competency Notes

EP 1b   Use reflection and self-regulation to manage personal values and maintain professionalism in practice situations. (p. 268)

      This exercise is designed to have students reflect about the composition and strengths of their families.

EP 7b   Apply knowledge of human behavior and the social environment, person-in-environment, and other multidisciplinary theoretical frameworks in the analysis of assessment data from clients and constituencies. (pp. 269)

      This section describes the family assessment tools of the eco-map and the genogram. The two exercises in this section focus on having students assess their families with the eco-map and the genogram.

EP 1b   Use reflection and self-regulation to manage personal values and maintain professionalism in practice situations. (p. 278)

      This exercise is designed to have students reflect about the problematic verbal communication patterns in their famines.

EP 1b   Use reflection and self-regulation to manage personal values and maintain professionalism in practice situations. (p. 279)

      This exercise is designed to have students reflect about the problematic nonverbal communication patterns in their families.

EP 1b   Use reflection and self-regulation to manage personal values and maintain professionalism in practice situations. (p. 280)

      This exercise is designed to have students reflect about the functional roles and problematic roles that members of their families play.

EP 1b   Use reflection and self-regulation to manage personal values and maintain professionalism in practice situations (p. 282)

      This exercise is designed to have students reflect about the personal goals, group goals, and hidden agendas of members of their families.

EP 1b   Use reflection and self-regulation to manage personal values and maintain professionalism in practice situations. (p. 284)

      This exercise is designed to have students reflect about the functional and problematic norms in their families.

EP 1b   Use reflection and self-regulation to manage personal values and maintain professionalism in practice situations. (p. 287)

This exercise is designed to have students reflect about the challenges being faced by their family members and to ponder what actions might help resolve these challenges.

EP 1b   Apply knowledge of human behavior and the social environment, person-in-environment, and other multidisciplinary theoretical frameworks in interventions with clients and constituencies. (pp. 292)

This exercise is designed to facilitate the development of family counseling skills in students.

EP 1b   Apply knowledge of human behavior and the social environment, person-in-environment, and other multidisciplinary theoretical frameworks in interventions with clients and constituencies. (pp. 294)

This exercise is designed to have students analyze their family dynamics in terms of the group concepts described in the text.

Key Term and Concept

Extended Family   In-Home Services   Out-of-Home Services
Family   Nuclear Family

Organizations, Communities, and Groups

ORGANIZATIONS

An organization is defined here as a collectivity of individuals gathered together to serve a particular purpose. The types of purposes (or goals) that people organize to achieve are infinite in number, ranging from obtaining basic necessities to eliminating the threat of worldwide terrorism or attaining world peace. In each case an organization exists because people working together can better accomplish tasks and achieve goals than one individual can.

Etzioni described the importance of organizations in our lives:

> We are born in organizations, educated by organizations, and most of us spend much of our lives working for organizations. We spend much of our leisure time paying, playing, and praying in organizations. Most of us will die in an organization, and when the time comes for burial, the largest organization of all—the state—must grant official permission.[1]

The importance of organizations for social work practice has been summarized by Netting, Kettner, and McMurtry:

> As social workers, our roles within, interactions with, and attempts to manipulate organizations define much of what we do. Clients often come to us seeking help because they are not able to obtain help from organizations that are critical to their survival or quality of life. In turn, the resources we attempt to gain for these clients usually come from still other organizations . . . Social workers with little or no idea of how organizations operate, how they interact, or how they can be influenced and changed from both outside and inside are likely to be severely limited in their effectiveness.[2]

Many disciplines (including business, psychology, political science, and sociology) have produced a prodigious amount of theory and research on organizations. However, in spite of the importance of organizations to social work practice, the amount of social work literature devoted to organizations is limited.

LO 1   Understand the Close Relationships between the Terms Group and Organization

THE RELATIONSHIP BETWEEN A GROUP AND AN ORGANIZATION

In Chapter 1, a group is defined as:

> two or more individuals in face-to-face interaction, each aware of his or her membership in the group, each aware of the others who belong to the group, and each aware of their positive interdependence as they strive to achieve mutual goals.[3]

An organization, as previously stated, is a collectivity of individuals gathered together to serve a purpose. How do these two terms relate?

There is considerable overlap between these two terms. Some organizations can also be considered groups and vice versa. For example, a social work student club can be considered to be both an organization and a group. Another example of both a group and an organization is a parent–teacher association at an elementary school.

However, a large organization is generally not considered a group. For example, the General Motors Corporation is considered an organization but not a group. One reason it is not referred to as a group is that its employees and owners (including stockholders) are so large in number that no one has personal contact with all the other members of the organization. In a similar manner, most other large organizations (such as the National Rifle Association and the American Medical Association) are not considered groups. Such associations are "gathered together" for a specific purpose. However, the term *gathered together* does not mean that everyone has personal contact with everyone else as do the members of a group.

Most small, informal groups with no specific purpose are not considered organizations. For example, a group of neighborhood children who occasionally meet to play with one another is not considered an organization.

EXERCISE 10.1   Refuting Our Organizational Myths

GOAL: Many students erroneously believe they have had very little involvement in an organization. This exercise is designed to demonstrate that you have participated in many organizations.

1. Make a list of the organizations you have participated in. These would include organizations such as the Boys and Girls Club, Girl Scouts, church groups, athletic organizations and teams, organizations you have volunteered for, organizations you have worked for, school organizations, student social work clubs, and day care centers you attended.

2. Select one organization that you particularly enjoyed participating in. Describe the goals of this organization. Also describe what you learned from participating in this organization and why you enjoyed participating in it.

3. Many students erroneously believe that organizational involvement is "distasteful." Now that you realize that you have already enjoyed participating in a variety of organizations, do you now look forward (more positively) to participating with organizations in the future?

LO 2   Identify Several Models of Organizations

EP 7b

MODELS OF ORGANIZATIONS*

The Autocratic Model

The autocratic model has been in existence for thousands of years. During the Industrial Revolution, this model was the prominent model of how an organization should function. The model depends on *power*. Those who are in power act autocratically. The message to employees is "You do this—or else," meaning that an employee who does not follow orders is penalized, often severely.

An autocratic model uses one-way communication—from the top to the workers. Management believes that it knows what is best. The employee's obligation is to follow orders. Employees have to be persuaded, directed, and pushed into performance, and this is management's task. Management does the thinking, and the workers obey the directives. Under autocratic conditions, the workers' role is obedience to management.

The autocratic model does work in some settings. Most military organizations throughout the world are formulated on this model. The model was also used successfully during

---

*   Material in this section is adapted from *The Practice of Social Work*, 7th ed., by Zastrow. © 2003. Reprinted with permission of Brooks/Cole.

the Industrial Revolution, for example, in building great railroad systems and in operating giant steel mills.

The autocratic model has a number of disadvantages. Workers are often in the best position to identify shortcomings in the structure and technology of the organizational system, but one-way communication prevents feedback to management. The model also fails to generate much of a commitment among the workers to accomplish organizational goals. Finally, the model fails to motivate workers to put forth effort to further develop their skills (skills that often would be highly beneficial to the employer).

The Custodial Model

Many decades ago when the autocratic model was the predominant model of organizational behavior, some progressive managers began to study their employees and soon found that the autocratic model often caused the employees to be filled with insecurity, frustration, and feelings of aggression toward management. Because the employees could not directly express their discontent, it was expressed indirectly. Some employees vented their anger on their families and neighbors, and the entire community suffered. Others sabotaged production. Davis and Newstrom described sabotage in a wood-processing plant:

> Managers treated workers crudely, sometimes even to the point of physical abuse. Since employees could not strike back directly for fear of losing their jobs, they found another way to do it. They *symbolically* fed their supervisor to a log-shredding machine! They did this by purposely destroying good sheets of veneer, which made the supervisor look bad when monthly efficiency reports were prepared.[4]

In the 1890s and 1900s, some progressive employers thought that if these feelings could be alleviated, employees might feel more like working, which would increase productivity. To satisfy the employees' security needs, a number of companies began to provide welfare programs; examples include pension programs, childcare centers at the workplace, health insurance, and life insurance.

EXERCISE 10.2   Working for an Autocratic Boss

GOAL: This exercise is designed to have you reflect on the merits and shortcomings of someone who is autocratic.

1. Briefly describe a job you held in which you worked for someone who was autocratic. (In essence, an autocratic boss uses one-way communication—does not want the workers' input on how to do the job.) If you have not worked for an autocratic boss, interview someone who has and then answer these questions.

2. How did you feel about working for someone who was autocratic—that is, someone who told you what to do and would not listen to your thoughts and concerns?

3. Were you motivated to do your best work? Why or why not?

4. Research has found that two-way communication is superior to one-way communication. Why do you believe that so many bosses, even today, use one-way communication?

The custodial approach leads to employee dependence on the organization. According to Davis and Newstrom, "If employees have ten years of seniority under the union contract and a good pension program, they cannot afford to quit even if the grass looks greener somewhere else!"[5]

Employees working under a custodial model tend to focus on their economic rewards and benefits. They are happier and more content than when working under the autocratic model, but they do not have a high commitment to helping the organization accomplish its goals. They tend to give **passive cooperation** to their employer. The model's most evident flaw is that most employees are producing substantially below their capacities. They are not motivated to advance to higher capacities. Most such employees do not feel fulfilled or motivated at their place of work. In summary, contented employees (which the custodial model is designed to generate) are not necessarily the most productive employees.

The Scientific Management Model

One of the earliest and most important schools of thought on the management of functions and tasks in the workplace was based on the work of Frederick Taylor.[6] Taylor was a mechanical engineer, an American industrialist, and an educator. He focused primarily on management techniques that would lead to increased productivity. He asserted that many organizational problems in the workplace involved misunderstandings between managers and workers. Managers erroneously thought that workers were lazy and unemotional, and they mistakenly believed they understood workers' jobs. Workers mistakenly thought that managers cared most about exploiting them.

To solve these problems, Taylor developed the **scientific management model**, which focused on the need for managers to conduct scientific analyses of the workplace. One of the first steps was to conduct a careful study of how each job could best be accomplished. An excellent way to do this, according to Taylor, was to identify the best worker for each job and then carefully study how he or she effectively and efficiently did the work. The goal of this analysis was to discover the optimal way of doing the job—in Taylor's words, the "one best way." Once this best way was identified, tools could be modified to better complete the work, workers' abilities and interests could be fitted to particular job assignments, and the level of production that the average worker could sustain could be gauged.

Once the level of production for the average worker was determined, Taylor indicated the next step was to provide incentives to increase productivity. His favorite strategy for doing this was the piece-rate wage, in which workers were paid for each unit they produced. The goals were to produce more units, reduce unit cost, increase organizational productivity and profitability, and provide incentives for workers to produce more.

Taylor's work has been criticized as having a technicist bias, as it tends to treat workers as little more than cogs in a wheel. No two workers are exactly alike, so the "one best way" of doing a job is often unique to the person doing it. In fact, forcing the same work approach on different workers may actually decrease both productivity and worker satisfaction. In addition, Taylor's approach has limited application to human services. Because each client is unique—with unique needs, unique environmental impact factors, and unique strengths and capacities—each human services case has to be individualized, and therefore it is difficult (if not impossible) to specify the "one best way" to proceed.

The Human Relations Model

In 1927, the Hawthorne Works of the Western Electric Company in Chicago began a series of experiments designed to discover ways to increase worker satisfaction and worker productivity.[7]

Hawthorne Works manufactured telephones on an assembly-line basis. Workers needed no special skills and performed simple, repetitive tasks. The workers were not unionized, and management sought to find ways to increase productivity. If job satisfaction could be increased, employees would work more efficiently and productivity would increase.

The company tested the effects on productivity of a number of factors: rest breaks, better lighting, changes in the number of work hours, changes in the wages paid, improved food facilities, and so on. The results were surprising. Productivity increased, as expected, with improved working conditions, but it also increased when working conditions worsened. This latter finding was unexpected and led to additional study.

The investigators discovered that participation in the experiments was extremely attractive to the workers. They felt they had been selected by the management for their individual abilities, and so they worked harder, even when working conditions became less favorable. In addition, the workers' morale and general attitude toward work improved, as they felt they were receiving special attention. By participating in this study, the workers were able to work in smaller groups and became involved in making decisions. Working in smaller groups allowed them to develop a stronger sense of solidarity with their fellow workers. Being involved in decision making decreased their feelings of meaninglessness and powerlessness about their work.

In sociological and psychological research, the results of this study have become known as the Hawthorne effect. In essence, when subjects know they are participants in a study, this awareness may lead them to behave differently and substantially influence the results.

The results of this study, and of other similar studies, led some researchers to conclude that the key variables affecting productivity are social factors. Etzioni summarized some of the basic tenets of the human relations approach:

- The level of production is set by social norms, not by physiological capacities.
- Noneconomic rewards and sanctions significantly affect the behavior of the workers and largely limit the effect of economic incentive plans.
- Workers do not act or react as individuals but as members of groups.
- The role of leadership is important in understanding social factors in organizations, and this leadership may be either formal or informal.[8]

Numerous studies have provided evidence to support these tenets.[9] Workers who are capable of greater productivity often will not excel because they are unwilling to exceed the "average" level set by the norms of the group, even if this means earning less. These studies have also found that attempts by management to influence workers' behavior are often more successful if targeted at the group as a whole, rather than at individuals. Finally, the studies have documented the importance of informal leadership in influencing workers' behavior in ways that can either amplify or negate formal leadership directives. This model asserts that managers who succeed in increasing productivity are most likely responsive to the workers' social needs.

One criticism of the human relations model is (surprisingly) that it tends to manipulate, dehumanize, oppress, and exploit workers. The model leads to the conclusion that management can increase productivity by helping workers become content, rather than by increasing economic rewards for higher productivity. The human relations model allows for concentrated power and decision making at the top. It is not intended to empower employees in the decision-making process or to assist them in acquiring genuine participation in the running of the organization. The practice of dealing with people on the basis of their perceived social relationships within the workplace may also be a factor in perpetuating the "good old boys" network; this network has disadvantaged women and people of color over the years. Another criticism of the human relations approach is that a happy workforce is not necessarily a productive workforce because the norms for worker production may be set well below the workers' levels of capability.

Theory X and Theory Y

McGregor developed two theories of management.[10] He theorized that management thinking and behavior are based on two different sets of assumptions, which he labeled Theory X and Theory Y.

Theory X managers view employees as incapable of much growth. Employees are perceived as having an inherent dislike for work and attempting to evade work whenever possible. Therefore, X-type managers believe they must control, direct, force, or threaten employees to make them work. Employees are also viewed as having relatively little ambition, wishing to avoid responsibilities and preferring to be directed. Theory X managers therefore spell out job responsibilities carefully, set work goals without employee input, use external rewards (such as money) to force employees to work, and punish those who deviate from established rules. Because Theory X managers reduce responsibilities to a level at which few mistakes can be made, work usually becomes so structured that it is monotonous and distasteful. These assumptions, of course, are inconsistent with what behavioral scientists assert are effective principles for directing, influencing, and motivating people. (Theory X managers are, in essence, adhering to an autocratic model of organizational behavior.)

In contrast, **Theory Y managers** view employees as wanting to grow and develop by exerting physical and mental effort to accomplish work objectives to which they are committed. These managers believe that the promise of internal rewards, such as self-respect and personal improvement, are stronger motivators than external rewards (money) and punishment. They also believe that under proper conditions, employees will not only accept responsibility, but will seek it. Most employees are assumed to have considerable ingenuity, creativity, and imagination for problem solving. Therefore, they are given considerable responsibility to test the limits of their capabilities. Mistakes and errors are viewed as necessary phases of the learning process, and work is structured so employees have a sense of accomplishment and growth.

Employees who work for Y-type managers are generally more creative and productive, experience greater work satisfaction, and are more highly motivated than employees who work for X-type managers. Under both management styles, expectations often become self-fulfilling prophecies.

The Collegial Model

A useful extension of Theory Y is the collegial model, which emphasizes the team concept. It involves employees working closely together and feeling a commitment to achieve a common purpose. Some organizations—such as university departments, research laboratories, and most human services organizations—have a goal of creating a collegial atmosphere to facilitate achieving their purposes. (Sadly, many such organizations are unsuccessful in creating such an atmosphere.)

EXERCISE 10.3   Working for Theory X versus Theory Y Managers

GOAL: This exercise is designed to assist you in understanding the merits and shortcomings of each of these two management styles.

1. Describe a job you had in which you worked for someone who used a Theory X style of management. Why would you categorize this person as having a Theory X style?

2. Describe a job you had in which you worked for someone who used a Theory Y style of management. Why would you categorize this person as having a Theory Y style? (If you have not worked for a Theory X or Theory Y manager, interview someone who has and then answer these questions.)

3. Compare your feelings about working for a Theory X versus Theory Y manager.

4. For which manager were you more motivated to do your best work? Indicate your reasons for this choice.

Creating a collegial atmosphere is highly dependent on management building a feeling of partnership with employees. When such a partnership develops, employees feel needed and useful. Managers are then viewed as joint contributors rather than as bosses. Management is the coach who builds a better team. Davis and Newstrom described some of the approaches to developing a team concept:

> The feeling of partnerships can be built in many ways. Some organizations have abolished the use of reserved parking spaces for executives, so every employee has an equal chance of finding one close to the workplace. Some firms have tried to eliminate the use of terms like "bosses" and "subordinates," feeling that those terms simply create perceptions of psychological distance between managers and nonmanagers. Other employers have removed time clocks, set up "fun committees," sponsored company canoe trips, or required managers to spend a week or two annually working in field or factory locations. All of these approaches are designed to build a spirit of mutuality, in which every person makes contributions and appreciates those of others.[11]

If the sense of partnership is developed, employees produce quality work and seek to cooperate with coworkers, not because management directs them to do so, but because they feel an internal obligation to produce high-quality work. The collegial approach thus leads to a sense of *self-discipline*. In this environment, employees are more apt to have a sense of fulfillment, to feel self-actualized, and to produce higher-quality work.

Theory Z

William Ouchi described the Japanese style of management in his 1981 best-seller *Theory Z*.[12] In the late 1970s and early 1980s, attention in the U.S. business world became focused on the Japanese approach to management, as markets long dominated by U.S. firms (such as the automobile industry) were being challenged for dominance by Japanese industries. Japanese industrial organizations had rapidly overcome their earlier reputation for poor-quality work and were setting worldwide standards for quality and durability.

Theory Z asserted that the theoretical principles underlying Japanese management went beyond Theory Y. According to Theory Z, a business organization in Japan is more than the profitability-oriented entity that it is in the United States. It is a way of life. It provides lifetime employment. It is enmeshed with the nation's political, social, and economic network. Furthermore, its influence spills over into many other organizations, such as nursery schools, elementary and secondary schools, and universities.

The basic philosophy of Theory Z is that involved and committed workers are the key to increased productivity. Ideas and suggestions about how to improve the organization are routinely solicited and implemented, where feasible. One strategy for accomplishing this is the *quality circle*, where employees and management routinely meet to brainstorm about ways to improve productivity and quality.

In contrast to U.S. organizations, Japanese organizations tend not to have written objectives or organizational charts. Most work is done in teams, and decisions are made by consensus. The teams tend to function without a designated leader. Cooperation within units and between units, loyalty to the organization, and organizational loyalty to the employee are all emphasized.

Experiments designed to transplant Japanese-style management to the United States have resulted in mixed success. In most cases U.S. organizations have concluded that Theory Z probably works quite well in a homogeneous culture that has Japan's societal values, but some components do not fit well with the more heterogeneous and individualistic character of the United States. In addition, some firms in volatile industries (such as electronics) have difficulty balancing their desire to provide lifetime employment with the need to adjust their workforces to meet rapidly changing market demands.

Management by Objectives

Fundamental to the core of an organization is its purpose, that is, the commonly shared understanding of the reason for its existence.

Management theorist Peter Drucker proposed a strategy for making organizational goals and objectives the central construct around which organizational life is designed to function.[13] In other words, instead of focusing on employee needs and wants or on organizational structure as the ways to increase efficiency and productivity, Drucker proposed beginning with the desired outcome and working backward. The strategy is first to identify the organizational objectives or goals and then to adapt the organizational tasks, resources, and structure to meet those objectives. This management by objectives (MBO) approach is designed to focus the organization's efforts on meeting these objectives. Success is determined, then, by the degree to which stated objectives are reached.

This approach can be applied to the organization as a whole, as well as to internal divisions or departments. When the MBO approach is applied to internal divisions, the objectives set for each division should be consistent and supportive of the overall organizational objectives.

In many areas, including human services, the MBO approach can be applied to the cases serviced by each employee. Goals are set with each client, tasks to meet these goals are then determined, and deadlines are set for the completion of these tasks. The degree of success of each case is then determined at a later date (often when a case is closed) by the extent to which stated goals were achieved.

An adaptation of the MBO approach, called strategic planning and budgeting (SPB), became popular in the 1990s and still is widely used. The process involves first specifying the overall vision or mission of an organization, then identifying a variety of more specific objectives or plans for achieving that vision, and finally adapting the resources to meet the specific high-priority objectives or plans. Organizations often hire outside consultants to assist in conducting the SPB process.

One major advantage of the MBO approach for an organization (or its divisions) is that it produces clear statements (made available to all employees) about the objectives and the tasks that are expected to be accomplished in specified time periods. This type of activity tends to improve cooperation and collaboration. The MBO approach is also useful because it provides a guide for allocating resources and a focus for monitoring and evaluating organizational efforts.

An additional benefit of the MBO approach is that it creates diversity in the workplace. Prior to this approach, those responsible for hiring failed to employ women and people of color in significant numbers. As affirmative action programs were developed within organizations, the MBO approach was widely used to set specific hiring goals and objectives. The result has been significant changes in recruitment approaches that have enabled a number of women and other minorities to secure employment.

Total Quality Management

Total quality management (TQM) has been defined as:

> the integration of all functions and processes within an organization in order to achieve continuous improvement of the quality of goods and services. The goal is customer satisfaction.[14]

TQM is based on a number of ideas. It means thinking about quality in terms of all functions of the enterprise and is a start-to-finish process that integrates interrelated functions at all levels. It is a systems approach that considers every interaction among the various elements of the organization. TQM asserts that management in many businesses and organizations makes the mistake of blaming what goes wrong in an organization as the fault of individual people, not of the system. TQM, instead, believes in the 85/15 Rule, which asserts that 85% of the problems can be corrected only by changing systems (structures, rules, practices, expectations, and traditions that are largely determined by management) and less than 15% of the problems can be solved by individual workers. When problems arise, TQM asserts that management should look for causes in the system and work to remove them before casting blame on workers.

EXERCISE 10.4   Applying Concepts of Models of Organizations

GOAL: This exercise is designed to assist you in understanding models of organizations and then applying some of their theoretical concepts.

1. Review the material in this chapter on the following models of organizations:

   - The autocratic model
   - The custodial model
   - The scientific management model
   - The human relations model
   - Theory X
   - Theory Y
   - The collegial model
   - Theory Z
   - Management by objectives
   - Total quality management

   Select an organization that you have worked for and describe the goals of this organization.

2. List the models that provide some useful concepts that assist you in understanding the behavior of the "boss/leader" and the "workers." Also summarize the theoretical concepts of these models that you found useful.

TQM asserts that quality includes continuously improving all the organization's processes that lead to customer satisfaction. Customer satisfaction is the main purpose of the organization. The customer is not the "point of sale." The customer is part of the design and production process, as the customers' needs must continually be monitored.

In recent years numerous organizations have adopted a TQM approach to seeking to improve their goods and services. One reason that quality is being emphasized more is that consumers are increasingly shunning mass-produced, poorly made, disposable products. Companies are realizing that in order to remain competitive in global markets, high quality is essential in their products and services. Ford's motto of "Quality Is Job One" symbolizes this emphasis on quality.

There are a variety of approaches to TQM because numerous theoreticians have advanced their own diverse approaches. A summary of these approaches is contained in *Principles of Total Quality*.[15]

With regard to human service agencies, the following are guiding principles of TQM:

- The first and major principle is to satisfy the customer. The customer is the one paying for the service (which may be the funding source, or if it is paying clients, then it would be these clients). Human service agencies satisfy customers by providing them value for funds they provide. The agencies that provide value for what the customers buy will get more repeat business and referral business and will have reduced complaints and reduced service expenses. Human service agencies should ask funders what they need and provide more of what they ask for.
- Human service agencies should instill pride into every employee. Helping every employee to enjoy his or her work will lead to higher motivation of employees to do well, which will result in these agencies becoming more productive. Agencies should provide a forum or seek to create high morale at work so that employees at all levels feel free to voice their opinions when they think they have good ideas. Agencies should review the suggestions and implement the best ones. Employees should be inspired and empowered to do their best. The number of layers of authority should be reduced to enhance employee empowerment. A focus of human service agencies should be to instill pride into every employee.
- Complaints from customers or from employees should be viewed as opportunities for improvement. In reviewing a complaint or a suggestion, the focus should be on quality evaluative information and data, rather than on opinions or egos.
- Supervisors should seek to keep their supervisees happy and productive by providing good task suggestions, the tools they need to do their job, and good working conditions. Supervisors should also reward productive employees with praise and good pay.
- Employees are an excellent source of continuous improvements. They often can provide suggestions on how to improve a system/process and eliminate waste or unnecessary work.

LO 3   Survive, and Thrive, in an Agency

EP 1b
EP 7b

THE RELEVANCE OF THEORY X AND THEORY Y FOR SOCIAL WORKERS

Two of the most relevant organizational theories for social workers are Theory X and Theory Y. These theories were described earlier in this chapter.[16] Theory X supervisors rely heavily on the threat of punishment to gain employee compliance. This managerial style is more effective when used to motivate a workforce that is not inherently motivated to perform.

Theory Y, in contrast, is characterized by considering the worker as being the most important asset of the organization. Theory Y supervisors assume that workers not only like their careers, but also are willing to take on some amount of professional responsibility. Theory Y supervisors seek input from workers on how the organization can make changes in order to better serve customers/clients.

It is critical for newly hired social workers in an organization to observe and determine if supervisors believe in a Theory X or Theory Y style of management. If a worker has Theory X supervisors, then that worker can best "survive" by doing what the supervisors tell him or her to do. That worker should make few (or no) suggestions for changes in the organization—because suggestions for changes will irritate the supervisors. To feel fulfilled/gratified as a person, such a worker should seek "recognition" from outside sources—such as a church, an athletic team that one joins, friends, or family members (Theory X organizations are not apt to give recognition to workers—such as promotions or praise—other than paying them.)

If a worker has Theory Y supervisors, then that worker can best "survive/thrive" by making suggestions for changes, as such suggestions are expected and appreciated. Also, workers can expect to be praised and promoted for work that is well done. When working for Theory Y supervisors, a worker is more apt to find recognition and become more ego-invested with that organization.

How can a new worker determine if his organization has primarily Theory X or Theory Y supervisors? *It is essential that new workers in a social service organization observe carefully the actions (and not the words) of their supervisors.* Theory X supervisors are apt to say they cherish suggestions for changes, "but the proof is in the pudding." I worked for an organization where the president/executive director said frequently that she cherished and invited suggestions for changes. However, if a worker made a suggestion for a change that appeared to be a little criticism of her, she made it her mission to either discharge that worker or make the job so distasteful that the worker left. (A president/executive director can make a job distasteful in a variety of ways—such as providing no pay increases, assigning heavy work responsibilities, assigning evening or weekend work, and rewriting that worker's job description to be more onerous.)

Servant Leadership and Theory Y   Servant leadership and Theory Y are closely related. Servant leadership is described in Chapter 3. The servant leadership approach was originally developed by Robert K. Greenleaf.[17]

A servant leader is someone who looks to the needs of the organization and to the needs of the employees. The servant leader administrator/supervisor asks herself how she can help the people she is supervising to solve problems and how she can best promote their personal development. A Theory Y supervisor has the same orientation. Readers may want to reexamine the characteristics of a servant leader that are identified in Chapter 3.

KNOPF'S BUREAUCRATIC SYSTEM MODEL AND THEORY X*

Knopf has developed a model of a bureaucratic system and its relevance for helping professionals (including social workers).[18] The model has a number of characteristics of Theory X. Knopf indicates a bureaucracy is a subcategory (or type) of organization. A bureaucracy can be defined as a form of social organization whose distinctive characteristics include a vertical hierarchy with power centered at the top; a task-specific division of labor; clearly defined rules; formalized channels of communication; and selection, compensation, promotion, and retention based on technical competence.

Knopf notes there are basic structural conflicts between helping professionals and the bureaucratic systems in which they work. Helping professionals place a high value on creativity and changing the system to serve clients. Bureaucracies resist change and are most efficient when no one is "rocking the boat." Helping professionals seek to personalize services by conveying to each client that "you count as a person." Bureaucracies are highly depersonalized, emotionally detached systems that view every employee and every client as a tiny component of a large system. In a large bureaucracy, employees *don't* count as "people" but only as functional parts of a system. Additional conflicting value orientations between a helping professional and bureaucratic systems are listed in the box titled "Value Conflicts between a Helping Professional and Bureaucracies."

---

*   Material in this section is adapted from *The Practice of Social Work*, 7th ed., by Zastrow. © 2003. Reprinted with permission of Brooks/Cole.

Value Conflicts between a Helping Professional and Bureaucracies

ORIENTATIONS OF A HELPING PROFESSIONAL	ORIENTATIONS OF BUREAUCRATIC SYSTEMS
Desires democratic system for decision making.	Most decisions are made autocratically.
Desires that power be distributed equally among employees (horizontal structure).	Power is distributed vertically.
Desires that clients have considerable power in the system.	Power is held primarily by top executives.
Desires a flexible, changing system.	System is rigid and stable.
Desires that creativity and growth be emphasized.	Emphasis is on structure and the status quo.
Desires that focus be client oriented.	System is organization centered.
Desires that communication be on a personalized level from person to person.	Communication is from level to level.
Desires shared decision making and shared responsibility structure.	A hierarchical decision-making structure and a hierarchical responsibility structure are characteristic.
Desires that decisions be made by those with the most knowledge.	Decisions are made in terms of the decision-making authority assigned to each position in the hierarchy.
Desires shared leadership.	System uses autocratic leadership.
Believes feelings of clients and employees should be highly valued by the system.	Procedures and processes are highly valued.

Any of these differences in value orientations can become an arena of conflict between helping professionals and the bureaucracies in which they work. Knopf summarized the potential areas of conflict between bureaucracies and helping professionals:

> The trademarks of a BS (bureaucratic system) are power, hierarchy, and specialization; that is, rules and roles. In essence, the result is depersonalization. The system itself is neither "good" nor "bad"; it is a system. I believe it to be amoral. It is efficient and effective, but in order to be so it must be impersonal in all of its functionings. This then is the location of the stress. The hallmark of the helping professional is a highly individualized, democratic, humanized, relationship-oriented service aimed at self-motivation. The hallmark of a bureaucratic system is a highly impersonalized, valueless (amoral), emotionally detached, hierarchical structure of organization. The dilemma of the HP (helping person) is how to give a personalized service to a client through a delivery system that is not set up in any way to do that.[19]

Numerous helping professionals respond to these orientation conflicts by erroneously projecting a "personality" onto the bureaucracy. The bureaucracy is viewed as being red tape, officialism, uncaring, cruel, the enemy. A negative personality is sometimes also projected onto the officials, who may be viewed as being paper shufflers, rigid, deadwood, inefficient, and unproductive. Knopf states:

> The HP (helping person) . . . may deal with the impersonal nature of the system by projecting values onto it and thereby give the BS (bureaucratic system) a "personality." In this way, we fool ourselves into thinking that we can deal with it in a personal way. Unfortunately, projection is almost always negative and reflects the dark or negative aspects of ourselves. The BS then becomes a screen onto which we vent our anger, sadness, or fright, and while a lot of energy is generated, very little is accomplished. Since the BS is amoral, it is unproductive to place a personality on it.[20]

A bureaucratic system is neither good nor bad. It has neither a personality nor a value system of its own. It is simply a structure developed to carry out various tasks.

A helping person may have various emotional reactions to these conflicts in orientation with bureaucratic systems. Common reactions are anger at the system, self-blame ("It's all my fault"), sadness and depression ("Poor me," "Nobody appreciates all I've done"), and fright and paranoia ("They're out to get me," "If I mess up I'm gone").

Knopf identified several types of behavior patterns that helping professionals choose in dealing with bureaucracies.

The *warrior* leads open campaigns to destroy and malign the system. A warrior discounts the value of the system and often enters into a win-lose conflict. The warrior generally loses and is dismissed.

The *gossip* is a covert warrior who complains to others (including clients, politicians, and the news media) about how terrible the system is. A gossip frequently singles out a few officials for criticism. Bureaucratic systems often make life very difficult for the gossip by assigning distasteful tasks, refusing to promote, giving very low salary increases, and perhaps even dismissing.

The *complainer* resembles a gossip but confines complaints to other helping people, to in-house staff, and to family members. A complainer wants people to agree in order to find comfort in shared misery. Complainers desire to stay with the system, and generally do.

The *dancer* is skillful at ignoring rules and procedures. Dancers are frequently lonely, often reprimanded for incorrectly filling out forms, and have low investment in the system or in helping clients.

The *defender* is scared; dislikes conflict; and therefore defends the rules, the system, and bureaucratic officials. Defenders are often supervisors and are viewed by others as bureaucrats.

The *machine* is a bureaucrat who takes on the orientation of the bureaucracy. Often a machine has not been involved in providing direct services for years. Machines are frequently named to head study committees and policy groups and to chair boards.

The *executioner* attacks people within an organization with enthusiasm and vigor. An executioner usually has a high energy level and is impulsive. An executioner abuses power by indiscriminately attacking and dismissing not only employees but also services and programs. Executioners have power and are angry (although the anger is disguised and denied). They are not committed to either the value orientation of helping professionals or the bureaucracy.

Knopf listed 66 tips on how to survive in a bureaucracy.[21] The most useful suggestions are summarized here:

1. Whenever your needs, or the needs of your clients, are not met by the bureaucracy, use the following problem-solving approach: (1) Precisely identify your needs (or the needs of clients) that are in conflict with the bureaucracy; this step is defining the problem. (2) Generate a list of possible solutions. Be creative in generating a wide range of solutions. (3) Evaluate the merits and shortcomings of the possible solutions. (4) Select a solution. (5) Implement the solution. (6) Evaluate the solution.

2. Obtain knowledge of how your bureaucracy is structured and how it functions. This knowledge will reduce fear of the unknown, make the system more predictable, and help in identifying rational ways to best meet your needs and those of your clients.

3. Remember that bureaucrats are people who have feelings. Communication gaps are often most effectively reduced if you treat them with as much respect and interest as you treat clients.

4. If you are at war with the bureaucracy, declare a truce. The system will find a way to dismiss you if you remain at war. With a truce, you can identify and use the strengths of the bureaucracy as an ally, rather than having the strengths be used against you as an enemy.

5. Know your work contract and job expectations. If the expectations are unclear, seek clarity.

EXERCISE 10.5   Your Orientation toward Bureaucratic Systems

GOAL: This exercise is designed to assist you in arriving at a realistic view of bureaucratic systems.

1. Examine the "orientations of a helping professional" and "orientations of bureaucratic systems" in the boxed feature "Value Conflicts Between a Helping Professional and Bureaucracies." Which set of orientations did you have prior to reading this material?

2. If you listed "orientations of a helping professional," do you now believe you need to view bureaucratic systems in terms of "orientations of bureaucratic systems"? Explain your views on this issue.

6. Continue to develop your knowledge and awareness of specific helping skills. Take advantage of continuing education opportunities (for example, workshops, conferences, courses). Among other advantages, your continued professional development will assist you in being able to contract from a position of competency and skill.

7. Seek to identify your professional strengths and limitations. Knowing your limitations will increase your ability to avoid undertaking responsibilities that are beyond your competencies.

8. Be aware that you can't change everything, so stop trying. In a bureaucracy, focus your change efforts on those aspects that most need change and that you have a fair chance of changing. Stop thinking and complaining about those aspects you cannot change. It is irrational to complain about things that you cannot change or to complain about those things that you do not intend to make an effort to change.

9. Learn how to control your emotions in your interactions with the bureaucracy. Emotions that are counterproductive (such as most angry outbursts) particularly

need to be controlled. Doing a rational self-analysis of unwanted emotions (see Appendix 1: Module 1) is one way of gaining control of your unwanted emotions. Learning how to respond to stress in your personal life will also prepare you to handle stress at work better.

10. Develop and use a sense of humor. Humor takes the edge off adverse conditions and reduces negative feelings.

11. Learn to accept your mistakes and perhaps even to laugh at some of them. No one is perfect.

12. Take time to enjoy and develop a support system with your coworkers.

13. Acknowledge your mistakes and give in sometimes on minor matters. You may not be right, and giving in sometimes allows other people to do the same.

14. Keep yourself physically fit and mentally alert. Learn to use approaches that will reduce stress and prevent burnout (see Chapter 11).

15. Leave your work at the office. If you have urgent unfinished bureaucratic business, do it before leaving work or don't leave.

16. Occasionally take your supervisor and other administrators to lunch. Socializing prevents isolation and facilitates your involvement with and understanding of the system.

17. Do not seek self-actualization or ego satisfaction from the bureaucracy. A depersonalized system is incapable of providing this. Only you can satisfy your ego and become self-actualized.

18. Make speeches to community groups that accentuate the positives about your agency. Do not hesitate to ask after speeches that a thank-you letter be sent to your supervisor or agency director.

19. If you have a problem involving the bureaucracy, discuss it with other employees; focus on problem solving rather than on complaining. Groups are much more powerful and productive than an individual working alone to make changes in a system.

20. No matter how high you rise in a hierarchy, maintain direct service contact. Direct contact keeps you abreast of changing client needs, prevents your approach from getting stale, and keeps you attuned to the concerns of employees in lower levels of the hierarchy.

21. Do not try to change everything in the system at once. Attacking too much will overextend you and lead to burnout. Start small and be selective and specific. Double-check your facts to make certain they accurately prove your position before confronting bureaucratic officials.

22. Identify your career goals and determine whether they can be met in this system. If the answer is no, then (1) change your goals, (2) change the bureaucracy, or (3) seek a position elsewhere in which your goals can be met.

LO 4   Comprehend the Impact of Structure and Leadership Competency on Organizations

ORGANIZATIONAL EFFECTIVENESS: STRUCTURE VERSUS LEADERSHIP COMPETENCY

Is it the structure of an organization or the competency level of the top leadership of an organization that primarily determines the overall performance level? (This author realizes that there are other factors that also affect overall performance level, such as the economic context—a serious recession, for example, is apt to lower overall performance.) Other factors include the level of expertise of employees and the morale of employees.

Yet two main factors that determine the overall level of performance are the bureaucratic structure and the competency level of the top leadership. Often, organizations spend considerable time internally debating whether a proposed change in structure will facilitate increased levels of performance.

It is the viewpoint of this author that, although structure is important, the competency level of the top leadership is more important in determining the overall level of performance.

The following hypotheses appear valid:

1. Competent and motivated top leadership can lead an organization with a restrictive structure to perform quite well.
2. Incompetent or even Machiavellian leadership (see Chapter 3) will usually result in an organization having a low level of performance—even when the organizational structure is designed to facilitate a high level of performance.

Why is it that when an organization is underperforming, usually initial efforts are focused on changing the organizational structure rather than making changes in who is occupying the top leadership positions? The answer appears to be that the top leadership is more willing to accept a change in the organizational structure than for them to voluntarily step down from their leadership positions. (In reality, maintaining incompetent people in leadership positions may be one of the worst decisions an organization can make.)

LO 5　Understand the Relationships between the Terms Group, Organization, and Community

COMMUNITIES, ORGANIZATIONS, AND GROUPS

A community has been defined as "a group of individuals or families that share certain values, services, institutions, interests or geographic proximity."[22] The term **institution** in this definition is sometimes rather difficult to comprehend. Barker has defined institution as "an organization established for some public purpose and the physical facility in which its work occurs, such as a prison."[23]

The reader will note that the terms **organization** and **community** are closely related. An organization was defined earlier in this chapter as a collectivity of individuals gathered together to serve a particular purpose. Some communities are also organizations. A nursing home can be considered both an organization (the residents and staff form a collectivity of individuals with a specific purpose) and a community (the residents and staff share certain values, services, physical facilities, interests, and geographic proximity).

But not all communities are institutions, and vice versa. The residents of a large city form a community, as they share certain services and institutions and have geographic proximity, but a large city is not an organization, as its residents are not gathered together to serve a particular purpose.

The owners and employees of a large multinational corporation (such as Philip Morris Corporation, which has offices in many countries and sells a variety of products, including tobacco and groceries) form an organization. However, the Philip Morris Corporation is not considered a community because the corporation is so large that its vast numbers of owners and employees do not engage sufficiently in "sharing" with one another to be considered a community.

A distinguishing characteristic of a group is that its members have personal contact with one another. A community, as stated earlier in this chapter, is "a group of individuals or families that share certain values, services, institutions, interests, or geographic proximity."[24]

In many cases a group and a community overlap, and the group can also be considered a community. The congregation of St. Peter's Catholic Church in Madison, Wisconsin, is both a group and a community. The members have personal contact with one another (characteristic of a group) and share the religious values of the Catholic Church (characteristic of a community).

There are a number of other examples in which a group is also a community. The small unincorporated village of Little Chicago, Wisconsin, is composed of one bank, three stores, one tavern, a restaurant, and five residential homes. The village is a community; its residents share geographic proximity, services, values, and interests and have personal contact with one another (a key characteristic of a group). Some of the interests and values that are shared are hard work, helping neighbors out in times of trouble, a belief in Christianity, and the cherishing of country living in rural America.

EXERCISE 10.6 Enjoying and Appreciating a Community

GOAL: Some students erroneously believe social work practice with communities is not rewarding. This exercise is designed to show students that community involvement has numerous rewards.

1. Describe a community that you have enjoyed participating in. This may be a sorority, a fraternity, the community you live in, a community you visited during a trip or vacation, a church group you are involved with, a residence hall that has become a community for you at this campus, and so on. In your description, seek to highlight the unique aspects of this community.

2. Specify the aspects of the community that you have enjoyed and appreciated.

3. Has this exercise moved you, at least a little, to conclude that community involvement (and yes, social work practice with communities) may be something you want to continue to pursue?

Many communities are so large that their members do not have personal contact with one another and therefore are not a group. For example, Roman Catholics throughout the world have a common set of values and therefore can be considered to be a community. However, no one has personal contact with everyone else, so they are not considered a group. The residents of New York City form a community, as they share geographic proximity (in fact, distinct geographic boundaries). But this community is not a group because no resident has personal contact with everyone else.

LO 6   Analyze a Community

EP 7b

Various frameworks have been developed for analyzing a community. The following framework presents an elementary approach:

1. *Community Members*: Who are the members of this community? How many members are there? What unique or distinct characteristics do these members have? What is their ethnic or racial composition? What is the age composition? Do the members have pride in their community? If "yes," what aspects do the residents have pride in?

2. *Economic Characteristics*: What are the principal economic characteristics of the community? What are the principal types of employment? What are the major industries? Have there been recent changes in the economic base? What is the unemployment rate?

3. *Community Values*: Does the community have a distinct set of values? If "yes," what are these values? Who set these values and why were they selected, or how did they develop? Have there been changes in these values over time? If "yes," what changes have occurred and for what reasons?

4. *Needs and Social Problems*: What do the members perceive as their most critical needs? Why are these needs perceived as critical? How effectively do the members perceive that their community is responding to their needs? Closely related to the previous questions are the following: What major social problems affect the members? Are subgroups of the population experiencing social problems of critical proportions? What data are available on these identified social problems, and what are the sources of these data?

5. *Oppression and Discrimination*: Are some subgroups of the population being victimized by oppression and discrimination? (Oppression can be defined as the unjust or cruel use of authority or power.) If "yes," the following questions are important: Why are oppression and discrimination occurring? How is the power structure in the community responding to the oppression and discrimination? What efforts are being made to combat this oppression and discrimination? Who are the leaders in these efforts?

6. *Power Structure:* Who holds the power in the community? What is the nature of the power—such as financial, military or police strength, election processes? How does the power structure maintain its power? Is the power fairly evenly distributed among the members, or is the power in the hands of a small segment of the members? What are the attitudes of the power structure toward those in the community with little or no power?

7. *Human Services:* What existing human service agencies and organizations are seen as the major service providers in the community? What primary human services are provided? Who are the major beneficiaries of these services? Are subgroups with critical needs being ignored? If "yes," why are their needs being ignored? What is the image of the social work profession in the community?

8. *Educational Services:* What are the major educational resources in the community? What educational services are being provided? Who are the major beneficiaries of these services? Are there subgroups whose educational needs are being ignored? If "yes," why are these needs being ignored?

EXERCISE 10.7   Analyzing Your Home Community

GOAL: This exercise is designed to assist you in learning how to apply a framework for analyzing a community.

1. Using the framework described in "Analyzing a Community," answer as many questions as you can about the community you live in at home. (There is no need to do much research—just answer in terms of what you now know about your home community.)

2. Summarize your thoughts about the merits and shortcomings of this framework for analyzing a community.

LO 7   Identify Three Models a Social Worker Can Use in Seeking Constructive Community Changes

EP 7b

MODELS OF COMMUNITY PRACTICE*

Various approaches have been developed for community practitioners to bring about community change. In reviewing these approaches, Rothman and Tropman have categorized them into three models: locality development, social planning, and social action.[25] It should be noted that these models are "ideal types." Actual approaches to community change have tendencies or emphases that categorize them in one of the previous models, yet most approaches also have components characteristic of one or both of the other models. Advocates of the social planning model, for example, may at times use community change techniques (such as wide discussion and participation by a variety of groups) that are characteristic of the other two models. At this point we will not attempt to deal with the mixed forms, but for analytical purposes will instead view the three models as "pure" forms.

Locality Development Model

Locality development (also called community development) asserts that community change can best be brought about through broad participation of a wide spectrum of people at the local community level. The model seeks to involve a broad cross-section of people (including the disadvantaged and the power structure) in identifying and solving their problems. Some themes emphasized in this model are democratic procedures, a consensus approach, voluntary cooperation, development of indigenous leadership, and self-help.

The roles of the community practitioner in this approach include enabler, catalyst, coordinator, and teacher of problem-solving skills and ethical values. The approach assumes that conflicts that arise between various interest groups can be creatively and constructively handled. It encourages people to express their differences freely, but assumes people will put aside their self-interests in order to further the interests of their community. The approach assumes people will put aside their self-interests through appeals to altruism. The basic theme of this approach is "Together we can figure out what to do and do it." The approach seeks to use discussion and communication between different factions to reach consensus about the problems to focus on and the strategies or actions to resolve these problems. A few examples of locality development efforts include neighborhood work programs conducted by community-based agencies; Volunteers in Service to America; village-level work in some overseas community development programs, including the Peace Corps; and a variety of activities performed by self-help groups. A case example of the locality development model is presented in the box "Case Example of the Locality Development Model."

Social Planning Model

The social planning approach emphasizes a technical process of problem solving. The approach assumes that community change in a complex industrial environment requires highly trained and skilled planners who can guide complex change processes. The role of the expert is stressed in this approach to identifying and resolving social problems. The expert or planner is generally employed by a segment of the power structure, such as area planning agency, city or county planning department, mental health center, United Way board, community welfare council, and so on. Because the social planner is employed by a segment of the power structure, there is a tendency for the planner to serve the interests of the power structure. Facilitating radical social change is generally not an emphasis in this approach.

The planner's roles in this approach include gathering facts, analyzing data, and serving as program designer, implementer, and facilitator. Community participation may vary from little to substantial with this approach, depending on the community's attitudes toward the problems being addressed. For example, an effort to design and obtain funding for a community center for the elderly may or may not result in substantial involvement by interested

---

* This section is adapted from *The Practice of Social Work*, 7th ed., by Zastrow. © 2003. Reprinted with permission of Brooks/Cole.

Case Example of the Locality Development Model

Robert McKearn, a social worker for a juvenile probation department, noticed in 1995 that an increasing number of school-age children were being referred to his office by the police department, school system, and parents from a small city of 11,000 people in the county served by his agency. The charges included status offenses (such as truancy from school) and delinquent offenses (such as shoplifting and burglary). Mr. McKearn noted that most of these children were from single-parent families.

Mr. McKearn contacted the self-help organization Parents Without Partners, the pupil services department of the public school system, the county social services department, some members of the clergy, and the community mental health center in the area. Nearly everyone he contacted saw an emerging need to better serve children in single-parent families. The pupil services department mentioned that such children were performing less well academically in school and tended to display more serious disciplinary problems.

Mr. McKearn arranged a meeting of representatives from the groups and organizations that were contacted.

At the initial meeting numerous concerns were expressed about the problematic behaviors being displayed by children who had single parents. The school system considered these children to be "at risk" for higher rates of truancy, dropping out of school, delinquent activities, suicide, emotional problems, and unwanted pregnancies. Although numerous problems were identified, no one at this initial meeting was able to suggest a viable strategy to better serve single parents and their children. The community was undergoing an economic recession; therefore, funds were unavailable for an expensive new program.

Three more meetings were held. At the first two, many suggestions for providing services were discussed, but all were viewed as either too expensive or impractical. At the fourth meeting of the group, a single parent representing Parents Without Partners mentioned that she was aware that Big Brothers and Big Sisters programs in some communities were of substantial benefit to children who were raised in single-parent families. This idea seemed to energize the group. Suggestions began to "piggy back." The group members, however, determined that funds were unavailable to hire staff to run a Big Brothers and Big Sisters program. However, Rhona Quinn, a social worker in the pupil services department, noted that she was willing to identify at-risk younger children in single-parent families and that she would be willing to supervise qualified volunteers in a "Big Buddy" program.

Mr. McKearn mentioned that he was currently supervising a student in an undergraduate field placement for an accredited social work program from a college in a nearby community. He noted that perhaps arrangements could be made for undergraduate social work students to be "Big Buddies" for their required volunteer experience. Rhona Quinn said she would approve of the suggestion if she could have the freedom to screen interested applicants for being "Big Buddies." Arrangements were made over the next 2 months for social work students to be "Big Buddies" for at-risk younger children from single-parent families. After a two-year experimental period, the school system found the program sufficiently successful that it assigned Ms. Quinn half-time to supervise the program, which included selecting at-risk children, screening volunteer applicants, matching children with "Big Buddies," monitoring the progress of each matched pair, and conducting follow-up to ascertain the outcome of each pairing.

community groups, depending on the politics surrounding such a center. Much of the focus of the social planning approach is on identifying needs and on arranging and delivering goods and services to people who need them. The change focus of this approach is "Let's get the facts and take the next rational steps." A case example of this approach is presented in the box "Case Example of the Social Planning Model."

Social-Action Model

The social-action approach assumes there is a disadvantaged (often oppressed) segment of the population that needs to be organized, perhaps in alliance with others, to pressure the power structure for increased resources or for treatment more in accordance with democracy or social justice. Social-action approaches at times seek basic changes in major institutions or seek changes in basic policies of formal organizations. Such approaches often seek redistribution of power and resources. Although locality developers envision a unified community, social-action advocates see the power structure as the opposition—the target of action. Perhaps the best-known social activist was Saul Alinsky, who advised, "Pick the target, freeze it, personalize it, and polarize it."[26]

The roles of the community practitioner in this approach include advocate, agitator, activist, partisan, broker, and negotiator. Tactics used in social-action projects include

Case Example of the Social Planning Model

In 1995 the board of directors of Lincoln County Social Planning Agency authorized its staff to conduct a feasibility study on establishing a centralized information and referral (I&R) center. Donald Levi (a social planner on the staff) was assigned to direct the study. Mr. Levi collected data showing the following:

- There were over 350 community service agencies and organizations in this largely metropolitan county of one-half million people. Not only clients but also service providers were confused about what services were available from this array of agencies.
- There was a confusing array of specialized I&R services being developed. (Specialized information and referral services provided I&R services in only one or two areas.) Specialized I&R services were developing in suicide prevention, mental health, cognitive disabilities, day care, adoption services, and alcohol and drug treatment.

Mr. Levi then designed a program model for a centralized information and referral service. The model described a service that would provide I&R services on all human and community services in the county. For example, I&R would provide information not only on what day care services were available, but also on where to find public tennis courts and whom to call to remove a stray cat killed in front of your house. The centralized information and referral service number would be widely publicized on television, radio, and billboards and in newspapers and telephone directories. A budget was developed by Mr. Levi for the program costs.

The board of directors of the Lincoln County Social Planning Agency concluded that such a centralized information and referral service would be more efficient and economical than the confusing array that had been developing. The board therefore authorized Mr. Levi to pursue the development of this centralized service.

Mr. Levi conducted a questionnaire survey of all the human service agencies and all the clergy in the county. The results showed that both groups strongly supported the development of a centralized I&R service. In addition, the Easter Seal Society felt so strongly that such a service was needed that it contacted Mr. Levi to indicate that the organization was willing to donate funds for the new program. Mr. Levi was delighted, and an arrangement was worked out for the Easter Seal Society to fund the program for a three-year demonstration period.

Only one barrier remained. The proposal for this new service needed to be approved by the county board of supervisors, as the proposal required the county to fund the program (beginning 3 years in the future) if the service proved to be effective during the 3-year demonstration phase. Mr. Levi and two members of the board of the Lincoln County Social Planning Agency presented the program proposal to the county board of supervisors. The presentation included graphs showing the savings of a centralized I&R service over specialized I&R services and contained written statements of support from a variety of sources, including city council members, the United Way, human service agencies, and members of the clergy. It was also indicated that there would be no cost to the county for a three-year demonstration period. At the end of that time, there would be an evaluative study of the merits and shortcomings of the program. Mr. Levi fully expected approval and was speechless when the county board of supervisors said "no." They turned the proposal down because they felt a centralized I&R meant that more people would be referred to county social service agencies, which would raise costs to the county, and because this board was opposed to making a commitment to funding any new social welfare program in the future.

The county continues to be served by less effective specialized I&R services. This case example realistically illustrates that some planning efforts are unsuccessful.

protests, boycotts, confrontation, and negotiation. The change strategy is one of "Let's organize to overpower our oppressor."[27] The client population is viewed as being a "victim" of the oppressive power structure. Examples of the social-action approach include boycotts during the civil rights movement of the 1960s, strikes by unions, protests by antiabortion groups, and protests by African American and Native American groups.

The social-action model is not widely used by social workers at present. Many workers find that being involved in social-action activities may lead their employing agencies to penalize them with unpleasant work assignments, low merit increases, and denial of promotions. Many agencies will accept minor and moderate changes in their service delivery systems, but are threatened by the prospect of radical changes that are often advocated by the social action approach.

An example of the social-action approach is presented in the box "Case Example of the Social-Action Model." Table 10.1 presents a summary of the three models that have been discussed—locality development, social planning, and social action.

Case Example of the Social-Action Model

Saul Alinsky, a nationally noted social-action strategist, provides an example of a creative social-action effort. The example also shows that social-action efforts are often enjoyable.

> I was lecturing at a college run by a very conservative, almost fundamentalist Protestant denomination. Afterward some of the students came to my motel to talk to me. Their problem was that they couldn't have any fun on campus. They weren't permitted to dance or smoke or have a can of beer. I had been talking about the strategy of effecting change in a society and they wanted to know what tactics they could use to change their situation. I reminded them that a tactic is doing what you can with what you've got. "Now, what have you got?" I asked.

"What do they permit you to do?" "Practically nothing," they said, "except—you know—we can chew gum." I said, "Fine Gum becomes the weapon. You get 200 or 300 students to get two packs of gum each, which is quite a wad. Then you have them drop it on the campus walks. This will cause absolute chaos. Why, with 500 wads of gum I could paralyze Chicago, stop all the traffic in the Loop." They looked at me as though I was some kind of nut. But about two weeks later I got an ecstatic letter saying, "It worked! It worked! Now we can do just about anything so long as we don't chew gum."

SOURCE: Alinsky, S. (1972). *Rules for Radicals* (pp. 145–146). New York: Random House.

TABLE 10.1   Characteristics of Three Models of Community Planning

Characteristic	Locality Development	Social Planning	Social Action
1. Goals	Self-help; improve community living, emphasize process goals	Use problem-solving approach to resolve community problems; emphasize task goals	Shift power relationships and resources to an oppressed group; create basic institutional change; emphasize task and process goals
2. Assumptions concerning community	Everyone wants community living to improve and is willing to contribute to that improvement	Social problems in the community can be resolved through the efforts of planning experts	Community has a power structure and one or more oppressed groups, so social injustice is a major problem
3. Basic change strategy	Broad cross-section of people involved in identifying and solving problems	Experts using fact-gathering and problem-solving approach	Members of oppressed groups organizing to take action against the power structure—i.e., the enemy
4. Characteristic change tactics and techniques	Consensus: communication among community groups and interests; group discussion	Consensus or conflict	Conflict or contest: confrontation, direct action, negotiation
5. Practitioner roles	Catalyst; facilitator; coordinator; teacher of problem-solving skills	Expert planner; fact gatherer; analyst; program developer; and implementer	Activist; advocate; agitator; broker; negotiator; partisan
6. Views of power structure	Members of power structure are collaborators in a common venture	Power structure is employers and sponsors	Power structure is external target of action, oppressors to be coerced or overturned
7. Views of client population	Citizens	Consumers	Victims
8. Views of client role	Participant in a problem-solving process	Consumer or recipient	Employer or constituent

LO 8   Understand Asset-Based Community Development

BUILDING AND SUSTAINING COMMUNITY ASSETS

Many communities have major social problems, such as high levels of poverty, homeless people, divorce, child abuse, battered spouses, unemployment, deteriorated housing, cancer and other health problems, crime, alcoholism and other drug abuse, school dropouts, and births outside of marriage. If we focus on these deficiencies and problems in a community, we are using the half-empty-glass approach. When we view the glass as half-empty, we focus on the negative aspects of life, and we are apt to become consumed with negativity and overcome with despair. Furthermore, if the focus is on problems and deficiencies, most members of that community will begin to despair. Despair becomes a self-fulfilling prophecy; members of the community will put little effort into developing themselves and little effort into developing the community.

Of critical importance, therefore, is to see the glass as half-full—that is, to focus on the positive elements in our lives and the positive elements in the community in which we live. Perception is reality. What we believe to be true often becomes the center of our thoughts so much that it really becomes true. By viewing the glass as half-full, we see the depth of the human spirit and the richness of the creative potential that exists in every community. We identify people who are talented and experienced in a variety of areas. The rate of unemployment in some communities may be high; let's say it's 17%—which means 83% of able-bodied adults are employed! There are strong social networks and associations in every community. There are many successful people in every community. There are beautiful landscapes where nature can be enjoyed. There are people getting things done that need to be done by using what is available. In other words, a focus on strengths and assets leads to vitality and positive actions. Every citizen has capacities that can be tapped to make life in the community better.

Social work has had a long tradition of practice-focused strengths and assets. For example, Dennis Saleeby and his colleagues at the University of Kansas School of Social Welfare have spent much of the last three decades developing, testing, and promoting a strengths perspective for social work practice.[28] The strengths perspective provides an orientation to practice that seeks to uncover and reaffirm people's talents, abilities, survivor skills, and aspirations. A focus on the strengths found in individuals, families, groups, and communities increases the likelihood that people will reach the goals they set for themselves. An asset approach is illustrated in the box "Case Example of Asset-Based Community Development."

SKILLS FOR MACRO PRACTICE

Macro practice involves social work practice with organizations and communities. Macro practice is aimed at bringing about improvements and changes in the general society. Activities include public education campaigns, the administration of social service agencies, some types of political action, and community organization. Additional activities include developing new resources when what clients need is unavailable and advocating to help clients get their due rights. Kirst-Ashman and Hull note:

> Macro practice targets "the system" to determine where and how changes need to be made. Numerous systems make up our "general society." They include political systems like town, country, state, and federal governments. They also include legal systems involving the police, legislature, and courts. Additionally, they involve social service delivery systems like county social service agencies, residential mental health facilities, and federal Veterans' Administration services.[29]

Social workers in macro practice need to be skilled at fulfilling the following roles: advocate, empowerer, activist, mediator, negotiator, educator, initiator, coordinator,

Case Example of Asset-Based Community Development

Many American (and foreign) cities have pockets of deeply troubled communities. These pockets have high rates of crime, violence, unemployment, welfare dependency, gangs, drug involvement, homelessness, and vacant and abandoned land and buildings.

There are two paths for seeking to find solutions for deteriorated communities; the deficiency-oriented model and the asset-based approach. Both of these approaches will be briefly described.

The deficiency model focuses attention on what is "wrong" with a community. A key instrument used in the deficiency model is a "needs" survey, which focuses on the deficits in a community. The deficiency model often leads to the creation of "client neighborhoods." The creation of a client neighborhood is often accelerated by the mass media with its focus on emphasizing the spectacularly problematic components of a client neighborhood. It is apt to lead residents in these neighborhoods to view themselves as deficient victims who are incapable of taking charge of their lives and of their community's future. Targeting resources based on a "needs map" directs funding to service providers rather than directly to the residents. The service providers, with the deficiency approach, then relate to the residents as "clients." This approach furthers the perception that only outside experts can provide "real help." Such an approach hinders the development of the leadership capacities of the residents. Furthermore, service providers are under funding pressure to provide annual evidence that problems continue to intensify in order for funding to be renewed. All of these factors tend to lead to the deepening of the cycle of dependence.

The asset-based model focuses on the development of policies and activities based on the assets, skills, and capacities of lower-income people and their neighborhoods.[a] The asset-based approach believes that significant community development only occurs when local community people are committed to investing themselves and their resources in improving the community. This approach believes sustainable development of a community must start from within the community—rather than waiting for significant help to arrive from outside the community. Instead of viewing the residents of a deteriorated neighborhood as being "clients," this model views residents as being "citizens"—who have untapped resources, assets, capabilities, and potential. The focus is on the community's assets, capacities, and abilities. In addition, every community has a number of citizens' associations—where the citizens assemble to share common interests and activities and to solve problems. (Every community has associations with religious, athletic, cultural, and recreational purposes.)

These associations are key instruments in having the potential for community development.

Additional assets in a community are private businesses; public institutions such as police and fire stations, parks, schools and libraries; social service agencies; hospitals; and medical clinics.

The key to asset-based community development is mobilizing the assets of individuals, associations, businesses, and public institutions to build a community from inside out

How can this mobilization be accomplished? Mathie and Cunningham edited a text that summarizes a number of successful efforts in many countries—in Egypt, Brazil, the United States, Ecuador, Vietnam, Canada, Morocco, India, South Africa, Kenya, and the Philippines.[b] The mobilization of one of these efforts, Building the Mercado Central in Minneapolis, will be summarized.[c]

The Mercado Central is located on Minneapolis' Lake Street. Historically this area was a commerce center. However, in the 1960s the area experienced serious deterioration. Established businesses began to close their doors. Homeowners fled this area. City services no longer were sufficient to upgrade the aging infrastructure. By 1970, this area was a "seedy" district with pawn shops, liquor stores, bars, and adult sex businesses.

Today, the Mercado Central is a thriving retail business cooperative that was developed by the Latino immigrant community in Minneapolis. More than 40 established businesses are located in this area. It is the hub of this community. It is a place of pride and culture for Latinos and for non-Latinos.

The Mercado Central is a central marketplace where people gather to socialize, shop, celebrate, share news, and share concerns. Traditional *mercados* in Latin American cities are in the center of a city and are designed to be an informal place for families to shop, socialize, and dine.

What led to the transformation of this "seedy area" in the 1970s to a thriving central market area that Latinos and non-Latinos now cherish? According to Sheehan, it began in 1990 when five Salvadoran immigrants asked Juan Linares, a social worker for Catholic Charities, to make St. Stephen's (the local Catholic church) available to community access during the week. The immigrants wanted a place to pray and gather during the week. (The church had been locked during the week.) Juan Linares had moved to the United States from Mexico City. Juan Linares' request that this church be opened during the week was granted. The Salvadoran immigrants then requested some church masses be held in Spanish. With the assistance of Isaiah (a multidenominational, congregation-based community-organizing coalition in Minneapolis) the first Spanish mass was conducted at St. Stephen's in 1991. The deacon,

(continued)

Carl Valdez, in this area (at the request of Juan Linares) then arranged for 12 bilingual priests to commit to a weekly rotation at St. Stephens. (From the 1970s to the 1990s this area of the city increasingly saw Latino immigrants settle in this neighborhood. These Latino immigrants were from Mexico, Central and South America, Cuba, and Puerto Rico.)

Deacon Valdez then visited over 200 families in the neighborhood to discuss their desire to build a spiritual community in this area. He also asked them whether they were willing to help build such a spiritual community. In 1995 a church was established in St. Stephen's Parish called Sagrado Corazon, which resulted in over 750 Latino families regularly attending this new Spanish-focused church. This church eventually became the center from which Latino residents would mobilize to build their local economy and to address community concerns.

From these church families, a "sponsoring team" of community members was formed to develop an action plan that addressed the community's concerns about what the community believed were unfair immigration practices of the Immigration and Naturalization Service (INS). This team wanted the INS to transform its interactions with Latino residents in ways that respected language barriers and other concerns.

Juan Linares and Salvador Miranda (one of Isaiah's community organizers) then began working with congregation members to develop a "Community Talent Inventory" (CTI) that was focused on developing entrepreneurial skills within the community and building relationships among community members. This CTI identified a desire for targeted entrepreneurial training.

Because an entrepreneurial training program in Spanish was already offered in the neighboring city of St. Paul, the provider of this training, Neighbourhood Development Center, agreed to offer this training to this geographic area in Minneapolis.

During this 16-week entrepreneurial training, the participants began to discuss how they could develop individual businesses that would be profitable without competing with one another. The participants agreed to develop a "cooperative" that would allow each business owner to make a profit, while working together and supporting each other's efforts.

Reflecting on their assets and cultures, this cooperative decided to build the Mercado Central, which is a central marketplace for people to gather, shop, and socialize.

The plan that emerged from the coordinating committee was fairly complex. A plan was developed for the Mercado Central. Land was purchased. A business development plan was formulated for the business start-ups. In addition, financing for the Mercado Central was obtained from about 25 sources—including banks, the city of Minneapolis, foundations, local corporations, nonprofit development organizations, and the Catholic Campaign for Human Development.

Many residents of this geographic area contributed their time, talents, capabilities, and assets to transform this geographic area from a "seedy district" into a thriving community that is a source of pride and a cultural treasure.

An asset-based community development has the potential to turn other deteriorated neighborhoods into communities that will prosper and flourish.

a. Kretzmann, J. P., & McKnight, J. L. (1993). *Building communities from the inside out*. Chicago, IL: ACTA Publications.
b. Mathie, A, & Cunningham, G. (Eds.) (2008). *From clients to citizens*. Warwickshire, UK: Practical Action Publishing.
c. Sheehan, G. (2008). Building the Mercado Central. In A. Mathie & G. Cunningham (Eds.), *From clients to citizens* (pp. 63–84). Warwickshire, UK: Practical Action Publishing.

public speaker, and staff supervisor. These roles are described in Chapter 2 of this text. Additional skills inherent in macro practice include the following: evaluating outcomes, fundraising, budgeting, working with the media, and conducting a needs assessment.

Evaluating Outcomes

Agencies and organizations in recent decades have assigned a high priority to evaluating the outcomes of provided services. Funding sources often require outcomes of services to be assessed. The following approaches to outcome evaluation are described in Chapter 13: single-subject design, task achievement scaling, and client satisfaction questionnaires.

Fundraising

Social programs cannot exist without financial support. Money is needed to pay staff, rent office space, and buy equipment and for transportation expenses, office supplies, and funds and services provided to clients. Many social programs depend on a combination of public funding and private donations to cover operating expenses.

For many people, asking for money is a distasteful task. Yet agencies cannot survive without fundraising. Fundraising involves a variety of approaches, including the following:

Writing a grant proposal to request funds for a specific service or project

Preparing a budget for anticipated service expenditures and submitting it to such funding sources as a town government, a city or county government, a state government, the federal government, or the United Way

Mail solicitations

Person-to-person solicitations

Telephone solicitations

Telethons

Budgeting

Closely related to fundraising is budgeting. A budget is a statement of probable income from all sources and expenditures during a specified time period. Every agency and organization have a budget regarding how much money it can spend and on what. When more money is spent than anticipated on one item, less money is available to spend on other items. One of the main tasks in administrating an agency is to prepare a realistic budget, seek approval from funding sources, and then monitor expenditures to ascertain that spending limits will not be exceeded.

Working with the Media

The news media include television, radio, and newspapers. Good communication with the media is an effective way to bring attention to one's cause and to influence decision makers of funding sources. For example, a homeless shelter in a community may contact a television station and ask that the station do a brief news program on the desperate plight of the homeless being turned away from the shelter in the winter because all existing beds are full—the aim being to initiate a fundraising campaign to expand the square footage of the shelter so as to increase the number of beds available.

Conducting a Needs Assessment

Needs assessment (NA) is a term that has acquired wide usage and a variety of meanings. It has been used to refer to a statewide comprehensive appraisal of problems and needs. It has also been used on a smaller scale to refer to assessment of a community's needs or an agency's assessment of its clients' needs. For example, a homeless shelter in a community may conduct a needs assessment of its clientele. On a large or small scale, needs assessment refers to efforts of acquiring and making sense out of information so it can be used as an aid in making decisions.

An NA is conducted for various reasons. A sponsoring group may know that a need exists, but without documentation, it will be difficult to convince decision makers and others of the necessity for action. In the same vein, an NA can increase the visibility of an issue or condition.

An agency or organization may conduct an NA to determine whether its efforts are addressing the most critical needs. Especially when new money is involved, NAs can be used to gain information about various problem areas to determine which area most needs attention.

NAs are frequently required by funding agencies. Various government and private funding organizations have policies that include a needs assessment as part of the proposal development process.

Two broad categories of data are used in NAs. One is already existing information, and the other is information that needs to be generated. Sources of existing information for every community include census records, state labor department and health department statistics, and agency records and reports. These data can serve as statistical indicators of the extent of problems or conditions. Another potential source of existing information is studies conducted at some previous time for a different purpose.

One good source of information is the regional planning commission that serves the given geographic area. In addition to possessing certain statistical information, individuals on planning commissions can be helpful in directing you to other sources. City and county planning units can also be valuable sources of information.

Sometimes information that is not presently available will need to be generated. This can be done in many ways—for example, community forums or interviews with selected individuals, community leaders, frontline workers, or clients.

One common way to generate data is the survey. Three survey techniques used to gather information are (1) the telephone interview, (2) the mailed questionnaire, and (3) the person-to-person interview.

Summary

The following summarizes the chapter's content in terms of the learning objectives presented at the beginning of the chapter.

1. Understand the close relationships between the terms group and organization.
An organization is a collectivity of individuals gathered together to serve a purpose. There is considerable overlap between a group and an organization. Some organizations can be considered groups and vice versa.

2. Identify several models of organizations.
Several models of organizations are described, including autocratic, custodial, scientific management, human relations, Theory X and Theory Y, collegial, Theory Z, management by objectives, and total quality management.

3. Survive, and thrive, in an agency.
Two of the most relevant organizational theories for social workers are Theory X and Theory Y. It is critical for newly hired social workers in an organization to determine if supervisors believe in a Theory X or Theory Y style of management, as it will assist workers in determining their roles in how to survive and thrive. Theory Y and servant leadership are closely related. Theory X and Knopf's bureaucratic system model are closely related. Knopf provides a number of suggestions on how to survive in a bureaucracy.

4. Comprehend the impact of structure and leadership competency on organizations. It is the viewpoint of this text that although structure is important, the competency level of the top leadership is more significant in determining the overall level of performance of an organization.

5. Understand the relationships between the terms groups, organization, and community.
A community is defined as a group of individuals or families that share certain services, values, interests, institutions, or geographic proximity. The terms *organization* and *community* are closely related. Some communities are also organizations. The terms *community* and *group* are also closely related. In many cases, a group and a community overlap, and the group can also be considered a community.

6. Analyze a community.
A framework is presented in this chapter for analyzing a community.

7. Identify three models a social worker can use in seeking constructive community changes.
Three models of community practice (different approaches to bringing about community change) are locality development, social planning, and social action.

8. Understand asset-based community development.

The asset-based approach believes that significant community development only occurs when local community people are committed to investing themselves and their resources in improving the community. This approach believes sustainable development of a community must start from within the community—rather than waiting for significant help to arrive from outside the community.

Group Exercises

EXERCISE A: Analyzing a Human Services Organization

EP 7a

GOAL: This exercise is designed to give students a framework for analyzing organizations.

Step 1. The leader divides the class into subgroups of five or six students. Each subgroup selects a human services agency to analyze. (Each subgroup should select a different agency.) Each subgroup will gather information through interviews at its agency and then give a report at a future class session covering the following questions:

1. What is the agency's mission statement?
2. What are its clients' major problems?
3. What services does the agency provide?
4. How are client needs determined?
5. What percentages of clients are people of color, women, gays or lesbians, elderly, or members of other at-risk populations?
6. What was the total cost of services for the past year?
7. How much money is spent on each program?
8. What are the agency's funding sources?
9. How much and what percentage of funds are received from each source?
10. What eligibility criteria must prospective clients meet before services will be provided?
11. What other agencies provide the same services in the community?
12. What is the organizational structure of the agency? For example, is there a formal chain of command?
13. Is there an informal organization (that is, people who exert a greater amount of influence on decision making than would be expected for their formal position in the bureaucracy)?
14. How much decision-making input do the direct service providers have on major policy decisions?
15. Does the agency have a board that oversees its operations? If yes, what are the backgrounds of the board members?
16. Do employees at every level feel valued?
17. What is the morale among employees?
18. What are the major unmet needs of the agency?
19. Does the agency have a handbook of personnel policies and procedures?
20. What is the public image of the agency in the community?
21. In recent years, what has been the rate of turnover among staff at the agency? What were the major reasons for leaving?
22. Does the agency have a process for evaluating the outcomes of its services? If yes, what is the process, and what are the outcome results?
23. What is the subgroup's overall impression of the agency? For example, if members of the subgroup needed services that this agency provides, would they want to apply at this agency? Why, or why not?

EXERCISE B: Understanding and Applying Models of Organizations

GOAL: This exercise is designed to increase students' knowledge of organizational models and to teach them how to apply the models.

Step 1. The leader should summarize the models of organizations described in this chapter: the autocratic model, the custodial model, the scientific management model, the human relations model, Theory X and Theory Y, the collegial model, Theory Z, management by objectives, and total quality management. (As an alternative, assign the students to read this material in the text.)

Step 2. Ask the students to form subgroups of about five members. Ask each subgroup to decide which models are currently most applicable to describing organizational behavior within the organization of social work faculty in the program. (If the number of social work faculty members is very small, the class may instead be asked to decide which models are currently most applicable to describing the organizational behavior of the departmental faculty of which the social work program is a component.)

Step 3. Have the members of each subgroup state their views on which models are most applicable and the reasons for their decisions. Seek to have a class discussion among the subgroups, because there are apt to be differences of opinion.

EXERCISE C: Theory X and Theory Y

GOAL: To become more aware of Theory X and Theory Y styles of management.

Step 1. The leader explains the purpose of this exercise and describes both theories of management, providing personal examples of employment under a manager who used one or the other style.

Step 2. Class members describe examples of their own employment held under these styles of management and then discuss their feelings about working under each system.

Step 3. Because Theory Y is apparently superior to Theory X in motivating employees to be creative and productive, students should discuss why Theory X is used by so many managers.

EXERCISE D: Appreciating Communities

GOAL: To have a greater appreciation of communities.

Step 1. The leader explains that at the next class session each student will be asked to briefly describe a community that she or he has lived in or visited. Each student should focus on the unique aspects of this community, as well as the positive aspects of this community. The leader may give an example of what is desired by describing a community.

Step 2. At the next class session, each student takes a turn in briefly describing his or her selected community.

Step 3. The leader may choose to end the exercise by summarizing positive aspects about the communities that the students described.

EXERCISE E: Analyzing a Community

GOAL: This exercise is designed to instruct students in understanding and analyzing communities.

Step 1. The leader begins by defining the term *community*. Subgroups of three or four students are then formed. Each subgroup selects a different community to analyze.

Step 2. Using the framework presented in this chapter in the section entitled "Analyzing a Community" (or some other framework chosen by the subgroup), each subgroup gathers information on the community it selected. At future class sessions, each subgroup makes a presentation to the class on its selected community.

EXERCISE F: Analyzing Community Change

GOAL: This exercise is designed to have students learn how to analyze community change efforts.

Step 1. The leader should describe the three models of community change developed by Rothman and Tropman. These models are locality development, social planning, and social action. In addition to describing these approaches, the leader should instruct the students to read the related material in this chapter.

Step 2. Have the class form subgroups of about three students each. Each subgroup should select a different community change or community planning effort to report on to the class. An example of a planning effort is a project by the social work student organization to plan an educational conference or workshop on a topic such as AIDS. Another example is the efforts of a community group to establish a homeless shelter.

Step 3. Each subgroup should gather information to answer the following questions about its selected community change effort. One way to gather the information is for the subgroup to interview the planners. In future class sessions each subgroup should give a presentation to the class on its selected planning effort.

Questions

1. What are the goals of the planning effort? How many planners are involved? Who are the planners, and what are their planning credentials? Why is this planning effort being undertaken?
2. Which of the three community change models is this planning group primarily using? What characteristics of this model (see Table 10.1) are being displayed by the planners? Does this planning effort have any characteristics of these other two models? If "yes," what characteristics of the other two models are being displayed?
3. What are the results of this planning effort—that is, to what extent are the goals being accomplished? What are the strengths and shortcomings of this planning effort?

Competency Notes

EP 7b   Apply knowledge of human behavior and the social environment, person-in-environment, and other multidisciplinary theoretical frameworks in the analysis of assessment data from clients and constituencies.

(pp. 299–309) The following models of organizations are described: autocratic, custodial, scientific management, human relations, Theory X and Theory Y, collegial, Theory Z, management by objectives, and total quality management.

EP 1b   Use reflection and self-regulation to manage personal values and maintain professionalism in practice situations.

EP 7b Apply knowledge of human behavior and the social environment, person-in-environment, and other multidisciplinary theoretical frameworks in the analysis of assessment data from clients and constituencies.

(pp. 309–314) Material is presented on surviving and thriving in an agency. It is critical for newly hired social workers in an organization to observe and determine if supervisors believe in a Theory X or Theory Y style of management. Servant leadership and Theory Y are closely related. Ron Knopf has developed a model of a bureaucratic system, which has a number of characteristics of Theory X.

EP 7b Apply knowledge of human behavior and the social environment, person-in-environment, and other multidisciplinary theoretical frameworks in the analysis of assessment data from clients and constituencies.

(pp. 317–318) A framework is presented for analyzing a community. An exercise allows students to apply this framework to their home communities.

EP 7b Apply knowledge of human behavior and the social environment, person-in-environment, and other multidisciplinary theoretical frameworks in the analysis of assessment data from clients and constituencies.

(pp. 319–322) Three models for community practitioners to bring about community change are presented: locality development, social planning, and social action.

EP 7b Apply knowledge of human behavior and the social environment, person-in-environment, and other multidisciplinary theoretical frameworks in the analysis of assessment data from clients and constituencies.

(pp. 328) An exercise is presented in which students analyze a human services organization according to a conceptual framework.

Key Terms and Concepts

Community	Needs Assessment	Passive Cooperation	Theory X Managers
Institution	Organization	Scientific Management Model	Theory Y Managers

11

Educational Groups: With a Focus on Self-Care

LO 1   Define an Educational Group

EP 1b
EP 1c
EP 7b
EP 8b

EDUCATIONAL GROUPS

An educational group is a group of people who are interested in becoming educated on a certain topic. Educational groups usually have a classroom atmosphere, involving considerable group interaction and discussion; a professional person with expertise in the area, sometimes a social worker, assumes the role of teacher. Although the topics covered vary widely, all education groups teach specialized skills and knowledge, such as classes on childrearing, stress management, parenting, English as a foreign language, assertiveness training, and self-care strategies. Orientations offered by social service organizations to train volunteers fall into this category as well.

This chapter will focus on the importance of social workers setting the highest priority on taking care of their own physical, emotional, intellectual, social, and spiritual well-being.

LO 2   Understand the Importance of Placing the Highest Priority on Self-Care

DEFINE SELF-CARE

Self-care for social workers involves social workers using intervention strategies to promote personal happiness, good physical health, a positive attitude, quality relationships with others, a gratifying career, intellectual sharpness, spiritual well-being, and emotional poise.

If social workers do not care for themselves, their ability to care for others will be sharply diminished or even depleted. This chapter will also describe a number of intervention strategies that social workers (and social work students) can and should use to maximize their own physical, emotional, intellectual, and spiritual well-being. Significantly, these intervention strategies are precisely the strategies that social workers should convey to their clients so that these clients can improve their lives.

Social work can be a high-stress occupation—a feature it shares with all helping professions. Some social work positions are more stressful than

LEARNING OBJECTIVES

Educational groups led by social workers are an important component of social work with groups. This chapter will help prepare students to:

LO 1
Define an educational group.

LO 2
Understand the importance of placing the highest priority on self-care.

LO 3
Better manage stress, burnout, and compassion fatigue.

others. Edelwich has identified the following factors in some social work positions that tend to be highly stressful[1]:

too many work hours	not enough money
too much paperwork	no support for important decisions
not sufficiently trained for job	powerlessness
not appreciated by clients	destructive office politics
not appreciated by supervisor	isolation from peers

Helping professionals, including social workers, are at risk of experiencing "compassion fatigue," which is the emotional reacting of exposure to clients' suffering that occurs as a result of traumatizing events—such as sexual abuse, physical abuse, combat in the military, domestic violence, suicide, and the unexpected death of a loved one.[2] Physical symptoms of compassion fatigue include sleep disruptions, hypertension, immune system malfunctions, and other stress-related illnesses; psychological symptoms of compassion fatigue include low self-esteem, fear, rage, cynicism, suspiciousness, anxiety, emotional numbing, and depression. Compassion fatigue has also been called "vicarious traumatization."

IMPORTANCE OF MANAGING STRESS

It is essential that students, social workers, and other helping professionals learn to manage stress in themselves and help their clients manage stress. Although some stress may be beneficial, stress is a contributing factor in a wide variety of emotional and behavioral problems, including anxiety, child abuse, spouse abuse, temper tantrums, feelings of inadequacy, physical assaults, explosive expressions of anger, feelings of hostility, impatience, stuttering, suicide attempts, and depression.[3]

Stress is also a contributing factor in most physical illnesses. These illnesses include hypertension, heart attacks, migraine and tension headaches, colitis, ulcers, diarrhea, constipation, arrhythmia, angina, diabetes, hay fever, backaches, arthritis, cancer, colds, flu, insomnia, hyperthyroidism, dermatitis, emphysema, Raynaud's disease, alcoholism, bronchitis, infections, allergies, and enuresis. Stress-related disorders have now been recognized as our number-one health problem.[4]

Becoming skillful at relaxation is important in treating and facilitating recovery from both emotional and physical disorders. The therapeutic value of learning to manage stress has been dramatically demonstrated by Simonton and Simonton, who have reported success in treating terminal cancer patients by instructing them on stress management.[5] People who have AIDS tend to live longer if they utilize stress management techniques.[6]

In fact, the increased recognition of the importance of stress management in treating physical and emotional disorders is gradually altering the traditional physician–patient relationship. Instead of being passive participants in treatment, patients are increasingly being taught by social workers and other health professionals how to prevent illness and how to speed up recovery by learning stress management strategies. People who are successful in managing stress have a life expectancy several years longer than those who are continually at high stress levels.[7] Moreover, effective stress management is a major factor that enables people to live fulfilling, healthy, satisfying, and productive lives.[8]

CONCEPTUALIZING STRESS

Stress can be defined as the physiological and emotional reactions to stressors. A **stressor** is a demand, situation, or circumstance that disrupts a person's equilibrium (internal balance) and initiates the stress response. Every moment people are alive, their bodies are responding to stressors that call for adaptation or adjustment. Their bodily reactions are continually striving for **homeostasis**, or balance. There is a nearly infinite variety of possible stressors: loss of a job, loud noise, toxic substances, value conflicts, arguments, death of a friend, getting engaged, getting married, heat, cold, pollutants, serious illness, moving away from home, and lack of purpose in life, to name a few.

EXERCISE 11.1 My Physiological Reactions to High Levels of Stress

GOAL: This exercise is designed to assist you in recognizing how you physiologically react to high levels of stress.

1. Specify two events that were very stressful to you—where you physiologically were in the alarm phase—in the past week.

2. What physiological reactions do you remember having? Review the material in this chapter on reactions to stress, then specify the physiological reactions that you remember having.

Reactions to Stress

Hans Selye, one of the foremost authorities on stress, found a three-stage physical reaction to stress—an alarm phase, a resistance phase, and an exhaustion phase.[9] Selye called this three-phase response the General Adaptation Syndrome.

In the **alarm phase** the body recognizes the stressor and responds by preparing for fight or flight. The body's reactions are numerous and complex and will be only briefly summarized here.[10] The hypothalamus (located in the brain) sends a message to the pituitary gland to release its hormones. These hormones trigger the adrenal glands to release adrenaline. The release of adrenaline and other hormones results in the following physical reactions:

1. Increased breathing and heartbeat rates
2. A rise in blood pressure
3. Increased coagulation of blood, which minimizes potential loss of blood in case of physical injury
4. Diversion of blood from the skin to the brain, the heart, and contracting muscles
5. A rise in serum cholesterol and blood fat
6. Decreased mobility of the gastrointestinal tract
7. Dilated pupils

These changes result in a huge burst of energy, improved vision and hearing, and increased muscular strength—all changes that increase a person's capacity to fight or to flee.[11] A major problem of the fight-or-flight reaction is that a threat cannot always be dealt with by fighting or fleeing. In our complex civilized society, fighting or fleeing generally violates sophisticated codes of acceptable behavior. The fight-or-flight response, appropriate and functional for humans in primitive societies who often had only these two courses of action when attacked by animals or other humans, is now seldom needed.

In the **resistance phase**, bodily processes attempt to return to homeostasis, and the body tries to repair any damage caused by the stressors. In handling most stressors, the body generally goes through only the two phases of alarm and repair. During a lifetime, these two phases are repeated thousands of times.

The third phase of **exhaustion** occurs only when the body remains in a state of high stress for an extended period and is unable to repair damage. If exhaustion continues, stress-related illness, such as high blood pressure, ulcers, or migraine headaches, may develop.

Stressors

A stressor has two components: (1) the experience or event encountered, and (2) our self-talk about the event.[12] Figure 11.1 presents a model of a stress response indicating both a sequence of events and reactions as they occur.

The following example shows how a person's thinking can turn a potentially positive event into a source of negative stress.

Stressor {

Event or experience: Sharon Kempers is asked out for a date by someone she has wanted to date for a long time.

Self-talk: *I'm really worried he won't like me. I'm not a good conversationalist, and he will now notice all the other faults I have. I really don't know what I should wear. He wants me to meet some of his friends, and I'm afraid they won't like me. I'm afraid I'm really going to blow this.*

Stress {

Emotional reactions: Anxiety, worry, alarm, tension

Physiological reactions: This alarm stage of the General Adaptation Syndrome is occurring. If sustained and intensive, conditions exist for a stress-related illness to develop.

The model in Figure 11.1 suggests two broad approaches for reducing stress: (1) either change the distressing event or (2) change the self-talk about the event. (These two approaches will be discussed at greater length in a later section.)

FIGURE 11.1   A Model of a Stress Response

Stressor {

Event or experience: Having to give a speech to a large group.

Self-talk: *What if I get stage fright? I've never done this before. I am really worried they won't like what I have to say. What if my voice sounds funny? I can feel my knees shaking. I'm afraid I'm going to bomb. I'm scared.*

Stress {

Emotional reactions: Fear, anxiety, worry, alarm

Physiological reactions: Alarm stage of General Adaptation Syndrome. The body prepares for fight or flight. Adrenaline and other hormones increase heartbeat and rate of breathing, increase perspiration, raise blood sugar levels, dilate the pupils, and slow digestion. The process results in greater muscular strength, a huge burst of energy, and better vision and hearing.

Stress-related disorder: If the body remains at a high level of stress for a prolonged time period, a stress-related disorder is apt to develop, such as an ulcer, insomnia, heart problem, or digestive problem.

EXERCISE 11.2   My Stress-Related Illnesses

GOAL: This exercise is designed to highlight the importance of learning and using stress management techniques.

1. Specify the stress-related illnesses that you have experienced. Also indicate (as best you can) the starting and ending times for these illnesses.

2. Rate the importance (1–5) for you of learning and using stress management strategies:

_____	_____	_____	_____	_____
Not important	Somewhat important	Fairly important	Very important	Absolutely essential

FIGURE 11.2   Level of Alarm Stage Response and Efficiency in Performing Tasks

It should certainly be noted that not all stress is bad. Life without it would be boring. Selye indicates that stress is often "the spice of life" and that it is impossible to live without experiencing stress.[13] Even dreaming produces stress. At times stress is beneficial because it stimulates and prepares individuals to perform tasks.

Optimal Levels of Stress

Virtually every task or activity requires some response from the alarm stage of the General Adaptation Syndrome, and for each task there is an optimal level of response. Students, for example, sometimes find that they need to be under moderate stress to study effectively for an exam. At too low a level of alarm stage response, they may have trouble concentrating and may even fall asleep. At too high a level of alarm stage response, they become anxious—which also interferes with concentration. Maximum levels of alarm stage response are needed only during emergencies when great physical strength is required—for example, when a heavy object has fallen on someone. At the opposite extreme, falling asleep requires relaxation—that is, an almost-zero level of alarm stage response. People who suffer from insomnia are not relaxed. They are still thinking about things that generate a moderate level of alarm stage response and keep them from dozing off. For a graphic illustration of this concept (see Figure 11.2).

Grasping this concept is important because self-talk can be altered and thereby increase or decrease levels of alarm stage response in order to bring it to an optimal level.

LONG-TERM DISTRESS

Selye calls harmful stress "distress."[14] Long-term distress generally results in a stress-related physical illness. Distress occurs when the stressors are prolonged so that a person enters the exhaustion phase of the General Adaptation Syndrome. There are a number of signals, presented in Table 11.1, that we can use to measure our level of stress. Most of us use the signals identified in Table 11.1 to judge whether our friends are under too much stress. But most of us fail to use these same signals to determine if our own stress level is too high. For our emotional and physical health, we need to give more attention to monitoring these signals in ourselves.

Long-term distress occurs when we continue to think negatively about events that have happened to us. When unpleasant events occur, we always have a choice to react negatively or positively. If we continue to think negatively about the situation, our thinking keeps our bodies under a high level of stress—which can then lead to a stress-related illness. On the other hand, if we think positively about the situation, our thinking enables the body to relax and repair any damage that was done. In addition, when we are relaxed, our natural immune system is much more effective in combating potential illnesses. There is substantial evidence that our self-talk (that is, our thinking process) has immense interaction with the functioning of the immune system. Our self-talk can function as both a slayer and a healer. If we **awfulize** (that is, think negative thoughts), we set off the alarm stage of the General

TABLE 11.1   Indicators of Stress Level

Positive Level	Level Too High
1. Behaviors	
Creative, making good decisions	High-pitched, nervous laughter
Friendly	Not creative
Generally successful	Poor work quality
Able to listen to others	Overdrink or overeat
Productive, getting a lot done	Smoke to excess
Appreciate others, sensitive to others, and recognize contributions of others	Stutter
Smile, laugh, joke	Unable to concentrate
	Easily startled by small noises
	Impatient
	Let little things bother you
	Unpleasant to be around
	Put others down, irritable
	Engage in wasteful activity
2. Feelings	
Confident	Resentful, bitter, dissatisfied, angry
Calm, relaxed	Timid, tense, anxious, fearful
Pleasure and enjoyment	Paranoid
Excitement and exhilaration	Weary, depressed, fed up
	Feeling inadequate
	Confused, swamped, overwhelmed
	Feeling powerless or helpless
3. Body Signals	
Able to sleep well	Loss of appetite, diarrhea, or vomiting
Absence of aches and pains	Prone to accidents
Coordinated body reactions	Sweating, frequent need to urinate
Unself-consciousness about body functioning	Trembling, nervous tics
In good health, stress-related illnesses absent	Feeling dizzy or weak
	Frequent colds and flu
	High blood pressure
	Tight or tense muscles
	Asthma or breathing irregularities
	Skin irritations, itches, and rashes
	Problems sleeping
	Upset stomach or ulcers
	Various aches and pains—muscle aches, backaches, neck aches, and headaches

Note: You have to use your own judgment based on these signals to determine whether a stress level is too high.

EXERCISE 11.3   Events and Self-Talk as Stressors

GOAL: This exercise is designed to assist you in recognizing current stressors and in realizing that stressors consist of distressing events and self-talk associated with those events.

1. Specify the events that are currently stressors in your life.

2. For each stressful event, specify your self-talk associated with it. (The self-talk may intensify, or decrease, your overall feeling of being under stress.)

3. Which form of a stressor (the event or the associated self-talk) do you believe is the major contributor to the level of stress that you experience? Explain your views on this issue.

Trauma and Stress Disorders

Physical trauma is an injury to the body caused by violence or accident, such as a fracture. Psychological trauma is an emotional wound or shock, often having long-lasting effects. Physical trauma often leads to psychological trauma.

Traumatic experiences often involve a threat to life or safety, but any situation that leaves one feeling overwhelmed and alone can be traumatic, even if it does not involve physical harm. It's not the objective facts that determine whether an event is traumatic, but one's subjective emotional experience of the event.

A stressful event is most likely to be traumatic if:
- It happened unexpectedly.
- One is unprepared for it.
- It happened repeatedly.
- One felt powerless to prevent it.
- Someone was intentionally cruel.

Trauma can come in a huge variety of ways. The following is a short list: serving in combat in the military, being physically or sexually abused, a sexual assault, an auto accident, the breakup of a significant relationship, a humiliating or deeply disappointing experience, and the discovery of a life-threatening illness or disabling condition.

People are more likely to be traumatized by a stressful experience if they are already under a heavy stress load or have recently suffered a series of losses. Not all potentially traumatic events lead to lasting psychological and emotional damage; some people rebound quickly from even the most shocking and tragic experiences, whereas others are devastated by experiences that appear on the surface to be "mildly upsetting."

Traumatic experiences in childhood can have a severe and long-lasting impact. Children who have been traumatized see the world as a dangerous and frightening place. When childhood trauma is unresolved, this sense of fear and helplessness carries over into adulthood, setting the stage for further trauma.

Emotional symptoms of trauma include:
- Denial, shock, or disbelief
- Anxiety and fear
- Withdrawing from others
- Feeling numb or disconnected
- Anger, irritability, and mood swings
- Confusion and difficulty concentrating
- Guilt, self-blame, and shame
- Feeling hopeless or sad

Physical symptoms of trauma include:
- Aches and pains
- Fatigue
- Muscle tension

- Being startled easily
- Racing heartbeat
- Agitation and edginess
- Difficulty concentrating

These emotional and physical symptoms gradually fade *if* the affected person makes progress in coming to terms with the trauma. But even if the person is progressing in resolving the trauma, he or she may be troubled from time to time by painful memories and emotions. Triggers for reliving the painful event include an anniversary of the event and sounds and images of the situation that remind the individual of the traumatic experience.

Two stress disorders are associated with severe traumas: acute stress disorder and posttraumatic stress disorder (PTSD). Acute stress disorder is an anxiety disorder in which fear and related symptoms are experienced soon after a traumatic event and last less than a month.

Posttraumatic stress disorder is an anxiety disorder in which fear and related symptoms continue to be experienced long after a traumatic event.

The primary symptoms of PTSD include flashbacks or intrusive memories, living in a constant state of "red alert," and avoiding things that remind the affected person of the traumatic event.

Working through trauma can be painful, scary, and potentially retraumatizing. The "healing" work is best done with a competent trauma expert. Trauma treatment involves:
- Processing the trauma memories and feelings
- Discharging the pent-up emotions/energy associated with the trauma
- Learning how to control strong emotions
- Rebuilding the capacity to trust other people

Treatment approaches for PTSD include the following:
- Cognitive-behavioral therapy, such as rational therapy (described in Module 1), in which the person learns to reframe the disturbing traumatic thoughts.
- Antianxiety drugs, which help control the anxieties and tensions associated with PTSD. Such medication provides some relief, but needs to be combined with a "talk" therapy approach.
- Eye movement desensitization and reprocessing (EMDR), which incorporates elements of cognitive-behavioral therapy, in which the affected persons move their eyes in a rhythmic manner from side to side while flooding their minds with images of the objects and situations they try to avoid. These back-and-forth eye movements are thought to work by "unfreezing" traumatic memories, which then can be processed and resolved.

Adaptation Syndrome. When we are in the alarm stage, our immune systems are depressed and do not function well. As a result, we are more susceptible to infections and diseases. On the other hand, when we think positive and relaxing thoughts, our bodies are in the resistance stage of the General Adaptation Syndrome. As a result, our immune systems are functioning at their optimal level and can fight off diseases and infections and assist in repairing any damage caused when our bodies were in the alarm stage.

Earlier it was indicated that our bodies react to positive stressors the same way they react to negative stressors. The reason negative stressors are much more likely to result in stress-related disorders is that we tend to stop thinking intensely about positive stressors (such as a romantic kiss) within a few hours after they occur, whereas we tend to intensify and dwell on negative stressors for several hours (or even days) after they occur. By thinking intensely about negative stressors, we keep our bodies under a moderate or high level of stress.

BURNOUT

Burnout is increasingly recognized as a serious problem affecting many people, particularly professionals employed in human services. Several books have been published on this subject.[15] Maslach and Pines have conducted extensive studies of burnout among social workers, psychiatrists, psychologists, prison personnel, psychiatric nurses, legal-aid attorneys, physicians, child-care workers, teachers, ministers, and counselors and have summarized a number of symptoms:

> Burn-out involves the loss of concern for the people with whom one is working. In addition to physical exhaustion (and sometimes even illness), burn-out is characterized by an emotional exhaustion in which the professional no longer has any positive feelings, sympathy, or respect for clients or patients. A very cynical and dehumanizing perception of these people often develops, in which they are labeled in derogatory ways and treated accordingly. As a result of this dehumanizing process, these people are viewed as somehow deserving of their problems and are blamed for their own victimization and thus there is a deterioration in the quality of care or service that they receive. The professional who burns out is unable to deal successfully with the overwhelming emotional stresses of the job, and this failure to cope can be manifested in a number of ways, ranging from impaired performance and absenteeism to various types of personal problems (such as alcohol and drug abuse, marital conflict, and mental illness). People who burn out often quit their jobs or even change professions, while some seek psychiatric treatment for what they believe to be their personal failings.[16]

Freudenberger describes the symptoms of burnout as follows:

> Briefly described, burn-out includes such symptoms as cynicism and negativism and a tendency to be inflexible and almost rigid in thinking, which often leads to a closed mind about change or innovation. The worker may begin to discuss the client in intellectual and jargon terms and thereby distance himself from any emotional involvement. Along with this, a form of paranoia may set in whereby the worker feels that his peers and administration are out to make life more difficult.

> Another sign is that the worker takes on a superior "know-it-all" attitude that borders on the condescending. He hardly communicates with others and tends to become a loner or withdrawn. On the other hand, he may go to the other extreme and hardly do any work because he is socializing most of the time. Other workers experiencing burnout may begin to limit their contact with their clients. They begin to speak of being bored with the work. . . . All is becoming too routine. They may also begin to verbalize a sense of helplessness as well as hopelessness about the clients and begin to speak of them in derogatory or flip terms.[17]

The term **burnout** has been applied to many different situations. A student who has been writing a term paper for three hours may feel burned out with writing but have plenty of energy to do something else. Some people who abuse their spouses or children may attempt to explain their actions by claiming they are under considerable stress and just burned out. Apathetic and cynical workers dealing with a frustrating job may claim they are burned out, and even some college and professional sports coaches claim the pressure to win is so intense that after several seasons they feel burned out.

EXERCISE 11.4   A Time When I Burned Out

GOAL: This exercise is designed to demonstrate that we all burn out, and it also helps us recognize what we can do when we experience burnout.

1. Describe a time in your life when you experienced burnout. When you were experiencing burnout, did you conclude (for a while)—"I just can't take this anymore"?

2. If you have recovered from feeling burned out, describe what helped you recover. If you are still feeling a sense of being burned out, speculate about what you need to do to make progress in recovering.

Structural Causes of Burnout

To understand the nature of burnout, it is useful to conceptualize it as one of several possible reactions to continuing high levels of stress. As suggested in Figure 11.3, burnout is caused *not only* by experiences that people encounter, but by what people tell themselves about these experiences. Examples of this kind of thinking are "I've had it"; "What's the use? Whatever I try won't work"; "I'm going to give up—I'm no longer going to make an effort." Other people encountering the same events will not burn out if they do not have such self-defeating thoughts.

FIGURE 11.3   Burnout as a Reaction to High Stress Level

The Helping Professions   Edelwich adds that people who seek a career in the helping professions are particularly vulnerable to burnout, as many enter this field with unrealistic expectations. Such expectations include the beliefs that (1) the services they provide will decisively improve the lives of their clients, (2) they will be highly appreciated by the employing agency and clients, (3) they will be able to substantially change bureaucracies to be more responsive to clients' needs, and (4) there will be many opportunities for rapid advancement and high status. In addition, Maslach has found that high caseloads in the helping professions are a major cause of stress and may lead to burnout:

> Burn-out often becomes inevitable when the professional is forced to provide care for too many people. As the ratio increases, the result is higher and higher emotional overload until, like a wire that has too much electricity flowing through it, the worker just burns out and emotionally disconnects.[18]

The frustrations experienced at work and the gradual recognition that many expectations are unrealistic contribute to stress and burnout.

Lack of Time Out   A lack of approved "time out" at work is another source of stress and may be a factor leading to burnout. Time out does not merely involve short coffee breaks but also opportunities for professionals to switch to less stressful tasks when they are having a difficult day. Break periods are possible in large agencies that have shared work responsibilities. Maslach notes:

> When institutional policies prevented the use of voluntary time-outs, we found lower staff morale, greater emotional stress and the inevitable consequence of more dissatisfied citizens, frustrated at not getting the care they needed.[19]

Clients   Certain types of clients are more apt to cause high levels of stress, particularly those whose problems are depressing or emotionally draining (such as terminally ill, belligerent, suicidal, and obnoxious clients, as well as incest and severe abuse cases).[20] Working with "chronic" clients who show no improvement (such as an alcoholic family in which the problem drinker denies a drinking problem) also may lead to frustration and high stress levels. Dealing with clients who remind the worker of current personal difficulties—for example, providing marriage counseling services when the worker is also having marital difficulties—is emotionally draining.

Personal Difficulties   Another important factor contributing to high stress and burnout at work is personal difficulties at home. Home responsibilities (for example, caring for a terminally ill parent, a child who is getting into trouble with the police, or dealing with an unhappy marriage) are stressful and may lead to burnout.

Other Causes   Additional causes include poor time management, inability to work effectively with other people, lack of purpose or undefined goals in life, and inability to handle emergencies effectively.[21]

Burnout and Compassion Fatigue

Burnout and compassion fatigue are closely related, but are not the same. Burnout at work results from stresses in the work environment. Burnout at a job can often be "treated" by leaving a stressful job and finding a different one.

Compassion fatigue is an emotional and physical reaction created by the trauma of helping others in distress, which leads to a reduced capacity for empathy toward suffering in the future.[22] A social worker who has compassion fatigue tells himself/herself the following:

"I don't have the resources to help traumatized clients, so why try"
"I have not been helpful to traumatized clients in the past"
"These clients are beyond help"
"The lives of these clients have been destroyed and there is no hope in the future for them"
"It is a mistake for me to get ego involved with these clients, I will just hurt myself emotionally if I get ego involved."

For a social worker suffering from compassion fatigue, changing jobs will usually not ease the problem; the compassion fatigue (having little or no empathy for suffering clients) will stay within the worker at the new job.

Interestingly, burnout is one type of emotional reaction to high stress levels, whereas compassion fatigue is another type of emotional reaction to high stress levels involving working with highly traumatized clients. The importance of this conceptualization is that stress management techniques can be used to manage stress, prevent and treat burnout, and combat compassion fatigue.

LO 3   Better Manage Stress, Burnout, and Compassion Fatigue

MANAGING STRESS

The following approaches have been useful for helping social workers, social work students, clients, and group members reduce stress, combat compassion fatigue, and prevent burnout. It is up to each individual to select the ones that will be most helpful. Managing stress is similar to dieting. It will work for those who put forth the effort. (For further reading on these approaches, see the endnotes of this chapter.) It should be noted these strategies can be taught in educational groups to clients and to social work students.

Goal Setting and Time Management

Stress and burnout can come from the feeling of "too much to do and too little time in which to do it." Often, this feeling is due to not having clear short-term and lifetime goals and not knowing how to manage time effectively to achieve them. Realistic goals and a plan for achieving them lead to increased self-confidence, improved decision making, a greater sense of purpose, and an improved sense of security.

One technique for stress management is to help group members define short-term and lifetime goals and teach them how to prioritize the tasks necessary to achieve them.[23]

Setting life goals is not an easy task. It requires considerable contemplation, reflection, and sifting through numerous options. But people who set life goals are generally more comfortable, happy, contented, and fulfilled. They know what brings them enjoyment and fulfillment and therefore can work toward accomplishing those goals. They tend to make decisions for themselves rather than having decisions made for them. When confronted with major decisions (such as marriage, having children, or a new job opportunity), they compare alternatives in terms of their life goals and arrive at a decision that will likely be in their long-term best interests.

Set Goals

The first step in a time management process is for individual group members to set personal goals. They should answer two questions:

1. What are my long-term goals?
2. What are my goals for the next six months?

Answers to each of these questions should be listed on separate sheets of paper. In identifying these goals, group members should recognize that their short-range and long-range goals will change over time. That is to be expected. Trapping themselves into working toward goals they no longer want is a mistake. As time passes, certain goals will be dropped or altered and others will be replaced.

In specifying short-range and long-range goals, group members should consider a variety of areas, including career, financial position, marital status, family goals, community involvement, religious goals, education, exercise, stress reduction, self-improvement, relationships, vacations, retirement, hobbies, and recreation and leisure.

Prioritize Goals

The next step is to prioritize these goals. Lakein recommends using three categories, assigning the letter "A" to high-value goals, "B" to medium-value goals, and "C" to those with low values.[24] Prioritizing should be done separately for both the short-range and the long-range goals. The A, or high-value goals, should be further prioritized by ranking them in order: A-l, A-2, A-3, A-4, and so on. With this process, group members will have identified just what it is they want to do with their lives at this time.

Long-term goals tend to change for a variety of reasons. A person could accomplish a number of them, such as graduating from college, getting married, or finding a career position. Some of the unattained goals may no longer be important or valuable. Therefore, it is advantageous to review and refine long-term goals periodically (perhaps annually). Because short-term goals are generally for six-month periods, they should be reviewed semiannually.

List Tasks for A Goals

The most important goals are A goals, and these should receive the bulk of attention and time. Because a group member cannot *do* a goal, the next step in the planning process is to list specific tasks that will help him or her move toward each short-range and long-range A goal.

A junior majoring in social work, for example, might have chosen "obtaining a social work job after graduation" as a longer-range goal. Specific tasks for reaching this goal might be listed as follows:

1. Studying carefully for exams and writing quality papers to get good grades
2. Doing volunteer work in social service agencies
3. Writing a résumé
4. Identifying areas in social work where vacancies are located and then taking elective courses related to these areas
5. Actively participating in the social work organization at this campus
6. Asking a social work faculty member whom I trust to give me feedback on my strengths and deficiencies for obtaining social work employment and on what I need to work on to improve my chances of getting a job
7. Selecting a field placement that will (1) best help me develop my social work skills and knowledge and (2) establish contacts with people who can help me get a job

Prioritize Tasks

If group members were conscientious in listing possible tasks for each goal, they would have too many tasks and not enough time for all of them. Therefore, they should prioritize each task into A, high-value tasks; B, medium-value tasks; and C, low-value tasks. A tasks for each A goal should then be further prioritized into A-l, A-2, A-3, A-4, and so on. (Readers will note that the method for prioritizing tasks is the same method that was used to prioritize goals.)

Schedule Tasks

If group members have faithfully followed the prioritizing process, they will have a clear vision of their important short-range and long-range goals and of the specific tasks that will help them achieve these goals. Daily work on each A task for each A goal is not possible, so group members need to select one or two (or a few more) daily tasks to focus on. If the A tasks a person selects seem too overwhelming (such as writing quality papers for each of his or her courses), they should be divided into smaller segments (such as doing library research for a policy paper).

In planning a schedule, time to achieve A tasks should be blocked out by designating specific hours or days for each task. Lakein suggests setting aside a special A time each day and banishing all C tasks and interruptions during this time period.[25] A weekly reminder calendar can help schedule meetings, exam dates, paper due dates, and other important tasks. By using a calendar, group members can block out times to do A tasks in a place free from interruptions and distractions.

EXERCISE 11.5   My High-Value Goals and Tasks

GOAL: This exercise is designed to assist you in specifying your short-range and long-range goals and to identify the tasks that will help you achieve these goals.

Note: If this process is conscientiously followed, you will have a clear vision of your goals in life and what you need to do to achieve these goals.

1. List your goals for the next six months on one sheet of paper and your long-range goals on another.

2. Prioritize your goals by assigning "A" to high-value goals, "B" to medium-value goals, and "C" to low-value goals. Next, the A's, or high-value goals, are further ranked in order: A-l, A-2, A-3, and so on.

3. List tasks needed to achieve the specified A goals.

4. Prioritize each task's value in achieving each of your A goals using the A, B, C, and so on approach.

Relaxation

Deep-breathing relaxation, imagery relaxation, progressive muscle relaxation, meditation, and biofeedback are effective techniques for reducing stress and inducing the "relaxation response" (becoming relaxed).[26] Each of these techniques is facilitated by sitting in a comfortable position in a quiet place and closing one's eyes.

Deep-breathing relaxation involves stopping thoughts about day-to-day concerns and concentrating on breathing processes. For 5 to 10 minutes, a group member may slowly and gradually inhale deeply and exhale while thinking something like "I am relaxing, breathing smoother. This is soothing, and I'm feeling calmer, renewed, and refreshed." Continued practice of this technique will enable a person to become more relaxed when confronting a tense situation.

By using **imagery relaxation**, a group member can switch his or her thinking from daily concerns to focusing on an ideal relaxation place for 10 to 15 minutes. This ideal setting might include lying on a beach by a scenic lake in the warm sun or relaxing in warm water in a bathtub while reading a magazine. The group member should savor all the pleasantness, the peacefulness, focusing on everything that he or she finds calming, soothing, and relaxing. The member will sense his or her whole body becoming refreshed, revived, and rejuvenated.

Progressive muscle relaxation is based on the principle that a person whose muscles are relaxed cannot be anxious.[27] The group leader instructs members to tighten and then relax a set of muscles. As they relax their muscles, they are asked to concentrate on the relaxed feeling while noting that the muscles are becoming less tense. The following is an excerpt of the first part of rather lengthy instructions to a group for progressive muscle relaxation:

> Make a fist with your dominant hand (usually right). Make a fist and tense the muscles of your (right) hand and forearm; tense it until it trembles. Feel the muscles pull across your fingers and the lower part of your forearm. . . . Hold this position for five to seven seconds, then . . . relax. . . . Just let your hand go. Pay attention to the muscles of your (right) hand and forearm as they relax. Note how these muscles feel as relaxation flows through (twenty to thirty seconds).[28]

The procedure of tensing and then relaxing the hand and forearm is repeated three or four times until they are relaxed. Next, other muscle groups are tensed and relaxed in the same manner, one group at a time. In succession, the muscle groups might include left hand and forearm, right biceps, left biceps, forehead muscles, upper lip and cheek muscles, jaw muscles, chin and throat muscles, chest muscles, abdominal muscles, back muscles between shoulder blades, right and left upper leg muscles, right and left calf muscles, and toes and arches of the feet. With practice, a group member can gradually develop the capacity to relax whenever anxious simply by visualizing the muscles relaxing.

There are a variety of **meditative approaches**—imagery relaxation and deep-breathing relaxation are two examples. Benson has identified four basic components in meditative approaches that induce the relaxation response.[29] These components are (1) being in a quiet environment free from external distractions; (2) being in a comfortable position; (3) having an object to dwell on, such as a word, sound, chant, phrase, or imagery of a painting[30]; and (4) assuming a passive attitude and not thinking about day-to-day concerns. This last component, Benson asserts, is the key element in inducing the relaxation response.

Biofeedback equipment provides mechanical feedback to a person about his or her level of stress. This equipment can inform people about levels of stress they are usually unaware of—until a markedly higher level is reached. For example, a person's hand temperature may vary 10 to 12 degrees in an hour's time, with an increase in temperature indicating increasing calm and relaxation. With biofeedback equipment, numerous physical conditions can be measured and fed back, such as blood pressure, hand temperature, muscle tension, heartbeat rate, and brain waves. With biofeedback training, a client is first instructed in using the equipment to recognize high levels of anxiety or tenseness. Then, he or she is instructed on how to reduce such high levels either by closing the eyes and adopting a passive, "letting go" attitude or by thinking about something pleasant and calming. Often relaxation approaches are combined with biofeedback to elicit the relaxation response.

Mindfulness

Mindfulness practice is another tool that social workers (and other persons) can readily use to reduce stress. Mindfulness meditations have increasingly been utilized in a variety of settings, including mental health agencies, schools, and medical settings.[31] Mindfulness is a state of consciousness with enhanced attention to moment-to-moment experience. Mindfulness involves maintaining a moment-by-moment awareness of our feelings, thoughts, bodily sensations, and surrounding environment. It involves acceptance; that is, paying attention to our thoughts and feelings without judging them. When we practice mindfulness, our thoughts tune into what we are sensing in the present moment, rather than rehashing the past or worrying about the future.[32]

Many people who are untrained in mindfulness focus their thoughts on ruminating about the past (in which they compulsively focus their attention on past distressing events; or they worry about the future; or they focus on trying to make decisions about courses of action they might take to alleviate distressing situations; or they focus on judging others; or they criticize themselves for things they did or failed to do. Such thought processes generally lead to anxiety, discomfort, being frustrated, and a high level of stress.

There are a number of benefits to mindfulness meditation. It has been found to reduce rumination (that is, reduce thinking negatively about past, present, or future events), reduce stress, boost working memory, improve affect, decrease depression, increase focus and suppress distracting information, increase cognitive flexibility, increase the ability to communicate one's emotions to a partner, enhance self-insight, increase intuition, decrease anxieties, increase physical well-being, increase information processing speed, promote empathy, increase compassion for others, improve self-concept, and increase quality of life.[33]

There are many different mindfulness exercises. The following is an example of an exercise you can try. Find a quiet, comfortable place to sit down. This might be on a chair or on a cushion on the floor. If it is a cushion on the floor, you may choose to cross your legs. Take a posture that is upright, but not rigid. Your back should be straight, with the curve in the lower back that is naturally there. For the next several minutes, just focus on your breathing. Your eyes may be closed or open. Do not try to control the flow of your breathing—just focus on the air going in and out of your body.

Notice how the air feels as it enters and exits. Notice how your stomach and rib cage rises and falls as you breathe in and then out. Also acknowledge your feelings, images, memories, and thoughts and allow them to float along, like a gentle moving white cloud on a very pleasant day. Allow your thoughts to come and go without judging them. Then focus again on your breathing. Expect your mind to wander—acknowledge the thoughts, images, and memories—without placing a judgment on them. Return to focus your attention on your breathing, and feel your body gradually relaxing as you breathe in and out. Remember that mindfulness meditation is about practicing being mindful of whatever happens. It is *not* about getting ourselves to stop thinking. With mindfulness, we are trying to be with ourselves as we already are, not trying to change ourselves into some preconceived notion of how we ought to be instead. Seek to practice this meditation technique a few times a day. Gradually, as the days pass, increase the time that you meditate to around 20 minutes at a time.

Two additional mindfulness exercises will be mentioned.

Body Scan   Start with your toes and focus your attention and awareness on whatever you sense in this body part. Gradually then focus your attention on your ankles and be aware of whatever you sense about this body part. Gradually do the same for calves, then your knees, then your thighs, then your pelvis, then your stomach, then your chest, then your neck, then your face, and finally the top of your head.

Walking Meditation   As you are taking a walk, focus on the movement of your body as you take step after step. Be aware of all of the movement that is taking place—perhaps first your heels, then your toes, then your ankles, then your calves, your knees, your thighs, your arms, and so on. (Mindfulness is closely related to relaxation techniques.)

Exercise

Stress prepares the body to move or become involved in large-muscle activity (including fight or flight). Large-muscle activity refers to the kinds of exercise involving many muscle groups at the same time, such as jumping rope. Through exercise, a group member can use up fuel in the blood, reduce his or her blood pressure and heart rate, and reverse the other physiological changes set off during the alarm stage of the General Adaptation Syndrome. Exercising helps a person keep physically fit and have more physical strength to handle crises. It also reduces stress and relieves tension. For these reasons group members should be encouraged to have a daily exercise program. A key to adhering to a daily exercise schedule is to select an enjoyable program. Many activities are available: walking, stretching, jogging, isometric exercises, jumping rope, swimming, playing tennis, dancing, housework, sex, gardening, or golf, for example.

Taking Care of Your Physical Self

In addition to exercising, it is important to have a nourishing diet, to take appropriate care of oneself, and to get enough sleep. Not only does a nourishing diet help keep people fit to resist stress, but research shows there are direct links between what individuals eat and how they feel emotionally. Some foods (such as coffee) produce tension, and overeating causes individuals to feel drowsy and even ill. Staying slim and trim helps a person feel good about himself or herself. Appropriate medical care also is a way to strengthen weak physical links that are vulnerable to stress-related illnesses.

Social Support Groups

Everyone needs to feel close to others. Support groups allow people to share their lives, have fun with others, and "let their hair down." These groups are also a resource for help when emergencies and crises arise. There are a variety of possible support groups that center on coworkers, a hobby or sports, a service (such as Rotary), a family, an extended family, a church, a community organization, a social club (such as Parents Without Partners), and so on. Essential characteristics of support groups are (1) the group meets regularly, (2) the same people attend, (3) there is an opportunity for spontaneity and informality, and (4) a feeling of closeness develops among members.[34]

Talking to Others

Every human needs someone with whom to share good times as well as personal difficulties. Sharing concerns with someone helps vent emotions, and talking a concern through often generates constructive strategies for resolving it. A good listener is someone who conveys caring and understanding, keeps the information confidential, is empathic, helps explore the difficulty in depth, helps arrive at alternatives for resolving the difficulty, and encourages the person to select and try out a resolution strategy.

Positive Thinking

When both anticipated and unanticipated events occur, people can choose to take either a positive or negative view of the situation. If they take a negative view, they are apt to experience more stress and alienate friends and acquaintances. If they take a positive view, they are likely to maintain their composure, stay relaxed, and cope with the situation quickly and easily, minimizing negative consequences. (This approach is described in the box "Positive Thinking.")

Akin to positive thinking is having a philosophy of life that allows you to take crises in stride and maintain a relaxed pace. When work is approached in a relaxed fashion, greater creativity is generated and stress is reduced. Leisure time should be enjoyed and used to develop oneself more fully as a person and to find enjoyment in each day.

When distressing events happen to you, it is psychologically therapeutic to view the event with the perspective of "Good luck? Bad luck? Who knows?" This perspective is indicated by the following story related by Anthony de Mello, SJ:

> There is a Chinese story of an old farmer who had an old horse for tilling his fields. One day the horse escaped into the hills and when all the farmer's neighbors sympathized with the old man over his bad luck, the farmer replied, "Bad luck? Good luck? Who knows?" A week later

Positive Thinking

- Give a smile to everyone you meet (smile with your eyes)—and you'll smile and receive smiles.
- Give a kind word (with a kindly thought behind the word)—you will be kind and receive kind words.
- Give appreciation (warmth from the heart)—you will appreciate and be appreciated.
- Give honor, credit, and applause (the victor's wreath)—you will be honorable and receive credit and applause.
- Give time for a worthy cause (with eagerness)—you will be worthy and richly rewarded.
- Give hope (the magic ingredient for success)—you will have hope and be made hopeful.

- Give happiness (a most treasured state of mind)—you will be happy and be made happy.
- Give cheer (the verbal sunshine)—you'll be cheerful and cheered.
- Give encouragement (the incentive to action)—you will have courage and be encouraged.
- Give a pleasant response (the neutralizer of irritants)—you will be pleasant and receive pleasant responses.
- Give good thoughts (nature's character builder)—you will be good and the world will have good thoughts for you.

SOURCE: Clement Stone, W. (1966). Be generous. In O. Mandino (Ed.), *A treasury of success unlimited* (pp. 9–10). New York: Hawthorne Books.

the horse returned with a herd of wild horses from the hills and this time the neighbors congratulated the farmer on his good luck. His reply was, "Good luck? Bad luck? Who knows?" Then, when the farmer's son was attempting to tame one of the wild horses, he fell off its back and broke his leg. Everyone thought this very bad luck. Not the farmer, whose only reaction was, "Bad luck? Good luck? Who knows?" Some weeks later the army marched into the village and conscripted every able-bodied youth they found there. When they saw the fanner's son with his broken leg they let him off. Now was that good luck? Bad luck? Who knows?[35]

Compassion Satisfaction

How to combat compassion fatigue? As mentioned earlier, compassion fatigue comes directly from thinking negative thoughts about working with highly traumatized clients; for example, "These clients are so traumatized, they will never get better—so why try?" The way to combat compassion fatigue is by compassion satisfaction. Radey and Figley note that it is meaningful, fulfilling, and uplifting for social workers to see their clients grow and change.[36] Compassion satisfaction results from recognizing these positive changes in clients and social workers then telling themselves such thoughts as:

"I am recognizing and excited about the positive changes that client X and client Y are making"
"There is no more valuable work than helping others who are suffering"
"I have the skills to help others improve, and I am doing a darn good job at what I do"
"Nothing else stirs my passion like this job"
"I often do not know when I am planting a seed that will inspire a client to make amazing life changes"

Compassion satisfaction is based on positive thinking. We always have a choice to think positively or negatively about life events. If we think positively, it will work wonders for us and for those we associate with. Learning to be positive for a person who has a history of negative thinking is not easy. An analogy comes to mind here—we know we should have a diet of healthy foods, but giving up the unhealthy eating habits is *so* difficult to do.

Changing Stress-Producing Thoughts

It is often erroneously believed that emotions, including feelings of tenseness and anxiety, are primarily determined by experiences—that is, by events that occur. However, cognitive therapies have shown the primary source of people's emotions to be what they tell themselves about their experiences.[37] An example will help clarify this important concept:

On the other hand, if Ms. Vogel tells herself something else, her emotions will be quite different.

This example illustrates two important concepts. First, a person's thoughts primarily determine his or her emotions. Second, by challenging and changing negative and irrational thinking, individuals can eliminate an unwanted emotion. Frequently, events cannot be changed, but individuals have the power to view such events rationally and positively and to control their emotions to a large degree.[38] (See Appendix 1: Module 1 for a fuller discussion.)

Law of Attraction

The Law of Attraction asserts that a person's thoughts (both conscious and unconscious) dictate the reality of that person's life, whether or not he or she is aware of it. The Law further asserts that if you really want something and truly believe it's possible, you'll get it. Furthermore, if you place a lot of attention and thought on something you don't want, you'll probably get that, too. For example, if you continue to worry and dwell on your belief that your romantic life "is in the pits," that belief system (along with the way you present yourself in accordance with this belief system) will lead you to have unhappy romantic relationships.

Think of the qualities you admire in others. A partial list might include honesty, a good listener, happy, contented, good sense of humor, charming, good problem solver, reliable, punctual, someone who helps you out when you need help, takes good care of her or his physical self, empathetic, perceptive, respectful of differences in others, usually has a smile, and focuses on the strengths of others.

The Law of Attraction asserts that we are always sending out vibes/vibrations of what we are thinking/feeling. If we are thinking bad thoughts, we will have bad feelings and will be sending out negative vibes. If we are thinking good/positive thoughts, we will have good feelings and will be sending out good vibes.

We like to be with people who send out good vibes—and who have the qualities you listed in Exercise 11.6. We generally do not like to associate with people who are sending out bad vibes.

EXERCISE 11.6   Qualities I Admire in Others

GOAL: This exercise is designed for you to identify the qualities you admire in others. (The exercise helps you actualize the Law of Attraction.)

1. List all the qualities that you admire in others. Feel free in your list to include some or all of the qualities that are listed in the description of the Law of Attraction in this chapter.

In order for salespeople to be successful, they need to be sending out good vibes so that customers will want to converse with them. In order for social workers to be effective with clients, they also need to be sending out good vibes so that clients will want to converse with them. This rule applies to most professionals: physicians, attorneys, psychologists, psychiatrists, guidance counselors, teachers, and so on.

The Law of Attraction asserts that if you present yourself as exhibiting the qualities you listed in Exercise 11.6, many doors will be opened up for you, and you will be successful, happy, contented, relaxed, and so on.

Are you willing to make a commitment to presenting yourself to others as having the characteristics you listed in Exercise 11.6?

Changing or Adapting to Distressing Events

There is a nearly infinite number of distressing events: the death of someone close, the breakup of a romantic relationship, being fired, having an unfulfilling job, failing some courses, getting into an argument, or having unresolved religious questions, for example. When distressing events occur, group members should be encouraged to confront them directly to try to improve the situation. If a person is grieving because of the death of someone else, he or she might find it helpful to talk about it within the group or seek professional private counseling. Terminated or fired employees should find out the reasons they were dismissed so they can deal constructively with them and begin to seek another job. If a person has unresolved religious questions, group discussion, followed by talking to a member of the clergy or taking a course on the philosophy of religion, may help.

Most distressing events can be improved by confronting them head on and taking constructive action to change them. However, a number of events cannot be changed. Group members may not be able to change the irritating habits of others. If a situation cannot be changed, the only constructive alternative is to accept it. It is counterproductive to nag, complain, and become upset. Acceptance of things that cannot be changed will leave an individual more relaxed and calm.

Personal Pleasures

Personal pleasures relieve stress, provide a change of pace, are enjoyable, make us feel good, and are (in reality) personal "therapies." What is pleasurable to one person may not be to another. Common pleasures are being hugged, listening to music, going shopping, taking a hot bath, going to a movie, having a glass of wine, family and religious get-togethers, taking a vacation, singing, and so on. Such "treats" remind individuals that they have worth; they also add spice to life.

Enjoyable activities beyond work and family responsibilities are also pleasures that relieve stress. Research has found that "stress reduces stress"; that is, an appropriate level of stressful activities in one area helps reduce excessive stress in others.[39] Getting involved in enjoyable outside activities switches a person's negative thinking about his or her daily concerns to positive thoughts about the enjoyable activities. Therefore, it is stress reducing to become involved in enjoyable activities such as golf, tennis, swimming, scuba diving, taking flying lessons, traveling, and so on.

Personal pleasures can also be used as "payoffs" to ourselves for jobs well done. Most of us would not shortchange others for doing well; we ought not to shortchange ourselves. Such rewards make us feel good and motivate us to move on to new challenges.

"Mental health time" is an indulgence that should be used when one is under extended stress. When a stress level has been too high for too long, relaxation is crucial to one's physical and emotional health. One should take a day off and do only what is pleasurable. (A number of agencies now allow employees a certain number of paid mental health days.)

OVERCOMING PROCRASTINATION

Procrastination is intentionally putting off doing something that should be done now; it is the thief of time. Once we develop the procrastination habit, we find plenty of ways to support it. We know we should be doing a certain A task, but instead we delay getting at it. We often squander our time by doing lesser-value tasks. For example, we know a paper is due in two days, but instead of writing it, we go shopping, spend hours talking to friends, wash clothes, or watch television. Sound familiar?

Procrastination is a major barrier to achieving short-range and long-range goals. The reason most people put off doing an A task is because it seems overwhelming or unpleasant. Overwhelming tasks are viewed as too complex or too time consuming. For example, you put off starting to write a 20-page paper due in one week because it seems that little can be accomplished in the short study time available. Unpleasant tasks, of course, generate negative emotions that may be difficult to deal with. For example, you put off telling your parents that you're failing a course because you fear their reactions and because you dread how you will feel after you inform them.

Swiss Cheese Approach

The key to getting an overwhelming A task under control is to poke holes in it by breaking it down into smaller tasks—the Swiss cheese approach. Completion of the smaller tasks nibbles away at the larger task until it is finally eliminated altogether.

For example, you have a research proposal to write for a class, and you feel overwhelmed because you have never written a proposal before and because you have few ideas for the proposal topic. Divide the task into smaller tasks. Begin by making a list of three or four research topics you're interested in. The next step is to formulate a research hypothesis in each of the areas. The third step might be to meet with your instructor to get his or her thoughts about the hypotheses. The fourth step might be to go to the Internet or to the library to examine what research has been done related to your hypotheses and to review what kinds of research designs have been used. Once you have done this, you will be ready to select a topic. And in reviewing the literature, you will in all probability have come across a design that you can adapt for writing your proposal. At this point, you may want to make a rough outline of your design that you can take to your instructor for feedback. After you make the changes suggested by your instructor, you are ready to sit down and write the research proposal.

EXERCISE 11.7   Ending My Procrastination

GOAL: This exercise is designed to assist you in ending your procrastination.

1. List the top three items that you are currently procrastinating about.

2. Examine these items and write down next to each one whether you are procrastinating because you view the task as "unpleasant," "overwhelming," or "both unpleasant and overwhelming."

3. For each task that needs to be done, list the strategies that you intend to use to stop procrastinating and to start doing these tasks.

Other Suggestions

Begin research: Unpleasant tasks can sometimes be made less unpleasant simply by learning more about them. Library research and interviews with experts or others knowledgeable in the field are good ways to begin.

Isolate parts of a task that can be done immediately: Completing several tasks early in the process provides initial success and motivation.

Set deadlines: Reasonable deadlines are a good way to avoid procrastination and build motivation.

Plan ahead: As parts of the project are completed, know the next step. This will keep the work moving forward.

Change of scene: If the work becomes boring or fatiguing, a change of pace or scene can often help. This approach simply means working for a while in the library, then in a dormitory room or even a student lounge. Such changes add variety and reduce boredom.

EXERCISE 11.8   Stress Management Techniques for Me

GOAL: This exercise is designed to familiarize you with available stress management techniques.

1. Review the material in this chapter on stress management techniques. List those techniques that you have used. Also, briefly describe whether each technique was beneficial to you in helping to reduce the level of stress you were experiencing.

2. Specify the stress management techniques that you are planning to use in the future.

EXERCISE 11.9   Developing a Self-Care Improvement Plan

GOAL: This exercise is designed to help you set goals for improving your self-care and to assist you in getting started to take better care of yourself.

1. Fill out this chart

Care Area	Specific Goals
Physical Care	Consider such goals as: • Improving diet • Improving sleep patterns • Physical exercise • Using stress management strategies • Reducing the use of alcohol and illegal drugs
Psychological Care	Consider such goals as: • Practicing mindfulness • Strategies to improve self-concept • Identifying your short- and long-term goals in life • Strategies to reduce your anxieties and feelings of being depressed • Identifying the characteristics of the kind of person you want to become • Specifying your sexual mores • Identifying your spiritual/religious beliefs
Social Care	Consider such goals as: • Improving relationships with family members • Improving relationships with friends and meeting new friends • Ending destructive or unfulfilling relationships • Becoming more assertive
Academic/Professional Care	Consider such goals as: • Identifying your career goals • Using time management to improve your use of time • Improving your study habits • Becoming involved in volunteer opportunities • Seeking to develop your career objectives that will lead to a career that is both gratifying and pays you sufficiently to lead the kind of lifestyle you desire • Seeking to establish "consistency" between your career goals and your marriage/family goals

2. A well-developed self-care improvement plan will facilitate your taking positive action to improve your well-being. To help ensure that your plan will "work" for you, please specify the time frames when you will review the progress you are making—such as every Sunday morning at 10:00 A.M.

Attack fear: Fear of failure or of a specific task can be a deterrent to even beginning work on a project. That fear can be attacked through a rational self-analysis (see Appendix 1: Module 1). This process can effectively neutralize fears and enable the project to proceed.

Consider the consequences: Delaying work can mean missed deadlines, hurried and thus inferior work, and poor grades. It can also mean missed opportunities. Contemplating the consequences of procrastination can be an effective motivator.

Consider the benefits: A personal reward system for completing a task—or parts of a task—is a good way to begin moving forward on a project.

Cut off escape routes: Common escapes from work include socializing, daydreaming, sleeping, and watching television programs. Escape routes can be blocked by removing the temptation or by working in a place or at a time when the temptations will not be available.

Summary

The following summarizes the chapter's content in terms of the learning objectives presented at the beginning of the chapter.

1. Define an educational group.

Educational groups in social work teach specialized skills and knowledge, such as classes on childrearing, stress management, parenting, English as a foreign language, self-care strategies, and assertiveness training. Educational social work groups usually have a classroom atmosphere, involving considerable group interaction and discussion.

2. Understand the importance of placing the highest priority on self-care.

If social workers do not care for themselves, their ability to care for others will be sharply diminished or even depleted. The self-care strategies that social workers learn and use are precisely the strategies that social workers should convey to their clients so that these clients can improve their lives.

3. Better manage stress, burnout, and compassion fatigue.

The following strategies are useful in reducing stress and combatting burnout and compassion fatigue: goal setting and time management, relaxation, mindfulness, exercise, taking care of your physical self, social support groups, talking to others, positive thinking, compassion satisfaction, changing stress-producing thoughts, Law of Attraction, changing or adapting to distressing events, personal pleasures, and overcoming procrastination.

Group Exercises

EXERCISE A: Resolving Current Stressors

GOAL: To identify and work on resolving current stressors.

Step 1. The leader describes what stressors are and indicates the goal of this exercise. The leader then instructs students to write their answers to the following questions. (These questions may be written on the blackboard.) The leader should inform students to feel free to write responses they want to keep private, as they will not be required to reveal anything they do not want to share.

1. What are the three most serious unresolved stressors that you are currently facing?
2. What attempts have you made to resolve each of these stressors?
3. Why have you not as yet been able to resolve each of these stressors?
4. Are you currently awfulizing about these stressors?
5. What constructive actions do you think you should now take to resolve each of these stressors?

Step 2. After the students write their answers to these questions, they form subgroups of three persons. In the subgroups, each member shares those responses that he or she comfortable in sharing. While a member is sharing his or her responses, the other two members focus on suggesting alternatives to resolving the stressors being discussed.

Step 3. After the subgroups finish their discussions, the leader asks if anyone (or any subgroup) has a complicated situation that he or she would like to share with the class. Such situations are discussed, with efforts being made to suggest alternatives to resolve the stressors. (If a distressing event cannot be changed, it is usually possible for the person involved to change his or her cognitions about the distressing event.) The exercise ends when no one has additional complicated situations to share.

EXERCISE B: Relaxation through Meditation

GOAL: To relax through meditating, thereby reducing stress and preventing burnout.

Step 1. The leader briefly describes what stress is and its causes and effects. He or she then explains that burnout is one of the reactions to high levels of stress and summarizes approaches for reducing stress and preventing burnout. (Preparing a handout that summarizes these approaches would be helpful.) The leader notes that it is important for each person to learn some ways to reduce stress.

Step 2. The leader explains that meditating is one way to reduce stress and then leads the group in the following meditative exercise. (The leader should feel free to modify and add to the following material).

I will now lead you in a meditation exercise. The purpose is to show you that through meditating you can reduce stress and anxiety. You can do this exercise by yourself whenever you are anxious or want to relax. You can do it, for example, before giving a speech in class, taking a crucial exam, or going to bed at night.

Herbert Benson, who wrote the book *The Relaxation Response*, has identified four key elements common to meditative approaches that help people relax. These four elements are (1) being in a quiet place; (2) getting in a comfortable position; (3) having an object to dwell on, such as your breathing or a phrase that you continually repeat silently to yourself; and (4) having a passive attitude in which you let go of your day-to-day concerns by no longer thinking about them. Having a passive attitude is the key element in helping you to relax.

Now, I want you form a circle. (Wait until a circle is formed.) I will lead you in three types of meditation. First, we will do a deep-breathing exercise. Then, we will move into repeating the word *relax* silently to ourselves. Third, I'll have you focus on visualizing your most relaxing place. We will move directly from the first to the second, and then from the second to the third, without stopping. When we do this exercise, don't worry about anything unusual happening. There will be no tricks. Concentrate on what I'm telling you to focus on, while taking a passive attitude where you let go of your everyday thoughts and concerns. Everyday thoughts and concerns may occasionally enter your mind, but seek to let go of them when they do.

Before we start, I want each of you to identity one of your most relaxing scenes. It may be lying in the sun on the beach or by a lake. It may be sitting in warm water in a bathtub reading a book. It may be sitting by a warm fireplace. Is there anyone who hasn't identified a relaxing scene? (Wait until everyone has identified one.)

OK, we're ready to start. (If possible, dim the lights or turn out some of them.) First, I want you to close your eyes and keep them closed for the entire exercise. Next, get in a comfortable position. If you want, you can sit or lie on the floor. (Take five or six minutes for each of the three meditative exercises. Speak softly and slowly. Pause frequently, sometimes for 20 seconds or more, without saying anything. Feel free to add material to the following instructions.)

First, I want you to focus on your breathing. Breathe in and out slowly and deeply. . . . Breathe in and out slowly . . . as you breathe out, feel how relaxing it feels. . . . While exhaling, imagine your concerns are leaving you . . . as you're breathing in and out, feel how you're becoming calmer, more relaxed, more refreshed. . . . Just keep focusing on breathing slowly in and out. . . . Don't try to be in sync when I'm talking about breathing in and out. . . . Find a breathing rhythm that's comfortable for you. . . . Breathe in slowly and deeply, and then slowly breathe out. . . . You've got the power within you to get more and more relaxed. . . . All you have to do is focus on your breathing. . . . Breathe in slowly and deeply, and then slowly breathe out. . . . If other thoughts happen to enter your mind, just let them drift away as effortlessly as possible. . . . The key to becoming more relaxed is to let go of your day-to-day concerns. . . . To do this, all you need to do is simply focus on your breathing. . . . Breathe in slowly and deeply, and then breathe out.

Now, we will switch to repeating silently to yourself the word *relax.* Keep your eyes closed . . . just keep repeating to yourself the word *relax.* . . . Keep repeating *relax* to yourself silently and slowly. . . . All of us encounter daily stressors. . . . It is impossible to avoid daily stressors. . . . The important thing to remember about stress management is not to seek to avoid daily stressors but to find ways to relax when we are under high levels of stress. . . . An excellent and very simple way to learn to relax is to sit in a quiet place, in a comfortable position, and silently repeat to yourself the word *relax . . . relax . . . relax.* . . . By simply repeating the word *relax* to yourself, you have the power within you to become more and more relaxed. . . . Find a nice comfortable pace for repeating the word *relax* to yourself. . . . The pace should be slow enough so that you can relax. . . . But not be so slow that thoughts about your day-to-day concerns enter your mind. . . . Remember, the key to relaxing is letting go of your day-to-day concerns. . . . If such concerns begin to enter your mind, focus more of your attention on repeating *relax* silently and slowly to yourself. . . . By repeating *relax* to yourself, you will find it will appear to have magical powers for you, as you will find yourself becoming more and more relaxed and refreshed. . . . Have the members repeat *relax* for five or six minutes.

Now, we will switch to focusing on your most relaxing scene. Don't open your eyes. . . . Focus on being in your most relaxing place. . . . Feel how good and relaxing it feels. . . . Just dwell on how relaxing it feels. . . . Enjoy everything about how calm and relaxing this place is. . . . Feel yourself becoming calmer, more relaxed. . . . Enjoy the peacefulness of this place. . . . Feel yourself becoming more relaxed, more renewed and refreshed. . . . Enjoy all the sights and sounds of this special place for you. . . . Notice and cherish the pleasant smells and aromas. . . . Feel the warmth, peacefulness, and serenity of this very special place for you. . . . Whenever you want to become more relaxed, all you have to do is close your eyes, sit quietly, and visualize yourself being in this very relaxing place. . . . The more you practice visualizing being in your relaxing place, the quicker you will find yourself becoming relaxed. . . . It will appear to you that your relaxing place has magical, relaxing powers for you, but in reality you are simply relaxing yourself by letting go of your day-to-day concerns and instead focusing on enjoying the peacefulness of your most relaxing place. . . . If you have to give a speech or are facing some other stressful situation, you can learn to reduce your level of anxiety by simply closing your eyes for a short period and focusing your thoughts on being in your most relaxing place. . . . You always have the power within you to reduce your level of anxiety. . . . All you have to do is close your eyes and visualize being in your very special relaxing place. . . . Continue to visualize, now, being in this very relaxing place. . . . Feel yourself becoming more relaxed, refreshed, and calm. . . . If you're feeling drowsy, that's fine. . . . Feeling drowsy is an indication that you're becoming more and more relaxed. ... You're doing fine. . . . Just keep on visualizing being in your very relaxing place. . . . You will become more and more relaxed by simply letting go of your day-to-day concerns and by enjoying this very special relaxing place. . . . (Pause for five or six minutes, then continue this exercise.)

Unfortunately, in a minute or so it will be time to return to this class. But there is no hurry. I will slowly count backwards from five to one, and then ask you to open your eyes shortly after we reach one. . . . (5) Enjoy how relaxed you feel. You may now feel warmer, drowsy, and so relaxed that you feel you don't even want to move a muscle. . . . Enjoy this very special feeling. . . . It is healthy to become this relaxed, as your immune system functions best when you are relaxed. . . . (4) Slowly begin to return to this class. . . . There is no rush. . . . There is no hurry. . . . Take your time to become more alert. Any time you want to relax, all you need to do is use one of these three meditative approaches. With practice you will gradually get better at relaxing by using these approaches. . . . (3) You should now focus on returning in a short time to this class. . . . Take your time . . . we still have a half-minute or so. . . . Examine whether you want to make a commitment to use relaxation exercises to reduce the daily stress you encounter. . . . (2) We are nearly at the time to return to this class. . . . You should now work toward becoming more and more alert. . . . (1) Slowly open your eyes. . . . There is no hurry. . . . Take your time to get oriented. A word of caution: if you have to drive someplace soon, please walk around for several minutes before trying to drive a car, as you may be so relaxed now that you may not be alert enough to drive safely.

Step 3. The leader then asks questions such as "What do you think of these three approaches?" "How relaxed did you get?" "Did any of you have trouble getting relaxed?" "If yes, why?" "Which of the three approaches did you like better and why?" (If the members are very relaxed and drowsy, they may feel they do not have the energy to respond to these questions. The leader should respect such a "mood" and not pressure members to respond.) *Note*: As an additional relaxation technique, the leader might play a muscle relaxation tape so that the class can experience this relaxation technique as well.

EXERCISE C: Setting High-Value Goals and Tasks

GOAL: To set short-range and long-range goals and to identify high-value tasks for accomplishing these goals.

Step 1. The leader begins by defining time management and describing the purpose of this exercise.

Step 2. Group members are asked to list their goals for the next six months on one sheet of paper and their long-range goals on another. A variety of areas should be considered, such as career, exercise and health, and education.

Step 3. After Step 2 is completed, group members prioritize their goals by assigning A to high-value goals, B to medium-value goals, and C to low-value goals, further ranking high-value goals in order: A-I, A-2, A-3, and so on.

Step 4. Group members then list the tasks needed to achieve the specific A goals.

Step 5. Group members then prioritize each task's value in achieving their A goals using the A, B, C approach. The leader explains that if this process is conscientiously followed, a person will have a clear vision of his or her important short-range and long-range goals and of the specific tasks that will help achieve these goals.

Step 6. The class discusses the merits and shortcomings of this process and what they learned from it.

EXERCISE D: Time Diagram

GOAL: To use a time diagram to determine how you are spending your time and whether this is the way you want to spend your time.

Step 1. The group leader explains that the way we spend our time can be viewed as a revolving stage, with each setting being a section. These settings can be diagrammed according to the amount of time we invest in each. The following examples should be provided.

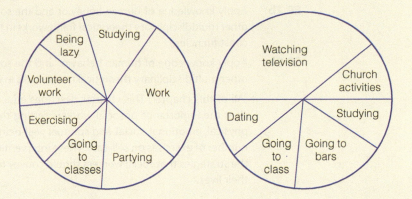

Note that the time spent sleeping is usually excluded from such diagrams, unless it is a specific time management problem.

Step 2. Students prepare diagrams showing how they spent their time for the past month. Each diagram should include the settings in which time was spent and the amount of time spent.

Step3. The class forms subgroups of three or four to share diagrams and comment on the following information:

1. Was this a typical month? If not, explain why.
2. Is this the way you *really want* to spend your time and energies?
3. Are you primarily directing your life, or is someone else? If someone else is primarily directing your life, who is this person, and what are your feelings about it?
4. If Exercise C has been done, the class discusses the extent to which the amount of time they are spending on high-value tasks is correlated to their use of time during the past month.

EXERCISE E: Ending Procrastination

GOAL: To develop strategies for doing the important tasks you are putting off.

Step 1. The group leader defines procrastination and explains that the main reason people procrastinate is that tasks are viewed as overwhelming or unpleasant. The leader then summarizes a number of strategies for ending procrastination. The leader may want to distribute a handout listing these strategies.

Step 2. Each person writes down answers to the following three questions on a sheet of paper.

1. What important tasks are not getting done because you're procrastinating?
2. Why are you procrastinating?
3. What specific strategies do you intend to use to stop procrastinating and to start doing these tasks?

Step 3. The class forms subgroups of three or four to share their responses and to suggest additional strategies for overcoming procrastination.

Step 4. The class discusses what they learned from this exercise.

Competency Notes

EP 1b   Use reflection and self-regulation to manage personal values and maintain professionalism in practice situations.

EP 1c   Demonstrate professional demeanor in behavior; appearance; and oral, written, and electronic communication.

EP 7b   Apply knowledge of human behavior and the social environment, person-in-environment, and other multidisciplinary theoretical frameworks in the analysis of assessment data from clients and constituencies.

EP 8b   Apply knowledge of human behavior and the social environment, person-in-environment, and other multidisciplinary theoretical frameworks in interventions with clients and constituencies.

(All of this chapter) This chapter describes educational groups. The chapter primarily emphasizes the importance of social workers setting the highest priority on taking care of their own physical, emotional, social, and spiritual well-being. The chapter has considerable content and a number of exercises on self-care. These intervention strategies to promote self-care are precisely the strategies that social workers should convey to their clients so that these clients can improve their lives.

Key Terms and Concepts

Alarm Phase	Burnout	Homeostasis	Progressive Muscle Relaxation
Awfulize	Deep-Breathing Relaxation	Imagery Relaxation	Resistance Phase
Biofeedback	Exhaustion	Meditative Approaches	Stressor

Treatment Groups

Treatment groups are designed to facilitate improvement in members who have emotional behavioral, or interpersonal challenges. This chapter will help prepare students to:

LO 1
Start, lead, and end treatment groups.

LO 2
Comprehend the therapeutic technique of motivational interviewing.

LO 3
Set professional boundaries with clients.

LO 4
Understand the therapeutic factors of treatment groups.

LO 5
Comprehend the merits and shortcomings of evidence-based practice.

LO 1   Start, Lead, and End Treatment Groups

EP 8b

STARTING, LEADING, AND ENDING TREATMENT GROUPS

Counseling people with personal problems is neither magical nor mystical. Although training and experience in counseling are beneficial, everyone has the potential to help another by listening and talking through difficulties. This is not to say that everyone will be successful at counseling. Helping professionals (such as social workers, psychiatrists, psychologists, and guidance counselors) have a higher probability of being successful, largely because they have received extensive training in counseling. But competence and empathy, rather than degrees or certificates, are the keys to effective counseling.

This chapter seeks to present a number of suggestions for how to effectively start, lead, and end treatment groups. Because experienced group facilitators may find this material to be rather obvious, the primary intended readers are those facilitators who are planning to lead their first groups and facilitators who have already led some groups but are seeking additional suggestions for improving their group skills.

PREPARATION AND HOMEWORK

Extensive preparation is needed for leading treatment groups. The leader should have considerable training in (1) assessing human behavior and human problems; (2) comprehensive therapeutic intervention approaches—such as reality therapy, behavior therapy, rational therapy, and feminist intervention;[1] (3) specialized therapeutic intervention techniques, such as assertiveness training and relaxation techniques;[2] (4) interviewing and counseling; and (5) principles of group dynamics, such as cohesion, task roles, social-emotional roles, and effects of authoritarian versus democratic styles of leadership. Baccalaureate and master's programs in social work generally provide considerable material in these areas.

For any treatment group, the leader also needs to study the literature on the causes of problems that members are experiencing, the most effective intervention strategies for these programs, the prognosis for positive changes, and expectations as to the length of time the intervention strategies need to be applied to induce positive changes.

When leading a group, extensive preparation is key to a successful group experience for the members (including yourself). Even experienced leaders have to carefully prepare for each group and for each time the group meets.

In planning for a new group, answers to the following questions need to be formulated. What are the overall purpose and general goals of the group? What are the ways in which these general goals might be accomplished? What are the characteristics of the members? What are the unique and individual needs of each member? What resources do the members need to have in order to help them better handle their personal problems? What should be the format for the first meeting? What are the individual therapeutic goals for each member? When the group first meets, should an ice-breaker exercise be used? If so, what? Should refreshments be provided? How should the chairs be arranged? What type of group atmosphere will best help the members solve their personal problems? What is the best available meeting place? Why have you been selected to lead the group? What do the members expect you to do?

As you plan for the first meeting, it is very helpful to view the group as a new member would view it. Questions and concerns that a new member may have are the following: Why am I joining? Will my personal goals be met in this group? Will I feel comfortable in this group? Will I be accepted by other members? Will the other members be radically different in terms of background and interests? If I do not like this group, can I get out of attending meetings? Will other members respect what I have to say, or will they laugh and make fun of me? What exactly will be discussed during these meetings? What will I be expected to say and do? Will pressures be put on me to make changes that I do not want to make? Through considering such concerns, the leader can plan the first meeting in a way that will assist the other members to feel comfortable and that will help clarify the members' questions as to the format and activities of the group.

When you are going to be a leader, it is *absolutely essential* that you do your homework prior to the first meeting to identify as precisely as possible what the members' needs and expectations are. The quickest way to fail as a leader is to allow a group to go in a different direction than the members desire.

There are a variety of ways to identify what the members want. It may be possible to discuss with each member, prior to the first meeting, what his or her expectations are and what each member can realistically expect to achieve in the group. If you are asked by someone else to lead the group, it is essential to ask that person what the expectations for the group are. The members should generally be asked at the first meeting to give their views as to what they desire to get out of the group. Another way to determine group members' expectations (which needs to be done for preparatory reasons anyway) is to obtain the following information about the group:

1. How many members are expected?
2. What are their characteristics (personal problems, ages, socioeconomic status, racial and ethnic backgrounds, gender mix, educational and professional backgrounds, and so on)? If you are involved in selecting who will be in the group, you will have to make some judgments regarding whom to include and whom to exclude. Two important criteria for including members in a treatment group are (1) the potential benefit of the group experience for each member and (2) the degree to which each member's presence is potentially beneficial to the other members in the group.
3. How knowledgeable and informed are the members about the issues the group will be dealing with?
4. What are apt to be the personal goals and agendas of the members?
5. How motivated are the members to accomplish the purposes for which the group is being formed? This can partly be determined by examining how voluntary the membership is. Involuntary members in a group (for example, members who have been court ordered to attend due to a conviction for driving while intoxicated) are apt initially to have little motivation to participate and perhaps may even be hostile that they are being forced to attend.
6. What are apt to be the underlying value systems of the members? A group of teenagers who have an eating disorder is apt to differ significantly from a group of adult parents who are mourning the death of a child. (However, it is important to remember to view the members in terms of being unique people rather than in terms of stereotypes.)

EXERCISE 12.1 My Concerns about Participating in a Treatment Group

EP 1b

GOAL: This exercise is designed to assist you in understanding the concerns of new members in becoming involved in a treatment group.

1. Imagine you have a serious emotional concern (such as being depressed) or have a behavioral difficulty (such as being bulimic). Also imagine you will soon be attending your first treatment group meeting. Specify your concerns about participating and revealing personal details of your issue in a treatment group.

2. What could the leader do or say to help alleviate these concerns?

In planning for the first (and additional) sessions, it is helpful to visualize (imagine) how you, as leader, want the session to go. For example, at the first session, the following scenario may be visualized:

> The members will arrive at various times. I will be there early to greet them, to introduce myself, to assist them in feeling comfortable, and to engage in small talk. Possible subjects of small talk that are apt to be of interest to these new members are _____ and _____.

> I will begin the session by introducing myself and the overall purpose of the group. I will use the following ice-breaker exercise for members to introduce themselves and to get acquainted with each other. I will ask the group to give me a list of four or five items that they would like to know about the other members. Then members will introduce themselves and give answers to the four or five items. I will also answer these items and encourage the members to ask further questions that they have about me and the group.

> After the ice-breaker exercise, I will briefly state the overall purpose of the group and ask if the members have questions about this. Possible questions that may arise are_____. If such questions arise, my answer will be_____.

> We will then proceed to an introductory exercise that is designed to encourage the members to begin sharing the personal problems they are experiencing. If this exercise fails to elicit much discussion after considerable probing on my part, I will present theoretical material on some of the psychological and societal dynamics of the personal problems they are experiencing.

The kind of group atmosphere I will seek to create is a democratic, egalitarian one. Such an atmosphere is best suited for encouraging members to share and problem-solve the issues they are experiencing. I will seek to do this by arranging the chairs in a circle, by drawing out through questions those who are silent, by using humor, and by making sure that I do not dominate the conversation.

I will end the session by summarizing what has been covered and what is planned for future sessions. During this summary, I will encourage members to give their suggestions for what should be dealt with in future sessions. We will set a time for the next session. Finally, I will ask if anyone has any additional comments or questions. Throughout the session, I will seek to establish a positive atmosphere, partly by complimenting the members on the contributions they make.

If a group has met one or more times, the leader needs to review the following kinds of questions:

- Has the overall format for the group been sufficiently decided upon and clarified? If not, what needs to be done in this clarification process?
- Is each member making adequate progress in problem solving? If not, what obstacles are preventing these members (and perhaps the group) from sufficiently progressing? Do these obstacles need to be confronted?

EXERCISE 12.2   My Concerns about Co-facilitating a Treatment Group

EP 1b

GOAL: This exercise is designed to assist you in identifying what you need to work on in order to be able to co-facilitate a treatment group.

1. Imagine you are an intern in a field placement and you will soon be co-facilitating a treatment group with an experienced treatment group facilitator. Specify your concerns about being a co-facilitator for a treatment group.

2. What can you do at the present time to alleviate some of these concerns?

- Are there more effective courses of action that might be considered that would benefit the group and certain members?
- What should be the format for the next session? What activities should be planned?
- Will successful completion of these activities move the group and the members toward accomplishing their overall goals? If not, perhaps other activities need to be selected.
- Does each member seem sufficiently interested and motivated to work on his or her problems, or are there some members who appear disinterested? If so, why do they appear disinterested, and what might be tried to stimulate their interests?

Guidelines and strategies for working with hostile and involuntary clients are presented below.

RELAXING BEFORE STARTING A SESSION

Before starting a session, you are apt to be nervous about how the session may go. Some anxiety is helpful in order to be mentally alert and to facilitate your attending to what is being communicated during the session. Some leaders, however, have too high a level of anxiety, which reduces their effectiveness. If your anxiety is too high, you can reduce it by engaging in activities that you find relaxing. Relaxation techniques are highly recommended (see Chapter 11). Other suggestions include taking a walk, jogging, listening to music you find relaxing, and finding a place where you can be alone to clear your mind. Effective group leaders generally learn they can reduce their level of anxiety through using one or more of these techniques. Through practice in leading groups, you will gradually build up your confidence.

CUES UPON ENTERING THE MEETING ROOM

It is important for you as leader to be on time—perhaps even a little early. By being early, you can check to see that everything is as you planned. You'll be able to do what needs to be done—such as checking to see that refreshments are available (if refreshments are planned), erasing the blackboard, arranging the chairs in the way you desire, and so on.

Strategies for Working with Hostile, Involuntary Members

Significant numbers of involuntary members are openly hostile in initial (and sometimes later) contacts with their assigned leader. What strategies can leaders use to develop rapport with such members and to motivate them to make positive changes? Six strategies are summarized here.

1. Treat such members with respect. Leaders need to understand that such members probably do not want to discuss their situation with the group. Modeling respect can help calm members and may then lead members to show respect for the leader and the other group members.
2. Allow members to vent their unhappiness over being forced to join the group. In many cases, it is useful to indicate as follows: "It is understandable that you are upset about having to be here—if the tables were turned and I was in your situation, I wouldn't want to be here either. It may help if we begin by you sharing your concerns about being forced to be here." Venting their concerns can have a calming effect.
3. Allowing members to vent concerns may also generate goals that the leader can help members work toward. For example, if a member is in a group because he physically abused his son while disciplining him, the leader can say, "I know you disciplined your child because you want the best for him—however, hurting a child is not acceptable. I wonder if we could explore some alternatives, like time outs for Timmy and anger management techniques?" *A key ingredient in working with involuntary members is establishing goals that are personally meaningful to them.* A leader should seek to limit the leader's goals for involuntary members to legal mandates and then seek to add

realistic goals that members desire. The strategy here is to search for common ground between the legal mandates and a member's personal goals. Often, redefining the problem in a way that adequately addresses the concerns of both the member and referral source reduces the member's resistance and makes a workable agreement possible.

4. Utilize the "disarming technique" (described in greater detail in Chapter 6), which involves finding some truth in what involuntary members are saying, even when the leader believes they are largely wrong, irrational, unfair, or unreasonable. There is always a grain of truth to be found. When the leader disarms members with this technique, the leader is offering respect; this may make members more cooperative. This technique also facilitates open (rather than defensive) communication.

5. Do not subject yourself to extensive verbal abuse. If hostile members become overly verbally abusive, postpone the contact with something like, "Sir, I'm treating you with respect, and in exchange I also have a right to be treated with respect. I see we presently are not getting anywhere. Let's postpone focusing on this issue until our next meeting—by that time we will hopefully be better able to more calmly discuss this."

6. If a member continues to be verbally abusive in subsequent meetings, the leader should meet with his or her immediate supervisor to discuss available options, such as terminating the member's participation in the group.

Being early will also give you an opportunity to observe the moods of the group members. If it is a group you have not previously met, being early gives you an opportunity to gain information about the interests of the participants from their age, gender, clothes and personal appearance, small talk, and the ways they interact with one another. An effective leader observes such cues and generally finds a way to join such participants.

SEATING ARRANGEMENTS

The seating arrangement is important for several reasons. It can affect who talks to whom and has an influence on who will play leadership roles. As a result, it can have an effect on group cohesion and group morale.

It is important in most groups for the members to have eye contact with one another. It is even more important that the group leader be able to make eye contact with everyone in order to obtain nonverbal feedback on what the members are thinking and feeling. A circle is ideal for generating discussion, for encouraging a sense of equal status for each member, and for promoting group openness and group cohesion.

When a group meets for the first time (and often later), members are apt to sit next to friends. If it is important that everyone in the group interact with one another, it may be desirable to ask people to sit next to people they do not know in order to counteract any cliquishness in the group and to encourage all members to get to know each other.

INTRODUCTION

During the introductions, the leader's credentials should be summarized in such a way that members gain a sense of confidence that he or she can fulfill their expectations. If the leader is introduced by someone, a brief concise summary of the leader's credentials for the expected role is desirable. If the leader is introducing himself or herself, important credentials should be summarized in a nonarrogant fashion. The summary should also be delivered in a way that creates the desired atmosphere—informal or formal, fun or serious, and so on. An excellent way in many groups to handle the introductions is to use an ice-breaker exercise.

In meeting with a group, it is highly desirable to learn the members' names as quickly as possible. This requires extra attention on the leader's part. Name tags facilitate this process for everyone. Members appreciate being addressed by name—it helps convey to them that they have importance.

It is generally advantageous for each member to introduce himself or herself, perhaps through using an ice breaker. It is often desirable during introductions that members state their expectations for the group. This helps uncover hidden agendas. If a stated expectation is beyond the scope of the group, the leader tactfully states and discusses it in order to prevent an unrealistic expectation from becoming a source of frustration or dissatisfaction for that member.

In treatment groups, as in individual counseling, there are two types of members: voluntary and involuntary. In voluntary groups, the facilitator can take a more casual, less directive approach to begin with. In such groups the facilitator may begin by involving members in small talk. This preliminary chit-chat may be about the weather, parking problems, baseball, something currently in the news, and so on. Casual conversation has the advantage of letting group members become acquainted with the facilitator and the other group members.

In involuntary groups, the facilitator may begin by introducing himself or herself and making a formal statement about the purpose of the group. Then members may be asked to introduce themselves. Generally, in involuntary groups, less is left up to the members themselves, as they have less motivation for being there and less commitment to the group's success.

With both voluntary and involuntary groups, it is sometimes helpful (after introductions) to begin a session with some factual information. This can be done in a brief presentation by the group leader or by showing a short film or videotape. For example, if the group members are involuntary clients who have been convicted of operating a motor vehicle while intoxicated, the leader may choose to show a film that vividly shows that as alcohol consumption increases, reaction times slow and the chance of serious accidents occurring dramatically increases. Such factual information is designed not only to provide educational material, but also to serve as a trigger to start a discussion. After factual information is presented, it is sometimes useful to involve the group members in an exercise related to the factual material.

If the group has met previously, the leader may choose to begin by bringing up for discussion a topic that was not fully discussed at the last meeting. Or, if "homework" assignments were given to some members, the leader may begin by saying, "Jim, at the last meeting you indicated you were going to do (such and such). How did that work out?"

CLARIFYING ROLES

As leader of a group, you must understand clearly your roles and responsibilities. In most situations it is a mistake for the leader to do the majority of the work. The group generally is most productive if all members make substantial contributions. The more members contribute to a group, the more they are apt to psychologically feel a part of the group.

The helper therapy principle is generally operative in groups.[3] With this principle, members at times interchange roles and sometimes become the helper for someone else's problems. In the helper role, members receive psychological rewards for helping others. Groups also help members to put their problems into perspective as they realize others have problems as serious as their own.

Even if you are fairly clear about what you would like your role to be, the other group members may be confused about what your role is, or may have different expectations of you. If there is a chance that the other members are puzzled about your role, you should explain carefully what you perceive your role to be. If members indicate they have different expectations, time should be devoted to clarifying the roles and responsibilities of the designated leader and other group members.

In explaining what you perceive your role to be, it is generally desirable to be straightforward about your skills and resources. Generally speaking, you want to come across as a knowledgeable person rather than as an authority figure who has all the answers.

Be prepared to explain the reasoning behind the things you do. For example, if you are doing an exercise, inform the group about the goals or objectives of that exercise. (If questions arise about whether the goals for the exercise are consistent with the overall goals for the group, be prepared to provide an explanation.)

The role that the leader assumes in a group will vary somewhat from situation to situation. For example, there are apt to be substantial differences in the responsibilities of the leader in an eating disorders group for teenagers versus an assertiveness group in a shelter for battered women.

Remember that leadership is a shared responsibility. Every member at times will take on leadership roles. Designated leaders should not seek to dominate a group, nor should they believe they are responsible for directing the group in all of its task functions and group maintenance functions. In fact, productivity and group cohesion are substantially increased when everyone contributes.

BUILDING RAPPORT

The facilitator tries to establish a nonthreatening group atmosphere wherein the members feel accepted and safe enough to communicate their troubles fully. During the initial contacts, the facilitator "sells" himself or herself (but not arrogantly) as a knowledgeable, understanding person who may be able to help and who wants to try. The tone of the facilitator's voice conveys the message that he or she understands and cares about group members' feelings. The facilitator is calm and never expresses shock or laughs when members begin to open up about problems. Emotional reactions, even if subtle, lead group members to believe that the facilitator is not going to understand or accept their difficulties, and they will usually stop discussing them.

A knowledgeable facilitator views group members as equals. New facilitators sometimes make the mistake of thinking that because someone is sharing intimate secrets with them, facilitators must be very important and end up assuming a superior position vis-a-vis their clients. If members feel that they are being treated as inferiors, they will be less motivated to reveal and discuss personal issues.

The facilitator should use a shared vocabulary with the members. This does not mean that the facilitator should use the same slang and the same accent as group members. If clients perceive that the facilitator is mimicking their speech patterns, they may feel seriously offended. To communicate effectively, the facilitator should use words that members understand and do not find offensive.

EXERCISE 12.3   The Helper Therapy Principle

GOAL: This exercise is designed to assist you in understanding the helper therapy principle.

1. Describe a time when you went out of your way to help someone.

2. Psychologically, how did you feel about yourself after you went out of your way to help someone?

The facilitator and other group members need to keep what members say confidential. Unfortunately, many people have nearly irresistible urges to share juicy secrets with someone else. If a group member discovers that confidentiality has been violated, that member's trust in the group will be quickly destroyed. It is essential that the facilitator explains the importance of the rule "what is said in the group, remains in the group."

Another important ground rule is emotional safety. The facilitator should state that if a member begins to share and he or she feels his or her disclosure is becoming too personal, the member should say, "This is becoming too personal." There should be no group pressure for that person to say more.

EXPLORING PROBLEMS IN DEPTH

How does a facilitator influence group members to share and then begin to problem-solve their issues? One way is to show a film, DVD, or videotape of a topic related to the issues of the members and then begin a discussion of the material after it is shown. Another way is for the facilitator to present some material on a topic involving the issues faced by the members and then encourage members to share their challenges with the topic. For example, if several members are struggling with depression, the facilitator may present theoretical material on the causes of and strategies to resolve depression and then ask members if some of the material might be pertinent to the challenges they are facing.

Another effective way for a facilitator to influence members to share and problem-solve their issues is for the facilitator to share a personal issue that is relevant to current challenges faced by group members that she or he is currently dealing with or has dealt with in the past. Possible topics are nearly infinite: grief management, ending a romantic relationship, creative financing, stress management, depression, becoming more assertive, letting go of a grudge, resolving an interpersonal dispute, and so forth. The facilitator should summarize the specifics of the issue she or he is facing and then discuss what she or he found useful in resolving (or working on resolving) this issue. The facilitator then asks if anyone in the group has experienced a similar issue and encourages volunteers to share. The facilitator should foster further discussion when a member shares a challenge he or she is facing by asking the group for ideas (strategies) on how to seek to resolve the challenges that have been raised. The merits and shortcomings of these strategies should then be discussed.

While exploring a member's problems in depth, the facilitator and group members examine areas such as the extent of the problem, how long the problem has existed, what the causes are, how the member feels about the problem, and what physical and mental capacities and strengths the member has to cope with the difficulty prior to exploring alternative solutions. A problem area is often multidimensional; that is, there are usually numerous problems involved. Explore all of them. A good way to decide which problem to handle first is to ask the group member which problem he or she perceives as most pressing. If it is a problem that can be solved, start by exploring it in depth and together develop a solution. Success in solving one problem will increase each group member's confidence in the leader and thereby further improve rapport.

Facilitators should convey **empathy**, not sympathy, and encourage group members to do so, too. Empathy is the capacity to understand and to share in another person's feelings. Sympathy also involves sharing feelings, but it results in offering pity. The difference is subtle. Empathy usually encourages problem solving, whereas sympathy usually encourages group members to dwell on the problem without taking action to improve the situation. For example, if a leader offers sympathy to a depressed person, that person will keep telling his or her sad story over and over, each time having the emotional outpouring reinforced by the leader's sympathy, without taking any action to improve the situation. Retelling the story only opens old wounds and prolongs the depression.

Facilitators should "trust their guts." The most important resources facilitators have are their own feelings and perceptions. Facilitators should continually strive to place themselves in members' shoes, understanding that members' values and pressures may be different from their own. It probably never happens that a group leader is 100% on target in an appraisal of a client's pressures, problems, and perspectives, but 70% to 80% is usually sufficient to allow the facilitator to be helpful. Empathizing is very useful in helping the facilitator determine what additional areas to explore, what should be said, and what possible solutions might be effected.

When a facilitator believes that a client has touched on an important area of concern, further communication can be encouraged in a number of ways. Showing interest nonverbally (by making and continuing eye contact, leaning forward, and raising the eyebrows slightly) encourages further sharing. Allowing for pauses is important. New facilitators usually become anxious when there is a pause and hasten to say something—anything—to keep the conversation going. This is usually a mistake, especially when it leads to a change in the topic. Although a pause often makes a group member anxious, it provides time to think about what areas of concern are most important and then usually motivates the member to continue the conversation in that area.

Neutral inquiries that do not control the direction of conversation but encourage further communication are helpful. For example, "Could you tell me more about it?" "Why do you feel that way?" and "I'm not sure I understand what you have in mind" all ask for further information, but just what kind is left up to the member. Reflecting feelings—for example, "You seem angry" or "You appear to be depressed about that"—works the same way. In your response, summarizing what a group member is saying shows not only that you are listening hut also that you have received the message the group member sent. An example is "During this past hour, you made a number of critical comments about your spouse; it sounds like you're fairly unhappy about certain aspects of your marriage."

Approach socially unacceptable topics tactfully. Tact is an essential quality of a competent facilitator. Try not to ask a question in such a way that the answer will put the respondent in an embarrassing position.

When pointing out a limitation that a group member has, also mention and compliment the member on any assets. When a limitation is mentioned, the person will feel that

---

EXERCISE 12.4   Using Tact in Treatment Groups

EP 1c

GOAL: This exercise is designed to assist you in tactfully confronting a group member about something she or he needs to be aware of.

A client (George) is a member of a treatment group you are facilitating. George recently received a master's degree in engineering. He has interviewed for a number of engineering positions, but someone else has always been hired. George has poor grooming habits and related body odor. There are vacant positions for engineers in your community. You and the other group members have exhausted in treatment with George all other explanations—it appears George is not being hired because of his grooming habits. Specify the words you would use in confronting George about his grooming habits. Also, would you confront George in the group or do the confronting in private?

something is being laid bare or taken away. Therefore, compliment him or her in another area to offer encouragement.

A competent leader watches for nonverbal cues and uses them to identify a sensitive subject, as the client will generally display anxiety by a changing tone of voice, fidgeting, yawning, stiff posture, or a flushed face. Some leaders claim that they can tell when a member's pupils dilate. (One of the reasons a member's pupils may dilate is because he or she is anxious or emotionally upset.)

Facilitators should be honest. An untruth may be discovered. If that happens, the group member's confidence in the facilitator will be seriously damaged and the relationship seriously jeopardized. Being honest goes beyond not telling lies. For example, the facilitator should point out shortcomings that are in the group member's best interest to correct. If a client is fired from jobs because of poor grooming habits, for example, this problem should be brought to the person's attention.

EXPLORING ALTERNATIVE SOLUTIONS

After a problem is explored in depth, the next step is to consider alternative solutions. The facilitator begins by asking something like "Have you thought about ways to resolve this?" The merits, shortcomings, and consequences of the alternatives thought of by the member are then tactfully and thoroughly examined. Next, the facilitator seeks to involve other group members by asking them if they are aware of any alternatives that may work for this situation. Those members who do suggest alternatives temporarily assume a "helper" role. In such a role the helper therapy principle operates as the member receives psychological rewards from helping others. If the facilitator has additional viable alternatives to suggest, they should then be mentioned. The merits, shortcomings, and consequences of the alternatives suggested by group members and by the facilitator are then thoroughly explored.

Group members usually have the right to self-determination, that is, to choose one course of action from possible alternatives. The facilitator's role is to help individuals clarify and understand the likely consequences of each available alternative, but usually not to give advice or choose the alternative for them. If a facilitator were to select an alternative, there are two possible outcomes: (1) the alternative may prove to be undesirable for the group member, in which case he or she will probably blame the facilitator for the advice and their future relationship will be seriously hampered or (2) the alternative may prove to be desirable for the person involved. This immediate outcome is advantageous. But the danger is that the group member will become overly dependent on the facilitator, seeking the facilitator's advice for nearly every decision in the future and generally being reluctant to make decisions.

The guideline of not giving advice means that the facilitator should suggest, not insist on, alternatives that a client has not considered. It is the facilitator's responsibility to suggest and explore all viable alternatives with a client. A good rule to follow is that when a facilitator believes a client should take a certain course of action, this should be phrased as a suggestion—"Have you thought about . . . ?"—rather than as advice, "I think you should."

Group treatment is done *with* group members, not *to* or *for* them. Each member should take responsibility for doing many of the tasks necessary to improve a situation. A good rule to follow is that each member should do those tasks that he or she has the capacity to carry out. Doing things for group members, similar to giving advice, brings with it the risk of creating a dependent relationship. Successful accomplishment of tasks by clients leads to personal growth and better prepares them for taking on future responsibilities.

A group member's right to self-determination should be taken away only if the selected course of action has a high probability of seriously hurting the client or others. For example, if it is highly probable that a group member may attempt to take his or her life, the facilitator should intervene (making arrangements for the member to receive in-patient psychiatric care if the risk of suicide is high), even if the group member objects to the intervention. For most situations, however, the group member should have the right to select a course of action even when the facilitator believes that another alternative is better. Frequently, a client is in a better position to know what is best, and if it turns out not to be the best, he or she will probably learn from the mistake.

Guidelines on Formulating a Contract

Contracts in social work practice specify goals to be accomplished and the tasks to be performed to accomplish them. In addition, contracts set deadlines for completion of the specified task and identify rewards for successful completion of tasks. Contracts also specify consequences for unsuccessful completion of tasks. A contract is, therefore, an agreement between a facilitator and one or more clients in their joint efforts to achieve specified outcomes. Formulating an explicit contract is directly related to a positive outcome for clients.

A contract, in outline format, should contain the following components:

1. Goals to be accomplished (ranked in order of priority)
2. Tasks to be accomplished by the client and by the facilitator (these tasks must be directly related to accomplishing the goals, so that accomplishing the tasks will result in successfully meeting the goals)
3. Time frame for completing the tasks
4. Means of monitoring progress toward accomplishing the tasks and the goals
5. Rewards for the client if the terms of the contract are met
6. Adverse consequences to the client upon nonfulfillment of the terms of the contract

Some facilitators prefer written contracts, and others prefer verbal contracts. A written contract has the advantage of emphasizing the commitment to the contract by both the facilitator and the client, and it also minimizes the risk of misunderstandings. A verbal contract has the advantage of avoiding the sterility of a written contract.

A verbal contract is generally as effective as the written contract with regard to the goals being successfully accomplished. If a facilitator chooses to use a verbal contract, the facilitator should still record the essential elements of the contract in his or her notes for future reference.

The most difficult element in formulating an effective contract is for the facilitator and the client to formulate goals. Goals specify what the client wishes to accomplish and should directly relate to the needs, wants, or problems being encountered by the client. Goals serve the following important functions:

1. Goals ensure that the facilitator and the client are in agreement about the objectives to be accomplished.
2. Goals provide direction to the helping process and thereby reduce needless wandering.
3. Goals guide selection of appropriate tasks (and interventions) that are focused on achieving the objectives.
4. Goals serve as outcome criteria in evaluating the extent to which the tasks (and interventions) are successful.

Useful guidelines when setting goals include:

1. *Goals must relate to the desired end results sought by the client.* The client must believe that accomplishing the selected goals will enhance his or her well-being. Therefore, the therapist needs to integrally involve the client in the process of selecting and specifying the goals.
2. *Goals should be stated in specific and measurable terms.* Nebulous goals (such as "Client gaining increased control over his emotions") are not sufficiently specific and often lead the client to drift or wander in the helping process. A specific goal (such as "The client will express his angry feelings with his mother in an assertive rather than an aggressive manner when they are having conflicts") is substantially more explicit. In addition, it is also measureable, whereas a nebulously stated goal is not. The client's mother (and others) can monitor the number of times over a specified period that the client expresses his or her angry feelings assertively as compared to aggressively. Clients tend to define goals more nebulously, so it is important for the therapist to assist clients in stating their goals in such a way that they are both specific and measurable.
3. *Goals should be feasible.* Unachievable goals set the client up for failure, which is then apt to lead to disappointment, disillusionment, and a sense of defeat. It is vital that the goals chosen can be accomplished by the client. For clients with grandiose tendencies, it is important for the facilitator to assist them (tactfully) in lowering their expectations to the upper level of what can reasonably be attained.

When arriving at feasible goal statements with a client, the facilitator should agree only to assist the client in working toward goals for which the facilitator has the requisite skills and knowledge. If the goal is beyond the facilitator's competence (for example, assisting the client in overcoming a complex sexual dysfunction), the facilitator has the responsibility to refer the client to a more appropriate resource in the community.

Once the client has settled on his or her goals, the final step in the process of negotiating goal statements is to assign priorities to the goals. The purpose of this step is to ensure that the initial change efforts are directed to the goal that is most important to the client.

The following example illustrates formulation of a contract. We begin with background information. Ray and Klareen Norwood have been married for three years. They join a treatment group composed of four married couples and a facilitator—the focus of the group is on improving their marital relationship. Klareen reveals that she is increasingly afraid of Ray's angry outbursts at her. Ray is physically and verbally abusive to her when he is angry. He has not hit Klareen yet, but she is afraid that Ray's escalating aggressiveness when they argue will lead to

(continued)

her being battered. Klareen is considering separating from Ray. She has already contacted an attorney to discuss divorce proceedings. Both partners, however, state that they want to maintain the marriage. The therapist and the other group members assist the Norwoods in formulating the following contract:

Goals: (1) Ray will cease being physically abusive to Klareen and will reduce by at least two-thirds the incidents of being verbally abusive to Klareen over the next 30 days. (This goal is rated number one.) (2) The Norwoods will begin discussing at some future date raising a family. (This goal is rated number two.) The Norwoods both agree to put off further discussion of it at this time, as Klareen says she first needs to make a decision about whether she wants to remain in the marriage.

TASKS OF THE PARTICIPANTS

Facilitator: The facilitator will instruct Ray in the following anger control techniques: (1) Ray learning to express his angry feelings to Klareen in an assertive rather than aggressive manner (see Appendix 1: Module 2); (2) Ray learning to reduce the intensity and frequency of his angry outbursts by countering negative and irrational self-talk underlying his anger with rational and positive self-talk (see Appendix 1: Module 1); (3) Ray learning how to counter his feelings of anger with deep-breathing relaxation (see Chapter 11); and (4) Ray learning to blow off steam nondestructively when he is angry through such physical activities as jogging or hitting a pillow (see Chapter 11). (Interestingly, the other group members also express interest in learning these anger control techniques during their group treatment sessions.)

Mr. Norwood: His main task is to use these techniques to cease being physically abusive to Klareen and to substantially reduce the incidents of being verbally abusive to Klareen. After 30 days, if Ray succeeds, a renegotiation of the terms of the contract will occur.

Mrs. Norwood: Klareen will seek to calmly discuss issues she has with Ray (in and outside the therapy sessions) to avoid provoking Ray's anger. Klareen also has the responsibility to record any incidents in which Ray is physically or verbally abusive to her in the next 30 days.

DURATION OF CONTRACT: 30 DAYS

Means of Monitoring Progress: Klareen will record incidents where Ray expresses his anger toward her in assertive or nondestructive ways. (This is designed to measure positive ways in which Ray is learning to express his anger.) Klareen will also record any incidents in which Ray is verbally or physically abusive to her.

Rewards for Ray and Klareen If Contract Is Met: They will continue their marriage, which is what both partners want.

Consequences for Ray and Klareen If Contract Is Not Met: If Ray hits Klareen one time in the next 30 days, she will separate. If Ray does not reduce by two-thirds the number of times he is being verbally abusive in the next month, she will separate. (To get baseline information, Klareen is asked to identify in the past week—taking each day at a time—the number of times Ray has been verbally abusive. Nine incidents are identified. As a result, Ray agrees he will, at most, be verbally aggressive to Klareen no more than 12 times in the next 28 days. If he exceeds this limit, it is agreed that Klareen will move in with her parents.)

If a group member fails to meet the terms of the contract, the facilitator should not criticize or accept excuses. Excuses let people off the hook; they provide temporary relief, but they eventually lead to more failure and to a failure identity. Simply ask, "Do you still wish to try to fulfill your commitment?" If the person answers affirmatively, another time deadline acceptable to the member is set.

When a group member selects an alternative, he or she should clearly understand what the goals are, what tasks need to be carried out, how to accomplish the tasks, and who will carry them out. Frequently, it is desirable to write a contract for future reference, with a time limit set for the accomplishment of each task. (The box "Guidelines on Formulating a Contract" shows how to formulate a contract with a client.)

Perhaps the biggest single factor in determining whether a group member's situation will improve is the motivation to carry out essential tasks. A facilitator tries to motivate apathetic group members. One way to increase a member's motivation is to clarify what will be gained by meeting a goal. When individuals meet commitments, facilitators should reward them, verbally or in other ways. Never criticize members for failing. Criticism usually increases hostility and rarely leads to positive, lasting change. Also, criticism serves only as a temporary means of obtaining different behavior; when a person believes that he or she is no longer under surveillance, that person will usually return to the destructive behavior. (The box "Motivational Interviewing" describes an approach for motivating clients to seek positive changes.)

LO 2 Comprehend the Therapeutic Technique of Motivational Interviewing

If a group member lacks confidence or experience, it may be helpful to role-play a task before the person actually attempts it. For example, if a pregnant single woman wants help in telling her partner about the pregnancy, role-playing the situation within the group assists the woman in selecting words and developing a strategy for informing him. The facilitator or another group member plays the woman's role and models an approach, letting the woman play the partner's role. Then the roles are reversed so that the woman practices telling her partner.

STAGES OF GROUP DEVELOPMENT

The group leader needs to be aware that treatment groups have stages of development. A useful model for understanding the developmental stages is the Garland, Jones, and Kolodny Model that was described in Chapter 1.[4] These stages will briefly be reiterated here.

The central focus of the model is emotional closeness among members, which is reflected in struggles that occur during the following five stages: preaffiliation, power and control, intimacy, differentiation, and separation.

In the first stage, **preaffiliation**, members are ambivalent about joining the group and interaction is guarded. Members test out whether they want to belong and continue on. They attempt to protect themselves from being hurt or taken advantage of by maintaining a certain amount of distance from other members and by attempting to get what they can from the group without taking many risks. During this first stage, the leader should seek to have the group appear as attractive as possible by allowing and supporting distance, using ice breakers, gently inviting trust, and gently indicating the likely benefits of continuing on. This first stage ends when the members gradually feel safe and comfortable within the group and when they realize that the potential rewards from participating are worth a tentative emotional commitment.

In the second stage, **power and control**, the character of the group begins to emerge. Alliances, patterns of communication, and subgroups begin to emerge. Members assume certain responsibilities and roles, norms develop for handling group tasks, and members more openly ask questions. Power struggles are apt to develop in which each member attempts to gain greater control over the rewards to be received from the group. The leader usually becomes a major source of gratification for the other group members, as the leader gives and withholds emotional and material rewards. The leader is also attractive to the members, as he or she influences the direction of the group. During this phase, group members realize the group is becoming important to them. A variety of power struggles may emerge. Does the group or the leader have primary control? To what extent will the leader use his or her power? Subgroups are apt to struggle with one another. Such struggles result in anxiety and considerable testing by group members—to gauge limits and establish norms for the power and the authority of both the leader and the other group members. Rebellions may occur, and the dropout rate is often highest at this phase. During these struggles, the leader should help the members to (1) understand that these struggles are a normal process of group development, (2) give emotional support to help members weather the discomfort, (3) problem-solve the issues that are emerging, and (4) assist in establishing norms to resolve the uncertainties. When members gradually trust the leader to maintain a safe balance of shared power and control, the members make a major commitment to become involved.

The third stage is **intimacy**. The group becomes more like a family. The likes and dislikes of intimate relationships are expressed. "Sibling rivalries" are apt to be exhibited, and the leader is sometimes viewed as a parent. Members more openly express and discuss feelings. The group becomes recognized as a place where growth and change are apt to take place. Members feel free to examine and make efforts to problem-solve their issues, concerns, and difficulties. There is more of a feeling of cohesiveness and "oneness." Members in the group examine "what this group is all about."

Motivational Interviewing

One of the biggest reality shocks of a "new" social worker is that many, perhaps most, clients are simply not motivated to make the necessary changes to improve their emotional and physical well-being. Examples are infinite. An alcoholic with accompanying serious health problems will often chose to continue to drink. A person who is depressed because his or her spouse recently attained a divorce will wallow in misery and not seek to make life changes that will bring happiness. A compulsive gambler who has lost a lot of money will continue gambling. A person with a stressful job will not seek to learn and practice stress management techniques. A person who is imprisoned for selling drugs may return to selling drugs again upon being released from incarceration.

A number of years ago it was thought that the best way to motivate a client who does not want to make constructive changes to improve his or her well-being was to hold an "intervention" with that person. For example, if one has a serious drinking problem, it was thought that his or her counselor should gather as much evidence as possible and enlist friends and relatives to have a meeting with the alcoholic to confront the person with all the evidence and incidents of the negative effects of drinking, which might include health challenges, relationship issues, loss of jobs, physical and verbal altercations, and arrests for driving under the influence. Sometimes such an intervention did prove beneficial, but often it did not. For alcoholics, drinking has become their "best friend," which they will not give up. So how does a social worker seek to motivate a client to make changes when that client denies that a problem exists and refuses to make changes?

Social workers need to recognize that people go through a process when they make positive changes in their lives. This process has been conceptualized by Prochaska and DiClemente as involving the following five stages[a]:

Stage 1.	PRECONTEMPLATION	A person is not seeing a need for a lifestyle change
Stage 2.	CONTEMPLATION	A person is considering making a change but has not decided yet.
Stage 3.	PREPARATION	A person has decided to make changes and is considering how to make them.
Stage 4.	ACTION	A person is actively doing something to change.
Stage 5.	MAINTENANCE	A person is working to maintain the change or new lifestyle. There may be some temptations to return to the former behavior or even small relapses.

The aim of motivational interviewing is to help clients who are in stages 1, 2, or 3 to move toward stages 4 and 5. It should be noted that clients are apt to move back and forth between these stages. Someone at stage 1, for example, may recognize that he does in fact have a problem and move, for a while, to stage 4 where he is actively making some constructive changes; then he may regress and return to stage 1 or 2; then move at a later date to stage 3 or 4; and so on.

Motivational interviewing is not a specific technique, but rather is a style of interacting with clients, with the objective of calmly encouraging clients to move toward stages 4 and 5. William R. Miller and Stephen Rollnick are generally recognized as the founders of motivational interviewing.[b] They developed this approach in their work with substance abusers who had high relapse rates while in treatment. Motivational interviewers seek to convey understanding of the challenges that clients face in recognizing they have an issue and being supportive of the efforts that clients need to make in order to make constructive changes. Motivational interviewing is now used with a wide variety of clients, including substance abusers, those with an eating disorder, depressed persons, those with a gambling addiction, persons with anger management issues, and those with a dysfunctional sexual addiction.

Key principles of motivational interviewing are the following:

- Express Empathy: The social worker needs to place himself or herself, as much as possible, into the "shoes" of the client. The social worker needs to focus on what a client who is resisting making positive changes is thinking and feeling and then convey his or her understanding of this. When clients feel they are being understood, they are much more apt to further open up and share their innermost thoughts, which may well lead them to start to move from stages 1, 2, or 3 to stage 4. When they feel support and understanding from the social worker, clients become more comfortable with examining their ambivalence about putting forth the efforts to make constructive changes. An example of a social worker's empathetic response to a client who has a drinking problem but is reluctant to taking action to reduce his drinking is the following, "In a sense, alcohol has become your best friend, as it helps to ease the pain of unwanted emotions that you feel; but are you aware that that there are other ways besides drinking that we might explore to help you make it through each day?"

- Develop Discrepancy: Clients tend to be more motivated to make constructive changes when they perceive a discrepancy between where they are and where they want to be. A social worker can assist a client in recognizing

(continued)

Motivational Interviewing (*continued*)

the discrepancies between where their current behavior is at and what their short- and long-term goals are by gently asking questions. For example, with a client who has a drinking issue, the social worker can ask questions like the following:

"Could you tell me some good things that drinking does for you?" After the client responds, the social worker asks, "Could you now tell me some less good things about your drinking?"

"Do you remember what your life was like before you started having problems with drinking?"

Do you believe your life might improve if you stopped drinking?"

"Have you thought about what your life might be like 10 years from now if you continue to drink as much as you do?"

- Roll With Resistance: The social worker expects resistance with motivational interviewing. The social worker does not fight the resistance, but seeks "to roll with it." Statements made by a client that indicate resistance are not challenged. Instead, the worker uses the client's momentum to further explore the client's views. A useful technique when a client is resisting change is using a reflection. A reflection enables the worker to respond to resistance with a nonresistant response by reflecting the client's statement in a neutral form. The following is an example with a client who drinks too much: "Let's talk about the incident when you spent the night in jail after receiving a citation for driving under the influence." The client responds, "What's to talk about? The police and you have already concluded that it was all my fault." The worker responds with the reflection "So you feel like your opinion does not matter?" instead of confronting the client with the facts contained in the police report.

Rolling with resistance avoids confrontations with clients on issues they have.

- Support Self-Efficacy: Self-efficacy is one's belief in one's ability to succeed in specific situations. One's self-efficacy plays a major role in how one approaches tasks, goals, and challenges. In motivational interviewing, the social worker focuses on helping clients stay motivated to put forth the efforts to move toward stages 4 and 5. A competent social worker knows and conveys to the client that there is no one right way to change. The worker wants the client to develop the argument for change and to also develop the courses of action to be taken for making changes. The more a client develops his or her own strategies for attaining change, the more the client will be committed to implementing those strategies.

One technique for assisting the client to assess his or her readiness for change is the following "Readiness to Change

Ruler": The worker shows the client the following scale and asks him or her to state the number that best reflects how ready, at the present time, he or she is to change his or her dysfunctional behavior:

Not Ready to Change	Thinking of Changing	Undecided/ Uncertain	Somewhat Ready	Very Ready to Change
1	2	3	4	5

It is important for the worker to identify the client's readiness to change, as the worker needs to focus his or her attention on the same level of readiness to change that the client is at in order to minimize resistance and gain cooperation. For example, if the client states he is "Thinking of changing his drinking behavior" the worker may make progress by gently asking, "What do you see as the benefits to reducing the number of drinks that you have?" And after the client responds, the worker may then ask, "Could you tell me your thoughts as to why you still want to continue drinking as much as you do?" Such communication may lead the client to further explore why he continues to drink to excess and may increase his chances of making a commitment to moving toward stage 4—taking some actions to reduce the amount of alcohol that he consumes.

- Encourages Supportive Relationships: The worker encourages the client to develop supportive relationships with friends and relatives who believe in the person's potential to improve. Also, self-help groups (such as AA for alcoholics) are a critical source of support. Members of self-help groups have experienced similar difficulties as the client and are on a similar journey of recovery; they can help the client develop coping strategies for the challenges that arise.
- Finding Meaning in Life: The worker assists the client in developing a sense of meaning to living, which is important in sustaining the recovery process.
- Developing Coping Strategies: The worker assists the client in developing coping and problem-solving skills to resolve other personal and family challenges that the client is facing.
- Being an Encouraging Person: The worker conveys to the client that he or she has the resources (internal strengths and social support networks) to conquer his or her issues and challenges. The worker has a nonjudgmental attitude so that the client no longer feels a need to lie, pretend, or wear a mask. The worker conveys to the client that she or he is genuinely interested in the client's progress and conveys that the client is an important, worthwhile person. The worker conveys sincere enthusiasm in the constructive interests, ideas, and risk-taking actions of the client. The worker takes

(continued)

the time to listen to and understand the client as fully as possible. Motivating a discouraged person takes a long, long, time; discouraged clients generally have a long history of failures. The worker reinforces efforts made by the client, even when the actions taken do not bring immediate success; the important thing is that the client tries to improve his or her life. The worker is a nonjudgmental listener so that the client's real thoughts and feelings can be expressed freely, without fear of censure.

a. Prochaska, J. O., & and DiClemente, C. C. (1982). Trans-Theoretical therapy toward a more integrative model of change. *Psychotherapy Theory, Research and Practice 19*(3), 276–288.
b. Miller, W. R., & Rollnick, S. (1981). *Motivational interviewing: Preparing people to change addictive behavior.* New York: Guilford Press.

The fourth stage is **differentiation**. Members are freer to experiment with new and alternative behavior patterns. Leadership is more evenly shared, members communicate more effectively, and roles are more functional. Power struggles are now minimal. Decisions are made on a more objective, less emotional basis. The differentiation stage is analogous to a healthy, functioning family in which the children have reached adulthood and are now becoming successful in pursuing their own lives. Relationships are now more egalitarian, and members are mutually supportive and able to relate to each other in more rational and objective ways.

The final stage is **separation**. Group goals have been achieved, and members have learned new behavioral patterns that are more functional for them. Termination is often a bittersweet experience. Some members may be reluctant to move on and may display regressive behavior to seek to prolong the existence of the group. Some members may express anger or may psychologically deny that termination is approaching. The leader in this phase must be able to let go. The leader needs to help members evaluate the merits and shortcomings of the group, problem-solve their fears and trepidation about the group ending, identify resources they can turn to when future issues arise, and assist members in recognizing their strengths and capacities to handle future challenges that may arise.

ENDING A SESSION

Ending is not always easy. Ideally, the facilitator and group members accept the fact that the session is ending, and subjects being discussed are not "left hanging." Abrupt endings are apt to be perceived by the group members as discourteous and rejecting.

There are some useful guidelines on how to terminate a treatment session. Initiate preparation for ending the session at the beginning of the session. Inform the members explicitly of the time the session will end. Unless an unusual situation develops, the leader assertively seeks to terminate at the scheduled time. When the allotted time is nearly up, the facilitator informs the group members by saying something like, "I see our time is just about up. Is there anything you'd like to add before we look at where we've come to and where we now go from here?"

It is often helpful to summarize what was discussed during the session. If the session focused only on exploring problems that the members have, another session can be set up for fuller exploration and to begin looking at alternatives for resolving the problems.

It is helpful to give members homework assignments between sessions. A couple who are having trouble communicating with each other might be encouraged to set aside a certain amount of time each evening to discuss their thoughts. At the next session, this "homework" assignment may be reviewed.

Ideally, the group members are emotionally at ease when the session ends. Therefore, the facilitator should not introduce emotionally charged content at the end of the session; just as it is sometimes advisable to begin a session with small talk, a short social conversation at the end may provide a transition out of the session. If a group member displays a reluctance to end a session, it is sometimes helpful to directly confront this by saying, "It appears to me that you wish we had more time." The reasons for the person's reluctance can then be discussed.

At times, a group session can be ended with a restatement of the way both the facilitator and group have agreed to proceed. Or, a more explicit summation may be made by the group leader of what was discussed, what decisions were arrived at, what questions remain to be resolved, and what actions will be taken. A somewhat different approach is to ask each group member to state one item that was discussed or learned from the session and/or what he or she now plans to do. Some treatment groups end by each member letting go of a bad feeling and taking home a good one to be acted upon during the week.

Sometimes concerns that were alluded to but not fully discussed might be mentioned in closing as topics that will be taken up at the next session. Some members reveal their most serious concerns for the first time at the end of a session, perhaps because they are ambivalent about whether they are ready to fully explore these concerns with the group. In these instances the facilitator has to make a professional judgment about whether to extend the session beyond the allotted time, or to set up an appointment to discuss these concerns privately, or to wait until the next group session.

Sometimes it is helpful to end a group session with a relaxation exercise (described in Chapter 11). A relaxation exercise helps members not only to relax but also to reduce their level of stress so that they can more objectively view and work on resolving their problems after they leave.

Closing is especially important because what occurs during this last phase is likely to determine the members' impressions of the session as a whole. Leave enough time for closing so that the members do not feel rushed, as that might create the impression that they are being evicted.

ENDING A GROUP

The ending phase of a group frequently offers the greatest potential for powerful and important work. Group members may feel a sense of urgency as they realize there is little time left, and this can lead them to reveal their most sensitive and personal concerns. Because the work remaining to be done is usually clearly identified at this point, members can focus their efforts on completing it. However, the relationship dynamics are also heightened in this phase, as the members prepare to move away from each other, and the termination of the group may evoke powerful feelings in members.

If group members have grown emotionally close to each other, the ending of a group will be interpreted as a loss and produce a variety of emotions. Kubler-Ross's stages of emotional reactions that people display when terminally ill resemble the reactions that people have to other important losses, including the ending of a successful and cohesive group.[5] Members may display denial by ignoring the imminent end of the group, anger and rage, or sadness and depression. They may attempt to bargain for an extension of the group in a variety of ways, such as urging that the group deal with additional problems. Ideally, members will ventilate and work through such feelings and gradually come to accept the ending of the group.

Other emotions may also be displayed. Some members may feel guilty because of adverse comments they made or because they believe they failed to take certain actions that would have benefited themselves or other members in the group. If a member left prematurely, some members may feel the group let him or her down. Members may want to share their feelings about the support system they will lose when the group ends. If certain members want the group to continue, they may interpret the ending of the group as a personal rejection. On the other hand, members who feel that the group was very successful may want to have a celebration to give recognition to the successes and to say goodbye.

In many ways the concluding sessions are the most difficult for the facilitator and the group members. Strong emotions are often generated and should be ventilated and worked through. It is painful to terminate a group when members have formed relationships to share their most personal and important concerns and feelings. Our society has done little to train us to handle such separations; in fact, some segments in our society have a norm of being strong and not expressing feelings.

The facilitator can help members accept the ending of a group in a number of ways. The process of terminating a group should begin during the early stages of the group. This guideline is particularly relevant for time-limited groups. The facilitator should attempt to prevent the formation of dependency relationships between the members and the facilitator.

The goal is independence and better functioning, and this should be reiterated whenever appropriate during group sessions.

The facilitator may summarize the emotional reactions that people have to group endings. An appropriate point for a discussion occurs when members display denial, anger, guilt, bargaining, or sadness. When discussing these feelings, the facilitator shares personal feelings and recollections, as the ending of the group has meaning for the facilitator as well. The facilitator can provide a model that may help members to express both their positive and negative concerns about the group ending. A problem-solving approach may be used to alleviate concerns; for example, if a group member is apprehensive about future problems, the facilitator might provide the member with several other counseling resources.

The ending process should provide enough time for the facilitator and the members to sort out their feelings and use the ending productively. A sudden ending cuts short necessary work and may not allow enough time for members to work through feelings and complete the remaining work. Sometimes, members indirectly express their anger by arriving late, appearing apathetic, being sarcastic, or battling over minor issues. In these situations the facilitator should respond directly to the indirect cues by saying something like, "I wonder if your recent critical remarks are related to your anger that this group is ending? I know you have invested a lot in this group and may dislike that our meetings are coming to an end." By helping members to recognize and articulate their feelings, a facilitator can help them express and work through them. Once such feelings are dealt with, members will be more productive during the remaining time.

At or near the end of a group, members may test new skills and do things independently. They may report having tackled a tough problem or dealt with an issue by themselves. The facilitator should acknowledge their independence and make positive remarks about the members' ability to "go it alone."

At times, the facilitator may be the person leaving the group, perhaps to take a job elsewhere. In this situation, the facilitator should create a smooth transition. If appropriate, involve the members in selecting the new leader. It may be helpful for the former leader and the new leader to be coleaders for a brief period.

The ending of a group is a transition to something else. The important element during the ending phase of a group is to work with all members to help them develop a game plan so that the transition enables them to work toward new goals. The transition should not stifle members; rather, it should help them to progress. It may be valuable to note that life is full of transitions and passages: from early childhood to kindergarten; from kindergarten to elementary school; from childhood to puberty; from puberty to dating; from school to the work world; from being single to being married; from having responsibility only for oneself to becoming a parent; from working to retirement; and so on. In a transition phase we have the potential to make choices that will affect our future; the choices we make and the efforts we put forth determine whether the transition is constructive or destructive for us. Helping each member to make productive, realistic plans for the future is a goal of the ending phase of many groups.

During the process of terminating a group, it is important that the facilitator spend time obtaining feedback on how to improve future groups. Usually this is done by having members fill out a brief evaluation at the last or next-to-last session. This evaluation is done anonymously by the members. The following questions apply to a variety of treatment groups. For the first seven questions use the following scale: (1) Strongly disagree, (2) Disagree, (3) Neutral or uncertain, (4) Agree, (5) Strongly agree.

1. I am very satisfied with what this group accomplished.

    1   2   3   4   5

2. My personal goals in this group have been attained.

    1   2   3   4   5

3. I truly enjoyed being a member of this group.

    1   2   3   4   5

4. The facilitator has done a superb job in leading the group.

    1   2   3   4   5

5. This has been one of the most rewarding groups I have participated in.
   1   2   3   4   5
6. I have grown extensively as a person through participating in this group.
   1   2   3   4   5
7. I have made substantial progress in resolving those personal problems that led me to join this group.
   1   2   3   4   5

The next three questions are open-ended:

8. The strengths of this group are:
9. The shortcomings of this group are:
10. My suggestions for changes in this group are:

Case Example: Therapy Group for Spouses of Adults with Cancer

Eight years ago Linda Sonsthagen's husband was diagnosed with cancer. Linda was a social worker, and her husband was a successful life insurance agent. They had two sons in grade school. Mr. Sonsthagen died four and a half years ago, after having gone through a variety of treatment programs and through considerable pain. He lost weight and his hair fell out. These years were extremely difficult for the Sonsthagens. Linda had to take a larger role in raising the children and was the primary caregiver to both her husband and the children. During these years, the Sonsthagens found that relatives and friends shied away from them—it took several months before they became aware that the reason was that friends and relatives saw cancer as something they didn't understand and wanted to avoid. Even more difficult was dealing emotionally with not knowing the course of the disorder, going through cycles of hope and then disappointment as different treatment approaches were tried. As her husband became more incapacitated, Linda found she had to assume more of his tasks—for example, home repairs, maintaining their two cars, disciplining the children, and other daily household tasks.

After her husband's death, Linda and the two children went through several months of mourning and grief. Linda also discovered it was somewhat awkward to go to social functions alone. Fortunately she had two single female friends with whom she increasingly socialized. These were very difficult years for Linda. She needed over two years after her husband's death to rebuild her life in such a way that she was again comfortable.

During these years she received some financial help from the local chapter of the American Cancer Society. She also met through this society another woman whose husband was dying of cancer. They gave each other emotional support and shared useful ideas for handling problems.

Eighteen months ago Linda proposed to the local chapter of the American Cancer Society that she was willing to volunteer her time to start a group for spouses of people with cancer and for spouses adjusting to a recent cancer death. The American Cancer Society gave their approval and endorsement.

Linda started with nine members. The objectives were to give emotional support, to help members handle the new responsibilities they had to take on, and to help them deal with their emotional reactions. Linda used primarily a combination of reality therapy and rational therapy (see Modules 1 and 3). Reality therapy helped the group members better understand and make decisions and plans for the problems they faced. For example, for the members whose spouses had cancer, one focus was how to inform and handle their friends' and relatives' reactions to illness. Survivors focused on rebuilding their lives. Rational therapy countered unwanted emotions. Common emotions included depression, guilt, anxiety, the feeling of being overwhelmed, and anger (particularly resulting from "Why does this have to happen to me?"). Members were instructed on how to do rational self-analysis (RSA; see Module 1) on their unwanted emotions, and members often shared and discussed their RSAs at group meetings.

Group members stated on several occasions that the group was very helpful. They mentioned that knowing others faced similar plights was beneficial in and of itself. Seeing how others handled difficult decisions inspired them and gave them useful ideas on how to handle crises they faced. When a member suffered a serious crisis (for example, a spouse hospitalized for a serious operation), other members were available for telephone contact and to lend physical assistance.

After eight months the local chapter of the American Cancer Society was so encouraged by the results that Linda was offered a full-time position to run additional groups and to be available for individual counseling for people with cancer and their relatives. Linda gave up her part-time job as a social worker at the YWCA and took this position. Her first effort was to divide her group, which was growing, into two groups. The definition of eligible membership was also expanded: One group was for adults who have a family member with cancer and the other for survivors. At this time Linda is leading one group of the first type and two groups of the second type.

At the final session, it is also desirable for the members to discuss what they got out of the group, the merits of the group, and suggestions for improving it. Members should be given a chance to bring up unfinished business. In some cases an extra session may be held to complete unfinished business items.

One final important suggestion will be given. Occasionally, a facilitator refers an individual to another group or facilitator or discusses a group member with another professional facilitator. The reason may be (1) the facilitator feels that he or she is unable to empathize with that group member; (2) the facilitator has extreme personal difficulty in accepting the fact that a member is choosing alternatives that the facilitator finds disgusting (such as continuing to abuse a family member); (3) the member's problems are of such a nature that the facilitator feels unable to provide the therapeutic help; and/or (4) a working relationship is not established with the member. A competent facilitator knows that he or she can work with and help some people, but not all. It may be in an individual's and a facilitator's best interests to refer a group member to someone else who can help.

CO-FACILITATING TREATMENT GROUPS

Even though many settings do not have the resources to allow two leaders to facilitate a group, some programs can afford this type of group facilitation. Also, many students in internships are given opportunities to co-facilitate groups with either their field instructor or some other professional at their agency. The co-facilitator approach has many advantages, including the following:

- Each facilitator can grow from working with, observing, and learning from the other.
- Group members can benefit from the different life experiences, insights, and perspectives of the two facilitators.
- The two facilitators can complement each other, thereby benefiting the group.
- The two facilitators can provide valuable feedback to each other by discussing what happened in a session and how to approach a complex issue.
- The two facilitators can serve as models for the members with respect to how they relate to and communicate with each other and to the group.
- If one of the leaders is female and the other is male, barriers that some members have involving gender can be more effectively confronted, explored, and resolved.
- While one facilitator is working with a particular member, the other facilitator can scan the group to get a sense of how the other members are reacting.
- Co-facilitating offers a certain safety, especially when practitioners are leading a group for the first time, as it is typical for beginning group facilitators to experience self-doubt and anxiety. Facing a group for the first time with a co-facilitator whom you respect and trust can turn what initially seems a frightening task into a delightful learning experience.

It should be noted that major disadvantages to co-facilitating a group occur when the facilitators fail to develop and maintain an effective working relationship with one another. To develop such a working relationship, it is essential that the two facilitators respect each other. The two facilitators are likely to have some differences in leadership style and may not always agree on or share the same perceptions and interpretations. However, when there is mutual respect, they will generally be able to communicate and discuss these differences, trust each other, and work cooperatively instead of competitively. If trust and respect between the facilitators are lacking, the members are bound to sense disharmony and the group is apt to be negatively affected. Power struggles between two incompatible co-facilitators may divide the group. Friction between the two facilitators can serve as a model for the other members to focus on negatives within the group and to subtly or overtly verbally hurt one another.

It is important for group facilitators to learn whom they can co-facilitate with and whom they cannot. Even secure, competent, and experienced facilitators who respect one another may not be able to work effectively together if their styles clash. For example, a facilitator who believes in leading by giving a great many suggestions aimed at providing quick answers for every problem expressed by group members is likely to clash with a facilitator who believes members best learn and grow by struggling and arriving at their own answers to their personal issues. If two facilitators discover that they cannot effectively work together, it does not necessarily mean that one is right and the other wrong or that one or both are incompetent. It may simply mean that their styles clash and that each would be better off making arrangements to work with someone who has a similar style.

It is important for co-facilitators to get together regularly (ideally shortly after the end of each session) to discuss where the group has come and where the group needs to go. Additional areas to be discussed include how the facilitators view the group and the individual members, how the facilitators feel about working with each other, and how to approach any complex issues that have arisen related to the group. The facilitators also need to make plans for the next session.

LEGAL SAFEGUARDS FOR GROUP FACILITATORS

Unfortunately, filing lawsuits has become a national pastime. To avoid a malpractice suit or to provide a defense if a lawsuit arises, a group facilitator should maintain reasonable, ordinary, and prudent (marked by wisdom or judiciousness) practices. Following are some guidelines for group leaders that are useful in translating the terms *reasonable*, *ordinary*, and *prudent* into concrete actions:

- Screen candidates for a group experience carefully. Many potential problems can be avoided by effective screening practices. The facilitator should select group members whose needs and goals are compatible with the goals of the group, who will not impede the group process, and whose well-being will not be jeopardized by the group experience.
- Adequately inform the members about the group process. Entrance procedures, time parameters of the group experience, expectations of group participation, goals of the group, intervention methods that will be used, rights of members, responsibilities of members and facilitator, methods of payment (where appropriate), and termination procedures should be explained at the outset of the group.
- Obtain written parental consent when working with minors.
- Obtain written informed-consent procedures at the outset of a group. Contracts signed by both the facilitator and the members are an example of such a procedure.
- Have a clear rationale for the techniques and exercises you employ in group sessions.
- Be prepared to concisely explain and defend the theoretical underpinnings of your techniques and exercises.
- Consult with your supervisor or an attorney on issues involving complex legal and ethical matters.
- Avoid becoming entangled in social relationships with group participants.
- Be aware of those situations in which you are legally required to break confidentiality.
- Carry malpractice insurance.
- Actively engage in keeping up with the theoretical and research developments that have a direct application to group therapy.
- Be knowledgeable about, and abide by, the codes of ethics for social workers. (In the United States, refer to the *National Association of Social Workers [NASW] Code of* Ethics, and in Canada refer to the Canadian Association of Social Workers' *Code of Ethics*.)
- Be aware of when it is appropriate to refer a group member for another form of treatment, and also be aware when group therapy might be inadvisable.
- Instruct members on how to evaluate their progress toward their individual goals. Also, routinely assess the general progress of the group.
- Write and maintain adequate records on the needs and goals of each member and the progress (or lack of it) made by each member in the group.
- Avoid promising members magical cures. Create reasonable expectations about what the group can and cannot achieve.
- Practice within the boundaries of your state and local laws.

- If you work for an agency, have a contract that specifies the agency's legal liability for your professional functioning.
- Abide by the policies of the agency that employs you. If you strongly disagree with agency policies and if they interfere with your ability to do your job, seek first to change these policies. If the policies cannot be changed, consider resigning.
- Define clearly to the members what confidentiality means and why it is important, and emphasize that what the members disclose must be kept confidential—even though the members should be aware that confidentiality cannot be guaranteed because some members may intentionally or unintentionally breach confidentiality.

LO 3   Set Professional Boundaries with Clients

EP 1a
EP 1b

SETTING PROFESSIONAL BOUNDARIES WITH CLIENTS

Is it appropriate for a social worker to have lunch or dinner with a client? Is it appropriate to attend a party where alcoholic drinks are being served where clients may be present? Is it appropriate to hug a client who is experiencing emotional distress? These are examples of boundary questions that arise in interactions with clients. Over the years I have seen a number of social workers and a number of social work interns subjected to severe disciplinary actions for failing to establish and maintain appropriate professional boundaries with clients. For example, a female intern was terminated at her field placement in a halfway house for chemically addicted correctional residents after she began dating one of the residents. A male social worker in a high school was dismissed for relating sexually explicit stories to the female clients he was working with.

Social workers have an obligation to establish appropriate boundaries in professional relationships with clients. The Canadian Association of Social Workers' *Code of Ethics* contains the following statements on these boundary issues:

> A social worker shall not exploit the relationship with a client for personal benefit, gain, or gratification.
>
> A social worker shall not become involved in a client's personal affairs that are not relevant to the service being provided.
>
> The social worker shall distinguish between actions and statements made as a private citizen and actions and statements made as a social worker.
>
> The social worker shall not have a sexual relationship with a client.
>
> The social worker shall not have a business relationship with a client, borrow money from a client, or loan money to a client.[6]

The NASW *Code of Ethics* contains these statements on boundary issues:

> Social workers should not take unfair advantage of any professional relationship or exploit others to further their personal, religious, political, or business interests.
>
> Social workers should not engage in dual or multiple relationships with clients or former clients in which there is a risk of exploitation or potential harm to the client. In instances when dual or multiple relationships are unavoidable, social workers should take steps to protect clients and are responsible for setting clear, appropriate, and culturally sensitive boundaries. (Dual or multiple relationships occur when social workers relate to clients in more than one relationship, whether professional, social, or business. Dual or multiple relationships can occur simultaneously or consecutively.)
>
> Social workers should under no circumstances engage in sexual activities or sexual contact with current clients, whether such contact is consensual or forced.
>
> Social workers should not engage in activities or sexual contact with clients' relatives or other individuals with whom clients maintain a close, personal relationship where there is a risk of exploitation or potential harm to the client. Sexual activity or sexual contact with clients'

EXERCISE 12.5   Boundaries with Clients

GOAL: This exercise is designed to assist you in determining appropriate boundaries with clients.

1. Is it ever appropriate for a worker to ask a client if she or he would like a hug? If you answer "yes," specify when it would be appropriate.

2. Are there situations where it would be appropriate for a social worker to go to lunch or dinner with a client? If you answer "yes," specify what those situations would be.

3. A social worker who facilitates a treatment group also has rental property. One of the clients in the group makes an offer to rent an apartment from the worker. What should the worker do?

4. You are a social worker at a high school. You are single but have been dating someone for three years. A 16-year-old niece of the person you are sexually involved with is a student at this school and comes to your office asking for counseling assistance for some personal dilemmas she is facing. Should you counsel her?

relatives or other individuals with whom clients maintain a personal relationship has the potential to be harmful to the client and may make it difficult for the social worker and client to maintain appropriate professional boundaries. Social workers—not their clients, their clients' relatives, or other individuals with whom the client maintains a professional relationship— assume the full burden for setting clear, appropriate, and culturally sensitive boundaries.

Social workers should not engage in sexual activities or sexual contact with former clients because of the potential for harm to the client.

Social workers should not provide clinical services to individuals with whom they have had a prior sexual relationship.

Social workers should not engage in physical contact with clients where there is a possibility of psychological harm to the client as a result of the contact (such as cradling or caressing clients). Social workers who engage in appropriate physical contact with clients are responsible for setting clear, appropriate, and culturally sensitive boundaries that govern such physical contact.[7]

It is impossible to develop additional guidelines that will answer all the questions that may arise when social workers set boundaries with clients. The following guidelines may be useful in resolving some boundary dilemmas:

- In your professional *and* personal life, try to be a role model for the values and principles of the social work profession.
- In relationships with clients, try to gain their respect and to exemplify the values and principles of the social work profession, rather than establish a friend-to-friend relationship.
- Never try to meet your personal needs or wants in relationships with clients.
- Try to increase your awareness of your own needs, feelings, values, and limitations so you become increasingly aware of how such factors may affect client relationships.
- When questions arise about the appropriateness of certain interactions with a client (such as whether to go to lunch), try to arrive at an answer by gauging whether the interaction will have a constructive impact on the client and your relationship. If a concrete beneficial impact cannot be objectively specified, do not engage in the interaction.
- Constructive professional relationships with clients require a certain amount of distance. If you have questions about whether contemplated social interactions will interfere with the boundaries of a professional relationship, consult your supervisor or a respected colleague.
- In your professional social work role with clients, be aware of any inappropriate behavior, inappropriate verbal communications, and inappropriate clothing on your part. For example, sharing details of your wild parties with teenage clients is unprofessional.

LO 4 Understand the Therapeutic Factors of Treatment Groups

THE THERAPEUTIC FACTORS: WHAT IT IS THAT HEALS

What are the therapeutic factors that lead to positive changes in clients who receive group treatment? The definitive factors are not yet fully known. This section will present two different frameworks, the first formulated by Dr. Albert Ellis, who developed rational therapy, and the second advanced by Dr. Irvin Yalom, a prominent group therapist.

Ellis asserts that any therapy technique that changes unwanted emotions or destructive actions is effective primarily because it changes a person's thinking from self-talk that is negative or irrational to self-talk that is more rational and positive. This approach is described at considerable length in Appendix 1: Module 1.

Yalom lists 12 factors that he thinks lead to positive changes in clients who receive group treatment (see Figure 12.1)[8]:

FIGURE 12.1   **Twelve Factors that Facilitate Positive Changes via Group Therapy**
   (According to Dr. Irvin Yalom)

1. *Instillation of hope:* Members are inspired and their expectations raised by contact with other group members who have trod the same path and then improved their lives.

2. *Universality:* Many members enter treatment with the erroneous notion that they are unique in their pain and suffering. Group treatment assists members in discovering that others have similar problems and have made progress in resolving their problems and improving their lives via group treatment.

3. *Imparting information:* Members receive useful information (including advice, suggestions, and direct guidance) from either the group leader or other group members. Members learn about psychic functioning, the meaning of symptoms, interpersonal and group dynamics, the process of treatment, and how to solve their problems more effectively.

4. *Altruism:* This concept is similar to the helper therapy principle. Members at times interchange roles and become the helper for someone else, which helps members put their own problems into perspective. Helping others makes a person feel good and worthwhile. Another, more subtle benefit of the altruistic act is that it gives additional meaning to life, particularly for those who complain of meaninglessness.

5. *The corrective recapitulation of the primary family group:* Many members in group treatment have a highly unsatisfactory experience in their primary family. Group treatment facilitates members gaining a better understanding of traumatic family experiences that occurred in the past. Members can interact with leaders and other members in ways reminiscent of how they once interacted with parents and siblings. Group treatment provides an opportunity for early familial conflicts to be relived and healed.

6. *Development of socializing techniques:* Social learning occurs in all treatment groups. Members receive social feedback from other members about their strengths and the challenges they need to work on. There are opportunities to try out more functional behaviors, for example, to be assertive instead of aggressive or nonassertive, or to be more communicative of one's thoughts and feelings, which is particularly beneficial for those with a pattern of being noncommunicative. Members also learn how to listen more effectively and to respond more helpfully to others. Many members learn methods of conflict resolution. Opportunities also exist for members to experience and express empathy.

7. *Imitative behavior:* Group leaders and other group members model constructive behavior (such as problem-solving skills, being assertive, being empathetic, being supportive) that is often imitated by members with issues in these areas. This phenomenon is sometimes referred to as *vicarious* or *spectator* treatment.

8. *Catharsis:* Group treatment provides members with an opportunity to ventilate. Through venting their feelings, fears, past traumatic events, and concerns, members gain a release of anxiety or tension, which often improves functioning. In groups, strong expression of emotions almost always enhances the development of group cohesiveness.

9. *Existential factors:* Members learn that there is a limit to the guidance they can get from others and that they bear the ultimate responsibility for their lives. They learn that everyone is thrown into the world alone and must die alone. Such isolation is partially countered by learning there is deep comfort and meaning to life through relating intimately to fellow travelers in the world.

10. *Group cohesiveness:* Considerable research indicates that positive changes in members are much more likely to occur when the treatment atmosphere creates trust, warmth, empathic understanding, and acceptance. In order for members to feel comfortable in revealing (and solving) their problems, it is essential that they trust other group members not to reveal their disclosures outside the group.

11. *Interpersonal learning:* The need to relate closely to others is as basic as any biological need and is equally necessary for survival. Many members have treatment goals of improving their interpersonal relationships. Group treatment often facilitates learning to communicate more effectively with others, to be more trusting and honest with others, and to learn to love.

12. *The group as social microcosm:* The group gradually becomes a microcosm of the world the participant members live in. Over time, group members begin to be themselves. They gradually interact with the other group members as they interact with others in their social sphere. Members will inevitably begin to display their maladaptive interpersonal behavior in the treatment group, presenting an opportunity for the leader and other group members to help that member acknowledge the maladaptive behavior. Furthermore, the other group members and the leader can assist that member to problem-solve and explore interacting with others in more functional ways.

SOURCE: Yalom, I. D. (1998). The therapeutic factors: What it is that heals. In *The Yalom Reader* (pp. 5–41). New York: Basic Books.

EXERCISE 12.6   What Causes Positive Changes through Counseling

GOAL: This exercise is designed to assist you in arriving at your conclusions as to what causes people with emotional issues or behavioral issues to make positive changes through counseling.

It is critical that social workers have an awareness of what causes positive changes in clients through counseling. We need to know the components that cause positive changes in counseling so that we will be certain to apply these when we are counseling someone. Rational therapy, developed by Ellis (see Appendix 1: Module 1), presents one explanation. Yalom, in the preceding material, presents another. Review these two explanations and then specify what you believe causes people with emotional or behavioral issues to make positive changes through counseling.

LO 5   Comprehend the Merits and Shortcomings of Evidence-Based Practice

EP 4a
EP 4b
EP 4c

SELECTING INTERVENTION STRATEGIES: EVIDENCE-BASED PRACTICE

In recent years, evidence-based practice (EBP) has become increasingly prominent in social work practice. EBP is the use of the best available scientific knowledge as one basis for guiding professional interventions and effective therapies, combined with professional ethical standards, clinical judgment, and practice wisdom.

EBP is an ideology (that is, a systematic body of concepts). The movement began in such disciplines as medicine, nursing, psychology, and social work to identify "treatments that work," using the results of research evidence. Another important aspect of EBP is to identify and end treatments that do harm to clients/patients. EBP seeks to supplement professional decision making with the latest research knowledge. It also seeks to provide beginning professionals with effective treatment strategies and a model for the continuing improvement and renewal of their professional practices.

Some EBP advocates argue that to treat anyone using treatments without known effectiveness is unethical. Also, some advocates assert that if one treatment program works better than other available treatment approaches, professionals have an ethical obligation to use it in order to best serve clients/patients.

Advocates of EBP have also asserted that only interventions with demonstrated effectiveness should be supported financially. Such an assertion links demonstrations of effectiveness with funding through managed care systems.[9]

There are seven steps in EBP:

Step 1: The professional first of all needs to be motivated to use EBP. On one hand, a professional may be motivated to use EBP because the approach fosters using effective treatment strategies. However, if a managed care system mandates the use of EBP, the professional may resent forced use.

Step 2: The professional needs to formulate a clear and answerable question that is based on the client's problems and needs. The question should cover such aspects as diagnosis, likely results of various treatment strategies, side effects, prognosis, likely benefits, and costs. An example of a question is "What are the most effective strategies to treat a 44-year-old recently divorced male who has a bipolar disorder?"

Step 3: Search the literature for relevant research that could help answer the question. EBP places greatest credibility on randomized control trials (RCTs). An RCT is an experiment in which participants are randomly assigned to either a treatment group or a control group. Ideally, neither the participant nor the treating professional knows which group is which. After a course of treatment (or control), improvement is measured by comparing pretreatment status with posttreatment status. If the treated group improves significantly more than the control group, the conclusion is that the treatment works (that is, it is better than no treatment).

Step 4: Carefully and critically appraise the research information for its validity and applicability to the client's needs and circumstances. Also to be considered in this appraisal process are (a) the client's wishes and needs (both stated and implicit) and (b) the professional's competencies to apply the various treatment strategies.

Step 5: Formulate and apply an intervention based on the appraisal in Step 4. The selected intervention is based on what has been called the "best available evidence."

Step 6: Monitor the intervention to verify that it was applied appropriately, and evaluate the benefits and side effects.

Step 7: The professional shares the results with others in order to add to the "best available evidence."

Some social work authorities have expressed concerns about an overemphasis on using EBP.[10] These concerns will be summarized here.

If EBP dictates what interventions will be used with clients, it takes the decision making away from the client and the social worker, denying the client's right to self-determination. EBP asserts that only *proven* intervention approaches should be used with clients, which may discourage the social worker and a client from trying an innovative (unproven) approach.

EBP tends to ignore one of the hallmarks of good social work practice: individualizing clients. Social workers do not simply treat the problem; they build a therapeutic relationship, identifying needs, goals, and resources as well as emphasizing mutuality in the relational context.

The relationship between worker and client, the therapeutic alliance, has been demonstrated to have significant influences across numerous studies.[11] Thus, nearly half of the outcome relies on fundamental skills and abilities that must be fostered in social workers, apart from the type of treatment offered. The therapeutic alliance has long been identified as the key to successful outcomes for clients. In fact, research on intervention outcomes suggest that four factors can account for much of the improvement in clients: client or extra-therapeutic factors (40%); relationship factors (30%); placebo, hope, and expectancy factors (15%); and model/technique factors (only 15%).[12] We need to ensure that social workers are learning to build these therapeutic relationships as a proven intervention.

EBP asserts the intervention approaches that are used should be based on the assessment/diagnosis of the client's symptoms and issues. EBP may work well in medicine, where the client's symptoms and issues are largely biological in nature. However, symptoms and issues of social work clients are more complex, involving bio/psycho/social/cultural/spiritual/environmental variables. Therefore, assessments and diagnoses of clients are a more inexact science than in medicine. With an inexact assessment/diagnosis in social work, it is much more difficult to identify the best EBP approach.

Summary

The following summarizes the chapter's content in terms of the learning objectives presented at the beginning of the chapter.

1. Start, lead, and end treatment groups.
   Treatment groups are designed to facilitate improvement in members who have emotional, behavioral, or interpersonal challenges. Numerous aspects are covered, including preparation and homework, relaxing before starting a session, cues upon entering the meeting room, seating arrangements, introductions, clarifying roles, building rapport, exploring problems in depth, exploring alternative solutions, stages of development, strategies for working with hostile members, ending a session, and ending a group.

2. Comprehend the therapeutic technique of motivational interviewing.
   One of the biggest reality shocks of a "new" social worker is that many, perhaps most, clients are simply not motivated to make the necessary changes to improve their emotional and physical well-being. Motivational interviewing has a number of conceptual suggestions on how social workers can inspire clients to want to make improvements in their lives.

3. Set professional boundaries with clients.
   Social workers have an obligation to establish appropriate boundaries in professional relationships with clients. The Code of Ethics of NASW and the Canadian Association of Social Workers' Code of Ethics have a number of guidelines for social workers in setting appropriate boundaries with clients.

4. Understand the therapeutic factors of treatment groups.
   What are the therapeutic factors that lead to positive changes in clients who receive group treatment? The definitive factors are not yet fully known. This chapter presents two different frameworks, the first formulated by Dr. Albert Ellis, who developed rational therapy, and the second advanced by Dr. Irvin Yalom, a prominent group therapist.
   Ellis asserts that any therapy technique that changes unwanted emotions or destructive actions is effective primarily because it changes a person's thinking from self-talk that is negative or irrational to self-talk that is more rational and positive. Yalom lists 12 factors that he thinks lead to positive changes in clients who receive group treatment.

5. Comprehend the merits and shortcomings of evidence-based practice.
   Evidence-based practice advocates using treatments that research has documented are beneficial. Furthermore, it urges that treatments that do harm to clients should be terminated. One shortcoming of evidence-based practice is that it may discourage a social worker from trying an innovative (unproven) approach.

Group Exercises

EXERCISE A: Developing Counseling Skills with Role-Playing

GOAL: To develop counseling skills through role-playing.

Step 1. The leader summarizes the following five phases of group counseling: (1) starting the meeting; (2) building a relationship; (3) exploring problems in depth; (4) exploring alternative solutions with clients and then trying one or more of the alternatives; and (5) ending the meeting. The purpose of the exercise is explained.

Step 2. Two students volunteer to play the role of clients with personal problems. These two students may be allowed to come up with their own contrived problem or be given one. A nearly infinite number of personal problems is possible, for example:

1. Two siblings are concerned about their dad living alone. Dad's wife recently died, and he has difficulty in getting around because of his arthritis. He tends to be gruff and not easy to live with.
2. A married couple has three children and is fairly content. The wife, however, wants to be a surrogate mother for a couple who wants a child. The husband does not want his wife to be a surrogate.
3. Two males or females have become sexually involved with each other. They do not know what the future will hold for their relationship and wonder whether they should inform their close friends and relatives.
4. A wife sometimes becomes so irritated at her two children that she physically abuses them. The husband wants the abuse to stop, but does not know why the abuse is occurring or what he can do to prevent it.
5. One person who does not drink is concerned that his friend has a drinking problem. The second person denies a problem exists. Both are seeking counseling to resolve this conflict.
6. A 16-year-old girl has informed her mother that sexual relations have been occurring frequently for the past three years with her stepfather. The mother is shocked; the teenager is embarrassed and afraid. Both are seeking counseling on how they can emotionally cope and what they should do.

Step 3. The group leader may do the counseling or ask one or two students to role-play the counselor. (If the group leader does the counseling, she or he should not be told what situation is being role-played prior to the interview.) It is useful to have two counselors for the role-play, so that one counselor isn't "stuck" not knowing what to say.

Step 4. Role-play the interview.

Step 5. The class discusses the merits and shortcomings of the counseling. The counseling may be analyzed in terms of the guidelines presented in the chapter.

Step 6. Additional situations may be role-played and then discussed.

EXERCISE B: Group Treatment in Action

GOAL: To give an experiential awareness of being in a group treatment session.

Step 1. The leader announces that at the next class period, a simulated group treatment session will be conducted and states the goal of the exercise. Each student is given the homework assignment of identifying one or two personal problems that a friend or relative currently has. Students are told that they should not reveal the identity of the person having the problem and that the personal problem should be that of a friend or relative *and not of themselves.*

Step 2. At the next class period, the leader begins by stating ground rules:

Today, we will have a simulated group treatment session in order to give you an experiential awareness of being in group treatment. Because this is a class, I strongly request that you do not reveal any personal information about any dilemmas or difficulties you are experiencing. Instead, describe one or two complicated personal dilemmas that a friend or relative is currently facing. For confidentiality reasons, please do not reveal the identity of the person whose problems you talk about. Remember, for reasons of confidentiality, what is said here stays here. Are there any questions about what we are going to do or about the ground rules?

If there are questions, try to answer them.

Step 3. Ask students to begin sharing concerns being faced by a friend or relative. If the class is reluctant to start, the leader initiates the process by specifically asking a normally vocal student to begin. When a student is sharing, the leader encourages the other students to probe with questions in order to further explore the problem and then encourages them to suggest realistic and creative courses of action to resolve the problem. (In group treatment sessions, each member will at times take on the role of facilitator.)

Step 4. After the dilemma revealed by one student is fully discussed and problem-solved, other students share dilemmas that are currently being experienced by their friends and relatives. The exercise continues until the end of the class period or until no one has anything further to share. At the end of the exercise, students are asked their thoughts about the benefits and shortcomings of the exercise and their suggestions for changes in the format of the exercise when it is again used. During the exercise, one or more of the students may begin talking about a personal problem he or she is facing. The leader at this point has to make a judgment as to whether to let the student continue. The leader should not allow students to divulge personal information that they are apt to later regret sharing.

EXERCISE C: Facilitating an Intervention Group

EP 8a
EP 8b

GOAL: To have each student in class develop skills at leading intervention groups.

Step 1. The instructor states the purpose of the exercise and indicates that a component of most class sessions will be the students taking turns in facilitating an intervention group. The instructor demonstrates an approach to doing this by sharing a personal issue that he or she is currently dealing with or has dealt with in the past. Possible topics are nearly infinite: depression, grief management, ending a relationship, creative financing, stress management, assertiveness, resolving an interpersonal dispute, and so on. The instructor then asks if anyone in the group has experienced a similar issue and encourages volunteers to share. The instructor then asks the group for ideas (strategies) on how to resolve dilemmas that have been raised. The merits and shortcomings of these strategies are then discussed. The instructor ends the exercise by summarizing important points that were made during the exercise.

Step 2. The instructor passes out a sign-up sheet where each student selects a date in class to lead the group in a similar fashion to the previous example. Each student should take 15 to 20 minutes to lead the group. Each student is graded on a pass/fail basis by the instructor. Those students who do not pass at first are given additional opportunities to lead a group in later class sessions. The instructor should inform those students who have to lead another session what they need to work on to improve. When students facilitate such intervention groups, it is advisable for the instructor to sit outside the circle of students so that the students attend to the facilitator rather than to the instructor. When sitting outside the circle, the instructor should evaluate the facilitator's strengths, note areas needing attention, and provide suggestions for changes. The instructor also informs the facilitator whether she or he has passed or whether another session has to be led. If someone should continue not to receive a passing grade after several tries, the student and instructor should meet privately to explore options. (Because it is important for social work students to be able to facilitate intervention groups, the instructor may choose to require that students receive a passing grade on this exercise in order to receive a passing grade in the class.)

Note: During these intervention exercises, two ground rules must be strictly followed:

1. Confidentiality— "What is said here, stays here" and should not be revealed outside the class.
2. Emotional safety—If someone begins to share and feels his or her disclosure is becoming too personal, the student should say, "This is becoming too personal," and there should be no group pressure for that person to say more.

EXERCISE D: Who Am I?

EP 1b

GOAL: To develop an improved sense of who you are and what you want out of life. (This exercise is sometimes used in treatment groups.)

Step 1. The leader indicates that the questions "Who am I?" and "What do I want out of life?" are probably the most important we will ever have to answer. Identity is the most important psychological need of an individual. Although the past has brought us to where we currently are, what we want out of the future, along with our motivation to achieve our goals, is more important than our past experiences in determining what our future will be.

Forming an identity essentially involves thinking about, and arriving at, answers to the following questions:

1. What do I want out of life?
2. What kind of person do I want to be?
3. Who am I?

These questions are not easily answered because they require considerable conscious contemplation and trial and error. However, the answers are important to the person who wants to lead a gratifying, fulfilling life based on direction and meaning. Without answers, individuals may muddle through life being passive responders to situations that arise, rather than continual achievers of their life's goals. To assist an individual in arriving at a sense of who he or she is and what he or she wants out of life, a series of more specific questions follows. As a person arrives at answers to these specific questions, he or she will simultaneously be arriving at an increased sense of personal identify.

Step 2. The leader distributes the following questions on a handout, with space for the students to write down their answers. The students take 20 to 30 minutes to outline their answers.

1. What do I find satisfying/meaningful/enjoyable? (Only after you identify what is meaningful and gratifying will you be able to be consciously involved in activities that will make your life fulfilling and avoid those activities that are meaningless or stifling.)
2. What is my moral code? (One possible code is to attempt to fulfill your needs and to find enjoyable experiences, as long as you do so in a way that does not deprive others of the ability to fulfill their needs.)
3. What are my religious beliefs?
4. What kind of career do I desire? (Ideally, such a career should be stimulating and satisfying to you and provide you with enough money to support your chosen lifestyle.) Also, what do I enjoy doing during my leisure time?
5. What are my sexual mores? (All of us should develop a consistent "comfortable" code that meets our needs without exploiting others. There is no one right code—what works for one may not work for another because of differences in lifestyles, life goals, and personal values.)
6. Do I wish to marry? (If yes, to what type of person and when? How consistent are your answers here with your other life goals?)
7. Do I want to have children? (If yes, how many and when? How congruent are these answers with other life goals?) .
8. What area of the country or world do I want to live in? (Variables to be considered are climate, geography, type of dwelling, rural or urban setting, closeness to relatives or friends, and characteristics of the neighborhood.)
9. What kind of image do I want to project to others? (A person's image is projected by style of clothes, grooming habits, emotions, personality, degree of assertiveness, capacity to

communicate, material possessions, moral code, physical features, and voice patterns. Strengths and shortcomings should be assessed honestly in this area and improvements made.)

10. What type of people do I enjoy being with, and why?
11. Do I hope to improve the quality of my life and that of others? If yes, in what ways? How can these goals be achieved?
12. What type of relationships do I want to have with relatives, friends, neighbors, and people I meet for the first time?
13. What are my thoughts about death and dying?
14. What do I hope to be doing 5 years, 10 years, 20 years from now?

Step 3. The leader asks for volunteers to summarize what they wrote down.

Step 4. The leader may end this exercise by summarizing the following. To establish a fairly well-developed sense of identity, group members need to have answers to most of these questions. Although few individuals have rational, consistent answers to every question, having answers to most of them will provide a reference for arriving at answers to questions that are as yet unanswered.

Honest, well-thought-out answers to these questions will assist members in defining their identity. Again, leaders should remind members that what a person wants out of life, along with his or her motivation to achieve these goals, will primarily determine his or her future. The foregoing questions are simple to state, but arriving at answers is a complicated, ongoing process. In addition, changes in life goals should be expected periodically. Just as group goals have to be continually reevaluated, an individual's identity has to be reassessed as short-term and long-term goals are reached. Environmental influences such as changes in working conditions and personal growth alter an individual's beliefs, attitudes, and values. If changes are accepted and a person's identity remains intact, life goals can be redefined so that continued direction predominates.

EXERCISE E: The Miracle Workers

GOAL: To identify physical and material characteristics that are important to you. (This exercise may be used in a treatment group.)

Step 1. The leader explains the purpose of the exercise, distributes on a handout the descriptions that follow, and explains to the students that their first task is to choose four miracle workers whose miracles they would most like to have.

THE MIRACLE WORKERS

The following group of miracle workers have gotten together and graciously decided to provide four of the following services to you. Whichever services you select, you are guaranteed to be 100% satisfied with them. It is up to you to select the four authorities whose services you most desire,

1. *Dr. Jean Olympic:* A famous athlete, she can make you an outstanding athlete in any one sport that you choose. If you select a well-paying sport, you will be guaranteed fame and fortune.
2. *Dr. Jane Adams:* A well-known social worker, she will train you to become a highly competent social worker, and you will gain a national reputation for your outstanding work.
3. *Dr. Joshua Methuselah:* This renowned gerontologist guarantees you a long life (beyond the age of 300) with the aging process slowed way down. For example, at age 100 you will look and feel like 25.
4. *Dr. Will Masters:* An expert in sexuality, he will guarantee you a perfectly happy sexual life. Every day or two, or as often as you wish, you will be in sexual heaven, without criticisms, without hassles, and without fear of a venereal disease.
5. *Dr. "Pop" U. Larity:* This charming gentleman guarantees that you will always have close friends who are honest and sincere and whom you will always enjoy being with.
6. *Dr. Ben Spock:* A family therapist, Spock guarantees you a happy family life, both with your parents and your children.

7. *Dr. Mary Monroe:* This acting coach guarantees you a famous film career. You will win an Academy Award and will also have a long-term series on television.

8. *Dr. Abe Lincoln:* The political guru guarantees you that you will become president of the United States. Although you will have some political hassles, you will go down in history as one of our best presidents.

9. *Dr. Gore Geous:* A famous plastic surgeon will guarantee you that you will look the way you want to as long as you live. You can have the weight, height, color and kind of hair, and physical appearance that you want.

10. *Dr. Act U. Puncture:* A medical expert, he will guarantee you perfect health and protection from physical injury, as long as you live.

11. *Dr. Al Einstein:* A famous scientist, he will guarantee you creativity and very high intelligence. You will eventually make some scientific discoveries that will benefit all humankind.

12. *Dr. H. Hughes:* A billionaire will give you the skills to earn fantastic sums of money. You will become one of the richest people in the world.

13. *Dr. Sig Freud:* A famous psychiatrist will guarantee you freedom from emotional problems and a positive self-concept.

14. *Dr. John Paul:* A famous religious leader will guarantee you a life in which you follow moral and religious values. Also, if a heaven exists, you will be guaranteed a reservation.

15. *Dr. Jon Dewey:* A famous educator will guarantee that you will graduate with highest academic honors from college. After graduating from college you will be guaranteed a high-paying job and will always have the capacity to think rationally.

Step 2. After the students have made their choices, they form subgroups of four or five people and each subgroup selects the four miracles it most desires.

Step 3. After the subgroups have reached their decisions, a representative from each subgroup states the miracles his or her subgroup wants and the reasons they selected the miracles.

Step 4. The students discuss their feelings about this exercise. Did the students have strong feelings about a subgroup choosing some miracles that were not their personal choices? Did this exercise help them to determine what, is really important in their lives?

EXERCISE F: Clients I Would Find Difficult to Work With

EP 1b

GOAL: Help students identify clients they would find difficult to work with and explore ways to become more effective in providing services to such clients.

Step 1: Students are given a sheet listing the following clients and asked to rank order them from 1 to 10 (with "1" being the hardest to work with). Students are told not to put their names on this sheet.

_____ A man who is in an incestuous relationship with his two daughters
_____ A woman seeking an abortion
_____ A husband who is abusing his wife
_____ A transsexual person
_____ A woman who frequently makes racist statements
_____ A woman who is a lesbian
_____ A religious zealot
_____ A man who frequently swears
_____ A woman who frequently is angry and yells in counseling sessions
_____ A man who is having an extramarital affair

Step 2: The sheets are handed in and a volunteer lists the rankings on a board.

Step 3: The five clients ranked as most difficult are identified. A class discussion is held on:

● Why these five are viewed as most difficult
● What might constructively be done to enable the social worker to be more effective in providing services to such clients

EXERCISE G: Feeling Good about Ourselves

GOAL: To feel good about yourself.

Step 1. The leader states the purpose of the exercise and has the students form subgroups of 7 to 10 persons. The leader indicates that each student will take a turn completing the sentence: "I'm not perfect at_____, but I'm slowly getting better by_____."

Some examples: "I'm not perfect at taking a positive view of things that happen to me, but I'm getting better by staying calmer and refraining from reacting angrily when someone cracks a joke about me" and "I'm not perfect at being assertive in classes, but I'm getting better by seeking to say something in each class that I attend."

Step 2. The class should reassemble, and the students should then discuss the merits and short-comings of this exercise.

EXERCISE H: Self-Fulfilling Prophecies

GOAL: To become aware that positive thinking and negative thinking often lead to self-fulfilling prophecies.

NOTE: Students should not disclose personal information.

Step 1. The leader explains the purpose of this exercise. The leader describes self-fulfilling prophecies as follows:

> A self-fulfilling prophecy occurs when a person's expectation of the outcome of an event makes the outcome more likely to happen than would otherwise have been true. Self-fulfilling prophecies occur frequently. We expect to have a miserable time at a social affair; therefore, we put little effort into conversing with others and end up having a miserable time. If an individual expects a low grade on a statistics exam, she sees little value in studying hard and ends up doing poorly on the exam. A person who feels very anxious about a job interview may then botch the interview because of her negative or anxious attitude. If a friend tells us that we won't like the person we are about to meet, the meeting will be focused on detecting things we don't like about the person and we may end up disliking her.
>
> There are two types of self-fulfilling prophecies. One type occurs when a person's expectations influence his behavior. A student can "feed" on becoming anxious during a class presentation, for example, and fear that he won't present himself well. This thinking leads him to become nervous during the presentation, and he does indeed present himself poorly. Players on sports team are well aware that if they have a defeatist attitude they won't be able to perform to the full extent of their capacities and will in all probability lose their contests. On the other hand, if a person thinks in terms of positive outcomes, he usually gives it his "best shot," which, in turn, improves his chances of doing well.
>
> A second type of self-fulfilling prophecy occurs when another's expectations govern a person's actions. Robert Rosenthal and Lenore Jacobson summarize a dramatic study of a self-fulfilling prophecy in the field of education:
>
>> Twenty percent of the children in a certain elementary school were reported to their teachers as showing unusual potential for intellectual growth. The names of these 20 percent were drawn out of a hat. Eight months later these unusual or "magic" children showed significantly greater gains in IQ than did the remaining children who had not been singled out for the teacher's attention. The change in the teacher's expectations regarding the intellectual performance of these allegedly "special" children had led to an actual change in the intellectual performance of these randomly selected children.[13]
>
> Apparently, the teachers communicated to these children, "You're bright and have a great future in store," which these children then accepted into their

self-concept. With a more positive self-concept, these children apparently studied harder and felt better about themselves, which led them to make marked intellectual advances. (If a group leader can infuse this type of positive thinking during group sessions, individual members may respond accordingly.)

This second type of self-fulfilling prophecy fits closely with Cooky's "looking-glass self." Namely, people will largely determine who they are in terms of how others relate to them. Through the looking-glass process, an individual often ends up fulfilling the expectations others have of him or her. To a large extent, we all become what others expect of us.

It should be noted that although self-fulfilling prophecies are an important factor in determining behavior, they are not the only factor. For example, a person may think he will really have a good day tomorrow, but unexpected events (such as an automobile accident) may make the day one that he would rather have skipped entirely.

Step 2. Students write down three examples from a friend's or relative's life of how positive or negative thinking has led to self-fulfilling prophecies.

Step 3. The students form subgroups of three persons and share what they wrote.

Step 4. Reassemble the class. Each subgroup shares one or two examples with the whole class.

Step 5. The exercise can be ended by summarizing the merits and cautions (outlined in the chapter) of positive thinking.

Competency Notes

EP 8b Apply knowledge of human behavior and the social environment, person-in-environment, and other multidisciplinary theoretical frameworks in interventions with clients and constituencies. (pp.)

This chapter presents substantial material on how start, lead and end treatment groups.

EP 1b Use reflection and self-regulation to manage personal values and maintain professionalism in practice situations. (p.)

This exercise is designed to assist students in understanding the concerns of new members in becoming involved in a treatment group.

EP 1b Use reflection and self-regulation to manage personal values and maintain professionalism in practice situations. (p.)

This exercise is designed to have students reflect about what they need to work on in order to be able to co-facilitate a treatment group.

EP 1c Demonstrate professional demeanor in behavior; appearance; and oral, written, and electronic communication. (p.)

This exercise is designed to assist students in tactfully confronting a group member about something she or he needs to be aware of.

EP 1a Make ethical decisions by applying the standards of the NASW *Code of Ethics*, relevant laws and regulations, models for ethical decision making, ethical conduct of research, and additional codes of ethics as appropriate to context;

EP 1b Use refection and self-regulation to manage personal values and maintain professionalism in practice situations. (pp.)

This section presents material on setting professional boundaries with clients, partly based on the NASW *Code of Ethics*. An exercise is presented that is designed to assist students in setting appropriate boundaries with clients.

EP 4a   Use practice experience and theory to inform scientific inquiry and research;

EP 4b   Apply critical thinking to engage in analysis of quantitative and qualitative research methods and research findings.

EP 4c   Use and translate research evidence to inform and improve practice, policy, and service delivery. (pp.)

Evidence-based practice (EBP) is described. EBP uses practice experience to inform scientific inquiry, and it uses research evidence to inform practice.

EP 8a   Critically choose and implement interventions to achieve practice goals and enhance capacities of clients and constituencies.

EP 8b   Apply knowledge of human behavior and the social environment, person-in-environment, and other multidisciplinary theoretical frameworks in interventions with clients and constituencies. (pp.)

Exercises A, B, and C are designed to facilitate the development of counseling skills in students and to further develop their capacities to lead treatment groups.

EP 1b   Use reflection and self-regulation to manage personal values and maintain professionalism in practice situations. (p.)

This exercise is designed to help students develop an improved sense of who they are and what they want out of life.

EP 1b   Use reflection and self-regulation to manage personal values and maintain professionalism in practice situations. (p.)

This exercise is designed to help students identify clients they would find difficult to work with and explore ways to become more effective in providing services to such clients.

Key Terms and Concepts

Differentiation	Intimacy	Power and Control
Empathy	Preaffiliation	Separation

13

Treatment Groups with Diverse and Vulnerable Populations

LO 1 Comprehend the Process of Designing Treatment Groups for Current and Future Clients

EP 6a
EP 6b
EP 8a
EP 8b

INTRODUCTION

The ability to design treatment groups for a wide variety of diverse and vulnerable populations is a critical knowledge and skill that is essential for social workers to acquire. In addition to the needed knowledge and skills that were identified in the prior chapter on treatment groups, the following knowledge and skills are needed in designing groups with diverse and vulnerable populations:

a. A thorough knowledge of the specific population that a social worker is working with
b. An in-depth knowledge of how to use group work with that population
c. Skills in designing group treatment exercises with that population

This chapter is focused on facilitating the reader's abilities in this area by illustrating group treatment approaches with the following five populations: adolescents, people who have an eating disorder, individuals affected by domestic violence, people who are grieving, and older adults. If a reader is working with any of these populations in the future, the reader may well be able to directly utilize this material. If the reader is working with other populations than those covered in this chapter, it is anticipated these illustrations will provide a "model" that the reader will be able to use to design treatment approaches with whatever populations he or she is working with. A major step for any reader to become an effective group treatment facilitator is to acquire the mental attitude that he or she is competent in designing and implementing group treatment programs with a wide variety of diverse and vulnerable populations. It is the aim of this chapter to assist the reader in developing the mental attitude that he or she can become competent in designing and implementing group treatment programs.

This chapter will use the following format for each of the five diverse and vulnerable populations that are presented: First, descriptive information about the population will be summarized. Second, group work with that population will be described. Third, some group exercises with that population will be presented. The reader will note that some of these exercises are specific to that group and would be inappropriate to use with students in a social work class. However, many of these exercises can be used with the selected population, as

LEARNING OBJECTIVES

Treatment groups can, and are, being used with a wide variety of diverse and vulnerable populations. This chapter provides illustrations of the wide variety of treatment groups that are being used. This chapter will help prepare students to:

LO 1 Comprehend the process of designing treatment groups for current and future clients.

well as with students in a social work class. (Readers will note that all of the exercises in this chapter are group exercises.)

Each of the following five sections (on adolescents, people who have an eating disorder, individuals affected by domestic violence, people who are grieving, and older adults) is written by an experienced group work practitioner.

GROUP WORK WITH ADOLESCENTS*

Working with adolescents can be one of the most rewarding activities a social worker can engage in. It can also be one of the most challenging. Teenagers often possess a tremendous amount of idealism, creativity, and unfiltered honesty. Their energy, enthusiasm, and passion can be very inspiring. However, their changing and unpredictable emotions, poor impulse control, and desire for independence can be very challenging for practitioners. Despite these challenges, working with adolescents is some of the most important work a social worker can undertake. Successful and safe completion of the adolescent developmental stage has lifelong implications for these soon-to-be adults. Social workers often have an opportunity to make a substantial impact on young people that may reverberate for many years to come. A positive adult role model may exert significant influence on many adolescents and provide important modeling of healthy identity and choices. For some vulnerable teens, the stakes truly are life and death. Social workers can feel very fulfilled and inspired about changing lives for the better through successful intervention with at-risk adolescents.

Adolescents often struggle with this difficult and sometimes stormy developmental stage. Characteristic emotional upheaval can be exacerbated by their still-emerging abstract reasoning skills, communication skills, ability to control impulses, family dynamics, and peer influences. There is a distinct learning curve as adolescents grapple with now adult-like brains and bodies. This can be made more difficult as growth is often uneven and sporadic. Teens tend to overemphasize rewards, downplay risks, and often give little consideration to long-term consequences. Social workers who work with adolescents need to have a good foundational understanding of the developmental process and the challenges that it brings. Teens often benefit from the group process as they navigate the changes they are experiencing. Involvement with school classes, sports, clubs, churches, and informal groups of friends are all groups where teens find support, engagement, learning, and opportunity for social development. Social work groups are merely more formal versions of such groups, with a goal of improving protective factors and reducing problems or challenges.

Beyond the physical and cognitive changes that adolescents struggle with, there are many other challenges and obstacles to overcome. Identity development is one such challenge that manifests on multiple levels. As teens develop a separate identity from their parents, they often struggle with understanding who they are and where they fit in the world. Issues of gender identity, sexual orientation, ethnic identity, and social status come to the forefront. Much conflict is often created as teens struggle to figure out how they fit in with their peers and family. These conflicts can sometimes create feelings of anxiety, depression, isolation, rejection, and at times anger. Their developmentally appropriate peer orientation magnifies the significance of peer status and interaction. Social and peer relationships can be simultaneously supportive/empowering and a tremendously negative influence. Teens' interactions with parents and adults can be conflictive as they emotionally detach from parents and explore an independent identity. Adolescents are apt to become oppositional and may make choices to demonstrate that adults cannot control them.

Today's adolescents are under pressure from a multitude of stressors that would be difficult even for mature adults. In addition to the stress of their physical, emotional, and cognitive development, teens must navigate the pressures of school, peers, family, and

---

* This section was written by Craig Mead, MSW, LSW, licensed social worker at Presence St. Mary and Elizabeth Medical Center, Chicago, IL.

outside activities. They may subsequently struggle with stress-related disorders, anxiety, depression, or alcohol and drug abuse. They may feel suicidal, take excessive risks, engage in premature sexual activity or criminal behavior, or display various other unhealthy behaviors. Groups targeted to teens often focus on these issues in addition to more treatment-specific issues that are often related to skill deficits. Many of these treatment-type groups are similar to other common treatment groups for adults (see Chapter 1) and address skill deficits in social interactions, anger management, impulse control, resisting peer pressures, developing healthy relationships, use of coping skills, and managing symptoms of mental illness.

Social workers are likely to encounter adolescent groups in a variety of settings and contexts. One of the first challenges that they're likely to encounter is that most adolescents are not self-referred. Often their participation in groups is at the behest of parents, schools, or courts. This often results in group participants who are at least initially less than enthusiastic and unmotivated to engage in the group process. This tendency can often be mitigated by group leaders through skillful engagement. Teens are much more likely to become engaged in the group if they are directly included in collaboration and decision making about the group's activities, structure, and goals. Although the hoped-for outcome of the group may be predetermined, group leaders generally have significant latitude as to how that outcome is reached. Achieving a positive outcome with adolescents will often depend on the extent that participants have "bought in" or taken ownership of the group. Their engagement can be enhanced by providing creative, interesting, novel, active, or fun activities that maintain attention and provide memorable experiences (see Exercise 13.1). Appropriately placed irreverence can also capture their attention (see Exercise 13.2).

Another important factor in group engagement with adolescents is the therapeutic skill level of the facilitator. We expect that adolescents will demand to have as much independence as allowed and will push back at perceived attempts to exert power and control over them. This often manifests as an authority problem, and adult social workers leading a group may be perceived as a representative authority such as a teacher or parent. A skilled facilitator will be able to balance maintaining authority, limits, and structure while fostering a collaborative, nonthreatening partnership with participants. Teenagers are acutely sensitive to disingenuousness, dishonesty, and hypocrisy. Leaders must make a strong effort to be completely genuine, caring, and empathic to facilitate a trusting atmosphere. The use of empathy, understanding, and validation is crucial to create that trusting environment with group participants. Group leaders need to create a safe, nonjudgmental, and trusting space where teens feel comfortable and are allowed an open conversation about issues that affect them. This will be critical if group goals are to be accomplished. Social workers who do not succeed in this step will likely find themselves with an uncooperative, guarded, and disengaged group of teens. However, social workers should not shy away from group work with teens. Skill is developed with practice. Each group you conduct will be an individual experiment. Keep what works and discard what doesn't. Every group will be an improvement on the last. It is not uncommon for a group idea simply not to work, but even in such circumstances teens often express that they took something useful away from the experience.

As much as adolescents dislike feeling controlled and subordinate, they need structure and limits. They are very aware of their own impulsivity and that of their peers. They know from experience that their peers can be judgmental, unkind, and verbally or physically aggressive. Teens actually feel safer when they know there are limits on behavior and adults are capable of enforcing rules. Structure and limits allow group leaders to create the needed physically and emotionally safe environment for the group to accomplish its objectives. It is not uncommon for teens to "act up" or draw attention to themselves when feeling unsafe. Leaders who experience acting up or verbal aggression by individual or groups of participants should explore if feeling emotionally or physically unsafe is driving the behavior. This behavior may be "fronting" behavior to demonstrate that they are capable of protecting themselves. Boys in particular may demonstrate excessive bravado or may make hyperbolic claims about their capabilities or experience.

EXERCISE 13.1   Anger Management Group

GOAL: To use novel and memorable methods to teach the importance of using anger management and healthy coping skills; to understand the dangers of bottling up feelings.

Materials needed: Balloons

1. Complete check-ins, and introduce the group topic: Talk about the nature of anger, taking a nonjudgmental approach that emphasizes anger as a natural emotion. Discuss how anger is often composed of many other feelings, such as disappointment, rejection, frustration, or fear.

2. Ask for volunteers to name things that make people angry. With each response, blow some air into a balloon. Continue until the balloon is quite full, nearly ready to pop. Tie off the balloon and hold it under one arm. Continue with a second balloon and place it under the other arm. Discuss how dangerous it is to walk around with all that anger, which could explode at any time. Enlist the help of an assistant to bump into you and then pop the balloons as he or she does so. Explode in playful anger at the assistant who bumped into you. Reinforce message that bottling up anger and walking around with it is a setup for conflict.

3. Follow the same procedure to fill up another balloon with things that make people angry. Instead of tying this balloon, let it go and let it fly around the room. Discuss how if we just let things out all at once it will be out of control. Fill another balloon and do not tie it. Ask the group to name coping skills that someone might use to help with anger. When someone gives a skill, let a little air out of the balloon, preferably making a loud squeaking noise. Discuss how using coping skills can let a little bit of anger out of the balloon at a time while still keeping control.

4. Pass out balloons to each group participant. Have volunteers name things that make them mad, blowing up their balloons as they go. When the balloon is sufficiently full, have them say what coping skills they could use. Instruct them to let a little air out of the balloon as they say each skill.

5. Engage the group in a closing discussion about what they learned. Allow participants to pop balloons, make noises, and then clean up the group room.

EXERCISE 13.2   "Own Your C.R.A.P."

GOAL: To challenge teens to take greater responsibility for their behavior and not blame others for their actions.

Materials needed: Large white board, handouts

1. Complete check-ins, and introduce the group topic: "Today we are going to talk about C.R.A.P."; explain that C.R.A.P. stands for control, revenge, anger, and power. Discuss how their own and other people's behavior is sometimes about "crap." Discuss how interpersonal conflicts are often driven by people's effort to engage in control, revenge, anger, and power. Make four sections on the board, one for each word. Assist the group with brainstorming behaviors that represent each—control, revenge, anger, and power. For example: engaging in passive-aggressive behavior in response to parental restrictions could be about power seeking or attempting to control. Giving someone the silent treatment is about control or revenge.

2. Pass out handouts with space to write what behavior they engage in that represents control, revenge, anger, and power. Ask for volunteers to share how they engage in "crap."

3. Discuss how we must all own and be responsible for our own "crap." Lead a group discussion about how they can do better at owning their own "crap," not blaming others for their behavior, and not using other's behavior as an excuse to behave in certain ways.

4. Engage the group in a closing discussion about what they learned.

Having reasonable but firm limits to behavior also prevents teens from needing to test limits. Group participants will feel more comfortable if they know exactly where the limits are and what the consequences will be. They will likely still initially test limits to see if the leaders are consistent and capable of enforcing established limits. Inexperienced clinicians often make the mistake of inconsistent limit setting or establishing unenforceable rules. They may subsequently find themselves with a very unruly group of teens. Working with group participants to establish their own set of group rules will improve compliance and self-policing of limits. When participants engage in inappropriate behavior, the leaders will have to use their clinical judgment as how to proceed. If the behavior is a deliberate disruption or simple attention seeking, ignoring the behavior may be an option. Some teens may wish to become the focus of attention or derail the group process. Focusing on their behavior may allow them to succeed in this goal. Conversely, engaging with these teens and focusing attention on them may establish what it is they need from the group. It is often beneficial to use the group for confrontations about disruptive or inappropriate behavior. This is often an opportunity for participants to practice their assertiveness and conflict resolution skills.

It is not uncommon for interpersonal conflicts to arise during group sessions. Group leaders will again need to use their best clinical judgment as to how to intervene. Participants should be supported in their effort to manage their own disagreements and be allowed the opportunity to independently problem-solve. These conflicts are excellent opportunities for teens to learn crucial interpersonal skills and be able to practice those skills in a safe and supportive environment. Group leaders who immediately jump in to resolve conflicts rob them of that opportunity. However, leaders should maintain limits and assist with demonstrating assertiveness, conflict resolution, and problem-solving skills when needed. One additional word of warning: leaders should pay close attention to signs that a verbal conflict may escalate beyond words. Teens are inherently impulsive and may react in unpredictable ways. A teen may explode with anger, become threatening, or spontaneously engage in physical aggression. Physical fights between group members may be more common in certain settings, but could happen even in the most benign groups. Every effort should be made to head off such potential before it escalates to the point of a physical fight. Individuals may need to be separated or temporarily removed from the group until emotions subside. In the event of a physical fight, group leaders should not get between the fighting teens or physically intervene unless appropriately trained and supported by sufficient staff to intervene safely. Teens do get into physical fights at times but rarely cause each other serious injury. Group leaders should focus on maintaining the safety of the other group participants, removing them from the area, and summoning assistance or emergency services. Agency standard operating procedure will dictate how such incidents are handled.

GROUP WORK WITH PEOPLE WHO HAVE AN EATING DISORDER*

Eating disorders continue to be a serious issue within the United States and other industrialized nations. Problems with this illness have now emerged in developing regions such as Asia, Latin America, and India, related to the possible impact of global economic development and the changing status of women in these cultures.[1] Although eating disorders primarily affect women, there is a growing concern with the rise in males affected with this illness.

Lasègue in 1873 and Gull in 1874 designated the term **anorexia nervosa** (AN) in separate cases in which they reported young females who were starving themselves. Descriptions of this illness became more frequent in the late 19th century.[2] Recent changes in the DSM-5 categorize anorexia nervosa as those individuals who restrict food intake resulting in low body weight outside of the norms for age, sex, development, and physical health.[3] Individuals with anorexia continually perceive themselves to be fat, despite a low body weight. In addition, these individuals exhibit an intense fear of gaining weight or becoming fat even when their body weight is significantly below the minimally normal range. Anorexia nervosa is subcategorized as being either the restricting type, in which individuals will severely limit their intake to only a few hundred calories per day and do not engage in bingeing and purging behaviors, or the binge-eating/purging type, which is characterized by those anorexics who frequently engage in binge-eating and purging behaviors. The primary age of onset is during early to mid-adolescence.[4]

Bulimia nervosa (BN), as noted in the current diagnostic criteria, was relatively obscure until the latter part of the 20th century.[5] BN is now considered more common than anorexia nervosa, and affected individuals strive to prevent weight gain or lose weight through binge/purge behaviors. BN is characterized by **binge eating**, in which an individual consumes large amounts of food within any two-hour period and lacks a sense of control over eating during this episode. Purging behaviors include self-induced vomiting; laxative, diuretic, or other medication misuse and abuse; food abstention; or excessive exercising following binge eating. These binge/purge incidents occur *at least once a week for a period of three months, but may be more frequent*. Body weight and shape heavily influence bulimics' self-evaluation. Binge eating frequently occurs in secrecy as shame drives the need to conceal the behaviors associated with bulimia nervosa. Some individuals experience dissociative symptoms such as depression and anxiety during and after binge-eating incidents.

---

* This section was written by Mary R. Weeden, MSW, LCSW, PhD, clinical therapist for eating disorders, Assistant Professor, University of Wisconsin-Oshkosh.

EXERCISE 13.3   Body Image Group

GOAL: To visually demonstrate how self-perceptions can sometimes be inaccurate. Body distortion is a key component with individuals suffering from anorexia nervosa and bulimia nervosa. Being able to visually demonstrate distortion can assist clients with this recognition.

Size of group: No more than six to eight people. Body image exercises can produce increased levels of anxiety, so smaller groups will allow for better processing of feelings and thoughts.

Materials needed: Magic markers, paper to make life-size drawings (butcher's paper or painting paper)

1. Clients should wear clothes that are tight fitting so that body images can be drawn with a fair degree of accuracy.
Place the paper on the floor. Divide the group into pairs. Have one individual lay supine (lying down with the face up) with his hands at his side. Have his partner mark the top of his head, feet, and hands. Then repeat the process for the second person.

2. At this point, individuals are instructed to draw themselves, as they perceive their bodies to look to others. This exercise is not about artistic talent. Clients may need to be gently refocused. Some clients feel a strong desire to add details such as eyes, clothing, and so on. Others may be upset because they do not feel they have adequate drawing skills. Remind them this is about their body images.

3. When everyone in the group has finished, have the clients return with their partners. One person lies down over his drawing, and the other person draws an outline as close to his body as possible. Then repeat this process for the second person.

4. Ask individuals what they see. How accurate is their perception of their body shape compared to what was actually drawn? What are their thoughts and feelings as they look at the comparisons? Encourage other members to offer feedback to one another.

Binge eating involves consuming food until feeling uncomfortable or even painfully full. As with anorexia nervosa, adolescence to young adulthood is the age range most commonly affected by bulimia nervosa. Multiple life-stressor events may occur as a precipitating risk factor in the onset of this illness.

Serious medical complications can arise with both disorders, and the incidence of death with AN appears to be higher when compared to individuals diagnosed with bulimia nervosa. Somatic comorbidity is a predictor of poorer outcomes. (Somatic comorbidity refers to the presence of one or more additional disorders, or diseases, co-occurring with the eating disorder.)

The mortality rates with the AN population have led to suggestions for staging (similar to stages of risk with cancer) the risk factors of AN patients in an effort to more effectively measure the incidence, progression, death risks, and intervention models in the treatment of this disease.[6] Cardiac abnormalities, neurological changes, osteoporosis, anemia, gastrointestinal problems, altered blood chemistry, and dermatologic issues may be seen in both anorexics and bulimics. Both disorders may exhibit symptoms of fatigue, sleep difficulties, and somatic comorbidity factors. In addition, individuals who binge and purge by vomiting often suffer from dental problems related to the loss of teeth enamel and gum disease

EXERCISE 13.4   Fear Food Group

GOAL: To have clients successfully eat a "fear food" to help them gain insight into how their thoughts and feelings guide their actions. This exercise also reaffirms the idea that eating a food will not lead to losing control. Individuals suffering from eating disorders often speak of trigger foods, that is, foods that will elicit feelings of wanting to binge (bulimia nervosa or binge-eating disorder) or foods that are considered taboo because of fear of weight gain (anorexia nervosa). Many of our experiences in life, good and bad, are often associated with food. Western society places a high value on rituals associated with food, leading some people to avoid eating in the presence of others, fearing they will be judged or lose control.

Size of group: Six to ten people

Materials needed: Everyone in the group is asked to bring their most feared food. Usually, this is something sweet such as candy, cookies, cake, or ice cream. This food may also be something salty, such as chips, French fries, or another high-calorie carbohydrate.

1. Have everyone gather in a circle. Discuss how anxiety about specific foods can often lead to fear of "losing control" if the item is consumed. Have each individual give a level of anxiety, using a Likert scale of "1" (no anxiety) to "10" (extreme anxiety). Encourage them to speak about their concerns and fears about the food using "I" statements. When was the last time they ate this food? What happened when they did?

2. After everyone has finished, have the members start eating the food items they brought. What are the smells and tastes associated with their food? What are their thoughts as they consume the item? Do they desire to just nibble the food, or do they want to consume it quickly? The facilitator needs to draw out responses from group members. Have members state their levels of anxiety while they eat the food. Encourage them to look at what they feel is causing a change in the level of anxiety. After everyone is finished consuming the food, have the group process what transpired. How did this exercise affect them? How did they feel about eating in front of other members? Did individuals have a desire to purge or restrict? Ask clients to describe their thoughts and feelings at that moment. At the end of this exercise, have clients measure their anxiety level one more time. Members who continue to have extreme anxiety can continue to process this event until their level of anxiety has decreased.

EXERCISE 13.5   Mirror Reflection Image Group

GOAL: To encourage members to focus on the positive qualities they possess and to use these strengths to focus on their recovery. A low self-esteem and body dissatisfaction are core symptoms of eating disorders. Clients often avoid looking at their reflection in a mirror, as this reinforces the self-loathing they feel about themselves. Having clients view themselves in a full-length mirror over a period of time helps to desensitize the negative feelings they associate with their bodies. Frequently, people only can recite the negative aspects of themselves and struggle to identify positive traits.

Group size: Six to eight members preferably, but no more than ten

1. Have each member stand before a full-length mirror. Instruct each individual to look directly into the mirror and make three positive self-statements. If the individual is unable to look at himself or herself or struggles to identify any positive qualities he or she possesses, the group leader may want to stand behind the person, offering verbal support to the group member. Other group members can offer suggestions and support. After this exercise, members might want to journal about their thoughts and feelings in doing this exercise. The Mirror Reflection exercise should be done at least weekly over a period of several months. Group members should write down their responses and track their thoughts and feelings after each session. Ideally, individuals will start to find looking at their image easier, and their positive self-statements will start to be more introspective as they develop awareness and move more toward self-acceptance.

because of hydrochloric acid in the vomitus. Although medical complications in anorexia nervosa are primarily due to weight loss and malnutrition, the complications for bulimia nervosa are attributed to the severity and modality of the purging behaviors. Many of the medical complications associated with anorexia nervosa and bulimia are reversible with early diagnosis and effective treatment.[7]

New to the DSM-5, binge-eating disorder (BED) is the most rapidly growing eating disorder diagnosis.[8] Similar to BN, binge eating is characterized by individuals who consume larger-than-normal amounts of food within a discrete, two-hour period and experience a lack of control over eating during this incident. Associated with the binge-eating episodes are three or more of the following: 1) eating rapidly compared to what would be deemed "normal"; 2) eating until feeling painfully full; 3) consuming large quantities of food despite not feeling physically hungry; 4) eating alone due to embarrassment over the quantity of food consumed; and 5) feelings of guilt, sadness, or self-loathing following a binge-eating episode. Distress due to the binge eating is present, and episodes occur *at least* weekly over a period of three months. Unlike BN, individuals who suffer from BED do not exhibit recurrent inappropriate compensatory purging behaviors following an episode of binge eating. Recent research suggests that BED is more prevalent compared to either AN or BN. Individuals with BED demonstrate a significant risk of experiencing additional psychiatric diagnoses.[9] Although the ratio of prevalence is greater for women than men, there is less disparity between genders compared to BN and AN.

Approximately 30% of individuals diagnosed with BED fall within their weight range.[10] The medical complications of BED include increased comorbidity with other mental health disorders. Physical health complications include obesity, hypertension, dyslipidemia, type 2 diabetes, gastrointestinal problems, and increased risk for coronary artery disease.[11]

Treatment options for AN and BN include inpatient, outpatient, group, individual, and residential therapies. Key factors for successful treatment often exist with the interprofessional approach, incorporating physicians, psychiatrists, nurses, social workers, and dieticians.[12] The goals of treatment include a resolution or reduction in maladaptive behaviors, addressing the psychological and physiological issues, and weight restoration for AN. Pharmacotherapy (drug therapy) combined with psychotherapeutic interventions appears to have the best outcome, especially with BN and BED. Cognitive-behavioral therapy continues to demonstrate the greatest empirical support, although research outcomes may not be as positive for BN individuals.[13] The cost of treatment is expensive—usually several thousand dollars—can take up to eight years or even longer, depending on the severity of the situation and the length of chronicity.[14]

GROUP WORK WITH INDIVIDUALS AFFECTED BY DOMESTIC VIOLENCE*

Domestic violence, also known as domestic abuse or intimate partner violence, is a significant public health concern in the United States and around the world. Historically, this is a crime that affects many, but often goes unreported and unnoticed. Domestic violence is an epidemic that does not discriminate against age, race, gender, ethnicity, sexual orientation, or socioeconomic status. Although violence has been found in every type of relationship throughout the course of history, from infanticide to spousal abuse, it has only been over the past few decades that the impact and lasting implications of these abuses have been brought into the spotlight. Attention to domestic violence was a grassroots movement, primarily led by women, and was highlighted by the women's movement of the 1970s. Prior to that time, domestic violence was considered to be a private, family matter and was rarely discussed. In recent years, more attention has been given to identifying the causes, implications, costs incurred, and treatment interventions related to domestic violence.

Domestic violence can be defined as any act that perpetuates fear and intimidation over another by utilizing elements of power and control. These willful acts of abuse can include physical abuse, emotional abuse, sexual abuse, psychological abuse, and economic abuse. The Power and Control Wheel (retrieved from http://www.ncdsv.org), developed by the Domestic Abuse Intervention Project, is a useful tool in understanding the overall pattern of abusive and violent behaviors that are used by a batterer to establish and maintain control.[15] The Power and Control Wheel identifies different ways that abusers inflict harm on their victims by utilizing things such as coercion and threats toward their victim; intimidation tactics; emotional abuse; isolation of the victim; minimizing, denying, and blaming for the violent behavior; using children to threaten the victim; and forms of economic abuse. This tool also identifies specific behaviors that may be demonstrated by the abuser, such as controlling what the victim does, abusing pets, keeping the victim from getting a job, threatening to take away the children, or blaming the victim for the violence that occurs. The Power and Control Wheel is a commonly used tool among service providers to educate both victims and offenders about the elements of domestic violence.

The Equality Wheel (retrieved from http://www.ncdsv.org), also created by the Domestic Abuse Intervention Project, can be used to provide psychoeducation to victims

---

*   This section on domestic violence was written by Rachel Dunn, MSW, LCSW. Ms. Dunn is a psychotherapist at Crossroads Counseling, Janesville, Wisconsin. She is also an associate lecturer at the University of Wisconsin-Madison.

and offenders.[16] The Equality Wheel identifies different elements of healthy and equal relationships, such as honesty and accountability of both partners, trust and support of one another, the use of nonthreatening behavior, shared responsibility within the household, and responsible parenting. This tool also identifies specific behaviors that can be demonstrated by partners to establish a healthy and equal relationship, such as communicating open and truthfully with each other, supporting each other's goals in life, being willing to compromise, making financial decisions together, and sharing parenting responsibilities.

Group work is one of many interventions that have proven to be beneficial in treating the victims and offenders of domestic violence, as well as those who witness these acts of violence, including children. It is important to note that the victims and offenders should be in separate groups to ensure each can safely address interpersonal issues affecting them and to reduce any additional harm or control by the offender.

Group Work with Victims of Domestic Violence

Domestic violence often goes underreported or unreported all together, making it difficult to collect and interpret accurate rates of domestic violence. Complicating matters even further is the fact that domestic violence is most likely to happen in the privacy of one's own home. Many people often assume that the victims of domestic violence are always the female partners in a relationship; however, some research suggests that rates of domestic violence are similar between men and women in relationships.[17] Women represent a substantial percentage of all injuries and fatalities from partner violence.[18] Many believe that although men are also victims of domestic violence, they are less likely to report for a number of reasons, including traditional gender roles, the stigma related to domestic violence, feeling embarrassed, or out of fear that no one would believe that the abuse was occurring. Research shows that women victims are often more likely to be injured as a result of domestically violent situations, often due to the means by which their male partner abuses them.[19] For example, women are more likely to use less aggressive means when attacking their partners, such as pushing, shoving, or kicking, whereas men are more likely to conduct more aggressive assaults, such as punching, choking, or utilizing weapons.

Victims of domestic violence are susceptible to suffering from a number of different symptoms that may manifest in physical, emotional, or mental health symptoms. These symptoms may include intrusive and anxious thoughts that interfere with their daily functioning. The victim may have difficulty eating, sleeping, or concentrating. Victims often suffer from a sense of constant hypervigilance, as their sense of personal safety has been violated, frequently on more than one occasion. Victims may also find themselves in situations where they feel dependent on their abuser physically, emotionally, and often financially. Victims may also experience adverse mental health symptoms or utilize maladaptive coping skills, such as substance use, as a result of their victimization.

Victims of domestic violence often lack the essential basic sense of safety, no matter what environment they are in. In all work done with victims of domestic violence, the element of safety should be the primary focus in an attempt to reestablish this key element of human survival. To do so, a victim must understand the elements of domestic violence. In a group setting, a victim has the ability to learn about the different elements of domestic violence by utilizing the Power and Control Wheel created by the Domestic Abuse Intervention Project.[20] Group participants can learn about and gain personal insight into the behaviors that their abusers may utilize to maintain power and control within the relationship. The Power and Control Wheel can assist victims in learning about the obvious abuses that may be occurring, but also about the less identifiable elements of abuse that they initially may not be aware of. The Equality Wheel, also created by the Domestic Abuse Intervention Project, can also be used in a group setting to provide psychoeducation to victims.[21] The Equality Wheel identifies elements of healthy relationships and outlines adaptive behaviors that make up healthy and equal relationships. Victims of domestic violence often feel betrayed, feel self-conscious, and may lack a sense of trust in themselves and others. Group work can be used with victims to reestablish these elements and allow the victims to empower their peers and to be empowered themselves.

Group Work Exercises with Victims of Domestic Violence

EXERCISE 13.6   Empowerment Role-Play

GOAL: To role-play to allow a victim to explore different topics and approaches to problem solving, assertiveness skills, and independent decision making in a safe and supportive environment. Within these roles, individuals can practice overcoming barriers that they may be encountering or foresee in their lives. By role-playing the situation, an individual is likely to feel more comfortable and confident in dealing with similar problematic situations in real time, leading to empowerment of the victim.

1. The group leader provides each pair in the group with a problematic scenario (informing a family member that they are leaving their relationship, issues in finding housing, barriers to opening a bank account, etc.).

2. In a pair, one member takes on the role of the victim and the other member plays the role of the service provider, family member, and so on.

3. The pair engages in a dialogue regarding the scenario presented, and the interviewer (service provider, family member, etc.) creates intentional barriers in the dialogue for the victim to problem-solve around.

4. The pair reverses roles and repeats Step 3.

5. The group leader reassigns scenarios, and Steps 2–4 are repeated in each pair.

6. As a group, each member discusses what it was like to encounter the problematic situation, how he or she handled it, and what he or she would do differently next time.

7. Collectively, the group and group leader provide praise and feedback for each participant related to his or her problem-solving techniques.

EXERCISE 13.7   Safety Planning

GOAL: To explore safety planning and develop a personal safety plan. Safety planning is a critical element to domestic violence intervention and is a practical guide that is intended to assist victims in remaining safe if they choose to stay in the relationship or decide to leave.

1. In a group setting, the group leader describes what a safety plan is, the elements of a safety plan, and why a safety plan is important to create.

2. Every participant prepares a safety plan. Safety plans are individualized and specific to each person's circumstances, so each group member is given time to fill out her or his own customized safety plan. The following safety plan template may be used. (If this exercise is being conducted in a social work classroom, the students should assume they are living with an abusive roommate and then fill out this safety template.)

Safety Plan Template

Name: _____

Date: _____

A. If a violent incident occurs, I will leave by: _____
_____

(Practice your escape plan—for example by leaving through a back door and going to a friend's place)

B. I will keep my purse/wallet and an extra set of car keys at (place) _____ in order to leave quickly.

C. I will teach my children how to call the police if violence erupts.

D. I will tell _____ and _____ about the violence in the past and request they call the police if they hear signs of violence from my residence.

E. I will use _____ as a code word to inform friends and relatives to call the police.

F. If I leave I will seek shelter at _____ for myself (and my children, if there are children).

G. (If you have children) My plan for removing the children from my current residence is

_____
_____
_____

H. I will take the following important items and documents with me (Please check the important ones):

_____ Checkbook and ATM card
_____ Driver's license and registration
_____ Money
_____ Social Security card
_____ Purse/wallet
_____ Personal identification
_____ My birth certificate
_____ My children's birth certificates
_____ Credit cards
_____ Keys to residence/car
_____ Medications (Please list the medications): _____

_____
_____

_____ Passport(s)
_____ Medical records
_____ Address book
_____ Pictures
_____ Jewelry
_____ Items of special sentimental value, which are: _____

_____
_____

_____ Insurance papers
_____ Other items and documents as indicated: _____

_____

Important contacts in my safety plan are the following (please check):

_____   Medical providers

_____   Lawyer

_____   School contacts

_____   Employer contacts

_____   Other, as follows: _____

_____

(These items and documents should be placed in one location so that you can grab them quickly if and when you leave.)

3. As a group, participants will walk through each element of their safety plans (safe people to contact when an unsafe situation occurs, safe ways to get out of one's home, locations that a victim can keep a bag of belongings, places to go to remain safe when leaving the relationships, etc.) and brainstorm ideas to include in their own safety plans.

4. Each member will further customize his or her safety plan to reflect these elements.

5. The group members will discuss safe places where they can keep their plans so they are easily accessible when needed.

6. The group leader will remind group participants that safety plans should be reviewed and updated often to ensure that they are applicable and able to be utilized when needed.

Group Work with Children and Other Witnesses of Domestic Violence

Although domestic violence occurs between two intimate partners, those who witness it may also suffer from the adverse effects of this abuse. Any person who directly observes, hears, or tries to get involved in a domestically violent situation is considered a witness and may also be considered a victim of the abuse.

Children are most likely to witness and become involved in domestically violent situations and are at risk for experiencing a number of different problematic issues as a result: emotionally, socially, physically, and behaviorally. These reactions can vary greatly and depend heavily on a child's age and developmental functioning at the time of the incident. Emotionally, children may experience a sense of shame or guilt and often think that they should be able to do more to stop the abuse from happening. Children may also experience symptoms of depression or anxiety, which could consequently interfere with their day-to-day functioning. Children who are exposed to domestic violence may isolate themselves socially or have trouble trusting others. They may also act out or demonstrate other behavioral issues. Many children report somatic complaints or feeling tired or lethargic. Personal hygiene issues, as well as incidents of self-abuse, may also be observed with children who have witnessed domestic violence.

Even if children are not directly injured as a result of domestic violence in the home, they can be negatively affected in other ways. The National Coalition Against Domestic Violence states that the strongest risk factor for transmitting violent behavior from one generation to the next is children who witness violence in the home. Consequently, boys who witness domestic violence are twice as likely to abuse their own partners and children when they become adults.[22] Thorough assessments and interventions are crucial elements in the working relationship to end this cyclical pattern of violence in families.

Children who have been exposed to domestic violence can gain a great deal from working in a group setting with their peers. Group counseling is one of the most efficient ways in which school mental health professionals can promote the growth and development of children exposed to domestic violence.[23] Children, as with adults, often find the group setting less threatening to address personal and often traumatic experiences because the group setting provides acceptance and support to participants.

Group work can be utilized in a number of ways to address the different developmental and cognitive levels of children exposed to domestic violence, and it is imperative that the practitioner takes these levels of functioning into consideration when determining appropriate interventions. In the safety and security of a group setting, children have the ability to interact with their peers and find a level of understanding. This interaction can assist in building one's empathy for others while establishing and empowering one to feel safe. Some practitioners use structured interventions in the group setting for feeling identification activities, role-plays, or games to identify and address what they have experienced in an attempt to assist them in processing this information. Providing young child witnesses with a supportive environment in which to share experiences, enhance social skills, identify and express feelings, and create personalized safety plans, as well as a focus on the strengths of each child, will help these child witnesses to cope with the domestic violence that they have witnessed.[24]

Play therapy is also a common technique used with children who have been exposed to domestic violence and can be conducted in an individual or group setting. Play has been identified as a natural form of communication for children and a way in which children are able to express themselves when they do not have the ability or willingness to do so verbally. Play therapy allows children to use play to directly or symbolically act out how they are feeling, what they may be thinking, or experiences that they have gone through. Play therapy can take many forms, including painting, drawing, puppet shows, storytelling, and work with sand trays. All of these activities may have a significant impact on a child's overall functioning, especially after a traumatic experience.

Group Work Exercises with Children and Other Witnesses of Domestic Violence

EXERCISE 13.8   Feeling Identification Exercise

GOAL: To assist children in correctly identifying, verbalizing, and processing the feelings that they experience at different times. In the group setting, children can learn about and discuss their feelings and how to express themselves in healthy and safe ways.

1. For younger children who have been exposed to domestic violence, the group leader can ask that the group come up with a list of feelings (happy, sad, mad, embarrassed, upset, etc.).

2. Each group participant picks a word from the list and is asked to act out that feeling for the other members to see and hear. For example, a participant may act out a person crying.

3. The group leader then asks the group participants to identify the last lime that they experienced that feeling and to describe what was occurring at that time ("I was sad when my mother was angry and yelling at my sister.").

4. The group leader validates and praises each participant for his or her response.

5. Each group member is then asked to describe the physical sensation experienced as a result of this feeling ("When I felt _____, my _____ hurt.").

6. The group leader validates and praises each participant for his or her response.

7. Each group member is then asked to describe how he or she reacted to experiencing this feeling ("When I was_____, I responded by_____.").

8. The group leader discusses the different feelings experienced by the group members, validates these feelings, and reviews healthy and safe ways to deal with these feelings.

Please note that this exercise can be used with older children and adolescents as well—perhaps utilizing more complex emotions (e.g., frustrated, anxious, satisfied, panic, jealous, apathy).

EXERCISE 13.9   Stress Relief and Deep-Breathing Exercise

GOAL: To teach deep-breathing skills that are useful for reducing anxiety and managing stress for individuals who experience problematic symptoms, including children. Deep breathing is the process of slow inhalation followed by slow and complete exhalation. Practicing deep breathing regularly has lasting effects on overall health and is a good tool for people of all ages to utilize.

1. The group leader explains that deep breathing is a useful tool to use when a person is feeling sad, mad, anxious, or experiencing stress of any kind in any situation. The group leader adds that deep breathing, or "belly breathing," can be used the next time a person experiences any of these emotions.

2. The group leader assures the children that this is a safe exercise and informs them that if they do not feel safe, they can end the activity at any time. The children are asked to lie on their backs and close their eyes, placing their hands on their abdomens.

3. The children are asked to keep their mouths closed and to breathe slowly through the nose. The group leader counts to eight out loud as the children breathe in for that count.

4. The children hold that air in the body while the group leader counts to two out loud.

5. The group leader then asks the children to slowly let the air out through the mouth or nose.

6. Steps 2–5 are repeated.

7. The group leader asks participants what they felt their bodies experience when they were using deep breathing. Please note that when deep breathing is done correctly, the abdomen should expand, not the chest, while doing the breathing, and that is why it is referred to as "belly breathing" when being taught to children.

8. Steps 2–5 are repeated with the group leader assisting the group participants in doing their own counting for breaths so they are able to utilize this technique independently.

Group Work with Offenders of Domestic Violence

Offenders of domestic violence, like victims, come from all walks of life, from all racial and ethnic backgrounds, may be male or female, and can be engaged in heterosexual or same-sex relationships. Offenders of domestic violence seek to have power and control over their victims. They seek to control all or most aspects of that victim's life. They will often blame their victims for their violent tendencies as well as excuse, minimize, or deny their own behaviors. Abusers often experience intense anger and rage. Offenders also adhere to rigid and stereotypical gender roles and expectations within their relationships.

Offender intervention programs are often utilized to address the dynamics of domestic violence in individual and group settings. Therapeutic interventions such as cognitive-behavioral interventions (see Modules 1 and 3), empathy training, and skills training programs are primary approaches utilized in offender treatment to ensure that the violence has stopped in the relationship, to hold the offender accountable, and to teach new skills to assist with continued safety.

Cognitive-behavioral treatment is often used for offenders of domestic violence and can be utilized in an individual and group setting. Cognitive-behavioral therapy is a short-term, evidence-supported therapeutic intervention that is used to focus on a specific problematic behavior. During the course of treatment, a person's thoughts and feelings are discussed and focused on, as these thought patterns and feelings are what trigger and influence the problematic behavior or action. By identifying these thoughts and feelings, cognitive-behavioral therapy assists people in changing the destructive or disturbing thought patterns that have a negative influence on behavior.

Group work provides an opportunity for offenders to engage in empathy training by gaining personal insight into their abusive behaviors and the ways in which these behaviors affect their victims. The Power and Control Wheel created by the Domestic Abuse Intervention Project can assist offenders in learning about the obvious abuses that may be occurring in the home, but also about the less recognizable forms of abuse that they may be engaging in but are not aware of. The Equality Wheel, also created by the Domestic Abuse Intervention Project, can be used in a group setting with offenders to identify and discuss elements of healthy and equal relationships that do not place either individual in jeopardy of harm.[25]

Offenders of domestic violence lack the ability to effectively and safely express their thoughts, feelings, and needs. Group work allows for offenders to learn, practice, and implement a new skill set that they do not have access to at the time the abuse occurs. Nonviolent and nonthreatening communication skills can be taught and practiced within the safety of the group setting (see Module 4). Problem-solving and resolution skills can also be explored and demonstrated (see Module 4). The group setting allows for participants to discover their maladaptive skills, to take ownership of their actions, and to learn how to avoid blaming their victims, while utilizing a new skill set that will be safe for both individuals in the relationship and others in the home.

Group Work Exercises with Offenders

EXERCISE 13.10   "Bail Out" Exercise

GOAL: To make offenders aware of the triggers and indicators that occur during any argument as evidence that the situation is escalating and that it is time for them to leave the situation, or "bail out," before someone gets hurt.

1. In a group setting, offenders are asked to discuss what different things trigger their anger or rage and what leads to incidents of domestic violence (e.g., "She did not make dinner for me, when she knows that is what I expect of her because she is home all day."). The group leader should note that some offenders will be aware of their triggers, whereas others will not.

2. The group leader makes a list of all of the different triggers identified for all of the participants to review and discuss.

3. Offenders are asked to identify the physical, emotional, or mental symptoms that they experience prior to, during, and after a violent incident (e.g., "I could feel my hands starting to sweat as she explained why she did not make dinner.").

4. The group leader makes a list of all of the different physical, emotional, or mental symptoms identified for all of the participants to review and discuss.

5. The group leader emphasizes that the purpose of this exercise is to learn a new skill set that allows offenders to identify their triggers and to be able to leave a situation while they are still in control of their emotions and able to act in a safe and responsible manner.

6. As a group, each participant picks one identified trigger or symptom he or she experiences and creates a plan how to respond and "bail out" when he or she experiences these things (e.g., "I know that I am becoming angry and escalating when my hands begin to sweat. Next time instead of yelling at my wife about why she didn't make dinner and then pushing her, I will leave the room when I begin to feel this.").

7. The group allows each offender to practice different techniques with his or her peers to leave a situation before the circumstances escalate to the point that someone may be in jeopardy of being hurt.

8. The group leader encourages participants to continue to practice "bailing out," or leaving a situation, every time they experience a trigger or a symptom that they know will escalate their behavior.

EXERCISE 13.11   Empathy Role-Play

GOAL: To give offenders insight or knowledge of the negative consequences that their actions have on their victims. Role-playing helps offenders get past the mistaken idea that their actions have little or no effect on people and gives offenders a chance to experience the situation and internalize feelings possibly experienced by their victims.

1. Group participants are asked to write out a scenario of the last violent incident that occurred between them and their partners. They are asked to identify what led up to the incident, who was involved, where this occurred, what actions they took, and how their partners reacted to this incident.

2. In groups of two or three, the group leader then assigns roles to each member of the group—as the victim, the offender, or the child witness. Please note that the offender should not be assigned to the offender role in his or her own scenario in an effort for the offender to experience what his or her victim was feeling at the time of the incident.

3. The groups are then asked to act out the scenarios they are given by assuming their assigned roles. They are asked to listen to and try to understand what each participant in the scenario experienced.

4. Following each scenario, each member is given a chance to speak about what he or she experienced in the assumed role. The participants who played the victim and the child witness in the scenario are encouraged to assume that role fully and express what their experiences were like to the offender.

5. The group leader provides additional information about being empathetic to one another and discusses strategies to handle situations differently in the future.

GROUP WORK WITH PEOPLE WHO ARE GRIEVING*

People in primitive societies handle death better than we do. Because the average age at which people die in primitive societies is lower and because members frequently witness the deaths of friends and relatives, people in primitive societies tend to view death as a natural occurrence.

In our society we tend to shy away from thinking about death. The terminally ill generally die in institutions (hospitals and nursing homes) away from home. Therefore, individuals are seldom exposed to dying people, and many avoid thinking about death by avoiding funerals and conversations about death. Many people act as if they believe they will live indefinitely.

In a very real sense everyone is terminal from birth, as everyone will die. If we become comfortable with the idea of our own eventual death, we will be better prepared for the deaths of close friends and relatives. We will then be better prepared to relate to the terminally ill and to help survivors who have experienced the death of a close friend or relative.

---

* This section was written by Charles Zastrow.

In practically any setting, social workers may encounter clients who are either grieving about the death of someone close or terminally ill. These clients are apt to be found in nursing homes, hospitals, and hospices, where death is more prevalent. In recent years social workers have become involved in a variety of settings in organizing and leading support groups for the terminally ill or for surviving friends and relatives. Social workers have also become involved in leading groups in educational settings that are designed to help people become comfortable with their own deaths and to learn how to better handle grief.

Nearly all of us are currently grieving a loss that we have had. It might be the end of a romantic relationship, moving away from friends and parents, the death of a pet, failing to get a grade we wanted, or someone's death.

Grieving over a loss does not end in a set amount of time, such as six months, a year, or three years. The "normal" grieving period is often the lifespan of the griever. When a loss of very high value is encountered, initially the grief is intense and shown through crying, depression, shock, and so on. Gradually, a person has hours, then days, then weeks, then months where he or she will not think about the loss and will not grieve. However, there will always be reminders of the loss—anniversaries, birthdays, and holidays—and the grief will surface again. The intense grieving periods will gradually become shorter, less frequent, and less intense.

Two models of the grieving process will be presented: the **Kübler-Ross model**[26] and the **Westberg model**.[27] Some people believe the Kübler-Ross model better describes the grieving process, whereas others assert that the Westberg model does. These models help us understand the grief we feel from *any* loss.

Kübler-Ross model: This model has the following five stages:

Stage One: Denial

During this stage, a person thinks, "No, this can't be. There must be a mistake. This just isn't happening." Denial is often useful because it helps cushion the impact of the loss.

Stage Two: Rage and Anger

In this stage, an individual reacts by asking "Why me? This just isn't fair." For example, terminally ill persons resent that they will soon die while other people remain healthy and alive. During this stage, God is sometimes a target of the anger.

Stage Three: Bargaining

During this stage, a person attempts to strike bargains to regain all or part of the loss. The terminally ill may attempt to bargain with God for more time. They promise to do something worthwhile or to "be good" in exchange for another month or year of life. Kübler-Ross indicates that even agnostics and atheists sometimes attempt to bargain with God during this stage.

Stage Four: Depression

During this stage, those having a loss tell themselves, "The loss is true, and it's really sad. This is awful." People at this stage become depressed and mourn the loss that has occurred. The depression may also be exacerbated by guilt or shame about acts of omission or commission.

Stage Five: Acceptance

Now the person fully acknowledges the loss. The terminally ill tell themselves, "I will die soon, and it's all right." Those close to the terminally ill person accept the loss and begin working on alternatives to cope with it and minimize it. By involving friends and relatives in the grieving process, dealing with required legal arrangements, and seeking spiritual counseling, the terminally ill person and surviving friends and relatives begin to restructure their lives.

WESTBERG MODEL

This model is diagrammed in Figure 13.1 and involves the following 10 stages:

Shock and Denial

Many people who are informed about a tragic loss are in such a state of shock that they are practically void of feeling. When emotional pain is unusually intense, it is possible that the human emotional system temporarily "blows out." This reaction insulates the person from emotions that are too intense. Denial is a way of avoiding the impact of a tragic loss.

Emotions Erupt

As the realization of the loss becomes evident, the person expresses the painful loss by crying, screaming, or sighing deeply.

Anger

At some point in time, the person usually experiences anger. The anger may be directed at God for causing the loss and perhaps for its unfairness. If the loss involves the death of a loved one, there is often anger at the dead person for "desertion" and for causing pain and problems by dying.

Illness

Grief may produce stress-related illnesses, such as a cold, flu, ulcers, tension headaches, diarrhea, rashes, insomnia, and so on. Intense grieving produces high levels of stress. If the stress is prolonged, stress-related illnesses are apt to develop.

Panic

Because the grieving person does not feel like his or her "old self," the person may panic and worry about going insane. Nightmares, unwanted emotions that appear uncontrollable, being less able to attend to family and work responsibilities, and having stress-related illnesses contribute to the panic.

Guilt

The grieving person may blame himself or herself for having done something that contributed to the loss, or feel guilty for not having done something that might have prevented the loss. The grieving person often unduly blames himself or herself.

Depression and Loneliness

At times, the grieving person may feel very sad, isolated, and lonely. He or she may also withdraw from others who do not seem supportive or understanding.

FIGURE 13.1   Westberg Model of the Grieving Process

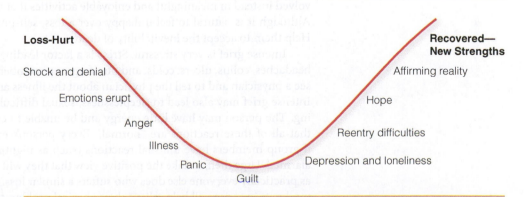

Reentry Difficulties

At this point, the grieving person makes efforts to put his or her life back together. Reentry problems arise: the person resists letting go of the past. Loyalties to memories hamper pursuit of new interests and activities.

Hope

Gradually, hope that one's life can be put back together returns and begins to grow.

Affirming Reality

The grieving person regains a feeling of having control of life. The reconstructed life is not the same as the old, and memories of the loss remain, but the reconstructed life is "OK."

In their models, Elisabeth Kübler-Ross and Granger Westberg note that some people continue grieving and never reach the final stage (Kübler-Ross's acceptance stage and Westberg's affirming reality stage of grieving). They also caution that not everyone will progress through these stages as diagrammed. There is often considerable movement back and forth among stages. For example, in the Kübler-Ross model, a person may go from denial to depression, to anger and rage, back to denial, then to bargaining, then to depression, back to anger and rage, and so on.

GRIEF MANAGEMENT IN GROUPS

A group leader can make a number of suggestions to help members who are experiencing loss cope with their grief. Crying is an acceptable and valuable expression of grief. Group members should be urged to cry if they feel the need in order to release the tension that comes as part of the grieving process.

Talking about a loss with friends, family, the clergy, a hospice volunteer, a professional counselor, or within a group is constructive. Explain to members that talking about their grief will ease their loneliness and allow them to ventilate their feelings and accept their loss so that they can make constructive plans for the present and future. Talking with close friends will offer them a sense of security and bring them closer to those they love. Talking with other group members who have experienced similar losses will help them put their problems into perspective and give them the chance to feel personal satisfaction by helping others.

Death often causes us to reexamine and question our faith or philosophy of life. Urge group members not to become discouraged if they begin questioning their beliefs, but to talk about them. A religious faith can help us accept loss. It is normal to question our basic beliefs about religion and the meaning of life in the process of grieving.

Writing out a rational self-analysis will help group members identify irrational thinking that contributes to grief (see Module 1). Once their irrational thinking is identified, much of their grief can be relieved through rational challenges to their irrational thinking. Advise group members not to dwell on their unhappiness. Suggest that they become involved instead in meaningful and enjoyable activities that will energize and motivate them. Although it is natural to feel unhappy over a loss, self-pity is a waste of time and energy. Help them to accept the inevitability of death.

Intense grief is very stressful. Stress is a factor leading to a variety of illnesses, such as headaches, colitis, ulcers, colds, and flu. If a group member becomes ill, urge that person to see a physician and to tell the physician about the illness and that it may be related to grief. Intense grief may also lead to sleeplessness, sexual difficulties, loss of appetite, or overeating. The person may have little energy and be unable to concentrate. Reassure the person that all of these reactions are "normal." Every person's experience of grief is different—if group members have unusual reactions (such as nightmares), they should not become alarmed. Urge them to take the positive view that they will get their lives back together, just as practically everyone else does who suffers a similar loss. A balanced diet, ample rest, and moderate exercise will help relieve their physical problems.

EXERCISE 13.12   Coping with a Loss

GOAL: To share the handling of grief experiences. Talking about these experiences is helpful because (1) it assists people who are still grieving to ventilate their concerns and (2) through sharing concerns, helpful suggestions may be given on how to handle present and future losses.

Note: It is advised that the instructor be the designated leader for the exercises in this section because they may generate strong emotions.

1. Summarize the Kübler-Ross and the Westberg models of the grieving process, as described in the chapter.

2. Inform the class that the following exercise is a visualization exercise to help them get in touch with a grief experience they have had. *Indicate that their feelings may become intense and if they become too intense it is certainly acceptable for them to leave the room temporarily.* If someone does leave, let him or her go, but talk to the person later to see if he or she wants to discuss the reasons for leaving. Dim the lights, if possible.

3. Ask the group members to close their eyes. Assure them that there will be no surprises. Read the following slowly, pausing frequently:

First, I want to have you get as relaxed and comfortable as possible . . . Take several deep breaths, while breathing in and out slowly . . . I want you now to focus on the greatest loss you have experienced . . . It might be the death of someone close to you . . . It might be the end of a romantic relationship . . . It might be moving away from friends and family . . . It might be the death of a pet . . . It might be not getting as high a grade on a test or in a course as you had hoped for . . . Whatever it is, concentrate on it . . . .

When you were first informed about the loss, were you in a state of shock? . . . Did you deny the loss? . . . Were you at times angry about the loss? . . . Did you at times seek to bargain about the loss? . . . If you did seek to bargain, whom did you seek to bargain with? . . . Were you at times depressed about the loss? . . . If you were depressed, why specifically were you depressed?

. . . Did you at times have some fears or concerns about the loss? . . . If you had fears or concerns, what were they? . . . Did you at times have guilt about this loss? . . . If you did feel guilty, what specifically did you feel guilty about? Did you cry about this loss? . . . If you cried, do you know why you cried? . . . If you didn't cry, do you know why you didn't cry? . . . If you cried, was it helpful? . . . How deeply has this loss hurt you? . . . How long have you been hurting about this loss? . . .

Are you still grieving about this loss? . . . Do you at times still grieve deeply about this loss? . . . Have you found that as time goes on you are grieving less deeply and that your intense grieving periods are shorter in duration? . . . Do holidays, anniversaries, birthdays, and special days still remind you of the loss? . . . If and when you are grieving deeply, how do you seek to handle this grief? . . .

Has the loss been so great that you thought about taking your life? . . . Many people think about taking their lives when they are grieving deeply . . . Have you made attempts to take your life? . . .

Have you had some physical reactions to the loss, such as difficulty in sleeping, stomach problems, headaches, anxiety attacks, sexual difficulties? . . . Grieving is very stressful, and it is common to have physical reactions . . . Do you dream about the loss? . . . For example, it is common for people who have lost a loved one to dream that the person is still alive . . . Often when someone awakes from such a dream, it is difficult to separate reality from the dream . . .

What aspects of the loss have you handled well? . . . What aspects could you have handled better? . . . What aspects are you still working on? . . . How have you gone about handling this loss? . . . How pleased are you with your efforts to handle this loss? . . . How have others close to you handled this loss? . . . How have you gone about helping them? . . . Have you grown from this loss experience? . . . What yet do you need to work on to handle this loss? . . . What specific efforts are you making to handle this loss? . . . OK . . . slowly open your eyes, and let's talk about grieving.

4. The instructor indicates that one of the best ways to handle grief is to talk about it. Then the leader asks if someone wishes to share a loss he or she has experienced and describe what helped him or her to handle this loss. If no one begins to share a grieving experience, the instructor describes a personal loss and how it was handled. (Caution: When doing this exercise, the instructor must be prepared to handle a variety of emotions and concerns that may he expressed.)

5. Student volunteers then describe whether the Westberg model or the Kübler-Ross model of the grieving process can better describe the grief they experienced.

6. The instructor summarizes material given in the chapter on how to handle grief.

EXERCISE 13.13   Recognizing That Life Is Terminal

GOAL: To have students become more aware of the thoughts and feelings they will have when their own deaths become imminent.

1. The leader begins by stating that many people do not like to attend funerals, nor do they like to think about their own eventual deaths. Many people avoid thinking about death—they have the irrational notion that their eventual deaths are so far in the future that they act as if they will live indefinitely. Yet grief management authorities assert we need to come to terms with our own deaths and that our daily lives will be more meaningful if we become more comfortable with the fact that life is terminal from birth—as we will all die. The leader then states the goal of this exercise.

2. The leader distributes to each student a packet of 12 slips of paper. The students are instructed to write on each of the small slips of paper one of the following 12 items:

- Three personal characteristics they are proud of
- Three activities they enjoy participating in
- The three possessions that they cherish most
- The names of the three people who are most important in their lives

Each student then arranges these 12 slips of paper in front of him or her on a desk or table so that all can be seen.

3. The leader states the following: Imagine that you haven't been feeling well for the past several months. You finally decide to see your doctor. The doctor administers a number of medical tests. Today you go in to hear the test results. As you walk in, the doctor has a very concerned look on her face. The doctor informs you that you have a terminal illness. *You have 30 seconds to tear up three of your slips of paper.* Tear up the three slips that are least important to you.

4. The leader states the following: You leave the physician's office in a state of shock. You return home. Who is there to greet you? Whom do you really *want* to find there? What do you say to these people? What do you want to hear from them? *Tear up another three slips of paper.*

5. The leader states the following: It is now two months later. You realize your health is deteriorating. Your symptoms are worsening, and you are feeling weaker. Where are you living now? Have you made changes in your lifestyle? Are there projects and loose ends in your life that you are seeking to complete? What are you thinking and feeling about your terminal illness? *Tear up another two slips of paper.*

6. The leader states the following: It is now four months after you were informed of your terminal illness. You are undeniably ill. You are in considerable pain, and you now need caregivers to stay alive. Where are you living now? Who is taking care of you? Who visits you? Who are the people you want to visit you and take care of you? *Tear up another two slips of paper.*

7. The leader states the following: Six months have now passed since you learned of your terminal illness. You have very little energy left. The smallest activity of daily living takes most of your energy. A caregiver now has to attend to you 24 hours a day. You can no longer bathe yourself. How do you now feel about yourself? Where are you living now? *Please turn over your remaining two slips of paper, and I will take one.* (The leader takes one from each student.)

8. The leader states the following: *Look at your last slip of paper, and then tear it up. You are now dead.*

9. The leader thanks the students for conscientiously participating in the first part of this exercise. The leader then asks the students to form subgroups of about three persons. The members of each subgroup are asked to share their reactions to the following questions, which should now be listed on the blackboard. (If a student chooses not to share, that is his or her right.)

1. Did the exercise seem real? If "yes," when did it become real? If "no," why didn't it seem real?
2. What emotional reactions did you have to this exercise?
3. What were the last two items on the slips of paper that you kept?
4. What were your thoughts, feelings, and reactions to the tearing up of the last slip of paper?

10. The class as a whole then discusses the merits and shortcomings of this exercise.

EXERCISE 13.14   Achieving Closure in a Lost Relationship

GOAL: To achieve closure in a relationship loss that has been experienced.

1. Explain that people who are grieving about a loss often feel guilty about things said or done—or things not said or done—that they believe may have contributed to the loss. Many people also feel guilty about not having resolved an interpersonal conflict before the death of someone close. People who experience a breakup of a romantic relationship often feel the need to obtain "closure" to the relationship by saying how they feel about the relationship ending or by finding answers to questions about why the relationship ended.

2. Ask each person to write down a number of items not resolved in a relationship on a sheet of paper. The relationship may have been with a person who died, a close friend or relative, or someone involved in a current conflict. Then ask each person to write down what he or she would say to resolve the conflict and then how he or she thinks the other person would respond. Indicate that this exercise has been found to be helpful in obtaining closure to relationships and in relieving guilt for survivors who have not obtained closure with someone who has died.

3. Ask the class to get together in groups of three to share what they wrote. *Indicate that if someone does not wish to share what was written, this request will be honored, as people have a right to privacy.*

4. Ask the class as a group to discuss their thoughts about the exercise and what they learned from it.

EXERCISE 13.15   Epitaphs

GOALS: To foster the discussion of death, to help you accept your own eventual death, and to provide some guidance on how to live.

1. Ask students to write down the epitaph they want placed on their tombstones. Explain that an epitaph is a brief statement or phrase meant as a remembrance. Indicate to the class that no names should be placed on the sheet and that the epitaphs will be read to the class. Several minutes will be needed to write this statement.

2. Collect the epitaphs in such a way that students will not be identified. Read the epitaphs to the class, making appropriate observations, such as: "It is interesting to note that hardly anyone mentioned wanting to be remembered for collecting material goods, yet so many people spend so much time trying to collect material things. These epitaphs provide some direction on how we should live our lives in order to be remembered in a way we would like."

Medication should be taken sparingly and only under the supervision of a physician. Grief should not be relieved with alcohol or other drugs because many drugs are addictive and may stop or delay the necessary grieving process. A group member may feel that he or she has nothing to live for and be considering suicide. Understand that many people who encounter severe losses feel this way. Seek to assure such people that a sense of purpose and meaning in life will return.

Guilt, real or imagined, is also a normal part of grief. Survivors often feel guilty about things they said or did to the deceased, or things they think they should have said or done. If members are experiencing intense guilt, suggest they share it with friends, with the group, or with a professional counselor. A rational self-analysis of the guilt might also be helpful. Reassure members that all humans make mistakes. If we didn't, we wouldn't be human. Ask them to learn to forgive themselves. Anger is another common reaction to loss. Urge members to express their anger constructively (see the exercise on expressing anger constructively in Module 2).

Grieving members may complain that friends and relatives appear to be shunning them. If this is happening, it is probably because of discomfort and uncertainty about what to say or do. Advise group members to take the initiative, to talk with their family members and friends about the loss, to tell them about ways in which they could be supportive.

Holidays and the anniversaries of a loved one's birth and death can be stressful to someone experiencing the loss of a loved one. These days should be spent with family and friends who will provide support. After a severe loss, major decisions should be put off until an individual is more emotionally relaxed. When a person is highly emotional, he or she is apt to make poor decisions.

GROUP WORK WITH OLDER ADULTS*

Introduction

The older adult population in the United States is one of the fastest growing populations, and this population is living longer because of great strides in the medical field. There are roughly 45 million people aged 65 and older, and with the "Baby Boom" population now reaching this age, the population is continuing to grow. According to U.S. Census Bureau projections, the number of persons aged 65 years and older will increase from 35 million to 66 million by 2030 and to 82 million by 2050.[28] Older adults face several challenges that younger generations may overlook or take for granted. Some of these challenges include housing issues, transportation, finances, health problems, and limited social supports.

Housing issues include finding affordable housing that fits within their monthly fixed income, but could also include having to maintain a home that they have lived in for years. Older adults often have a hard time moving in to new settings, and often the biggest challenge for a child or other caregiver maybe getting an older adult to accept that she or he can no longer live in her or his home safely. It could be for a variety of reasons, including too many steps, too many obstacles, lack of space to maneuver a wheelchair, or inability to keep up on general maintenance of the yard and interior of the home.

Transportation is a huge contributor to a person's independence. Whether it is access to their own vehicles or to public transportation, there are costs associated with transportation. For older adults, there are also safety factors to consider in driving a vehicle. These mainly have to do with physical health issues that may arise, such as loss of or poor vision. Factors contributing to this could include cataracts or glaucoma. Another cost includes

---

* This section was written by Jacob Dunn, MSW, LCSW. Mr. Dunn is a social worker at Stoughton Hospital Geriatric Psychiatry Unit. He is also an associate lecturer at the University of Wisconsin-Madison.

paying to insure a vehicle, and as one gets older, these costs increase. As stated earlier, older adults are often on a fixed income, and most do not have the ability to afford these things. Even public transportation has considerations that older adults need to keep in mind that younger generations may not. For instance, if an older adult is mobility impaired, she or he has to make sure the bus, cab, or train has the ability to accommodate a wheelchair or walker. If an older adult is living in a rural setting, she or he may have a long distance to go to catch a bus, if the route even comes to her or his home. Transportation companies that provide rides to older adults may charge more to pick someone up who resides in a rural community.

Many older adults rely solely on their Social Security and pensions for their income. Many older females may have never worked, or their primary occupation was as a home-maker. For several years older adults did not receive any increases in their Social Security payments, and, as we know, the amount of money in the Social Security fund is dwindling at a very high rate; many believe that younger generations may not be able to count on this as income when they retire. The struggle this has posed for older adults is that their groceries, medical bills, prescription medications, and other expenses have all increased. Unfortunately, many older adults are left with the choice at the end of the month of whether to buy food or fill one of their medications. This, in turn, may lead to additional health problems.

Health concerns are a major issue faced by older adults. Many older adults have more than one major medical issue and often face issues of comorbidity (physical and mental health issues). Common physical health disorders that older adults face are arthritis, heart disease, hypertension (high blood pressure), diabetes, obesity, and dementia. Any one of these disorders can lead to a decrease in independent functioning, and often to depression. Other issues that can lead to a decrease in functioning are falls and psychosocial issues that lead to stress affecting an individual's ability to perform activities of daily living (ADLs). ADLs include bathing, grooming, dressing, and eating. Losing the ability to perform ADLs leads to a loss of independence and can lead to depression, as one is not able to perform tasks she or he used to take for granted. Depression often exacerbates physical health problems.

In older adulthood, individuals are also faced with loss. Loss of social supports can lead to isolation for an older adult. Studies have demonstrated an association between increased levels of social support and reduced risks for physical disease, mental illness, and mortality.[29] Social support includes real or perceived resources provided by others that enable a person to feel cared for, valued, and part of a network of communication and mutual obligation. Social support can be critical for those older adults who rely on family, friends, or organizations to assist them with daily activities, provide companionship, and care for their well-being.

How Group Work Can Be Used with Older Adults

One way for social workers to help address some of the issues that older adults face is providing support to them in a group setting. In a group setting, older adults will develop a sense of belonging and form new meaningful relationships with other peers. There has been a shift in the theory of group work with older adults from institutions to more home- and community-based options.[30] Factors that Haight and Gibson say should be considered when setting up groups in the community include:

- Cultural characteristics
- Health and social service needs
- Training, ethics, and values of staff
- Objectives of agency
- Financial resources available for programs[31]

The main intentions are to build and strengthen an individual's abilities; foster mutual aid; and promote well-being, stability, change, and education.

One of the most common types of groups for older adults is treatment groups.[32] These groups provide an environment to change beliefs and influence behavior, and members often face similar difficulties, problems, or challenges. Treatment groups also offer companionship, opportunities to give and receive information, and opportunities to contribute and benefit as equals. These groups often use a multidisciplinary approach and are facilitated by nurses, activity therapists, physical and occupational therapists, and social workers. Settings for treatment groups can include skilled nursing facilities, community-based residential facilities (CBRFs), memory care facilities, adult day service programs, and senior centers. Other types of groups that exist for older adults include psychotherapeutic groups, where the focus is on changing relationships, feelings, or behavior and managing life stress or other problems. Mutual aid groups focus on members sharing a common experience, need, and/or interest. Task-centered groups can focus on fundraising, social action, or other issues. Action-oriented groups focus on empowerment, social change, and campaigns. Problem-solving groups, brief solution-focused groups, psychoeducational groups, and activity groups are other common forms of groups for older adults.

Issues to consider when facilitating groups with older adults include using a direct approach, where there is an active leadership role. This is effective in answering specific questions, providing information, and sharing information about oneself.[33] Having a supportive leader can increase confidence among members and promote cohesiveness. Another major component when working with older adults is good communication. Poor communication can lead to confusion, ill feelings, and lack of interest in the group and among the members.[34] The following are illustrations of the various types of groups involving older adults.

Reality Orientation

Haight and Gibson discuss reality orientation (RO) groups, which are commonly used for older adults affected by dementia.[35] They are designed to assist confused, disoriented, and forgetful older adults to remain oriented. RO groups should not have more than four members because of the demands this population places on the group leader. There is typically a large board posted in the group meeting room that has updates, such as date, weather, and when the next meal will be served. The main focus is on time, place, and person.

Validation Therapy

Validation therapy is based on Erikson's theory[36] and focuses on caregivers of disoriented persons understanding their behaviors. Four stages are outlined by Naomi Feil[37]: malorientation, time confusion, repetitive motion, and vegetative state. Malorientation is characterized by defensive behavior. Time confusion includes lack of awareness of time, the day, and the month. Repetitive motion is when the members are only oriented to themselves and not to others around them. Vegetative state is when motion is stopped, eyes are closed, and the end of life is near.

Remotivation Therapy

The focus of remotivation therapy is for older adults who have been isolated and dependent on others. The group leader sets up a structured environment with props to facilitate discussion among members on specific topics so that members discuss their own experiences in relation to the topic. The goal is for members to start interacting with one another and ask questions when some of them may have not spoken in quite some time.

Reminiscence Groups

Reminiscence groups are one of the most commonly used group modalities for older adults. They are typically theme based and are designed to have six or eight members so that each person can explore memories about the specific topic. Group leaders encourage sharing memories that range from happy to sad, lighthearted to serious, and include all stages of life.

Topic-Specific Groups

Haight and Gibson talk about common topic-specific groups such as music, art, poetry, reading, and writing therapy.[38] Music groups can include sing-along, listening, and instrumental. They are designed to improve the quality and enjoyment of daily living, encourage movement, and increase reminiscing through familiar music among the group members. Art and poetry groups encourage expression among members who may not be able to express themselves otherwise. Reading groups promote reading aloud to facilitate energizing older adults and their interacting with one another. Writing therapy benefits members by allowing them to self-express, enhance self-esteem, encourage reminiscing, and increase social interaction.

Health-Related Groups

Settings for health-related groups are often nutrition centers, retirement homes, senior centers, and assisted living communities. They are often led by a variety of different leaders who specialize in a specific area[39] to provide education to individuals. The main reason for these groups is to teach prevention. The format could be a lecture in a large-group setting or a small discussion-based group.

Groups for Family Members

Group work with family members can be extremely beneficial and can be offered for a variety of reasons. Such groups reduce hostility, anxiety, and guilt among the family. They also help educate the family about the aging process and often increase family members' interest in the progress of the relative. They can also provide a network for families by providing insight and support. These groups can be held at a variety of settings and can be led by administrators of a facility, social workers, clergy, nurses, or psychologists.

Psychotherapy Groups

Group psychotherapy is one of the more preferred treatments for older adults because it is cost effective and an efficient use of time for the therapist. Members feel a sense of belonging, and they can assist older adults in adjusting to loss by increasing their support network. Haight and Gibson outline 14 rationales for using a group setting for psychotherapy:

1. Assist in problem solving later-life challenges
2. Reduce social isolation, depression, and loneliness
3. Reduce feelings of inadequacy
4. Change sense of anonymity
5. Provide opportunity for camaraderie
6. Provide opportunity for social exercise
7. Provide opportunity for meaningful interpersonal interactions
8. Provide forum for personal feedback
9. Work through unresolved conflicts
10. Transference is "divided"; not as intense as in standard psychotherapy
11. Offer cognitive stimulation
12. Offer emotional responsiveness
13. Reduce feelings of being rejected by family
14. Offer almost immediate relief[40]

EXERCISE 13.16   Things That Go Together

GOAL: To facilitate reminiscing and socialization among a group of older adults.

1. The group leader first starts by finding out the backgrounds of the residents. For example, if many of the members are from farming communities, topics that are selected may include the county fair, things on a farm, and gardening. Topic cards are then prepared, for example, things on a farm.

2. The leader then prints off five items that would fall under that topic. For the "Farm" topic, the leader could choose a cow, a tractor, a barn, a chicken, and a pig. These items are listed—one on a card—and each of these cards will be called an "item card." The leader prepares five item cards for each topic card. For each "game," there are three to four topic cards and five item cards for each topic.

3. The leader then puts all the topic cards in his or her hand and places all of the item cards face down in the middle of a table. Each player (there should be about three to seven players) takes three to five item cards (the larger the number of players, the fewer the number of item cards that are taken). The players turn up their item cards and place the cards in front of them.

4. One member picks a topic card from the leader's hand. That member reads it out loud to the others. The members have to select their item cards that correspond to the selected topic card. The leader goes around the table to see if anyone has an item card that fits the topic card. If someone is having trouble putting her or his cards into a category, the leader can assist by picking up two cards from the member's selection (one that fits and one that doesn't) and have the individual choose between them.

5. During the game the leader may ask the members about the item cards they have and ask them to share any personal stories about something that happened to them related to their item cards.

6. This continues until all of the cards are gone.

- *Variations:* The group leader can have the members tell the group about the topic card before going around the table. For example, the leader can ask them to use all their senses and describe what a farm smells like, what they would hear on a farm, or what they would see on a farm.
- Another way to play the game is to play it backward. Remove all the topic cards and set them aside. Put all the item cards in the middle of the table face up. Have the members find cards that go together and have them tell the leader why they go together. When the cards are put into categories, the leader brings out the topic cards, and the members put them together with the five item cards.
- *Other topics:* Other topics could include "Transportation," "At the Beach," "Holidays," and "School Days."

EXERCISE 13.17   Would You Rather?

GOAL: To facilitate reminiscing and socialization among a group of older adults.

1. The leader puts pictures in a photo album of various topics, such as fall to summer, spring to winter, country to city, pie to cake, or cat to dog.

2. For each topic, the group leader asks a member "Would you rather. . . "? For example, the group leader would ask the member, "Would you rather have a cat or a dog?"

3. The player can then choose her or his preference, and the group leader and members can discuss topics such as if they ever had pets, what kind of pets, their names, and their favorite memories of their pets.

EXERCISE 13.18   Balloon Pop and Reminisce

GOAL: To facilitate reminiscing and interaction among a group of older adults. Equipment needed: Balloons, scissors or pin, paper and pencil

1. Begin by writing a variety of reminisce questions/statements on small slips of paper with one question or statement on each slip.

Examples are:

- What do you remember most about high school?
- Tell us about your best childhood friend.
- What do you remember about your grandparents?
- Who taught you how to drive?
- Tell us about your first date.
- Describe the house you grew up in.
- What was your first job?

2. Place one slip into each balloon. The group members are then seated in a circle with balloons on the floor in the middle.

3. Have one resident pick a balloon. The group leader pops the balloon with the scissors and the group member answers the question.

4. The game continues by going around the circle, having all residents answer that question.

5. The next group member then selects a balloon and the process continues.

Summary

The following summarizes the chapter's content in terms of the learning objective presented at the beginning of the chapter.

This chapter is focused on facilitating the readers' abilities to design treatment groups for a wide variety of diverse and vulnerable populations. It is so important for social workers to develop the knowledge and skills to be able to design and implement treatment groups for a wide variety of diverse populations. This chapter illustrates group treatment approaches with the following five populations: adolescents, people who have an eating disorder, individuals affected by domestic violence, people who are grieving, and older adults.

Group Exercises

EXERCISE A: Designing a Group Treatment Exercise

GOAL: To further develop the capacity of students to design group treatment exercises.

Step 1. The leader divides the class into groups of three to four students in each subgroup. Each subgroup first selects a population for which it will design a group treatment exercise. (Many examples of group treatment exercises are presented in this chapter.)

Step 2. Each subgroup then designs a group treatment exercise for its selected population.

Step 3. The subgroups present their selected populations and their group treatment exercises to the class. The exercise ends with the class discussing the merits and shortcomings of using group treatment exercises with diverse and vulnerable populations.

Competency Notes

EP 6a Apply knowledge of human behavior and the social environment, person-in-environment, and other multidisciplinary theoretical frameworks to engage with clients and constituencies.

EP 6b Use empathy, reflection, and interpersonal skills to effectively engage diverse clients and constituencies.

EP 8a Critically choose and implement interventions to achieve practice goals and enhance capacities of clients and constituencies.

EP 8b Apply knowledge of human behavior and the social environment, person-in-environment, and other multidisciplinary theoretical frameworks in interventions with clients and constituencies. (pp. 400–450)

This chapter is focused on facilitating students' abilities to design treatment groups for a wide variety of diverse and vulnerable populations.

Key Terms and Concepts

Anorexia Nervosa	Bulimia Nervosa	Westberg Model of Grieving
Binge Eating	Kübler-Ross Model of Grieving	

14

Termination and Evaluation of a Group

LEARNING OBJECTIVES

Termination and evaluation are among the most important phases of a group. This chapter will help prepare students to:

LO 1
Effectively terminate a group.

LO 2
Conduct a process evaluation of a group.

LO 3
Conduct three approaches to evaluating the outcome of a group.

Through reading this text, participating in the exercises, and leading some of the exercises, it is hoped that you have developed the skills needed to become an effective group leader and member. Your verbal and nonverbal communication in groups and active listening skills should have improved. Having gained an understanding of why controversy is desirable for groups, you should be able to use problem-solving and decision-making approaches to foster group effectiveness. You should be able to lead a brainstorming group and a nominal group and have some familiarity with parliamentary procedure.

Groups can be used to help members control unwanted emotions, manage grief, become more comfortable with death, become more assertive, manage stress, treat chemical dependency, prevent burnout, improve time management, develop a positive self-identity, and improve close relationships. At the end of this class, you should be better able to lead a variety of social work groups. Effective functioning in groups helps us accomplish our personal goals, furthers our personal growth, and improves our interpersonal relationships. Acquiring group skills and knowledge facilitates our capacities to function effectively in organizations, communities, families, and society. Now that we have reached the end of this class and the end of this text, we need to focus on how to end a group.

LO 1 Effectively Terminate a Group

TERMINATION

The process of ending a treatment group has already been described in Chapter 12. This section will describe the process of termination for a broad array of groups.

Inherent in termination is separation from the group and from group members. Separation typically involves mixed feelings that vary in intensity according to a number of factors, several of which will be discussed here. The more emotionally close and emotionally invested a member is in a group, the greater will be that member's feeling of loss. The greater the feeling of success of members in accomplishing their goals via the group, the greater will be their feelings of "sweet sorrow"—sweetness from feeling that they have grown and had success, and sorrow because of separation from the group that has come to be an important and meaningful part of their lives.

451

EXERCISE 14.1   The Emotions Involved in Leaving a Group That Is Important to You

GOAL: This exercise is designed to assist you in understanding the emotions involved when members leave a group that has become emotionally important to them.

1. The emotions that members experience when leaving a group that is important to them are comparable to the emotions you experienced when you ended participation in something that was emotionally important to you. Describe an experience that you had in which you ended participation in something that was emotionally important to you. It might be leaving a group (such as Girl Scouts or a baseball team), or moving away from your family and friends to go to college, or leaving high school, and so on.

2. Describe your feelings about leaving and "moving on." Specify both positive and negative feelings. Perhaps this experience of leaving was "bittersweet"—sadness about leaving but sweetness about positive memories and positive feelings about moving on to another phase in your life.

3. If you felt really sad (or other negative emotions) about leaving, have you let go of these feelings? If "yes," what helped you to let go? If "no," what do you still need to work on, and what is your strategy to assist in letting go?

The more emotionally dependent a member has become on a group, the more he or she is apt to feel anger, rejection, and depression over termination. The more a member has experienced difficulties in separating in the past from significant others, the more likely it is that the separation will be experienced as difficult, as the pattern of reacting to separations is apt to be repeated.

There are a variety of types of termination, which include:

1. Termination of a successful group
2. Termination of an unsuccessful group
3. A member dropping out
4. Transfer of a member
5. The leader's leaving

Each of these types will be briefly described.

Termination of a Successful Group

A successful group is one in which the group and its members have generally accomplished their goals. Termination of such a group is apt to generate the "sweet sorrow" reaction. The members are apt to be delighted with their accomplishments. The accomplishments are apt to increase their levels of self-confidence and self-esteem. Members are also apt to experience a feeling of loss (varying in intensity) due to separating from a group in which they have become emotionally invested. Such a group may desire to dine together or have some other ceremony to commemorate and recognize the group and its accomplishments.

In terminating a successful group, it is essential that formal termination begin one or more meetings before the final meeting. Ideally, the date of the last meeting should be discussed and agreed upon by the members well in advance of the final meetings. (For some groups the final meeting is scheduled even before the group begins to meet.) Sufficient time has to be allowed in terminating a successful group so that (1) progress made in accomplishing the tasks and goals of the group and its members can be evaluated; (2) plans can be made for continued work by the members on remaining problems; (3) work can be done on unresolved, last-minute issues that are identified by members; (4) emotional reactions of members to terminating can be handled; and (5) members have time to discuss whether they want to plan for a special social event for the group's ending.

Although goodbyes are often sad, the negative feelings can be offset by emphasizing what members have given and received, the ways they have grown, the skills they have learned, and what the group has accomplished. In some cases, an extra session could be held to complete unfinished business items. The members may decide to have "class reunions" periodically or social get-togethers in the future.

Termination of an Unsuccessful Group

An unsuccessful group is one in which most or all of the goals of the group and its members are largely unmet. The reactions of members to the lack of progress may vary considerably: anger, frustration, disappointment, despair, guilt (for unproductive efforts or over lack of effort), scapegoating, blaming, and apathy. In rarer cases, it is possible for an unsuccessful group to be fairly pleased and accepting of its efforts. For example, a group that is formed to write a grant (when there is limited hope of funding) from the federal government may be pleased with its efforts and with the new relationships with others that were formulated and only mildly disappointed to learn that the grant will not be funded.

In planning the termination of an unsuccessful group, it is essential that formal termination be as well planned as with successful groups. The date of the last meeting should be discussed and agreed upon by the members well in advance of the final meeting. Sufficient time has to be allowed in terminating an unsuccessful group so that (1) reasons for the lack of progress of the group can be assessed and analyzed; (2) discussions can be held of alternatives for the group and its members to reach their goals (such alternatives may involve changing the format of the present group, referral of members to other groups, and alternatives involving individual actions rather than group efforts); (3) emotional reactions of members to terminating and their reactions to the lack of progress made by the group can be handled; (4) members have time to work on unresolved, last-minute issues; and (5) members have time to discuss whether they want to plan for a special social event for the group's ending.

At times the ending of an unsuccessful group is chaotic and abrupt. For example, a group that has been appointed to write a grant may be nearly finished when members are informed the funding organization has had a financial shortfall and is therefore withdrawing its request for funding proposals. Such a group may end abruptly in despair. Or, in a group of involuntary members (such as at a prison or at an adolescent residential treatment facility), the leader may decide it is counterproductive to continue a group in which the members are continually "goofing off" and not putting effort into achieving the goals of the group. In every case, the reasons for the group's ending should be fully explained, and time should be given to dealing with the reactions of the members to the closing. If there is insufficient time at the final meeting for dealing with the tasks involved in ending a group, it is sometimes advisable either to have another session or for the leader to meet individually with each member to discuss their reactions to goals being unmet, alternatives for reaching their goals, reactions to the group ending, and unresolved concerns they may have.

When an unsuccessful group ends abruptly, some group members may be highly critical of the leader, of other group members, or of experiences that occurred in the group. If the leader contacts members to gain their thoughts about the group, he or she needs to be prepared to respond to highly critical feedback. One way the leader can prepare is to "visualize" possible criticisms and then formulate a positive and realistic response to each anticipated criticism.

A Member Dropping Out

When a member drops out, that person no longer attends, even though the group continues. A member may drop out for a variety of reasons. The member may become disenchanted with the group and feel that the group will not accomplish the goals that have been set. The member may have a disagreement with or dislike another group member. The member may be a parent who has to provide child care at the time the group meets. The member may start a new job with work hours that conflict with the meeting time. And there are numerous other reasons.

When a group member drops out without informing the group as to the reasons, the leader should contact the person to ascertain the reasons for terminating. In some instances it is desirable for the leader to explain that deciding to leave is a major decision that should not be made abruptly and that the leader would like the opportunity to explore the reasons that led to the decision. If the member has a conflict with another group member, perhaps the conflict can be resolved so that the member decides to return. Perhaps action can be taken to enable the member to return. For example, if child care is a problem for a parent, childcare arrangements can be made.

If the member decides not to return, the reasons for leaving should be explored. Perhaps the member may raise legitimate concerns that need to be dealt with so that other members do not also become discouraged and leave. If a person drops out of a treatment group, a sensitivity group, or an educational group and still has unresolved personal concerns, a referral to another group or to one-to-one professional help may be advisable.

Whenever a member drops out, the leader needs to inform that member of his or her positive contributions to the group. Dropping out of a group is often viewed as a personal failure, and therefore the person needs to be thanked for positive contributions to soothe the sense of personal failure.

When a member drops out, the remaining members may experience a variety of emotions. Some may feel they failed this member. Some may feel guilt for what they said

EXERCISE 14.2   The Experience of Being Rejected

GOAL: This exercise is designed to give you increased awareness of what a member of a group is apt to feel when he or she is asked to leave a group that is emotionally important.

1. Describe an event when you were rejected. The rejection event should be something that was emotionally important to you.

2. What feelings did you experience? (Such feelings are perhaps comparable to those of a group member when she or he is asked to leave an important group.)

3. Have you successfully dealt with your negative feelings over being rejected? If "yes," what helped you let go? If "no," what is your strategy to emotionally let go?

or did—or feel guilt for failing to do or say what they believe would have led the person to stay. Some may feel relief or joy over the member leaving, as they may view the member as unworthy of the group or as an obstacle in the group's efforts to accomplish its goals. Some may feel sadness for the member dropping out and be concerned that something tragic has happened to that member. Some members may experience anger toward the person for leaving, as they feel he or she is abandoning the group. A few may feel personally rejected. Often, when a member drops out, rumors begin to circulate as to the reasons. Therefore, it is essential that the group be informed about the reasons for the person's decision to leave. A member's leaving can be devastating to group morale. If several members depart, the group's survival may be jeopardized.

Ideally, the person who leaves should inform the group about the reasons, either in person or in writing. If the member does not do this, the leader or some other group member should contact the person to ascertain the reasons for leaving and then inform the group.

Transfer of a Member

A transfer of a group member to another group or to some other type of professional services generally involves a planned arrangement between the group leader and the member. The transfer may occur for a variety of reasons. In a problem-solving group, the employing agency may decide the group member's talents and skills could be better used in some other capacity. In a therapy group, the leader and group members may jointly decide the member would be better served by receiving more specialized services in some other therapeutic format. A group member may transfer from any kind of a group because of a conflict that cannot be resolved between that group member and other group members. The conflict may severely interfere with goal accomplishment within the group. (For example, there may be a serious and insurmountable gap in mutual understanding and communication caused by differences in religious beliefs, values, or language.)

When a transfer occurs, the leader does everything possible to keep the transfer from being unexpected or abrupt. The member being transferred should clearly understand the reasons for the transfer and be accepting of the transfer. In addition, the group should receive an explanation as to the reasons for the transfer. Ideally, the member should explain to the group why he or she is transferring. This allows the other group members an opportunity to wish the member well and to gain a sense of closure to the member leaving the group.

The Leader's Leaving

Sometimes a group leader must terminate work with a group because of reassignment, change of employment, health reasons, or family crises. Such a termination is difficult for both the group leader and the members. Emotional reactions may be intense, and adequate time for working through these reactions may not be available. Members who feel vulnerable and dependent upon the leader may feel devastated. Some may personalize the leader's leaving as due to something they said or did. Some may feel angry and betrayed because they made a commitment to the group, confided in, and trusted the leader and then the leader left when their goals and the group's goals were only partially accomplished.

The leader, too, may experience intense emotions, including guilt for not following through on the implicit commitment to lead the group until its goals were accomplished.

When a leader leaves, he or she should encourage the members to express their feelings. The leader may want to initiate this expression by fully explaining why he or she is leaving, listing a number of positive things about the group, and expressing feelings of sadness and guilt over leaving. Before leaving, the leader (or group) should select a new leader. If the new leader is not a member of the group, the leader who is leaving should inform (outside a group meeting) the new leader about the goals, characteristics of members, current tasks and difficulties, and progress toward goals that the group has made. This new leader should be introduced to the group by the leader who is leaving. As much as possible, a smooth transition is the goal in shifting responsibilities from the former leader to the new leader.

EXERCISE 14.3   The Experience of a Significant Person Leaving

GOAL: This exercise is designed to assist you in being aware of what group members emotionally feel when a valued leader leaves the group.

1. Describe an experience where a valued person did not reject you but geographically moved away from you.

2. How did you feel about this person leaving?

EP 4a
EP 4b
EP 4c
EP 9a
EP 9c
EP 9d

EVALUATION

In the past few decades, accountability has become a major emphasis in social welfare. Funding sources demand research evidence that funds allocated are having a beneficial effect. An essential component of accountability is evaluation.

In broad terms, evaluation is designed to assess whether services provided were effective and efficient. Services provided in which goals and objectives are unmet are neither effective nor efficient. In evaluating the services provided by a group, there are two dimensions of evaluation: process evaluation and outcome evaluation.

LO 2   Conduct a Process Evaluation of a Group

PROCESS EVALUATION

A **process evaluation** is an assessment, generally by group members, as to the aspects of the group that were useful or detrimental. Feedback about techniques and incidents that blocked or enhanced progress is of immense value to the group leader. With this information, the leader can hone certain skills, eliminate some materials, and give direction for approaches and materials to add. Such feedback can aid confidence. If the feedback is highly critical, it can be humbling and even devastating. It is far better to make changes suggested

EXERCISE 14.4   Your Process Evaluation of a Group

GOAL: This exercise is designed to familiarize you with a process evaluation.

1. Describe a group that you participated in, which has now ended.

2. Summarize the following:

(a) Strengths of this group:

(b) Shortcomings of this group:

(c) Suggestions for how this group could have been improved:

by the evaluation than to reject and "deny" the feedback and repeat the same mistakes in future groups. Group leaders need to welcome criticism and be prepared to respond to it constructively, which is the way that social workers expect clients to take constructive criticism.

A process evaluation can be conducted orally by asking the group members to discuss the aspects, techniques, materials, and incidents that were constructive and those that were counterproductive. An advantage of such an oral evaluation is that most members enjoy a verbal discussion. A disadvantage is that some may be inhibited from giving negative feedback verbally, as there is a social norm in such situations to focus on the positives.

A process evaluation can also be accomplished by a brief questionnaire. Three key questions follow:

1. Summarize the strengths of this group. (Cite specific materials and incidents. Also cite skills and techniques used by the leader.)
2. Summarize the shortcomings of this group. (Cite specific materials and incidents. Also cite skills and techniques used by the leader.)
3. Briefly outline your specific suggestions for changes.

In process evaluations, group members typically cite positive factors more than negative ones.[1] Such positive feedback not only has a "stroking value," but also enables leaders to be more aware of their strengths so that they are apt to increase the use of these strengths in the future.

Negative feedback is as valuable as, and often more valuable than, positive feedback. It informs the leader of aspects that need improvement, which the leader can then attend to. Hepworth and Larsen note, "As with clients, awareness precedes change."[2]

Another way of evaluating process is by **peer review**, a form of quality control. A peer review is conducted by having one or more "peers" (usually other group leaders) periodically sit in on a group. (Some agencies have one-way mirrors so that the group can be unobtrusively observed.) Prior to a peer review, the agency or organization should agree upon a set of principles or criteria that reflect quality group leadership. A peer review is a review of a small portion of the total functioning of the group. That small portion may be typical or atypical of the total functioning of the group. (Many colleges and universities use a peer-review process in which tenured faculty in a department sit in on some of the classes of recently hired faculty.)

A variation of the peer-review process is taping (either audio or video) a meeting. That tape is played back and reviewed by the leader and a peer (or by the leader's supervisor). Prior to taping a meeting, the leader should explain the reasons for wanting to tape the meeting, indicate who will view the tape, and then ask the members for their permission to tape the session.

LO 3   Conduct Three Approaches to Evaluating the Outcome of a Group

OUTCOME EVALUATION

Outcome evaluation involves assessing the extent to which the goals have been accomplished that were formulated when the group began. Specific approaches to measure goal attainment are single-subject design, task achievement scaling, and **satisfaction questionnaire**.

Single-Subject Design   **Single-subject design** has become increasingly popular in the helping professions in the past two decades. There are more than a dozen variations of single-subject design, some of which are very complex and rigorous.[3] Fortunately, the simpler designs can be used by entry-level social workers in many direct practice situations. The basic elements of the design are described here.

Single-subject design has been identified by several other terms—single-system design, single N or N = 1 research, intensive or ideographic research, single case-study design, single-organism research, time-series research or design, and single-case experimental design.[4] The phrase **single-subject** indicates a focus of research attention on a single client—which is usually an individual but can be a small group or a family.

In a single-subject design, the client becomes the control group. For this reason, the approach is relatively easy to incorporate into a practitioner's usual services.

The steps in the research process involve:

1. Specifying the outcome
2. Selecting a suitable measure
3. Recording baseline data
4. Implementing an intervention and monitoring the outcome
5. Assessing change
6. Inferring effectiveness[5]

The first step in single-subject design is to specify the outcome of interest. The selected outcome should reflect the needs of the client and what is realistic to achieve. It also must be an outcome that can be defined specifically and measured. For a client with bulimia who is binging and purging, an appropriate outcome may be cessation of purging. For a family in which there are frequent heated arguments, an appropriate outcome may be a sharp reduction in heated arguments.

The second step in the design process is to select a suitable measure. The target behavior that the practitioner and client hope to change (such as reduction in heated arguments) must be specified in such a manner that it can be measured in some reliable way. There are many ways to measure client outcomes, including direct observation, self-reports from the client, and standardized measures. Standardized measures include tests, questionnaires, rating scales, inventories, and checklists. Many standardized measures have been developed to evaluate variables such as self-esteem, level of assertiveness, level of depression, anxiety level, degree of marital satisfaction, burnout, amount of stress, potential for suicide, and generalized contentment.

The third step is to record baseline data. Baselining involves collecting data for a period of time before implementing the intervention. The objective of baselining is to establish the base rate of the outcome measure before intervention occurs. This baselining rate can then be used to provide a basis of comparison for the occurrence of the target behavior (behavior to be changed) before, during, and after intervention.

The fourth step is to implement the intervention and monitor the outcomes. For example, for a client who is generally nonassertive, the intervention may be to have the client participate in an assertiveness training group.

The fifth step is to assess change. This step involves a comparison of the occurrence of the target behavior before, during, and after treatment. Often the occurrence of the target behavior during these three time periods can be displayed on a graph, as shown in Figure 14.1.

The sixth step in the process is to infer effectiveness. This step involves demonstrating logically and empirically that the intervention is the only reasonable explanation for the observed change in client outcome. In essence, this stage involves ruling out other possible explanations for the observed change. The primary criterion for inferring causality is concomitant variation; that is, the observed change in the outcome must occur at (or soon after) the time the intervention is implemented. If positive changes begin during the baseline period, then logically we have to conclude that something other than the intervention may have contributed to the positive changes. Likewise, if change occurs too long after intervention, then other possible factors may be responsible for the change. If we examine the chart for the intervention results for a client with bulimia (Figure 14.1), we can logically conclude that the intervention had

FIGURE 14.1   **Intervention Results for a Client with Bulimia**

a positive effect, as the number of purges per week declined sharply during and after intervention. However, the usual goal with clients with bulimia is complete cessation of purging. Because the client is still purging periodically, additional interventions may be advisable.

In some situations in single-subject research, it is necessary to use a multiple baseline, which indicates the use of more than one baseline as a means of measuring change. Sheafor, Horejsi, and Horejsi summarize an example of where a multiple baseline might be used:

> In work with a child having trouble in school, one baseline might focus on frequency of school attendance, a second on grades received for weekly assignments, and a third on a teacher's weekly rating of the student's level of cooperation in the classroom. Unless the target behavior is highly specific, multiple baselines are usually necessary in order to capture the impact of an intervention.[6]

There are a couple of ways to use single-subject design in therapeutic, sensitivity, and educational groups. One way is to construct a single-subject design for each member. If the group is living together (for example, in a group home) and members have interpersonal problems (such as heated arguments), a single-subject design can be constructed on the group as the client. For example, if decreasing the number of heated arguments is the target behavior, the number of heated arguments per week among group members can be counted by the staff members during the three time periods of baseline, intervention, and after intervention.

Task Achievement Scaling   The objective of this approach is to gauge the degree to which group members and/or the leader have completed agreed-upon intervention tasks. In this approach, the work toward the goals of the members and of the group is broken down into many separate actions or tasks. The tasks are selected by mutual agreement of the members, and each member is assigned or selects specific tasks to reach his or her goal and the overall goal of the group. Usually, a deadline is set for the completion of each task. **Task achievement scaling** refers to a procedure for rating the degree to which each agreed-upon task has, in fact, been achieved.

EXERCISE 14.5   Applying Single-Subject Design to Alleviating One of Your Bad Habits

GOAL: This exercise is designed to assist you in understanding and applying single-subject design.

1. Identify a bad habit that you have and that you want to reduce in frequency or eliminate entirely. It might be, for example, drinking fewer alcoholic beverages or quitting smoking.

2. For alleviating this habit, specify the following:

  (a) Your desired outcome:

  (b) A suitable measure to determine progress:

  (c) Your baseline data:

(d) Implementing intervention and monitoring the outcome:

(e) Assessing change:

(f) Inferring effectiveness:

3. Being realistic, after completing this evaluation, do you have a commitment to alleviating your undesired habit?

EXERCISE 14.6 Applying a Satisfaction Questionnaire to a Group You Participated In

GOAL: This exercise is designed to assist you in applying a satisfaction questionnaire.

1. Describe a group that you participated in that has now ended.

2. Answer the questions from the satisfaction questionnaire that appears in Figure 14.2 for the group you identified.

Reid and Epstein, in using this approach, utilize a four-point scale to record progress on each task[7]:

4 = Completely achieved
3 = Substantially achieved, action is still necessary
2 = Partially achieved, considerable work needs to be done
1 = Minimally achieved or not achieved

Where appropriate, they have a fifth rating: "No," for "No opportunity to work on task." With this approach, only results are rated—not effort, motivation, or good intentions. The appealing features of this approach are its simplicity and the fact that it can be used when more rigorous procedures are not feasible because of insufficient time, insufficient data, or difficulties in finding a suitable way to measure changes in the target behavior. The approach also has limitations. For example, if the tasks are erroneously conceptualized to be constructive in resolving the client's problems, then completing the tasks may have little effect on resolving the client's problems.

Satisfaction Questionnaire   Still another way to assess the outcome of a group is to have group members fill out a questionnaire that measures level of satisfaction. An example of such a questionnaire is the group member satisfaction questionnaire shown in Figure 14.2.

FIGURE 14.2   Group Member Satisfaction Questionnaire

Thank you for taking a few minutes to evaluate your experiences in our group. Your answers to this brief questionnaire will help us improve future groups. Feel free to offer your comments. To assure anonymity, please do not sign your name

1. Did you accomplish what you expected when you joined the group?
   _____ Yes, completely
   _____ Mostly
   _____ No real progress
   _____ Worse off now than before
   Comments _____

2. Do you feel the group accomplished its goals?
   _____ Yes, completely
   _____ Mostly
   _____ No real progress
   _____ The group was an utter failure
   Comments _____

3. How do you feel about the group leader?
   _____ Very satisfied
   _____ Satisfied
   _____ No feelings one way or another
   _____ Dissatisfied
   _____ Very dissatisfied
   Comments _____

4. How do you feel about the other members in the group?
   _____ Satisfied with everyone
   _____ Satisfied with some, and dissatisfied with others
   _____ No feelings one way or another
   _____ Dissatisfied with most of the other members
   _____ Dissatisfied with all of the other members
   _____ Very dissatisfied with all of the other members
   Comments _____

Such a questionnaire is a relatively simple and inexpensive way to measure the members' satisfaction level with the group. The questionnaire can be filled out at the last meeting of the group or can be mailed to members some time after the last meeting. Questions that evaluate process (described earlier in this chapter) can be added to this questionnaire.

Summary

The following summarizes the chapter's content in terms of the learning objectives presented at the beginning of the chapter.

1. Effectively terminate a group.

Termination and evaluation are among the most important phases of a group. The ending of a group for many members typically involves mixed feelings that vary in intensity. Some members experience feelings of "sweet sorrow"—sweetness for the accomplishments and from the feeling that they have grown, and sorrow because of leaving a group that has come to be an important part of their lives. This chapter discusses the dynamics of termination of a successful group, termination of an unsuccessful group, a member dropping out, transfer of a member, and the leader's leaving.

2. Conduct a process evaluation of a group.

There are two dimensions of evaluation of a group: process evaluation and outcome evaluation. A process evaluation is an assessment, generally by group members, as to the aspects of the group that were useful or detrimental.

3. Conduct three approaches to evaluating the outcome of a group.

Outcome evaluation involves assessing the extent to which the goals have been accomplished that were formulated when the group began. Specific approaches to measuring goal attainment are single-subject design, task achievement scaling, and satisfaction questionnaires.

Group Exercises

EXERCISE A: Evaluating and Ending the Class

GOAL: To bring closure to a group.

Note: The instructor of the course should lead this exercise.

Step 1. The instructor begins by expressing a number of positive thoughts and feelings that she or he has about the group. The instructor may also mention a few memorable experiences.

Step 2. The group sits in a circle, and the instructor asks: "Is there anything that anyone wants to express before the class ends? Is there any unfinished business that we should deal with?"

Step 3. The instructor leads a discussion in which the group reflects upon the course through questions such as: "Do you believe this course has helped prepare you to lead groups in social work?" "What else might have been done to better prepare you to lead groups?" "What exercises or materials have helped you grow as a person?" "What do you see as the strengths of this course?" "What do you see as the shortcomings of this course?" "How might this course be improved?" (An alternative to a verbal discussion of the questions in this step is to have the students record their responses anonymously on a sheet of paper and then hand them in.)

Step 4. The members express what they will most remember about this course and/or what they feel they have learned. Each member should be given an opportunity to express this.

Step 5. Each member expresses nonverbally how she or he felt about being in this class at the first session and how she or he now feels about having been in the class. (This step is optional.)

Step 6. The leader asks each member to give an imaginary gift to the person on his or her right. Each person should take a turn so everyone can hear what the gifts are. When giving or receiving the gifts, the members extend their hands to symbolize the giving or receiving of the gifts. Examples of such gifts are the time management key to ending procrastination, a warm sun for a smiling personality, a heart for happier relationships, positive and rational thinking for handling unwanted emotions, and the gift of meditation for reducing stress. (This step is optional.)

Step 7. The instructor may end the class by administering a student course evaluation, by saying some final words, or in some other appropriate way. A positive, optional, way to end the class is for the instructor to distribute a small container (such as a small paper bag) to each student, with a magic marker. Each student then writes her or his first name on the container. The instructor then distributes a packet of papers (each sheet about 2 inches by 3 inches) to each student. Each student then writes something positive to each of his or her classmates and then places the comments in the respective container for each classmate. After the distribution is completed, each student then reads (silently) the comments that were placed in his or her container.

EXERCISE B: Final Exam, Leading a Treatment Group*

GOAL: To evaluate the ability of students to develop their own treatment groups given a real-life situation.

Note: Students must have access to the Internet (using computers or smartphones) during the class.

Step 1: Instructor should break students into groups of three or four.

Step 2: Instructor informs students that they have been placed into an internship (field) agency. As part of their role, they have been sitting in treatment groups at the agency. The group leader called to report he or she is stuck in court for an emergency hearing and will not be able to lead a group that starts in 60 minutes. The supervisor stated he or she knows the students have the skills to lead the treatment group independently. It is the students' responsibility to develop a program agenda to lead the treatment group meeting, as no one else in the agency is able to cover this responsibility, because the supervisor knows the students are prepared, and because the students have developed a relationship with the treatment group members.

Step 3: Students are allowed to pick from three different scenarios:

Scenario A: The students have been a part of a weekly treatment group on parenting. The treatment group consists of single parents who have been involved with a child welfare agency over concerns of physical abuse of a child. Last week was the first week. All of the members are court ordered to belong to the treatment group. The only topic covered was introductions and rule setting. The students must develop a program agenda related to the topic of effective parenting.

Scenario B: The students have been a part of a weekly treatment group in a residential center for adolescent boys (ages 12 to 15). The topic scheduled to be addressed this week is anger management. The treatment group has been meeting for the past three months; however, the adolescents remain difficult to engage and have had difficulty paying attention in group.

Scenario C: The students have been working at a domestic violence shelter for women. Women enter and leave the shelter on a rotating basis. Women have a treatment group three times a week. The women range in length of time at the shelter (from 1 day to 2 months) and in motivation to change.

---

*   Sarah Hessenauer, MSW, PhD (chair of the Social Work Department, University of Wisconsin-Whitewater; Associate Professor) wrote this exercise.

Step 4: Students are to use class time to complete the following activities:

1. Pick one of the scenarios.
2. Determine a relevant topic to cover in the treatment group based on the scenario.
3. Develop an agenda for the treatment group.
4. Identify goals for their treatment group meeting.
5. Identify activities for the treatment group related to the topic. This will involve identifying your treatment group topic and finding relevant information. The students must share what they will be teaching.
   a. This is where the Internet will be the most useful. This treatment group is required to have an educational component.
   b. The students must be specific and detailed in their plan (what topic they plan to address, provide definitions related to the topic if applicable, describe what activities they will include, develop a timeline for the group, identify which students will do what, etc.).
6. Develop an evaluation plan for the treatment session. You want to ask yourself, "How will we know if this session is successful?"
7. Students must write out their detailed plan and share with the instructor before they leave class and "go to lead their treatment group."

PART 1 OF EXAM

The instructor may choose to give a "group grade" for each subgroup, based on what is developed.

PART 2 OF EXAM

Please answer the following questions. (This part of the exam allows the instructor to assign an individual grade to each student).

GROUP DEVELOPMENT

Did you experience any of the stages of group development as described in the text? If so, identify and describe the stage (s). Say why these fit.

LEADERSHIP

Did anyone take on a leadership role? If yes, what qualities did this individual possess that allowed him or her to take on this role? If you took on the role, why do you feel the group allowed you this role? Did power play a role in the leadership role? If yes, describe how.

ROLES

Describe the roles taken on by each group member. Did the roles assigned facilitate the completion of the task? Would you have assigned roles any differently? What role did you play and why?

GROUP NORMS

Did any group norms develop during this exercise? Did any groupthink occur? Please describe.

COMMUNICATION

Examining both verbal and nonverbal communication, how did your group communicate with each other? What communication enhanced the group attaining the final goal? What communication detracted from the group attaining the final goal?

USE OF TECHNOLOGY

How did the use of technology aid your group in meeting the final goal? Do you believe your group used technology efficiently? Did your group find the resources you needed on your computer? Did you face any obstacles related to the use of technology?

RESOURCES

Do you believe your group found adequate resources to lead your treatment group? If no, what resources would you have needed to be more effective? Did you use any evidence based resources? What additional resources would have been useful?

TERMINATION

Was your group ready to terminate and go lead your treatment group? Why or why not? How did the time allotted affect your termination? Did you use your time wisely? Explain.

GOAL ATTAINMENT

Do you believe that your group is ready to present to your treatment group? Did all group members contribute to the success of the group? Why or why not? What other factors led to your success or what other factors hindered it? Explain your answer.

PLAN FOR EVALUATION

Do you believe you have a good plan for evaluating the success of your session? Why or why not?

PERSONAL REFLECTION

How active were you or how much did you contribute to the group process? What was this group experience like for you? How has your confidence in leading a treatment group changed since the beginning of the semester? Have you grown? How? If not, why not? Would you be ready to lead your treatment group on your own (without your classmates' help)? What did you learn about yourself?

Please note: Your group analysis should be typed, double-spaced, and 5 to 10 pages in length.

Competency Notes

EP 4a   Use practice experience and theory to inform scientific inquiry and research.

EP 4b   Apply critical thinking to engage in analysis of quantitative and qualitative research methods and research findings.

EP 4c   Use and translate research evidence to inform and improve practice, policy, and service delivery.

EP 9a   Select and use appropriate methods for evaluation of outcomes.

EP 9c   Critically analyze, monitor, and evaluate intervention and program processes and outcomes.

EP 9d   Apply evaluation findings to improve practice effectiveness at the micro, mezzo, and macro levels. (pp. 457–466)

Material is presented on process evaluation and outcome evaluation. Outcome evaluation measures include single-subject design, satisfaction questionnaires, and task achievement scaling. Exercises on process evaluation and single-subject design are included that allow students to apply these evaluation techniques.

Key Terms and Concepts

Outcome Evaluation
Peer Review

Process Evaluation
Satisfaction Questionnaire

Single-Subject
Task Achievement Scaling

1

Group Treatment Theories Resource Manual (GTTRM)

In this manual you will find four prominent theories of group treatment intervention. Use it as a reference guide in your future practice and as a primer in your current coursework.

An effective group treatment leader needs knowledge of prominent group treatment theories. An effective group treatment leader generally knows several treatment approaches and, depending on the problems being presented by group members, is able to pick and choose from a "bag of tricks" an intervention strategy likely to have the highest probability of success. The material in the group treatment theories resource manual (GTTRM) summarizes four prominent group treatment theories (rational therapy, behavior therapy, reality therapy, and dialectical behavior therapy) that group treatment leaders commonly use. Case examples illustrate how each is used. Before presenting these theories, we will first compare and contrast "counseling" and "therapy/psychotherapy."

COUNSELING VERSUS THERAPY/PSYCHOTHERAPY

One of the reviewers of this manuscript commented that this author needs to make it clear that graduates of accredited baccalaureate social work programs can counsel clients, but they cannot provide therapy/psychotherapy to clients. As far as the profession of social work is concerned, it is accurate that only licensed clinical social workers can be reimbursed by third-party payers (which are usually health insurance companies) for providing psychotherapy. (Other helping professionals, such as clinical psychologists and psychiatrists are also reimbursed for providing psychotherapy.)

The question arises: What differentiates "counseling" from "therapy" or "psychotherapy"? This author believes this question is very critical because graduates of accredited baccalaureate programs should limit the services they provide to "counseling." This author researched a variety of sources to seek a definition that would differentiate "counseling" from "therapy" and "psychotherapy," including three state licensing/certification boards in social work and the Association of Social Work Boards. This author also asked baccalaureate social work educators who are on the Baccalaureate Program Directors (BPD) listserv to respond to this question.

A variety of definitions of these three terms were received. For instance, Dictionary. com defines these terms as follows:

Counseling—Professional guidance in resolving personal conflicts and emotional problems.[1]

Therapy—The treatment of physical, mental, or social disorders or diseases.[2]

Psychotherapy—The treatment of psychological disorders or maladjustments by a professional technique, such as psychoanalysis, group therapy, or behavioral therapy.[3]

From the BPD listserv, I received a variety of responses regarding what differentiates "counseling" from "therapy" or "psychotherapy." The following are illustrative of the types of responses received:

- The licensed professions should limit the use of the term *psychotherapy* to only the licensed mental health professions for the protection of the public.
- In this state, there is no control of therapy/psychotherapy. We may think that these terms convey work that is done by only the most skilled professionals. However, in reality anybody off the street can perform the duties of a therapist/psychotherapist.

- There is no difference among them.
- Although psychotherapy and counseling overlap considerably, there are also some differences. The work with clients may be of considerable depth in both modalities; however, the focus of counseling is more likely to be on specific problems or changes in life adjustment. Psychotherapy is more concerned with the restructuring of the personality or self.
- Although both psychotherapists and counselors work with a wide variety of clients, psychotherapists are more likely to work very intensively with more deeply disturbed individuals who are seen more frequently over a longer period.
- Counseling is an educative modality, and therapy is an emotional, understanding, restorative modality.
- Counseling is problem solving, and therapy/psychotherapy deals with deeper psychological or mental health issues.
- Psychotherapy is concerned with some type of personality change, whereas counseling is concerned with helping individuals utilize full coping potential.
- Counseling is best for routine maintenance, and psychotherapy is best for a major overhaul of the client's personality.
- The distinction between counseling and psychotherapy is murky at best, even at the master's and doctoral levels.

Given this list, what can be concluded? There is definitely considerable overlap between "counseling" and "therapy/psychotherapy." At the present time, there appears to be no major clear-cut distinctions between these terms.

Some key unanswered questions are the following: First, are there some intervention techniques (such as hypnosis) that are beyond the limit of authority for a BSW graduate to use? If so, what are these? Finally, how do we determine if a BSW graduate has gone beyond his or her limit of authority?

I asked this last question of a social worker in my state who is a member of the state social work certification/licensing board. This person responded, "To date, the board has only concluded that a BSW person is acting outside the scope of his or her certification when that person states in a résumé or in an ad that she or he provides psychotherapy."

1 # Rational Therapy in Groups

LEARNING OBJECTIVES

EP 7a
EP 7b
EP 7c
EP 8a
EP 8b

Rational therapy asserts that unwanted emotions and dysfunctional behaviors are primarily determined by our thought processes rather than by external events. This module will help prepare students to:

LO 1
Comprehend rational therapy.

LO 2
Use rational therapy in groups.

ALBERT ELLIS*

The founder of rational therapy, Albert Ellis (1913–2007), practiced psychoanalytic approaches to therapy during the late 1940s and early 1950s but became disenchanted with both the results and the approach. Ellis observed that even when patients achieved incredible insight into their childhood and unconscious processes, they continued to experience emotional difficulties.

Ellis developed a new approach, *rational therapy* (also called *rational-emotive therapy*), in which he treated clients by challenging and changing their irrational beliefs.[1]

In 1959, Ellis established the Institute for Rational Living in New York City, which provides adult education courses in rational living and a moderate-cost psychotherapy clinic for clients. In 1968, Ellis founded the Institute for Advanced Study in Rational Psychotherapy, which provides helping professionals with extensive training in rational therapy and provides seminars and workshops throughout the country. Ellis is also recognized nationally as an authority on sexuality.

In addition to running workshops and seminars and being a practicing psychotherapist, he has written 54 books and over 600 articles!

Rational therapy has had an enormous impact on both professionals and the public. The principles of rational therapy have been applied to such areas as assertiveness training, sexuality, adolescence, law and criminality, religion, executive leadership, children's literature, music, feminism, philosophy, personal problems, alcoholism, marriage and the family, and sex adjustment and therapy.

The approach has the potential to enable those who become skillful in rationally analyzing their self-talk to control or get rid of their undesirable emotions and dysfunctional behaviors.

LO 1   Comprehend Rational Therapy

THEORY OF RATIONAL THERAPY

Most people erroneously believe that our emotions and our actions are primarily determined by our experiences (that is, by events that happen to us). On the contrary, rational therapy has demonstrated that the primary cause of all our emotions and actions is what we tell ourselves about events that happen to us.

All feelings and actions occur according to the following format:

Event: (or experiences)
↓
Self-talk: (Self-talk is the set of evaluating thoughts you give yourself about facts and events that happen to you.)
↓
Emotions: (May include remaining calm)
↓
Actions:

---

* This history is adapted from *The Practice of Social Work,* 9th ed., by Zastrow. ©2010, Brooks/Cole.

An example will illustrate this process.

Event:	Cheryl, the 5-year-old daughter of Mr. and Mrs. Shaw, is playing with her brother and knocks over and breaks a lamp.
↓	
Mr. Shaw's self-talk:	*"That lamp was our favorite: we bought it on our honeymoon— it's irreplaceable. This is awful."*
	"Spare the rod and spoil the child—some stiff discipline will make her shape up."
	"As head of this household it's my duty to make her shape up. I'll teach her a lesson she'll never forget by giving her the spanking of her life."
	"She's always breaking things. I think this might have been intentional! I'll teach her to have respect for me and for our valuable items."
↓	
Emotions:	Anger, disappointment, frustration.
Actions:	Spanking and yelling at Cheryl, with the severity of the spanking bordering on abuse.

If, on the other hand, Mr. Shaw gives himself a different set of self-talk, his emotions and actions will be quite different.

Event:	Cheryl, the 5-year-old daughter of Mr. and Mrs. Shaw, is playing with her brother and knocks over and breaks a lamp.
↓	
Mr. Shaw's self-talk:	*"This was a lamp we cherished, but I know she didn't break it intentionally. It was an accident. My getting angry at this point won't help."*
	"I might have prevented this accident by informing Cheryl and our son that they can horse around in the house only in the rec room and in their bedrooms."
	"With young children some accidents are bound to happen."
	"The most constructive thing I can do at this point is to say that I understand that it was an accident, that all of us are disappointed that the lamp broke, and tell them in the future their horsing around should be limited to the rec room and the bedrooms."
↓	
Emotions:	Some disappointment but generally remaining calm.
↓	
Actions:	Talking to the children in an understanding fashion and expressing his thoughts in line with his self-talk.

The most important point about this process is that our self-talk determines how we feel and act; by changing our self-talk, we can change how we feel and act. Generally, we cannot control events that happen to us, but we have the power to think rationally and thereby change *all* of our unwanted emotions and ineffective actions.

The rehabilitative aspect of this conceptualization of self-talk is that any unwanted emotion and any ineffective behavior can be changed by identifying and then changing the underlying self-talk.

The self-talk we give ourselves about specific events that happen to us is often based on a variety of factors, including our beliefs, attitudes, values, wants, motives, goals, and desires.[2] For example, the self-talk a married woman might give herself on being informed by her husband that he wants a divorce would be influenced by her desire (or lack of desire) to remain married, by her values and beliefs about being a divorcée, by her attitudes toward her husband, by how she believes getting a divorce would be consistent or inconsistent with her present goals, and by her beliefs about the reasons why her husband says he wants a divorce.

Another important thing about self-talk is that with repeated occurrences of an event, a person's emotional reaction becomes nearly automatic because the person rapidly gives himself or herself a large set of self-talk gradually acquired through past experiences. For example, a few years ago I counseled a woman who became intensely upset and depressed every time her husband came home intoxicated. In examining her emotional reactions, it became clear that because of the repeated occurrences she would rapidly tell herself the following on seeing him inebriated:

> "He's making a fool of himself and of me."
> "He's foolishly spending money we desperately need."
> "For the next few hours I'm going to have to put up with his drunken talk and behavior—this is awful."
> "He loves drinking more than he loves me because he knows I do not want him to get drunk."
> "Woe is me."

EXERCISE M1.1   Our Self-Talk Causes Our Emotions*

GOAL: This exercise is designed to illustrate that it is primarily our self-talk (rather than the event) that causes our emotions.

1. Specify a negative emotion that you recently experienced.

---

* The M1.1 in this exercise designates this as the first exercise for Module 1. Similar designations will be used for additional exercises in these modules.

2. Describe the event associated with this emotion.

3. Specify your self-talk associated with this event.

4. Review the material on self-talk being the primary source of our emotions. Is it not true that if you had given yourself a different set of self-talk about this event, you would have felt differently?

5. Do you now believe that self-talk is the primary source of our emotions? Explain your views.

Another prominent developer of cognitive therapy is Aaron T. Beck,[3] an American psychiatrist. He pioneered cognitive theories that are widely used in the treatment of clinical depression.

Beck examined automatic thoughts and schemas. Automatic thoughts are images or mental activity that occur as a response to a trigger (like an action or event). They are automatic and seem to "pop up" or "flash" in our mind without conscious thoughts. Automatic thoughts are often thoughts that we have that appear to us as being in the form of phrases or sentences. The following is an example:

Carl has been dating Julie for several months. Julie almost always calls Carl every Tuesday morning around 9:00 A.M. She fails to call this Tuesday morning. Carl has the automatic thought, "She is angry with me," and he then feels "sad and fearful."

Automatic thoughts have the following attributes:

- They can be words, a memory, an image, an imagined sound, or based on our intuition.
- We tend to automatically believe our thoughts, usually not stopping to question their validity. Automatic thoughts are not necessarily true, accurate, or helpful.
- They usually pop into our heads, often without our noticing them.
- They tend to be habitual and persistent. Our thoughts tend to repeat over and over, and the more they repeat, the more we tend to believe (often erroneously) that they are valid and accurate.
- Because of our upbringing, or previous experiences, or our culture, or our religious beliefs, or our family values, we may well have different interpretations of events and situations than someone else does.

Where do automatic thoughts come from? They come from "schemas." A schema is a cognitive framework or concept that helps us organize and interpret information. Schemas are useful when they allow us to take shortcuts in interpreting the vast amount of information that is available in the environment. However, schemas can also be counterproductive. Certain schemas may cause us to exclude pertinent (and valid) information that then lead us to focus instead on things that confirm our preexisting (perhaps erroneous) ideas and beliefs. Schemas may contribute to us using negative stereotypes that make it difficult for us to retain new information that does not conform to our established ideas about the world.

Prejudice is one example of schema that prevents us from seeing the world as it is and inhibits us from taking in new information. By holding certain erroneous beliefs about a particular group of people, prejudice may cause us to interpret situations incorrectly.

Our schemas often develop in early childhood. They are influenced by our education, parents, peers, the media, major life events, and our culture. They can evolve and change over time based on our exposure to new information and experiences.

Schemas are the foundation of our (and our clients') personal beliefs and values. We, and our clients, screen options for change through these value systems—and most readily apply change strategies that are congruent with existing beliefs.

In a very real sense, positive changes in counseling occur when clients examine their automatic thoughts and schemas and then make decisions to change their inaccurate automatic thoughts and schemas in a rational direction. Such changes are the essence of effective counseling.

CHANGING UNWANTED EMOTIONS

Rational therapy is increasingly being used to change unwanted emotions. Because this is a primary focus of rational therapy, the methods used to change unwanted emotions will be specified in this section.

Rational therapy asserts that all emotions are primarily determined by self-talk, even the emotion of love. Individuals often believe that love is a feeling beyond their control. The language of love reinforces this erroneous belief: "I just *couldn't help it*, he swept me off my feet," "*I fell* in love," and "*It was* love at first sight." In reality, even the emotion of love is based primarily on self-talk. The following format illustrates this process:

Event:	A woman's ideal date is a man who is tall and athletic, has dark hair, is a good conversationalist, and likes pop music. She meets a man in one of her classes who is 6 feet tall, a football player, has dark hair, is personable, and likes pop music.
Her self-talk:	*I can hardly believe I've finally met someone I'm really attracted to. This person is really handsome, charming, the kind of person I'd really like to get to know better and to go out to dinner with.*
Her Emotion:	Feelings of infatuation.

There are five ways to change an unwanted emotion. Three are constructive: getting involved in a meaningful activity, changing the negative and irrational thinking underlying the unwanted emotion, and changing the distressing event. Each can be learned and practiced within a group setting. Two are destructive: abuse of alcohol, drugs, and food and suicide. We will discuss each of the five in turn.

Meaningful Activity

Practically everyone encounters day-to-day frustrations and irritations—having a class or two that aren't going well, working at a job that's unpleasant, or coping with a dull social life. Dwelling on such irritations will spawn such unwanted emotions as depression, anger, frustration, despair, or feelings of failure. Which of these emotions a person has will directly depend upon the person's self-talk.

Meaningful, enjoyable activity, however, produces satisfaction and a healthful distraction from unwanted emotions. Group members can learn the value of meaningful activity by writing an "escape" list of activities they find motivating, energizing, and enjoyable—taking a walk, playing golf or tennis, going to a movie, shopping, doing needlework, visiting friends, and so on. By having an "escape" list of things they enjoy doing, group members can nip unwanted emotions in the bud. By getting involved in things they enjoy, they can use enjoyable activities to take their minds off their day-to-day concerns and irritations. The positive emotions they experience will stem directly from the things they tell themselves about the enjoyable things they are doing.

In urging group members to compile and use an escape list, rational therapy is not suggesting that members avoid doing something about unpleasant events. If something can be done to change a distressing event, all constructive efforts should be tried. However, we often do not have control over unpleasant events and cannot change them. Although we cannot change unpleasant events, we always have the capacity to control and change what we tell ourselves about the unpleasant events. It is this latter focus that is often helpful in learning to change our unwanted emotions.

CHANGING SELF-TALK

A second approach to changing unwanted emotions is to identify and then alter the negative and irrational thinking that leads to them. Maultsby has developed an approach entitled rational self-analysis (RSA) that is useful for learning to challenge and change irrational thinking.[4] An RSA has six parts, as shown in Figure M1.1.

The goal in doing an RSA is to change an unwanted emotion (anger, love, guilt, depression, hate) by recording the event and one's self-talk on paper. Under Part A (facts and events), group members state the facts or events that occurred. Under Part B (self-talk), they write all of their thoughts about the events in Part A. Group members number each statement in order (1, 2, 3, 4, and so on), and write "good," "bad," or "neutral" after each self-talk statement to show themselves how they believe each Part B statement reflects on themselves as individuals. Under Part C (emotional consequences), they write simple statements describing their gut reactions/emotions stemming from the self-talk in Part B.

EXERCISE M1.2   Using Meaningful Activities to Change Unwanted Emotions

GOAL: This exercise demonstrates that when we are awfulizing about something and thereby feeling bad, we can alleviate the unwanted emotions by getting involved in meaningful activities.

1. Describe a time when you were awfulizing about something and thereby feeling bad and then alleviated the unwanted emotions by getting involved in something you enjoyed doing.

2. Reflect on this experience. Is it not true that getting involved in enjoyable activities stopped you from awfulizing (that is, you stopped thinking about an unpleasant event and instead switched to thinking about an activity you were enjoying)? Also, is it not true that when you stopped awfulizing, you then alleviated your unwanted emotions?

FIGURE M1.1   Format for Rational Self-Analysis (RSA)

A	D(a)
Facts and events	Camera check of A
B	D(b)
Self-talk	Rational debate of B
1 _____	1 _____
2 _____	2 _____
etc.	etc.
C	E
Emotional consequences of B	Emotional goals and behavioral goals for similar future events

Part D(a) is to be written *only* after Parts A, B, and C have been completed; Part D(a) is a "camera check" of Part A. Group members reread Part A and ask themselves, "If I had taken a moving picture of what I wrote was happening, would the camera verify what I have written as fact?" A moving picture would probably have recorded the facts but not personal beliefs or opinions. Personal beliefs or opinions belong in Part B. A common example of a personal opinion mistaken as a fact is: "Karen made me look like a fool when she laughed at me while I was trying to make a serious point." Under D(a), camera check of A, group members correct any opinions by stating only the factual part: "I was attempting to make a serious point when Karen began laughing at what I was saying." Then, the personal opinion part of the statement should be added to B (that is, "Karen made me look like a fool").

Part D(b) determines whether the self-talk statements in B are rational. Each B statement should be taken separately. Group members read B-1 first and ask themselves if it is consistent with rational thinking. It is *irrational* if it does one or more of the following:

1. *Does not fit the facts:* For example, when a person *feels* unloved after a lover has ended their relationship, even though several close friends and relatives love that person
2. *Endangers one's life:* For example, when someone takes drugs to escape from a problem
3. *Keeps one from achieving short- and long-term goals:* For example, when a person wants to do well in college but decides to go out socializing instead of studying before exams
4. *Causes significant trouble with other people:* For example, when a person challenges others to a fight when feeling insulted
5. *Leads one to feel emotions that one does not want to feel*

If the self-talk statement is rational, group members should merely write "that's rational." If, on the other hand, the self-talk statement is irrational, group members should then think of an alternative self-talk to that B statement. This new self-talk statement is of crucial importance in changing an undesirable emotion (and dysfunctional behavior that is associated with the unwanted emotion) and needs to be (1) rational and (2) a self-talk statement a group member is willing to accept as a new opinion for himself or herself. After jotting down this D(b)-1 self-talk in Part D(b), group members consider B-2, B-3, and so on in the same way.

Under Part E, the new emotions group members desire in similar, future A situations should be noted. In listing these new emotions, members should keep in mind that they will follow from their self-talk statements in Part D(b). This part may also contain a description of specific actions they intend to take to help them achieve their emotional goals when they encounter future A events.

To make a rational self-analysis work, group members must challenge their negative and irrational thinking with rational debates. With effort, they can learn to change any unwanted emotion, and this capacity is one of the most important abilities a person can have. (Once members become adept in RSA, they will be able to do the process mentally, without having to write it out.)

Challenging negative and irrational thinking *will* change unwanted emotions if members put the needed effort into it. Just as dieting is guaranteed to result in a loss of weight, so this approach is guaranteed to change unwanted emotions. Both, however, require effort and a commitment to use the processes in order to make them work.

Changing the Distressing Event

A third way to change unwanted emotions is to change the distressing event. There is a nearly infinite number of distressing events: losing a job, the breakup of a romantic relationship, receiving failing grades, being in an automobile accident, and so on. In some cases,

Example of a Rational Self-Analysis: Combating Unwanted Emotions Following the Ending of a Romantic Relationship

A. FACTS AND EVENTS

A. For 2 months I dated a guy whom I really thought I liked. I knew something was not quite right with our relationship. I was unable to figure out what it was until he finally said that he had been dating another girl for 2 years and was still seeing her. However, he promised that they would break up soon and urged me to "hang on" for a little while. Three weeks passed, and then I saw them speaking to each other one night. When she left, I went over to talk to him and he seemed to be in a bad mood. I tried to get out of him what the matter was. Then, we began to talk about the other girl, and he said he could not break up with her for a while and we were not going to see each other at all for a while. Then I started to yell at him for various things, and the crying began.

B. SELF-TALK

B 1. I hate him! (bad)

B 2. How could I be such a sucker for the last 2 months? (bad)

B 3. All guys are jerks. (bad)

B 4. I'll never date anyone else again. (bad)

B.5. I'm glad I know now where I stand for sure. (good)

B 6. What did I ever do to him to be treated like this? (bad)

B 7. No one loves me. (bad)

B 8. I'm a failure. (bad)

B 9. I'll never find anyone I loved as much as him to date. My life is ruined. (bad)

B 10. This guy just used me and took what he could get. (bad)

B 11. My life is over. I'll never find happiness again. (bad)

B 12. This is awful! This is the worst thing that could happen to me. (bad)

C. MY EMOTIONS

Outward emotions were crying and yelling. Inner emotions were feeling angry, hurt, depressed, embarrassed, a failure, and unloved.

D(A). CAMERA CHECK OF A

D(a). All of this is factual.

D(B). MY RATIONAL DEBATES OF B

1. I don't really hate him. He was good to me, and we did enjoy the times we had together.

2. I should not feel as if I was a sucker because I did not know about the other girl until he finally told me.

3. Guys are not all jerks. I have many male friends who are far from being jerks: In fact, I do not even know what a "jerk" is. I've never seen a jerk. Guys are humans, not jerks. It is irrational to label someone a "jerk" and then to relate to that person as if the label were real.

4. I know I will date again, because I always have after other breakups.

5. That's rational.

6. He told me I never did anything to have this happen. It was just a situation he got himself into and now he needs time to work things out.

7. How can I say that! I have a lot of close friends and relatives, and I know several guys who think highly of me.

8. I'm not a failure. I'm doing well in college and at my part-time job.

9. My life is certainly not ruined. I'm accomplishing many of my goals in life. With 2 million eligible guys in the world there are certainly many other worthy guys to form a relationship with. I told myself the same erroneous things a few years ago when I broke up with someone else. I will eventually get involved in another relationship with someone else I love. I need to think positively and dwell on the positive things I've learned in this relationship.

10. Neither of us "used" the other. I'm even uncertain what "used" means. We enjoyed being together and had a lot of good times. He told me he has a lot of positive feelings toward me. He was forced to make a choice between two people, both of whom he enjoyed being with.

11. My life is certainly not over. I have many positive things happening to me right now, and there are many things I enjoy doing. I also have a number of close relatives and friends who'll be there when I need them.

12. Life is full of ups and downs. It is a mistake to "awfulize" and to exaggerate how this breakup will affect my future. There are many other more dreadful things that could happen—such as a terminal illness.

E. MY EMOTIONAL AND BEHAVIORAL GOALS

To be able to change my unwanted emotions so that I no longer am angry, depressed, and hurt about this breakup. Also, I would like to talk to him in private and apologize for my behavior. After I become more comfortable with this breakup, I will gradually be interested in dating someone else in the future.

Explaining How to Change an Unwanted Emotion to a Client

The following is a step-by-step guide for a counselor to use in using rational therapy concepts with a client who has an unwanted emotion:

Step 1: Introductions are made between the counselor and the client. (The counselor may engage in some small talk to facilitate forming a therapeutic relationship.)

Step 2: The counselor asks the client to summarize why he (we will assume the client is a male) came in today. We will also assume the client indicates he has an unwanted emotion that he is struggling with. The unwanted emotion may be depression, anger, anxiety, frustration, or some other painful emotion.

Step 3: The counselor asks the client what he believes is the cause of the unwanted emotion. Practically all clients will indicate the cause is due to external events. For illustrative purposes, let us take the example of the client saying, "I am really sad because my wife is ending our marriage."

Step 4: The counselor briefly summarizes that, in almost all cases, it is not so much the external event, but what he is telling himself about the event, that is the cause of his unwanted emotion. (Expect the client to be puzzled by this statement.) To clarify, ask the client to ponder the following: Are you thinking some of the following thoughts about the impending divorce: "I love her so much—I don't want her to leave." "My life is ruined without her." "I'll never find anyone as good as her." "My life is no longer worth living." "I am such a loser—I drove her away." "I'm just not a lovable person."

You may want to ask the client in this situation: "Would you not feel very different if you were thinking the following about her leaving: "This is good—I will find someone better than her." "Thank God she is leaving; we've haven't gotten along for the past few years." "There are plenty of other fish in the sea."

Step 5: Spend time clarifying with the client that it is our self-talk (thoughts) that are the major source of unwanted emotions, perhaps with additional examples. Add that we have the power to change our thoughts, which will then lead to our painful unwanted emotion going "poof"—that is, leaving us.

Step 6: Indicate there are only three constructive approaches to making an unwanted emotion go "poof." The first is to seek to change the external event. For example, ask the client if he thought offering to go to marriage counseling with his wife may lead the wife to decide to work on maintaining their marriage. It should be noted that some events can be changed, whereas others can't. For example, an event that cannot be changed is being involved in a bad car accident. An event that may be changed is going to marriage counseling instead of seeking a divorce.

Step 7: Indicate the second option for changing an unwanted emotion is to change one's self-talk about the external event. One way of doing this is for the client to write out a rational self-analysis in which he specifies the external event, his self-talk about that event, his unwanted emotions that he is feeling, his rational debates of his irrational self-talk, and his emotional and behavioral goals. (An example is provided in this module.) It is generally helpful to have a copy of an RSA that can be given to the client for illustrative purposes.

Step 8: Indicate that the third option is to make the unwanted emotion go "poof" by getting involved in some meaningful activities. Ask the client to indicate what activities he truly enjoys, that would then stop him (at least for while) from thinking about his wife leaving. Indicate, "We sometimes cannot control external events, but we always have the power to change our thoughts." For example, "If you are awfulizing about your wife leaving you, and suddenly you are informed you had just won a lottery, would you not think happy thoughts for a while?"

Step 9: Ask the client to summarize the three constructive options for seeking to change an unwanted emotion. (If the client has a few challenges in summarizing these options, help him with this.)

Step 10: Ask the client which of these three options or strategies he wants to try. The client may choose a combination of these three strategies, which is "good."

Step 11: Wish the client the best with his strategies, and check back with him in a week or two as to how he is doing.

constructive action can be taken to change the distressing event. For example, if a man is terminated from a job, he can seek another; when he finds one, he will feel better. If a student is getting failing grades, a conference with the instructor may give the student some ideas about how to improve the grades. If the suggestions appear practical and have merit, the student will feel better.

Not all distressing events can be changed. For example, a woman may have a job that she needs and be forced to interact with other employees who display behaviors

EXERCISE M1.3   Changing Unwanted Emotions with a Rational Self-Analysis

GOAL: This exercise demonstrates that writing (and then using the rational debates) will change unwanted emotions.

1. Review the material on a rational self-analysis. Write a rational self-analysis on an unwanted emotion you recently experienced.

2. Do you believe that if you apply rational debates to your negative and irrational self-talk, you will be able to change unwanted emotions? Explain your views.

she dislikes. If that individual cannot change the behaviors of the others, the only other constructive option is to "bite the bullet" and adapt to the circumstances. However, when it is practical to change distressing events, they should be changed. When constructive changes in events are made, a person is then apt to feel better because he or she will then (in all likelihood) be having more positive self-talk related to the constructive changes that have been made.

EXERCISE M1.4   Changing Unwanted Emotions by Changing Events

GOAL: This exercise demonstrates that unwanted emotions can be changed by changing the event that is associated with your unwanted emotion.

1. Describe a time in your life when you were awfulizing about something and thereby feeling bad and you then changed the event—which resulted in your stopping to awfulize. For example, you may have had an unpleasant job, which you then changed. Or, you may have been in an abusive relationship, which you then ended.

2. Is it not true that you stopped feeling bad after changing the unpleasant event because you stopped awfulizing and then had more positive self-talk related to the constructive changes that you made? Explain your views on this.

Destructive Ways of Dealing with Unwanted Emotions

There are two destructive ways to deal with unwanted emotions that, unfortunately, some people use. (I want to make it clear that I strongly discourage using either of the following two ways. I present them only in order to complete the list of ways to deal with unwanted emotions.) One method is to temporarily relieve intense unwanted emotions through the use of alcohol, other drugs, or food. When the effects of a drug wear off, the person's problems and unwanted emotions remain, and there is a danger that through repeated use the person will become dependent on the drug. Some people overeat for the same reasons—loneliness, insecurity, boredom, and frustration. The process of eating and the feeling of having a full stomach provide temporary relief from intense unwanted emotions. Such people are apt to become overweight or bulimic—or both.

The other destructive way to relieve unwanted emotions is suicide. This is the ultimate destructive approach to dealing with unwanted emotions. If you know of someone who is contemplating suicide, you have a legal right and an ethical obligation to seek to connect that person with professional help—even when the suicidal person requests that you do not inform anyone else of his or her intentions.

EXERCISE M1.5 Changing Unwanted Emotions by Abusing Alcohol, Other Drugs, or Food

GOAL: This exercise demonstrates that unwanted emotions can temporarily be changed through the abusive use of alcohol, other drugs, or food.

1. Describe someone you know who emotionally was feeling bad and turned to abusive use of alcohol, other drugs, or food. If you do not know anyone who did this, describe a time in your life where you were feeling bad and resorted to the abusive use of alcohol, other drugs, or food.

2. Is it not accurate that the abusive use of alcohol, other drugs, or food only provides temporary relief? Give a short explanation of your views on this question.

ASSESSING AND CHANGING DYSFUNCTIONAL BEHAVIOR

Our self-talk is the primary determinant not only of our emotions, but also of our actions, as illustrated in the following diagram:

Events

↓

Self-talk

↓

Emotions

↓

Actions

In a nutshell, our actions are primarily determined by our self-talk (cognitions). Our thoughts determine our actions. To demonstrate this principle, reflect on the last time you did something bizarre or unusual. What self-talk statements were you giving yourself (that is, what were you thinking) prior to and during the time when you did what you did?

Rational therapy maintains that the reasons for any dysfunctional act (including crime) can be determined by examining what the offender was telling himself or herself prior to and during the time when the act was being committed. Two examples of cognitions that lead to dysfunctional behavior are the following:

Cognition: A 16-year-old sees an unlocked Corvette and thinks, "Hey, this is the ulti-
↓   mate car to drive. Let me cross the starting wires and take it for a ride."

Behavior: Car theft.

Cognition: A 23-year-old male is on his third date with the same woman. He brings
↓   her to his apartment and thinks, "She is really sexy. Since I've wined and
                  dined her three times, now it's time for her to show her appreciation. I'll
                  bet she wants it as much as I do. I'll show her what a great lover I am. If
                  she says, 'Don't,' I know she really means 'Don't stop. 'I'll use a little force
                  if I have to. When it's over, she'll really love me."

Behavior: Date rape.

It should be noted that the cognitions underlying each dysfunctional behavior may vary considerably among perpetrators. For example, possible cognitions for shoplifting a shirt might be the following. "This shirt would look really nice for the wedding I'm going to on Saturday. Because I'm buying a number of other items from this store, they still will make a profit from me even if I take this without paying for it." Another may be: "This will be a challenge to see if I can get away with taking this shirt. I'll put it on in the fitting room and put my own shirt and coat on over it, and no one will even see me walk out of the store with it. Because I've taken a number of things in the past, I'll act real casual as I walk out of the store." Or: "My son really needs a decent shirt. He doesn't have any nice ones to wear. I don't get enough money from public assistance to buy my children what they need. I know my son is embarrassed to wear the rags that he has. I'll just stick this shirt under my coat and walk out with it."

Assessing *human behavior is largely a process of identifying the cognitions that underlie unwanted emotions or dysfunctional behavior.* The stages of this process are as follows:

1. Identify as precisely as possible the unwanted emotions and/or dysfunctional behavior that a client has.
2. Identify the cognitions or thinking patterns that the client has during the time when the client is having unwanted emotions or is displaying dysfunctional behavior. There are two primary ways of identifying these cognitions. One way is to ask the client what he was thinking prior to and during the time when the client was having unwanted emotions or displaying dysfunctional behavior. If this approach does not work (perhaps

because the client refuses to divulge what he was thinking), a second approach is to obtain information about the client's life circumstances at that time. Once these life circumstances are identified, the professional conducting the assessment needs to place herself mentally into the life circumstances of the perpetrator and then reflect on the kinds of cognitions that would lead this client to have his specific unwanted emotions or dysfunctional behavior. For example, if the client is a 16-year-old female who has run away from home and is unemployed, it is fairly easy to identify (to some extent) the kinds of cognitions that would lead such a person to turn to prostitution.

A deduction of the principle that thinking processes determine dysfunctional behaviors and unwanted emotions is that *in order to change dysfunctional behaviors or unwanted emotions, it is necessary for the affected person to change his or her thinking patterns.* These concepts are illustrated in the box "Our Thinking Determines Our Behaviors and Our Emotions."

WHAT REALLY CAUSES PSYCHOLOGICAL CHANGES VIA PSYCHOTHERAPY?

Client-centered therapy, psychoanalysis, rational therapy, feminist intervention, behavior therapy, transactional analysis, reality therapy, hypnosis, meditation, and crisis intervention have all been used to treat a wide range of emotional and behavioral problems. Practically all of these approaches have been used to treat people who are depressed or lonely; have marital or other interpersonal relationship problems; have disabling fears and phobias; are overly aggressive; have drinking problems; or suffer from grief, shame, or guilt. Each of the therapies differs substantially from every other in treatment techniques and in terms of explaining why therapeutic change occurs. Yet each approach is used by various practitioners who are able to provide case examples that each of these approaches leads to positive changes.

How can all these distinct and diverse psychotherapeutic approaches produce positive changes in clients? What is it that produces positive changes in therapy? Is there a single explanation that will describe psychotherapy changes that are produced by diverse therapies? (The explanation presented here is one that is advanced by rational therapists. This explanation has not as yet been universally accepted.)

Rational therapy asserts that unwanted emotions and dysfunctional actions arise primarily from our self-talk, generally self-talk that is negative or irrational. If this conceptualization is accurate, an important corollary is that *any therapy technique that is successful in changing emotions or actions is effective primarily because it changes a person's thinking from self-talk that is negative or irrational to self-talk that is more rational and positive.* In other words, self-talk appears to be the key therapeutic agent in all approaches that produce positive changes in our emotions and our behaviors.

Our Thinking Determines Our Behaviors and Our Emotions

A few years ago I was describing to a class the concept that our thinking primarily causes our emotions and our actions. A male student voluntarily self-disclosed the following:

What you're saying makes a lot of sense. It really applies to something that happened to me. I was living with a female student whom I really cared about. I thought, though, that she was going out on me. When I confronted her about it, she always said I was paranoid and denied it.

Then one night I walked into a bar in this town and I saw her in a corner hugging this guy. I told myself things like "She really is cheating on me. Both of them are playing me for a fool." Such thinking led me to be angry.

I also told myself "I'm going to set this straight. I'm going to get even with them. I'll break the bottoms off these two empty beer bottles and then jab each of them with the jagged edges." I proceeded to knock off the bottoms on the bar and then started walking toward them. I got to within 8 feet of them, and they were still hugging each other and didn't see me. I began, though, to change my thinking. I thought that if I jabbed them, the end result would be that I would get 8 to 10 years in prison, and I concluded she isn't worth that. Based on this thinking I decided to drop the beer bottles, walk out, and end my relationship with her—which is what I did.

EXERCISE M1.6   Our Actions Are Determined by Our Thoughts

GOAL: This exercise demonstrates that most of our actions are determined by what we think.

1. Describe something quite embarrassing that you did.

2. Describe what you were thinking that led you to do the embarrassing thing that you described.

3. Can you identify any actions that you engaged in that were not partially influenced by what you were thinking? If "yes," specify such actions.

4. In criminal court proceedings, prosecuting attorneys are expected to identify the motive as to why the defendant committed the alleged crime. Is not the search for the motive, in actuality, a search to identify the thinking patterns that led the defendant to commit the alleged crime? Explain your views.

5. Is it not true that in order to stop someone from engaging in dysfunctional or deviant behavior that person needs to change the thought patterns underlying the dysfunctional behaviors? Explain your views.

6. As an example, what intervention might be used to change the abusive behavior of a husband who abuses his wife?

EXERCISE M1.7   The Key Therapeutic Change Agent

GOAL: This exercise is designed to have you reflect about whether the key therapeutic change agent, common to any psychotherapy technique that is effective, is changing the client's thinking from self-talk that is negative or irrational to self-talk that is more rational and positive.

1. Summarize your thoughts on what causes unwanted emotions.

2. Summarize your thoughts on what causes dysfunctional behaviors.

3. How can unwanted emotions be changed?

4. How can dysfunctional behaviors be effectively changed?

5. Do you believe the key therapeutic change agent, common to any psychotherapy technique that is effective, is changing the client's thinking from self-talk that is negative or irrational to self-talk that is more rational and positive? Explain your thoughts.

LO 2   Use Rational Therapy in Groups

USING RATIONAL THERAPY IN GROUPS

Rational therapy asserts that learning how to think rationally (and thereby countering unwanted emotions and dysfunctional behaviors) is an educational process. Clients can learn how to analyze and change irrational self-talk in a variety of ways: instructions by the therapist, viewing videotapes and films on rational therapy, reading books and pamphlets, and attending workshops or seminars on rational therapy.

In group therapy, the therapist first teaches clients the basic concepts of rational therapy. Group members are then assisted in identifying their unwanted emotions and dysfunctional behaviors, identifying the irrational and negative self-talk that causes their unwanted emotions and dysfunctional behaviors, and developing more rational and positive thinking processes to counter their negative and irrational self-talk. Group members also are assisted in other ways to change their unwanted emotions and dysfunctional behaviors—for example, by getting involved in meaningful activities and by changing distressing events. One common strategy in rational therapy groups is to give each member the homework assignment of writing a rational self-analysis (RSA) on an unwanted emotion or dysfunctional behavior that he or she wants to change. At future group sessions, these RSAs are shared and discussed.

Summary

The following summarizes the module's content in terms of the learning objectives presented at the beginning.

1. Comprehend rational therapy.
   The founder of rational therapy is Albert Ellis. Rational therapy asserts that unwanted emotions and dysfunctional behaviors are primarily determined by our thought processes rather than by external events. The theory asserts there are three constructive ways to change unwanted emotions:
   a. Getting involved in meaningful, enjoyable activities
   b. Challenging and changing negative self-talk to more positive and rational self-talk
   c. Changing the distressing event

   Rational therapy asserts that assessing human behavior is largely a process of identifying the cognitions that underlie unwanted emotions or dysfunctional behavior. Rational therapy asserts that the key therapeutic change agent in any therapy technique is changing a person's thinking from self-talk that is negative or irrational to self-talk that is more rational and positive. Rational therapy is a cognitive-behavioral approach to therapy.

2. Use rational therapy in groups.
   In group therapy, the therapist first teaches clients the basic concepts of rational therapy. Group members are then assisted in identifying their unwanted emotions and dysfunctional behaviors, identifying the irrational and negative self-talk that causes their unwanted emotions and dysfunctional behaviors, and developing more rational and positive thinking processes to counter their negative and irrational self-talk. Group members also are assisted in other ways to change their unwanted emotions and dysfunctional behaviors—for example, by getting involved in meaningful activities and by changing distressing events.

Group Exercises

EXERCISE A: Changing Unwanted Emotions with Self-Talk

GOAL: To learn that unwanted emotions stem primarily from negative and irrational self-talk and that they can be relieved by positive, rational self-talk.

Note: It is advised that the instructor be the designated leader for the exercises in this module, as the exercises may generate strong emotions in the participants. Students should not divulge sensitive personal information.

Step 1. Ask the students to think about the last time they were depressed or angry and then to relate what made them depressed or angry. List three or four responses on a blackboard under the two headings "Angry" and "Depressed." (I've conducted this exercise over 50 times, and people will always provide events or experiences that they believe cause their unwanted emotions.) After making the list, point out that events cannot generate an emotion; instead a person's thoughts about these events cause the unwanted emotions.

Elaborate on this by suggesting certain self-talk statements that may have led students to be angry or depressed. For example, if someone says "I became depressed because my boyfriend didn't send me flowers on Valentine's Day," you might say, "Was your self-talk something like, 'He really doesn't love me. He didn't even remember me on Valentine's Day. This is the pits. This is awful. I feel so hurt. I put so much time into this relationship and it appears he doesn't think very much of me"? (As an alternative to guessing at self-talk, you can ask students to tell the class what their thoughts were about the events.) Diagram the self-talk process to the class, illustrating that unwanted emotions arise from our self-talk about events.

Step 2. Ask the students what their self-talk would be if the following event occurred: Someone they have been dating for 3 years says the relationship is over. This event is listed on the blackboard under the heading "A-Event." List each of the self-talk statements given by the students on the blackboard under a B section (B-l, B-2, etc.). For each, self-talk statement, the students discuss what emotions would result. (For example, if a student says, "I'll never find anyone else," the resulting emotions might be depression and despair.) Write the emotions on the blackboard under a C section (C-l, C-2, etc.)

Step 3. Explain that all unwanted emotions can be changed by challenging each negative and irrational self-talk statement with a rational debate. Ask the students to give a rational debate for each of the negative and irrational self-talk statements listed in the B section.

EXERCISE B: Writing a Rational Self-Analysis

GOAL: To demonstrate how to write a rational self-analysis.

Explain that all emotions arise primarily from self-talk and that unwanted emotions can be changed by identifying the negative and irrational self-talk and then challenging this self-talk with rational debates. Distribute a handout of a rational self-analysis (the example in this chapter will work) to show how an RSA is written. Have each person in the class write an RSA on an unwanted emotion they have experienced in the recent past. Then, complete the exercise by having the students discuss the merits and shortcomings of writing a rational self-analysis.

EXERCISE C: Using Positive Affirmations

GOAL: To provide another way to change negative and irrational thinking.

Step 1. Indicate that some people find writing a rational self-analysis to be too time consuming and cumbersome. An alternative is to use a positive affirmation—a positive assertion that helps one achieve emotional and behavioral goals. The process of writing a positive affirmation also enables a person to identify negative and irrational thinking that the person may not be aware of.

Step 2. Each student selects a realistic emotional or behavioral goal that he or she wants to achieve. The following are examples:

"I believe I am a person of worth."
"I will no longer be depressed about _____."
"I will no longer get angry and aggressive when _____ occurs."
"I will lose 15 pounds in 2 months."
"1 will stop smoking today."
"I will limit my drinking of alcohol to two drinks when I go out."
"I will no longer feel guilty about _____."
"I believe I am an attractive person."
"I will assertively express myself when _____ occurs."

Step 3. Have each student start writing on a sheet of paper one positive affirmation over and over. When negative thoughts enter their minds, have them record those thoughts and then continue writing the positive affirmation according to the following format:

POSITIVE AFFIRMATIONS	NEGATIVE THOUGHTS
I will lose 15 pounds in 2 months.	I overeat when I'm bored, depressed, or lonely.
I will lose 15 pounds in 2 months.	
I will lose 15 pounds in 2 months.	I will need to develop an exercise program, which I hate to do.
I will lose 15 pounds in 2 months.	
I will lose 15 pounds in 2 months.	
I will lose 15 pounds in 2 months.	One reason I'm fat is that I snack between meals.
I will lose 15 pounds in 2 months.	I will have to limit the number of beers that I have when I go out—beer is putting a lot of weight on me.
I will lose 15 pounds in 2 months.	I wonder if I really want to make all the changes that I will have to make to lose 15 pounds.
I will lose 15 pounds in 2 months.	
I will lose 15 pounds in 2 months.	
I will lose 15 pounds in 2 months.	

Step 4. Allow the students to write for 10 to 15 minutes. Ask for volunteers to share what they wrote. Have the class discuss the merits and shortcomings of writing positive affirmations. One advantage of repeatedly writing the affirmation, for example, is that it trains the mind to more readily accept the positive affirmation.

EXERCISE D: Assessing and Changing Dysfunctional Behavior

GOAL: To facilitate students' learning how to assess and change dysfunctional behavior.

Step 1. The leader indicates that rational therapy asserts that thinking processes primarily determine behavior. This approach maintains that the reasons for unusual or dysfunctional behavior can always be identified by determining what the perpetrator was thinking prior to and during the time when the act was being committed. Divide the class into subgroups of about four people. Hand each subgroup a card that identifies a perpetrator who has engaged in dysfunctional behavior. Each subgroup should have a different dysfunctional behavior to focus on. Examples of character types to distribute to students include:

1. Alcoholic
2. Spouse abuser
3. Child abuser
4. Bulimic
5. Anorexic
6. Date rapist
7. Compulsive gambler
8. Embezzler
9. Adulterer
10. Arsonist

Step 2. Each subgroup seeks to specify the cognitions that would lead its assigned perpetrator to engage in the indicated dysfunctional behavior. After the subgroups identify the cognitions through a discussion, each subgroup is instructed to specify the interventions that it believes would be most effective in changing the thinking patterns of its assigned perpetrator and curbing the dysfunctional behavior. (Examples of interventions include individual and group therapy, support groups, legal intervention, and family therapy.) The subgroup then selects a spokesperson to summarize the cognitions and list of interventions for the class.

Step 3. Each subgroup specifies to the whole class the type of perpetrator it was assigned to focus on, and the spokesperson then summarizes the cognitions and interventions listed. After each subgroup presents this information, the remainder of the class has an opportunity to suggest cognitions and interventions that the subgroup may have overlooked.

Step 4. The exercise is ended by the class discussing the merits and shortcomings of the assertion by rational therapy that cognitions determine behavior, and that changing negative and irrational cognitions in a positive and rational direction is the key psychotherapeutic agent in changing dysfunctional behavior.

EXERCISE E:	Improving Your Self-Concept

GOAL: To improve your self-concept.

Step 1. The leader asks each student to list on a sheet of paper her or his good qualities— what she or he likes about herself or himself.

Step 2. The leader asks each student to then list what he or she dislikes about himself or herself.

Step 3. The leader then asks each student to write down for each negative quality listed in Step 2 what positive things he or she will tell himself or herself whenever this student starts "awfulizing" about a negative quality. (The refuting positive quality may be a quality listed in Step 1.)

Step 4. The leader explains that a negative self-concept stems from negative and irrational self-talk that people give themselves. One way to improve a negative self-concept is to identify the underlying negative self-talk and then challenge this self-talk with positive thoughts about oneself.

Competency Notes

EP 7a Collect and organize data, and apply critical thinking to interpret information from clients and constituencies.

EP 7b Apply knowledge of human behavior and the social environment, person-in-environment, and other multidisciplinary theoretical frameworks in the analysis of assessment data from clients and constituencies.

EP 7c Develop mutually agreed-on intervention goals and objectives based on the critical assessment of strengths, needs, and challenges within clients and constituencies.

EP 8a Critically choose and implement interventions to achieve practice goals and enhance capacities of clients and constituencies.

EP 8b Apply knowledge of human behavior and the social environment, person-in-environment, and other multidisciplinary theoretical frameworks in interventions with clients and constituencies. (pp. 473-495)

Rational therapy is a cognitive-behavioral approach for assessing, intervening, and evaluating interventions with individuals, families, and groups. Several exercises are presented in which students are instructed in using meaningful activities to change unwanted emotions; are instructed in changing unwanted emotions with a rational self-analysis; are instructed in changing unwanted emotions by changing events; learn that their actions are primarily determined by their thoughts; reflect on the assertion that the key psychotherapeutic change agent is changing the client's thinking from self-talk that is negative or irrational to self-talk that is more rational and positive; and learn to improve their self-concept.

MODULE 2 Behavior Therapy in Groups

LEARNING OBJECTIVES

Behavior therapy approaches are based on learning theories. This module helps prepare students to:

EP 7a
EP 7b
EP 7c
EP 8a
EP 8b

LO 1

Comprehend three learning processes.

LO 2

Understand the following behavior intervention techniques that are used by social workers in groups: assertiveness training, token economies, behavioral contracting, and cognitive-behavioral techniques.

No one person is credited with the development of behavioral approaches to psychotherapy. Behavior therapists vary considerably in both theory and technique. The main assumption of this therapy system is that maladaptive behaviors are primarily acquired through learning and can be modified through additional learning.

Historically, learning theory has been the philosophical foundation for behavior therapy, even though there has never been agreement as to which learning theory is the core of behavior therapy. Authorities have advanced somewhat different theories of how people learn. Ivan Pavlov, a Russian who lived between 1849 and 1936, was one of the earliest. Other prominent learning theorists include Edward Thorndike, E. R. Guthrie, C. L. Hull, E. C. Tolman, and B. F. Skinner.[1]

Many behavior therapists have achieved international recognition for developing therapy approaches based on learning principles. Some of these therapists include R. E. Alberti and M. L. Emmons, A. Bandura, B. F. Skinner, J. B. Watson and R. Rayner, and J. Wolpe.[2]

In spite of the wide variation in behavioral therapy approaches and techniques, there are some common emphases. One is that the maladaptive behavior (such as bed-wetting) is the problem and needs to be changed. This approach is in sharp contrast to the psychoanalytic approach that views the problematic behavior as being a *symptom* of some underlying, subconscious causes. Although psychoanalysts assert the underlying, subconscious causes must be treated to prevent the substitution of new symptoms or the return of old symptoms, behavior therapists assert that treating the problematic behavior will not result in symptom substitution.

Another common emphasis of behavior therapists is the assertion that therapy approaches must be tested and validated by rigorous experimental procedures. Such a focus requires that the goals of therapy be articulated in behavioral terms that can be measured. Baseline levels of problematic behaviors are established prior to therapy in order to measure whether the therapy approach is producing the desired change in the rate or intensity of responding.

LO 1 Comprehend Three Learning Processes

TYPES OF LEARNING PROCESSES

The three major types of learning processes postulated by learning theory are operant conditioning, respondent conditioning, and modeling. These three learning processes are briefly described in the following sections.

Operant Conditioning

Much of human behavior, according to learning theory, is determined by positive and negative reinforcers. A *positive reinforcer* is any stimulus that, when applied following a behavior, increases or strengthens that behavior. Common examples of such stimuli are food, water, sex, attention, affection, and approval. The list of positive reinforcers is inexhaustible and highly individualized. Praise, for example, is a positive reinforcer when, and only when, it maintains or increases the behavior with which it is associated (for example, efforts to improve one's writing skills).

A synonym for negative reinforcer is aversive stimulus. A *negative reinforcer* (or aversive stimulus) is any stimulus that a person will terminate or avoid if given the opportunity. Common examples of negative reinforcers are frowns, electric shock, and criticism. (It should be noted that the same stimulus—for example, the smell of Limburger cheese—can be a positive reinforcer for one person and a negative reinforcer for another.)

There are four basic learning principles involving positive reinforcers and aversive stimuli:

1. If a positive reinforcer (for example, food) is presented to a person following a response, the result is positive reinforcement. With positive reinforcement, the occurrence of a given behavior is strengthened or increased.
2. If a positive reinforcer is withdrawn following a person's response, the result is punishment.
3. If an aversive stimulus (for example, an electric shock) is presented to a person following a response, the result is punishment. (As can be seen, there are two types of punishment.)
4. If an aversive stimulus is withdrawn following a person's response, the result is negative reinforcement. In negative reinforcement, a response (behavior) is increased through removing an aversive stimulus (for example, fastening one's seat belt in a car to turn off the obnoxiously loud and annoying buzzer).

In sum, positive and negative reinforcement increase behavior, and punishment decreases behavior. Principles of operant conditioning are used in three behavioral techniques that are described in this chapter (assertiveness training, token economies, and contingency contracting). Operant conditioning principles are also used in aversive techniques (such as administering an electric shock when a client engages in maladaptive behavior). Aversive techniques will not be described in this chapter, as they are seldom, if ever, used by social workers. Positive *reinforcement (reward) approaches are generally more effective than those based on punishment. Punishment is often counterproductive, as it can result in the client's becoming hostile about the treatment procedures. Also, punishment may have only temporary effects. When clients realize they are no longer under surveillance, they may return to exhibiting the maladaptive behavior.

Respondent Conditioning

Respondent learning has also been called classical or Pavlovian conditioning. Widely ranging everyday behaviors are considered to be respondent behaviors—including many anxieties, fears, and phobias. A key concept in respondent learning is "pairing"; that is, behaviors are learned by being consistently and over time paired with other behaviors or events. In order to explain respondent conditioning, we will begin by defining the following key terms:

Neutral stimulus (NS): A stimulus that elicits little or no response
Unconditioned stimulus (UCS): A stimulus that elicits an unlearned or innate response
Unlearned or innate response (UR): A response that is innate—for example, the response of salivating to having food in the mouth
Conditioned response (CR): A new response that has been learned
Conditioned stimulus (CS): An originally neutral stimulus that through pairing with an unconditioned stimulus now begins to elicit a conditioned response

Respondent learning asserts that when a neutral stimulus *(NS)* is paired with an unconditioned stimulus *(UCS)*, the neutral stimulus will also come to elicit a response similar to that being elicited by the UCS. That new response is called a *conditioned response (CR)* because it has been learned; the originally neutral stimulus, once it begins to elicit the response, becomes the conditioned stimulus (CS). Thus, it is possible for an

EXERCISE M2.1   Operant Conditioning

GOAL: This exercise is designed to assist you in understanding and applying operant conditioning.

1. Describe an experience where a behavior of yours was increased by a positive reinforcer.

2. Describe an experience where a behavior of yours was decreased by a negative reinforcer.

event that originally elicited no fear whatsoever (for example, being in the dark) to come to elicit fear when it is paired with a stimulus that does elicit fear (for example, horrifying stories about being in the dark). This learning process is indicated in the following paradigm:

1. UCS (horrifying stories about being in the dark) $\longrightarrow$ elicits UR (fear)

2. NS (being in the dark)

$\quad\quad\downarrow$

(paired with)

UCS $\longrightarrow$ elicits $\longrightarrow$ CR (fear)

3. NS becomes CS $\longrightarrow$ elicits CR (fear)

EXERCISE M2.2   Pavlovian Conditioning

GOAL: This exercise is designed to assist you in understanding and applying respondent conditioning.

1. Describe an experience where a behavior of yours was shaped by respondent conditioning.

The *CS-CR* bond can be broken by *respondent extinction* or by *counterconditioning*. Respondent extinction involves continuing presentation of the conditioned stimulus without any further pairing with the unconditioned stimulus. Respondent extinction gradually weakens, and eventually eliminates, the CS-CR bond.

Counterconditioning is based on the principle that the CS-CR bond can be broken by using new responses that are stronger than and incompatible with old responses that are elicited by the same stimulus. For example, it is possible to teach a person to relax (new response) instead of becoming anxious (old response) when confronted with a particular stimulus (for example, the prospect of flying in a small plane). (One way of teaching a person to relax is instructing the person to use the deep-breathing relaxation technique.)

Modeling

Modeling refers to a change in behavior as a result of the observation of someone else's behavior—that is, learning by vicarious experience or imitation. Much of everyday learning is thought to take place through modeling—using both live models and symbolic models (such as films). Modeling has been used in behavior modification to develop new behaviors that are not in a person's repertoire; for example, showing a youngster how to swing a bat. Modeling has also been used to eliminate anxieties and fears—for example, through using a model in assertiveness training. Anxieties and fears are reduced or eliminated through modeling in assertiveness training by exposing fearful observers to modeled events in which the model performs feared activity without experiencing any adverse effects and even enjoys the process.

EXERCISE M2.3   Modeling

GOAL: This exercise is designed to assist you in understanding and applying the principles of modeling.

1. Describe an experience where you learned a new behavior by modeling.

THEORY OF BEHAVIOR THERAPY

Behavior therapy is based on the assumption that all behavior occurs in response to stimulation, internal or external. The first task of the behavior therapist is to identify the probable stimulus-response (S-R) connections that are occurring for the client. This part of the therapy process is called the behavioral or functional analysis. The following is an illustration of an S-R connection: For a person who has a fear of heights, the stimulus (S) of flying in a small plane would have the response (R) of intense anxiety and seeking to avoid the stimulus.

Prior to and during the time when the therapist is doing the behavioral analysis, the therapist is also attempting to establish a working relationship. During the behavioral analysis, the therapist attempts to determine the stimuli that are associated with the maladaptive responses. Through this analysis both the client and the therapist arrive at an understanding of the problem and generally how it developed. This insight, although it does not treat the problem, is useful because it reduces some of the client's anxiety and the client no longer feels possessed or overwhelmed by unknown, mysterious forces. It should be noted that errors about hypothesized S-R connections at this diagnostic stage usually lead to ineffective treatment, as the treatment will then be focused on treating S-R connections that are *not* involved in perpetuating the maladaptive behavior.

The therapist begins a behavioral analysis by taking a detailed history of the presenting problem, its course, and particularly of its association with current experiences. In making such an analysis it is crucial to obtain specific, concrete details about the circumstances in which the presenting problem arises. If, for example, a client is shy in some situations, it is important to identify the specific interactions in which the client is shy. Furthermore, it is important to determine the reasons why the client is shy: Is it because the person does not know how to express himself or herself, or is it because the person has certain fears? The treatment chosen depends on such information.

If the clients do not know how to express themselves, a *modeling* approach through role-playing might be used. On the other hand, if clients have the response potential but are inhibited because they do not think they have the right to assertively express themselves, reframing (described later in this module) might be used to change their thinking processes so that they realize that everyone has the right to express thoughts and feelings.

The objective in doing a behavioral analysis is to identify the antecedent stimuli that are generating the maladaptive responses. Once these connections are identified, they are discussed with the client to help the client gain insight and to obtain the client's feedback on possible erroneous connections. The client and the therapist then agree upon the goals for the treatment. The process of how therapy will proceed (along with the techniques to be used) are described to the client. This provides the client with an idea of his or her role in treatment, and Orne and Wender have found that this knowledge fosters positive outcomes and reduces the dropout rate.[3]

Chambless and Goldstein describe the sources of information for making a behavioral analysis:

> The behavior therapist may base the functional analysis on interviews with the client and important people in the client's life or on information gained by having the client keep a journal. Questionnaire data are often useful. Interpersonal problems may be more clearly defined if the therapist and client role play interactions with which the client reports difficulty. When the therapist has a difficult time making the analysis, observing the client in the situation where the problem occurs may lead to a wealth of information. Obviously, there are times when this would be impossible or in poor taste, but direct observation is used much less frequently than it should be.[4]

LO 2 Understand the Following Behavior Intervention Techniques That Are Used by Social Workers in Groups: Assertiveness Training, Token Economies, Behavioral Contracting, and Cognitive-Behavioral Techniques

BEHAVIOR THERAPY TECHNIQUES

The remainder of this module is focused on presenting behavior therapy techniques that are commonly used by social workers. These techniques include assertiveness training, token economies, behavioral contracting, and cognitive-behavioral techniques.

ASSERTIVENESS TRAINING

Assertiveness training has become the most frequently used method in modifying unadaptive interpersonal behavior. It is particularly effective in changing both timid behavior and aggressive behavior. Wolpe originally developed this approach,[5] and it has been further developed by a variety of authors, including Alberti and Emmons, and Fensterheim and Baer.[6]

Assertiveness problems range from extreme shyness, introversion, and withdrawal to inappropriate rages that can alienate others. A nonassertive person is often acquiescent, fearful, and afraid of expressing his or her real feelings spontaneously. Frequently, resentment and anxiety build up, which may result in general discomfort, feelings of low self-esteem, tension headaches, fatigue, and perhaps a destructive explosion of anger and aggression. Some people are overly shy and timid in nearly all interactions; however, most encounter occasional problems in isolated areas where it would be to their benefit to be more assertive. For example, a young man might be quite effective and assertive in his job as a store manager but still be awkward and timid in a social situation.

Nonassertive, Aggressive, and Assertive Behaviors

There are three basic styles of interacting with others—nonassertive, aggressive, and assertive—and they have been summarized by Alberti and Emmons as follows:

> In the *nonassertive* style, you are likely to hesitate, speak softly, look away, avoid the issue, agree regardless of your own feelings, not express opinions, value yourself "below" others, and hurt yourself to avoid any chance of hurting others.

> In the *aggressive style,* you typically answer before the other person is through talking, speak loudly and abusively, glare at the other person, speak "past" the issue (accusing, blaming, demeaning), vehemently expound your feelings and opinions, value yourself "above" others, and hurt others to avoid hurting yourself.

> In the *assertive style,* you will answer spontaneously, speak with a conversational tone and volume, look at the other person, speak to the issue, openly express your personal feelings and opinions (anger, love, disagreement, sorrow), value yourself equal to others, and hurt neither yourself nor others.[7]

The following examples describe two typical situations in which an assertive response could be used effectively. In the first situation, the level of intimacy is low because the situation occurs with a business associate. However, in the second instance, the social situation involves a husband and wife and a much more intimate relationship. Group leaders should note that just as it is more difficult to say "no" to a friend than to a stranger who wants to borrow $50, it is more difficult to deal with assertive behavior on an intimate than on a superficial level.

1. You are driving with a business associate to a distant city for a conference. The associate lights up a pipe; you soon find the smoke irritating and the odor somewhat stifling. What are your choices?

> *Nonassertive response:* You attempt to carry on a cheery conversation for the 3-hour trip without commenting about the smoke.
>
> *Aggressive response:* You become increasingly irritated until you explode, "Either you put out that pipe or I'll put it out for you—the odor is sickening."
>
> *Assertive response:* In a firm, conversational tone, you look directly at the associate and state, "The smoke from your pipe is irritating me. I'd appreciate it if you would put it away."

2. At a party with friends, your husband subtly puts you down by stating, "Wives always talk too much." What do you do?

> *Nonassertive response:* You don't say anything, but feel hurt and become quiet.
>
> *Aggressive response:* You glare at him and angrily ask, "John, why are you always criticizing me?"
>
> *Assertive response:* You carry on as usual, waiting until the drive home to calmly look at him and say, "When we were at the party tonight, you said that wives always talk too much. I felt you were putting me down when you said that. What did you mean by that comment?"

Assertiveness training is designed to lead one to realize, feel, and act on the assumption that one has the right to be oneself and express one's feelings freely. Assertive responses are generally not aggressive responses, and the distinction between these two types of interactions is important. If, for example, a woman has an overly critical mother-in-law, the woman may intentionally do things that will upset her (not visiting, serving food she dislikes, not cleaning the house), urging her husband to tell his mother to "shut up," and getting into loud arguments with her. On the other hand, an effective assertive response would be to counter criticism by saying: "Jane, your criticism deeply hurts me. I know you're trying to help when you give advice, but I feel that you're criticizing me. I know you don't want me to make mistakes, but to grow, I need to make my own errors and learn from them. If you want to help me, let me do it myself and be responsible for the consequences. The type of relationship I'd like to have with you is a close adult-to-adult relationship and not a mother-child relationship."

Assertiveness Training in Groups

All of us are nonassertive in some situations where it would be to our benefit to be assertive. Many of us are aggressive in some situations in which it would be more constructive to be assertive. Assertiveness training groups are ideal settings to learn to be more assertive, for they allow members to test new assertive behaviors through interactions with others. Assertiveness training groups also allow members to learn new assertive strategies through observing effective assertive responses that are modeled by other group members. The following material summarizes a step-by-step approach for facilitating an assertiveness training program within a group setting.[8]

Examining Group Interactions The first step to implementing assertiveness training in a group is for each member to examine his or her interactions. Aggressive, assertive, and nonassertive behavior are defined by the group leader, and examples are provided. Then, group members are asked by the leader to silently and privately arrive at answers to the following questions:

1. Are there situations that you would like to handle more assertively?
2. Are there situations in which you habitually withhold opinions and feelings that you want to express?
3. Are there situations in which you habitually become angry and lash out at others, only to regret your aggression later?

Selecting Areas for Improvement Group members individually and privately select interactions (identified in the preceding step) in which it would be to their benefit to be more assertive. These may include situations in which they were overpolite, too apologetic, timid, or allowed others to take advantage of them while inwardly harboring feelings of resentment, anger, embarrassment, fear, or self-criticism for not having the courage to express themselves or overly aggressive interactions in which they exploded in anger or walked over others. For *each* set of nonassertive or aggressive interactions, group members can become more assertive, as shown in the next steps. The group leader should add at this point that the members will not be required to reveal the situations in which they have habitually been nonassertive or aggressive.

Visualizing an Incident Group members are instructed to concentrate on a specific incident involving their problematic interactions. They close their eyes for several minutes and vividly imagine the details, including specific conversations and feelings. As part of this visualization process, the leader indicates that nonverbal communication is as important as verbal communication. The leader then asks the members to silently arrive at answers to the following questions:

1. *Eye contact:* "Did you look directly at the other person in a relaxed, steady manner? Looking down or away suggests a lack of self-confidence. Glaring is an aggressive response."
2. *Gestures:* "Were your gestures appropriate, free-flowing, relaxed, and used to emphasize your message effectively? Awkward stiffness suggests nervousness; other gestures, such as an angry fist, signal an aggressive reaction."
3. *Body posture:* "Did you show the importance of your message by facing the other person, leaning forward, holding your head up, and sitting or standing appropriately close?"
4. *Facial expression:* "Did your facial expression show the firmness of purpose and self-confidence consistent with an assertive response?"

5. *Voice tone and volume:* "Was your response stated in a firm, conversational tone? Shouting may suggest anger. Speaking softly suggests shyness; a cracking voice suggests nervousness."

6. *Speech fluency:* "Did your speech flow smoothly, clearly, and slowly? Rapid speech or hesitation in speaking suggests nervousness."

7. *Timing:* "Were your verbal reactions to a problem stated at the appropriate time? Generally, spontaneous expressions are the best, but certain situations should be handled at a later time—for example, challenging some of your boss's erroneous statements in private rather than in front of the group he is addressing."

8. *Message content:* "Which of your statements were aggressive, which assertive, and which nonassertive? Why do you believe you responded nonassertively or aggressively? Have you habitually responded nonassertively or aggressively in this situation?"

Visualizing an Assertive Model   The leader instructs the group members to continue to keep their eyes closed. The leader states; "We will now focus on coming up with some alternative approaches for being assertive that you can use in your problematic situation. One way to do this is to visualize how someone you view as being fairly assertive would handle this situation. What would this assertive model say? How would this person be assertive nonverbally in this situation?" (Pause)

Alternative Assertive Approaches   The leader continues the visualization exercise by asking group members to come up with several alternative approaches for being assertive in this situation. Members then are instructed to visualize using each of these approaches. For each approach, members should think through what the full set of interactions would be, along with the consequences. (The leader pauses frequently while group members are visualizing these alternatives.) The leader then instructs members to select an approach, or combination of approaches, that each believes will work best in his or her situation. Through imagery, members should continue practicing this approach until they feel comfortable with it.

If anyone has difficulty in thinking of a strategy to use, the leader indicates that it may be helpful after this visualization exercise ends to have someone else in the class role-play an assertive approach for this situation. Group members continue, through imagery, to practice their chosen strategy until they feel ready to use it when their problematic situation occurs again. The leader informs the members that when a real-life situation occurs they should expect to be somewhat anxious when they first try to be assertive. Members are also informed that after trying out their assertive strategy in a real-life situation, they should reflect on its effectiveness by asking themselves the following questions:

1. Considering the nonverbal and verbal guidelines for being assertive, which components of your responses were assertive, which were aggressive, and which were nonassertive?

2. What were the consequences of your effort?

3. How do you feel after trying out this new set of interactions?

The leader explains that some success is to be expected but not complete personal satisfaction with these initial efforts. Learning to be more assertive is a continuing process. Also, group members should be told: "Pat yourself on your back for the progress you made in being more assertive—you've earned it! Learning to be more assertive is an exhilarating experience. But you should also identify the areas where you need to improve, and then continue to work on becoming more assertive by using the above mentioned steps in the assertiveness process." Finally, members should be informed that the visualization exercise is drawing to a close and should now open their eyes.

Role-Playing   The leader distributes note cards and asks members to write down anonymously one or two problematic situations they would like others in the class to role-play. After the cards are handed in, the leader selects an interesting situation and asks volunteers to role-play it. Generally, there are two people in the situation, and one role involves using an assertive strategy. After the situation is role-played, the class discusses what was done well and what else might have been done. Another role-play situation is then selected, and the process continues.

The Assertiveness Model   After several situations are role-played, the leader summarizes how one becomes more assertive:

1. Identify a problematic situation in which you are habitually nonassertive or aggressive.
2. Visualize a problematic incident and identify your nonverbal and verbal communication.
3. Develop alternative approaches for being assertive in this situation. A few approaches may be arrived at by visualizing how an assertive model would act.
4. Select an assertive strategy and continue to practice it through imagery.
5. Role-play an assertive strategy to gain confidence, or watch someone else role-play the strategy. After watching someone else, role-play the approach yourself.
6. Try out the assertive strategy in a real-life situation.
7. Analyze what you did well and what you still need to work on to become more assertive.

Comments   The leader may want to supplement the previous material by showing one or more films or videotapes on assertiveness training. If a group member is still afraid of attempting assertive behavior, he or she should repeat the modeling, visualizing, and role-playing steps. For those few individuals who fail to develop the needed confidence to try out being assertive, seeking professional private counseling is advised, as being able to express oneself and have effective interactions with others is essential for personal happiness.

The leader should add that it is a mistake to seek to be assertive in all situations. There are some situations in which it is best to be nonassertive. For example, if two large muscular people are physically fighting, it may be a mistake for a small person to assertively intervene. There are also some situations where it is best to be aggressive. For example, if you observe someone being sexually assaulted, it may be advantageous to intervene by aggressively seeking to stop the perpetrator.

The format of the technique in assertiveness training is relatively simple to comprehend. Considerable skill (common sense and ingenuity), however, is needed to determine what will be an effective assertive strategy when a real-life situation arises. The joy and pride obtained from being able fully to express oneself assertively is nearly unequaled.

TOKEN ECONOMIES

Tokens are symbolic reinforcers, such as poker chips or points on a tally sheet, which can later be exchanged for items that constitute direct forms of reinforcement, such as candy or increased privileges (for example, an adolescent in a group home being allowed to go to movies). An economy involves an exchange system that specifies exactly what the tokens can be exchanged for and how many tokens it takes to get particular items or privileges. The economy also specifies the target behaviors (such as going to school or making a bed) that can earn tokens and the rate of responding that is required to earn a particular number of tokens. For example, attending school every day for 2 weeks earns 10 tokens at an adolescent group home, and 10 tokens can be exchanged for attending a sports event.

Token economies have been successfully used in a wide variety of institutional settings, including mental hospitals, training schools for delinquents, classrooms for students with emotional problems, schools for people with a cognitive disability, rehabilitation centers for people with a physical or cognitive disability, and group homes for adolescents. There is more evidence to support the effectiveness of token economies than for almost any other behavioral technique.[9] Token economies have been used to effect positive changes in a wide variety of behaviors, including personal hygiene, social interactions, job attendance and performance, academic performance, domestic tasks such as cleaning, and personal

EXERCISE M2.4   Becoming Assertive

GOAL: This exercise is designed to assist you in understanding and applying the principles of assertiveness training.

1. Describe a behavior of yours where you are routinely nonassertive and you instead want to be more assertive.

2. Review the material on assertiveness training. Visualize yourself being assertive in this situation. Describe what you will say, and describe what you want to communicate with your nonverbal behavior.

3. Describe a behavior of yours where you are routinely aggressive and you instead want to be more assertive.

4. Visualize yourself being assertive in this situation. Describe what you will say, and describe what you want to communicate with your nonverbal behavior.

5. When these problematic situations again arise where you have been either nonassertive or aggressive, are you committed now to seeking to be assertive?

appearance. At times, clients not only earn tokens for desired behaviors but also lose tokens for undesired behaviors (for example, instigating a fight).

Effective token economies are much more difficult to establish than it appears at first glance. Prochaska summarizes some of the most important factors that need to be given attention in establishing a token economy:

> Some of the more important considerations include staff cooperation and coordination, since the staff must be more observant and more systematic in their responses to clients than in a noncontingent system. A variety of attempts at establishing token economies have failed because the staff did not cooperate adequately in monitoring the behavior of residents. Effective token economies must also have adequate control over reinforcements, since an economy becomes ineffective if residents have access to reinforcements by having money from home or being able to burn a cigarette from a less cooperative staff member. Problems must be clearly defined in terms of specific behaviors to be changed in order to avoid conflicts among staff or patients. Improving personal hygiene, for example, is too open to interpretation by individuals, and parents may insist that they are improving their hygiene even though staff members may disagree. There is much less room for misunderstandings if personal hygiene is defined as clean fingernails, no evidence of body odor, clean underwear, and other clear-cut rules. Specifying behaviors that are positive alternatives to problem behavior is very critical in teaching residents what positive actions they can take to help

themselves, rather than relying on just a negative set of eliminating responses. Perhaps most important for more lasting effectiveness of token economies is that they be gradually phased out as problem behaviors are reduced and more adaptive responses become well established. Obviously the outside world does not run according to an institution's internal economy, and it is important that clients be prepared to make the transition to the larger society. Using an abundance of social reinforcers along with token reinforcers helps prepare clients for the fading out of tokens, so that positive behaviors can be maintained by praise or recognition rather than by tokens. Also encouraging patients to reinforce themselves, such as by learning to take pride in their appearance, is an important step in fading out tokens. Some institutions use transitional wards where clients go from token economies and learn to maintain adaptive behaviors through more naturalistic contingencies, such as praise from a fellow patient. In such transitional settings, backup reinforcers are available if needed, but they are used much more sparingly than in the token economies. Without the use of fading, taken economies can become nothing more than hospital management procedures that make the care of patients more efficient without preparing patients to live effectively in the larger society.[10]

It is interesting to note that the system of employers hiring employees to work has many components of a token economy. Employers pay cash to employees to do tasks that are

EXERCISE M2.5   Token Economy

GOAL: This exercise is designed to assist you in understanding a token economy.

1. Describe a token economy that you participated in. Perhaps it was a token economy that a former teacher used with the class. Perhaps it was a system that your parents used to pay you for you doing work that they wanted completed.

2. What do you see as the strengths and shortcomings of the token economy that you participated in?

specified by the employer. Employees then decide what products and services they will then purchase with the cash they received.

BEHAVIORAL CONTRACTING

Closely related to token economies is behavioral contracting. Behavioral contracts provide the client with a set of rules that govern the change process. Contracts may be unilateral; that is, a client may make a contract with himself or herself. For example, a woman with a weight problem may limit herself to a certain calorie intake, with a system of rewards being established for staying within the calorie limit. Contracts may also be bilateral and specify the obligations and the mutual reinforcements for each of the parties.

Helping professionals are finding it very useful to develop behavioral contracts with clients. Formulating contracts with clients in both one-to-one settings and group settings has a number of advantages. The contracts serve as guides to clients as to the specific actions they need to take in order to improve their problematic situations. Contracts tend to have a motivational effect because when people commit to the terms of a contract, they usually feel a moral obligation to follow through on the commitments they make. In addition, reviewing whether or not commitments made in contracts are being met provides therapists and clients with one method for measuring progress. If a client's commitments are usually fulfilled, positive changes are probably occurring. If commitments are generally unfulfilled, it suggests that positive changes are not occurring.

Contracts in social work practice specify goals to be accomplished and the tasks to be performed to accomplish them. In addition, contracts set deadlines for completion of the specified task and identify rewards for successful completion of tasks. Contracts also specify consequences for unsuccessful completion of tasks. A contract is, therefore, an agreement between a social worker and one or more clients in their joint efforts to achieve specified outcomes. Formulating an explicit contract is directly related to a positive outcome for clients.[11]

A contract, in outline format, should contain the following components:

1. Goals to be accomplished (ranked in order of priority).
2. Tasks to be accomplished by the client and by the worker. (These tasks must be directly related to accomplishing the goals, so that accomplishing the tasks will result in successfully meeting the goals.)
3. Time frame for completing the tasks.
4. Means of monitoring progress toward accomplishing the tasks and the goals.
5. Rewards for the client if the terms of the contract are met.
6. Adverse consequences to the client upon nonfulfillment of the terms of the contract.

Some workers prefer written contracts, and others prefer verbal contracts. A written contract has the advantage of emphasizing the commitment to the contract by both the worker and the client, and it minimizes the risks of misunderstandings. A verbal contract has the advantage of clients being apt to view it as being more "humane" than a written contract. Research comparing the effectiveness of written versus verbal contracts shows that the verbal contract is generally as effective as the written contract with regard to the goals being successfully accomplished.[12] If a worker chooses to use a verbal contract, the worker should still record the essential elements of the contract in his or her notes for future reference.

The most difficult element in formulating an effective contract is for the worker and the client to formulate goals. Goals specify what the client wishes to accomplish and should directly relate to the needs, wants, or problems being encountered by the client. Goals serve the following important functions:

1. Goals ensure that the worker and the client are in agreement about the objectives to be accomplished.
2. Goals provide direction to the helping process and thereby reduce needless wandering.
3. Goals guide selection of appropriate tasks (and interventions) that are focused on achieving the objectives.
4. Goals serve as outcome criteria in evaluating the extent to which the tasks (and interventions) are being successful.

Useful guidelines when setting goals include:

1. *Goals must relate to the desired end results sought by the client:* The client must believe that accomplishing the selected goals will enhance his or her well-being. Therefore, the worker needs to integrally involve the client in the process of selecting and specifying the goals.

2. *Goals should be stated in specific and measurable terms:* Nebulous goals (such as "Client gaining increased control over his emotions") are not sufficiently specific and often lead the client to "drift" or wander in the helping process. A specific goal (such as "The client will express his angry feelings with his mother in an assertive rather than an aggressive manner when they are having conflicts") is substantially more explicit. In addition, it is measurable, whereas a nebulously stated goal is not. The client's mother (and others) can monitor the number of times over a specified period that the client expresses his angry feelings assertively as compared to aggressively. Clients tend to define goals more nebulously, so it is important for the worker to assist clients in stating their goals in such a way that they are both specific and measurable.

3. *Goals should be feasible:* Unachievable goals set the client up for failure, which is then apt to lead to disappointment, disillusionment, and a sense of defeat. It is vital that the goals chosen can be accomplished by the client. For clients with grandiose tendencies, it is important for the worker to assist them (tactfully) in lowering their expectations to the upper level of what can reasonably be attained.

When arriving at feasible goal statements with a client, the worker should agree only to assist the client in working toward goals for which the worker has the requisite skills and knowledge. If the goal is beyond the worker's competence (for example, assisting the client in overcoming a complex sexual dysfunction), the worker has the responsibility to refer the client to a more appropriate resource in the community.

Once the client has settled on his or her goals, the final step in the process of negotiating goal statements is to assign priorities to the goals. The purpose of this step is to ensure that the initial change efforts are directed to the goal that is most important to the client. The example presented in Chapter 12 illustrates the formulation of a behavioral contract.

COGNITIVE-BEHAVIORAL TECHNIQUES*

Cognitive-behavioral therapy (CBT) techniques are some of the most popular and common evidenced-based practices used by social workers and mental health professionals today. Significant research has been conducted in the last 30 years that validates this variation of behavior therapy, which recognizes the role of cognition (thinking processes) in human behavior. Following the observations of cognitive therapists such as Ellis and Beck, cognitive-behavioral therapists have embraced the notion that changing the content of one's thoughts will often change one's feelings and behavior.[13] The focus of intervention is primarily on distorted thinking patterns, which are sometimes called thinking errors or cognitive distortions. These maladaptive thinking patterns and the beliefs that drive them are believed to be the source of unwanted feelings that lead to problematic behavior. They often fuel interpersonal conflicts and self-destructive behavior choices. The goal of treatment is help clients understand how their thought patterns influence their feelings and behaviors and then to identify and change those patterns. Instead of focusing on changing stressors or situations beyond their control, clients are encouraged to modify the one thing they can control: how they interpret and deal with situations that are causing them distress.

CBT differs from the traditional paradigm of behavior therapy, which looks at behavior in terms of S (stimulus) → R (response). Cognitive-behavioral therapists insert an additional step in this paradigm: S (stimulus) → O (cognitions of organism) → R (response).[14]

---

* The first part of this section on cognitive-behavioral techniques (up to "Thought Stopping and Covert Assertion") was written by Craig Mead. MSW, LSW, licensed social worker at Presence St. Mary and Elizabeth Medical Center, Chicago, IL

EXERCISE M2.6   Contingency Contracting

GOAL: This exercise is designed to assist you in understanding and applying contingency contracting (which is a type of a behavioral contract).

1. Identify a behavior of yours that you want to change (such as quitting smoking, stopping procrastination on a project, or only having two alcoholic beverages when you go out).

2. State your behavioral goal.

3. Specify what you need to do to accomplish your goal.

4. State your time frame for accomplishing the tasks.

5. Specify the means of monitoring progress toward accomplishing the tasks and goals.

6. Specify how you will reward yourself if you accomplish your goal.

7. Specify what you will do whenever you engage in   inconsistent with your goal (such as donating $5 to a charity).

This variation of behavior therapy is still very goal oriented and problem focused. It is time limited and focused on the present. The therapist actively engages in collaborative problem solving with the clients, who are often given homework or practice exercises to improve their use of coping skills and ability to more effectively self-manage problems. They may be asked to log their "automatic thoughts" when problems arise, which may help identify negative thought patterns, misperceptions, or irrational beliefs. Clients may be holding erroneous beliefs such as feeling worthless, unloved, not cared for, stupid, weak, or unworthy. They are encouraged to "reality test" these negative beliefs, which are reframed as hypotheses instead of facts. Clients can then experiment and gather evidence to see if these beliefs are, in fact, true. They may then be able to restructure their thought patterns to eliminate these negative biases that lack objective evidence. Clients are encouraged to take an active role in making small but consistent changes in how they think and behave in daily situations.

Sometimes clients have limited or poor insight into how or why their behavior is maladaptive or self-destructive. They may blame other people, themselves, or situations for the problem. In order to change a thought, feeling, or behavior, one must first acknowledge and accept responsibility for it. For those clients, a CBT therapist may start with helping clients make an honest and objective assessment of their behavior. This involves nonjudgmentally framing or labeling the behavior so clients can begin to see the behavior as problematic and perhaps make it a focus of change. Therapists have come up with various problem names that they may teach clients to help them identify and categorize certain behaviors. Following are some of the more common problem names.

PROBLEM NAMES

1. LOW SELF-IMAGE: Has poor opinion of self; feels worthless and of little value; gives up or quits easily; focused on feeling sorry for self; blames self for problems when unwarranted; discounts own strengths or ability.

2. INCONSIDERATE TO SELF: Makes choices that are against own best interest; allows others to intrude or impose on him or her; avoids or denies his or her problems, engages in behaviors that are harmful or damaging to self; self-sacrifices or accepts blame for others; denies injury from others.

3. INCONSIDERATE OF OTHERS: Does things that are harmful or damaging to others; behaves selfishly; little consideration for the needs of others; puts down, demeans, or emotionally injures others; invalidates others' feelings, ideas, or opinions; takes advantage of others; disrespectful to others or their property; fails to meet family, work, school, or social expectations or fulfill responsibilities.

4. AUTHORITY PROBLEM: Resents being managed by others, confrontational over minor issues with authority; doesn't like to be told what to do; dislikes advice; passive-aggressive or seeks to circumvent authority; feels powerless or weak when given limits.

5. EASILY ANGERED: Often irritable; gets upset over minor issues or conflicts; sensitive to negative feedback or criticism; reacts excessively to failure or disappointment; excuses behavior as part of temperament; blames others for making angry.

6. AGGRAVATES OTHERS: Deliberately annoying or irritating others, uses put-downs, criticism, or teasing to make others feel bad; oppositional, hostile, or contrary to obstruct others; uses payback threatening, or bullying.

7. MISLEADS OTHERS: Encourages others to engage in negative or harmful behavior; manipulates; attempts to draw others into getting into trouble; toys with people for intellectual amusement; blames others for being misled and denies responsibility.

8. EASILY MISLED: Easily influenced by others; engages in negative or harmful behavior to go along with others; indecisive and allows others to make decisions; allows others to manipulate him or her.

9. LYING: Dishonest, untrustworthy, and untruthful; misleads others through false impression; uses denial to avoid responsibility; may enjoy manipulating others

or get a thrill from successful lies; lacks ego strength to accept consequences of actions.

10. FRONTING OR FALSE SELF: Avoids feeling vulnerable, weak, or powerless by putting up false facade; puts on act instead of being genuine; may try to bluff or con others; may use fronting to distract from an issue or deny a problem; may use fronting to avoid showing real feelings.

11. DRUG OR ALCOHOL PROBLEM: Continued use despite harmful effects and consequences; may use as coping skill or self-medication; may deny problems that are a result of use; may minimize or blame others for use and/or resultant problems.

While cognitive-behavioral therapists work with clients to identify unwanted, unhealthy, or self-destructive thoughts, beliefs, feelings, or behaviors, they often discover common cognitive distortions or thinking errors that contribute to and support these thoughts, feelings, and behaviors. Often clients are not aware that they are using these types of erroneous thinking patterns. Other times they may be used consciously or unconsciously to avoid taking responsibility due to the client not being ready for change. CBT therapists educate their clients about these distorted thinking patterns so they may begin to identify and change them on their own. Following are descriptions of some of the most common types of thinking errors.

COGNITIVE DISTORTIONS AND THINKING ERRORS

1. AWFULIZING or CATASTROPHIZING: Magnifying the importance or consequences of events, actions, or situations; exaggerating possible or hypothetical negative outcomes; viewing solvable problems as disasters; discounting his or her ability to manage stressors.

2. BLAMING: Assigning responsibility for choices on someone else; attributing feelings to others' actions; attributing failures to others while discounting own role.

3. MINIMIZING: Discounting or understating negative consequences of events or actions; invalidating others' perceptions of events or actions; downplaying positive events; avoiding problems through labeling as "no big deal."

4. MAKING EXCUSES: Offering rationalizations for choices; discounting own ability to make choices; using justification to avoid responsibility.

5. ALL-OR-NOTHING (BLACK-AND-WHITE) THINKING: Seeing things one way or another; believing in only extreme polarities or outcomes; excessive rigidity that doesn't allow for middle ground.

6. OVERGENERALIZING: Extrapolating single events to make broad conclusions based on minimal evidence; using anecdotal evidence as basis of believed facts.

7. SHOULDS AND MUSTS: Having rigid beliefs about how things should be; believing that certain situations or actions are intolerable; failing to account for human fallibility; holding unrealistic expectations.

8. ASSUMING THE WORST: Using negative predictions and jumping to conclusions; making a negative interpretation or conclusion with little or no evidence to support it; fortune telling and prophesizing failure; mind reading and making negative assumptions about others; believing minor failures predict impossible outcomes.

9. DENIAL: Discounting or ignoring clear evidence to avoid facing facts; refusing to acknowledge problems; using distraction to divert attention away from actions or feelings.

10. POOR ME: Personalizing injury caused by others; feeling sorry for oneself; assuming responsibility and blame for events when unwarranted; excessive guilt; seeing self as a victim.

11. SELF-CENTERED: Thinking and acting only for self; ignoring how actions affect others; believing own needs are more important than the needs of others; feeling others are solely focused on him or her.

12. PLAYING THE VICTIM: Portraying self as victim to avoid responsibility for own actions; using false victimhood for attention; distorting own emotional injury as being greater than that of others.

13. CONFIRMATION BIAS OR MENTAL FILTER: Only seeing what he or she wants to see in situations; ignoring evidence that doesn't reinforce what he or she already believes; focusing on negative feedback and discounting the positive; dismissing evidence that has clear validity.

14. LABELING: Giving self or others a negative label instead of focusing on a specific behavior; using mistakes or poor choices as evidence of character flaws; using judgmental labels for actions.

15. EMOTIONAL REASONING: Belief that feeling something makes it true; belief that emotions are an accurate reflection of reality; "If I feel unloved, then I am unloved."

The next section summarizes the techniques that have been developed to change cognitions: thought stopping and covert assertion, diversion techniques, and reframing.

Thought Stopping and Covert Assertion

Thought stopping is used by clients whose major problems involve obsessive thinking and ruminations about events that are very unlikely to occur (such as worrying that a plane they will be taking in 2 weeks will crash, or worrying that they are becoming mentally ill).

In thought stopping, the client is first asked to concentrate on and express out loud obsessive, anxiety-inducing thoughts. As the client begins to express those thoughts, the therapist suddenly and emphatically shouts "Stop." This procedure is repeated several times until the client reports that the thoughts are being successfully interrupted. Then the responsibility for the intervention is shifted to the client, so that the client now says "Stop" out loud when he or she begins to think about the troubling thoughts. Once the overt shouting is effective in stopping the troubling thoughts, the client then begins to practice saying "Stop" silently whenever the troubling thoughts begin.

Rimm and Masters supplemented the thought-stopping technique with a *covert assertion* procedure.[15] In addition to interrupting obsessive thoughts by saying "Stop," the client is encouraged to produce a positive, assertive statement that is incompatible with the content of the obsession. For example, a client who worries about becoming mentally ill (when there is no basis for such thinking) may be encouraged to add the covert assertion "I'm perfectly normal" whenever he or she interrupts the obsessive thinking with "Stop."

Mahoney successfully used thought stopping and covert assertion as part of a comprehensive program for overweight clients.[16] Mahoney first instructed clients to become aware of such self-statements as, "I just don't have the willpower" and "I sure can taste eating a strawberry sundae." The clients were then trained to use thought stopping and covert assertion to combat these thoughts.

Diversion Techniques

Diversion techniques are used with clients who have strong, unwanted emotions— such as loneliness, bitterness, depression, frustration, and anger. As indicated in Module 1, unwanted emotions stem primarily from negative and irrational thinking. By becoming involved in physical activity, work, social interactions, or play, these clients will usually switch their negative cognitions to cognitions related to the diversion activities they are involved in. Once they focus their thinking on the diversion activities that they find meaningful and enjoyable, they will experience more pleasing emotions.

Diversion techniques are used in both rational therapy (see Module 1) and CBT. Rational therapy and cognitive-behavioral therapy are closely related. In fact, rational therapy is sometimes classified as a cognitive-behavioral approach.

EXERCISE M2.7   Applying Thought Stopping and Covert Assertion

GOAL: This exercise is designed to demonstrate how to use thought stopping and covert assertion.

1. This may sound strange, but start awfulizing about a current problem in your life. Awfulize for about 5 minutes about this problem.

2. After 5 minutes, yell "Stop" to yourself (either out loud or silently). Also think of a positive, assertive statement that is incompatible with the content of the obsession. Now, whenever you start awfulizing about your problem, yell "Stop" and also use your covert assertion.

3. Specify what you were awfulizing about.

4. Specify the covert assertion you used.

5. Indicate whether the thought-stopping and covert assertion approach worked for you.

6. If the technique did not work very well, indicate why you believe it did not work very well for you.

EXERCISE M2.8   Applying the Diversion Technique

GOAL: This exercise is designed to demonstrate that most people can change an unwanted emotion by the diversion technique.

1. Think about a situation in your past that you tended to awfulize extensively about and then used a diversion technique to stop the awfulizing—and thereby changed an unwanted emotion related to the awfulizing. (For example, you may have awfulized about someone breaking up with you.)

2. Specify what you were awfulizing about. Also indicate your resulting unwanted emotion(s).

3. Describe the diversion technique that you used.

4. Describe the results of using your diversion technique.

5. Are you willing to try the diversion technique the next time you start awfulizing?

Reframing

Reframing involves helping a client change those cognitions that cause unwanted emotions or dysfunctional behaviors. There is a nearly infinite variety of categories of cognitions that may be reframed. The following categories are illustrative.

One focus of reframing is on *positive thinking*. When unpleasant events occur (such as receiving a lower grade on an exam than anticipated), we can choose to think positively or to think negatively. If we take a positive view and focus on problem solving, we are apt to identify and initiate actions to improve the circumstances. On the other hand, if we think negatively, we develop unwanted emotions (such as depression and frustration) and fail to focus on problem solving. With negative thinking, we generally do not do anything constructive and may even engage in destructive behavior.

When a client is thinking negatively, a therapist can use reframing to assist the client in realizing that he or she is thinking negatively. At times it is helpful to say to the client that both negative and positive thinking often become self-fulfilling prophecies, then, through asking the client to name some positive aspects of the situation, the therapist seeks to assist the client in thinking more positively. (If the client is unable to identify any positives, the therapist may suggest some positive aspects.) The client may be encouraged to tell himself or herself to "stop" whenever negative thinking occurs and instead to focus on self-talk about positive aspects of the situation.

Some people take a negative view of most events that happen to them; for such people, reframing through using positive cognitions is more difficult and time consuming. However, if they are successful in learning to think positively, they often make substantial gains.

A second closely related way in which reframing is used is *deawfulizing*. When distressing events occur, most of us tend to awfulize—we exaggerate the negatives. Think about how you reacted when someone with whom you were romantically involved broke up with you, or when you received a parking or speeding citation. Did you awfulize the situation and as a result feel angry, hurt, or depressed? When we awfulize, we focus only on the negatives and do not identify constructive actions to improve the situation. When a client is awfulizing, a therapist can usually help the client identify such thought processes by simply inquiring, "I wonder if you're awfulizing?" The therapist can then assist the client, as described in the material on reframing with positive thinking, to suggest cognitions that are more positive and oriented toward problem solving.

A third reframing focus involves *decatastrophizing*.[17] Decatastrophizing is used when clients are worrying about anticipated feared events. Decatastrophizing involves continually asking clients "what if an anticipated, undesired consequence occurs. For example, the following is a dialogue with a 21-year-old college student who feared expressing his thoughts and feelings in class:

> *Therapist:* What do you think will happen if you begin expressing your views in your classes?
> *Client:* My voice may crack, and the others may laugh at me.
> *Therapist:* It is unlikely that your voice will crack. But even if it does and the students happen to laugh a little, is that really worse than your anger and frustration over not sharing your thoughts?
> *Client:* I don't know.
> *Therapist:* Which is worse when you're asked a question in class: shrugging your shoulders and appearing tongue-tied, or responding as best as you can even though your voice may crack?
> *Client:* I hear what you're saying.
> *Therapist:* What other negative consequences might occur if you begin expressing yourself in class?
> *Client:* (pause) None that I can think of.
> *Therapist:* What positives may come from your speaking up in class?
> *Client:* I'd probably get more out of the class and feel better about myself. Enough of this. I get the message loud and clear. I will commit myself to speaking up at least once a week in each of my classes.

People who catastrophize usually exaggerate the anticipated feared consequences. Decatastrophizing is designed to demonstrate to clients that even if feared consequences occur (which they seldom do), those consequences are not as severe as feared.

A fourth focus of reframing is to assist clients in *separating positive intents from negative behaviors,* so that the positive intents become linked to new, positive behaviors. A parent who is physically abusive to a child has the positive intent of raising the child well, but when the parent is under stress and the child is misbehaving, that parent may not be aware that there are other options that are much more constructive than physically beating the child. A therapist can assist such a parent by helping the parent to reframe thoughts so that when the child misbehaves the parent can focus his or her thinking processes on alternative responses. For example, the stressed parent can ask his or her spouse to handle the child's misbehavior or punish the child with a time-out. An example of this type of reframing is given in the box "Case Example: Reframing Cognitions That Cause Dysfunctional Behaviors."

Redefining is a fifth focus of reframing that is used for clients who believe a problem is beyond their personal control.[18] For example, a bored person who believes "Life is boring" may be encouraged to think, "The reasons I'm bored are I don't have special interests and I'm not initiating activities. It's not life that is boring—it's my thinking processes that are leading me to feel bored. What I'm going to do is get involved in activities I enjoy and initiate interactions with people I like to be with." Redefining is accomplished by the therapist first demonstrating that emotions, such as being bored, primarily stem from self-talk (see Module 1). The therapist demonstrates that if the client thinks more positively and realistically, he or she will feel better. Together, the client and the therapist identify the client's negative thinking

Case Example: Reframing Cognitions That Cause Dysfunctional Behaviors

A 28-year-old woman came into treatment because she wanted her husband to stop drinking so much. She indicated that 1 or 2 nights a week her husband would stop off at a bar with other construction workers. She indicated he would usually be 2 or 3 hours late for dinner and would be quite intoxicated when he arrived home. She would then chastise him for being late, for spending their scarce money on alcohol, and for ruining her evening by his "foolish talk." Her husband generally reacted with name-calling and by verbally abusing his wife in other ways. The woman added that generally there were problems in the marriage only when her husband was drinking. She also stated that her husband denies he has a drinking problem and refuses to join /her in counseling. The counselor reframed the positive intent of her behavior in the following manner:

> It appears you and your husband get along well, except when he's been drinking. When he comes home drunk,

you definitely want to make the best of the situation. Up until now your wanting to make the best of the situation has led you to respond by verbally getting on his case for drinking. At that point he probably feels a need to defend himself, and a "blow-up" occurs. Because you want to avoid the heated exchanges with him when he's drunk, I'm wondering if there aren't other actions you can take—such as taking a walk by yourself, going shopping, or going to visit someone when he is intoxicated?

The woman thought about this for a while and concluded that such suggestions might well work. In the next session a month later, she reported that the strategy of leaving the house for a couple of hours when her husband came home intoxicated was working out well. Because she realized she did not have the capacity to stop her husband from drinking, she stated that reducing the difficulties the drinking created was her next best choice.

EXERCISE M2.9   Applying Reframing

GOAL: This exercise is designed to assist you in understanding and applying reframing.

1. Specify an unwanted emotion you are currently (occasionally) experiencing, or a dysfunctional behavior you sometimes engage in.

2. Specify the cognitions that underlie your unwanted emotion or dysfunctional behavior.

3. Specify a "reframe" for each of these cognitions.

4. When you have this unwanted emotion in the future or are tempted to engage in your dysfunctional behavior, do you think it will be useful to focus your thinking on using your specified "reframes"? Explain your views.

patterns that cause him or her to believe the problem is beyond personal control. Finally, they identify new cognitions that the client can make a commitment to use to counter the cognitions that are (in actuality) causing the unwanted emotions and ineffective behaviors.

I enjoy and initiate interactions with people I like to be with." Redefining is accomplished by the therapist first demonstrating that emotions, such as being bored, primarily stem from self-talk (see Module 1). The therapist demonstrates that if the client thinks more positively and realistically, he or she will feel better. Together, the client and the therapist identify the client's negative thinking patterns that cause him or her to believe the problem is beyond personal control. Finally, they identify new cognitions that the client can make a commitment to use to counter the cognitions that are (in actuality) causing the unwanted emotions and ineffective behaviors.

Decentering is a sixth focus of reframing that is used with anxious clients who erroneously believe that they are the focus of everyone's attention.[19] Decentering occurs by having such clients observe the behaviors of others rather than focusing on their own anxiety; thereby, they come to realize they are not the center of attention. Beck and Weishaar give an example:

> One student who was reluctant to speak in class believed his classmates watched him constantly and noticed his anxiety. By observing them instead of focusing on his own discomfort, he saw some students taking notes, some looking at the professor, and some daydreaming. He concluded his classmates had other concerns.[20]

Summary

The following summarizes the module's content in terms of the learning objective presented at the beginning.

1. Comprehend three learning processes.
   Behavior therapy approaches are based on learning theories. The three major types of learning processes postulated by learning theory are operant conditioning, respondent conditioning, and modeling.

2. Understand the following behavior intervention techniques that are used by social workers in groups: assertiveness training, token economies, behavioral contracting, and cognitive-behavioral techniques.
   Behavior therapy has advanced a number of behavior therapy techniques that are commonly used by social workers. These techniques include assertiveness training, token economies, behavioral contracting, and cognitive-behavioral techniques. Cognitive-behavioral techniques include thought stopping and covert assertion, diversion techniques, and reframing.

Group Exercises

EXERCISE A: Role-Playing Assertive Behavior

GOAL: To provide practice in being assertive.

The leader asks the group if there is a situation involving assertiveness they would like to see others in the class role-play. If members suggest some situations, volunteers role-play these. If no situations are suggested, volunteers role play some of the following:

1. Someone is smoking near you, and you find the smoke very annoying. Request the smoker to put out the cigarette.
2. Ask someone to turn down a stereo that is too loud.

3. Ask for a date or refuse a request for a date.
4. Inform your parents you want to be treated as an equal, rather than as a child, continually being told what to do.
5. Refuse to lend an item that someone is trying to borrow. (Before doing this one, ask, the "refuser" to identify the possession he or she does not want to lend.)
6. You are a female, and a male is making derogatory sexist comments. Assertively request that he stop.

Another approach is for group members to write down (anonymously on note, cards) a situation they would like, others in class to role-play. The members should place their note cards in a container in such a way that anonymity is maintained.

After each situation is role-played, the class discusses the strengths of the approach and what else could have been done.

EXERCISE B: Giving and Receiving Compliments

GOAL: To learn to give and receive compliments assertively.

Step 1. The group leader begins by stating the following:

The purpose of this exercise is to learn how to give and receive compliments assertively. We all seek to receive compliments and very much appreciate it when we do receive them. Yet when we receive a compliment, we often say things that discourage the giver of the compliment from giving us additional compliments. For example, if someone compliments you by saying "That's a good-looking sweater that you're wearing," you may discourage future compliments by saying something like, "Oh really? I've had the thing for years. I don't really like it." Or future compliments may be discouraged by a comment like, "Of course it looks good on me. I look good in everything." Now, I'd like to begin the exercise by having you tell me some other negative things people have said that would discourage the giver of the compliment from giving another compliment.

These negative statements are written on the blackboard and then discussed.

Step 2. The leader states:

Although people are frequently seeking positive compliments and recognition from others, they often fail to give them. Also, compliments are sometimes offered in less than a positive fashion. For example, "Most people may not like that coat that you have, but I do." Now, as the second part of this exercise, I'd like to hear statements you've heard that were intended as compliments but that came out sounding critical.

The group leader then lists these statements on the blackboard; class discussion follows.

Step 3. The class sits with name cards visible if the members do not know each other's names. The leader states the following:

Now, let's practice giving and receiving sincere and assertive compliments. I'll start by giving a compliment to someone in the group. That person should assertively receive the compliment by saying something like "Well, thank you, I really appreciate your saying that." Each time, the receiver should vary his or her response to the compliment given. After the receiver acknowledges the compliment, the receiver gives a compliment to someone else—who acknowledges it, and then gives a compliment to someone else. We'll just keep going at this until I say "Stop."

Step 4. After Step 3, the group discusses the positive ways in which compliments were given and received.

EXERCISE C: Expressing Anger Constructively

GOAL: To learn how to express anger constructively.

Step 1. The leader states the following:

Many of us have been taught that getting angry is bad and that anger should not be expressed. It is true that violent and aggressive expressions of anger are generally dangerous and destructive. Yet, feeling angry is not evil. All of us get angry at times, and anger is a normal human emotion. We have a right to get angry, but unfortunately, some people tell us we should not. How many times have you been told not to get angry by a parent, teacher, or authority figure? Others may try to convince us that we should not be angry when we are, but even if we try to comply, the unexpressed angry feelings will still exist. When angry feelings are not expressed assertively, they tend to be expressed indirectly in destructive ways. Turning anger inward can lead to depression. Being angry, but failing to express it, can lead to anxiety. It can also lead to guilt (punishing ourselves for getting angry when we erroneously believe we should not). Some people seek to relieve their angry feelings through self-destructive excessive drinking or overeating. So, the question should not be, "Is anger acceptable?" The question should be, "How can we express anger constructively?"

Step 2. The leader explains that there are constructive ways to express anger. These ways include the following:

1. Taking responsibility for your angry feelings by admitting when you are angry. Only you can make yourself angry; do not blame getting angry on someone else. Remember, you have a right to your emotions, including anger.
2. Expressing your anger at the time you become angry so that you do not "stew" about it. If you delay expressing anger, the hostility may build up until you explode.
3. Expressing your angry feelings assertively so that no one is hurt in the process. Seek to use "I-messages" in which you nonblamingly communicate your feelings. For example, "When you make comments like that, I become angry because I feel I don't have your respect." Expressing anger in a nonblaming way does not put the other person on the defensive. Instead, it gives the other person a chance to understand why you are upset, and provides that person with an opportunity to voluntarily change those actions that he or she now realizes are upsetting you. (I-messages have been farther described in Chapter 5.)
4. Attempting to blow off steam nondestructively through such physical activity as running, hitting a punching bag or pillow, or tearing up paper, especially if your anger is intense and you feel like you are going to explode.
5. Analyzing your rational and irrational self-talk by writing out a rational self-analysis (see Module 1).

Step 3. The leader requests that each student write out answers to the following three questions on a sheet of paper:
1. Three things that make me angry are:
2. When I am angry, I usually:
3. Things I can do to express anger more constructively are:

The class has 5 or 10 minutes to complete the answers.

Step 4. The class divides into groups of three people to share what they wrote and to receive suggestions on how they could express anger more constructively. If someone does not want to share what she or he wrote, that is acceptable.

Step 5. The students share the constructive approaches to expressing anger that they came up with and discusses what they learned or discovered from this exercise.

EXERCISE D: Identifying and Accepting Rights

GOAL: To learn to identify and accept one's personal rights.

Step 1. The leader states the following:

Often, people are not assertive because they are unclear about what rights they have and what rights others have. The basic interpersonal right that individuals have is the right to express and act upon their beliefs, opinions, needs, and feelings as long as they do not violate the rights of others. For example, we have the right to express our opinions here, but we do not have the right to tell others to "shut up."

Step 2. The class lists the personal rights they can think of on a blackboard. The leader might begin by giving a few examples from the following list:

RIGHTS

to get angry	to change one's mind
to make requests	to try and to fail
to refuse requests	to pursue one's own goals
to say no	to make mistakes
to be treated with respect	to choose not to assert oneself
to disagree	to decide what happens to one's body

Step 3. Each student silently selects one of the rights he or she feels most uncomfortable accepting (or a right that he or she has experienced problems with in the past) in preparation for a visualization exercise. The leader gives the following instructions:

Close your eyes . . . take a couple deep breaths. . . . Breathe in and out slowly. . . . Get as comfortable as possible . . . there are no surprises in this exercise. . . . Now imagine that you have the right that you chose from the list. . . . What situations or circumstances in the past were troublesome for you because you did not know that you had this right? . . . Vividly imagine all the details of these situations. ... If you really believed you had this right, what would you now do or say differently? . . . If you assert yourself in having this right, how will you feel about yourself? . . . How would life change for yon if you accepted this right?

This visualization continues for about 2 minutes. The leader pauses, and then says:

Now let's do a switch. . . . Imagine that you do not have this right. . . . How would your interactions with others change if you could not express this right? . . . What would be the consequences to you if you could not express this right? . . . How would you feel about yourself? . . . How would you feel about other people? . . . OK, gradually open your eyes.

Step. 4. The leader explains that it is acceptable not to share a visualization. The class members divide into groups of three people to discuss the following questions:

1. What right did you choose?
2. What situations in the past have been troublesome for you because you were uncertain you had this, right?
3. How did you feel when you visualized yourself having this right?
4. What do you intend to say or do differently in the future because you now know you have this right?
5. How did you feel when you visualized that this right was taken away from you?

(If someone does not want to share what she or he wrote, that is acceptable.)

Step 5. The students discuss what they learned from this exercise, and the leader asks if members have questions about the personal rights listed on the blackboard. The leader asks it anyone would like to see a situation related to personal rights role-played.

EXERCISE E: Behavioral Contracting

GOAL: To demonstrate the principles of behavioral contracting by applying the principles to one's own behavior.

Step 1. Describe the goal of this exercise and explain the principles of behavioral contracting.

Step 2. Ask each student to prepare a contract about an area of behavior he or she would like to change. The behavior may involve an area such as eating less, drinking less, exercising more, ending procrastination, studying more, or increasing contact with parents and other relatives. In preparing the contact, ask the students to write on a sheet of paper answers to the following questions. (Indicate that the students will not be required to reveal what they wrote.)

1. What behavior do you want to change? (Be as specific as possible.)
2. What is your behavior goal?
3. What specifically will you do to achieve this goal?
4. What are your deadlines for doing these tasks?
5. How will you reward yourself for doing the tasks necessary to reach this goal?
6. What adverse consequences will you apply to yourself if you fail to do the tasks?

Step 3. Ask for volunteers to share what they wrote. Have the class discuss the merits and shortcomings of writing such a behavioral contract.

Step 4. As an added component of the exercise, students may discuss whether they want to attempt to fulfill the conditions they have written into then contracts. If the class decides to do this, a future date (such as 4 weeks later) may be set for the students to describe their successes and failures in fulfilling the conditions of their contracts.

EXERCISE F: Reframing

GOAL: To demonstrate how to reframe cognitions involving awfulizing

Step 1. Describe the concepts of reframing and awfulizing. To illustrate the process of awfulizing, the leader indicates a few examples in which he or she has awfulized in the past.

Step 2. Instruct each student to record his or her responses to the following, questions and instructions on a sheet of paper. Students will not be required to reveal their responses.

1. Briefly describe a distressing event that occurred in your life and that you awfulized over.
2. Specify the awfulizing cognitions that you gave yourself about this distressing event.
3. For each awfulizing cognition, specify a more positive and realistic cognition that you could give yourself about this event. (Ideally, many of these countering cognitions should also facilitate problem solving.)
4. Indicate the approximate length of time that you awfulized over this event.
5. Are you still awfulizing about this event?
6. Do you believe countering the awfulizing cognitions with more positive and realistic cognitions would have shortened the time you spent awfulizing?

Step 3. Ask for volunteers to share their responses to these questions. The exercise can be ended by asking students to indicate their thoughts on the merits and shortcomings of using reframing in therapy.

Competency Notes

EP 7a   Collect and organize data, and apply critical thinking to interpret information from clients and constituencies.

EP 7b   Apply knowledge of human behavior and the social environment, person-in-environment, and other multidisciplinary theoretical frameworks in the analysis of assessment data from clients and constituencies.

EP 7c   Develop mutually agreed-on intervention goals and objectives based on the critical assessment of strengths, needs, and challenges within clients and constituencies.

EP 8a   Critically choose and implement interventions to achieve practice goals and enhance capacities of clients and constituencies.

EP 8b   Apply knowledge of human behavior and the social environment, person-in-environment, and other multidisciplinary theoretical frameworks in interventions with clients and constituencies. (pp. 496–528)

Behavior therapy presents a number of techniques to assess and intervene with individuals, families, and groups. These techniques include assertiveness training; token economies; behavioral contracting; and the cognitive-behavioral techniques of thought stopping and covert assertion, diversion techniques, and reframing, Some exercises are presented on these techniques that allow students to use them in resolving the personal challenges they face.

3

Reality Therapy in Groups

Reality therapy is based on choice theory. The approach emphasizes the importance of relationships and asserts that there are dynamic interactions between our thoughts, emotions, actions, and physiology. This module will help prepare students to:

EP 7a
EP 7b
EP 7c
EP 8a
EP 8b

LO 1
Comprehend reality therapy.

LO 2
Use reality therapy in groups.

WILLIAM GLASSER

The founder of reality therapy is William Glasser (1925–2013). Glasser developed two variations of reality therapy. The first was developed in the 1960s and was based on identity theory.[1] The second has been developed in the past two decades and is based on choice theory.[2] This second version will be described in this module.

William Glasser is an internationally recognized psychiatrist. He graduated from Case Western Reserve Medical School in Cleveland, Ohio, in 1953. In 1956, he became a consulting psychiatrist to the Ventura School for Girls, a California state institution for the treatment of delinquent girls.

Glasser had grown skeptical of the value of orthodox psychoanalysis. At the Ventura School for Girls, he set up a new treatment program based on the principles of his *reality therapy*. The program showed promise, and participants expressed enthusiasm.

In 1966 Glasser began consulting in the California school system and applied the concepts of reality therapy to education. His emphasis on the need for schools to highlight involvement, relevance, and thinking continues to have a profound impact on the education system.

Glasser does not believe in the concept of mental illness. He has written over 20 books. In 1967, he founded the Institute for Reality Therapy, which has trained over 60,000 people worldwide in reality therapy.

In recent years, Glasser's major focus has been to teach the world his views on choice theory, a new psychology that is described in this module.

LO 1   Comprehend Reality Therapy

CHOICE THEORY

A major thrust of choice theory is that we carry around pictures in our heads, both of what reality is like and of how we would like it to be. Glasser asserts, "All our behavior is our constant attempt to reduce the difference between what we want (the pictures in our heads) and what we have (the way we see situations in the world)."[3]

Some examples will illustrate this idea. Each of us has a detailed idea of the type of person we would like to date or form a relationship with; when we find someone who closely matches these characteristics, we seek to form a relationship. Each of us carries around a picture album of our favorite foods; when we're hungry, we select an item and go about obtaining that food.

How do we develop these pictures/albums/ideas that we believe will satisfy our needs? Glasser asserts that we begin to create our albums at an early age (perhaps even before birth) and that we spend our whole lives enlarging them. Essentially, whenever what we do gets us something that satisfies a need, we store the picture of it in our personal albums.

Glasser gives the following example of this process by describing how a hungry child added chocolate chip cookies to his picture album:

> Suppose you had a grandson and your daughter left you in charge while he was taking a nap. She said she would be right back, because he would be ravenous when he awoke and she knew you had no idea what to feed an eleven-month-old child. She was right. As soon as she left, he awoke screaming his head off, obviously starved. You tried a bottle, but he rejected it—he had something more substantial in mind. But what? Being unused to a howling baby, and desperate, you tried a chocolate-chip cookie and it worked wonders. At first, he did not seem to know what it was, but he was a quick learner. He quickly polished off three cookies. She returned and almost polished you off for being so stupid as to give a baby chocolate. "Now," she said, "he will be yelling all day for those cookies." She was right. If he is like most of us, he will probably have chocolate on his mind for the rest of his life.[4]

When this child learned how satisfying chocolate chip cookies are, he placed the picture of these cookies in his personal picture album.

By the term *pictures*, Glasser means *perceptions* from our five senses of sight, hearing, touch, smell, and taste. The pictures in our albums do not have to be rational. Anorexics picture themselves as too fat and starve themselves to come closer to their irrational picture of unhealthy thinness. Rapists have pictures of satisfying their power needs, and perhaps sexual needs, through sexual assault. To change a picture, we must replace it with one that will at least reasonably satisfy the need in question. People who are unable to replace a picture may endure a lifetime of misery. Some battered women, for example, endure brutal beatings and humiliations in marriage because they cannot picture themselves as worthy of a loving relationship.

Glasser notes that whenever the picture we see and the one we want to see differ, a *signal* generated by this difference leads us to behave in a way that will obtain the picture we want. We examine our behaviors and select one or more that we believe will help us reduce this difference. These behaviors not only include straightforward problem-solving efforts but also manipulative strategies such as anger, pouting, and guilt. People who act irresponsibly or ineffectually have either failed to select responsible behaviors from their repertoires or have not yet learned responsible courses of action.

Glasser believes we are driven by five basic, innate needs. As soon as one need is satisfied, another need (or perhaps more than one acting together) pushes for satisfaction. Our first need is *survival*. This includes such vital functions as breathing; digesting food; sweating; regulating blood pressure; and meeting the demands of hunger, thirst, and sex.

Our second need is *love and belonging*. We generally meet this need through family, friends, pets, plans, and material possessions.

Our third need is *power*. Glasser says this need involves getting others to obey us and to then receive the esteem and recognition that accompanies power. Our drive for power is sometimes in conflict with our need to belong. Two people in a relationship may struggle to control it rather than create an equalitarian relationship.

Our fourth need is *freedom*. People want the freedom to choose how they live their lives, to express themselves, to read and write what they choose, to associate with whom they select, and to worship or not worship as they believe.

Our fifth need is *fun*. Glasser believes learning is often fun; this gives us a great incentive to assimilate what we require to satisfy our needs. Classes that are grim and boring are major failings of our educational system. Laughing and humor help fulfill our needs for fun. Fun is such a vital part of living that most of us have trouble conceiving of life without it.

Choice theory is an *internal control psychology;* it explains why and how we make the choices that determine the course of our lives. By internal control psychology, Glasser asserts we choose everything we do.[5]

Axioms of Choice Theory

1. The only person whose behavior we can control is our own. No one can make us do anything we do not want to do as long as we are willing to endure the consequences—punishment for not doing what others want us to do. If we choose to do what others want us to do under the threat of severe punishment, we tend to be passive-aggressive by not performing very well. When we try to force others to do what they do not want to do, they may choose not to do it—or choose to also be passive-aggressive by not performing well.

2. All we can give or get from other people is information. How we deal with that information is our, or their, choice. A teacher, for example, can assign readings to students but is not responsible if some students choose not to do the readings. The teacher, therefore, should not feel personally responsible for those students who choose not to do the readings. The teacher can choose, of course, to give consequences to those students who fail to follow the reading instructions— such as giving a lower grade to those students.

3. All we can do from birth to death, according to Glasser, is "behave." Glasser indicates that all behavior is "total behavior" and is made up of four inseparable components: acting, thinking, feeling, and physiology. Each of these components interacts and affects the three other components. (The next two axioms elaborate on this interaction.)

4. All long-lasting psychological problems are relationship problems. Relationship problems are also a partial cause of many other problems, such as fatigue, pain, weakness, and autoimmune diseases (such as fibromyalgia and rheumatoid arthritis). Glasser states:

   > Most doctors believe that adult rheumatoid arthritis is caused by the victims' immune systems attacking their own joints as if these joints were foreign bodies. Another way of putting it is that their own creative systems are trying to protect these people from a perceived harm. If we could figure out a way to stop this misguided creativity, millions of people who suffer from this disease and a host of other relentless diseases, called autoimmune diseases, could be helped.[6]

   > Our usual way of dealing with an important relationship that is not working out the way we want it to is to choose misery—emotional misery and physical misery.

5. Human brains are very creative. A woman who has frequently been sexually abused as a child may develop a dissociative identity disorder to psychologically shield herself from the emotional pain of the abuse. Glasser asserts that almost all medical problems for which physicians are unable to identify the cause are partially created by the ill person's brain to deal with unhappiness that she or he is experiencing. Unhappiness is the force that inspires the creativity inherent in the brain to be a partial cause of symptoms described in the American Psychiatric Association's *DSM-5*, aches and pains (such as migraine headaches), and physical illnesses (such as heart disease, cancer, adult asthma, and eczema).[7]

   In regard to the brain creating the symptoms in the *DSM-IV*, Glasser describes how unhappiness may lead the brain to create hallucinations:

   > Suppose, instead of your creativity presenting an idea to you as a thought, it created a voice uttering a threat or any other message directly into the auditory cortex of your brain. You would hear an actual voice or voices; it could be a stranger or you might recognize whose voice it was. It would be impossible, just by hearing it, for you to tell it from an actual voice or voices.[8]

   Because we can hear voices, our brains can create voices that we hear when no one else is around. Because we can see, the brain can create visual hallucinations. Because

EXERCISE M3.1   Seeking to Change Someone and Being Controlled by Someone

GOAL: This exercise is designed to illustrate that we are prone to attempting to change others and that others sometimes attempt to control us. The consequences of attempting to control others and of others attempting to control us are also examined.

Note: Isn't it interesting? We think we have a right to attempt to change irritating behavior of people we are dating, but we don't like to have others attempt to change us!

1. Describe a situation where you attempted to change the behavior of someone else. (It might be your attempting to change irritating actions of someone you were dating.)

2. Were you successful in changing the behavior of this person? Also, what were the emotional reactions of this person to your attempting to change him or her?

3. If the person did change the behavior that you found irritating, do you think this person changed because you forced him or her to change or because this person "chose" to change?

4. Describe a situation where someone (perhaps a parent or someone you were dating) sought change your behavior that he or she found irritating.

5. Did you change your behavior? Also, how did you feel about someone trying to change (or control) you?

6. If you did change your behavior, did you change because someone forced you to change or because you "chose" to change?

we can feel pain, it can create pain—perhaps in greater severity and duration than what we experience from an injury or illness. Because we are able to fear, it can and does create disabling phobias. See Figure M3.1.

6. Barring untreatable physical illnesses or severe poverty, unsatisfying relationships are the primary source of crimes, addictions, and emotional and behavioral disorders.

7. It is a serious mistake (and irrational) to seek to control others by nagging, preaching, punishing, or threatening to punish them. As indicated earlier, the only person we can effectively control is ourselves. To progress in improving human relationships, we

---

FIGURE M3.1   Our Thoughts Affect Our Physiological Functioning: Healing Thoughts Versus Disease-Facilitating Thoughts

Diseases and medical conditions are caused by a variety of factors: what we eat; exposure to germs, viruses, and bacteria; genetics; too much or too little sun; lack of exercise; lack of sleep; and thoughts. The following are examples of how our thoughts impact our physiological functioning:

1. Under hypnosis, "I will feel no pain" —> **painless surgery without anesthesia.**
2. Under hypnosis, "Something hot is burning my arm" —> **blister.**
3. Deep breathing relaxation, "I am relaxing" —> **painless dental drilling without anesthesia.**
4. "I no longer want to live"—> **death in a few years.**
5. "I don't want to die yet" —> **ravaged by cancer, person continues to live.**
6. When having a cold, "I must get all these things done —> **cold lingers for weeks. When having a cold, "I will take time off to rest and relax" —> cold ends after a few days.**
7. Hangover, "This pain is killing me"—> **intense pain.** Hangover, "I will relax and ignore the pain" —> **pain soon subsides (the same is true for most other headaches).**
8. "I am worried about such and such," or "I have SO much to do tomorrow" —> **inability to fall asleep.**
9. "I will have serious complications if I have this surgery" —> **greater likelihood of complications.**
10. "This plane I'm going to fly on is going to crash" —> **anxiety, panic attacks. (Panic attacks, if frequent, will lead to a variety of illnesses, including hypertension and heart problems.)**
11. A woman thinking she's pregnant, but she isn't —> **morning sickness and enlarged stomach.**
12. Thinking relaxing thoughts —> **immune system functions well, fights off illnesses, and facilitates healing.**
13. Thinking alarming thoughts (such as I miss—SO much!" —> **high stress level —> a variety of illnesses—such as heart problems, colitis, stomach problems, skin rashes, ulcers, aches and pains, headaches, cancer, colds, flus, and so forth. (Immune system is suppressed when a person is under high levels of stress.)**
14. "I will do well today in this sport, by focusing on —"—> **being good at tennis, golf, bowling, baseball, and so forth.**
15. "I am too fat; by controlling my eating, I can control part of my life" —> **anorexia and a variety of health problems.**
16. "By throwing up after eating I can maintain my weight and figure, and also enjoy the good taste of food" —> **bulimia and a variety of health problems.**
17. "I need several drinks each day to get through the day and numb my pain" —> **alcoholism.**
18. "I love food SO much, I don't care what happens to me" —> **compulsive overeating, obesity, diabetes, and a variety of other health problems.**
19. Are certain thought processes involved in autoimmune diseases, such as multiple sclerosis, rheumatoid arthritis, fibromyalgia?
20. "I need to get more work done, in a shorter time, for the next 10 years" —> **Type A personality, hypertension, heart problems, and strokes.**
21. "I will never forgive—for what she or he did," or "I'll get even with her/him if it's the last thing I do in life" —> **hostility, and heart problems and strokes.**
22. "Sex is disgusting," or "My partner stinks," or "My partner is inept at lovemaking" —> **lack of sexual, arousal, and other sexual dysfunctions.**

Note: Module 1 demonstrates that all our emotions and all our actions/behaviors are largely determined by our thoughts. This module suggests that our thoughts have a major impact on our physiological functioning. It appears that our thoughts have a major impact on our lives!

need to give up seeking to control others through nagging, preaching, putting down, or threatening punishment.

8. The unsatisfying (problematic) relationship is always a current one. We cannot live happily without at least one satisfying relationship. In a quality relationship between two people, each person seeks to meet his or her needs and wants, and those of the other person.

9. The *solving circle* is a good strategy for two people who know choice theory to use in redefining their freedom and improving their relationship. Glasser advocates its use in marital and dating relationships. Each person pictures the relationship inside a large circle, called the solving circle. An imaginary circle is drawn on the floor. Both people take a seat on a chair within the circle. The two people are told there are three entities in the solving circle: the two people and the relationship. The two people are asked to agree that maintaining the relationship takes precedence over what each person wants. In the circle, each person tells the other what he or she will agree to do to help the relationship. Within those limits, the two people must reach a compromise on their conflicts.

10. Painful events that happened in the past have a great deal to do with who we are today, but dwelling on the painful past can contribute little or nothing to what we need to do now—which is to improve an important, present relationship.

11. It is not necessary to know our past before we can deal with the present. It is good to revisit the parts of our past that were satisfying, but it is even better to leave what was unhappy alone.

12. We can satisfy our basic needs only by satisfying one or more pictures in our quality worlds. Our quality worlds consist of three kinds of need-satisfying pictures: (1) people (such as parents), (2) things (such as a car and clothes), and (3) beliefs (such as our religious and political beliefs). The most freedom we ever experience is when we are able to satisfy one or more pictures in our quality worlds. We are giving up part of our freedom when we put pictures into our quality world that we cannot satisfy.

13. When we have difficulty in getting along with other people, we usually make the mistake of choosing to employ *external control psychology* in which we attempt to coerce or control others by nagging, preaching, moralizing, criticizing, or by using put-down messages.

14. Because relationships are central to human happiness, improving our emotional and physical well-being involves exploring how we relate to others and looking for ways of improving how we relate to others (particularly those people who we feel closest to).

15. It is therapeutic to view our "total behavior" in terms of verbs. For example, it is much more accurate to say to oneself "I am choosing to depress" instead of thinking "I am suffering from depression" or "I am depressed." When we say "I am choosing to depress," we are immediately aware that we are actively choosing to depress and have the choice to do and feel something else (such as "I will go golfing and enjoy the day"). People who instead say "I am depressed" mistakenly tend to believe the depressing is beyond their control. (In addition, they are apt to mistakenly believe the depressing has been caused by what someone else has done to them.) To recognize that we have power to choose to stop depressing (or to stop angering or frustrating, etc.) is a wonderful freedom that people who adhere to the view that they are largely controlled by others will never have.

16. All total behavior (thinking, feeling, acting, and physiology) is chosen, but we have direct control over only the acting and thinking components. We do, however, control our physiology and our feelings through how we choose to act and think. It is not easy to change our actions and thoughts, but it is all we can do. When we succeed in coming up with more satisfying actions and thoughts, we gain a great deal of personal freedom.

EXERCISE M3.2 The Creativity in Our Brains

GOAL: This exercise is designed to assist you in understanding that our mental thoughts are a factor in causing our somatic problems, emotional difficulties, and behavioral dysfunctions.

1. Identify a somatic problem (such as migraine headaches) of unknown physical cause that you have or someone close to you has. Speculate on the way mental thoughts may be a factor in causing the somatic problem.

2. Identify an emotional or behavioral problem that you have or that someone close to you has. Speculate on how this person's mental thoughts contributed to this emotional or behavioral problem.

17. Whenever you feel as if you don't have the freedom you want in a relationship, it is because you, your partner, or both of you are unwilling to accept a key axiom of choice theory: *You can only control your own life.* The more both you, and your partner, learn choice theory, the better you will get along with one another. Choice theory supports the golden rule (do unto others as you would have them do unto you).

EXERCISE M3.3   The Effects of Nagging and Preaching

GOAL: This exercise is designed to increase your awareness of the effects of nagging, preaching, putting down, or threatening punishment.

1. Describe a situation where someone tried to control you by nagging, preaching, putting down, or threatening punishment.

2. How did you feel about someone else attempting to control you with these external control strategies?

3. Did you change your behavior? If you did change, was it because you were forced to change or because you "chose" to change?

4. Describe a situation where you attempted to change someone by nagging, preaching, putting down, or threatening punishment.

5. How did that person emotionally react to your external control attempts?

6. Did that person change his or her behavior? If the person did change, was it because you forced him or her to change or because he or she "chose" to change?

EXERCISE M3.4   Improving an Unhappy Relationship

GOAL: This exercise is designed to assist you in improving, through problem solving, a significant relationship in your life.

1. Identify and briefly describe a significant relationship in your life that you would like to improve.

2. Do you believe the unhappy components in this relationship may be having an adverse impact on your physical or mental well-being? Please explain. (If you cannot identify a problematic current relationship, describe a past unhappy relationship and indicate how it negatively affected your physical and mental well-being.)

3. Speculate on what you might do to improve a current problematic relationship.

EXERCISE M3.5   Letting Go to Grudges

GOAL: This exercise is designed to assist you in letting go of severe feelings of being wronged by others in the past.

1. Describe a situation in which you felt that someone severely wronged you and about which you currently still awfulize.

2. Does it do you any good to continue to awfulize about this? Research shows that hostility toward others is a major factor in heart disease and other stress-related illnesses.[9] By holding a grudge, are you not adversely affecting your physical and mental well-being? Speculate on how holding a grudge may currently be affecting you.

3. Speculate on what you can do to let go of this grudge.

EXERCISE M3.6   Expressing Our Negative Emotions in Terms of Verbs

GOAL: This exercise is designed to demonstrate that expressing our negative emotions in terms of verbs assists us in recognizing that we are choosing to feel this way and that we can choose to feel positive emotions instead.

1. List all of the negative emotions you have felt in the past week.

2. Rephrase all of these negative emotions in terms of verbs (for example, "I am depressing" instead of "depressed").

3. Does this exercise help you understand that we *choose* to feel negative emotions and that we have the choice to feel positive emotions instead? Explain your thoughts on this.

EXERCISE M3.7   Changing Our Feelings and Improving Somatic Problems

GOAL: This exercise is designed to demonstrate that our negative emotions can be changed, and some of our somatic problems can be improved, by changing our thoughts and actions.

1. Describe how you changed a negative emotion by changing your thoughts or actions.

2. Describe how you improved on a somatic problem (perhaps a headache) by changing your thoughts or actions.

18. People choose (although some are unaware of their choice) to play the mentally ill roles that are described in the *DSM-5*.[10] These people have the symptoms described in the *DSM-5*, but they are not mentally ill (if mental illness is defined as a disease of the mind). These people do not have an untreatable or incurable mental illness. The symptoms are only an indication that these people are not as healthy as they could learn to be. (See boxes "Does Mental Illness Exist?" and "Case Example: Reality Therapy.")

Does Mental Illness Exist?

Thomas Szasz, in the 1960s, was one of the first authorities to assert that mental illness is a myth—that it does not exist. Beginning with the assumption that the term *mental illness* implies a "disease in the mind," Szasz categorizes all of the so-called mental illnesses into three types of emotional disorders and discusses the inappropriateness of calling such human difficulties "mental illnesses":

1. *Personal disabilities*, such as excessive anxiety, depression, fears, and feelings of inadequacy. (Another term for personal disabilities is "unwanted emotions.") Szasz says such so-called mental illnesses may appropriately be considered "mental" (in the sense that thinking and feeling are considered "mental" activities), but he asserts they are not diseases.

2. *Antisocial acts*, such as bizarre homicides and other social deviations. Homosexuality used to be in this category but was removed from the American Psychiatric Association's list of mental illnesses in 1974. Szasz says such antisocial acts are only social deviations, and he asserts they are neither "mental" nor "diseases."

3. *Deterioration of the brain with associated personality changes*. This category includes the "mental illnesses" in which personality changes result following brain deterioration from such causes as arteriosclerosis, chronic alcoholism, Alzheimer's disease, general paresis, or serious brain damage due to an accident. Common symptoms are loss of memory, listlessness, apathy,

and deterioration of personal grooming habits. Szasz says these disorders can appropriately be considered "diseases" but are diseases of the *brain* (that is, brain deterioration specifies, the nature of the problem) rather than being diseases of the *mind*.

Szasz, in "The Myth of Mental Illness," asserts that the notion that people with emotional problems are mentally ill is as absurd as the belief that the emotionally disturbed are possessed by demons:

> The belief in mental illness as something other than man's trouble in getting along with his fellow man, is the proper heir to the belief in demonology and witchcraft. Mental illness exists or is real in exactly the same sense in which witches existed or were real. (p. 67)

The point that Szasz and many other writers are striving to make is that people do have emotional and behavioral problems, but they do not have a mystical mental illness. These writers believe that terms that describe unwanted emotions and dysfunctional behaviors are very useful: for example, *depression, anxiety, obsession, compulsion, excessive fear, hallucinations*, and feelings *of being a failure*. Such terms describe personal problems that people have. But mental illness terms (such as schizophrenia and psychosis), they assert, are not useful because there is no distinguishing symptom that would indicate whether a person has, or does not have, the "illness."

---

19. A mentally healthy person enjoys being with most of the people he or she knows— especially the important people such as family and friends. A mentally healthy person likes people and is more than willing to help an unhappy friend, colleague, or family member to feel better. A mentally healthy person laughs a lot and leads a mostly tension-free life. He or she enjoys life and has no trouble accepting others who are different. He or she does not focus on criticizing others or try to change others. He or she is creative. A mentally healthy person, when unhappy (no one can be happy all the time), knows why she or he is unhappy and will attempt to do something about it.

PRINCIPLES OF REALITY THERAPY

1. It is what you choose to do in a relationship, not what others choose to do, that is the focus of reality therapy.
2. People choose the behaviors that have led them into therapy because these behaviors are always perceived by them as being their best effort to deal with either an unsatisfying relationship or with no relationship at all.
3. The task of the counselor is to help unhappy clients choose new relationship-improving behaviors. These new behaviors will also help clients satisfy one or more of their five basic needs: love and belonging, power, freedom, fun, and survival.

Case Example: Reality Therapy

A number of years ago when I [the author] was employed as a social worker at a maximum-security hospital for the criminally insane, my supervisor asked me to develop and lead a therapy group. When I wondered aloud who should be in the group and what its objectives should be, my supervisor indicated those decisions would be mine. He added that no one else was doing group therapy at the hospital and that the hospital administration thought it would be desirable to develop such a program.

Being newly employed at the hospital and wary because I had never been a group leader before, I asked myself, "Who is in the greatest need of group therapy?" and "If the group members do not improve, or even deteriorate, how will I be able to explain this—that is, cover my tracks?" I concluded that I should select those identified as being most ill (those labeled as chronic schizophrenics). Because such patients are generally expected to show little improvement, I felt I would not be blamed if group members did not improve. However, if they did improve, I thought it would be viewed as a substantial accomplishment.

First I read the case records of all the residents (11) who were diagnosed as chronic schizophrenics. I then met individually with each of these residents to invite them to join the group. (To my surprise, each of the residents appeared to be very different from the impressions I received from reading the case records.) I explained the purpose of the group and the probable topics to be covered. Eight of the 11 who were contacted decided to join; some frankly stated they would join primarily because it would look good on their records and increase their chances for an early release.

In counseling these group members, the approach I used was based on reality therapy. I began the first group meeting by stating I knew what the "key" was to their being discharged from the hospital and asked if *they* knew what that might be. This statement got their attention. I indicated that the key was very simple—they had to learn to "act sane" so that the medical staff would think they had recovered. At the first meeting the purpose and the focus of the group was presented and described. Our purpose was not to review the past but to make life in the present more enjoyable and meaningful and to plan for the future. Various topics would be covered: how group members could convince the hospital staff they no longer needed hospitalization, how they could prepare for returning to their home communities (for example, learning an employable skill while at the institution), and what to do when they felt depressed or some other unwanted emotion or had an urge to do something that would get them into trouble again after their release. Also to be covered were discussions on how to improve relationships with people who were important to them. Occasionally films covering some of these topics would be shown and discussed. The group would meet for about 1 hour each week for 12 weeks.

This focus on improving the current circumstances of the group members stimulated their interest, but soon they found it uncomfortable and anxiety producing to examine what the future might hold for them. They also became uncomfortable after being told they had considerable control over their future. They reacted to this discomfort by stating that they were "mentally ill" and therefore had some internal condition that was causing their strange behavior. Further, because no cure for their schizophrenia had yet been found, they believed they could do little to improve.

I told them that their excuses were "garbage" (stronger terms were used) and spent a few sessions convincing them that the term "chronic schizophrenic" was a meaningless label. I spent considerable time in explaining the myth of mental illness: that people do not have a "disease of the mind," although they may have emotional problems. I went on to explain that what had gotten them locked up was their deviant behavior. The only way for them to get out was to stop such behavior and convince the staff that they would not exhibit it if released.

The next excuse they tried was that the broken homes or inferior schools or broken romances or other misfortunes had "messed up" their lives for good, and they could do little about their situation. "Garbage," I told them. True, their past experiences were important. But, I emphasized, what they *wanted* out of their future and the motivation they had to achieve then goals, were more important in determining the future.

Finally, after working through a number of excuses, we focused on how they could better handle specific problems: how to handle being depressed, how to stop exhibiting behavior considered "strange," how to present themselves as being "sane" in order to increase their chances of an early release, and how to adjust to returning to their home communities. We also focused on what kind of work or career they desired upon their release and how they could prepare themselves for their selected careers by learning a skill or trade while at the institution. Another focus was to help them examine what they wanted out of the future and the specific steps they would have to lake to achieve their goals. Also discussed was how they could improve relationships important to them.

The results of this approach were encouraging. Instead of idly spending much of the time brooding about their situations, group members became motivated to take action. At the end of the 12 weeks, the eight members spontaneously stated that the meetings were making a positive change in their lives and requested that another social worker from the hospital be assigned to continue the group after I left to return to school. This was arranged. Three years later on a return visit to the hospital, I was informed that five of the eight group members had been released to their home communities and two of the others had shown improvement. One group member's condition was described as "unchanged."

SOURCE: Szasz, T. (1961). The myth of mental illness. In J. R. Braun (Ed.), *Clinical psychology in transition* (p. 27). Cleveland, OH: Howard Allen.

EXERCISE M3.8 A Mentally Healthy Person

GOAL: This exercise is designed to help you identify what you need to work on to improve your mental well-being.

1. Review Glasser's definition of a mentally healthy person. Describe components of your current life that are consistent with mental well-being.

2. Identify components in your life that you need to work on in order to improve your mental well-being.

3. For the components that you need to work on, speculate about courses of action that you should take in order to improve your mental well-being.

EXERCISE M3.9   The Solving Circle

GOAL: This exercise is designed to have you speculate about the merits and shortcomings of the solving circle.

1. Specify difficulties you are currently having in a relationship that is significant to you.

2. Review the material on a solving circle. Do you believe that using a solving circle with the person you are currently having difficulties with would be useful? (If possible, try to become involved in an actual solving circle with this person.) Speculate about the merits and shortcomings of the solving circle.

4. Satisfying the need for love and belonging is the key to satisfying the other four needs, as the five basic needs can only be satisfied when we have good relationships with other people.

5. Because love and belonging (like all of the basic five needs) can be satisfied only in the present, reality therapy focuses almost entirely on the here and now.

6. Although most of us have been traumatized in the past, we are only victims of our past if we currently choose to be. The solution to our problems is rarely found in explorations of the past; one exception may be a focus on past successes.

7. The symptoms or the pain that clients choose (because of their unhappiness) is not important to the counseling process. The focus in counseling needs to be on improving present relationships. (It is usually a fruitless endeavor to seek to determine why one discontented person may choose to depress, another to drink, a third to obsess, and a fourth to go crazy.)

8. A continuing goal of reality therapy is to create a choice theory relationship between the counselor and the client. By experiencing a satisfying relationship, the client can learn a lot about a model relationship and how to improve the troubled relationship that brought him or her into counseling.

9. As long as clients continue to use the choice theory concepts they've learned in counseling, the therapy never ends.

10. With marriage or couple counseling, Glasser urges that *structured reality therapy* be used.[11] This approach emphasizes that marriage is a partnership and the only way to help a troubled couple is to focus on what's best for their marriage, not on what may be best for one or the other. Any marital counseling that allows one partner to blame the other will only harm the marriage. Couples are urged to never say or do anything in a relationship that experience indicates will drive the two further apart. They are urged to only say and do what will bring them closer or keep them close. Couples are also instructed to extensively use the solving circle (which was described earlier).

11. Reality therapy is a "doing" approach. Clients are guided in the direction of actually doing something about their problems.

12. In this newer approach to reality therapy, the original term "responsibility" (in the first version of reality therapy) is now replaced with the more explicit idea that we choose all our behaviors because we can't be anything but responsible for all we choose to do. In this way, the possible argument over what is responsible, and what is not, is avoided.

13. The therapist looks for every opportunity to teach choice therapy to clients and their families so that everyone involved can begin the process of replacing external control psychology with choice theory.

EXERCISE M3.10   Symptoms as a Cry for Help

GOAL: This exercise is designed to assist you in recognizing that emotional difficulties, dysfunctional behaviors, somatic problems, and relationship problems are cries for help.

1. Describe how someone you know is demonstrating that his or her emotional difficulties, relationship problems, dysfunctional behaviors, or somatic problems are cries for help.

14. A symptom is a cry for help. People use symptoms to avoid situations that they fear will increase their frustration.

15. Good or bad, happy or sad, people choose everything they do all day long.

CAN OUR THOUGHTS ALTER OUR GENETIC CODE?

Dr. Bruce Lipton is a former medical school professor (University of Wisconsin) and research scientist (Stanford University School of Medicine). He has conducted a number of experiments on the molecular mechanisms by which cells process information. He has found genes do not, in fact, control our behavior; instead, genes are turned on and off by influences outside the cell. These influences include our thoughts, perceptions, and beliefs. Dr. Lipton asserts that our thoughts and beliefs, true or false, positive or negative, affect genetic activity and actually alter our genetic code. He further asserts that we can retrain our consciousness to create healthy thoughts and beliefs and that doing so will result in a profoundly positive impact on our bodies and on our lives.[12]

LO 2   Use Reality Therapy in Groups

USING REALITY THERAPY IN GROUPS

Reality therapy has been found to be effective with clients in one-to-one situations and in groups. Reality therapy focuses on the importance of improving relationships with people who are significant to us. The approach emphasizes the importance of the interactions between our thoughts, actions, emotions, and physiology. By changing our negative thoughts and dysfunctional behaviors, we can improve our emotions and alleviate some somatic problems.

Various approaches can be used to apply reality therapy to groups. Members can read about the concepts of the approach prior to group meetings and then discuss the concepts in groups. Members can do the exercises in this module (either prior to group meetings or during group meetings) and then share and discuss what they wrote. The leader can assist members in treatment sessions by first having members specify the emotional, behavior, relationship, or somatic problems they are facing and then assisting them in identifying specific courses of action they can take to attempt to alleviate these difficulties.

An example of the use of reality therapy is presented in the box "Case Example: Reality Therapy" found earlier in this module. Reality therapy is an approach that is rich in psychodynamic concepts. It has the potential to assist people in improving their physical and emotional well-being, and in helping people to eliminate their ineffective and dysfunctional behaviors.

Summary

The following summarizes the module's content in terms of the learning objectives presented at the beginning.

1. Comprehend reality therapy.

   The founder of reality therapy is William Glasser. Glasser also developed choice theory. A major thrust of choice theory is that we carry around pictures in our heads, both of what reality is like and of how we would like it to be. We are: constantly involved in attempting to reduce the differences between what we want (the pictures in our heads) and what we have (the way we see situations in the world).

   Assertions/principles of reality theory and control theory are the following.

   • Our lives are largely determined by the choices we make.
   • We have five basic, innate needs: survival, love and belonging, power, freedom, and fun.

- The only person whose behavior we can control is our own.
- Our cognitions primarily determine our feelings, behaviors, and physiological functioning.
- All long-lasting psychological problems are relationship problems. Unsatisfying relationships are the primary sources of crimes, addictions, and behavioral disorders.
- It is a serious mistake to seek to control others by nagging, preaching, punishing, or threatening to punish them.
- The solving circle is a good strategy for two people to use to improve their relationship.
- Dwelling on a painful past will contribute little or nothing to what we need to do now to improve our lives. We need to let go of grudges.
- It is therapeutic to view our total behavior in terms of verbs.
- Mental illness is a myth. People choose to play a mentally ill role.

Reality therapy is a cognitive-behavioral approach to therapy.

2. Use reality therapy in groups.

Various approaches can be used to apply reality therapy to groups. Members can read about the concepts of the approach prior to group meetings and then discuss the concepts in groups. Members can do the exercises in this module (either prior to group meetings or during group meetings) and then share and discuss what they wrote.

The leader can assist members in treatment sessions by first having members specify the emotional, behavior, relationship, or somatic problems they are facing, and then assisting them in identifying specific courses of action they can take to attempt to alleviate these difficulties.

Group Exercise

EXERCISE A: Mental Illness Debate

GOAL: To identify the arguments as to whether mental Illness exists.

Step 1. At a class session, certain (not all) students in the class form two panels—one that will argue that mental illness exists, and the other that will argue that mental illness is a myth. Panel members are given a few days to gather information and prepare their arguments. Panel members may interview counselors and therapists in the community and read reference materials.

Step 2. At the selected class date, a debate is held. At the end of the debate, the students uninvolved in the debate summarize the strong points made by the debaters.

Competency Notes

EP 7a   Collect and organize data, and apply critical thinking to interpret information from clients and constituencies;

EP 7b   Apply knowledge of human behavior and the social environment, person-in-environment, and other multidisciplinary theoretical frameworks in the analysis of assessment data from clients and constituencies;

EP 7c   Develop mutually agreed-on intervention goals and objectives based on the critical assessment of strengths, needs, and challenges within clients and constituencies;

EP 8a   Critically choose and implement interventions to achieve practice goals and enhance capacities of clients and constituencies;

EP 8b   Apply knowledge of human behavior and the social environment, person-in-environment, and other multidisciplinary theoretical frameworks in interventions with clients and constituencies. (pp. 529–550)

Reality therapy is based on choice theory. Choice theory asserts there are dynamic interactions between our thoughts, emotions, actions and physiology. Choice theory and reality therapy present a number of axioms for assessing and intervening with individuals, groups, and families. Examples of these axioms are: The only person whose behavior we can control is our own; it is a serious mistake to seek to control others by nagging or preaching; and it is beneficial to our physiological health to let go of grudges. Choice theory also asserts that people choose (although some are unaware of their choice) to play mentally ill roles. Choice theory facilitates viewing reality from divergent perspectives. Numerous exercises are presented in the chapter that facilitate students applying reality therapy and choice theory to their personal lives.

Dialectical Behavior Therapy in Groups*

LEARNING OBJECTIVES

EP 7a
EP 7b
EP 7c
EP 8a
EP 8b

Dialectical behavior therapy is a newer form of therapy. This module will prepare students to:

LO 1
Comprehend dialectical behavior therapy (DBT).

LO 2
Understand how to use DBT in groups.

LO 1   Comprehend Dialectical Behavior Therapy (DBT)

INTRODUCTION AND HISTORY

Dialectical behavior therapy, or DBT, is a contemporary evidenced-based treatment approach that has become increasingly popular in the last 20 years. DBT is part of the newest evolution, or third generation, of cognitive-behavioral therapy (CBT) that has generated considerable enthusiasm among researchers, psychologists, and social workers. Third-generation CBT therapies theorize a benefit from a decreased emphasis on controlling or changing thoughts and emotions. Instead, they are more focused on changing the ways we think about and deal with emotions rather than changing our thought content. Unwanted thoughts and emotions can be placed in a different context and managed without necessarily changing them. DBT is one of the first successful treatment interventions developed for borderline personality disorder (BPD) and offers a novel therapeutic style that presents a different way for clinicians to relate to clients. Included is a unique set of psychosocial skills with wide-ranging applicability. Several research studies to date have shown statistically significant improvements in clients treated by DBT,[1] although some researchers caution that we do not yet have sufficient data to prove its effectiveness or validate the underlying theory.[2] Others have questioned whether Eastern mindfulness practices can be blended with traditional CBT without destroying the integrity of CBT as a theory.[3] Despite these misgivings, many researchers feel we have only begun to explore the potential usefulness of this type of treatment approach. Empirical evidence continues to be gathered supporting its use, which is now recommended by the American Psychological Association (APA). Researchers and clinicians are currently testing DBT with an expanded range of populations with similar characteristics and treatment challenges as those with BPD. Because DBT represents a rather significant shift in traditional CBT, we will need to spend some time understanding its theoretical underpinnings. Later we will look at how DBT is used in a group context. First we need to learn exactly what DBT is and where it came from.

DBT was pioneered by psychologist Dr. Marsha Lineham of the University of Washington to treat her BPD patients. This population had proven to be very resistant to treatment with standard therapeutic approaches. Clients with BPD have sometimes been referred to as "emotional third-degree-burn patients"[4] and can cause frequent burnout of clinicians due to their resistance to standard therapies, high level of need, and frequent crises. Many frequently attempt suicide, make suicidal gestures, or self-injure, resulting in a constant state of crisis that must be managed by clinicians as a matter of priority. Dr. Linehan used her own personal struggle and experience with BPD to develop a unique therapeutic method of encouraging positive change within individuals in this population.[5] She continues to research DBT's effectiveness with comorbid disorders within BPD clients, which has subsequently opened the door for experimentation with similar populations. DBT is now being explored with non-BPD clients with significant suicidality, mood and bipolar disorders, complex traumas, post-traumatic stress disorder (PTSD), alcohol and substance

---

* This module was written by Craig Mead. MSW, LSW, licensed social worker at Presence St. Mary and Elizabeth Medical Center, Chicago, IL.

dependence, eating disorders, and attention-deficit/hyperactivity disorder (ADHD). Other groups, such as domestic violence victims and perpetrators, adolescent self-injurers (cutters), persons with a developmental disability, and various adult and adolescent forensic and institutional populations.[6] It has also been used for family psycho-education to reduce caregiver stress and enhance client skill transference. DBT adaptations have been showing up in a variety of settings that a social worker may encounter, such as community-based outpatient clinics, inpatient psychiatric units, partial inpatient and intensive outpatient programs, eating disorder programs and clinics, domestic violence programs, substance abuse centers and 12-step programs, adolescent and adult residential centers, halfway houses, prisons, and juvenile detention centers. Many clinicians and researchers are hopeful that these expanded efforts will demonstrate expanded positive results.

DBT is a somewhat abstract and complex therapeutic strategy that requires clinicians be fully trained in its structure, philosophies, and concepts. This module is not designed to be sufficient training for you to implement a DBT program in your practice. It is designed for you to gain a fundamental understanding of its basic philosophy, structure, concepts, and skill sets. Some research has demonstrated that advanced clinical training is needed in order for DBT to be effectively implemented with positive outcomes.[7] A DBT individual therapy component should not be attempted without sufficient training. Social workers

Case Example

A major child and adolescent behavioral health provider in northern Illinois provides a high-end (most restrictive) 18- to 24-month community-based residential treatment program for male juvenile sex offenders age 13 to 19. Admission to the program requires that youth be accused of sexual aggression or have engaged in sexually problematic behavior, often directed at other children or minors. Youth are also required to have a history of problems with anger/aggression and have failed to improve in other treatment settings. This is a long-standing program that previously used a fairly standard cognitive-behavioral therapy program for adolescents considered to be the "worst of the worst." The social worker and staff at this program began to notice a pattern of new admissions with substantially greater histories of complex trauma, PTSD, emotional dysregulation, suicidality, self-injury (cutting), and parasuicidal gestures. It should be noted that juvenile sex offenders are often sexual abuse victims first and then repeat the behavior toward siblings, relatives, or other minors. Most have long histories of abuse, neglect, foster placements, and mental health treatment.

The program milieu began to experience a significant increase in interpersonal conflicts, peer-on-peer aggression, suicide attempts, self-injury, parasuicidal gestures, physical restraints, borderline tendency behavior, and subsequent psychiatric hospitalizations. The unit social worker and therapist decided to implement a DBT program to improve the residents' abilities to manage their feelings, to reduce suicidal gestures and self-injury, and to improve their abilities to resolve interpersonal conflicts. There had been some empirical

evidence of DBT success with this population. The milieu staff was instructed on the basic theories of DBT and 12 selected skills. They were encouraged to begin to use the theories and skill sets with themselves and in their daily interactions with residents. The mindfulness and DBT skills also had the added benefit of reducing burnout among the staff. The unit therapist (who was fully trained in DBT) began using DBT in individual therapy sessions and conducted a DBT skills group twice weekly. One skill was introduced during each group session and residents were required to complete diary cards as homework that logged their use of skills as they learned them. Residents were not allowed to attend group meetings without their diary cards. There was a strong incentive to complete homework, as milieu, and recreational privileges were dependent on group participation. The milieu staff co-facilitated and participated in these groups, learning alongside with, the residents. They were also able to incorporate DBT skills into their other therapeutic groups and crisis interventions. Everyone participated in learning the skill sets and provided feedback and encouragement to enhance skill acquisition.

This group of residents was able to achieve a moderate reduction in problematic behavior, aggression, conflicts, and suicidality that required hospitalization. The staff was also able to achieve a much-needed reduction in daily stress, compassion fatigue, and burnout. Although DBT did not prove to be a magic cure, significant improvement was attained. The DBT skills proved to be a needed addition and worthwhile, adaptation to the changing needs of this particular population of residents.

should be mindful of the ethical contraindication of operating beyond the scope of their training. Well-meaning but uninformed clinicians can do more harm than good and hinder a client's progress. However, social workers may be called upon to assist with implementation of a DBT program with somewhat minimal instruction. A DBT psychosocial skills training group is a significant component of this strategy and well within the skill level of even an entry-level social worker. These groups are primarily educational in nature and emphasize skill acquisition. Later in the module, we'll specifically discuss DBT groups.

These concepts may also be highly useful in other areas of individual and group practice. The core components and individual skill sets are a great set of tools that you might adapt for use in a variety of group settings with many different populations. Social workers and clinicians often work with significantly challenging populations. You may also find DBT an important self-care tool to help prevent the burnout and compassion fatigue especially common among less experienced clinicians. Using DBT skills in your practice and personal life is a great way to help manage your stress and give you the ability to teach from genuine personal experience.

WHAT IS DIALECTICAL BEHAVIOR THERAPY?

Describing dialectical behavior therapy poses several challenges due to its complexity. Its abstract nature and joining of disparate ideas make it difficult to synthesize a comprehensive explanation. There are many nuances that often require frequent review to gain a comprehensive understanding. You are encouraged to continue to study this theory in order to fully grasp its theory beyond the foundation this text presents. DBT is an evolution and adaptation of cognitive-behavioral therapy that blends several other ideas, such as despiritualized, Eastern mindfulness (Zen Buddhist) concepts, Hegelian dialectic philosophy, and motivational enhancement approaches. It emphasizes empowering clients to have the lives that they want to live and offers concrete skills to achieve greater happiness, peace, and stability.[8] These concepts are also applied equally to the therapist and the therapeutic relationship. DBT clinicians don't merely teach DBT skill sets, but also structure their therapeutic relationship and interventions using its philosophies. Effective DBT requires that you fundamentally believe in the concepts and use them daily. You probably will recognize many of these ideas in things you already do or know. It's highly likely you are already using DBT in your life but just haven't recognized it. Let's now look at how Dr. Linehan has blended dialectics and Zen philosophy into CBT to create this new approach.

Dialectics form the foundation of DBT therapy. Linehan[9] describes dialectics as applicable in two ways: as "the fundamental nature of reality" and a "treatment approach or strategy used by the therapist to effect change." It is adapted from ancient Western philosophy where opposing arguments (thesis and antithesis) were synthesized into one incorporated truth that maintains the values of both without contradiction. Two dichotomous forces are simultaneously balanced and combined to create a new whole based on a compromised middle path. Another way to think of it is as two opposites that are integrated into something new that incorporates both disparate parts. DBT itself is a therapeutic approach based upon seemingly opposing forces. DBT is a balance of two dichotomous philosophies: (a) modern Western psychology with its emphasis on thinking and analytic logic and (b) ancient Eastern religion that emphasizes balance and harmony through an absence of analysis, judgment, and logic. DBT creates a synthesis of opposites to create a new balanced philosophy toward life. Life is full of oppositions that need to be navigated in order to achieve a healthy balance and homeostatic state of equilibrium. Living in any extreme polarity can create emotional distress and dysfunction. DBT proposes that we move toward a middle state of existence to lessen the extremes of life's challenges. Following are some of life's dialectical challenges. Each dialectic challenge contains within itself its own opposition. Take a moment to think about how you balance these challenges. See if you can think of your own examples.

Allowing your children to be independent while protecting them from harm.
Liking yourself as you are but wanting to make changes and improvements.
Wanting something but avoiding the work necessary to achieve it.

Meeting work expectations while taking care of family needs.
Reacting based on emotion but thinking before acting.
Hoping for the best but planning for the worst.
Wanting intimacy but fearing rejection.
Having strong values but tolerating differences.
Having a problem but struggling to find a solution.
Wanting to solve your own problems but needing help.
Wanting to prove a point but wanting to avoid conflict.
Wanting something for ourselves but needing to sacrifice for others.
Having unconditional positive regard for clients but pushing them to change themselves.

Synthesizing a balance between opposing forces can be challenging, and emotional reactions often occur when one force is dominant. For example, relationship conflicts often result if we rigidly focus on our own needs and fail to balance those with the needs of our significant other. Harmony is not achieved unless there is a balanced synthesis between both people's needs. Likewise, learning to balance thoughts and emotions is skill that many struggle to achieve. You can probably think of someone you know who is overly analytical and somewhat emotionless. Or perhaps you know someone who is very emotionally reactive and acts impulsively on emotions without giving thought to the consequences of his or her actions. DBT encourages clients to balance their emotions and thinking. The force of negative emotion can often be diminished by positive and rational thinking. Negative thoughts can be balanced by positive ones or by achieving a positive emotional state. Significant stress reduction can be achieved by increasing a sense of control over oneself through synthesizing dialectic balance. However, permeating this strategy is a dialectic of wanting change but fearing it at the same time. Change itself creates a new set of challenges as a result of that change. Becoming adaptable to change is a fundamental goal of DBT. To help clients, DBT clinicians must navigate several fundamental therapeutic dialectics. We must completely accept clients as they are while simultaneously motivating and nurturing change. Additionally, clinicians must balance validating clients' emotional responses and unhealthy behavior choices as adaptive while focusing on problem solving new healthier ways to adapt.[10] These strategies must be effectively balanced to achieve successful intervention. If the balance is tipped too far in either direction, our efforts may become counterproductive, as some clients may become defensive or, alternatively, complacent.

Pseudo-Zen-Buddhist concepts such as mindfulness, acceptance, tolerance, willingness, and nonjudgment are adjunctive to dialectics and encourage creating these types of balances. Kabat-Zinn[11] conceptualizes mindfulness as "paying attention on purpose, in the present moment, and nonjudgmentally to the unfolding of experience moment by moment." According to Linehan,[12] increasing mindfulness of current emotional experience functions as an informal exposure to negative emotions, which over time helps extinguish maladaptive avoidance responses. This also improves clients' ability to improve their sense of self through observation. Part of mindfulness is learning to be focused on the here and now and staying present in the moment. Distress is often created by ruminating or worrying about the past or future and subsequent internal judgments. Being present in the moment prevents this type of rumination, as we merely move from moment to moment in an endless string of "nows." The past is unalterable and the future unwritten. Past events must be accepted as they are and must not prevent us from creating the now that we want. DBT psychosocial skill education does not include rummaging through a client's past to assist a client in gaming insight. Clients may have had very bad luck in the past, but must now work on creating a present and future they want. If the future is perceived as uncertain or scary, then the best we can do is take things one moment or day at a time. Focusing on problem solving in the moment will prevent you from worrying about future events. Distressing events and feelings that are happening in the moment can be merely acknowledged and ultimately tolerated while we seek out solutions. Often one must only wait and the moment will pass. You might imagine your grandmother saying "this too shall pass." It's important to remember that distressing emotions have come and gone many times without disaster or annihilation.

Clients can learn to wait for the emotion to pass and ride out their distress. We don't have to like certain feelings but can learn to tolerate them nonetheless and keep them in the proper context. Having a feeling doesn't mean we need to act upon it. If clients are unhappy with their current circumstances, they may need to tolerate things while working on finding solutions. Giving up is not a solution but working harder is. Many things are beyond our control. We need to accept and tolerate other people, as we can only control ourselves. Giving up on efforts to control things beyond us must be done in a radical way. We also need to surrender willful attempts to change others and events beyond our control and be willing to take another approach. Many of these concepts are very similar to 12-step programs or the serenity prayer but have been de-spiritualized for more of a universal application.

The concept of willingness is threaded throughout these philosophies. Clients must move in the direction of being willing to change perspectives and try new ways of adapting. Being willful, on the other hand, is repeatedly engaging in ineffective responses, yet hoping for a different result. Interpersonal conflicts are often perceived in black-and-white terms. Clients are taught to be willing to compromise and find common ground. Problems are born out of a win-lose mentality. Solutions can be found through compromise and finding a middle path. Nonjudgment is another key. Positive and negative judgments that we assign to people, events, and emotions contribute to our feelings. These things are neither fundamentally good nor bad; they just are. Emotions are often the direct result of these judgments. The experience of the observer is dependent upon whether the judgment is positive or negative. You've probably noticed how two people can have completely different emotional reactions to a single event. One person may have a very negative feeling and the other is quite neutral or positive. The negative person may then eliminate the negative feeling by merely talking to the positive person and seeing a different perspective. Much distress also comes from a perception or judgment that people, situations, and feelings are intolerable and unbearable. Telling ourselves we can't stand something often makes us overly focused on the emotion. This can create the perception that the feeling is more intense or worse than it is. It is possible to be overly mindful and focused on a feeling. Making negative judgments about ourselves is another significant source of distress. How we feel about ourselves has a profound influence on how we feel overall. Learning to accept ourselves (warts and all) is a universal human lesson that many of us struggle with. However, learning to have a nonjudgmental healthy perception of ourselves can alleviate substantial negative emotions. Stress can occur because we have negative feelings about the fact that we have negative feelings. Emotions are part of the human experience. We run into trouble when we place a judgment upon those feelings and what it says about us as people. There are no bad or wrong feelings. It's important to self-validate our feelings and our right to have them. We must accept that having feelings is part of who we are as humans. Feelings can be merely noticed and appreciated for what they are. Unhealthy attempts to avoid feelings usually reinforce them and force that energy to come out in other ways. Unhealthy behavior choices as a result of our feelings should be a greater focus of intervention. However, let's throw in some dialectics and remember that it's OK to not like certain feelings and put some effort into changing those feelings. It's understandable why we feel the way we do based upon given circumstances, but we can change the way our thoughts drive our emotions.

It's important to remember that DBT is merely another form of CBT. It might be easier to think of it as basically CBT with dialectics and mindfulness philosophies strapped on. Fundamentally, it is CBT and has a primary emphasis on the client's current thoughts and behavior choices. Clients are encouraged to recognize how their thoughts, behavior patterns, and choices can be unhealthy and counterproductive, or cause unwanted emotions. Notice we are going to avoid the word *maladaptive* because in DBT all behavior is considered an attempt to adapt, regardless of its success or dysfunctional nature. All of the traditional CBT strategies discussed in other chapters and texts are applied. These strategies will include cognitive restructuring, reframing, reinforcement, modeling, shaping, practice, repetition, and education. However, here we are going to throw in yet another dialectic. We are going to balance changing and reframing unwanted thoughts and feelings with tolerating them when needed. Clients are assumed to want change and desire the ability to avoid emotional pain but are merely unable to muster the resources or skills to affect that change themselves. Behavior chain analysis is used to analyze exact sequences of triggers, thoughts, feelings, and behaviors. These thoughts, feelings, and behaviors are validated as reasonable given the client's unique biology, experience, and situation but are recognized as ineffective nonetheless. No judgment is placed on their responses other than recognizing what does or does not work. Clients are encouraged to change from ineffective to effective responses to those thoughts, feelings, situations, and challenges. However, this push for change is tempered with an ongoing opposing validation of client's feelings as an understandable but ineffective effort to cope. This is an important distinction between traditional CBT and DBT. Remember that DBT was designed for a much more emotionally vulnerable population that might view a clinician's push for change as invalidation. Clients are viewed as doing the best that they can at any given moment even when engaging in destructive and unhealthy coping mechanisms. Clients are accepted as they are while being encouraged to change. This type of clinical philosophy can reduce defensiveness in clients and frustration in clinicians. Later in this module we'll learn more about conducting a behavior chain analysis.

Motivation enhancement is utilized throughout to assist clients to recognize that they have the power to choose how they respond to life's challenges. Pros and cons of using new DBT skills versus prior ineffective methods of coping are repetitiously evaluated. How we think, feel, and act are choices. We can choose to use old ineffective coping mechanisms or we can try our new DBT skills. Clients must be met where they are at in their stage of change. For example, those in the pre-contemplative stage (see motivational interviewing in Chapter 12) should be first assisted with recognizing how their ineffective coping skills are problematic and don't achieve a desired outcome. Reducing ambivalence to change is a primary goal. The client's stage of motivation to change will be continuously assessed and addressed individually and in group settings.

Traditional DBT has four core parts: individual therapy, group therapy, phone support, and clinical supervision. Individual and group sessions are utilized for motivation, skills training, and learning healthier behaviors and responses. For some clients, individual sessions may also be used to process and integrate past trauma, gain insight, and address personality and psychiatric issues. Group therapy is primarily educational but also addresses motivation to use new skills. Clients also have an opportunity to practice their new skills during the group process. Phone support assists clients with skill transference: to natural environments, motivation, and generalizing skill use. Clinical supervision assists the therapist with maintaining boundaries, avoiding burnout, and recognizing therapy-interfering behaviors. Individually and in groups, clients learn new skills for managing stress, regulating emotions, problem solving, and improving interpersonal relationships. Skills are taught to replace unhealthy and destructive coping strategies. Skills are repetitiously practiced in sessions and groups. Homework is utilized for clients to track their use of new skills and identify barriers or motivational problems. Clinician modeling and sharing of personal examples of using DBT reinforces the validity and reliability of the skills.

LO 2   Comprehend How to Use DBT in Groups

DBT GROUPS

The primary focus of DBT groups is skill or "ability" development. The emphasis is placed on learning new effective ways to respond to life's challenges. Linehan[13] describes this as follows: "Effectiveness is gauged by both direct and indirect effects of the behavior. Effective performance can be defined as those behaviors that lead to a maximum of positive outcomes with a minimum of negative outcomes." Additionally, practice is an essential behavioral component of skill development. Group leaders serve as skills trainers and coaches. Once taught the skills themselves, leaders need to practice the skills to enhance their ability to teach as well as model work skill use during group work. Skill practice is emphasized and demonstrated to improve clients' understanding. This has the added benefit of demonstrating effectiveness and applicability in the moment. For example, if a conflict arises during the group, a DBT skill teaching moment is created. Clients are generally required to use diary cards or worksheets to record when and how well they practiced each skill. This may even be homework that is required for group admittance. Clients may be asked to record when they used the skill, for what occurrence, and whether it was successful or not. A DBT group is frequently very unlike other social work groups. The leader will often take a much more directive role and may set an agenda with little input from group members. Groups may be set up more like a classroom and feature more of a classroom lecture style by the group leader. Feedback and support from individual group members may be discouraged, at least in the initial phase of each skill module. The first individual skill session will likely focus on discussing skill relevancy, applicability, and motivation followed by practice demonstration. Subsequent group sessions may briefly begin with "check-ins" and address attendance-interfering behaviors. Half of the group time may then be devoted to homework review and individual group members discussing how they did in practicing the newly learned skills from the last session. To maintain the group schedule, the group leader may have to be more direct to prevent drift and to limit sharing as well as feedback. However, all members should be asked to share which skills they practiced outside of group. This type of dialog is also important for group members to see how others handle problems and potentially extrapolate the relevancy to their own lives. Failures are equally important during these discussions to learn how to more effectively problem-solve. Problems are also an opportunity for clients to seek out support when faced with challenges. A client's lack of comprehension may also become apparent when discussing ineffective skill use.

Linehan[14] encourages the use of an open group for practicality reasons as well as the benefits of "learning to cope with change in a relatively stable environment." This allows for group members to practice their new skills during transitions. Only when all skills are learned will a group be allotted time for interpersonal processing. Some DBT adaptation groups may encourage group members to assist each other in understanding each skill and learning how to use it. Individuals may be able to give examples of how they might use the skill, which could assist their peers' understanding. It could also be useful for peers to encourage each other to weigh the pros and cons of using the skill. Group leaders may choose to use other creative and novel methods to improve understanding. Worksheets are often utilized to improve clients' understanding and provide a concrete visual reminder of the skills and can be kept in a special DBT binder or workbook. Many worksheets ask clients to list pros and cons of using or not using a specific skill. The duration of a DBT group will likely vary by context and members' needs. Groups may run as short as a few weeks in inpatient settings to over a year in other settings.

Group leaders may choose to introduce only one or two skills per group session depending on the developmental level and ability of the group as a whole. Overwhelming clients with too many skills at once could be counterproductive. How many and which different skills are taught is a decision that the team should make based upon the specific group's needs. Often one or two skills are introduced and clients are charged with practicing the skill until the next session. DBT groups often face many of the same challenges as other groups. However, clients in DBT skills groups likely struggle with emotional reactivity, mood disturbances, anger problems, or social skill deficits. If the DBT group is composed of those with BPD (borderline personality disorder) or borderline tendencies, substantially more skill may be required by group leaders. Leaders should be mindful that the group process (discussing personal problems, or listening to other's difficulties) can be very stressful and even traumatic for some group participants. The end of a group session should be devoted to returning clients to baseline with relaxation exercises or mood-enhancing activities.

Skill sets are broken down in this module into four major divisions: core mindfulness, emotional regulation, distress tolerance, and interpersonal effectiveness. Mindfulness is generally taught first and then integrated throughout the other skill sets. Next you'll find a small sampling of some of the more common skills, although many others have been developed. These are all fundamentally based upon the work of Dr. Linehan, but individual skills have been developed by others and given various names.

Mindfulness Skills

Mindfulness is considered the core skill of DBT. Many of the Zen concepts are included here, such as focusing on the present moment, being nonjudgmental, and keeping a balance between our feeling and thinking minds. Mindfulness emphasizes being more attentive of our bodies, emotions, and behaviors. While learning new skills, it's important that we pay attention to the processes involved. Mindfulness uses "what skills" and "how skills." "What skills" include being able to step outside of yourself and observe what is happening, putting that observation into words, and participating while paying attention. We should remind ourselves that thoughts and feelings are separate from events. Feeling like we are being attacked is not the same as being attacked. Feeling scared doesn't mean we are in danger. These skills allow us to pay attention to exactly what is happening inside and outside of ourselves. "How skills" assist with learning how to do the "what skills." These skills teach us to take a nonjudgmental approach, choose effective responses, and slow down our focus.

Moment to Pause   Moment to pause is a skill that helps us use the mindfulness skill. It reminds us to stop, notice what's happening, and take a break before reacting. This is especially important when we have intense emotional reactions to situations or events. It prompts us to stop and think before acting based upon emotion. When we take a moment to pause, we will take a breath and notice what's happening inside of us. Then we take another breath and notice what's happening around us. Now we can make a better decision about how to respond effectively. This skill prevents flying off the handle and impulsive reactions.

Wise Mind   This skill emphasizes that often we are using either the thinking mind or our emotional mind. The thinking mind is when we use logic, reasoning, and think rationally. This involves using logical, nondistorted facts to make reasonable conclusions and responding in a logical and dispassionate manner. The emotional mind involves being ruled by our emotional reactions to situations, with limited logic and reasoning. Our actions may be reactionary based upon the emotion involved. A wise mind balances the two minds and allows us to respond to triggers without reacting to them. It allows us to have greater control over our behavior and slows down rash decision making based on emotional reactions. We are most effective when we balance our thinking and emotional minds. Being unbalanced in either direction can create distress and problems.

One Mind   One mind is about focusing on one thing at a time and staying in the moment. You often use this skill when you are reading. You are solely focused on reading and ideally are not distracted by outside stimuli. Using one mind encourages us to concentrate and do one thing at a time. This even includes worrying. If you are going to worry, allow yourself a certain amount of time to do so fully. Then move on and focus on another activity—keep your focus and don't allow yourself to be distracted with worry.

Turtling   The turtling skill teaches how to act more like a turtle. Turtles retreat into their shells when they sense danger. When they are in their shells, things roll off and they can easily protect themselves while ignoring the outside world. If they get turned upside down, they self-right themselves. They walk slowly and deliberately, taking one step at a time. Retreating into a protective shell may be needed when no other options are available. It also allows us time to stop and think instead of reacting. It's then easier to use the one mind and wise mind skills.

Focused Breathing   Focused breathing allows us to slow ourselves down and observe. Breathe in for 4 seconds then breathe out for 4 seconds. Repeat four times. The key to this skill is using mindfulness to focus only on our breathing and observing the feelings in our body. Being focused on our breathing prevents our minds horn running away from us and triggering additional unwanted feelings. This is a way to rebalance ourselves and remind us about using our other mindfulness skills. It relaxes our minds and bodies so we can step outside ourselves, control emotions, and make effective choices.

Effectiveness Being effective involves doing what works in any given situation. This skill reminds us that we can choose the path of least resistance and do what is needed rather than shooting ourselves in the foot with responses that harm us. Sometimes we need to choose between being right and solving problems or getting along with others. We also need to be willing to give up responses that simply don't work and result in us not getting what we want. Our actions should be focused on what makes us feel better, not worse. This also involves being skillful in our interactions. We should not adjust our choices for any given situation on how we feel things should be. We need to let go of anger and resentment and instead focus on the goal at hand.

Radical Acceptance. Radical acceptance teaches us to refocus our energy on things that we can control. The bottom line is that we can only control ourselves, which includes our thoughts, feelings, and choices. We must be willing to give up attempts to control other people and events. We can try to influence these things but we will never control them. Sometimes life is unfair and we must accept some things as they are. We can choose to be unhappy about it or move on to the things we can control. "Shoulds" and" "musts" are the enemy here. Ultimately, we must accept reality as it is, not as we would like it to be. This skill reminds us to take a radical step and completely let go of what is out of our control.

Nonjudgmental This skill reminds us that deciding something is "good" or "bad" is a choice. Mistakes happen, but that doesn't mean that we are bad people or failures. Other people make mistakes too. It doesn't mean they dislike us or are deliberately trying to hurt us. Ineffective choices are simply that. We don't have to assign greater meaning or label things one way or another. Negative judgments set us up to feel bad and lay blame. Excessively positive judgments can lead to disappointments as well. Let's also not forget to avoid judging the fact we catch ourselves judging. This skill is about separating fact from opinion and eliminating positive and negative evaluations. Acknowledgment is our target, not judgment.

Willingness Willingness is a skill that overlaps almost every other skill. It involves being amendable to try something that works and is effective. Stubbornness is the enemy here. We can choose to continue to make the same responses we have in the past. However, we must reconcile the fact that those responses may have not gotten us what we want. If we are unhappy about circumstances or ourselves, we must be willing to make a change and consider other possibilities. This includes a willingness to be wrong. This skill reminds us that we have the power to control our own internal experiences. We also have power over the choices we make.

Middle Path The middle path skill teaches us to find the path of least resistance in all interactions. Sometimes our "shoulds" and "musts" get in the way of compromise. These internal pictures of what we think things should be prevent us from accepting the reality of a situation. Willfully trying to swim against the stream because we are "right" reduces our effectiveness with other people. Sometimes we don't recognize when we are thinking in black-and-white terms. A "my way or the highway" or win-lose mentality can create conflict, emotional upset, and distress. There is almost always a middle path of compromise that will produce a happier balanced existence and better outcomes. The middle path skill does require that we use our willingness skill to be more effective with ourselves and others. This is also in keeping with being more balanced and avoiding extremes.

Emotional Regulation Skills

These skills emphasize responding (not reacting) emotions, changing unwanted feelings, and waiting for emotions to pass before acting. Through observation and proper labeling, we learn to understand our emotions. Negative labels and judgments create distressing emotions. There are things that we can do to diminish unwanted emotions if we are willing. Notice we used the word *unwanted* instead of *negative*. The word *negative* is a judgmental label. We must also accept that sometimes there is nothing that we can currently do about a certain circumstance. Sometimes the best we can do is ride it out and wait for it to pass. These skills will help us reduce our vulnerability to unwanted emotions and increase positive ones.

Lemons to Lemonade This skill reminds us that everyone can get lemons at some point in their lives. Everyone has burdens to bear. Life can be unfair and bad things happen. Everyone gets a bad hand now and then, but we do have a choice of how we deal with it. As the saying goes, "it's not what happens to you but how you deal with it." Almost every weakness can be turned into a strength. Failures and setbacks can be reframed and transformed into something positive. We can choose to ruminate about how unfair or awful something is or we can make something good from it. Positive attitude is key here. This skill teaches that we have a choice how we handle things and what label we put on them.

Opposite Emotion Opposite emotion teaches us that every emotion has an opposite. This opposite emotion is our best defense and antidote for unwanted feelings. Many times we can change our emotions if we are willing to take action. Doing something that makes us happy is the best counterweight to sadness. Laughter almost always reduces anger. Using this skill improves our ability to balance emotions and feel more empowered over our experiences. It may sound simple, but it really does work. This skill requires that we improve our self-awareness of our emotional states and be willing to try a new, more effective choice. A wise person knows his or her limits and takes action to make a change.

Ride the Wave Sometimes emotions are beyond our control, like ocean waves that come and go regularly. We can choose to be overwhelmed by them or we can choose to ride them out and wait for them to pass. Almost everyone has at some point in their lives experienced a full range of emotions, from terrified to exhilarated. Regardless of the emotion experienced, we are still standing at the end of the day. One thing we know for sure is that feelings are fleeting and generally don't last. Sometimes we need to simply wait it out and tolerate the feeling while we work on finding a solution. This involves observing and acknowledging the feeling without judgment. Feelings are an experience we must own as part of who we are. They are not things other people give us or assault us with. This skill teaches us to simply observe our feelings and not act on them.

Please Master

> **PhysicaL**
> **Eating**
> **Altering drugs**
> **Sleep**
> **Exercise**
> **Mastery**

PLEASE MASTER teaches us to achieve mastery over our bodies, which will help us feel better and be less at risk for emotional upsets. Physical illness can be distressing. Being ill can make us irritable and have a lower frustration tolerance. It's important to listen to our bodies and treat illness when needed. Eating right can go a long way to improving our emotions. A healthy and balanced diet can improve how we feel day to day. Excessively heavy and starchy food can slow us down and lead us to feel lethargic. Mood-altering drugs compromise our ability to maintain a balanced and healthy lifestyle. Illicit drugs can alter moods and increase mood swings. Some can exacerbate underlying psychological problems such as depression. Even caffeine can alter how we feel and drag down our mood when it wears off. Sleep is important to help us feel rested and have the energy we need day to day. Lack of sleep can make us tired, irritable, and less able to handle daily stressors. Exercise produces feel-good endorphins and neurotransmitters. It can boost our mood and make us feel better overall. Sleep and the immune system are improved with exercise. Proper exercise helps us have the energy needed to handle our daily lives. Mastery is about being more effective and skillful in how we take care of our bodies.

Distress Tolerance Skills

These skills emphasize how we handle daily stressors, problem-solve, tolerate challenges, and give up attempts to control. These skills are about coping with unwanted emotions and learning strategies to help us handle things when we cannot change certain distressing situations. Many problems require time to resolve, so we need skills to be able to manage our feelings. This buys us time to problem-solve and make effective choices. These skills can provide a distraction from our feelings, remind us we have the power to self-soothe, and offer alternatives to self-destructive behaviors.

Self-Soothe First Aid Kit A self-soothe first aid kit helps giving us the tools we need to cope with unwanted emotions and distressing events. The kit should only include things that are effective and helpful. This kit might include things that help us improve mindfulness or activate all five senses. This could include sensory items such as things to smell (for example, a scented candle), music we like, or pictures that make us feel happy or remind us of our goals. Special foods we like is another option. Tactile activities such as using a stress ball or taking a bath would be good options as well. This kit could also include activities that we enjoy that are distracting. Finding enjoyable activities or hobbies is an important skill to help us recharge our batteries and manage stress. Using our mindfulness skills will improve the effectiveness of this kit.

Crisis Survival Network A crisis survival network is a list of people, including phone numbers, and resources that can provide support in times of crisis. This could include counselors, friends, family, mentors, teachers, self-help groups, and online resources. Everyone needs to have a support system and people they can rely on to provide emotional support, validation, and comfort. Sometimes venting emotions can be cathartic and allow us to reduce rumination. It also can help us step outside ourselves and gain needed perspective. It is important to not overuse individuals on your list to avoid overtaxing any one resource. We should also be willing to provide others support when they need it as well.

Half-Smile The half-smile skill teaches us to pay more attention to our level of physical tension and how our bodies are responding to stressful situations. Research shows that we feel better when we smile, and there is a distinct mind–body connection between smiling and emotions. Having even a half-smile about something distressing can go a long way toward reducing stress and unwanted emotions. We could also use our willingness skill to find some positive thing to smile about in even the worst situation. This skill is about reminding ourselves to keep a positive attitude and find the good in any situation. Emotions are heightened when we focus on how intolerable things are.

Interpersonal Effectiveness Skills

These skills improve our ability to navigate relationships in a healthy way, maintain balance and reciprocity, learn assertiveness, and get what we want from others. Relationships require work and skill to avoid conflicts. Relationships can also be demanding, which may require that we be assertive in expressing our needs and establishing boundaries. This includes the ability to say no to unreasonable requests and effectively ask for what we need.

Dear Man
 Describe
 Express
 Assert
 Reinforce
 Mindful
 Appear confident
 Negotiate

DEAR MAN is a guideline to improve our ability to assertively ask others for what we want or need. Confrontation can be difficult and cause anxiety for many people. This skill allows us to think out a plan before making our request. It also gives us reminders to use in the moment to improve our effectiveness. Describe involves verbalizing and plainly expressing exactly what the problem is. The nature of a problem is not always self-evident. Express is verbalizing exactly what your thoughts, feelings, needs, and opinions are. Here is where we should be using "I" statements and avoiding blame and judgment. Assert is about plainly asking for what you need or want to happen. Don't assume the other person knows what you want. Asserting does not involve aggression. Reinforce is about expressing the pros and cons of what you want or need. Express what positive reinforcement may come from getting what you want and what the reward will be. Mindful reminds us to stay on task and focused on our objective. Here you may need to use the broken record skill to assist you in staying on track. It may also be necessary to ignore distractions, diversions, and (discussed later) negative feedback. Appear confident is part of being assertive. Making eye contact and appearing to believe in what we want makes a good impression. Hesitation and appearing indifferent may prevent you from getting what you want. Negotiate is the final step. Being willing to compromise and accommodate the other's needs is important. No-lose problem solving is the best way to negotiate a successful request. The middle path skill applies here.

Give

Gentle
Interested
Validate
Easy manner

The GIVE skill assists us with asking for what we want and need from others in an effective manner. Give stands for being gentle in interactions by being considerate, nonaggressive, and nonjudgmental. Being gentle doesn't involve using verbal aggression, threats, or manipulation. Acting interested involves using active and reflective listening skills to understand another person's perspective or opinion. Empathy skills are the key to acting interested. Validate is about acknowledging someone else's feelings, needs, and opinions. This may involve verbally using your nonjudgmental skills. Easy manner is about being cooperative, approachable, and flexible. A little humor goes a long way. The phrase "you'll attract more flies with sugar than vinegar" applies here.

Making Repairs   Making repairs is about putting in the work needed to maintain relationships. Sometimes we need to make an effort to repair a relationship that we may have damaged by our choices. Many people find a simple act of apology difficult for them. Conversely some have a difficult time accepting apologies. Acknowledging when we hurt someone and expressing regret can go a long way toward improving relationships and participating in an effective manner. Sometimes we have to be willing to let certain things go in order to improve a relationship. Making repairs involves acknowledging our mistakes and the harm caused, apologizing, and taking positive steps to repair the relationship.

Broken Record   Broken record teaches us to keep coming back to our values, needs, and desires for ourselves. We may need to repeatedly remind ourselves what kind of life we would like and what we want our present and future to be. This includes our commitment to use our DBT skills. It also involves having a commitment to being effective in our choices and our desire to make relationships work. Sometimes it may be necessary to be firm in our requests of others to get what we need. We may need to keep asserting ourselves with those who may try to avoid needed discussions.

Skill Group Example
Lemons to Lemonade Skill Group
Goal

This exercise is designed to assist you in turning your weakness into strengths.

Group supplies: Lemonade Worksheet, Styrofoam or plastic cups, pitcher of water, one bottle lemon juice, sugar, spoons

Step 1: *Introduction and check-in* (5 minutes). Briefly complete a group check-in. Ask all participants to briefly say how they're feeling today and how they've been since the last group session. This allows the clinician to assess clients' emotional state and any stressors that may interfere with their participation and learning, it can also be useful to incorporate this information into the skill instruction and discussion. For example, if a client states she is feeling depressed today and worried about a family member, the clinician can later explain how the chosen skill could help with feelings of sadness or worry.

Step 2: *Review of diary cards* (20 minutes). Ask each group member to tell the group about one event on his or her diary card. Encourage them to briefly explain the situation, what skill they used, and whether they were effective or ineffective. Group leaders provide positive feedback and encouragement for using a skill and encourage clients to analyze, problem-solve, and address the causes of skill failures. Group members may be allowed to give positive or negative feedback. Not using a skill for a problem could also be a focus of discussion.

Step 3: *New skill introduction—lemons to lemonade* (15 minutes). The group leader introduces and explains the lemons to lemonade skill. The skill should be explained in a variety of different ways to facilitate participant understanding and using language that is understandable for the developmental level of the group. Use worksheets that also explain the skill and provide a reminder for clients to keep in their DBT binders. The leader should use a personal example of how he or she has used the skill in his or her life. Check for understanding by asking participants to express in their own words how they could explain and use the skill. Sometimes participants explain things in ways that make more sense to their peers.

Step 4: *Elaborate on the lemons to lemonade skill.* This skill involves turning your weakness (challenges in life) into strengths. The following are some examples:

- You are fired from a job and then find a job that you enjoy much more.
- You are "dumped" in a romantic relationship and then find a new partner with whom you are much happier being with.
- You are majoring in a discipline in college that you find "unfulfilling"; you discontinue that major and find one that you are much more passionate about.
- You are arrested for driving under the influence, which leads you to make a decision to drink much less and to lead a healthier lifestyle.

Fill out the following worksheet (15 minutes). Then ask for volunteers to share what they listed.

Step 5: *Group activity and closing* (10 minutes). Novel and fun activities enhance participants' understanding of concepts and make skills more memorable. Pass out cups and put a capful of lemon juice in each cup. Encourage participants to taste the lemon juice and note how bitter it tastes. Add water to the cups and then 1 teaspoon sugar. During this time, ask for volunteers to share what lemons they currently have and how they might make lemonade out of challenging circumstances in their lives. Encourage exploration of making a strength out of a weakness. Note the tremendous difference in taste from the lemon juice to the lemonade. Remind group members to use this skill and note in their diary cards for next week.

Behavior Chain Analysis

Behavior chain analysis is part of cognitive restructuring that helps clients recognize thought and behavior patterns that lead to their distress and ineffective behavior choices. The goal is for clients to be able to conduct their own analysis and self-evaluate their own inner workings to improve their ability to manage and control themselves. Clients are then empowered to recognize and alter counterproductive patterns as needed. As with all social work, the clinician's goal is to prepare the client so that he or she longer needs the social worker to assist with managing day-to-day functioning. The key to behavior chain analysis is dissecting ineffective patterns by breaking down an exact chain of events. Each link in the chain is evaluated individually and then as a sequence. It may be helpful to think of yourself as a detective as you investigate each step. The first step is to choose a problem behavior or unwanted emotion. The next step is to analyze the sequential chain of events that lead to it.

Lemonade Worksheet

Turning your shortcomings into strengths is the skill of turning lemons into lemonade.

Step 1: List the ways you have made lemonade in the past.

_____

_____

_____

_____

_____

_____

Step 2: List some of your current lemons (challenges you are facing).

_____

_____

_____

_____

_____

_____

Step 3: List your strategies for making your current lemons into lemonade.

_____

_____

_____

_____

_____

_____

_____

EXERCISE M4.1   Lemons to Lemonade

GOAL: This exercise is designed to assist you in understanding and applying the lemons to lemonade skill.

1. Fill out the Lemonade Worksheet that appears in this chapter.

2. Specify your thoughts on the merits and shortcomings of this strategy.

Vulnerability Many things might make us more vulnerable to unwanted emotions or behaviors. It's important to identify and evaluate factors that contribute to increased vulnerability. Oftentimes these things appear unrelated to a problem but are actually contributing factors. Biological factors can play a role, such as lack of sleep, alcohol and drug use, illness, poor eating habits, or lack of exercise. Stressful events (such as interpersonal or relationship conflicts) can drain our resources, which makes us more vulnerable. Emotional arousal or the presence of strong emotions can make it more likely that certain events will trigger certain thoughts or feelings. Vulnerability factors are the first links in the chain because they set us up for certain outcomes.

Precipitating Event The next link in the chain is referred to as the precipitating event or trigger. Clients are not always aware of an accurate precipitating event and may need assistance with verbalizing an exact starting point. It's important to explore what the true trigger or activating event is in order to accurately analyze subsequent steps in the chain. Sometimes the actual trigger takes place earlier than clients may recognize. This step is also important for clients to be able to assemble a list of their more common triggers. The precipitating event will include the who, what, when, where, and why of the situation. Look carefully at everyone's part, including what you were thinking, feeling, and expecting. There may also be environmental factors that contributed to the situation.

Thoughts, Feelings, and Actions The precipitating event leads directly to the next link, which could be a thought, feeling, or behavior. Often there is first a thought followed by a feeling and then an action. But this is not always the case. Sometimes emotions happen rapidly, before we even have a chance to think about them. Behaviors can be impulsive as well. Regardless of which come first, these thoughts, feelings, or behaviors often lead to subsequent thoughts, feelings, and behaviors. Often several links are made here as you react to your reactions. These thoughts, feelings, or behaviors can be positive or negative. However, the focus of attention is on the resulting unwanted feelings or ineffective or problematic behaviors.

Consequences There are always natural consequences for our behavior choices. Sometimes these are internal and sometimes they are external or environmental. Even unhealthy or ineffective behavior can have positive payoffs for us, even if temporary. When looking at the consequences, we must ask ourselves if we got what we wanted, were effective, or have achieved results that meet our goals. Some emotional reactions and behaviors may feel good at the moment but have negative impacts on our relationships or goals and harm others. Often we add more links to the chain as we then think and feel negatively about our actions and behavior choices.

Alternative Strategies and Vulnerability Reduction. When we look at each link in the chain we can identify alternative strategies to counteract events, thoughts, feelings, or behaviors. When effective, this can prevent the chain from proceeding to the next link. Often it is helpful to use a piece of paper divided in half. On one side list the links in the behavior chain and on the other side list strategies, solutions, or skills that may help. Again we look at desired outcomes, goals, and being more effective as motivation to try new ways to cope with unwanted thoughts, feelings, and behaviors.

Behavior Chain Analysis Example Problem: Molly cuts her arms and thighs with a razor when she's feeling overwhelmed or has an argument with her boyfriend.

CHAIN LINKS	ALTERNATIVE STRATEGIES
Vulnerability: Molly was stressed out about missing assignments at school and stayed up late texting her friend.	Molly could make sure she's taking time each day to do homework and keep a regular bedtime. (PLEASE MASTER skill)
Precipitating event: Molly's boyfriend posts a flirtatious message on a friend's Facebook page. Molly immediately saw this post because she checks her boyfriend's page several times per day.	Molly could make an effort to not check her boyfriend's posts as often per day or ask him not to post those types of messages. (DEAR MAN, nonjudgmental, radical acceptance skills)
Thoughts, feelings, and actions: Molly felt hurt when she saw the message, then thought "It must mean he's breaking up with me." She then felt sad, rejected, and unloved. Molly then chose to write a mean message on his Facebook page. Her boyfriend reacted by calling her names. She then felt angry and defensive. She thought the relationship was over and didn't know what to do to fix it. She was angry with him but afraid of losing him at the same time. Feeling overwhelmed, she cut herself to relieve the stress.	Molly could have used her moment to pause skill to think before acting. She could try talking to her boyfriend before jumping to conclusions about their relationship. She could use her self-soothe first aid kit or crisis network when she was feeling overwhelmed. (Wise mind and turtling skills)
Consequences: Molly feels badly that she cut again. She had made a promise to herself and her mother that she wouldn't do that anymore. She worries her mother will find out and tell her therapist. Her mother will be disappointed and her therapist may say she needs to go back to the psychiatric hospital.	Molly could remind herself not to judge herself. She could review her DBT skills with her therapist and make a commitment to use her skills more. (Nonjudgmental, one mind, and making repairs skills)

EXERCISE M4.2 Conducting a Behavior Analysis

GOAL: This exercise is designed to familiarize you with conducting a behavior analysis.

1. Identify an unwanted feeling or behavior that you want to change.

2. Identify what vulnerability factors contribute to that unwanted feeling or behavior. List some alternative strategies to counteract those factors.

3. Identify a precipitating event or trigger that initiates the problem. List some alternative strategies and DBT skills to counteract the event.

4. Identify a sequence of thoughts, feelings, and actions that result from that event. What are the subsequent thoughts, feelings, and actions? List some alternative strategies and DBT skills that might counteract those thoughts, feelings, and actions.

5. Identify what consequences and outcomes result from the identified sequence of thoughts, feelings, and actions. List some alternative strategies and skills that might repair these consequences and prevent the chain from happening again.

Summary

The following summarizes the module's content in terms of the learning objectives presented at the beginning.

1. Comprehend dialectical behavior therapy (DBT).
Dialectical behavior therapy is a contemporary therapeutic approach that blends cognitive-behavioral therapy with aspects of Eastern philosophies and Zen Buddhism. It teaches clients specific mindfulness and psychosocial skills that help with emotional regulation, distress tolerance, and interpersonal effectiveness.

2. Understand how to use DBT in groups.
DBT uses the group process to teach skill sets, enhance motivation, and improve skill acquisition through practice. These skills have wide-ranging applicability with a variety of contexts and settings. DBT encourages and empowers clients to take a proactive role in working toward desired outcomes through effective self-intervention. Considerable material on how to use DBT in groups is presented in this chapter.

Group Exercise

EXERCISE A: Conducting Your Own DBT Skills Group

GOAL: This exercise is designed to assist you with preparing and facilitating your own DBT group.

Step 1. Choose a DBT skill from the list in this module.

Step 2. Describe how you would explain this skill to group participants using a variety of different wordings and examples. Include a personal example of how you have used the skill yourself.

Step 3: Describe how you would enhance participants' motivation to use the chosen skill.

Step 4: Describe what materials or novel methods you would use to enhance participants' understanding of the concepts.

Step 5: Create a skill handout or worksheet to improve, participants' understanding of the skill. (The following two worksheets are examples of what might be prepared.)

Step 6: The instructor asks for volunteers to share with the group what they have prepared. The group then discusses the merits of what each volunteer has prepared.

Radical Acceptance Worksheet

Radical acceptance teaches us to refocus our energy on things that we can control. The bottom line is that we can only control ourselves, which includes our thoughts, feelings, and choices. We must be willing to give up attempts to control other people and events.

1. Some examples where I have unsuccessfully tried to control others (with the results being not what I wanted) are:

    _____

    _____

    _____

    _____

    _____

    _____

    _____

2. In the future, I will stop trying to control others by no longer doing what (such as nagging, preaching, criticizing)?

    _____

    _____

    _____

    _____

    _____

    _____

    _____

3. The only person I can control is myself. I will focus my energies on improving my life by:

    _____

    _____

    _____

    _____

    _____

    _____

    _____

Nonjudgemental Worksheet

1. A problematic judgment for me is _____

_____

_____

_____

_____

_____

_____

_____

2. This judgment is problematic because _____

_____

_____

_____

_____

_____

_____

_____

_____

3. I will replace this judgment by instead telling myself the following:

_____

_____

_____

_____

_____

_____

_____

Competency Notes

EP 7a   Collect and organize data, and apply critical thinking to interpret information from clients and constituencies.

EP 7b   Apply knowledge of human behavior and the social environment, person-in-environment, and other multidisciplinary theoretical frameworks in the analysis of assessment data from clients and constituencies.

EP 7c   Develop mutually agreed-on intervention goals and objectives based on the critical assessment of strengths, needs, and challenges within clients and constituencies.

EP 8a   Critically choose and implement interventions to achieve practice goals and enhance capacities of clients and constituencies.

EP 8b   Apply knowledge of human behavior and the social environment, person-in-environment, and other multidisciplinary theoretical frameworks in interventions with clients and constituencies. (pp. 551–572)

DBT blends cognitive-behavioral therapy with aspects of Eastern philosophies and Zen Buddhism. It teaches clients a variety of skills that help with distress tolerance, emotional regulation, and interpersonal effectiveness. The group process is used to assess and teach skill sets, enhance motivation, and improve skill acquisition through practice.

2 Answers to Group Exercises D–F in Chapter 6

EXERCISE D

1. Twenty; 9, 19, 29, 39, 49, 59, 69, 79, 89, 90, 91, 92, 93, 94, 95, 96, 97, 98, 99.
2. They're playing with different partners.
3. Two hours.
4. The water will never reach the top of the ladder because the boat keeps rising with the tide.
5. Of course.
6. He's still alive.
7. Six.
8. The bear is white because it is a polar bear. The house is located at the North Pole.
9. Three minutes.
10. Car A travels 1,200 miles; Car B travels 800 miles from the point of origin.
11. One haystack.
12. Karen is Jill's mother.
13. Four dollars.

EXERCISE E

Task 1:

Task 2:

Task 3:

Task 4:

Task 5:

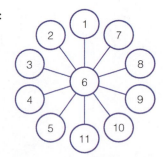

EXERCISE F

1. Sandbox
2. Man overboard
3. I understand
4. Reading between the lines
5. Long underwear
6. Crossroads
7. Downtown
8. Tricycle
9. Split level
10. Three degrees below zero
11. Neon lights
12. Circles under the eyes
13. High chair
14. Paradise
15. Touchdown
16. Six feet underground
17. Mind over matter
18. He's beside himself
19. Backward glance
20. Life after death
21. G.I. overseas
22. Space program
23. See-through blouse
24. Just between you and me
25. Empty

Notes

CHAPTER 1   Groups: Types and Stages of Development

1. Euster, G. L. (1980). Group work. In D. Brieland, L. B. Costin & C. R. Atherton (Eds.), *Contemporary social work* (2nd ed., p. 100). New York: McGraw-Hill.
2. Ibid., p. 100.
3. Stroup, H. (1986). *Social welfare pioneers* (p. 9). Chicago: Nelson-Hall.
4. Becker, D. G. (1968) Social welfare leaders as spokesmen for the poor. *Social Casework 49*(2), 85.
5. Stroup, *Social welfare pioneers,* pp. 1–29.
6. Ibid., pp. 255–280.
7. Ibid., p. 297.
8. Euster, Group work, p. 100.
9. Johnson, D. W., & Johnson, F. P. (2009). *Joining together: Group theory and group skills* (10th ed.). Boston: Allyn and Bacon.
10. Barker, R. L. (2003). *The social work dictionary* (5th ed., p. 165). Washington, DC: NASW Press.
11. Katz, A. H., & Bender, E. I. (1976). *The strength in us: Self-help groups in the modern world* (p. 9) New York: Franklin Watts.
12. Powell, T. J. (1987). *Self-help organizations and professional practice.* Silver Spring, MD: National Association of Social Workers.
13. Post, S. G. (2008). Updating the helper therapy principle. Retrieved from http://www.psychologytoday.com/blog/the-joy-giving/200809/updating-the-helper-therapy-principle.
14. Euster, Group work, p. 103.
15. Lewin, K. (1952). Group decision and social change. In G. E. Swanson, T. M. Newcomb, & E. L. Hartley (Eds.), *Readings in social psychology* (pp. 459–73). New York: Holt.
16. Ibid.
17. Tubbs, S. L. & Baird, J. W. (1976). *The open person ... self-disclosure and personal growth* (pp. 48–50). Columbus, OH: Charles E. Merrill.
18. Ibid., p. 48.
19. Rogers, C. (1970). *Carl Rogers on encounter groups* (pp. 40–41). New York: Harper & Row.
20. Shostrom, E. L. (1969). Group therapy: Let the buyer beware. *Psychology Today 2*(12), 38–39.
21. Lieberman, M. A., Yalom, E. D., & Miles, M. B. (1973). Encounter: The leader makes the difference. *Psychology Today, 6,* 11.
22. Toseland, R. W., & Rivas, R. F. (2009). *An introduction to group work practice* (6th ed.). Boston: Pearson.
23. Slater, P. E. (1958). Contrasting correlates of group size. *Sociometry 21,* 137–138.
24. Toseland & Rivas, *An introduction to group work practice.*
25. Hansen, J. C., Warner, R. W., & Smith, E. M. (1980). *Group counseling: Theory and process* (2nd ed.). Chicago: Rand McNally College Publishing.
26. Toseland & Rivas, *An introduction to group work practice.*
27. Ibid.
28. Ibid.
29. Garland, J. A., Jones, H. & Kolodny, R. (1965). A model for stages of development in social work groups. In S. Bernstein (Ed.), *Explorations in group work* (pp. 12–53). Boston: Milford House.
30. Garland, J. A., & Frey, L. A. (1973). Applications of stages of group development to groups in psychiatric settings. In S. Bernstein (Ed.), *Further explorations in group work* (p. 3). Boston: Milford House.
31. Ibid., p. 5.
32. Ibid., p. 6.
33. Tuckman, B. (1065). Developmental sequence in small groups. *Psychological Bulletin 63*, 384–399.
34. Northen, H., & Kurland, R. (2001). *Social work with groups* (3rd ed.). New York: Columbia University Press.
35. Ibid., p. 288.
36. Bales, R. F. (1965). The equilibrium problem in small groups. In A. Hare, E. Borgatta, & R. Bales (Eds.), *Small groups: studies in social interaction* (pp. 444–476). New York: Knopf.

CHAPTER 2   Social Group Work and Social Work Practice

1. For a summary, see Zastrow, C. (2010). *The practice of social work* (9th ed.). Belmont, CA: Brooks/Cole.
2. Published 1982. National Association of Social Workers, Inc. Reprinted with permission from *Standards for the Classification of Social Work Practice,* Policy Statement 4, p. 5. Copyright National Association of Social Workers, Inc.
3. Pincus A., & Minahan, A. (1973). *Social work practice: Model and method* (p. 54). Itasca, IL: Peacock.
4. Retrieved from http://www.socialpolicy.ca/cush/ml/ml-t3stm.
5. Published 1982. National Association of Social Workers, Inc. Reprinted with permission, from *Standards for the Classification of Social Work Practice,* Policy Statement 4, p. 5. Copyright National Association of Social Workers, Inc.
6. BPD, "Definition of Generalist Practice," discussed and advanced by the BPD Social Work Continuum Committee and approved by the BPD Board of Directors, 2006.
7. *Educational Policy and Accreditation Standards* (EPAS), (Alexandria, VA: Council on Social Work Education, 2015).
8. Masters, W. H., & Johnson, V. E. (1970). *Human sexual inadequacy.* Boston: Little, Brown.
9. Jackson, D. D. (1965). The study of the family. *Family Process 4*, 1–20.
10. Comer, R. J. (2005). *Fundamentals of abnormal psychology* (4th ed., pp. 251–260). New York: Worth Publishing.
11. Ibid.
12. Stuart, R. B. (1970). *Trick or treatment.* Champaign, IL: Research Press.

13. National Association of Social Workers, *Standards for the Classification of Social Work Practice* (Washington, DC: National Association of Social Workers, 1982), p. 17.
14. *Educational Policy and Accreditation Standards* (EPAS), 2015.
15. Ibid.
16. Billingsley, A. (1993). *Climbing Jacob's ladder: The enduring legacy of African-American families.* New York: Simon & Schuster.
17. Saleeby, D. (1997). *The strengths perspective in social work practice* (2nd ed., pp. 12–15). New York: Longman.
18. Ibid., p.12
19. Stevie Wonder Page. Retrieved from http://www.soulwalking.co.uk /StevieWonder.html.

20. Grandin, T. (2011). *The way I see it* (2nd ed.). Arlington, TX: Future Horizons.
21. Hepworth, D. H., & Larsen, J. (1986). *Direct social work practice: Theory and skills* (2nd ed., p. 563). Pacific Grove, CA: Brooks/Cole.
22. Riessman, F. (1965). The "helper therapy" principle. *Journal of Social Work 2,* 27–34.
23. Barker, R. (2003). *The social work dictionary* (5th ed., p. 84). Washington, DC: NASW Press.
24. Reprinted with permission from *Educational Policy and Accreditation Standards* (EPAS) (Alexandria, VA: Council on Social Work Education, 2015).

CHAPTER 3   Group Dynamics: Leadership

1. Krech, D., Crutchfield, R. S., & Ballachey, E. L. (1962). *Individual in society* (pp. 428–431). New York: McGraw-Hill.
2. Toseland, R. W., & Rivas, R. F. (2009). *An introduction to group work practice* (6th ed.). Boston: Pearson.
3. Davis, J. S., & Hare, A. P. (1956). Button-down collar culture: A study of undergraduate life at a men's college. *Human Organization 14,* 13–20.
4. Toseland & Rivas, *An introduction to group work practice.*
5. Johnson, D. W., & Johnson, F. P. (1987). *Joining together: Group theory and group skills* (3rd ed., p. 43). Englewood Cliffs, NJ: Prentice Hall.
6. Ibid., p. 44.
7. Christie, R., & Geis, F. (1970). *Studies in Machiavellianism.* New York: Academic Press.
8. Lewin, K., Lippitt, R., & White, R. K. (1939). Patterns of aggressive behavior in experimentally created social climates. *Journal of Social Psychology 10,* 271–299.
9. Toseland & Rivas, *An introduction to group work practice.*
10. Retrieved from http://www.greenleaf.org/whatissl/.
11. Retrieved from http://www.regent.edu/acad/global/publications /sl_proceedings/2005/spears_practice.pdf.
12. Bales, R. F. (1950). *Interaction process analysis: A method for the study of small groups.* Reading, MA: Addison-Wesley.

13. Johnson, D., & Johnson, F. P. (1975). *Joining together: Group theory and group skills* (pp. 26–27). Boston, MA: Allyn and Bacon.
14. Hersey, P., & Blanchard, K. (1977). *Management of organizational behavior: Utilizing human resources* (3rd ed.). Englewood Cliffs, NJ: Prentice Hall.
15. French, J. R. P., & Raven, B. (1968). The bases of social power. In D. Cartwright & A. Zander (Eds.), *Group dynamics: Research and theory* (3rd ed., pp. 259–269). New York: Harper & Row.
16. Toseland & Rivas, *An introduction to group work practice.*
17. Halle, L. J. (1967). Overestimating the power of power. *New Republic 10,* 15–17.
18. Cartwright, D., & Zander, A. (1968). Power and influence in groups. In D. Cartwright & A. Zander (Eds.), *Group dynamics* (3rd ed., pp. 215–235). New York: Harper & Row.
19. Deutsch, M. (1969). Conflicts: Productive and destructive. *Journal of Social Issues 25,* 7–43.
20. Alinsky, S. (1972). *Rules for radicals.* New York: Vintage.
21. Ibid., pp. 143–144.
22. Toseland & Rivas, *An introduction to group work practice.*
23. Wright, M. (2002). Co-facilitation: Fashion or function? *Social Work with Groups 25,* 77–92.
24. Rath, T., & Conchie, B. (2008). *Strengths based leadership.* New York: Gallup Press.

CHAPTER 4   Group Dynamics: Goals and Norms

1. Johnson, D. W., & Johnson, F. P. (2009). *Joining together: Group theory and group skills* (10th ed.). Boston: Allyn and Bacon.
2. Johnson, D. W., & Johnson, F. P. (1975). *Joining together: Group theory and group skills* (p. 103). Englewood Cliffs, NJ: Prentice Hall.
3. Johnson & Johnson, *Joining together* (10th ed.).
4. Ibid.
5. Ibid.
6. Ibid.
7. Kelly, H. H., & Stahelski, A. J. (1970). Social interaction basis of cooperators' and competitors' beliefs about others. *Journal of Personality and Social Psychology 16,* 66–91.
8. Johnson & Johnson, *Joining together* (10th ed.).
9. Delbecq, A. L., & Van de Ven, A. (1971). A group process model for problem identification and program planning. *Journal of Applied Behavioral Science 7,* 466–492.
10. Van de Ven, A., & Delbecq, A. L. (1971). Nominal versus interacting group processes for committee decision-making effectiveness. *Academy of Management Journal 14,* 205.

11. For an illustration of the nominal group approach in developing social programs, see Zastrow, C. (1973). The nominal group: A new approach to designing programs for curbing delinquency. *Canadian Journal of Criminology and Corrections 15,* 109–117.
12. For an additional discussion of using the nominal group approach to identify course content, see Zastrow, C. & Navarre, R. (1977). The nominal group: A new tool for making social work education relevant. *Journal of Education for Social Work 13,* 112–118.
13. Van de Ven & Delbecq, Nominal versus interacting group processes, p. 205.
14. Ibid.
15. Napier, R. W., & Gershenfeld, M. K. (1981). *Groups: Theory and experience* (2nd ed., p. 134). Boston: Houghton Mifflin.
16. Sherif, M. (1935). A study of some social factors in perception. *Archives of Psychology 187.* 1–27; Sherif, M. (1936). *The psychology of social norms.* New York: Harper; and Sherif, M. (1961). Conformity— Deviation, norms and group relations. In I. A. Berg and B. M. Bass (Eds.). *Conformity and deviation* (pp. 159–198). New York: Harper.

17. Asch, S. E. (1951). Effects of group pressure upon the modification and distortion of judgments. In H. Guetzkow (ed.), *Groups, leadership, and men* (pp. 177–190). Pittsburgh: Carnegie; Asch, S. E. (1955). Opinions and social pressure. *Scientific American 193*(5), 31–35; and Asch, S. E. (1956). Studies of independence and conformity: A minority of one against a unanimous majority. *Psychological Monographs 70*(9), 1–70.

18. Schachter, S. (1959). *The psychology of affiliation*. Palo Alto, CA: Stanford University Press; and Schachter, S., & Singer, J. (1962). The theory of social comparison. *Psychological Review 69*, 379–399.

19. Johnson & Johnson, *Joining together* (10th ed.).

20. Milgram, S. (1963). Behavioral study of obedience. *Journal of Abnormal and Social Psychology 68*, 371–378.

21. Hollander, E. P. (1958). Conformity, status, and idiosyncrasy credit. *Psychological Review 65*, 117–127.

22. Bach, G. R., & Wyden, P. (1981). *The intimate enemy*. New York: Avon.

23. Gordon, T. (2000). *Parent effectiveness training: The proven program for raising responsible children*. New York: Random House.

CHAPTER 5   Verbal and Nonverbal Communication

1. Quoted in Adler, R. B., & Towne, N. (1981). *Looking out/Looking in* (3rd ed., p. 253). New York: Holt, Rinehart and Winston.

2. Scott, C. R. (2001). Communication, social support, and burn out, a brief literature review. *Micro Organizational Communication Theory and Research* Fall.

3. Johnson, D. W., & Johnson, F. P. (2009). *Joining together: Group theory and group skills* (10th ed.). Boston: Allyn and Bacon.

4. McGregor, D. (1967). *The professional manager*. New York: McGraw-Hill.

5. Zahn, M. (2008, Nov. 23). Court leaves deaf parents in the dark. *Journal Sentinel*, P. 3.

6. Atieno Okech, J. E., Pimpleton, A. M., Vannetta, R., & Champe, J. (2015). Intercultural communication: An application to group work. *The Journal for Specialists in Group Work* 268–293.

7. Adler, R. B., & Towne, N. (1981). *Looking out/Looking in* (3rd ed., p. 171). New York: Holt, Rinehart and Winston.

8. Ibid., p. 178.

9. Ibid.

10. Ibid., p. 180.

11. Gibb, J. R. (1961). Defensive communication. *Journal of Communication 11*, 141–148.

12. Adler & Towne, *Looking out*, p. 38.

13. Jourard, S. M. (1971). *The transparent self*. New York: Van Nostrand Reinhold.

14. Ibid, pp. 47–63.

15. Luft, J. (1969). *Of human interaction*. Palo Alto, CA: National Press Books.

16. Kadushin, A. (1983). *The social work interview* (p. 188). New York: Columbia University Press.

17. Ibid., p. 190.

18. Gordon, T. (2000). *Parent effectiveness training: The Proven program for raising responsible children*. New York: Random House.

19. Reamer, F. G. (2013). Social work in a digital age: Ethical and risk management challenges. *Social Work* 163–172.

20. Conan Doyle, A. (1974). A scandal in Bohemia. In *The Adventures of Sherlock Holmes*. London: John Murray.

21. Adler & Towne, *Looking out*, p. 257.

22. Knapp, M. L., & Hall, J. A. (2009). *Nonverbal communication in human interaction* (6th ed.). Belmont, CA: Wadsworth.

23. Ekman, P., & Friesen, W. V. (1975). *Unmasking the face*. Englewood Cliffs, NJ: Prentice Hall.

24. Adler & Towne, *Looking out*, p. 266.

25. Hess, E. H., & Polt, J. M. (1960). Pupil size as related to interest value of visual stimuli. *Science 132*, 349–350.

26. Scheflen, A. E. (1974). *How behavior means*. Garden City, NY: Anchor.

27. Renninger, L., Wade, J., & Grammer, K. (2004). Getting that female glance: Patterns and consequences of male nonverbal behavior in courtship contexts. *Evolution and Human Behavior 25*, 416–431.

28. Kraus, M. W., & Keltner, D. Rich Man, Poor Man: Study Shows Body Language Can Indicate Socioeconomic Status. Retrieved from http://www.psychologicalscience.org/media/releases/2009/kraus.com.

29. Spitz, R. (1945). Hospitalization: Genesis of psychiatric conditions in early childhood. *Psychoanalytic Study of the Child 1*, 53.

30. Montagu, A. (1971). *Touching: The human significance of the skin*. New York: Harper & Row.

31. Quoted in Adler & Towne, *Looking out*, p. 279.

32. Hoult, R. (1954). Experimental measurement of clothing as a factor in some social ratings of selected American men. *American Sociological Review 19*, 324–328.

33. Adler & Towne, *Looking out*, p. 281.

34. Hall, E. T. (1969). *The hidden dimension*. Garden City, NY: Doubleday.

35. Knapp & Hall, *Nonverbal communication in human interaction*.

36. Ibid., p. 323.

37. Ibid.

38. Mehrabian, A. (1981). *Silent messages* (2nd ed.). Belmont, CA: Wadsworth.

39. Singer, J. E. (1964). The use of manipulative strategies: Machiavellianism and attractiveness. *Sociometry 27*, 128–151.

40. Mills, J., & Aronson, E. (1965). Opinion change as a function of the communicator's attractiveness and desire to influence. *Journal of Personality and Social Psychology 1*, 73–77.

41. Widgery, R. N., & Webster, B. (1969). The effects of physical attractiveness upon perceived initial credibility. *Michigan Speech Journal 4*, 9–15.

42. Solender, E. K., & Solender, E. (1976). Minimizing the effect of the unattractive client on the jury: A study of the interaction of physical appearance with assertions and self-experience references. *Human Rights 5*, 201–214.

43. Knapp & Hall, *Nonverbal communication in human interaction*.

44. Ibid.

45. Ibid.

46. Ibid.

47. Ibid.

48. Ibid.

49. Ibid.

50. Maslow, A. H., & Mintz, N. L. (1956). Effects of esthetic surroundings. I. Initial effects of three esthetic conditions upon perceiving "energy" and "well-being" in faces. *Journal of Psychology 41*, 247–254.

51. This story by Samuel J. Sackett, entitled "Tin Lizzie," appears in Johnson, D. W., & Johnson, F. P. (1975). *Joining together: Group therapy and group skills* (pp. 327–328). Englewood Cliffs, NJ: Prentice Hall.

CHAPTER 6   Task Groups

1. Toseland, R. W., & Rivas, R. F. (2009). *An Introduction to group work practice* (6th ed., p. 153). Boston: Pearson.
2. Ibid., p. 323.
3. Johnson, D. W., & Johnson, F. P. (1975). *Joining together: Group therapy and group skills* (p. 257). Englewood Cliffs, NJ: Prentice Hall.
4. Mooney, L. A., Knox, D., & Schachl, C. (2013). *Understanding social problems* (8th ed.). Belmont, CA: Wadsworth/Cengage Learning.
5. Henley, A. B., & Price, K. H. (2004). The interdependency of task and relationship conflict over time. *A Coding of Management*, A1–A6.
6. See Napier, R. W., & Gershenfeld, M. K. (1981). *Groups: Theory and experience* (2nd ed., p. 384). Boston: Houghton Mifflin.
7. See Vroom, V. H., Grant, L. D., & Cotton, T. S. (1969). The consequences of social interaction in group problem solving. *Journal of Organizational Behavior and Human Performance 4*, 79–95; and Collaros, R. A., & Anderson, L. (1969). Effects of perceived expertness upon creativity of members of brainstorming groups. *Journal of Applied Psychology 53*, 159–164.
8. Bouchard, T. J. (1972). Training, motivation and personality as determinants of the effectiveness of brainstorming groups and individuals. *Journal of Applied Psychology 56*, 324–331.
9. Napier & Gershenfeld, *Groups*, p. 385.
10. Johnson & Johnson, *Joining Together*, p. 139.
11. Moore, C. W. (1986). *The mediation process* (p. 158). San Francisco, CA: Jossey-Bass.
12. Gordon, T. (2000). *Parent effectiveness training: The proven program for raising responsible children.* New York: Random House.
13. Ibid.
14. Deutsch, M. (1969). Conflicts: Productive and destructive. *Journal of Social Issues 25*, 7–43.
15. Rokeach, M. (1960). *The open and closed mind.* New York: Basic.
16. Johnson, D. W. (1971). Role reversal: A summary and review of the research. *International Journal of Group Tensions 1*, 318–334.
17. Moore, *Mediation process*, p. 21.
18. Ibid., pp. 21–22.
19. Ibid., p. 22.
20. Ibid., p. 23.
21. Ibid., p. 6.
22. See Moore, *Mediation process*, for a review.
23. Blades, J. (1985). *Mediate your divorce.* Englewood Cliffs, NJ: Prentice Hall.
24. Moore, *Mediation Process*.
25. Johnson, D. W., & Johnson, F. P. (2009). *Joining together: Group therapy and group skills* (10th ed.). Boston: Allyn and Bacon.
26. Ibid.
27. Mooney, Knox, & Schacht, *Understanding social problems*.
28. Ibid.
29. Ibid.
30. Ibid.
31. Ibid.
32. Johnson & Johnson, *Joining together* (10th ed.), p. 60.
33. Ibid., p. 75.
34. Toseland, R. W., & Rivas, R. F. (2009). *An introduction to group work practice* (6th ed.). Boston: Pearson.
35. Janis, I. L. (1971). Groupthink. *Psychology Today* 43–46, 74–76.
36. Watts, J. (2013). Why hyper bonding occurs in the learning community classroom and what to do about it. *Learning Communities Research and Practice 3*, 1–16.

CHAPTER 7   Working with Diverse Groups

1. *Code of Ethics* of the National Association of Social Workers, National Association of Social Workers (Washington, DC: NASW Press, 2008).
2. Ibid.
3. Merton, R. (1949). Discrimination and the American creed. In R. M. MacIver (Ed.), *Discrimination and national welfare.* New York: Harper & Row.
4. Council on Social Work Education. (2015). *Educational policy and accreditation standards.* Alexandria, VA: Council on Social Work Education.
5. Ibid.
6. Barker, R. L. (2003). *The social work dictionary* (5th ed., pp. 404–405). Washington, DC: NASW Press.
7. Council on Social Work Education, *Educational Policy and Accreditation Standards*.
8. Mor Barak, M. E. (2005). *Managing diversity: Toward a globally inclusive workplace.* Thousand Oaks, CA: Sage Publications.
9. Barak, M. E. (January 3, 1998) Model minority doesn't tell? *Chicago Tribune*, P. 18.
10. Sadar, Z. (2001, July 30). More Hackney Than Bollywood. *New Statesman*, PP. 14–16.
11. Mooney, L. A., Knox, D., & Schacht, C. (2015). *Understanding social problems* (9th ed.) Stanford, CT: Cengage Learning.
12. Ibid.
13. Council on Social Work Education, *Educational Policy and Accreditation Standards*.
14. Murphy, Y., Hunt, V., Zajicek, A., Norris, A., & Hamilton, L. (2009). *Incorporating intersectionality in social work practice, research, policy, and education.* Washington, DC: NASW Press.
15. Excerpted from a speech by Abraham Lincoln in Charleston, Illinois, in 1858, as reported in Hofstader, R. (1948). *The American political tradition* (p. 116). New York: Knopf.
16. Hyde, J. S., & DeLamater, J. (2011). *Understanding human sexuality* (11th ed., pp. 313–337). Boston: McGraw-Hill.
17. Ibid.
18. Ibid.
19. Ibid.
20. Kinsey, A., Pomeroy, W. B., & Martin, C. E. (1948). *Sexual behavior in the human male.* Philadelphia, PA: Saunders.
21. Hyde & DeLamater, *Understanding human sexuality*, pp. 313–337.
22. Bell, A. P., Weinberg, M. S., & Hammersmith, S. K. (1981). *Sexual preference.* Bloomington, IN: Indiana University Press.
23. Mizio, E. (1972). White worker-minority client. *Social Worker 17*, 82–86.
24. Sager, C. J., Brayboy, T. L., & Waxenberg, B. R. (1970). *Black ghetto family in therapy: A laboratory experience* (pp. 210–211). New York: Grove Press.
25. Lewis, R. G., & Keung Ho, M. (1975). Social work with Native Americans. *Social Work 20*, 378–382.
26. Sinclair, L. G. (2003). Sex counseling and therapy. In Zastrow, C. (Ed.), *The practice of social work* (7th ed., p. 492). Pacific Grove, CA: Brooks/Cole.
27. Shaefer, R. T. (2015). *Racial and ethnic groups* (14th ed.). Upper Saddle River, NJ: Pearson.
28. Ibid.
29. Ibid.
30. Wright, B. A. (1960). *Physical disability: A psychological approach* (p. 259). New York: Harper & Row.

31. Ibid.
32. Weinberg, N. (1980). Rehabilitation. In D. Brieland, L. Costin, & C. Atherton (Eds.), *Contemporary social work* (2nd. ed., p. 310). New York: McGraw-Hill.
33. Ibid.
34. Kalyanpur, M., & Harry, B. (1997). A posture of reciprocity: A practical approach to collaboration between professionals and parents of culturally diverse backgrounds. *Journal of Child and Family Studies 6*, 487–509.
35. Ibid., p. 493.
36. Norton, D. G. (1978). Incorporating content on minority groups into social work practice courses. In *The dual perspective* (p. 22). New York: Council on Social Work Education.
37. Hull, Jr., G. H. (1995). Social work practice with diverse groups. In C. Zastrow (Ed.), *The practice of social work* (5th ed., p. 359). Pacific Grove, CA: Brooks/Cole.
38. Delgado, M., & Humm-Delgado, D. (1982). Natural support systems: Source of strength in Hispanic communities. *Social Work 27*(1), 83–89.
39. Kadushin, A. (1972). *The social work interview.* New York: Columbia University Press.
40. Davis, L. E. (1979). Racial composition of groups. *Social Work 24*, 208–213.
41. Good Tracks, J. G. (1973). Native American noninterference. *Social Work 18,* 30–34.
42. Moses, A. E., & Hawkins, R. O. (1982). *Counseling lesbian women and gay men: A life-issues approach.* St. Louis, MO: C. V. Mosby.
43. Gramick, J. (1983). Homophobia: A new challenge. *Social Work 28*(2), 137–141.
44. Devote, W., & Seblesinger, E. G. (1998). *Ethnic-sensitive social work practice* (5th ed.). Needham Heights, MA: Allyn & Bacon.
45. Norton, D. G. (1978). Incorporating content on minority groups into social work practice courses. In *The dual perspective.* New York: Council on Social Work Education.
46. Devore & Schlesinger, *Ethnic-sensitive social work practice.*
47. Ibid.
48. Barker, *The social work dictionary,* p. 142.
49. Dhopper, S. S., & Moore, S. E. (2001). *Social work practice with culturally diverse people.* Thousand Oaks, CA: Sage.
50. Ibid.
51. National Association of Social Workers. (2008). *NASW code of ethics.* Washington, DC: NASW.
52. Council on Social Work Education. (2015). *Educational policy and accreditation standards* (EPAS). Washington, DC: CSWE.
53. Dhopper & Moore, *Social work practice with culturally diverse people;* National Association of Social Workers. (2001). *Standards for cultural competence in social work practice.* Washington, DC: NASW; and National Association of Social Workers. (2015). *Standards and indicators for cultural competence in social work practice.* Washington, DC: NASW.
54. Council on Social Work Education, *Educational Policy and Accreditation Standards.*
55. Reichert, E. (2007). *Challenges in human rights: A social work perspective.* New York: Columbia University Press.
56. Ibid.
57. United Nations. (1948). *Universal declaration of human rights.* Adopted December 10, 1948. General Assembly Resolution, 2200 AXXI. New York: United Nations.
58. Reichert, *Challenges in human rights,* p. 8.
59. Davis, L. E., Galinsky, M. J., & Schopler, J. H. (1995). RAP: A framework for leadership of multiracial groups. *Social Work 40*(2), 155–165.
60. Barker, *The social work dictionary,* p. 161.
61. Ibid.
62. Kirst-Ashman, K., & Hull, Jr., G. H. (1993). *Understanding generalist practice* (p. 427). Chicago: Nelson-Hall.
63. Van Den Bergh, N., & Cooper, L. B. (1987). Feminist social work. In *The encyclopedia of social work* (pp. 610–618). Washington, DC: National Association of Social Workers; Kirst-Ashman & Hull, *Understanding generalist practice;* and Van Den Bergh, N. (1992). Feminist treatment for people with depression. In K. Corcoran (Ed.), *Structuring change* (pp. 95–110). Chicago: Lyceum Books.
64. Kirst-Ashman & Hull, *Understanding generalist practice,* p. 613.
65. Van Den Bergh, Feminist treatment for people with depression, p. 103.
66. Ibid., p. 101.
67. Ibid., p. 104.
68. Ibid., p. 104.
69. Van Den Bergh & Cooper, Feminist social work, p. 617.
70. Ibid.
71. Van Den Bergh, Feminist treatment for people with depression, pp. 95–110.
72. Ibid., p. 105.
73. Kirst-Ashman & Hull, *Understanding generalist practice,* p. 427.
74. Schiller, L. Y. (1995). Stages of development in women's groups: A relational model. In R. Kurland & R. Salmon (Eds.), *Group work practice in a troubled society: Problems and opportunities* (pp. 117–138). Binghamton, NY: Haworth Press.
75. Ibid., p. 117.
76. Ibid., p. 122.
77. Ibid., p. 122.
78. Ibid., p. 122.
79. Ibid.

CHAPTER 8 Self-Help Groups

1. Bonds, G. et al., (1979). Growth of a medical self-help group. In M. A. Lieberman, L. D. Borman, and Associates (Eds.). *Self-help groups for coping with crisis* (pp. 43–66). San Francisco, CA: Jossey-Bass.
2. Borman, L. D., & Lieberman, M. A. (1979). Conclusion: Contributions, dilemmas, and implications for mental health policy. In Lieberman et al. (Eds.), *Self-help groups for coping with crisis: Origins, members, processes, and impact* (p. 408). San Francisco, CA: Jossey-Bass.
3. Lieberman, M. A., & Borman, L. D. (1979). Overview: The nature of self-help groups. In Lieberman et al (Eds.), *Self-help groups for coping with crisis* (p. 2). San Francisco, CA: Jossey-Bass
4. Hepworth, D. H., Rooney, R. H., Rooney, G. D., Strom-Gottfried, K., & Larsen, J. (2010). *Direct social work practice: Theory and skills* (8th ed., p. 275). Belmont, CA: Brooks/Cole.
5. Reissman, F. (1987). Foreword. In T. J. Powell, *Self-help organizations and professional practice* (pp. ix–x). Silver Spring, MD: National Association of Social Workers.
6. Katz, A. H., & Bender, E. I. (1976). *The strength in us: Self-help groups in the modern world.* New York: Franklin-Watts.
7. Ibid., p. 38.
8. Ibid.
9. Powell, T. J. (1987). *Self-help organizations and professional practice.* Silver Spring, MD: National Association of Social Workers.
10. Riessman, F. (1965). The "helper therapy" principle. *Journal of Social Work,* 27–34.
11. Hepworth & Larsen, *Direct social work practice,* p. 549.
12. Borman, L. (1979). New self-help and support systems for the chronically mentally ill. Paper presented at the Pittsburgh Conference on Neighborhood Support Systems, Pittsburgh, PA.

13. Kurtz, L. F. (1997). *Self-help and support groups: A handbook for practitioners* (p. 13). Thousand Oaks, CA: Sage.
14. Maguire, L. (1981). Natural helping networks and self-help groups. In M. Nobel (Ed.), *Primary prevention in mental health and social work* (p. 41). New York: Council on Social Work Education.

15. Hepworth, D. H., & Larsen, J. (1986). *Direct social work practice: Theory and skills* (p. 550). Homewood, IL: Dorsey Press.
16. Lieberman & Borman, Overview, p. 31.
17. Kurtz, *Self-help and support groups,* p. 187.

CHAPTER 9   Social Work with Families

1. Hepworth, D. H., Rooney, R. H., Rooney, G. D., Strom-Gottfried, K., & Larsen, J. (2010). *Direct social work practice: Theory and skills* (8th ed.). Belmont, CA: Brooks/Cole.
2. Mooney, L. A., Knox, D., & Schacht, C. (2013). *Understanding social problems* (8th ed., p. 136). Belmont, CA: Wadsworth/Cengage Learning.
3. Komblum, W., & Julian, J. (2011). *Social problems* (14th ed., p. 330). Boston: Pearson.
4. Council Social Work Education. (2015). *Educational policy and accreditation standards (EPAS).* Alexandria, VA: Council on Social Work Education.
5. Hartman, A. (1978). Diagrammatic assessment of family relationships. *Social Casework 59,* 465–476.

6. Kerr, M. E., & Bowen, M. (1988). *Family evaluation: An approach based on Brown's theory.* New York: Norton.
7. Wegscheider, S. (1981). *Another chance: Hope and health for the alcoholic family.* Palo Alto, CA: Science & Behavior Books.
8. Congress, E. P. (2004). Cultural and ethical issues in working with culturally diverse patients and their families: The use of the culturagram to promote cultural competent practice in health care settings. In *Social work visions from around the globe: Citizens, methods, and approaches* (pp. 249–262). Binghamton, NY: Haworth Press.
9. Thorman, G. (1982). *Helping troubled families: A social work perspective* (p. 65). New York: Aldine.
10. Suppes, M. A., & Wells, C. (2009). *The social work experience: An introduction to social work and social welfare* (5th ed.). Boston: Pearson.

CHAPTER 10   Organizations, Communities, and Groups

1. Etzioni, A. (1964). *Modern organizations* (p. 1). Englewood Cliffs, NJ: Prentice Hall.
2. Netting, F. E., Kettner, P. M., & McMurtry, S. L. (1998). Social *work macro practice* (2nd ed., pp. 193–194) New York: Longman.
3. Johnson, D. W., & Johnson, F. P. (2003). *Joining together: Group theory and group skills* (8th ed., p. 19). Boston: Allyn and Bacon.
4. Davis, K., & Newstrom, J. W. (1989). *Human behavior at work* (8th ed., p. 31). New York: McGraw-Hill.
5. Ibid.
6. Taylor, F. (1947). *Scientific management.* New York: Harper & Row.
7. Roethlisberger, F. J., & Dickson, W. J. (1939). *Management and the worker.* Cambridge, MA: Harvard University Press.
8. Etzioni, *Modern organizations,* pp. 34–35.
9. Netting, Kettner, & McMurtry, *Social work macro practice,* pp. 202–203.
10. McGregor, D. (1960). *The human side of enterprise.* New York: McGraw-Hill.
11. Davis & Newstrom, *Human behavior at work,* p. 34.
12. Ouchi, W. (1981). *Theory Z: How American business can meet the Japanese challenge.* Reading, MA: Addison-Wesley.
13. Drucker, P. F. (1954). *The practice of management.* New York: Harper.
14. Omachony, V. K., & Ross, J. E. (1994). *Principles of total quality* (p. 1). Delray Beach, FL: St. Lucie Press.

15. Ibid.
16. McGregor, D., *The human side of enterprise.*
17. Retrieved from http://www.greenleaf.org/whatissl/.
18. Knopf, R. (1979). *Surviving the BS (bureaucratic system)* (pp. 21–22). Wilmington, NC: Mandala Press.
19. Ibid., p. 25.
20. Ibid.
21. Ibid.
22. Barker, R. L. (2003). *The social work dictionary* (5th ed., p. 83). Washington, DC: NASW Press.
23. Ibid., p. 219.
24. Ibid., p. 83.
25. Rothman, J., & Tropman, J. E. (1987). Models of community organization and macro practice perspectives: Their mixing and phasing. In F. Cox, J. Erlich, J. Rothman, & J. E. Tropman (Eds.), *Strategies of community organization* (4th ed., pp. 3–26). Itasca, IL: F. E. Peacock.
26. Alinsky, S. (1972). *Rules for radicals* (p. 27). New York: Random House.
27. Alinsky, S. (1969). *Reveille for radicals* (p. 42). New York: Basic Books.
28. Saleeby, D. (2009). *The strengths perspective in social work practice* (5th. ed.). Boston: Allyn & Bacon.
29. Kirst-Ashman, K. K., & Hull Jr., G. H. (2006). *Understanding generalist practice* (4th ed., p. 109). Belmont, CA: Brooks/Cole.

CHAPTER 11   Educational Groups: With a Focus on Self-Care

1. Edelwich, J. (1980). *Burn-Out* (pp. 44–142). New York: Human Sciences Press.
2. Cox, K., & Steiner, S. (2013). *Self-care in social work.* Washington, DC: NASW Press; Smullens, S. (2015). *Burnout and self-care in social work.* Washington, DC: NASW Press.
3. Davis, M., Eshelman, E. R., Mckay, M., & Fanning, P. (2008). *The relaxation & stress reduction workbook.* Oakland, CA: New Harbinger.

4. Sapolsky, R. (1998). *Why zebras don't get ulcers: An updated guide to stress, stress related diseases and coping.* New York: W. H. Freeman.
5. Simonton, O. C., & Matthews-Simonton, S. (1978). *Getting well again.* Los Angeles: J. P. Tarcher.
6. Gauzer, B. (1990, June 10). What we can learn from those who survive AIDS. *Parade Magazine,* 4–7.
7. Pelletier, K. R. (1977). *Mind as healer, mind as slayer.* (p. 310). New York: Dell.

8. Tubesing, D. A. (1981). *Kicking your stress habits*. Duluth, MN: Whole Person Associates.
9. Selye, H. (1956). *The stress of life* (pp. 25–46). New York: McGraw-Hill.
10. For an expanded description of the physiological reactions involved in stress, see Sapolsky, *Why zebras don't get ulcers*.
11. Ibid.
12. Ibid.
13. Selye, H. (1974). *Stress without distress* (p. 83). New York: Signet.
14. Ibid.
15. Smullens, *Burnout and Self-Care in Social Work*; Edelwich, *Burn-Out*; Pines, A., & Aronson, E. (1981). *Burn-out*. New York: Free Press; Freudenberger, H. (1980). *Burn-out*. Garden City, NY: Anchor; and Maslach, C. (1982). *Burnout—The cost of caring*. Englewood Cliffs, NJ: Spectrum.
16. Maslach, C., & Pines, A. (1977). The burn-out syndrome in the day care setting. *Child Care Quarterly 6*, 100–101.
17. Freudenberger, *Burn-out*, pp. 90–91.
18. Maslach, C. (1976). Burned-out. *Human behavior 5*, 19.
19. Ibid., p. 20.
20. Maslach, C. (1978). The client role in staff burn-out. *Journal of Social Issues 34*, 111–124.
21. Pines & Aronson, Burn-out syndrome, pp. 45–81.
22. Cox & Steiner, *Self-care in social work*; Smullens, *Burnout and self-care in social work*.
23. Lakein, A. (1973). *How to get control of your time and your life*. New York: Signet.
24. Ibid., p. 44.
25. Ibid., p. 71.

26. These relaxation techniques are more fully described in Naparstek, B. (2004). *Invisible heroes: Survivors of trauma and how they heal*. New York: Bantam.
27. Jacobson, E. (1938). *Progressive relaxation* (2nd ed.). Chicago: University of Chicago Press.
28. Watson, D. L., & Tharp, R. G. (1973). *Self-directed behavior* (pp. 182–183). Pacific Grove, CA: Brooks/Cole.
29. Benson, H. (1975). *The relaxation response*. New York: Avon.
30. Because any neutral word or phrase will work, Herbert Benson, in *The Relaxation Response* (New York: Avon, 1975), suggests repeating the word *one* silently to oneself.
31. Follette, V., Palm, K., & Pearson, A. N. (2006). Mindfulness and trauma: Implications for treatment. *Journal of Rational-Emotive & Cognitive-Behavior Therapy 24*(1), 45–62.
32. Kabot-Zinn, J. (2012). *Mindfulness for beginners: Reclaiming the present moment—and your life*. Boulder, CO: Sounds True.
33. Ibid.
34. Sapolsky, *Why zebras don't get ulcers*.
35. de Mello, A. (1978). *Sadhana: A way to God* (p. 140). Garden City, NY: Image Books.
36. Radey, M., & Figley, C. R. *(2007)*. The social psychology of compassion. *Clinical Social Work Journal 35*, 207–214.
37. Ellis, A., & Harper, R. (1997). *A guide to rational living*. Chatsworth CA: Wilshire.
38. For case examples demonstrating how to change unwanted emotions, see Ellis & Harper, *A guide to rational living*.
39. Seaward, B. L. (2009). *Managing stress* (6th ed.). Sudbury, MA: Jones & Bartlett.

CHAPTER 12   Treatment Groups

1. These therapy approaches are summarized in Chapter 7 and Appendix 1: Modules 1, 2, and 3.
2. These therapy approaches are described in Corsini, R. J., & Wedding, D. (2008). *Current psychotherapies* (8th ed.). Belmont, CA: Thomson Learning; and Sharf, R. S. (2008). *Theories of psychotherapy and counseling* (4th ed.). Belmont, CA: Thomson Learning.
3. Riessman, F. (1965). The "helper therapy" principle. *Journal of Social Work* 27–34.
4. Garland, J. A., Jones, H., & Kolodny, R. (1965). A model for stages of development in social work groups. In Bernstein, S. (Ed.), *Explorations in group work* (pp. 12–53). Boston: Milford House; and Garland, J. A., & Frey, L. A. (1973). Applications of stages of group development to groups in psychiatric settings. In Bernstein, S. (Ed.), *Further explorations in group work* (p. 3). Boston: Milford House.
5. Kübler-Ross, E. (1969). *On death and dying*. New York: Macmillan.
6. Canadian Association of Social Workers (2005). *Social work code of ethics*. Ottawa: Canadian Association of Social Workers.
7. National Association of Social Workers. (2008). *Code of ethics*. Washington, DC: National Association of Social Workers.

8. Retrieved from http://www.mapl.com.au/evidence/evidence/3.htm.
9. Gambril, E. (1999). Evidence-based practice: An alternative to authority-based practice. *Families in Society: Journal of Contemporary Human Services 80*(4), 341–350.
10. Adams, K. B., Matto, H. C., & Lecroy, C. W. (2009). Limitations of evidence-based practice for social work education. Unpacking the complexity. *Journal of Social Work Education 45*(2); and Mullen, E. J., & Streiner, D. L. (2004). The evidence for and against evidence-based practice. *Brief Treatment and Crisis Intervention 4*, 111–121.
11. Norcross, J. C., & Lambert, M. J. (2006). The therapy relationship. In J. C. Norcross, L. E. Beufler, & R. F. Levant (Eds.), *Evidence-based practices in mental health: Debate and dialogue on the fundamental questions* (pp. 208–217). Washington, DC: American Psychological Association; and Wampold, B. (2001). *The great psychotherapy debate: Models, methods and findings*. Mahwah, NJ: Erlbaum.
12. Duncan, B. L., & Miller, S. P. (2000). *The heroic client*. San Francisco: Jossey Bass.
13. Rosenthal, R., & Jacobson, L. (1968). *Pygmalion in the classroom*. New York: Holt, Rinehart and Winston.

CHAPTER 13   Treatment Groups with Diverse and Vulnerable Populations

1. Gordon, R. A., (2001). Eating disorders East and West: A culture-bound syndrome unbound. In M. Nasser, M. A. Katzman, & R. A. Gordon (Eds.), *Eating disorders and cultures in transition* (pp. 3–4). New York: Taylor & Francis, Inc.
2. Silverman, J. A. (1997). Anorexia nervosa: Historical perspective on treatment. In D. M. Garner & P. E. Garfinkel (Eds.), *Handbook of treatment for eating disorders* (pp. 4–5). New York: Guilford Press.

3. American Psychiatric Association. (2013). *Diagnostic and statistical manual of mental disorders* (DSM-5) (5th ed.). Washington, DC: APA.
4. Ibid.
5. Russel, G. F. M. (1997). The history of bulimia nervosa," In D. M. Garner & P. E. Garfinkel (Eds.), *Handbook of treatment for eating disorders* (p. 20). New York: Guilford Press.

6. Treasure, J., Stein, D., & Maguire, S. (2015). Has the time come for a staging model to map the course of eating disorders from high risk to severe enduring illness? An examination of the evidence. *Early Intervention in Psychiatry 9*, 173–185.

7. Westmoreland, P., Krantz, M. J., & Mehler, P. S. (2016). Medical complications of anorexia nervosa and bulimia. *The American Journal of Medicine 129*(1), 30–37.

8. American Psychiatric Association, *Diagnostic and statistical manual of mental disorders* (DSM-5).

9. Citrome, L. (2015). a primer on binge eating disorder diagnosis and management. *CNS Specirums20*(S1), 41–51.

10. Dingemans, A. E., & van Forth, E. F. (2012). Binge eating disorder psychopathology in normal weight and obese individuals. *The International Journal Of Eating Disorder 45*(1), 135–138.

11. Sheehan, D. V., & Herman, B. K. (2015). The psychological and medical factors associated with untreated binge eating disorder. *The Primary Care Companion for CNS Disorders 17*(2). Retrieved from www.ncbi.nim.nih.gov/pme/aiticles/FMC4560195.

12. Crow, S. (2014). The economics of eating disorder treatment. *Current Psychiatry Reports 16*(7), 1–3.

13. Harrington, B. C., Jimerson, M., Haxton, C., & Jimerson, D. C. (2015). Initial evaluation, diagnosis, and treatment of anorexia nervosa and bulimia nervosa. *American Family Physician 91*(1), 46–52.

14. Crow, The economics of eating disorder treatment.

15. Domestic Abuse Intervention Project (1984). Power and Control Wheel. Retrieved from http://www.ncdsv.org.

16. Domestic Abuse Intervention Project (1984). Equality Wheel. Retrieved from http://www.ncdsv.org.

17. Loseke, D. R., Gelles, R. J., & Cavanaugh, M. M. (2005). *Current controversies on family violence* (2nd ed.). Thousand Oaks, CA: Sage.

18. Ibid.

19. Hampton, R. L. (1999). *Family violence prevention and treatment* (2nd ed.). Thousand Oaks, CA: Sage.

20. Domestic Abuse Intervention Project, Power and Control Wheel.

21. Domestic Abuse Intervention Project, Equality Wheel.

22. National Coalition Against Domestic Violence, Public Policy Office. (2007). Domestic Violence Facts. Retrieved from http://www.ncadv.org.

23. Thompson, H. E., & Trice-Black, S. (2012). School-based group interventions for children exposed to domestic violence. *Journal of Family Violence*. Advanced online publication. Doi: 10.1007/sl0896-012-9416-6, 2012.

24. Ibid.

25. Domestic Abuse Intervention Project, Equality Wheel.

26. Kübler-Ross, E. (1969). *On death and dying*. New York: Macmillan.

27. Westberg, G. (1962). *Good grief*. Philadelphia: Fortress.

28. Crowther, M., Norton, M., & Scogin, F. (2010). Treating the aged in rural communities: The application of cognitive-behavioral therapy for depression. *Journal of Clinical Psychology* 502–512.

29. Seeman, T. E. (2000). Health promoting effects of friends and family on health outcomes in older adults. *American Journal Health Promotion 14*, 362–370.

30. Haight, B., & Gibson, F. eds. (2006). *Burnside's working with older adults: Group processes and techniques* (4th ed.). Sudbury, MA: Jones and Bartlett.

31. Ibid.

32. Ibid.

33. Ibid.

34. Ibid.

35. Ibid.

36. Erikson, E. H. (1963). *Childhood and society* (2nd ed.). New York: Norton.

37. Fell, N. (2002). *The validation breakthrough: Simple techniques for communicating with people with Alzheimer's-type dementia*. Baltimore, MD: Health Professions Press.

38. Haight & Gibson, *Burnside's working with older adults*.

39. Ibid.

40. Ibid.

CHAPTER 14   Termination and Evaluation of a Group

1. Hepworth, D. H., & Larsen, J. (1986). *Direct social work practice: Theory and skills* (2nd ed., p. 590). Homewood, IL: Dorsey Press.

2. Ibid.

3. Bloom, M., Fischer, J., & Orme, J. G. (2009). *Evaluating practice: Guidelines for the accountable professional* (6th ed.). Upper Saddle River, NJ: Prentice Hall.

4. Sheafor, B. W., & Horejsi, C. R. (2007). *Techniques and guidelines for social work practice* (8th ed.). Boston: Allyn & Bacon.

5. Gingerich, W. J. (2010). Evaluating social work practice. In Zastrow, C. (Ed.), *The practice of social work* (9th ed., pp. 314–342). Belmont, CA: Brooks/Cole.

6. Sheafor & Horejsi, *Techniques and guidelines for social work practice*, p. 394.

7. Reid, W., & Epstein, L. (1972). *Task-centered casework*. New York: Columbia University Press.

APPENDIX 1   Group Treatment Theories Resource Manual (GTTRM)

INTRODUCTION

1. Retrieved from http://Dictionary.com.

2. Ibid.

3. Ibid.

MODULE 1: RATIONAL THERAPY IN GROUPS

1. Ellis, A., & Harper, R. A. (1997). *A guide to rational living*. Chatsworth, CA: Wilshire; and Maultsby, Jr., M. C. (1975). *Help yourself to happiness*. Boston: Herman.

2. Zastrow, C. (1993). *You are what you think: A guide to self-realization*. Chicago: Nelson-Hall.

3. Beck, A. T. (1975). *Cognitive therapy and the emotional disorders*. Philadelphia, PA: University of Pennsylvania Press.

4. Maultsby, *Help yourself to happiness*.

MODULE 2: BEHAVIOR THERAPY IN GROUPS

1. Thorndike, E. (1913). *The psychology of learning*. New York: Teachers College Press; Guthrie, E. R. (1935). *The psychology of learning*. New York: Harper & Row; Hull, C. L. (1943). *Principles of behavior*. New York: Appleton-Century-Crofts; Tolman, E. C. (1932). *Purposive behavior in animals and men*. New York: Appleton-Century-Crofts; and Skinner, B. F. (1938). *The behavior of organisms*. New York: Appleton-Century-Crofts.

2. Alberti. R. E., & Emmons, M. L. (2001). *Your perfect right: A guide to assertive behavior* (8th ed.). San Luis Obispo, CA: Impact Publishers; Bandura, A. (1969). *Principles of behavior modification.* New York: Holt, Rinehart and Winston; Skinner, B. F. (1948). *Walden two.* New York: Macmillan; Watson, J. B., & Rayner, R. (1920). Conditioned emotional reaction. *Journal of Experimental Psychology 3*(1), 1–14; and Wolpe, J. (1958). *Psychotherapy by reciprocal inhibition.* Stanford, CA: Stanford University Press.

3. Ome, M. T., & Wender, P. H. (1968). Anticipatory socialization for psychotherapy: Method and rationale. *American Journal of Psychiatry 124,* 1201–1212.

4. Chambless, D. L., & Goldstein, A. J. (1979). Behavior psychotherapy. In R. Corsini (Ed.), *Current psychotherapies* (2nd ed., pp. 244–245). Itasca, IL: Peacock.

5. Wolpe, *Psychotherapy by reciprocal inhibition.*

6. Alberti & Emmons, *Your perfect right;* and Fensterheim, H., & Baer, J. (1975). *Don't say yes when you want to say no.* New York: Dell.

7. Alberti, R. E., & Emmons, M. L. (1975). *Stand up, speak out, talk back!* (p. 24). New York: Pocket Books.

8. These training steps are a modification of assertiveness training programs developed in Alberti & Emmons, *Your perfect right* and in Fensterheim & Baer, *Don't say yes when you want to say no.*

9. Kazdin, A. (1977). *The token economy.* New York: Plenum.

10. Prochaska, J. O. (1979). *Systems of psychotherapy* (pp. 324–325). Homewood, IL: Dorsey Press. Reprinted by permission of Wadsworth Publishing Co.

11. Hepworth, D. H., Rooney, R. H., Rooney, G. D., Strom-Gottfried, K., & Larsen, J. (2010). *Direct social work practice: Theory and skills* (8th ed.). Belmont, CA: Brooks/Cole.

12. Ibid.

13. Ellis, A., & Harper, R. A. (1997). *A guide to rational living.* Chatsworth, CA: Wilshire; and Beck, A. T. (1976). *Cognitive theory and the emotional disorders.* New York: International Universities Press.

14. Note that the paradigm of cognitive behavior therapists [S (stimulus) → O (cognitions of organism) → R (response)] is similar to the following paradigm of rational therapists (Events Self-Talk → Emotions and Actions].

15. Rimm, D., & Masters, J. (1974). *Behavior therapy.* New York: Academic Press.

16. Mahoney, M. J. (1973). Clinical issues in self-control training. Paper presented at the meeting of the American Psychological Association, Montreal.

17. Beck, A. T., & Weishaar, M. E. (1989). Cognitive therapy. In R. Corsini & D. Wedding (Eds.), *Current psychotherapies* (4th ed., p. 309). Itasca, IL: Peacock.

18. Ibid., pp. 309–310.

19. Ibid., p. 310.

20. Ibid.

MODULE 3: REALITY THERAPY IN GROUPS

1. Glasser, W. (1965). *Reality therapy.* New York: Harper & Row.

2. Glasser, W. (1998). *Choice theory: A new psychology of personal freedom.* New York: Harper Perennial.

3. Glasser, W. (1984). *Control theory* (p. 32). New York: Harper & Row.

4. Ibid., p. 19.

5. Glasser, *Choice theory.*

6. Ibid., pp. 137–138.

7. American Psychiatric Association. (2013). *Diagnostic and statistical manual of mental disorders* (5th ed.). Arlington, VA: APA.

8. Glasser, W. (2003). *Warning: Psychiatry can be hazardous to your mental health* (p. 114). New York: HarperCollins.

9. Leyden-Rubenstein, L. (1998). *The stress management handbook.* New Canaan, CT: Keats Publishing.

10. American Psychiatric Association, *Diagnostic and statistical manual.*

11. Glasser, W. (2000). *Reality therapy in action.* New York: HarperCollins.

12. Lipton, B. H. (2008). *The biology of belief.* Carlsbad, CA: Hay House.

MODULE 4: DIALECTICAL BEHAVIOR THERAPY IN GROUPS

1. Lynch, T. R., & Cozza, C. (2009). Behavior therapy for nonsuicidal self-injury. In M. K. Noek (Ed.), *Understanding nonsuicidal self-injury: Origins, assessment, and treatment.* Washington, DC: American Psychological Association.

2. Lynch, T. R., Trost, W. T., Salsman, N., & Lineban, M. M. (2007). Dialectical behavior therapy for borderline personality disorder. *Annual Review of Clinical Psychology 3,* 181–205.

3. Kliem, S., Kröger, C., & Kosfelder, J. (2010). Dialectical behavior therapy for borderline personality disorder: A meta-analysis using mixed-effects modeling. *Journal of Consulting and Clinical Psychology 78*(6), 936–951.

4. Blennerhassett, R. C., & O'Raghallaigh, J. W. (2005). Dialectical behavior therapy in the treatment of borderline personality disorder. *British Journal of Psychiatry 186,* 278–280.

5. Scheel, K. R. (2000). The empirical basis of dialectical behavior therapy: Summary, critique, and implications. *Clinical Psychology Science and Practice 7,* 68–86.

6. Harrington, N., & Pickles, C. (2009). Mindfulness and cognitive behavioral therapy: Are they compatible concepts? *Journal of Cognitive Psychotherapy 23*(4), 315–323.

7. Linehan, M. M. (1993). *Cognitive behavioral treatment of borderline personality disorder.* New York: Guilford Press.

8. Carey, B. (2011, June 23). Expert on mental illness reveals her own fight. *The New York Times.*

9. Feigenbaum, J. (2007). Dialectical behavior therapy: An increasing evidence base. *Journal of Mental Health 16*(1), 51–68.

10. Miller, A. L., Rathaus, J. H., & Linehan, M. M. (2007). *Dialectical behavior therapy with suicidal adolescents.* New York: Guilford Press.

11. Kabat-Zinn, J. (2003). Mindfulness-based interventions in context: Past, present, and future. *Clinical Psychology: Science and Practice 10,* 144–156.

12. Linehan, M. M. *Cognitive behavioral treatment of borderline personality disorder.*

13. Linehan, M., (1993). *Skills training manual for treatment borderline personality disorder.* New York: The Guilford Press

14. Ibid.

Index